Introduction to Anthropology

Introduction to Anthropology

Joseph B. Aceves
VIRGINIA POLYTECHNIC INSTITUTE AND STATE UNIVERSITY

H. Gill King
EASTFIELD COLLEGE, DALLAS

GENERAL LEARNING PRESS
Scott, Foresman and Company

Manufactured in the United States of America
Library of Congress Catalog Card Number 78-63034
ISBN 0-382-18053-4
For information write to:
General Learning Press
250 James Street
Morristown, N.J. 07960

Contents

Preface

Anthropology, perhaps more than any other discipline, illuminates the human experience. Anthropologists introduce us to societies in every quarter of the globe; tell us about the lifestyles, customs, and world views of social groups other than our own; and thus enable us to test our theories of humanity as well as our preconceptions of other people. It is the purpose of this book to introduce the student to this cross-cultural approach to the study of human values and behavior.

The text also presents the story of human evolution. It describes how members of the human family, and their forebears, developed physically as they adapted to a wide variety of environments. It also describes our cultural evolution from the earliest cultures represented by crude stone tools to those that gave birth to the first cities.

Students who look carefully at the cultures presented here will begin to discover not only the universals but also the varieties of human experience. They will realize that every culture chooses from among different alternatives and makes different adaptations to resolve such questions as "How will we maintain order?" or "How will we deal with our natural resources?" Human values and behavior are part of an ongoing process, a process that probably began in Africa millions of years ago—when the first members of the human family appeared—and continues in modern complex societies.

Organization

This text is divided into seven parts which deal with the four subdivisions of anthropology—cultural anthropology,* physical anthropology, prehistoric archeology, and linguistics.

PART 1: INTRODUCTION.   In the first chapter, the subject matter of anthropology is presented along with many of the classic theories of the discipline. Chapter 2 discusses the concept of culture and the relationship of a culture to the life of the people whose heritage it is. The first part, then, consists of explanations of what anthropology is and the various ways we might think about and organize the subject matter.

---

*The American Anthropological Association uses the terms *social anthropology* and *ethnology* rather than *cultural anthropology*. The terms are, however, largely interchangeable. We have used the latter one throughout the book, because most college courses are still labeled *cultural anthropology*.

PART 2: ORGANIC EVOLUTION. This section deals with physical anthropology and explores the evolution of the human family. Chapter 3 discusses the nonhuman primates. Chapter 4 covers the basic principles of evolutionary theory as they pertain to all living things. Chapter 5 examines the fossil remains of our predecessors and discusses how evolutionary forces have shaped human physical development. Chapter 6 centers on the ways evolution has produced physical variation among modern human groups.

PART 3: EVOLUTION OF CULTURE. This section investigates the discoveries that archeology has given the world. In Chapter 7, the earliest human cultures and their artifacts are examined. Chapter 8 probes the factors that gave rise to the earliest domesticators of plants and animals. Chapter 9 examines the appearance of the earliest cities, and the important sociocultural developments that they produced.

PART 4: SOCIAL ADAPTATION. This section is devoted to economics and political organization. In Chapter 10 the concept of cultural ecology—the adaptation of a culture to a specific environment—is explained, and the different subsistence types are described. In Chapters 11 and 12

the economic and political arrangements of the different subsistence types are discussed.

PART 5: SOCIAL GROUPS AND IDENTITY. The smaller social groups within a society are examined in this section. Chapter 13 is concerned with the importance of marriage and family in all societies and with kinship as a cohesive force. In Chapter 14 groups larger than the family—groups of people with a common ethnic or cultural background—are examined.

PART 6: EXPRESSIVE ASPECTS OF CULTURE. Every culture includes various means for people to express themselves. Chapter 15 is devoted to the most basic means of all, language. Chapter 16 is devoted to the arts: painting and sculpture, music, and the language arts. Religion is examined in Chapter 17 in terms of the function it plays in people's lives and in cultures as a whole.

PART 7: CONTEMPORARY DIMENSIONS OF ANTHROPOLOGY. This part covers the current condition of the small-scale societies that traditionally have been the subject matter of anthropologists. Many investigators are now studying small-scale groups from the perspective of the impact of the modern industrial states upon them. Chapter 19 investigates two topics that are increasingly capturing the interest of anthropologists—medical and urban anthropology. Chapter 20 includes a discussion of the responsibilities of anthropologists to the people who constitute the subject matter of their work. This chapter also raises several issues that are being seriously debated among anthropologists today. We do not necessarily agree with all of the views presented here, but we believe that students should be made aware of them.

Features

PART OPENERS.   Each part of the text opens with a discussion of the topics to be covered in that section. The purpose of the part openers is twofold. First, each relates the theoretical orientation of the text—that is, that all cultures choose from among many alternatives and arrive at different adaptations to maintain their social organization—to the subject matter of the part. The second purpose of the openers is to provide an overview of the material and a continuity from part to part. Each opener typically includes an example of an anthropological phenomenon that fulfills this purpose. The opener

for Part 4, for example, investigates some of the events that took place when European nations switched from wood to coal as the chief source of energy. The opener points out the social, economic, and technological adaptations that this changeover entailed.

CAPSULE STUDIES AND ETHNO- GRAPHIES.   Each chapter opens with either a capsule study or a capsule ethnography—a portion of a published study of a small-scale society. These introductions have been chosen for their relevance to the chapter that follows. The capsule ethnography in Chapter 11 (Economic Anthropology), for example, is from Malinowski's study of the *kula* trade ring in eastern New Guinea, and examples from this study are used within the chapter to reinforce certain points. In this fashion, students not only become familiar with the actual work of anthropologists but also can attach real meaning to abstract concepts and theories.

FIELD PROJECTS.   In order to give students a better understanding of the ways anthropologists go about their work, this text has included some projects to be done outside the classroom. Each one consists of a research problem similar to problems encountered by anthropologists in the field. However, these field projects, such as gathering a life history, can be done within the confines of the campus or a local community.

PEDAGOGICAL AIDS. Each chapter is accompanied by a summary, review questions, and an annotated list of suggested readings. The summary and review questions are designed to offer students an opportunity to check their understanding of the chapter and to help them prepare for examinations. At the end of the book we have included a glossary of commonly used anthropological terms and an index. In addition, there are two appendices: one that covers archeological methodology, and another on kinship terminology.

Acknowledgments

This book is the product of several hundred people, each of whom brought some special expertise to the enterprise. Some of these people are colleagues in anthropology, others are specialists in publishing: all of them merit our sincere thanks for their help.

We especially would like to thank the reviewers whose names are listed opposite the title page and Jeanine Aagaard, who assisted us with the linguistics material. The people at General Learning Press have poured an immense amount of time and skill into this book. The overwhelming bulk of the work was handled by Walter Kossmann and Judy Green. It would be impossible for us to give them all the thanks they deserve.

We also were helped by the editorial contributions of Susan Rothstein and Teresa Weinert. Although not directly involved in the book, Janet Barrett of General Learning Press did a great deal to help us through her clerical work.

Thanks also go to Rodie Siegler (Editor-in-Chief); Daniel Liberatore (Project Editor); Rena Lederman (Editorial Consultant); Ruth Zaslavsky (Copy Editor); Eileen Max (Production Manager); Ellen Klugherz (Photo Research); Pyramid Composition Company, Inc., and Ro-Mark Typographic Company, Inc. Special thanks go to Gloria Priam (Art Director), who executed the fine drawings that help illuminate difficult topics in the chapters on physical anthropology and archeology. The book was designed by Melanson Associates of Boston. The cover photograph is by courtesy of the United Nations.

We hope that our efforts together with the efforts of all the publishing personnel involved will meet with the approval of our readers.

Joseph B. Aceves   H. Gill King
Blacksburg, Virginia   Dallas, Texas

PART ONE

Anthropology is a unique discipline, attempting as it does to explore human behavior in every kind of setting, historical as well as contemporary. Anthropologists examine the similarities and differences among the world's peoples and then describe patterns and produce generalizations concerning these similarities and differences. To arrive at these cultural universals, anthropologists use the comparative method—they place one society beside another to contrast the behavioral patterns of each. In so doing, they seek to discover how each society adapts to its environment and why each chose, from among the alternatives available, its own characteristic adaptation.

Anthropologists observe human groups from a number of vantage points. Thus, anthropology is part social science, part biological science, and part history. For example, anthropologists study humans as animals, with emphasis on the biological features that help them adapt to their physical environment. They are interested, too, in human evolution, as well as in the cultural adaptations of humans. They search for the physical remains of our ancestors and their relatives in an attempt to trace the evolution of human physical development. Anthropologists as archeologists analyze the cultural remains of past societies: the temples, tools, and houses that helped ancient peoples to exploit their environment most effectively. In this way, they reconstruct cultural systems on the basis of cultural remains that have survived to the present. But they are also aware of the biological aspects of human adaptations.

Of primary interest to many anthropologists, however, is culture, the learned behavior of a given society. In adapting to its environment, each society employs particular kinds of behavior, beliefs, and material products. The investigator observes these phenomena, notes the interrelationships among them, and attempts to make a theoretical statement about the culture. In studying a particular religious ritual, for example, the researcher would record the ritual, including its participants, the objects used, the purpose of the ritual, and the circumstances under which it is performed. By observing these phenomena and noting how they relate to other components of the culture—its political and economic organization, for example—the researcher can get a clear picture of many adaptive aspects of the society.

The purpose of this section of the text is to introduce the student to the discipline of anthropology. Chapter 1, for example, offers an overview of the field, showing the extent of the subject and describing its branches, ideas, techniques, and data base. It also briefly sketches the development of anthropology, noting how the discipline itself has adapted to changing physical and social environments over time.

Introduction

Chapter 2 focuses on culture and the individual. It points out the way in which the culture of each society is a strategy for adapting to and exploiting the resources of a given environment. Different environments call for different adaptive responses, resulting in different cultures. Thus, the culture of the Eskimos, who used the kayak and harpoon to hunt seals, is considerably different from that of the Cheyenne Indians of the North American Plains, who used the horse, spear, and bow and arrow to hunt the buffalo.

Chapter 2 also makes clear that human personality—the individual's integrated system of behavior—is acquired as an individual interacts with the physical and cultural environment. Each society demands patterns of behavior from its young, who must respond in accordance with these expectations or face sanctions. As a result, we learn to become who we are. An example is seen in the case of the Alorese of the southwest Pacific. A few weeks after giving birth, Alorese mothers go off and work in the fields, leaving their infants virtually unattended—the children are cared for only by any adults who may be present. Largely as a result of this lack of maternal attention and affection, the Alorese grow up to be anxious, suspicious, pessimistic, uncreative, and lacking in confidence.

This philosophy contrasts with that of the Iatmul, a tribe of New Guinea headhunters whose society is based on aggression and warfare. These people encourage their children to fight for their basic needs so that they may grow up into confident, proud, fierce warriors. Child-rearing practices, then, like culture and personality, appear to be adaptive: they are devised to produce the kind of people best suited to adapt not only to their physical environment but to the culture of the society in which they must live as adults.

At the same time, each society offers its members a number of behavioral alternatives: an individual may choose from a number of strategies the best way to behave in a given situation. But these choices are limited for the individual by his or her culture. The capsule ethnography that introduces Chapter 2, for instance, indicates that the Cheyenne Indians emphasized aggression and warfare. As a result, the values of masculine vitality, courage, self-control, and endurance were instilled in the young males of the tribe. Those rare men who could not adapt to these demands could avoid them by becoming transvestites. But they had to do this in a way that was acceptable to Cheyenne society, by assuming women's social roles and performing women's work. These *berdaches*—half men, half women—were taught medical skills and may even have been allowed to play roles in certain tribal ceremonies. As we progress through the text, we will meet many examples of such adaptations and alternatives. And we will see how these behavior patterns forged many of the planet's cultures, including our own.

Chapter 1

Introducing Anthropology

MEETING THE YANOMAMÖ

NATIVE NAME: Yanomamö (also Shiriana and Waica)

POPULATION: Approximately 10,000 distributed in 125 villages

ENVIRONMENT: Dense jungle of the Orinoco River basin in southern Venezuela, and northern Brazil, South America. People cultivate up to 80 percent of the food they eat, the rest coming from hunting, fishing and collecting.

FIELDWORK: Data on the Yanomamö were collected during numerous field trips during the 1960s and are based on participant observation and interviews.

ETHNOGRAPHIC PRESENT: 1960s

We arrived at the village, Bisaasi-teri, about 2:00 P.M. and docked the boat along the muddy bank at the terminus of the path used by the Indians to fetch their drinking water. It was hot and muggy, and my clothing was soaked with perspiration. It clung uncomfortably to my body, as it did thereafter for the remainder of the work. The small, biting gnats were out in astronomical numbers, for it

Source: From Napoleon A. Chagnon, *Yanomamö: The Fierce People*, 2nd ed. (New York: Holt, Rinehart and Winston, 1977), pp. 4-6. Copyright © 1968, 1977 by Holt, Rinehart and Winston, Inc. Reprinted by permission of Holt, Rinehart and Winston.

was the beginning of the dry season. My face and hands were swollen from the venom of their numerous stings. In just a few moments I was to meet my first Yanomamö, my first primitive man. What would it be like? I had visions of entering the village and seeing 125 social facts running about calling each other kinship terms and sharing food, each waiting and anxious to have me collect his genealogy. I would wear them out in turn. Would they like me? This was important to me; I wanted them to be so fond of me that they would adopt me into their kinship system and way of life, because I had heard that successful anthropologists always get adopted by their people. I had learned during my seven years of anthropological training at the University of Michigan that kinship was equivalent to society in primitive tribes and that it was a moral way of life, "moral" being something "good" and "desirable." I was determined to work my way into their moral system of kinship and become a member of their society.

My heart began to pound as we approached the village and heard the buzz of activity within the circular compound. Mr. Barker commented that he was anxious to see if any changes had taken place while he was away and wondered how many of them had died during his absence. I felt into my back pocket to make sure that my notebook was still there and felt personally more secure when I touched it. Otherwise, I would not have known what to do with my hands.

The entrance to the village was covered over with brush and dry palm leaves. We pushed them aside to expose the low opening to the village. The excitement of meeting my first Indians was almost unbearable as I duck-waddled through the low passage into the village clearing.

I looked up and gasped when I saw a dozen burly, naked, filthy, hideous men staring at us down the shafts of their drawn arrows! Immense wads of green tobacco were stuck between their lower teeth and lips making them look even more hideous, and strands of dark-green slime dripped or hung from their noses. We arrived at the village while the men were blowing a hallucinogenic drug up their noses. One of the side effects of the drug is a runny nose. The mucus is always saturated with the green powder and the Indians usually let it run freely from their nostrils. My next discovery was that there were a dozen or so vicious, underfed dogs snapping at my legs, circling me as if I were going to be their next meal. I just stood there holding my notebook, helpless and pathetic. Then the stench of the decaying vegetation and filth struck me and I almost got sick. I was horrified. What sort of a welcome was this for the person who came here to live with you and learn your way of life, to become friends with you? They put their weapons down when they recognized Barker and returned to their chanting, keeping a nervous eye on the village entrances.

We had arrived just after a serious fight. Seven women had been abducted the day before by a neighboring group, and the local men and their guests had just that morning recovered five of them in a brutal club fight that nearly ended in a shooting war. The abductors, angry because they lost five of the seven captives, vowed to raid the Bisaasi-teri. When we arrived and entered the village unexpectedly, the Indians feared that we were the raiders. On several occasions during the next two hours the men in the village jumped to their feet, armed themselves, and waited nervously for the noise outside the village to be identified. My enthusiasm for collecting ethnographic curiosities diminished in proportion to the number of times such an alarm was raised. In fact, I was relieved when Mr. Barker suggested that we sleep across the river for the evening. It would be safer over there.

As we walked down the path to the boat, I pondered the wisdom of having decided to spend a year and a half with this tribe before I had ever seen what they were like. I am not ashamed to admit, either, that had there been a diplomatic way out, I would have ended my field work then and there. I did not look forward to the next day when I would be left alone with the Indians; I did not speak a word of their language, and they were decidedly different from what I had imagined them to be. The whole situation was depressing, and I wondered why I ever decided to switch from civil engineering to anthropology in the first place. I had not eaten all day, I was soaking wet from perspiration, the gnats were biting me, and I was covered with red pigment, the result of a dozen or so complete examinations I had been given by as many burly Indians. These examinations capped an otherwise grim day. The Indians would blow their noses into their hands, flick as much of the mucus off that would separate in a snap of the wrist, wipe the residue into their hair, and then carefully examine my face, arms, legs, hair, and the contents of my pockets. I asked Mr. Barker how to say "Your hands are dirty"; my comments were met by the Indians in the following way: They would "clean" their hands by spitting a quantity of slimy tobacco juice into them, rub them together, and then proceed with the examination.[1]

● ● ● ● ● ● ● ●

6

By American standards, the Yanomamö Indians of Venezuela and adjacent northern Brazil are not "nice" people. The major characteristic of their way of life is constant violence and aggressiveness. However, the Makiritare Indians who are the neighbors of the Yanomamö are described by Napoleon Chagnon, who studied them as well as the Yanomamö, as being "very pleasant and charming" and lacking the extreme aggressiveness of their fierce neighbors. How does one explain this difference? Can it be accounted for by the few kilometers of forest that separate the two groups? Is aggressiveness "inborn," or instinctive? Or is it something that must be learned? Americans and Canadians (like any other people) have definite standards of what is "nice" and what is not. Do these standards have any relevance in trying to understand the Yanomamö?

Questions such as these, and many others, are the subject matter of anthropology. These kinds of questions are what keep anthropologists at their task of describing, preserving, and understanding the ways of life of various groups of human beings.

What Is Anthropology?

Anthropology is the comparative study of humans and their cultures. It is not necessary to travel to the forests of South America, or Africa, or New Guinea to pursue anthropology. Modern anthropologists may be found at work in cities throughout the world and in situations that are familiar to almost every college student. For example, two anthropologists, a man and a woman, made a bar and its barmaids in an American city the locus of their research.[2] Like Chagnon, they employed what has become known as the outstanding methodological characteristic of anthropology—*participant observation.* Using this technique, the investigator lives among the subjects he or she is studying, taking part in the activities of their daily lives and studying their social interactions. Brady's Bar, a college hangout of sorts, provided the raw data for James Spradley and Brenda Mann's analysis of how women's roles are perceived by men. In Brady's Bar, certain jobs were done by men and certain others by women. The bartenders who mixed the drinks were always male; the people who took the orders and delivered the drinks to the customers were always female. Among the Yanomamö, as among the habitués of Brady's Bar, the women do the heavy work (gathering firewood is one of the major chores of Yanomamö) and must cater to the desires of the men by, among other things, serving them food and drink. Thus anthropologists not only study small-scale groups in faraway places untouched by Western culture, but they also study small groups in modern cities. Brady's Bar is just as valid a place in which to study

1. From Napoleon Chagnon, *Yanomamö: The Fierce People,* 2nd ed., pp. 4–6. Copyright © 1977 by Holt, Rinehart and Winston. Reprinted by permission of Holt, Rinehart and Winston.

2. James Spradley and Brenda Mann, *The Cocktail Waitress: Woman's Work in a Man's World* (New York: John Wiley, 1975).

An anthropologist may study town life—the intermingling of different people, the economic function of the town for the hinterland, or even the relationship of the local architecture to the culture of a group.

human behavior as is a tribal village in New Guinea. Anthropology can be done wherever there are groups of people.

The data from the Yanomamö and Brady's Bar allow us to speculate whether a division of labor by sex is found, in one form or another, in all human groups throughout the world. The data may also provide a basis for making certain gen-

eralizations about male-female relationships. The validity of such generalizations should be tested by comparing male-female relationships in many different groups. Such work is the province of cultural anthropology. But before pursuing a discussion of the subject matter, aims, and methods of cultural anthropology, it is best to look at the discipline as a whole.

The Discipline of Anthropology

Anthropologists usually divide the study of their discipline into four specialties: physical anthropology, cultural anthropology, anthropological linguistics, and archeology. All four specialties have the study of the human species as their subject matter; each field uses the holistic approach. In other words, anthropologists study the entire aspect of human behavior as a whole—hence the use of the term *holistic*. Suppose, for example, an anthropologist were interested in the dance. The strategy would not be to record the music and the steps, bring home a reproducible choreography, and perhaps perform it or publish a text with pictures. Rather, the anthropologist would study the whole culture of a group, record the music and steps of the dancing, and relate the dance to every aspect of the culture: Under what circumstance is the dance performed? by whom? at what time of year? to what purpose? The result would be an entire account of the group with a special emphasis on their dancing.

Human biology, psychology, and sociology—the disciplines closest to anthropology—are all concerned with the human species. Anthropology, however, is the only discipline that studies people in the light of their entire culture; in every area of the world; among industrialized people or those with the most minimal technol-

Affection between mother and daughter seems to be a universal. Is the warm and relaxed feeling shown by this Senegalese family unusual or common in their culture?

ogy; in every historical epoch; from primate beginnings to the present day.

Physical Anthropology

Let us consider physical anthropology first. Human beings are animals, and all animals have certain features that help them adapt to their physical habitat. Physical anthropologists study human genetics as well as physical variations among human populations. In this respect, physical anthropology is quite close to biology. Indeed, a physical anthropologist must be as well versed in many aspects of human biology as a member of that discipline. Physical anthropologists also study the evolution of humankind's ancestors—and of the modern primates, the contemporary animal species that share a common ancestry with human beings. Such phenomena as genetic mutations, disease resistance, human physical variations in such areas as growth and development, sex differences, and the behavior of non-human primates are merely a few of the concerns of physical anthropology.

As far as we can tell from the available evidence, humankind has been on this earth for several million years. During this time, human organisms have undergone significant biological changes. Increased brain size, decline in importance of certain teeth, and an improved capacity for standing upright are examples of these changes. The physical anthropologist can tell us about our biological heritage and make an estimate of our possible further development.

Whatever the field of expertise, the physical anthropologist is concerned with biology in relation to behavior in a society. A physical anthropologist studying the Yanomamö would ask such questions as, for example, Is there a genetic explanation for their violent ways? What is the effect of their diet on the development of their bodies? What are the physiological mechanisms that allow them to adapt to life in a tropical environment? What is their biological relationship to neighboring peoples? In the last case, studies of blood types and physical features of the people (shape of the head, hairiness of the body) might allow the physical anthropologist to determine that the Yanomamö are biologically close to other Indians in the area. Or have they, perhaps, migrated into the area in recent times, which might offer an explanation for their aggressiveness? A major contribution of anthropology centers on the idea of adaptation. Anthropologists have explained how humans have adapted to their environments through physiological changes that have developed in a definite evolutionary sequence.

A related contribution is being made now as physical anthropologists learn more about the biological and genetic factors that affect certain kinds of behavior. Chapters 3 through 6 are devoted to physical anthropology.

Cultural Anthropology

Cultural anthropologists are interested in cultural similarities and differences. As Franz Boas noted, "Cultures are many but Man is one." Traditionally, the way of life of so-called primitive peoples has been the province of cultural anthropology. Perhaps the most important contribution of cultural anthropology has been the realization that there is nothing particularly primitive about these peoples except their technology. In fact, the peoples themselves, upon closer examination, turned out to be much like ourselves. Great intelligence and resourcefulness are required to survive, as do the Yanomamö, in an inhospitable environment with a cultural heritage which includes only a few tools.

By the use of the *comparative*, or *cross-cultural method*, in which practices in one society are compared and contrasted to those in other groups, it becomes possible to determine what is universal to all people. Universal personal and group characteristics are what we mean when we refer to "human nature"—those emotions, those behaviors, those ways of relating to others in the group that can be found among all people everywhere. If some kind of marriage is found among all peoples, the assumption is that it is universal that people should marry. What about religion, play, ornamentation, music, and dance? Is such behavior universal among human beings? Consider other characteristics often defined as universal in our own society, such as war, money for exchange purposes, and competition. Do we find them universally in every society studied by anthropologists? How are issues settled without recourse to violence? How do people obtain needed items from others without money? How do you know who is "best" without competition? Anthropology has learned much from the study of other societies—even those that at first glance seemed backward in their technology. These valuable lessons can be highly useful to students seeking to learn about their own society.

The cultural anthropologist studies living peoples, although he or she will usually require some knowledge of a people's past in order to place their current situation in a proper historical perspective. Many aspects of people's lives are studied:

In Togo, Africa, as in many places, care of the child is often turned over to an older sister.

religious beliefs and behavior, political organization, kinship, family life, technology, arts and crafts, and subsistence patterns are but a few of these. However, a researcher interested in one of the above aspects—for example, political organization—will not study it in isolation from all other aspects of life in that society. To the contrary, the unique perspective of the anthropologist requires that she or he place an interest in political organization within the context of the culture of the group. Do powerful families gain further political control by alliances reinforced by marriages between family members? If this is the case, the anthropologist must study kinship and marriage to determine the extent of alliances or to be able to evaluate politically a particular marriage. Is political power based on economic control in a society? The researcher must study the economy and technology of the group in order to understand its political organization.

Cultural anthropologists do not limit themselves to the study of groups with simple technologies. As we have seen, today they study urban and industrial peoples as well. But as in the study of Brady's Bar, they generally limit themselves to small segments of complex societies in a holistic way—that is, they study the ways of relating and behaving in one environment within an urban society, be it a bar, a street corner, or a small town. Chapter 19 deals with modern urban anthropology. All branches of anthropology are concerned with all of humankind, not just "natives" in a tropical forest far away from "civilization."

Chagnon's study of the Yanomamö involved a detailed examination of all facets of the people's lives as well as special study of the role of violence in their everyday life. The problems encountered by the cultural anthropologist in meeting a strange group are made inescapably clear in the capsule ethnography that opened this chapter. Fortunately, however, not all first encounters are so unpleasant. Indeed, many anthropologists find living with a people who have a different way of life a congenial and highly rewarding personal experience.

Anthropological Linguistics

Language is a phenomenon studied by a variety of specialists ranging from historical philologists to literary critics. The *anthropological linguist* is concerned primarily with languages that have no written form, although written languages are not ignored by any means. The anthropological linguist analyzes a language and its sound system and describes its grammar, structure, and vocabulary. By means of a special set of symbols, a linguist can reduce any language to a written form that can be read by anthropologists from any society.

Anthropological linguists also study the historical relationships among various languages. These relationships, when uncovered, are useful in detailing the historical

The logos of the multinational corporations offer a common vocabulary throughout the world.

development of different cultures, and can be analyzed to provide a means to estimate the time at which one group split off from another. The English language, for example, has its base in a Germanic language, but also includes elements from French as brought by the Normans in 1066. Historical analyses of English show that elements have been added or dropped from usage over a period of time. The relationship that English has with other languages in the Indo-European language family can also be demonstrated.

A detailed linguistic analysis of the Yanomamö is not given in Chagnon's ethnography. However, we do know from other sources that the Yanomamö language is related to languages spoken by other Indians in Venezuela and Brazil. A linguistic analysis of Yanomamö would reveal what things are important in Yanomamö life. For example, the terms that are applied to various kinds of kinfolk might tell us a great deal about social interaction.

Using an instance from the Eskimo language, we note that most Eskimo bands have approximately twenty different words for snow—terms for wet snow, dry powder snow, and so on. Although we all know that snow is important to Eskimos, it is interesting to note the attention the substance is given in the language. Closer to home, most North Americans have a preoccupation with money, hence the many terms used for money: "bread," "dough," "moolah," "bucks," "cash," and so on. We will discuss anthropological linguistics within the broader context of the relation of language and culture in Chapter 15.

Archeology

To the general public, archeology is the field of anthropology most widely known, and perhaps least understood. *Archeology* is the scientific study of the unwritten history of a people based on the excavation and analysis of material remains. Just as physical anthropologists analyze the biological heritage of a people by examining human remains such as bones and teeth, the archeologist explores their cultural heritage by examining material remains such as projectile points (arrowheads), stone tools, or the remains of houses or other forms of shelter. Usually archeologists and physical anthropologists work closely together, especially if the archeologist happens to unearth human remains.

There are two general categories of archeologists: classical and anthropological. Classical archeologists study the remains from our historical past of the great civilizations of the Middle East, Asia, and Europe, such as Sumer or Rome. Classical archeologists are particularly interested in reconstructing historically important sites and finding objects with aesthetic value. The anthropological archeologist, on the other hand, although not indifferent to any *objets d'art* that may be found, seeks out the more commonplace remains—of great and small cultures. The anthropologist searches for the minutiae of daily life from which not only to determine how the site looked when it was occupied, but to reconstruct the culture of the people who inhabited the site at different periods of time. This type of archeology is being done at Indian sites all over the United States and Canada. The goal of modern anthropological archeology is to determine from the remains of people long since gone the nature of their way of life, including their technology and even their kinship system.

Archeologists reconstruct the behavior patterns of past cultures by analyzing cultural remains. Here, an archeologist on a dig removes cultural objects from an excavation trench.

To our knowledge, no archeological examination of the Yanomamö has ever been done. If, however, such a task were to be undertaken, it would greatly increase our understanding of these contemporary Indians. An excavation of an ancient settlement could give us a good idea of migrations of the people within their physical habitat. If it were possible to determine significant matters such as kinship systems from the excavated artifacts, this would allow anthropologists to see if and how the early Yanomamö differed from the present-day Yanomamö. Since the Yanomamö, like many peoples, have not developed a written language, their history comes to us through the tales and myths passed down from generation to generation. Archeological data might provide additional knowledge of the history of these people. Chapters 7 to 9 are devoted to archeology, and archeological methods are covered in Appendix A.

An Interdisciplinary Approach

In practice, anthropologists ignore the boundaries between the different specialties. In accordance with the holistic view, it is usual for anthropologists to need and use knowledge that "belongs" to a field or area of specialization that is not their own. The proliferation of knowledge in recent years has made it virtually impossible for any one anthropologist to know all that can be known about a given human population or a given topic. Hence, specialists in the different areas of anthropology frequently collaborate with each other; likewise, anthropologists frequently collaborate with specialists from fields outside of anthropology. For example, one author of this book, Joseph Aceves, has been working since 1966 on a study of rural development programs in a number of villages in central Spain.[3] The problem in which he is interested centers on the refusal of the farmers to join agricultural cooperatives while at the same time acknowledging that cooperatives would benefit them in many ways. In this work, he has used the knowledge and assistance of a number of different specialists.

Although his area of specialization is cultural anthropology, Aceves used some archeological data to help put the history of the village and its area in the proper time perspective. Part of the research involved tracing the development of agricultural practices; evidence obtained from nearby villages by Spanish archeologists, for example, indicated that wheat was introduced into the area about 2,000 years ago. Data from physical anthropology indicated that people were physically smaller and weighed less in the eighteenth century than today, a fact that was useful in understanding certain construction practices the villagers had used in building their houses. The use of anthropological linguistics was helpful in examining the

basic values of the villagers. For example, prior to any understanding of why the villagers rejected farm production cooperatives, it was necessary to understand what Spaniards meant by such frequently used words as *serio*. This word, literally translated into English, means "serious," but in Spanish it implies much more; *serio* as an adjective suggests a certain dignity in speaking, dressing, and interacting with social equals, superiors, and inferiors. Perhaps cooperatives were not a sufficiently weighty or socially appealing enterprise for the Spanish farmers of El Pinar.

During the course of the research, a Spanish psychologist was consulted for information about the use of psychological tests to examine various personality traits of the people. The same psychologist, a daughter of a local physician, later helped to interpret the test results. Several physicians provided information about dietary habits. Many villagers suffered from severe gastrointestinal ailments. These could be traced to a diet consisting mainly of carbohydrates and insufficient protein.

Forestry specialists provided information on the effects of certain conservation practices the villagers used in the pine forest surrounding the town. Since many villagers earned their income working in the woods extracting raw resin from pine trees that would later be refined into resin derivatives such as turpentine and tar, it was imperative for the anthropologist to understand the technology associated with forest use.

The history of an area can shed light on current practices, and so a number of Spanish historians provided data on how the village had been governed in the past. These data were useful in contrasting what had happened in the past with current

3. Joseph Aceves, *Social Change in a Spanish Village* (Cambridge, Mass.: Schenkman Publishing, 1971).

Chapter One

events in the village. A Spanish rural sociologist, involved in a land reform project in the area of the village, provided information on the major demographic characteristics of the village and its region, data that included birth rates, death rates, migration into and out of the village, and a wealth of statistical information on almost every aspect of village life. Some of the results of Aceves' research are given in Chapter 18 as part of the discussion of cultural change.

Gaining knowledge is the anthropologist's prime concern, and most anthropologists, regardless of their special interests, are eclectic. In other words, they use whatever knowledge and research techniques are available in order to solve the problems they are investigating.

Fieldwork Methods in Anthropology

The cultural anthropologist studies people by direct observation. Relying for the most part on his or her eyes and ears, the investigator listens, watches, and makes careful notes. It is the most ancient method of collecting data. Five hundred years before the birth of Christ, Herodotus, the Greek historian, watched and listened to different peoples of the ancient world and recorded their myths, religious rituals, their seemingly quaint and bizarre customs, noted their dress, their agricultural practices, and their manufactures. Not only was Herodotus the first historian to leave a written record, but he was perhaps the first anthropologist. He saw the history of a people within the context of their culture and traditions.

Today cultural anthropologists go out "into the field" just as Herodotus did. The "field" may be the highlands of New Guinea, the *barrios* of Mexico City, or the ghettos of Washington, D.C. The method, though it is generally adapted to the individual anthropologist, is the same in each case.

In addition to eyes and ears, the anthropologist may use a tape recorder, movie and still cameras, and other recording devices. The principal aid, however, is the intimate knowledge of a people that comes from living among them for a long period of time. Fieldwork is distinct from the laboratory experiment of the psychologist. In such an experiment, the investigator places subjects in situations requiring the performance of certain tasks. The investigator then introduces factors designed to affect the subject's performance, and finally measures the effect of these factors on the behavior of the subject. The anthropologist, by contrast, "goes native" and studies people in their natural habitats. Cultural anthropology is people-oriented, relying far less than, for example, sociology on statistics and abstractions. Fieldwork in cultural anthropology is based on face-to-face contact and the participation of the researcher in the everyday life of the people being studied. It is essential, therefore, that the investigator learn the language of the group he or she is living with. In addition to being able to communicate with informants, knowing the language enables the anthropologist to pick up the innuendos that an interpreter cannot convey, and to listen to gossip that reveals much about the culture.

Fieldwork in physical anthropology is extremely different, and some of these differences are discussed below. The field methods of the archeologist are described in Appendix A.

Fieldwork in Cultural Anthropology

Rather than enumerate a long list of general and specific do's and don't's about operating in the field, it may be well to discuss some of the common problems and techniques within the context of a specific research project. This project was begun by Aceves during 1966–1967 and has continued to the present day through shorter periods of fieldwork. The work was done in a Spanish peasant district in the province of Segovia and involved fourteen villages of the district that were undergoing a series of fairly rapid and extensive technological and social changes. The basic scientific aim was to study patterns of resistance to change in agriculture.

The project has several aspects worth discussing in detail; it is more or less typical of fieldwork as far as personal adaptations, problems with informants, and general methodology are concerned. In general, the types of research tactics used were those fairly common to researchers in all kinds of cultures, from the most remote small-scale society to the most complex urban neighborhood. Indeed, similar problems had been encountered in a Puerto Rican neighborhood in Massachusetts, a rural county in Illinois, and a rural area of Texas.

PREPARING FOR THE FIELD. The first step in fieldwork is to get into the field. For some people this may involve a short train, plane, or automobile trip. Some urban anthropologists commute from their homes to their area of study on the other side of town. It is preferable, however, to live in the neighborhood being studied.

It is often quite expensive just to travel from one's home to the field. The other major expense is that of maintaining oneself for a year or more without an income. Thus, most cultural anthropologists have their research subsidized in whole or in part by grants from various government agencies, such as the National Science Foundation, or from private foundations, such as the Wenner-Gren Foundation for Anthropological Research. This requires the preparation of a grant proposal that outlines the theoretical significance of the research, the location, the methods to be used, the time period of the research, and a budget to cover the expenses of the researcher and assistants, if any. The writing of the grant proposal requires that researchers do a great deal of preparation. Such preparation can prove useful when they go into the field. They must read up on everything available about their topic and about "their people." Fieldworkers supplement this "book" knowledge by talking to or corresponding with anthropologists or others who have firsthand knowledge of the area and the people. Most anthropologists are cooperative and willing to share their knowledge with a colleague. Only a few refuse such help or, even worse, attempt to keep a prospective researcher out of "their" area, sometimes with good reason, sometimes not. There is a kind of unwritten code in the profession that one does not work on another person's "turf," at least not without that person's approval. This code is waived when a long period of time has passed since the original research in the area was done. One of the problems arising from this attitude is that restudies of communities by scholars who did not participate in the original research are rare, and all too often all that we know about a people is based on the work of one anthropologist. Assuming, then, that the proposal has been approved and funds are available, the fortunate cultural anthropologist is ready to leave for the field.

ENTERING THE FIELD.   We shall skip over the specifics regarding travel and supplies, except to note that usually some problem crops up about how to get to a place and what supplies to take. Since Aceves was going to an accessible location with readily available supplies, he took only clothing, a camera, and a small portable typewriter. He traveled by air to Geneva, where he picked up a Volkswagen and drove for several days down to El Pinar, the Spanish village in which he would live. A researcher going to a more remote area might have to pack in supplies, hire porters, and worry about the erratic schedules of local transportation companies.

After the researcher finds a place to live and food to eat, the important problem becomes that of explaining the reason for being there. This latter has three related components: *Why* are you here?, Why are *you* here?, and Why are you *here*?

Here the researcher faces a dilemma: What do you say? The answer is to tell the truth in such a way that those to whom you are talking can understand it. Aceves's explanation was that he was interested in studying how the village had changed since 1949, when he first went there, and that he wanted his people in America to know how Spaniards really live. These responses proved satisfactory to his audience and had the further advantage of being the truth. But how could he afford to do this, they asked. Except for local

schoolteachers and a few professionals, nobody in the district understood about research grants, and they actually refused to believe that part of Aceves's expenses were paid from a fund set up by the Rockefeller family. Why, they asked, would a Rockefeller give him money to come over here? An explanation based on the value of scientific research was not widely accepted. Why does Rockefeller care about us with all the money he has? Aceves then explained income tax write-offs and said that if the Rockefellers did not do things like this, the money would be taken by the government in taxes. That they understood.

There are times when one claims status as an anthropologist and finds that it works against him. This is particularly true in American Indian groups where the American Indian movement has made inroads and where the anthropologist is seen as a tool of the dominant white groups who use anthropological knowledge to keep the Indians "in their place" or to exploit them. Some other anthropologists have been suspected by local people of being spies or tax assessors. This was no problem in Spain—at least not for Aceves, even in villages where he was unknown at first.

The fact is that few people, even in the United States, England, or Canada, know what an anthropologist is or does. In the southwestern United States, anthropology is thought by the public to mean digging up Indian ruins. In Europe, the term "anthropology" is synonymous with what Americans call physical anthropology, and several educated people asked Aceves if he was measuring heads. Others, knowing that anthropologists deal with so-called primitives, felt insulted and demanded that Aceves go "to Africa" to do his research. In addition to these kinds of misunderstandings, there are some that seem highly improbable—until they happen. Aceves was introduced by a friend to a group of men, mostly fairly elderly civil servants, and one of the older men asked what he did. In his best Spanish, Aceves said he was *un antropólogo*. There was a definite stir in the group as the man looked rather taken aback and, after a pause, inquired, "Are there many of you in your country?" Aceves's answer was that there were probably only about seven or eight thousand people like him in the world. Aceves's friend, seeing something was wrong, took the man aside to see what was troubling him about the anthropologist. It turned out he had a hearing problem and thought Aceves said he was *un antropófago*, that is, an anthropophage or a cannibal. The mixup was straightened out, but thereafter Aceves simply said he was a professor who was writing a book and left out the details unless specifically asked for them.

What is an appropriate role for the anthropologist in a community? In El Pinar and surrounding villages, the role had to be defined mutually by Aceves and the people, with the latter having the larger say in the definition. Their definition was made in accordance with his activities; therefore an anthropologist is a foreigner, who does, however, speak good Spanish, who is writing a book about the people and who gets his material doing strange things, like helping people who don't belong to his family thresh wheat for no pay, driving all over the area asking people all sorts of questions, sitting half the late afternoon in the bars playing cards with the old men, and doing weirder things such as constantly whipping out a tape measure to measure adobe bricks or the width of the road through the forest. Until Aceves started doing his typing for several hours during the *siesta*, his status was defined as one who did not really work. It was difficult for the farmers to conceive of what he was doing as real work. But the fact that his typewriter could be heard while others rested and that he acted as though he were working soon led them to accept him as one who did, in fact, have to work to earn a living.

Aceves's fullest acceptance by the people of the district came after they made the judgment that he had learned enough about their way of life so that ignorance was not acceptable as an excuse for his blunders. Aceves knew that such a judgment was made when one day he was told by some older men that he had no need to put up with the mulish behavior of the town plumber, who would never come to fix the drains despite repeated promises to do so. Taking the hint, Aceves verbally chastised him and thereby gained his respect and the respect of the others in El Pinar. The incident is trivial in itself, but it has symbolic significance in that it marked Aceves's transition. In the eyes of the community he had moved from childhood and adolescence to adulthood in their world: he could thenceforward be regarded as a man.

Fieldwork in Physical Anthropology

Some physical anthropologists specialize in unearthing the fossil remains of our early ancestors. These *human paleontologists* dig in the earth for skeletons which they then reconstruct. They may also work with physicists and geologists, using various chemicals and radioactive substances, to determine the ages of the specimens removed from the earth. Other physical anthropologists are more closely related to biochemists in that they do the bulk of their work in laboratories, analyzing substances found in the bodies of primates, including humans. These scientists use microscopes and other laboratory equipment to study blood, urine, and other biochemicals. Their aim is to find variations in these substances—and the causes of the variations—among different human and nonhuman primates.

Some anthropologists may live in a tropical jungle for years at a time, studying the behavior and social lives of chimpanzees, gorillas, or other primates. These *primatologists* are seeking clues about the ways our early ancestors may have adapted to similar environments and the effects such adaptations may have had on anatomy and behavior. These investigators use many of the techniques of the cultural anthropologists—natural observation that sometimes includes participant observation, pen and pencil, tape recorders, cameras, and other recording devices.

Other physical anthropologists focus on *anthropometry,* which is concerned with techniques to measure various parts of the human body, including head, face, trunk, and skeleton. The results of such studies are helpful in designing clothing for large groups of people, as well as for the design of furniture, automobiles, airplanes, and other similar products. A related specialty is the study of those aspects of human biology concerned with our development and growth from the prenatal state through old age and death. *Biological anthropologists* work with biologists, embryologists, and other life scientists, using microscopes, radioactive chemicals, and X-rays to study physical changes in the human body (weight, height, and body composition and build, for example) over time.

The Anthropological Perspective

Basic to each discipline is a set of assumptions about the world and about the subject matter of the discipline. Anthropology, like other disciplines, is based on concepts and sets of assumptions concerning these concepts. The purpose of this book is to acquaint the reader with the major concepts of the field. *Culture* is one such concept, and the most widely used one in anthropology.

Culture as an anthropological concept refers to all the learned behavior of any human being and the products of such behavior. As you progress through the text, the meanings that anthropologists attach to the concept *culture* will become increasingly clear. There are, however, certain assumptions about culture by anthropologists which must be made explicit.

1. Cultural anthropologists make the cultures of different human groups their chief object of study. They make culture the object of research, although a great deal of any culture exists in the minds of people. Cultural anthropologists have evolved the aforementioned *fieldwork* methods to observe and record the various manifestations of a culture.

2. Anthropologists submit that the average member of any human group has the same potential for learning a culture as the member of any other human group; that skin color or sex does not affect intellectual capacity.

3. Most anthropologists assume that no group of people can be condemned for their culture; that no culture is intrinsically good or bad. This doctrine is called *cultural relativism*. However, many anthropologists do make value judgments. In her autobiography, *Blackberry Spring*, for example, Margaret Mead stated that any culture that actively rejected infants was a bad culture.

This issue will be discussed briefly below, but will be encountered repeatedly throughout the book.

Ethnocentrism

One could argue that the history of anthropology has been the history of the struggle to achieve greater objectivity by obtaining greater understanding of other societies and other cultures. For the most part, systematic inquiries into human nature have been colored by *ethnocentric* explanations, that is, explanations in which the scholar's own moral system formed the basis by which other phenomena were judged. Implicit in ethnocentrism is the notion that one's own system of doing things is usually better than some other group's system. Thus, the Spanish conquistadores under Cortez could look at Tenochtitlán, the Aztec capital (a city with a population of more than 100,000, with a complex system of streets, canals, and sewage disposal facilities as well as a complex system of laws governing the inhabitants' behavior) and still call the Aztecs "savages." They made such a judgment at a time when Spain was in chaos and Madrid was a remote, rural adobe village with a population of approximately 3,000.

Ethnocentrism interferes with understanding others and with the ability to look at one's own culture with any degree of objectivity. Ethnocentrism is a cultural universal, but one of the contributions of anthropology has been to develop a less ethnocentric perspective. An aspect of this perspective is that anthropologists find it just as valid and important to study the religious, political, or economic behavior of a small-scale society consisting of 100 souls as to study the behavior of a complex society of many millions.

The Yanomamö provide another example of ethnocentrism. According to their mythology they were the first people to be created. They view other peoples as a degeneration of the Yanomamö. Of course, it is not humanly possible for any social scientist to be totally free of any ethnocentric bias. Ethnocentrism in varying degrees is a feature for which even some of the most outstanding theorists in anthropology have been criticized. The opposite of ethnocentrism is cultural relativism.

Cultural Relativism

In 1724 a French priest, Father J. F. Lafitau, described the culture of North American Indians. Although it contains many factual errors, this report is significant today because of its point of view, which was considered radical at the time it was written. Father Lafitau insisted that alien ways of life should be observed and described not according to the prevailing European standards of what is proper and moral, but by a consideration of the conditions under which these ways of life exist.

This notion, *cultural relativism*, holds that the culture of a people should be approached with respect although it·may differ from one's own. Evaluations of a people's way of life are outside the realm

This photograph, "Answering the Signal," by Rodman Wanamaker, made in the early 1900s of a people already ravaged by industrial society, forms part of the record of the Plains Indian culture.

of a scientific discipline. For example, the practices and customs of one people, such as the Yanomamö, can be understood only within the context of that people's culture. The ferocity of the Yanomamö, however repugnant to an American, makes sense to the Yanomamö in the context of their specific cultural situation. To further a basic understanding of people such as the Yanomamö—or to further people's understanding of themselves, for that matter—anthropologists try to avoid value judgments in their professional research and reporting. Cultural relativism will be discussed at greater length in Chapter 2.

An Ideological Perspective

The study of human behavior is biased by the philosophy of the individual. This philosophy, in turn, is biased by the standards and traditions of the human group of which an individual is a member. Pure objectivity is impossible to achieve, since any view of humankind is filtered through the perspective of the culture of any single individual, modified by that person's own idiosyncrasies. Even a scientific viewpoint is biased, because science itself makes certain assumptions about the nature of reality. One assumption of science, for example, is that there is an order to the

Introducing Anthropology

universe which can be discovered and explained.

There is nothing wrong with such biases, especially since they are unavoidable. To use a less emotionally loaded term than "bias," we can say that anthropologists and other scientists operate within an ideological framework. *Ideology*, as we use the term, means a set of ideas about the nature of reality. Since everyone, including anthropologists, has a set of ideas —concepts, assumptions, ideologies— about the nature of the world, it seems best to state them at the outset rather than to claim objectivity.

The *ideological perspective* taken in this book is that humans—as individuals and as groups—have developed ways of adapting to their physical and social habitats. Furthermore, individuals and groups are able, in many cases, to choose from among alternative modes of behavior in given situations. We will use the words *adaptations* and *alternatives* in reference to this anthropological perspective. We will deal in detail with these concepts in Chapter 2. While the ideology that we outline may not be useful or valid in every attempt to explain why people do what they do, we feel that it provides a useful and thought-provoking introduction to anthropology.

The Historical Background of Anthropology

The ideologies of anthropology—and there are more than one—have deep roots in the past. Before we can use the ideological perspective of adaptations and alternatives, we need to know something about these earlier views, some of which are quite valid and have survived today in more sophisticated forms. Anthropology is the child of what is called the Western tradition, that is, the interrelated set of ideas about humankind that developed in the Greek, Roman, and Western European areas of the world, with some input from Arabic sources. What follows, then, is a brief outline of some of the major ideologies, and of the major scholars who have contributed to the development of the discipline and have advanced it to where it is today.

The Beginnings

Anthropology is a relatively new science. Although speculations about the nature of humankind and of human experience date back to the beginning of written history, anthropology did not come into being until the latter part of the nineteenth century.

Stimulated by the discoveries of exotic groups by various explorers in the two preceding centuries, nineteenth-century scholars became concerned with human evolution—the stages by which humankind presumably had made a physical and cultural transition from a "state of nature" to civilization. While the influence of Charles Darwin's *On the Origin of Species*, published in 1859, was enormous, Darwin's main contribution had been to apply natural selection to biological evolution and to provide evidence for natural selection in nature. Darwin's ideas are discussed in detail in Chapter 4. The notion of cultural evolution itself actually predated Darwin by several centuries. Virtually all of these evolutionary theories were based on unilinear cultural evolution. *Evolutionism* is the idea that there was a set of "stages" through which all groups or peoples had passed or would pass, from the simplest to the most complex level.

For example, a Spanish priest, José de

Acosta, who had been in the New World during the 1570s and 1580s, postulated a three-stage cultural evolutionary scheme. Civilization was the highest stage, characterized by a system of writing and well-organized political system; as an example, de Acosta cited China. The stage below civilization was barbarism, of which the Aztecs were an example. The lowest stage, savagery, was typified by the Carib Indians who had neither writing nor a complex political system. The Yanomamö, had they been known at the time, certainly would have been classified as savages.

This three-part scheme was restated in various ways by scholars who were probably unfamiliar with the rather obscure work of de Acosta. Among the most important of these evolutionists were Lewis Henry Morgan, an American lawyer, and Sir Edward Tylor, a British scholar. While Morgan's scheme is nearly identical to de Acosta's, Tylor's focus was primarily on the development of religious systems. According to Tylor, religious systems also "evolved" from the lowest stages of animism (which holds that nature is alive), to polytheism (belief in more than one god), and finally to monotheism (belief in one god).

The years from 1860 to 1900, a significant period of colonial expansion, saw a great surge of evolutionary thought, primarily in England and the United States. The whole notion quickly became wrapped in ethnocentric judgment: Victorian gentlefolk held civilization to be normally superior to barbarism and barbarism to be better than savagery.

SOCIAL DARWINISM. After Darwin's publication of *On the Origin of Species*, a number of scholars became concerned with the idea that social life was a struggle for existence, with victory going to the "fittest" individuals in a given society. Those who subscribed to this view were dubbed, appropriately enough, *social Darwinists*. Among the most prominent of the social Darwinists was the British philosopher and sociologist Herbert Spencer (1820–1903). Spencer believed that natural selection acted on individuals in a particular society; those who competed best survived and produced offspring. As a result of this continued reproduction of superior individuals at the expense of the inferior, the society gradually improved. Thus, said the social Darwinists, societies, like plants and animals, evolve through the agency of natural selection.

An obvious conclusion to be drawn from this theory was that some societies were better than others and that all of the peoples of the world could be arranged on an evolutionary continuum according to their stages of technological and social development. A hierarchy of races became generally accepted in Europe and North America wherein the "white" race was seen as superior to the "yellow" race, which, in turn, was seen as superior to the "black" race. The race to which an individual belonged was determined by measuring certain physical factors, such as the size and shape of the head or the amount and type of hair on the body. The whole system of such measurements became so intricate that quite frequently two brothers could be classified as members of different racial groups.

Today, this type of racism is generally regarded by anthropologists as an idiocy of the past, but until the impact of modern genetic studies by biologists and physical anthropologists, race served as an "explanation" for differing behaviors by different peoples until the 1940s. However, some scholars still feel that there is a racial or genetic basis for behavior. These questions are dealt with in Chapter 6.

DIFFUSIONISM. In addition to evolutionism and social Darwinism, the nineteenth-century anthropologists also emphasized the notion of *diffusion*—that is, the spread of various elements of culture, behavioral and material, from one human group to another. The diffusionists were especially prominent in Great Britain, where such scholars as G. Elliot Smith and W. H. R. Rivers argued that higher levels of civilization originated in ancient Egypt and then spread to other parts of the world.

The basic notion underlying diffusionism was that human beings are essentially unimaginative and uninventive. The British diffusionists thus rejected the possibility that similar inventions could rise independently of each other in different parts of the world. They denied, for example, the independent origins of agriculture (see Chapter 8) and the first civilizations (see Chapter 9). Instead, they argued for a single invention—in one place and at one time.

Modern-day diffusionism admits the probability that different peoples may arrive at similar or parallel inventions in different places and at different times without cultural exchange. This concept is known as *independent invention*. Indeed, the concept of diffusion, stripped of its nineteenth-century focus, is used today in discussions of social, historical change.

Twentieth-Century Trends

At around the turn of the century, the "line of descent" of anthropology in Britain began to diverge from that in America. Perhaps the single most influential figure in American anthropology was Franz Boas (1858–1942), a German scientist, who came to North America as a graduate student with the intention of studying the color of sea water. Boas pursued his studies in the Arctic, where he observed the Eskimo and Indian groups of the region. Captivated by the customs of these peoples, he soon gave up physics to pursue *ethnology*, the collection of empirical data about the technology and culture of groups.

Boas was aghast at the theories that had sprung from the minds of the nineteenth-century evolutionists. He believed that much of their data were useless and inaccurate since they came from second- and even third-hand sources, such as explorers, missionaries, and traders. Boas thought that cultural similarities might be the product of dissimilar historical, environmental, and psychological factors. Therefore, it was crucial to collect as much historical material as possible. He advocated first-hand research and the gathering of detailed data before making any generalizations about people's ways of life. Furthermore, in his book, *The Mind of Primitive Man* (1911), he demonstrated that differences among humans arise from cultural characteristics rather than from inherent racial characteristics. These contributions gave American anthropology an anti-evolutionary bias that dominated the field until the end of World War II.

FUNCTIONALISM. While Boas and his students were reshaping anthropology in the United States, another major development in this discipline was taking place in

*Few cultures remain intact today, unaffected by the modern industrial states.
This game of checkers, for example, is being played by two Hawaiians in a
re-created village in Honolulu.*

France and Britain. This was the rise of *functionalism.* The functionalist orientation is considered by many investigators to be basic to contemporary anthropology, particularly to ethnology. In very general terms, the functionalist position states that each trait and institution within a culture performs a specific task which serves to hold the social system together. The theory also holds that the structure of a society is determined by the way in which traits and institutions fulfill its needs.

Herbert Spencer was an evolutionist. But he was the first to use "function" as a technical term for the analysis of society. In keeping within the evolutionary tradition, he compared the development of human societies to that of biological organisms with respect to the differentiation of functions required to sustain the proper working of the organisms. In this comparison, the individual members of the society correspond to the cells of an organism.

Later writers drew their analogies from the organs of the human body. The foremost proponent of the organic model was the French sociologist Emile Durkheim (1858–1917). Durkheim was concerned with the concepts of social unity and solidarity. In *The Division of Labor* (1893), he systematically explored the sources of unity that are to be found in the nature of the legal and moral codes ingrained in every society. In smaller tribal societies organized around a simple division of labor based on age and sex differences, all members are bound by a "collective conscience." He called this type of unity *mechanical solidarity*. In complex societies, solidarity results from the interdependence of different parts of society, not from the homogeneity of the whole. Durkheim referred to this unity as *organic solidarity*. Thus, he tried to show that all societies are functionally integrated wholes, with the needs of various parts being satisfied by other parts of the same society.

The two most celebrated proponents of functionalism in British social anthropology have been Bronislaw Malinowski (1884–1942) and A. R. Radcliffe-Brown (1881–1955). Each claimed that his particular brand of functionalism provided a key to the understanding of societies and cultures as wholes, as well as to the understanding of particular institutions.

Malinowski was a Polish anthropologist who had studied in England prior to World War I. When the war broke out, Malinowski was interned as an enemy alien. He was sent to the Trobriand Islands in the western Pacific, where the Australian government allowed him to study the native peoples.

Malinowski's original training had been in physics and mathematics, with subsequent work in psychology. Like Boas, he was an ardent advocate of firsthand field research or participant observation. Whereas Victorian scholars depended on data gathered by secondhand sources, Malinowski believed in observing the natives with his own eyes. He lived with the Trobrianders, spoke their language, and tried to see the world in their terms.

The basic doctrine of functionalism as stated by Malinowski is: "The functional view of culture insists upon the principle that every type of civilization, every custom, material object, idea, and belief fulfills some vital function, has some task to accomplish, represents an indispensable part within a working whole."[4]

The essence of functionalism lies in the notion of a systemic relationship of elements within a whole. Using the functionalist approach, seemingly bizarre customs of "simple" peoples make sense—they are logical extensions of the people's need to adapt to each other and to their environment.

The Englishman A. R. Radcliffe-Brown also developed a form of functionalism. He stated that the function of a custom, or of any other element present in a people's way of life, is to contribute to, or maintain, that way of life. In brief, everything that is functional has a purpose and that purpose is to promote and maintain the social life of the people. Both Malinowski's and Radcliffe-Brown's brands of functionalism have been modified over the years by other scholars, but the basic notions are still very much a part of anthropological theory today.

STRUCTURALISM. An anthropological school of thought that is quite different from functionalism is *structuralism*. This school of thought holds that subconscious mental processes, or "mental structures,"

---

4. Bronislaw Malinowski, "Anthropology," *Encylopedia Britannica*, vol. 1 suppl. (Chicago: Benton, 1926), p. 132.

are the forces behind human behavior. *Structuralism* is most often associated with the writings of the French anthropologist Claude Lévi-Strauss. The word itself is borrowed from structural linguistics. This science is particularly concerned with the "deep structure"—or subconscious mental processes—that influence and determine our use of language. Lévi-Strauss applied the deep structure idea to anthropology, seeking to discover the "mental structures," or ideas, that are responsible for human behavior.

The obvious problem is, how does one discover these immaterial will-o-the-wisps? The key to these structures, says Lévi-Strauss, is in the language of the subjects, The mental structures are revealed in the concepts of *binary opposites*—pairs of opposed ideas which represent the struggle of the mind to impose order on reality and to come to grips with it. Examples of such polar pairs include right versus left, up versus down, cold versus hot, and so on. By analyzing the ways in which a society used such terms, the anthropologist could ferret out important information that would shed light on its cultural beliefs and practices and social organizations. Thus, Lévi-Strauss is interested primarily in cognitive or mental processes. In this respect, then, he is more of a psychologist than an anthropologist. Yet, like his British and French counterparts, he still studies culture—but culture as it is reflected in the native's mind, rather than "culture" on the ground and observable by a fieldworker.

One of Lévi-Strauss's chief theories is that the deep structure of the mind is universal, the same for all people. To support this contention, the French anthropologist embarked on a huge, four-volume study of myths. He believes that myths show the universality of the processes of the mind because a great many myths from different cultures and different periods of time carry the same motifs and structures. It is statistically impossible, he asserts, that so many similar ideas could have been independently produced by so many different cultures. For example, consider creation myths—those that explain how the world came into being. Many creation myths involve the contradictory notion that the earth existed simultaneously before the creation of the universe and was created at the same time as the rest of the universe. Similarly, many myths of origin also tell of a pair of first parents from whom the human race is descended. Moreover, the mythologies of numerous cultures contain some variant of the myth of the great flood which swallowed up all but a few living creatures.

NEOEVOLUTIONISM AND CULTURAL ECOLOGY. In the 1930s, the American anthropologist Leslie A. White (1900–1975) revived the concept of evolution originally held by nineteenth-century scholars. For this reason, White and his followers were labeled *neoevolutionists* by other anthropologists. White's major contribution to evolutionary thought was to relate the development of culture to the amount of energy expended in that culture by means of technology. Thus, White's brand of cultural evolution differs from that of his Victorian predecessors in one important respect: it provides a criterion —the amount of energy generated by a culture in a specific period of time— which can be used to distinguish a culture at one stage of evolution from other cultures at a different stage. White's energy-focused approach generated much controversy at the time. This was due in part to the difficulty of measuring energy utilized in times past. Another criticism centered on the fact that his approach cannot explain why some societies evolve to a high state of complexity, whereas others become extinct.

Like White, Julian Steward (1902–1972) was interested in the relationship between culture and environment. But Steward's idea of cultural evolution was on a much smaller scale than White's. Steward was more interested in *specific* cultures, or groups of cultures, than in *culture* conceived in White's broader terms. Steward called White's theory an example of universal evolution; he then went on to propose a method for dealing with cultural differences and similarities, which he called *multilinear evolution*. This approach enables one to compare parallel sequences of cultural development over widespread and differing geographic and ecological zones. In this way, the investigator can spot similar culture patterns that may have been produced by the same evolutionary processes. Such processes could then be formulated as general evolutionary laws and applied to the development of other cultures. For example, Steward compared the evolution of five areas where civilization is first thought to have appeared: Mesopotamia, Egypt, China, Peru, and Mexico. He noticed that irrigation, flood control, and other water-management techniques associated with intensive agricultural systems were important for the rise of each of the five early civilizations. Furthermore, the religious, social, and military systems of each state were similar and had developed in more or less the same order. This discovery enabled

Winnowing to separate the chaff from the grain can still be observed in Africa today.

him to propose an evolutionary scenario for the five areas consisting of three general stages: the *formative* era, during which the states first appeared and began developing; the *classic* era, during which they expanded and flourished; and the *postclassic* era, during which each state began its decline.

Steward was able to dispel the diffusionist misconception that humankind was essentially uninventive and that all cultures owed their origin to one central source. Because of his insistence on the importance of considering the adaptive relationship between culture and environment, he has come to be known as the founder of cultural ecology.

Cultural ecology is concerned with adaptation on two levels. First, it is the study of the way cultural systems adapt to their total environment. Second—as a consequence of this systematic adaptation—it is the study of the way institutions of a given culture adapt to one another. By focusing on these processes, one can see how different cultural patterns emerge, are maintained, and become transformed. The cultural ecology approach is more fully discussed in Chapter 10.

One school of thought that is closely related to cultural ecology is *cultural materialism*. This approach holds that the maintenance and evolution of a culture depend upon how efficiently it uses its technology, or material products, in adapting to its environment. Anthropologists who call themselves cultural materialists have been inspired primarily by the writings of Karl Marx.

Capitalism, says Marx, is rooted in the unequal control and distribution of material resources. By seeking to understand the nature of the evolution of capitalism as a universally dominant economic system, we can begin to understand the sources of other systems of social stratification and inequality as well. Under the influence of contemporary evolutionists and functionalists, Marx formulated a "law" of cultural evolution. According to Marvin Harris, this law contains a number of major ingredients.[5] The first of these is a division of all societies into an economic base which supports the social organization and ideology of the culture. Second, the social organization and the ideology of a society are explained as

adaptive responses to its economic conditions. Third, all three parts of this system interact with and influence one another in a systematic fashion. Thus, a change in any one of them produces changes in the other two. If a new way of farming is introduced, for example, the new practice will have important effects on the social organization and cultural beliefs of the society.

CULTURE AND PERSONALITY. The 1920s marked the beginning of the encounter between anthropology and the psychoanalytic theories of Sigmund Freud. In essence, anthropologists working in the tradition of culture and personality, under the influence of Freud's theory of human development and psychodynamics, take the view that the personality of individuals is shaped to a great extent by the culture of their society. They are particularly interested in child-rearing practices. Cultures that emphasize different aspects of the human experience will produce different kinds of people. It is the view of the world, as given by the culture, that is important. (See Chapter 2 for a more detailed discussion of personality and culture.) Two of the forerunners of this new approach, which stresses the influence of culture on the personality of the individual members of a society, were Malinowski, and the psychoanalyst Geza Roheim.

Margaret Mead, a student of Boas, wrote on the question of cultural patterning in such areas as differentiation of sex roles and child development. Eventually, two schools of thought about culture and individual personalities emerged. The first approach tried to delineate the so-called *basic personality structure* of a group by looking at its culture, institutions, and

---

5. Marvin Harris, *The Rise of Anthropological Theory* (New York: Thomas Y. Crowell, 1968), p. 240.

projections of itself in fantasy, religion, and art. The second approach, called *modal personality structure*, characterized groups statistically through the analysis of data on individuals, individual documents, behavior, interviews, and psychological tests. This theory was developed by Anthony Wallace in 1952.

Summary

1. Anthropology is divided into four subdisciplines: physical anthropology, cultural anthropology, anthropological linguistics, and archeology. Each subfield uses the holistic approach, studying all facets of human behavior as a whole.

2. Physical anthropologists study the genetics and physical variation among human populations, as well as the evolution of humankind's ancestors.

3. Cultural anthropologists use the holistic method to explore every aspect of people's lives, including religious beliefs and practices, politics, kinship, and family life.

4. Anthropological linguistics is concerned primarily with languages that have no written form. Archeology is the scientific study of the unwritten history of a people based on the excavation and analysis of cultural remains.

5. Specialists in different areas of anthropology frequently collaborate with one another and with specialists from fields outside anthropology.

6. Fieldwork in cultural anthropology is based on face-to-face contact and the participation of the researcher in the everyday life of the people being studied.

7. Fieldwork in physical anthropology is different in a number of respects. Some physical anthropologists are paleontologists who study

fossils, some are interested in the hereditary differences in such physical characteristics as blood types, resistance to disease, the number and kinds of proteins in the body, and so on. Primatologists study the behavior of chimpanzees, gorillas, and other primates in their natural habitats. Finally, biological anthropologists work with other life scientists to study various biological aspects of the human body.

8. Culture as an anthropological concept refers to all learned behavior and the products of such behavior. The notion of cultural relativism holds that the culture of a people should be approached with respect, no matter how different or bizarre it may seem.

9. Ethnocentrism, a notion peculiar to early anthropology and to all human societies, involves the formulation of explanations in which the investigator's own moral system forms the basis on which other cultures are judged.

10. Opposed to ethnocentrism is cultural relativism, the ideological perspective of modern anthropology which holds that humans have developed many different and valid ways of adapting to their physical and social habitats.

11. The earliest anthropologists were interested in discovering how human society developed from the simplest "state of nature" to the most complex civilization. Social Darwinism produced a simplistic view that race provided an explanation for the differing behaviors of different peoples.

12. Believing that human beings are unimaginative and uninventive, the nineteenth-century diffusionists thought that behavioral and material elements of culture arise in unique situations and then spread to other societies in all parts of the world.

13. Franz Boas demonstrated that the contrasts between groups were the result not of racial but of cultural characteristics. His work gave American anthropology its decidedly anti-evolutionary bias in the first half of the twentieth century.

14. English and French anthropologists led by Bronislaw Malinowski developed the theory of functionalism. They believed that every ele-

ment of a culture serves a vital purpose in fulfilling the needs of the society.

15. Structuralists such as Claude Lévi-Strauss concern themselves with the cognitive and mental processes that underlie human behavior. This "deep structure" is universal, they believe, and it is essential for anthropologists to listen to the natives' point of view as well as to make objective observations.

16. According to Leslie White and the neo-evolutionists, the development of culture is related to the amount of energy expended in the culture. Julian Steward and the cultural ecologists have observed cross-cultural seqences of development which reflect the adaptive nature of the relationship between culture and environment.

17. In the cultural materialism of Marvin Harris, culture is regarded as an expression of the interactions of economy, social organization, and ideology. Margaret Mead and others interested in the relation between culture and personality have explored the implications of psychiatric theory for the study of anthropology.

Review Questions

1. Name and define the four subdisciplines of anthropology.

2. The anthropologist frequently uses knowledge from all four specialties of his or her discipline. Give an example of this approach.

3. Explain fieldwork in cultural anthropology. How does it differ from the way psychologists conduct their research? How does it differ from the fieldwork of a physical anthropologist?

4. What are the assumptions that anthropologists make about the concept of culture?

5. What is the connection between cultural relativism and ethnocentrism?

6. Anthropologists today have tried to abandon ethnocentrism in studying preliterate cultures. Explain the ideological perspective of modern anthropology.

Suggested Readings

Anderson, Robert T. *Anthropology: A Perspective on Man.* Belmont, Calif.: Wadsworth, 1972.

This is a humanistic approach to the nature of anthropology and what anthropologists do.

Casagrande, Joseph, ed. *In the Company of Man: Twenty Portraits by Anthropologists.* New York: Harper and Row, 1960.

In this fascinating book, twenty well-known anthropologists describe their encounters with the people they studied. In particular, they each draw a portrait of their main informant, mostly with gratitude and wonder at the understanding and patience each gave to the stranger in their midst.

Frantz, Charles. *The Student Anthropologist's Handbook.* Cambridge, Mass.: Schenkman Publishing. 1972.

In this book, Frantz talks of the professional aspects of anthropology as a career and provides a wealth of information for anyone interested in a career in anthropology.

Golde, Peggy, ed. *Women in the Field: Anthropological Experience.* Chicago: Aldine, 1970.

A dozen American women anthropologists present their personal observations about their work—what they do, how they do it, and how they feel about it.

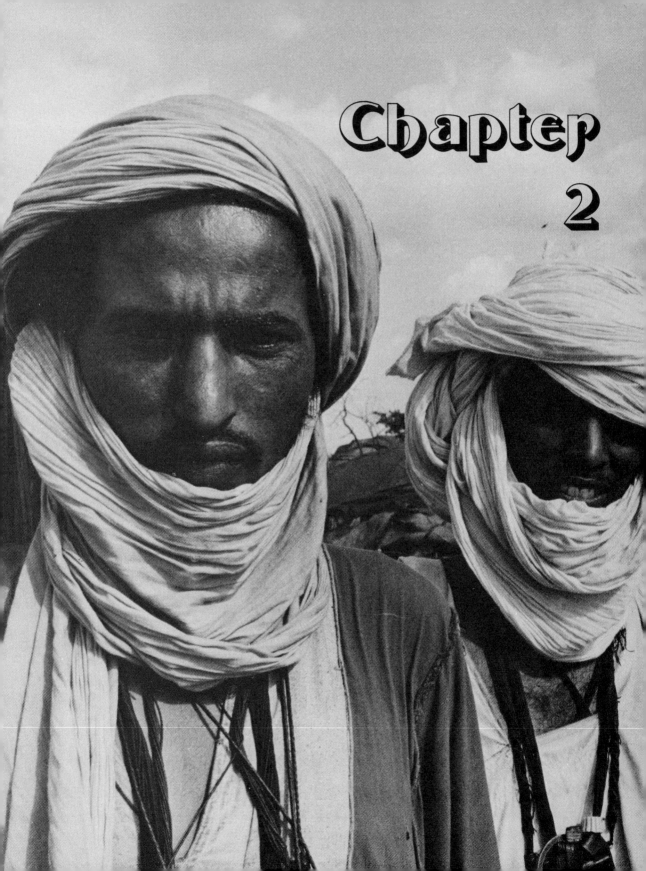

Chapter 2

Culture, Society & the Individual

PERSONALITY STRUCTURE IN THE PLAINS

NATIVE NAME: Cheyenne or Tsistsistas (meaning "the people")
POPULATION: Not known; perhaps 50,000 in the pre-1800 period
ENVIRONMENT: Presently western Montana, eastern Wyoming, and northwest Nebraska. At the high point of the horse culture, during the late 1700s, they lived on the Great Plains, open country west of the Mississippi River and east of the Rockies. Originally the Cheyenne were farmers living in the eastern woodland areas near the Great Lakes.
FIELDWORK: Gladwin based his comparison on work done by E. A. Hoebel in 1935–36 among the northern Cheyenne. Hoebel's fieldwork was based on interviews with older informants. Gladwin also used firsthand accounts by George B. Grinnell, who wrote *The Cheyenne Indians* in the late 1800s.
ETHNOGRAPHIC PRESENT: Approximately 1840–60

Until the horse spread through [the High Plains of North America] often in advance of the white men who had introduced it on this continent, the High Plains were only sparsely populated outside of the few river valleys. Although game, and particularly buffalo, was

---

Source: From Thomas Gladwin, "Personality Structure in the Plains," *Anthropological Quarterly* 30, no. 4 (1957): 111–124. Copyright 1957 by the Catholic University of America Press. Reprinted by permission.

abundant, hunters could not subsist in any numbers in most of the area because of the great distances which separated the sources of water. Hunters wandering in search of a herd could well die of thirst before they made contact with it. There were seasonal hunts carried out into the Plains by those who lived on their peripheries and a few tribes, such as the Querecho described by Coronado's expedition, apparently did live all year in some sections of the area. But the difficulties of traversing the Plains on foot were enough to discourage most of the surrounding tribes from capitalizing on the resources of food represented by the vast herds of buffalo.

The horse removed these limitations. Now it was possible to camp near a stream, range widely each day, probably bring down a few buffalo or antelope, and carry the meat back packed on the horse. The lure of an assured food supply in a free and open country was irresistible. Almost overnight, during the 17th and early 18th Centuries, thousands of people flowed in from all sides to fill the vacuum. As each tribe emerged into this swirling, shifting potpourri of peoples, they repeatedly made contact with others they had never seen before, many of them groups of very different origin from themselves. Occasionally they made peace and an alliance, however informal, with another tribe, though this was rare; the Cheyenne and the Arapaho are an example. More commonly they fought. The horse provided not only the means but a major incentive for highly mobile warfare. This was characterized by hit and run raids, whose principal goals were acquiring honor and stealing horses. All the tribes of the Plains participated in this warfare; it was the most striking common feature of their various cultures, and provided the basic orientation of all of these societies. Whatever may have been their prestige structure before their emergence onto the Plains, in every tribe the people now centered their attention upon the young men of fighting age. . . .

Few of these peoples were culturally equipped for dealing with the problems of horse nomadism before they left their home territories. As a result, they borrowed these skills from their neighbors; despite the state of almost constant hostility which characterized practically all intertribal relations, each new technique which was developed by one group spread rapidly to all the others. Thus in a short time a whole new way of life was evolved and as rapidly taken up by all the Plains tribes. Not only were the technical aspects of warfare and hunting methods so diffused, but also many associated beliefs and attitudes and values, as well as their characteristic social organization in bands, and even ceremonies, of which the Sun Dance is the most familiar.

They apparently acquired the habit of borrowing and could not stop. By the beginning of the 19th century, when the Plains peoples entered their Golden Age of thirty or forty years of untrammelled freedom, all these tribes of so diverse origin shared what was almost a common culture, whose principal values centered on warfare and whose subsistence was based almost exclusively on the vast herds of buffalo (bison) which roamed the prairie.

Mooney, in writing of the Cheyenne, summarizes graphically the degree of transformation undergone by the culture of one of the tribes usually considered to be among the most typical of the Plains societies. He describes the Cheyenne as:

> A sedentary and agricultural people cut off from the main body of their kindred and transformed by pressure of circumstance within the historic period into a race of nomad and predatory hunters, with such entire change of habit and ceremony that the old life is remembered only in sacred tradition and would seem impossible of belief but for the connected documentary proof of fact. . . Practically all that they have today of tribal life and ceremony, excepting the Medicine Arrow rite, has been acquired in the course of this migration, and the oldest things date back not more than two centuries.

With their cultures so uniform and yet so new to each, the question naturally arises whether this new life had the same meaning for all of the Plains peoples. In other words, did they shed their old personalities at the same time that they abandoned their old ways of life?

In order to explore this question, I have selected two of the better known of the typical Plains tribes for examination, the Comanche and the Cheyenne. . . . The Comanche were originally one of the western Plateau Shoshonean tribes, whose home was in southern Wyoming, and whose former humble way of life is still followed by many of the Shoshoni and Paiute, who until recently eked out a bare and rude existence by simple hunting and the gathering of wild berries and roots and seeds. The people wandered in very small economically self-sufficient groups throughout the year, coming together with other bands very briefly in the summer; the need for social organization and social controls was at a minimum. The Comanche carried with them into the Plains this extremely fluid, unstructured and informal way of life.

The Cheyenne, on the other hand, were an Algonkin people, previously sharing the general Woodland culture of the western Great Lakes area. During the 18th century they had moved down to the Missouri River; before they took up the nomad's life they had been for some time in close association with the Mandan, a well-organized agricultural village people like themselves. They brought with them a more structured social and political organization, and a far greater emphasis on ritual and etiquette.

After their establishment among the nomadic horsemen of the Plains, with the revolutionary adaptation to the new cultural patterns and way of life this entailed, it is not surprising to find that the Comanche and Cheyenne also came to share in common a number of new cultural determinants of personality, which we would expect to have had a strong influence in shaping their personalities toward a common pattern. In both we find, as might be expected from their major orientation toward warfare, an emphasis on masculine vitality and courage, which found its ultimate vindication in the terrifying and uncertain moments of the attack. Although in the Cheyenne a very few men could take up the homosexual role of the *berdache*, neither society offered to the majority of youths any approved means of avoiding this test, nor to the adult any permanent respite from the hazardous trials of warfare without shame and loss of status.

In both Comanche and Cheyenne, the major burden of the up-bringing of small children devolved upon their grandparents and their older siblings, real or classificatory, especially sisters. These were the people primarily responsible for imposing disciplines and restraints, though in this respect the Cheyenne leaned rather more heavily than did the Comanche on the grandparents, the older siblings being responsible primarily for only the physical care of Cheyenne infants and children. It might be concluded from the fact that in the Cheyenne siblings had less disciplinary functions than among the Comanche, sibling hostility would be less pronounced in the former than in the latter. However, in keeping with the generally more restrictive nature of Cheyenne social controls, a severe taboo was placed on all relations between adult brothers and sisters in this society, amounting to a ban on even speaking to each other in ordinary circumstances. Consequently, neither hostility nor its opposite could be expected to find overt expression in this relationship.

In keeping with the shifting of the disciplinary functions to siblings and grandparents, the Cheyenne and Comanche parents treated their children not as a different order of beings, but simply as smaller and not yet fully competent adults. The first animal a boy killed in either society was the occasion for great acclaim and compliments from his parents and other adults, as great as if he had brought down a buffalo bull. This pattern was retained for all childhood accomplishments, so that the parents were consistently rewarding agents, while others did the punishing. Not only did this reduce ambivalence in the child's attitude toward those upon whom he was most dependent, his parents, but it also made the transition into adult life extremely easy: there was, to use Benedict's concept, no discontinuity of role between childhood, adolescence, and adulthood. There were no puberty ceremonies for boys in either tribe, though adult status was considered achieved only after the first war party. The psychological effects of this experience were undoubtedly more severe, however, for the Cheyenne boy than the Comanche, for in the former he went out when he was fourteen or fifteen, as against seventeen or eighteen in the latter, and sex experience was denied him until this time, a restriction not imposed upon the Comanche youth.

Despite these several important parallels in childhood development, there was one crucial respect in which they differed fundamentally. Kardiner found that probably the most striking single characteristic of Comanche childhood, adolescence, and adulthood was the almost complete freedom of expression granted to the individual, aggressively, sexually, or otherwise. Sexual conquests provided a major source of adolescent diversion, and even adults found a number of possible channels for such activity. Fights within the group, leading even to killings, were the concern only of the principals and perhaps their close friends and relatives. In the Cheyenne, on the other hand, repression and moderation of all overt emotional expression within the group was the rule, enforced from earliest childhood. These differing points of view found their expression in every aspect of daily life, and it is in consequence of these that we would expect to, and actually do, find the greatest differences between these peoples at the personality level.

The Cheyenne child though enthusiastically rewarded for any achievements reflecting technical skills was severely condemned for any aggression or even undue affection shown in interpersonal relations; at the same time a constant stream of advice and admonitions, particularly from the grandparents but echoed by the parents, served to build up the anxieties associated with such behavior. Though information on childhood sexuality is lacking, it seems almost certain that this too was repressed; we do know that the grandparents began early to warn the child of the calamity for the family if the child, and particularly the daughter, did not marry in the formal and respectable manner through family gift exchange. Such a marriage was made impossible not only if the girl chose to elope, but even if she were unchaste. To be unchaste a girl did not have to have intercourse with a boy; she was defiled if he touched her genitals, or even her breasts. For this reason, a Cheyenne girl after her first menstruation donned a rope and rawhide cover which acted quite effectively as a chastity belt. The woman whose account Michelson published remarked:

> My mother would always tell me that the main purpose of her teaching me, as well as the object of my owning my own bed, was to keep me at home, and to keep me from being away to spend my nights with my girl chum [and hence away from parental supervision]. This was done so that there would be no chance for gossip by other people. . . .
>
> After I was married I thought I would have more freedom in going around with my girl friends, but my mother watched me more closely and kept me near my husband, day and night. This was done to prevent any gossip from my husband's people.

We may contrast this with Linton's comment on the Comanche:

> Sexual play between children began at an early age, and was carried on quite freely as long as the two children were not brother and sister. The Comanche paid no attention to virginity; they took these childhood relations more or less for granted.

The Cheyenne repression of self-expression was particularly emphasized in dealing with parents and other adults. The child was, to use our phrase, to be seen but not heard; he had always to speak quietly, respectfully, and politely in the presence of adults. A breach of this rule brought down the wrath not only of the people involved, but also of the supernatural. . . . Practically the only outlet the society provided the children was in play groups, which during later childhood included both sexes, whose principal activities were elaborate imitations of adult activities, including home life, warfare, and hunting. These play groups were similarly organized in both Comanche and Cheyenne but we may be fairly sure that the anxieties inculcated by the adults carried over into the play situations of the Cheyenne children. . . . Despite these reservations, it seems doubtful that a Cheyenne child could have grown to adulthood with even the limited capacity for self-expression he did show without the warmth of these playmate relationships and the opportunities for ego development they provided. . . .

The concept of the guardian spirit, the personal supernatural helper, was known to both, as it was to all Plains tribes, but their interpretations were totally different. The guardian spirit came to a Cheyenne through suffering: he fasted and prayed, often alone, and frequently inflicted tortures on himself. Even then the vision of the helper, usually an animal, bird or reptile, did not always come; and even when it did come, more often than not it gave advice or foretold the outcome of a projected activity, and left, never to return. Only rarely could a Cheyenne rely upon a guardian spirit of his own to help him in a succession of difficulties. On the other hand, practically every Comanche had his own guardian or "power," upon whom he could call at will; this helper was his for life. And he did not have to suffer to get it. Though a few who wished to obtain the power of a great man already dead spent a night by his grave waiting for the power to come, enduring nothing worse than fright, the usual practice was to ask a man who had the desired power to share it, giving a present in return; occasionally it came uninvited in a dream. Thus the Comanche asked for what he wanted and got it, and could rely upon his power thenceforward; the Cheyenne suffered desperately for the same thing, and was often not rewarded. . . .

Moving into the early adult level of the Cheyenne, we see these childhood and adolescent anxieties concerning interpersonal relationships and particularly sex expressed again in courtship and marriage. Courting techniques were extremely tentative, and even then frightening. The hero of Grinnell's biography stood by the trail covered with a blanket for days just to catch a glimpse of his sweetheart as she went out with the other women to get water. Finally one day she lagged behind and he dared reveal himself. "She stopped and we stood there and talked for a little while. We were both of us afraid, we did not know of what, and had not much to say, but it was pleasant to be there talking to her, and looking at her face. . . . After that, I think she knew me whenever I stood by the trail, and sometimes she was late in coming for water, and I had a chance to speak to her alone." At this time he had already been out on a war party, penetrating to the middle of an enemy camp alone, and was in the society's eyes a man. He went through several more years of indecision before finally marrying her. Again, we may compare Linton's account of the Comanche:

> Boys often talked under the tipi edge to a favorite girl, then pulled out a tipi stake and crawled in to spend a large part of the night in her bed, getting away before dawn if he did not want to marry her. These contacts ended variously. If the couple suspected the opposition of the parents, or if some man had a previous claim, the couple would elope and return after a short time. Generally the marriage would then be accepted. If no opposition was expected, the boy simply slept late in bed with the girl, and the proper behavior for the father when he found them was to make the boy a brief and friendly speech —that is, that he was glad his daughter had found a husband —and invite him to breakfast.

Even after marriage, it was not unusual for a Cheyenne girl to continue to wear her chastity ropes for several weeks. The woman of Michelson's account said, "We had our first child after we had been married a year. It was at this time that I really began to love my husband." The ideal couple did not have a second child for ten years or so, meanwhile remaining continent.

For a Cheyenne girl, the prospect of marriage was often made doubly forbidding by her parents' attempts to marry her off to a man she found personally distasteful. While she could refuse, there was great pressure upon her to avoid the shame for her family which would result from such a refusal, or, even worse, an elopement. The admonitions and veiled threats of years had led up to this moment; most girls gave in, but some, feeling that they would be outcasts from their own family anyway, eloped with someone else, while many were forced into suicide.

An additional fear also colored a Cheyenne boy's attitude toward courtship and marriage: these were only possible after he had been subjected to the terrifying ordeal of going on his first war party; the association between the two was inescapable. The Comanche placed no restrictions on a boy's relations with girls as we have seen, so that the first war party, while perhaps no less frightening, carried no identification with women as threatening creatures.

The anxieties of the Cheyenne were inevitably expressed in unconscious hostility between the sexes, and found clear . . . expression in . . . the custom, described by Llewellyn and Hoebel whereby a man punished an unfaithful wife. Inviting his entire soldier society to a "feast" on the prairie, he brought out the offending girl, and "gave" her to them. All the men who were not related to her raped her in succession; though there are no cases of a death resulting, the girl apparently seldom fully recovered, physically or socially. The authors conclude that "as a gang of individuals reinforcing each other in some off-the-line activity, also possibly, as a release of sex antagonisms by which men could make a woman suffer for her defiance of male authority, it was possible for men to do collectively that which they did not individually hold to be honorable." . . .

Some outlets for aggression were socially sanctioned for the Cheyenne, the most obvious of these being the outward expression of aggression in warfare. But even here there is a contrast with Comanche, for Cheyenne warfare was surrounded with ritual and etiquette, and the highest achievement was not in killing an enemy, but in touching him on the field of battle—counting coup—irrespective of who killed him or even of whether he was dead. Comanche warfare was on a much more free-for-all basis, and most Comanche bands did not count coup at all, striving only to kill the enemy and steal his horses. . . .

In contrast again to the Comanche, if in-group aggression ever became so severe among the Cheyenne that a murder within the tribe resulted, the whole tribe was affected. The sacred medicine arrows were sullied, and a special ceremony had to be performed to renew them before any hazardous undertakings could be made by anyone. The murderer was an outcast within his group, and often fled to the Arapaho until things cooled off. Even on his return he remained in the lowest possible status for the rest of his life; such degradation applied even to war chiefs. These extreme sanctions not only represent another repressive mechanism, but bear witness to the implicit recognition by the Cheyenne of the chaos and carnage which would result if their suppressed hatreds were ever given an opportunity for free expression.

Sorcery is frequently interpreted as symptomatic of aggressive anxieties in a society, and the contrast between these tribes in their attitudes toward sorcery and sorcerors is revealing. While there were sorcerors recognized by the Comanche, they were little feared; if they became too troublesome, an excuse was found and they were simply killed. On the other hand, only a few very powerful medicine men dared practice sorcery among the Cheyenne; but the people greatly feared those who did, and were powerless against them.

It is characteristic of strong hostility at an unconscious level that when its outward expression is blocked, it often turns inward upon the individual in the form of masochism. It is no accident that the Cheyenne reached a peak for the Plains in self-mutilation and torture. The extreme forms consisted in attaching ropes to skewers passed through holes cut in the flesh. These ropes usually ran from a pole to skewers on the chest, and the man would swing about the pole for hours, leaning against the rope and trying to pull out the skewers by breaking the loop of flesh. Or they might be attached to his back, and used to drag a collection of heavy buffalo skulls about. These ordeals were reserved for times of greatest anxiety: for a young man before he led his first war party, or in response to a vow made in requesting supernatural aid during the serious illness of a close relative. They were often performed during the Sun Dance, when power was running high; but they might also be done on a lonely hill, with a vision as a possible reward. For occasions of somewhat lesser anxiety, the cutting of strips of skin from the arms with accompanying ritual sufficed; the typical Cheyenne male had both arms covered with scars from such offerings. In either case the correlation of masochism with increased anxiety and its attendant rise in hostility is clear.

Thus with aggression, as with sex and interpersonal relations in general, we see the Cheyenne deeply inhibited and frustrated, while the Comanche gave full reign to their feelings. Why then, when each took on the common culture, did they interpret it in such diametrically opposite ways?

As we have already seen, the Comanche came onto the Plains with an extremely loose social organization and an almost complete lack of social controls, made possible by the very small social groups typical of Plateau life. When they fell heir to the potentially highly destructive attitudes and techniques of the Plains, most of the aggression which might have been disastrous for their now somewhat larger groupings was directed outside, and their free system permitted what was left to dissipate itself without major damage within the community. . . . The freedom in sexual expression, while not so pronounced for adults as for adolescents, was still sufficient to make marriages highly unstable; however, the organization into still fairly small shifting bands on the Plateau pattern, with an option for families to live alone, was sufficiently fluid to prevent disastrous disruption.

The Cheyenne, on the other hand, emerged from a highly knit agricultural village culture with well structured social controls and an integrated social organization. Faced with the increased potentialities for aggression of warrior life, they channellized and circumscribed their hostilities now just as they had before channellized those which arose from the lesser frictions of sedentary village life, and rigid repression of in-group aggression resulted. Much the same processes were operative in regard to sex, for the informal and unregulated nature of nomadic life made the disruptive potentialities of casual sex relations far greater, and the society had to fortify the superego to compensate for the decreased effectiveness of external sanctions.

These two cultures, though representative, are not all of the Plains; nor have we explored all the ramifications of Kardiner's analysis of the Comanche with which comparisons could be made. But it is clear that the Plains people, for all their cultural homogeneity, were anything but identical in their basic personality structure.[1]

●　●　●　●　●　●　●　●

The capsule ethnography points out some of the ways in which the activities, beliefs, values, and psychology of the Cheyenne changed when they abandoned their agricultural villages to take up the life of nomadic hunters and warriors. The changes reached into every aspect of life; courting, raising children, worshipping the gods. Yet, because of their old traditions, the Cheyenne adapted to their new life in ways that differed from those of their neighbors, the Comanche. Although various groups may have certain activities or objects in common, these elements play different parts in the overall pattern of each group.

The pattern of activities, beliefs, and artifacts that is characteristic of a group is called the *culture* of that group by anthropologists. We may define culture as the totality of the learned and shared patterns of belief and behavior of a human group. This definition is similar to that proposed by the American anthropologist E. A. Hoebel, who defined culture as "the integrated system of learned behavior patterns which are characteristic of the members of a society and which are not the result of biological inheritance." [2] In these definitions of culture, note the following words: totality, learned, shared, belief, behavior; and note the opposition of culture to biological inheritance. Each of these is

important and will be discussed in turn.

Culture is an attribute of a *society*. The arrows of the Cheyenne were a manifestation of their culture; the Cheyenne people constituted a society. Thus, a society means people: a permanent group of people who share a common culture. Each society, by definition, is possessed of a culture. Moreover, each culture is, to a certain extent, unique, differing in its total configuration from all other cultures. For example, although the Cheyenne and the Comanche lived in similar ways, they attached entirely different meanings to almost all aspects of their lives because their cultural traditions differed so greatly.

For the most part, the culture of a society exists in the minds of the members of that society. Artifacts and other products of behavior, such as arrows, irrigation ditches, or burial grounds, are material expressions of a culture. The cultures of different societies form the subject matter of anthropologists, who observe the behavior, beliefs, and artifacts of people in a given society in order to describe their culture.

Characteristics of Culture

All people have certain physiological needs which must be met if they are to survive. Among these are their needs for food and drink and for protection from the extremes of the environment. And in order to develop as human beings, with the ability to communicate conceptually and interact with other human beings, young people need to be cared for, nurtured, and educated by others—needs as important as the physiological ones. A child left alone to survive without the support of other humans does not become human, in the sense

1. From Thomas Gladwin, "Personality Structure in the Plains," *Anthropological Quarterly* 30, no. 4 (1957): 111–124. Copyright 1957 by the Catholic University of America Press. Reprinted by permission.

2. E. Adamson Hoebel, *Anthropology: The Study of Man* (New York: McGraw-Hill, 1972), p. 6.

of knowing a language, having personal and emotional ties to others, and knowing how to behave according to the cultural definitions of his or her own society.[3]

Culture Is Learned

In a vital sense, human beings are born incomplete, that is, without a complete set of instincts to guide them in the ways of living that will enable them to survive. One can say people are "completed" in the process of becoming socialized, a process that anthropologists call *enculturation*. Rather than look for universals—similar patterns or needs that might be the basis for all human behavior—most anthropologists believe that a universal basis for human behavior is the capacity for enculturation—that is, the ability of humans to learn to live according to their own culture.[4]

All humans inherit two means for coping with the challenge of survival. One is *instinctive behavior*, which we receive from our parents along with the capacity and limitations of the human mind and body. The other is *learned behavior*, derived from the cultural traditions of our group. What distinguishes us from nonhumans is not the capacity for learning but the cultural heritage that enables us to benefit from the creativity and the wisdom, as well as the foibles and mistakes, of the generations that preceded us in our own society. Enculturation, then, includes all those learning processes by which a human being, a member of a given society, obtains a working knowledge of the culture of that society.

In many small-scale societies, such as that of the Cheyenne, young people learn appropriate behavior almost entirely from parents and relatives. Not only do parents tell their children what they should do, but children learn values and skills by observing the activities of adults in their society. Children also learn a great deal from grandparents and other relatives, who may tell tales and stories to illustrate approved and disapproved behavior. And children in all cultures learn much from their siblings and peers as well as from their elders. In industrial societies, however, although enculturation is started by the parents and other relatives, it is usually carried on through a system of formal education. It is further complicated by a wide variety of instructions and models made available by advanced communications and technology. The influence of peers may be more important than in the simpler societies.

The way we are enculturated determines to a great degree how we go about satisfying our individual needs. We eat what we have been taught to think of as "food." For Americans, hamburgers are food, whereas grubs and ants are not. We consider milk to be the "perfect food," although a French premier was almost laughed out of office for suggesting that the French drink milk at the table instead of wine. We may have a need for intimacy with a person of the opposite sex, but whom we choose depends on how we are taught. In some societies, one prefers to marry a maternal cousin; in other

3. J. A. L. Singh and R. M. Zingg, *Wolf-Children and Feral Man* (New York: Harper, 1942).

4. Clifford Geertz, "The Impact of the Concept of Culture on the Concept of Man," in *Man in Adaptation: The Cultural Present*, ed. Yehudi Cohen (Chicago: Aldine Publishing, 1968), pp. 16–29.

Humans are not the only primates to learn social rituals that bind a group of individuals together into a cohesive unit.

groups such a marriage is considered incest. Within recent history, we have seen the marriage pattern in many European families change from one of arranged marriage, in which affection between the partners was irrelevant, to one of romantic love, in which it is assumed that all practical considerations are of little consequence.

Culture Is Shared

If one person has an unusual idea or way of doing something—belongs to the Flat Earth Society and thinks the world is flat, or prefers to sleep during the day and work at night—we think he or she has a personal idiosyncrasy, or a habit. But many ideas and habits are shared by a group of people—are part of the culture. Some patterns of ideas and types of behavior may be shared by large numbers of people, over wide areas; other patterns may be shared by a group of families, or by people of a similar historical back-

These Thais have in common many patterns of behavior that together make up their shared culture.

ground. When we speak about the shared customs or ways of doing things of a society, we are speaking about the culture of that society. If we talk about the shared beliefs of a certain group within that society, we speak of a *subculture*, such as that of Italian-Americans or the Canadian Hutterites. Cultures such as those of Western Europe, which have shared many historical developments, may be thought of as having a general cultural background, which so far has only been called "Western European culture," but which can be contrasted with the general historical and cultural patterns of Asia, for example.

People who live as members of the same society and who share a common culture are able to predict with some reasonable degree of accuracy how others will behave in given situations. This is a necessity if some orderly form of social life is to be possible. Only by successfully predicting other people's responses can we choose our own behavior.

Culture Is Symbolically Expressed and Transmitted

More than any other species, humans rely on symbols to communicate shared knowledge, behavior patterns, and values. Language, of course, is the primary medium for the transmission of cultural values and knowledge about the world. By means of language, each new generation benefits from the knowledge, experience, and inventions of the generations that went before. If this were not the case, each of us would have to start from scratch. Tribal story-tellers are little different in this respect from government archives and scientific records. Folk music and oral history transmit tribal culture just as the concert repertoire and the library catalogue transmit our culture. Both shape and are shaped by, reflect and are influenced by, the cultural legacies of the society they serve.

Aside from language, there are other symbolic systems at work in any culture. An object like a national flag has a special meaning to the people of a particular country—a meaning that has little to do with the piece of colored cloth. In the same way, a word like "democracy" evokes for many emotions that cannot be seen or heard in the mere series of sounds. All groups of people have created symbols like these to express values, beliefs, and emotions. In short, *symbols* are forms, sounds, objects, or ideas which through time and experience come to stand for and evoke meanings beyond the objects or words themselves.

The symbolic aspect of culture is being emphasized by many anthropologists today. Clifford Geertz[5] and others see culture as a system of symbols, coherent in a logical way. Some of these symbols represent aspects of a culture's value system;

The way these Australian aborigine dancers paint their body gives added symbolic dimension to their art.

for example, the masochistic practices of the Sun Dance represent the Cheyenne value of self-control. These historically developed meanings are assigned to objects as well as actions.[6] In this way,

---

5. Clifford Geertz, "Ritual and Social Change: A Javanese Example," in *Reader in Comparative Religion*, ed. William A. Lessa and Evon Z. Vogt (New York: Harper and Row, 1965), pp. 547–559.

6. Felix M. Keesing, "Anthropological Use of the Term 'Culture'," in *Make Men of Them*, ed. Charles C. Hughes (Chicago: Rand McNally, 1972), p. 186.

the arrows were a symbol of the unity of the Cheyenne people, as well as a tool for hunting. The meanings that are assigned to reality reflect and shape the world in which the members of a culture live, and they form a kind of blueprint for daily action, a reference system for people to live by. Moreover, the more people respond to symbols, the more the symbols themselves take on powerful emotional significance, which strengthens the unity of the group sharing those symbols.

We must emphasize, however, that no symbolic system is more important to a society than its language. Some anthropologists feel that language is so important, in fact, that it actually shapes the way people see the world. Benjamin Whorf, an early linguist, felt that the grammatical categories of a language would determine the way the speakers of a language would understand the world, because "agreement is reached by linguistic processes, or else it is not reached." [7] He felt, for example, that the Hopi Indians would develop a different kind of physics, because their language describes things—houses, flames, and clouds—as processes, whereas English tends to make processes into fixed things. Whorf and modern anthropologists like Dorothy Lee [8] see cultural symbols as help-

7. Benjamin Lee Whorf, "Science and Linguistics," in *Make Men of Them*, ed. Charles C. Hughes (Chicago: Rand McNally, 1972), pp. 129–134.

8. Dorothy Lee, "Symbolization and Value," in *Symbols and Values: An Initial Study*, Thirteenth Symposium of the Conference on Science, Philosophy and Religion, ed. Lyman Bryson, Louis Finkelstein, R. M. MacIver, and Richard McKeon (New York: Harper, 1954), pp. 73–85.

ing to create a world of meanings in which people live.

Culture Is Adaptive

Whether we see it as symbols that guide behavior or as the patterns of behavior themselves, a cultural system is a means by which a group of people survives, raises its children, and continues. Because this is true, many anthropologists see culture as a means of adaptation to the environment. We can say that the culture of each society is an *adaptive strategy*. Each adaptive strategy consists of the human, technological and natural resources of the group that enable it to survive.

Different environments require different adaptations, and this is one reason that cultures may differ. In the simplest sense, for example, the Cheyenne way of living would not be effective in the environment of the Eskimo. The Cheyenne directed their activities to exploiting the buffalo of the prairies with the horse, spear, and bow and arrow. They made the most of their environment by moving with the game, scattering in winter, and gathering in summer. They were not often hungry, although the margin was thin. The Cheyenne had been farmers in the past. Undoubtedly as they moved into a new way of life, they developed new patterns of behavior and new ways of thinking which were suited to the hunt. As we saw in the capsule ethnography, adaptation to the hunting life, which stressed aggression, independence, and close organization, created certain conflicts for some Cheyenne. They had to be not only nonaggressive and cooperative in the camp, but independent and assertive in the hunt. Thus, what is adaptive for the whole may not be completely adaptive for the individual. Nonetheless, the society and culture must meet the needs of most individuals, or the group will not survive.

Culture Is Functional

When anthropologists study the culture and daily activities of a group, they usually assume that most social patterns and cultural values have some purpose. Generally, *functionalists* believe that the culture of a group meets the needs of individuals for food, support, and shelter, and that it serves to keep the group intact and continuing. With this in mind, a functionalist would examine the role of witchcraft, for example, and explain it in terms of channeling and resolving tensions in African societies.[9] Another example might be the long taboo on sex after the birth of a child that exists in many tropical societies. This might be explained as a means of preventing the birth of a new baby, and thus guaranteeing a milk supply for the last child in an area in which other protein sources are scarce or lacking.[10] Thus, the functionalist interpretation assumes there is a reason for the existence of the features of a culture; each feature meets some human need.

Culture Is Integrated

A culture is not a "thing of shreds and patches." It is a dynamic arrangement of interrelated ideas and activities that are continually interacting with each other. We have seen that the Cheyenne culture

---

9. E. E. Evans-Pritchard, *Witchcraft, Oracles and Magic among the Azande* (Oxford: Clarendon, 1937).

---

10. John M. Whiting, "Effects of Climate on Certain Cultural Practices," in *Explorations in Cultural Anthropology*, ed. Ward Goodenough (New York: McGraw-Hill, 1964), pp. 129–134.

was organized around patterns of male dominance, self-control, and bravery. Men as well as women were expected to be sexually continent for long periods of time, even-tempered, and generous within the group. The values of the Cheyenne were in keeping with their way of life, which revolved around hunting the buffalo and raiding other groups for horses. Correct behavior was rewarded and violations of the social order were dealt with firmly. The group was the *unit of survival*. The individuals were expected to subordinate their behavior to the group's ideas of right conduct.

As in most cultures, change and new ideas from other groups were not adopted casually. They were first debated and evaluated. A form of wife-stealing, for example, was rejected when introduced from another Plains group, because it was inconsistent with Cheyenne views of sexual morality. In another case, the tribal council decided to give a man formal permission to disobey the tribal restriction on hunting alone in a time when hunting was done by the entire group. But they also decided to deprive the individual of his rights as a member of the Cheyenne, since he had chosen to disobey the rules of the group.

The idea that culture is integrated, then, means that people seem to try to make their ideas and behavior consistent. One role of cultural systems is to give us a sense of an integrated, orderly, and meaningful world.

Culture Is Dynamic

Although cultural systems are more or less integrated, they also change. They vary with changes in the environment and with contact with other groups and ideas. They must adjust in order to cope with new

This little boy in Upper Volta is playing a traditional game of his tribe— with the substitution of a metal barrel hoop for the more usual wooden one.

problems. The Cheyenne, for example, had lived in villages and had been an agricultural people before they came down to the Plains. They must have lived quite differently before they became hunters. With the coming of the horse their lives changed again, and later, with the arrival of the U.S. Army, they found themselves in new, and generally bitter, situations. They were forced to settle in areas far from where they had lived, decimated by disease and military defeats. Again they adjusted to a new environment, but at a cost of terrible human misery.

Not all changes, of course, are like those suffered by the Cheyenne, but changes do seem to challenge the creative abilities of the people involved. The crises of our own nation and period are certainly such challenges today. Because changes in one area, such as a resource or an area of technology, can upset activities in other areas of a culture, there may follow a period of difficult readjustment. Some cultural groups will not survive—as human history shows.

Every Culture Has Its Deviants

Cultures continue through time because young people are taught to think and behave in ways similar to those of their parents. Most groups allow some sorts of individual variation, but all put limits on what differences in thought and action can be tolerated. In our own society, certain types of murders are punishable by death; others are considered lamentable, but justifiable. Among the migrant shepherds of northern Greece, the Sarakatsani, adultery or premarital sex relations on the part of a woman are punishable by death. Other societies have alternate ways of dealing with those who deviate from the acceptable patterns of behavior. Sometimes, deviants are accused of witchcraft, as in the Azande of Africa. In that society, those who would not share, or who quarreled too much with others, or who otherwise would not abide by the rules for sociable conduct might be accused of witchcraft. Similar accusations and gossip were directed against deviants among the Hopi of the American southwest.

Among the Cheyenne of the Plains, there were some options for certain kinds of deviants. In a society that valued masculine valor, self-control and endurance, those few men who could not cope with the demands made on them could dress like women and perform the work of women. These men were the *berdaches*, "half men—half women" who often acquired medical skills and ceremonial responsibilities. The Cheyenne also recognized a few individuals called Contraries, because they did everything backwards—shivered when hot, went away when summoned, and so forth. The Contraries rejected conventional sexual behavior in favor of a supermale role that was demanding, isolated, and respected.

Among the Cheyenne, however, certain other forms of deviance, which included sexual deviance and murder within the group, could result in the death or exile of the offender. Crimes against the group rather than against a particular individual or family were not tolerated.

Ideal and Real Culture

One aspect of culture is that it embodies ideals and values that determine what ought to go on in a society. Many anthropologists call this *ideal culture*, because it exists mainly as ideals in the minds of people. As we know, what people say is the correct way to do something is not always the way they actually do it. To know what really takes place, anthropologists have to observe what people do in the society they are studying. What actually goes on is often called *real culture*.[11]

Anthropologists refer to the organized patterns of actual behavior as *social organization*.[12] Sociologists and many anthropologists stress this aspect of human behavior—the systematic network of ongoing relationships, obligations, and responsibilities between people who share a similar view of the world. Sociologists and social anthropologists call the rules for right behavior in a given society *norms*. A Cheyenne norm, for example, might be for a man to give freely of his property to the poor. As we can see, there is considerable overlap between the ideals that some anthropologists call "values" and the rules that others call "norms." This fuzziness is not accidental. The viewpoints that em-

11. Felix M. Keesing, "The 'Abstract' or 'Construct' Nature of Anthropological Concepts," in *Cultural Anthropology: The Science of Custom*, ed. Felix M. Keesing (New York: Holt, Rinehart and Winston, 1958).

12. Raymond Firth, *Elements of Social Organization* (Boston: Beacon Press, 1951).

phasize cultural ideals and values, and those that stress description and explanation of what actually happens, are simply two points of view from which to observe the same reality.

The Concept of Society

In casual conversation we often use the term *society* as almost synonymous with culture. However, by society anthropologists mean a permanent group of people who share a common culture.[13] The members of a society depend on each other for their survival and well-being. They share institutions (or patterns of organized activity), values, and goals. The needs of the individuals are met within the society.

By these criteria, the Cheyenne were indeed a society: all the families and groups of families were seen as valued but subordinate parts of the social whole, which was to be preserved from disruption—even if that meant the exile of some individuals. The Cheyenne families depended on each other for aid in hunting and in the sharing of meat. Knowledge, practical and ritual, was shared and taught in the group. Individual actions were evaluated as they affected the group as a whole.

Social Relations and Social Structure

Another tool of the anthropologist is the concept of *social relationship*, which derives from our original notion of society. Social relationships are the struc-

This family group (in a polygamous tribe) is the basic social unit that structures society.

tured ways in which people behave when other people are the objects of that behavior.[14] The social relationship between husband and wife, for example, refers to the way husbands and wives behave toward each other in a specific society. In fact, they act quite differently toward each other in different societies, as a comparison between Cheyenne marriages and a modern "open" marriage can show.

By *social structure* we mean the totality of the different groups within the society—families, administrative bodies, legal bodies,

13. David F. Aberle, A. K. Cohen, A. K. Davis, M. J. Levy, Jr., and F. X. Sutton, "The Functional Prerequisite of a Society," *Ethics* 60 (January 1960): 100–111.

14. John Beattie, *Other Cultures* (New York: Free Press, 1964), pp. 35–36.

defense groups, religious groups, and work groups—which interact in systematic ways to make up a whole. We have seen an example of social structure in our capsule ethnography. Cheyenne society is a composite tribe made up of bands, which are in turn made up of related families. These have informal representatives in the religious and decision-making bodies of the society as a whole. In the communal hunts, men and women together participated in surrounding the herds of buffalo, with the military societies making sure that no individual scared off the prey. The meat was shared by all, again under the policing supervision of the military societies. These groups also took care of defense—from the small war parties of the early days to the major military operations made necessary by the incursions of the white man. Bound together by these ties of family, common belief, and membership in overlapping organizations, the Cheyenne considered themselves an integrated whole.

Culture and Personality

Anthropologists study culture and society by observing individuals. It is individuals—who work and love and fight—who make and implement decisions. So we are faced with an apparent contradiction: the culture is greater than the individual behavior, but the group or society of individuals is the concrete manifestation of the abstraction we call culture.

The Cheyenne certainly illustrate this point. Decisions were made by groups, such as the Council of 44, who had authority to decide matters of law and conduct. All men, however, had the right to speak and be heard. All groups con-

cerned in a decision were consulted. Individual excellence was continually recognized. Brave, restrained, and selfless men became eligible for positions of military, political, or religious leadership. Women were honored for virtue and given ritual positions as well. Their achievements in crafts or lodge-making were occasions for celebrations in the whole group. Men or women who broke the laws of the tribe were punished but, except in the case of a woman convicted of adultery, they were almost always given the opportunity to rehabilitate themselves.

This interplay between the society and the individual has interested anthropologists since the early decades of the twentieth century. In order to perpetuate itself, a society must be made up of people who, if they are not all alike, at least have similar ways of interpreting situations and acting. And although members of a society see great differences in behavior and outlook among themselves, they often seem to have similar characteristics to an outsider. Many of us would agree to the generalizations, for example, that Americans and Canadians are more easy-going and friendly than the British, and that even the British are less formal than the Japanese. Similarly, southern Europeans seem, to the average American, emotional and prone to take offense. On the other hand, many of these same Italians, Greeks, and Spaniards feel that Americans are too open about personal matters —weak and without honor or self-respect.

Anthropologists have been interested in the differences in the personal characteristics of different societies. This is the field that is known as *culture and personality*, or as *psychological anthropology*. Bear in mind, however, that even in per-

54

sonality studies, anthropologists do not focus on the individual per se, as psychologists do. Anthropologists always consider the individual in the context of the culture in which he or she lives.

Personality

As each society finds ways of meeting the needs of the new generation, it also demands patterns of behavior from the young. As Erich Fromm noted, it is better if the members of a society want to act as they have to act. In the enculturation process, they are taught to behave in a way the society agrees is socially necessary.[15] The patterns of feelings and behavior which are created in individuals in the process of growing up are called their *personality*. Personality may be defined as an integrated system of behavior, learned and unlearned, characteristic of an individual.

The personality of each individual is the result of many interacting factors. Each person is born with certain physical characteristics, and, perhaps, levels of activity and responsiveness. To some degree, these are unique. In addition, the physical environment affects both the culture of the individual and, to some extent, his or her own adjustment as well. As far as we know, however, probably the most important influences on the formation of personality come from the social and cultural reality in which we grow up—although each of us experiences our culture in a unique way.

Early Anthropological Approaches to Personality

Some of the best-known early studies of

personality and culture were those done in the first decades of the twentieth century by Margaret Mead and Bronislaw Malinowski.[16] Although neither then had an explicit theory of culture and personality, they set about testing then-popular assumptions, based on the work of Sigmund Freud, that personalities everywhere developed in similar ways. In the Trobriand Islands of the Pacific, Malinowski tested the Freudian hypothesis about the Oedipus complex (in which the young boy desires his mother and feels hostile toward his father, whom he perceives as a rival). He found that in societies where the mother's brother had authority over a boy, the boy resented the uncle rather than the father. In the Trobriand Islands, where there was a severe brother–sister incest taboo, boys had incestuous longings, not for their mothers, but for their sisters, who seemed to them mysterious and forbidden figures. Their myths and dreams reflected this, as those of Western people reflect the Oedipal urge. Thus, Malinowski discovered the Oedipus complex to be a cultural phenomenon, not a psychological universal.

Margaret Mead studied groups in various islands of the Pacific.[17] She tested the prevailing psychological view that the storm and stress of adolescence were caused

15. Erich Fromm, "Individual and Social Origins of Neurosis," *American Sociological Review* 9 (1944): 380–434.

16. Margaret Mead, *Sex and Temperament in Three Primitive Societies* (1935; reprint ed., New York: William Morrow, 1963), and Bronislaw Malinowski, *Sex and Repression in Savage Society* (1927; reprint ed., New York: Humanities Press. 1953).

17. Margaret Mead, *Coming of Age in Samoa* (1928; reprint ed., New York: William Morrow, 1961).

by physiological changes and thus universal. She was interested in seeing where biology left off and where culture became important. She relied on her observations of behavior and her impressions of the feelings and emotions of the people she studied, rather than using the psychological testing methods of later anthropologists. She described how, in Samoa, adolescence was an easy period of casual relationships between the growing children, their families, and their lovers. There was no conflict in the movement from childhood to adulthood, no potentially frustrating quest for status or sex, no difficult choices to make, no disruption of tradition or revision of expectations. It was a group-oriented, cooperative society with no fear of failure or rejection. In the large extended families of Samoa, children grew up with no intense feelings of love or competition. Hence adolescence as we know it hardly seemed to exist.[18]

In her work in New Guinea, Mead found that Western stereotypes of male and female behavior were no more universal than those concerning adolescence. The Arapesh men and women both acted in a way that many of us would expect women to act—mild, even-tempered, and nurturing. Mundugumor men and women, on the other hand, both behaved according to the masculine stereotype—with independence, competitiveness, self-assertion, aggressiveness, and even violence. Tchambuli men, however, were like the American female stereotype—vain, catty, and gossiping—while their women were energetic, comradely, and forthright.

In the same period, Ruth Benedict, a poet as well as an anthropologist, approached the question of culture and personality in a way that is often called configurational. She saw cultures as integrated around certain psychological and cultural *configurations*. These patterns were impressed on the members of a society as ideals that were to be striven for. The ideal person, then, was equated with an abstract character structure. As a demonstration of her theory, she compared the configurations of different Indian groups in North America.

In *Patterns of Culture*, Benedict described the Plains Indians as Dionysian.[19] Like Dionysus, the Greek god of wine, these Indians indulged in what members of other cultures might consider excessive behavior. They would on occasion torture themselves, go into orgies of grief, fast, and seek religious intoxication. Another group, the Kwakiutls, were also Dionysian, but they expressed Dionysian tendencies in other ways. They were prone to extravagant boasting, they indulged in rage rather than grief, and they went on wild rampages during which property was destroyed. Sometimes the Kwakiutls went on head-hunting expeditions. Some committed suicide. There were even incidents of cannibalism among them.

In contrast with these Dionysian groups, Benedict found the Pueblo Indians striving for the golden mean of moderation and called these people Apollonian. They sought sobriety and quiet dignity. Their lives were characterized by restraint. Their ceremo-

---

18. Margaret Mead, *From the South Seas: Studies of Adolescence and Sex in Primitive Societies* (New York: William Morrow, 1939).

19. Ruth Benedict, *Patterns of Culture* (1934; reprint ed., Boston: Houghton Mifflin, 1961).

We all like to think that we are special individuals, our own creation, but much of what we consider personality is shaped by culture.

nies were elaborate and formal, and they encouraged sober cooperation within the group. Unlike the Plains Indians, these people were never known to commit suicide or to go into violent rages.

Where, then, would the ideal Cheyenne personality fit into Benedict's two patterns? The Cheyenne admired self-control and encouraged cooperation and nonaggression. These characteristics would suggest the Apollonian type. But the excesses of the Sun Dance, with its self-mutilation, and the rigors of the adultery taboo, with its gang-rape punishment, are in contrast to the moderation of the Apollonian ideal. Perhaps the Cheyenne do not fit neatly into either pattern.

Although many of Benedict's conclusions have been questioned, her more general approach to culture and personality had lasting influence. Many important researchers still use the idea of general personality types, such as the "peasant personality," and speak about cultural "themes" which seem to organize wider areas of belief and behavior.

The early studies laid the basis for further research. Rather than rely on generalized Freudian stages of development, later researchers have looked to more general psychological processes, to see how they interact with cultural forms. They have often used standardized psychological tests, such as the Rorschach test and the Thematic Apperception Test, as a source of data. Their goal has been to test more precisely the relationships between cultural processes and individual psychology.

Basic Personality and Modal Personality

The idea of *basic personality structure* originated with the configurational concept of the ideal personality. Abram Kardiner, a psychoanalyst interested in culture, formulated in 1936 a theory to explain the basic personality structure.[20] Kardiner, who drew on the ideas of Freud, thought that the people in a given society could be understood by analyzing the development of individual personalities within that society. By focusing on child-rearing in a society, Kardiner and those anthropologists who worked with him set about to determine the way culture acts upon personality.

They studied such universal drives as hunger, sex, and aggression, by concentrating on processes such as weaning and toilet-training. They theorized that because child-rearing in a small-scale society is similar for all, individuals share common childhood experiences and probably have similar means for expressing their emotions about them. In other words, similar childhood experiences lead the members of a society to possess a common basic personality.

Child-Rearing and Personality

How do personality differences come about? As human infants, our needs are met through the actions of adults who feel responsible toward us. The ways in which they treat us teach us, in actions and words, the sort of persons they think we are. To a great degree, we learn to become who we are.

In her study of three New Guinea societies, Mead found that the Arapesh care for their children lovingly and indulgently.[21] The Iatmul headhunters, on the other hand, tend to push small children aside, allowing them to cry at length before feeding them, encouraging the children to fight aggressively for what they want. In a group that stresses aggression in war, Iatmul children are encouraged to demand and seize what they need.

One of the most famous studies of the relation between child-rearing and adult personality was that done in the southwest Pacific islands of Alor by Cora Du Bois, a colleague of Kardiner's.[22] To collect her materials, she used psychological tests and life histories, techniques developed by psychologists for the study of individual personality.

Alorese mothers go back to work in the fields several weeks after giving birth. The infants are left virtually unattended, only inconsistently cared for by any adults who are present. The mothers return at the end of the day, and only then do they nurse their babies. According to one commentator, "The only compensating feature of Alorese childhood is permissive sexuality,

20. Abram Kardiner, "The Concept of Basic Personality Structure as an Operational Tool in the Social Sciences," in *The Science of Man in the World Crisis*, ed. Ralph Linton (New York: Columbia University Press, 1957). See also Kardiner, *The Psychological Frontiers of Society* (New York: Columbia University Press, 1945).

21. Mead, *Sex and Temperament in Three Primitive Societies*.

22. Cora A. DuBois, *People of Alor: A Social-Psychological Study of an East Indian Island* (Cambridge, Mass.: Harvard University Press, 1960).

The amount of time parents spend with their children, and the emotional tone of their relationship (both culturally prescribed), greatly influence the personality development of the next generation of the social group.

including masturbation. . . ." [23]

Du Bois gave her psychological material to several psychoanalysts and psychologists, none of whom knew the identity of the subjects. They had not read Du Bois' original ethnography, nor did they know Du Bois' conclusions. Nonetheless, their interpretations of the biographies, dreams, Rorschach responses, and children's draw-

ings were amazingly similar to Du Bois' descriptions. The typical Alorese adult personality was characterized by anxiety, suspicion, pessimism, lack of self-esteem, confidence, and ambition, lack of imagination and creativity, inability to sustain a love relationship or a friendship based on voluntary trust, and a tendency to collapse and wait for death in the event of even a mild illness or injury. The Alorese exhibited indirect aggression in the form of preying on their neighbors, lying, and chicanery. The principal causes of this kind of personality structure are usually ex-

---

23. Gerald Berreman et al., eds., *Anthropology Today* (Del Mar, Calif.: CRM Books, 1971), p. 361.

plained by psychologists as the result of maternal neglect, inconsistent handling at an early age, the lack of even a single relationship of trust and dependence, and sporadically-given help and security—all features of Alorese infancy and childhood.

Kardiner and Du Bois did not investigate systematically the development of these patterns of child-rearing among the Alorese. Later anthropologists and psychologists, however, have used statistical comparisons of different cultures to test propositions such as those of Kardiner about relationships between child-rearing institutions (Kardiner's *primary institutions*) and the modal personality types. These studies have found certain relationships between child-rearing practices and patterns of subsistence. Many anthropologists now believe that child-rearing practices are adaptive: they are geared to produce the kinds of people best suited to do the work necessary for the survival of the society. As Whiting and Child say, "The economic, political and social organs of a society—the basic customs surrounding the nourishment, sheltering and protection of its members—seem a likely source of influence on child training practices." [24]

Personality and Other Aspects of Culture

Kardiner believed that basic personality patterns established early in life would carry over to, or influence, the larger institutional structures of a society, such as the religion, folk tales, and art. He found, for example, that the oral deprivations of Alorese childhood were reflected in their religion. Alorese gods and ancestors were a good deal like Alorese parents: they had to be placated, and not much could be expected from them. They were neither revered nor exalted. On the contrary, when they had to be fed, lest they become angry in an emergency, it was done grudgingly. Religious art—chiefly effigies of the gods—was careless and shoddy, and it was quickly discarded. Even the Alorese folk tales centered on parental frustration and hatred.

Alorese patterns of warfare similarly reflected their basic and modal personality structures. An Alorese war was no more than a disorganized and vengeful means of getting even, or a sort of irritable gesture, a cowardly assault carried out by trickery and with stealth. Women as well as men might be the victims of such a raid.

PERSONALITY AND SOCIAL CHANGE. Although the personality of an individual is somewhat fixed as a pattern early in life, people are often faced with the necessity of coping with changes in their ways of living. The sorts of personalities they have affect the ways they may respond to change. In a comparative study of Navajo and Zuñi veterans of World War II,[25] it was found that the Navajo men found it easier to leave their homes and families and later return to them. They and their society were able to accept changes. The Zuñi, however, resisted changes, and those who remained at home during the war often rejected the men who were returning from "outside."

24. John W. M. Whiting and Irvin L. Child, *Child Training and Personality* (New Haven, Conn.: Yale University Press, 1953), p. 310.

25. John Adair and Evon Vogt, "Navajo and Zuñi Veterans: A Study of Contrasting Modes of Culture Change," *American Anthropologist* 51 (October–December 1949): 547–560.

The Otavalo Indians of Ecuador have replaced their more traditional games with volleyball, but the new game serves the same old function.

Change was felt as a threat.

We know now that patterns of child-rearing are not set for all time: parents who recognize a changing situation may decide to change the way they bring up their children, at least to some degree, hoping that the children will be better able to cope with change. Several studies have been done on Russian national character and child-rearing, comparing them with reconstructions of what they were before the Revolution.[26] They indicate that younger Soviet citizens are less oriented to tradi-

26. Alex Inkeles, Eugenia Hanfman, and Helen Beier, "Modal Personality and Adjustment to the Soviet Socio-Political System," *Human Relations* 11 (1958): 3–22.

Chapter Two

tion; they are more political, intellectual, and oriented to self-expression.

It is obvious that the Cheyenne were able to make radical changes when they moved from their settled agricultural existence to the nomadic hunting life described in our capsule ethnography. With the coming of the white man, further adaptation was required.

Freedom and Constraint

We have grown up in a society which stresses personal freedom and alternative ways of doing things. An examination of these beliefs, however, may be revealing. Freedom is referred to as a quality or fact pertaining to individuals, who may make choices about certain ways of behaving in a situation. All cultures, to some degree, offer such behavioral alternatives in some areas. Ironically, we as individuals may choose only from a set of alternatives allowed by the culture. I may choose to be a Catholic or a Protestant. I may not, as an American, choose to be a cannibal, or to ritually kill sheep on my suburban front lawn. In fact, choices are *culturally constrained*, or defined, for us.

How do we define freedom, then? All cultures allow some choices in making a living, or in personal style, because not all people have similar personalities—even in simple societies. Generally, however, these variations exist within culturally defined limits. Thus, a Cheyenne may be a homosexual, but he must do it in the way acceptable to the society. If he merely wishes to avoid women as a *Contrary*, there is a way to do it—but only one way. Thus, in order to create and maintain cultural cohesion, limits are set. Within the urban areas of the world, there are more choices available to the individual. But this is a question still to be settled, and an important one. How different, how creative, can an individual be?

Just as individuals have a conditioned kind of freedom, we may speak of the freedom for cultures and societies to develop in different ways. We have discussed cultures as adaptive strategies, organized in a particular way to deal with the realities of the environment. Cultures may also be *creative* solutions to the problem of making a living in nature—gathering or extracting energy from the habitat. However, the environment also imposes certain constraints on people, given the tools they have on hand for survival. For an Eskimo family to change its way of life, it must adopt new technologies to deal with the environment. The Eskimo have the choice of adopting the rifle and the snowmobile—when they are made available by another group which has been able to develop them. Without such outside help, it is unlikely that the Eskimo would have been able to develop that technology themselves. In that way, they were not free to change.

On the other hand, human groups have indeed seized opportunities to change the ways they live, as our study of adaptations will show. Humans are free, in certain moments and places, to find new ways to grow. This is not by accident or whim, because human survival hangs or falls on it, and it is a possibility which is uniquely human. In just that way, then, we may have to think about the possible freedom we may have, as individuals and as members of a culture in a time of rapid and critical change.

Summary

1. Culture refers to the integrated system of beliefs, artifacts, and behavior patterns which are learned and shared by the members of a society. These patterns are developed through time and expressed symbolically.

2. The process of learning the knowledge and the ways of behaving of one's group is called enculturation.

3. The shared beliefs of a group within a society may be called a subculture.

4. All human groups have created symbols to express ideas, values, beliefs, and emotions. Symbols are forms, sounds, objects, or ideas that stand for and evoke meanings beyond the objects or ideas themselves.

5. Culture may be seen as a system of symbols, "blueprints for action," which create a world of meaning for those who share them.

6. Each culture can be seen as an adaptive strategy for survival in nature. A culture may be integrated around its survival techniques.

7. Cultural systems are dynamic. They change with the environment, innovations, and contact with other groups.

8. Ideals, or values about what should go on in a society, are called ideal culture. What actually occurs is often called real culture.

9. Ongoing networks of actual behavior are sometimes called social organizations. The rules that govern these patterns are called norms.

10. A society is a self-reproducing whole, made up of interdependent people, sharing institutions, values, and goals. An institution is made up of human relationships patterned around specific needs and goals.

11. Social relationships are the structured ways people interact with each other. A social structure refers to a totality of interrelated human institutions.

12. Personality is the configuration of feelings and behavior created in an individual in the process of growing up.

13. Early important studies in the relationship between culture and personality were done by Mead, Malinowski, and Benedict.

14. Kardiner felt that similar childhood experiences would tend to create similar personalities in the people of a society. He called this basic personality.

15. Modal personality refers to those personality characteristics that occur most frequently in a society.

16. Personalities differ because children are raised differently. Child-rearing is adaptive, varying with ecological differences, economic practices, social position, or social change.

17. Basic personality patterns and conflicts can be reflected in expressive institutions such as war, art, religion, magic, and games.

18. All societies allow some personal freedom for individuals, and also set limits on the range of acceptable behavior. Each cultural strategy entails some choices and some constraints.

Review Questions

1. What are the characteristics of culture?

2. What is a symbol? Give an example of a symbol, and explain its significance.

3. Why would ethnocentric attitudes make it difficult for an anthropologist to work? Give a possible example.

4. What is a norm? Can you describe three norms of the society in which you live?

5. What are some of the factors that seem to affect the rearing and the personalities of children?

Suggested Readings

Benedict, Ruth. *Patterns of Culture.* 1934. Reprint. New York: New American Library, 1959.

This famous classic depicts societies as having cultural configurations somewhat like personalities. Benedict describes what she saw as the configurations of three societies.

DuBois, Cora. *The People of Alor: A Social-Psychological Study of an East Indian Island.* 1944. Reprint. Cambridge, Mass.: Harvard University Press, 1960.

This is the most rigorous of the early field studies of basic personality structure.

Kroeber, A. L. *The Nature of Culture.* Chicago: University of Chicago Press, 1952.

Written by one of the most distinguished anthropological scholars of the twentieth century, this is a collection of papers on the concept of culture.

Mead, Margaret. *From the South Seas.* New York: William Morrow, 1939.

Three of Mead's famous studies are included in this volume. The studies examine "nature versus culture" in sex roles and adolescence in societies of Samoa and New Guinea.

Radcliffe-Brown, A. R. *Structure and Function in Primitive Society.* 1952. Reprint. New York: Free Press, 1965. This is a series of basic essays by one of the foremost figures of British anthropology. Essays on function, social structure, and kinship present some of the most important concepts of the structural–functional approach.

FIELD PROJECT
Life History

This is the first of four field projects. Their purpose is not only to give you a sense of what doing anthropological fieldwork is like, but also to help you to see your own society from an anthropological point of view. As we saw in the fieldwork done in El Pinar, anthropological research typically involves living for an extended period with the people whose lives one is studying. It also involves comparison: often anthropologists study people who live differently from themselves. Anthropologists can then compare what is happening around themselves with the way the same things are done in their own societies. It is important, then, for anthropological fieldwork, that anthropologists heed the warning, "know thyself." Only in this way can they hope to be critical of the biases and presuppositions which they bring with them when they study other people's lives. And only in this way can they learn to use their own experiences productively.

In these projects, you will not be asked to live any differently than you presently do. Instead, you will be asked to observe your own circumstances more closely than you might otherwise—to be a "participant observer" in your own society—and then to compare what you observe with what you will be reading about in the text.

This exercise concerns the use by researchers of the *life history*. In Chapter 2, you read about the relationship between the individual and society and learned that culture is shared. That is, a portion of any individual's experience and knowledge is held in common with other people of the same culture. When we study an individual life history, then, we can learn much about the culture in which that individual grew up and lives.

In its essence, life history research is just one kind of *interview*, one in which the researcher listens to and questions one individual at length about his or her biography. Anthropologists use interviews—systematic questioning—to learn facts which they could not pick up by observing the normal course of life. Some interviews are designed to collect detailed and specific information on a particular subject—for example, marketing activities or kinship relationships—from a large number of informants. (*Informants* is the anthropological term for people in the society being studied from whom an anthropologist has gotten information.) Life history interviews focus on a single individual and collect information about that person's life experiences. Such life experiences may be interesting to the anthropologist for a number of reasons. For example, the person may be an outstanding leader, artist, etc., who has an atypical but illuminating perspective on his or her society, or who may have affected his or her society's history in some way. For example, in 1832, B. B. Thatcher published *Indian Biography: Or, An Historical Account of Those Individuals who Have Been Distinguished among the North American Natives as Orators, Warriors, Statesmen and Other Remarkable Characters.*

On the other hand, as with the case of anthropologist Paul Radin's *Crashing Thunder* (originally written in 1920 under the title *The Autobiography of a Winnebago Indian* for the University of California's Publications in American Archaeology and Ethnology), life histories may be collected of typical representatives of a culture. The purpose of such interviews is to get a close look at what living in a particular culture is like. Another reason for collecting a life history is that it might be one of the few sources of information about a way of life that no longer exists in an independent and viable form. Much American Indian research, especially during the 1925–1945 period was carried out in this spirit.

In general, however, life histories are particularly valuable for anthropologists interested in "personality and culture" studies (see Chapter 2).

Selecting an Informant

Ideally, one would live in a community for a while to get a feel for life there before selecting an informant. For this project, find an older person, preferably someone who comes from a culture different from your own. This might be someone who was born and raised in another country, or whose religious background is quite different from your own. You might interview one of your own grandparents or a grandparent of a friend, or an older person whom you happen to know. Tell the person what you intend to do, explaining in general terms the subject matter with which you hope to deal. After the person agrees to be interviewed, arrange when and where and how long the first interview will be. You might make arrangements for several interviewing sessions after you see how the first one goes.

Getting Ready for the Interview

You will need a pad and pen and/or a tape recorder (if you can obtain one). Before going to meet your informant for your first session, prepare by reading whatever you can on topics related to your informant's background. If your informant left Tsarist Russia in 1904 to come to the United States at the age of fifteen, you might read a bit about turn-of-the-century Russia, and about attitudes toward immigrants in the United States in the early 1900s. If your informant is a Mormon, you might read about the Mormon religion. You might also look at Lewis Langness's book, *The Life History in Anthropological Science* (Holt, Rinehart and Winston, 1965) for ideas. This reading will help you to formulate intelligent questions to put to the person you will be interviewing.

Before going to the interview, you might also draw up a list of questions. In general, when seeking a life history, most of the talking ought to be done by the informant, with the interviewer merely reassuring, listening carefully, and taking notes. Too many interruptions might discourage the informant and stop the flow of ideas and associations. Keep a list of follow-up questions as they occur to you, and use them when the informant seems to be running out of things to say. Otherwise, lead into the interview with the most general of questions, and then listen. Some examples of the kinds of questions one might be prepared to ask are:

1. What was life like when you were a child?
2. What was your family (town, country) like?
3. Why did you come to the United States? What was it like to adjust to a new country?
4. How did you come to marry your husband/wife? (Add other questions about significant life events, such as jobs, births, or deaths.)

The Interview

In the beginning, or even during the interview, you might find it helpful, in order to encourage the informant to talk and to make your relationship with him or her more reciprocal, to talk about yourself and your own background. During the interview, too, you might decide that it would be interesting to encourage the informant to go into detail on one specific topic, especially if your informant has had an unusual life. It is important, in an interview situation, to be flexible and to follow up leads whenever this is possible. You should also arrange to conduct the interview in a setting in which both you and your informant feel comfortable and are relatively undisturbed. Interviewing your informant in his or her home might be ideal, since it would provide you with some clues as to how the person lives.

Evaluating Your Results

You should listen to your interview tapes or read your notes after you have completed your interviews.

1. Write a life history summarizing the information, perhaps organized chronologically.

2. Did your background reading help you in formulating questions or understanding what your informant was saying? Do you have any suggestions as to how an interviewer ought to prepare?

3. What comments can you make about the problems of interviewing in terms of types of questions to ask, establishing informant–inter-

viewer rapport, guiding the interview to solicit useful information, and so on?

4. What can you say about the reliability of the information you obtained? What are some ways of checking the information?

5. Anthropologists rarely interview only one person in their research about a culture, because any one individual is bound to have only a partial view of the culture as a whole. What were some of your informant's cultural biases? For example, did you feel that your informant's sex or wealth or religion or political belief shaped the answers given? How? What could be done to acquire a more rounded view of the culture as a whole?

6. How were your informant's early life experiences different from your own? How were your informant's values different from yours? Do you think that these differences affected the success of the interview? How?

7. Have you learned anything new about the informant's culture as a result of the interview? Have you learned anything new about your own prejudices and biases? about your own culture?

PART TWO

"Human Teeth in China Dated at 1.7 Million Years," read a recent headline in *The New York Times*. Such finds have long been considered newsworthy because they add another episode to the drama of human life on earth. The teeth mentioned above belonged to an early member of the human family known as *Homo erectus*. They are important because they push back by one million years the date when *Homo erectus* was previously thought to have lived.

Stories such as this often unloose a flood of questions in the mind of the lay reader. When did humans first appear on earth? Where did they come from? How did they become thinking, feeling beings? Such topics are the province of physical anthropology, the subject of this section.

Cultural anthropology studies humans as cultural beings, whereas physical anthropology focuses on the fact that humans are members of the animal kingdom, subject to the laws of nature. Like all other animals, humans have arrived at their present position by adapting to their surroundings and by changing—in structure, physiology, and behavior—over time. Such changes constitute *organic evolution*, the basics of which are discussed in Chapter 4.

The principle of organic evolution through natural selection is one of the great organizing concepts of modern physical anthropology and biology. The other major principle is that of *ecology*, the idea that all organisms in a specific environment are interrelated to one another and to their environment. Thus, the major thrust of this section is how the human species has adapted to its environment, gradually evolving into the dominant life form in the ecology of the planet.

But why begin the story of human evolution with baboons, chimpanzees, and the like, as does Chapter 3? Anthropologists study these beasts for a number of reasons. First, they study the entire primate order—that group of animals which includes tarsiers, monkeys, chimpanzees, and humans. Nonhuman primates are our closest relatives in the animal world. Indeed, they descended with us from a common ancestor that lived about 80 million years in the past.

Millions of years ago, the human line split from the other primates. After studying the physical remains of early primates, most researchers have concluded that the split took place at least 10 million years ago. However, other workers, notably V. Sarich and A. Wilson, have analyzed certain biochemicals in the blood proteins of living primates and concluded that humans separated from other primates about 4 million years ago. This "evolutionary distance" between different species was arrived at by assuming that the blood biochemicals have evolved at a constant rate for each primate lineage, and that this rate is measurable.

Since our ancestors left us no written records, their evolution must be partly inferred from indirect sources. Anthropologists study the anatomy and behavior of modern monkeys and apes because the adaptations of these primates are thought to resemble those of our predecessors.

Organic Evolution

More important clues to human adaptation are found in fossils—the bones and other physical remains of creatures who lived eons ago. The fossils of apes and members of the human family are the subject of Chapter 5. An anthropologist coming upon the remains of one of our early ancestors tries to discover the importance of the find for human evolution. Did the creature that was attached to this leg bone walk upright on two legs? Were these molar teeth used to chew meat foods or plant foods? Was the brain housed by this skull large and complex enough to think as humans do? The answers to such questions help the investigator to discover how our ancestors adapted, and to fix their place in our family tree.

At first, our forebears lived mostly in tropical areas. As they became more human, they developed technologies (shelter, clothing, and fire, for example) that enabled them to spread into many diverse environments. In the process, they had to adapt to a wide range of climates, foods, and even diseases. As a result, human groups became physically different from one another. Such variation is examined in Chapter 6. There, we will see that anthropologists investigate the ecological, or adaptive, factors that forged evolutionary changes. Investigators want to know, for instance, why people who live in tropical regions have darker skin than natives of cooler areas.

The study of such factors leads to the consideration of an entirely different kind of evolution, one that was wrought by human minds and hands. This is called cultural evolution. As a mechanism for human adaptation, cultural change is far more efficient than the biological variety. Moreover, it produces change much faster. We shall see in Chapter 5, for instance, that once our early ancestors learned to master their environment with fire and efficient tools, the tempo of human cultural evolution accelerated greatly.

Not surprisingly, our cultural evolution has also affected our biological evolution. For example, children in industrial nations have been reaching sexual maturity earlier than past generations. They have also been growing taller. Both examples of biological evolution apparently are the result of better nutrition and health care, which are cultural factors. Some investigators have speculated that this evolutionary trend may mean that these youngsters are also maturing faster emotionally and intellectually. One interesting implication of these events for American college youth is that the university system is geared for adolescents and has remained unchanged, whereas students are coming of age earlier. As a result, the system may be out of step with the attitudes and emotions of modern college students.

For human development, then, organic evolution alone has ceased to play the paramount role it once played. For good or ill, biocultural evolution will guide the destiny of future generations of humankind.

Chapter 3

The Primate Order

CHIMPANZEES IN AN AFRICAN FOREST

While many details of their social behavior were hidden from me by the foliage, I did get occasional fascinating glimpses. I saw one female, newly arrived in a group, hurry up to a big male and hold her hand toward him. Almost regally he reached out, clasped her hand in his, drew it toward him, and kissed it with his lips. I saw two adult males embrace each other in greeting. I saw youngsters having wild games through the treetops, chasing around after each other or jumping again and again, one after the other, from a branch to a springy bough below. I watched small infants dangling happily by themselves for minutes on end, patting at their toes with one hand, rotating gently from side to side. Once two tiny infants pulled on opposite ends of a twig in a gentle tug-of-war. Often, during the heat of midday or after a long spell of feeding, I saw two or more adults grooming each other, carefully looking through the hair of their companions. . . .

At about noon the first heavy drops of rain began to fall. The chimpanzees climbed out of the tree and one after the other plodded up the steep grassy slope toward the open ridge at the top. There were seven adult males in the group, including Goliath and David Graybeard, several females, and a few youngsters. As they reached

Source: Jane van Lawick-Goodall, *In the Shadow of Man* (New York: Dell Publishing, 1971), pp. 44, 66–67, 83, 109, 129–130. Copyright 1971 by Hugo and Jane van Lawick-Goodall. Reprinted by permission of Houghton Mifflin Company and William Collins Sons & Co. Ltd.

the ridge the chimpanzees paused. At that moment the storm broke. The rain was torrential, and the sudden clap of thunder, right overhead, made me jump. As if this were a signal, one of the big males stood upright and as he swayed and swaggered rhythmically from foot to foot I could just hear the rising crescendo of his pant-hoots above the beating of the rain. Then he charged to, flat-out down the slope toward the trees he had just left. He ran some thirty yards, and then, swinging round the trunk of a small tree to break his headlong rush, leaped into the low branches and sat motionless.

Almost at once two other males charged after him. One broke off a low branch from a tree as he ran and brandished it in the air before hurling it ahead of him. The other, as he reached the end of his run, stood upright and rhythmically swayed the branches of a tree back and forth before seizing a huge branch and dragging it farther down the slope. A fourth male, as he too charged, leaped into a tree and, almost without breaking his speed, tore off a large branch, leaped with it to the ground, and continued down the slope. As the last two males called and charged down, so the one who had started the whole performance climbed from his tree and began plodding up the slope again. The others, who had also climbed into trees near the bottom of the slope, followed suit. When they reached the ridge, they started charging down all over again, one after the other, with equal vigor.

The females and youngsters had climbed into trees near the top of the rise as soon as the displays had begun, and there they remained watching throughout the whole performance. As the males charged down and plodded back up, so the rain fell harder, jagged forks or brilliant flares of lightning lit the leaden sky, and the crashing of the thunder seemed to shake the very mountains. . . .

It happened most unexpectedly. I had taken Hugo up to show him the peak and we were watching four red colobus monkeys that were evidently separated from their troop. Suddenly an adolescent male chimpanzee climbed cautiously up the tree next to the monkeys and moved slowly along a branch. Then he sat down. After a moment, three of the monkeys jumped away—quite calmly, it appeared. The fourth remained, his head turned toward the chimp. A second later another adolescent male chimp climbed out of the thick vegetation surrounding the tree, rushed along the branch on which the last monkey was sitting, and grabbed it. Instantly several other chimps climbed up into the tree and, screaming and barking in excitement, tore their victim into several pieces. It was all over within a minute from the time of capture. . . .

Evered, as he climbed through a tree, suddenly stopped and, with his face close to the bark, peered into what looked like a small hollow. He picked a handful of leaves, chewed them for a moment, took them out of his mouth, and pushed them down into the hollow. As he withdrew them we saw the gleam of water. Quickly Evered sucked the liquid from his homemade sponge and poked it down into the hollow once more. At that moment Gilka came up and watched him closely. When he moved away she made a tiny sponge and pushed it into the hollow, but it seemed that all the water had gone. She dropped her sponge and wandered off. Later we saw the same behavior many times, for we had made an artificial water bowl in a fallen tree trunk in camp. Always the chimpanzees first crumpled and chewed the leaves, and that of course made their sponge much more absorbent. It is, in fact, another example of tool*making*. . . .

A chimpanzee community is an extremely complex social organization. Only when a large number of individuals began to visit the feeding area and I could make regular observations on their interactions one with another did I begin to appreciate just how complex it is. The members who compose the community move about in constantly changing associations, and yet, though the society seems to be organized in such a casual manner, each individual knows his place in the social structure—knows his status in relation to any other chimpanzee he may chance upon during the day. Small wonder there is such a wide range of greeting gestures, and that most chimpanzees do greet each other when they meet after a separation. Figan, going up to an older male with a submissive pant-grunt, is probably affirming that he remembers quite well the little aggressive incident of two days before when he was thumped soundly on the back. "I know you are dominant. I admit it; I remember" is probably the sort of communication inherent in his submissive gesturing. "I acknowledge your respect; I shall not attack you just now" is implicit in the gentle patting movement of Mike's hand as he greets a submissive female.

As Hugo and I became increasingly familiar with Mike's community we began to learn more and more about the variety of relationships which existed between different adult chimpanzees. Some individuals only interacted when chance—such as a fruiting tree or a sexually attractive female—threw them together. Others moved about together frequently and showed an affectionate tolerance and regard for each other which we felt could best be described as friendship. . . . And the more we learned, the more we were impressed by the obvious parallels between some chimpanzee and some human relationships.[1]

The Primate Order

Primate Classification

As Jane Goodall points out, certain aspects of chimpanzee social life resemble that of humans. From a biological standpoint, too, these apes, with orangutans and gorillas, are our closest relatives in the animal kingdom. To understand the meaning of this statement requires some knowledge of the family tree that shows how each member of the animal kingdom is related to all others in body structure, function, and evolutionary development. The science that holds the rules for such classification is *taxonomy.*

The originator of the basic system of classification was Carolus Linnaeus (1707–1778), a Swedish botanist and naturalist. Linnaeus devised a hierarchical system that classifies animals and plants according to their biological relationships to one another. He placed organisms that were structurally similar in the same category. Linnaeus's other achievement was to give every organism two Latin names, a system known as *binomial nomenclature,* which enables scientists the world over to recognize any organism referred to in a piece of scientific writing. Linnaeus's two names are the *genus* and the *species.* For example, humans belong to the genus *Homo* (which in Latin means "man") and the species *sapiens* (wise).

Linnaeus also created other categories, or *taxa* (singular, *taxon*). Eventually, seven basic hierarchies were established. These are the *kingdom, phylum, class,*

1. Jane van Lawick-Goodall, *In the Shadow of Man* (New York: Dell Publishing, 1971), pp. 44, 66–67, 83, 109, 129–130.

order, family, genus, and *species.* The kingdom is the most general, or most inclusive category, whereas the species is the least inclusive. This means that a kingdom contains all the phyla that are related to one another by anatomical structure and evolutionary development, a phylum includes all the classes that are related, and so on. As knowledge of living things accumulated, these levels were expanded. Thus, an existing taxon could be subdivided, creating, for example, the suborder or the superfamily. Goodall's chimpanzees would be classified in this system as follows:

Kingdom *Animalia* (chimpanzees are animals)

Subkingdom *Metazoa* (they are multicellular)

Phylum *Chordata* (they have an internal skeleton)

Subphylum *Vertebrata* (they have a segmented spine)

Class *Mammalia* (they are warm-blooded and give birth to live young)

Order *Primates* (they are members of one of the eighteen subdivisions of the Class *Mammalia*)

Superfamily *Hominoidea* (a category that includes apes and humans)

Family *Pongidae* (a category that includes only apes)

Genus *Pan* (to differentiate from the other chimpanzee genus, *Paniscus*)

Species *Troglodytes*

Besides being a classificatory device, the taxonomic hierarchy illustrates evolutionary trends. The various taxa within the primate order may be related to an evolutionary timetable, for each taxon represents a collection of features which first appeared within the order at a particular point in evolutionary history. A *trend* is the tendency of a species to evolve the characteristics that separate it from other organisms. For example, in the course of human evolution a tendency has been observed toward movement on the two hind limbs rather than on all four limbs. This is the trend toward *bipedalism,* or "two-leggedness."

The Primate Order

The order of primates is believed to contain more than 200 species, which are grouped in 58 *genera* (plural of *genus*). The order consists of two large suborders, the prosimians and the anthropoids. Prosimians, sometimes referred to as lower primates, encompass the lemurs, lorises, galagos, and tarsiers. The anthropoids contain four large groups—New World monkeys, Old World monkeys, apes, and humans.[2] There has been some debate as to whether tree shrews, too, should be included among the primates. However, many investigators believe these animals to be transitional forms between insectivores (small, insect-eating mammals such as the mole) and primates. Nevertheless, we have included them in the diagram of the primate family tree (Figure 3–1) to show where they are believed to fit.

The Primate Pattern

All primates are beings of the forest in the sense that their physical structures are the product of a long period of adap-

2. J. R. Napier and P. H. Napier, *A Handbook of Living Primates* (New York: Academic Press, 1967).

tation, or adjustment, to life in the trees. Indeed, virtually all primates today live in trees. As a result of this *arboreal* adaptation, primates developed a series of traits involving the sense organs and brain, locomotor and postural structures, and reproductive system. For example, life in the trees favored the evolution of long, flexible digits with nails instead of claws, enabling the hands and feet of the animal to grasp tree limbs and branches as it traveled through them. Eventually, freely moving digits evolved to permit most primates to oppose the thumb to the other four digits. (A pinching movement serves as a good illustration of this trait.) The act of circling an object with the thumb on one side and the four fingers on the other is referred to as *digital prehension.* Two types of digital prehension are possible for most primates: the *precision grip,* in which the thumb is opposed to the forefinger for precise manipulation of an object, and the *power grip,* in which the entire hand is used to grasp an object such as a flashlight or tree branch (see Figure 3–2). These grips permit the animal to manipulate objects in the environment quite extensively. The mobile upper limb, complete with prehensile hand, eventually made a great contribution to the environmental mastery that is characteristic of our species. More than any other animals, primates pick up objects, turning them around to examine them from all angles. Morover, unlike most other animals, primates also use their hands to transport food to their mouths.

Additional modifications in the tips of the primate digits include moisture-secreting glands, which add traction, and increased numbers and types of nerve endings, which send information about the animal's surroundings to the brain. These help the animal adapt to the problems of movement in an arboreal environment.

Accompanying these modifications was the evolution of stereoscopic vision, which enables the primate to perceive better its surroundings in three dimensions. Not surprisingly, this is a valuable trait to possess if one travels through the trees at high speeds, as some primates do. An animal that misjudges the distance between one tree limb and another could end up on the ground, injured, or at the mercy of prowling predators.

Most higher primates (monkeys, apes, and humans) are able to perceive their environment in color. Color vision is probably related to the fact that most primates are *diurnal*—that is, they are most active

Figure 3–1   *A classification of the primate order showing the theoretical evolutionary relationships of each type, from prosimians through humans. (After Napier, 1968)*

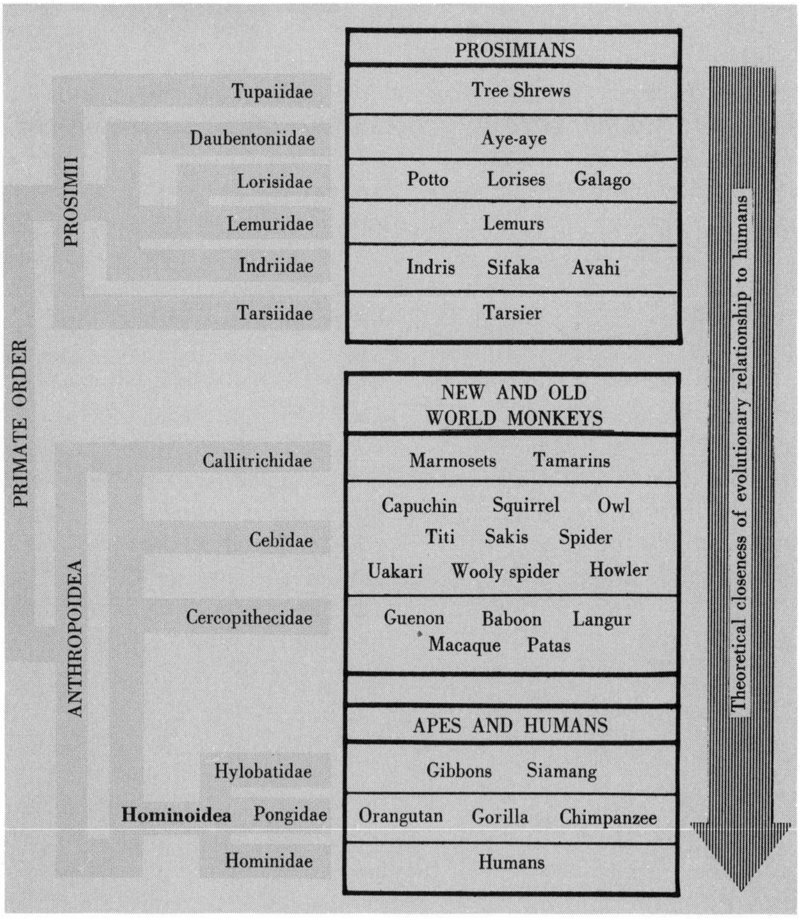

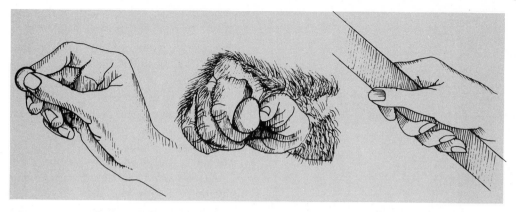

Figure 3–2   *Their fully opposable thumbs make humans more capable of fine manipulation of objects than other primates. Chimpanzee precision grip is shown at center and human power grip at right.*

during daylight hours when differences in color in the environment are most apparent. Color vision helps the animal discriminate among many types of food, as well as poisonous snakes.

Life in the trees also called for an advanced system of muscular and sensory coordination, a reflection of the fact that split-second decisions were often necessary. One result of this was the development of certain areas of the brain. The area involved with vision, for example, expanded, whereas that concerned with *olfaction* (smell) decreased (see Figure 3–3). The reasons for the reduction of the olfactory area are twofold. First, odors tend to remain close to the ground and smell usually serves lower mammals, especially *terrestrial* (ground-dwelling) animals, as a kind of distant early warning system which helps the animal defend itself against, or avoid, its predators. Second, the sense of smell in lower mammals helps them find food and recognize one another for mating and for other purposes. Tree-dwelling primates, not liv-

ing so close to the ground, did not require such a developed sense of smell because the wind wafting through the trees dispersed the odors. Moreover, a developed olfactory sense would not tell the tree-dwelling animal the location of the nest branch and its distance from the one the animal happened to be occupying.

As a result of the increased dexterity of the hands, those parts of the brain concerned with the motor and sensory functions of the hand became enlarged. And as the feet became important with the development of bipedalism (walking erect on two feet), the regions of the brain controlling the feet also grew larger. This is particularly true in humans. Indeed, perhaps the most successful single feature of the primate order is the marked increase in size of the wrinkled outer layer of the brain, called the *cortex*. This gray matter contains both motor and sensory nerve cells; in humans and the higher primates it is responsible for memory, learning and, most notably, social behavior. Primate brains are generally large

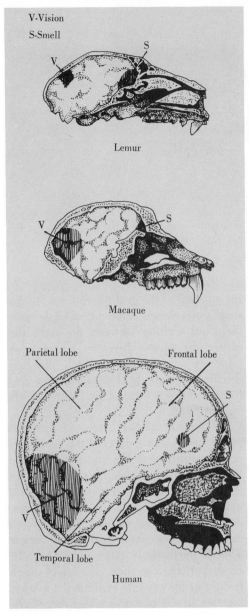

V-Vision
S-Smell

Lemur

Macaque

Parietal lobe

Frontal lobe

Temporal lobe

Human

Figure 3–3   *In higher primates,
the smell center of the brain
decreases in size, whereas the
visual center increases. Similarly,
the cortex becomes increasingly
wrinkled and more complex.*

in proportion to the overall size of the animal, and structurally are quite complex. The most significant consequence of this development is the rich variety of behaviors seen in the order.

Although they first evolved in the trees, primates occupy a wide range of habitats, including tropical jungles, open grasslands, mountainous areas, temperate woodlands, and even snowy regions. The animals are able to sit, stand, walk, swing, and leap in a variety of ways, in the trees or on the ground if necessary. Throughout the anthropoid suborder, primates have evolved postures which free the upper limbs (arms and hands). They have also developed bipedal locomotion. This trait is primitive in lower forms and increasingly evident as one moves upward toward humans, who are typically bipedal. All primates are capable of at least some temporary degrees of erect posture, and thus at least some use of the forelimbs. The principal advantage of freed upper limbs lies in the fact that this enables many primates to manipulate the environment in new ways, using the hands as extensions of the brain. In animals which are exclusively *quadrupedal* (who travel about on four limbs), the mouth must be the principal device for manipulating the environment: it is used to carry objects, to obtain food, and to threaten or attack others.

Another important primate trait is the collarbone, or *clavicle*. This structure adds stability to the shoulder girdle while allowing the upper limbs a wide range of motion.

As for reproduction, primates typically give birth to only one offspring at a time. One advantage of the single birth is that it allows the tree-dwelling mother to concentrate all her attention on her infant, which in turn contributes to the survival odds of the infant.

Primates, like nearly all mammals, are born with their brains in an incomplete state of development. But the degree of such development is greater in primates than in other mammals. This trend has resulted indirectly in longer periods of behavioral and physical dependence on primate mothers by their offspring following birth. If the brain of the fetal primate were fully developed in size and organization at birth, the mother and her offspring would be in considerable danger as this large structure passed through the body outlet formed by the mother's pelvic girdle. Incomplete development of the brain results in a prolonged period of infant dependence upon the mother while the brain continues to grow, until the newborn is capable of fending for itself. Again, this characteristic trend is most developed in humans, who spend 20 percent of their total life spans acquiring the maturity and social knowledge necessary to survive on their own (see Figure 3–4).

As we shall see, not all primates have all of these characteristics. As one ascends the evolutionary ladder, the traits become more apparent. The thumbs, for

Figure 3–4   *As these comparative primate age spans indicate, each stage of life is longer in duration in the higher primates. (After J. R. Napier and P. H. Napier, 1967)*

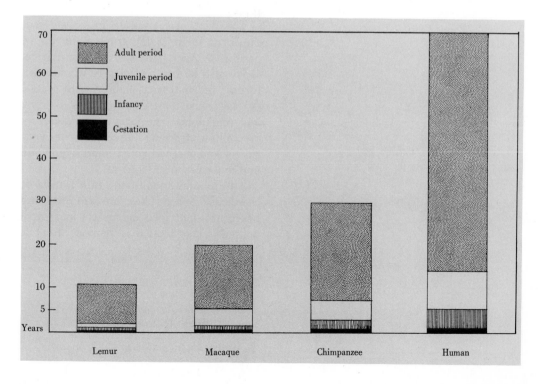

The Primate Order

example, become more opposable, posture becomes more erect, the brain becomes larger and more complex, and so on.

Prosimians

The word *prosimian* means "early monkey." The members of this group are quite primitive among the primates.

The lemurs live in Madagascar and the Comoro Islands, off Africa. The size of the lemur varies from the 4-ounce, 6-inch mouse lemur to the dog-sized indris. Most

The tarsier has large eyes and ears that are adaptations to its nocturnal lifestyle.

lemurs are *vegetarians,* subsisting on flowers, leaves, and some fruits. Although most are primarily arboreal, some lemurs do spend a fair amount of time on the ground, where they move about by bipedal locomotion. Some are *nocturnal,* active only at night; others are diurnal. Some are quadrupeds and some (the indrises) are *vertical clingers and leapers*—they cling to tree limbs in a vertical position and cover great distances as they leap from one trunk to another. Lemurs are also *scent markers,* stamping their habitat and other lemurs with urine and glandular secretions. Finally, lemurs are said to be *territorial* animals: they live in a specified area which they defend against invasion by other lemurs. Such a spacing mechanism prevents one area from being overpopulated by members of the same species who might rapidly deplete the food supply.

The next prosimian to be considered, the loris, inhabits the tropical forests of Southeast Asia and sub-Saharan Africa. It is entirely arboreal, nearly wholly nocturnal, and marks its habitat with scents. Its diet consists of insects, fruits, flowers, and vegetables. The loris moves about by creeping up trees and along branches very slowly and methodically, hand over hand and foot over foot.[3]

The tarsiers inhabit the rain forests of Southeast Asia.[4] They are arboreal and nocturnal, and feed on insects and small animals. The tarsier is named after its

3. Stephen I. Rosen, *Introduction to the Primates: Living and Fossil* (Englewood Cliffs, N. J.: Prentice-Hall, 1974).

4. Rosen, *Introduction to the Primates.*

Figure 3–5	**Summary of Prosimian Characteristics**

Thirty-six teeth
Show numerous specializations—for example, in body type and size (mostly small)
Do not superficially resemble most higher primates
Increasing trend toward color vision and stereovision
Large eyes and ears, lapping tongues, projecting muzzle, and expressionless faces
Variety of locomotor styles (quadrupedal, clinging, and leaping)
Demonstrate rudimentary social behavior and territoriality
Both diurnal and nocturnal forms, but mostly diurnal
Digits act in unison, rather than separately

elongated tarsal ankle bones which help it to leap great distances, as much as 7 feet in a single bound. Figure 3–5 summarizes the major prosimian characteristics.

The Anthropoids

The anthropoids—the so-called higher primates—are divided into three major groups: New World monkeys (*Ceboidea*), Old World monkeys (*Cercopithecoidea*), and apes and humans (*Hominoidea*).

NEW WORLD MONKEYS. New World monkeys live in the tropical forests of South America and some parts of Central America.[5] Like humans, most are *omniverous*, eating plants, fruits, insects, and small animals. All possess tails, which in some species are prehensile—that is, the tails serve as a kind of extra limb that can be wrapped around tree limbs and

other objects. All are arboreal, and all but the owl monkey are diurnal. Moreover, they have one premolar tooth more than all the anthropoids and, like the prosimians, possess a total of thirty-six teeth.

OLD WORLD MONKEYS. These monkeys range from Africa to Southeast Asia and Gibraltar, adapting even to the foothills of the Himalayas. Some live in trees in tropical forests, some on African savannas, some in snowy areas of the Japanese islands, some in cities around the temples in India. They lack prehensile tails, and most are larger than the American monkeys. Largely on the basis of habitat and diet, the Old World monkeys are divided into two subfamilies. The colobine monkeys, represented by colobus monkeys, Asian langurs, and several other species, are largely arboreal leaf-eaters. They rely on flight in the face of danger, are quick and agile, and have labyrinthine digestive systems. The cercopithecine monkeys, by contrast, are omniverous and largely ter-

5. Napier and Napier, *A Handbook of Living Primates.*

Figure 3–6	Summary of Characteristics of New and Old World Monkeys	
NEW WORLD MONKEYS	**OLD WORLD MONKEYS**	
Thirty-six teeth	Thirty-two teeth	
Platyrrhine noses	Catarrhine noses	
Variety in physical forms	Great differences between arboreal and terrestrial species	
Greater variety in locomotor patterns	Somewhat less variation in locomotor patterns	
Entirely arboreal	Terrestrial and arboreal	
All possess a tail which in some species is prehensile	No prehensile tail	
Slightly mobile digits, but more mobile than prosimians	Highly mobile digits	
Little sexual dimorphism	Marked sexual dimorphism in terrestrial forms	
No cheek pouches	Cheek pouches	

restrial. Many are also *sexually dimorphous*—that is, the secondary sexual characteristics (body size and build, for example) which develop after puberty show marked differences in males and females. For example, the males of some species are twice as big as the females. Moreover, the main structural defenses of the males—the daggerlike canine teeth—are larger and fiercer looking than those of the female. A summary of the differences between New World and Old World monkeys is shown in Figure 3–6.

APES. With humans, apes are members of the superfamily *Hominoidea*, which means "manlike." The apes are further subdivided into the hylobatids (gibbons) and pongids (orangutans, gorillas, and chimpanzees). The former are sometimes called lesser apes and the latter, great apes. The *Hominoidea* are distinguished from other primates by the fact that most are larger in size, do not possess a tail, and have relatively large, complex brains. Of all the *Hominoidea*, the humans are the only group that typically moves about by means of bipedal locomotion. Although apes sometimes stand or walk bipedally for short periods, their typical posture is better described as semierect. On the ground, chimpanzees and gorillas get about by means of *knuckle-walking*—the animal walks on all fours, using the middle portions of each finger to support the weight of its upper body.

Of all the apes, the agile *gibbon* is the only full-time *brachiator*—which means he swings hand over hand from one tree branch to the next. As a result, the arms of this primate are quite large, about one and one-half times the length of its trunk. The gibbon is wholly arboreal, living in the tropical rain forests of Southeast Asia, Sumatra, Java, and Borneo. The adult gibbon weighs from 10 to 20 pounds and

The agile gibbon, the king of the brachiators among apes, can cover up to 30 feet in a single leap.

semibrachiator, the orangutan, or "old man of the forest," is entirely arboreal and eats only plants and other vegetable matter. They build nests with a roof of leaves for protection from the elements. Males may weigh more than 150 pounds and females about 75 pounds, with marked sexual dimorphism. Orangs travel alone, in pairs with offspring, or occasionally in groups of five to ten animals. The red hair of these primates sets them apart from other apes, as do their unusual facial features—fat cheek pads which dominate the face of the adult male, and a balloonlike air sac that hangs from the neck and is used in vocalization. Orangs are shy and gentle. They are also an endangered species, being nearly hunted out of existence by humans.

The largest and heaviest of the primates, the *gorilla,* weighs up to 450 pounds in the wild. Gorillas live in the tropical forests and mountains of equatorial Africa. In comparison to other apes, gorillas have large hands and feet, a wide chest, a high forehead, and a face that appears to consist of shiny black leather—all of which contribute to its menacing appearance. However, the "King Kong" story notwithstanding, and as George Schaller discovered in his extensive studies of these beasts,[7] they are really quite shy. They spend most of their day eating leaves and other plant matter. For the

reaches up to 3 feet in height. The chief item in its diet is fruit, but it is also quite fond of fledgling birds, insects, and leaves. Unlike other apes, it does not build nests, and mature males and females often pair off and remain together for life. There is little sexual dimorphism among these most numerous of all apes.[6]

Orangutans are neighbors of the gibbon and live in Borneo and Sumatra. A

6. Rosen, *Introduction to the Primates.*

7. George Schaller, *The Year of the Gorilla* (Chicago: University of Chicago Press, 1964), and Schaller, "The Behavior of the Mountain Gorilla," in *Primate Behavior: Field Studies of Monkeys and Apes,* ed. Irven DeVore (New York: Holt, Rinehart and Winston, 1965).

most part, these gentle giants are terrestrial; each night they fashion sleeping nests of branches and twigs. Some of the smaller animals, particularly the females and young, sleep in tree nests and spend some waking time in the trees.

We have already met the most familiar member of the nonhuman primates, the *chimpanzee*. Although the adult of this species weighs only up to 150 pounds and stands barely 5 feet tall, it is quite powerful—equal in strength to five adult men.[8] Chimpanzees are partly terrestrial, partly tree-dwellers; at night they build sleeping nests in the trees. And like humans, they are *omniverous*, eating virtually anything —including plants, insects, fruit, small reptiles, and mammals. As we saw in the introductory capsule, they even devour

---

8. Rosen, *Introduction to the Primates*.

A gorilla knuckle-walking through its habitat. These ferocious-looking primates are actually docile animals that spend much of their day eating plant foods. At night, they build sleeping nests.

Figure 3–7   **Summary of Ape Characteristics**

Increasingly complex brains, particularly in chimpanzees and gorillas
All, except chimpanzees, are vegetarians
Mixed locomotor styles (all brachiate; knuckle-walking in African forms)
Wide variations in size
Extended period of infant dependency with tight mother–child bond
All fear water and so cannot swim
Great apes build nightly nests
All lack external tails

---

larger animals, such as monkeys, which they sometimes hunt cooperatively. Even more surprising is the fact that some chimpanzees apparently murder one another. Jane Goodall found that one group of chimps divided into two colonies. Shortly thereafter, the larger colony systematically attacked and wiped out the smaller one.[9] Figure 3–7 summarizes the trends in the evolution of the apes.

Primate Lifestyles

From the moment of birth, many primates spend the bulk of their time interacting with others of their kind. Some primates (gibbons, siamangs, and humans) live in small families, consisting of only two adults or a mother and her infant, whereas others (Japanese macaques) belong to groups having as many as 1,600 members. The average size of the primate group, however, lies somewhere between ten and seventy or eighty individuals. Chimpanzees, for example, usually travel in groups of thirty to eighty members.

In general, there are three types of primate groups. The most common is the multimale group, in which live two or more adult males, two or more adult females, plus juveniles and infants of both sexes. Macaques, many langurs, most baboons, and the majority of New World monkeys fall into this category, as do the chimpanzees. Second, is the one-male group, consisting of a single adult male and several females with their young. This type of group prevails among patas monkeys and certain species of baboons and prosimians. The third group is the monogamous single pair, bonded together almost like husband and wife. The gibbons, siamangs, and the New World titi monkeys maintain this type of relationship.[10]

The important point about the various kinds of primate social structures is that each represents an adaptation to some particular environment. One reason these

---

9. "Animal Behaviorist Finds Chimpanzees Take Others' Lives," *New York Times*, April 20, 1978, p. A-19.

10. Hans Kummer, *Primate Societies* (Chicago: Aldine Publishing, 1971).

adaptations are studied is that they may shed light on the ways in which our earliest ancestors adapted to their environments. An examination of some representative primate lifestyles will show the importance of the habitat for the social structure and behavior of these animals.

The Social Behavior of Old World Monkeys

Old World monkeys are closely related to humans, more so than their New World counterparts. Some terrestrial species may have made the same adaptations to their environments as our early ancestors. For this reason, they are studied extensively for hints about the forces that shaped our own evolution. Anthropologists have found one species of Old World forms—the savanna baboons of Africa—of special interest.

The Savanna Baboons

Baboons are members of the family *Cercopithecidae* and the genera *Papio* and *Theropithecus*. The five species of the genus *Papio* are the chacma, yellow, Guinea, olive, and hamadryas baboons. The first four groups are commonly referred to as savanna, or open-country, baboons because of their habitat—grasslands which contain scattered trees.

The open-country baboon lives in multimale social units called *troops*. The size of the troop ranges from twelve to 185 individuals, with an average of thirty to fifty animals. Like most other primates, baboons wander throughout a *home range*, the area in which the troop members spend their adult lives. The size of this area varies, depending on such factors as

troop size, food supplies, and the location of sleeping sites and neighboring troops. K. R. L. Hall and I. DeVore, for example, found that the home range for one troop of eighty-seven baboons was about 14 square miles, compared to 2 square miles for another troop of twelve.[11] The notion of home range must not be confused with that of territoriality. *Territory* is that space within a home range that a group will defend against invasion by others of its species. In most open-country species, territoriality does not appear to exist. There are no fights, for example, when one baboon troop encroaches on the territory of another. As we have seen, some primates living in lusher, more protected environments are territorial; this spacing mechanism helps prevent them from exhausting the food supply of any one area. Within the home range is the *core area* where the baboons normally eat, sleep, and carry out the activities of their daily round. One twenty-eight-member troop observed by Hall and DeVore,[12] for example, had three core areas totaling about 3 square miles within a 15.5-square-mile home range.

Baboons are basically vegetarians, some troops eating as many as ninety-four species of plant foods. They also consume insects, reptiles, shellfish, eggs, and small animals. Some catch and devour rabbits,

---

11. K. R. L. Hall and Irven DeVore, "Baboon Social Behavior," in *Primate Behavior: Field Studies of Monkeys and Apes*, ed. Irven DeVore (New York: Holt, Rinehart and Winston, 1965).

12. Hall and DeVore, "Baboon Social Behavior."

young gazelles, and vervet monkeys. At night, they sleep in trees and cliffs for protection against predators.

SOCIAL ORGANIZATION. The outstanding feature of savanna baboon social organization is the dominance hierarchy centered on the adult males. The hierarchy ranks all the adult males with respect to one another and determines who gets first choice of scarce resources, such as food. Generally, older and stronger individuals rule over the weaker ones, and males are usually dominant over females of the same age.[13] Dominance is also revealed in a number of other situations. A subordinate male, for example, will move if he occupies a choice sitting or sleeping position desired by a dominant male. This action is known as *supplantation*. Often, too, a subordinate male will approach a dominant animal by *presenting* his hind quarters to the superior baboon, a way of saying, "I don't want trouble." Typically, the dominant animal may then briefly *mount* the other—that is, assume the mating posture—to show that he has accepted the submissive gesture.

Each member learns his rank in the dominance hierarchy—usually during play activity as a subadult. Such ranking keeps peace by preventing fights over resources. Troop members know one another's strength and rank order, and a low-ranking individual typically will not challenge a high-ranking one. Despite this tight organization, however, tension runs high in savanna baboon troops. There is always a great deal of harassment, bickering, and quarreling—which sometimes accelerate to skirmishes—with growling, slapping,

and canine flashing. In most cases, however, the *yawn threat*, in which one animal yawns to expose its canine teeth, is often sufficient to put another troop member in its place.

Along with dominance behavior, there is a high degree of sexual dimorphism among baboons. The male appears to outstrip the female in those characteristics that enable him to put up a good fight. The male, for instance, is larger in body size, generally more muscular and, of course, has larger canine teeth. The dominant males protect troop members from dangerous predators. When a baboon troop is on the move across the open savanna, it assumes a specific configuration—the dominant males accompany females with infants at the center of the troop. The younger males, who are expendable, form a protective barrier at the

The yawn threat of this baboon warns other troop members that he means business.

---

13. Kummer, *Primate Societies*.

flanks, and older males make up the front and rear guard. When the troop confronts a predator, such as a cheetah, the adult males of most savanna species quickly place themselves between the predator and the rest of the troop. While the big males flash their canines and bark loudly at the enemy, the rest of the troop scrambles to safety.

The dominant male of the troop also has other tasks. It is he, for example, who breaks up destructive and wasteful infighting among juveniles, females, and low-ranking males. Such *policing* is a way of assuring that troop members save their energy for confrontations with predators. The dominant male also protects mothers with infants from harassment by other members, and generally helps lead the troop; with the cooperation of other members, he decides when to rise in the morning, when and where to forage for food, and where to bed down for the night.

Many anthropologists believe that these traits—tight social organization, including a rigid dominance hierarchy, a high level of controlled intragroup aggression, and pronounced sexual dimorphism— probably represent adaptations to a hostile open-country environment. Life on the open ground more or less leaves the animal to its own devices. A terrestrial animal without some kind of large teeth, claws, or other weapon (such as intelligence or a tightly controlled social organization) with which to protect itself would be quickly decimated by predators.

The same is generally not true for arboreal forms, first, because few predators enter the trees, and second, because it is relatively easy for the agile primates to escape from those that do. Since arboreal primates do not have to stand and fight their enemies, there is no reason for the males to be larger than the females or to have a social structure that is organized around protection. Some investigators point out, however, that this theory does not always apply. Orangutans, for example, are sexually dimorphous, but arboreal, with little or no intragroup aggression.

The idea that the dominance hierarchy is an adaptation to the harsh environment is exhibited in times of food scarcity. At such times, dominant males will have priority in taking food, the subordinate animals often going without. In this way, the survival of the older, superior animal— who is more socially knowledgeable, experienced, and reproductively active—is guaranteed at the expense of the more expendable younger animals.[14]

It is interesting to note that baboons entering the protected environment of the forest (where humans have killed off their natural predators) assume a looser social organization: there is far less intragroup aggression, the females are less subordinate, and the tight dominance hierarchy appears to diminish as the principal shaper of social organization.[15] Indeed, one instance has been reported in which an old male with broken canines led a forest-dwelling troop. But when the same troop moved back into the open country, the dominance-oriented pattern was resumed. This suggests that the behavior observed in open-country primates is probably not *species-specific*—that is, it is not practiced by all baboon species. Instead, social

---

14. Kummer, *Primate Societies.*

15. Thelma E. Rowell, "Forest-living Baboons in Uganda," *Journal of Zoology* 149 (1966) : 344–364.

structure and behavior are probably *environment-specific,* or related to the environment in which the animals live.

The Social Behavior of Apes

As the passage that opened this chapter demonstrates, some apes display behavior that is similar to that of humans. The species of ape to be examined here is the forest-dwelling chimpanzee studied by Jane Goodall.[16]

The Forest Chimpanzee

The chimpanzees discussed by Goodall live in the forests of the Gombe Stream Research Center in Tanzania, East Africa. About sixty to eighty chimps make their home in this area where food is abundant and available all year. These animals are nomadic, following apparently irregular patterns as they search for food by day and for sleeping places at night.[17] Although they are mostly quadruped knuckle-walkers, chimpanzees have been observed standing erect and running on their hind legs for short distances. They also spend time in the trees, where they move about either quadrupedally or by brachia-tion. Chimpanzees travel in small heterosexual groups which consist of individuals of all ages. The mother-child group is the only stable bond among these animals.

By the age of one year or so, the youngster begins to play with other children. Running, jumping, and wrestling are some of the play activities. As with all other primates, play among the young chimpanzees is an important learning activity. During these periods, the animals learn to sharpen physical and social skills, as well as their places in the dominance hierarchy. By interacting with peers in these nonchallenging situations, they also absorb the correct behavioral codes of chimpanzee society.

Indeed, the growing years are important in the life of the primate because they are a period of *learning.* At this formative time, the young animal explores its surroundings, observing and imitating the behaviors of others that will enable it to survive and be a successful member of the group. In many other species, the young depend primarily on *instinct* for survival—complex and stereotyped behavior patterns are wired into their hereditary materials. The animals are able to perform these behaviors virtually from birth. A young spider, for example, is able to spin a web without ever having seen it done before. Chimpanzee babies, and those of other primates, however, lack such detailed genetic instructions: they must learn most of their survival behaviors by imitation and by trial and error. Their behaviors are sufficiently flexible to invent—and to learn from other inventors—techniques that will enable the animals to adapt successfully to their surroundings.

This is not to say, however, that all

---

16. Jane Goodall, "Chimpanzees of the Gombe Stream Reserve," in *Primate Behavior: Field Studies of Monkeys and Apes,* ed. Irven DeVore (New York: Holt, Rinehart and Winston, 1965), and Jane van Lawick-Goodall, *In the Shadow of Man* (New York: Dell Publishing, 1971).

---

17. Goodall, "Chimpanzees of the Gombe Stream Reserve," and van Lawick-Goodall, *In the Shadow of Man.*

primate behavior patterns are learned. Some are *innate,* or instinctive. Among the most dramatic of these is probably the gorilla's chest-beating display, performed by the adult male to reinforce its dominance or to frighten off an enemy. The dramatic ritual, as George Schaller describes it, has nine components performed in a definite sequence.[18] These include hooting, throwing vegetation around, vigorously pounding its chest, running sideways on all fours, shaking branches, and breaking off tree limbs.

Like most other primates, chimpanzees engage in *grooming*—scratching and cleaning one another's fur, removing dirt, parasites, and other debris. Besides keeping one another clean, primate grooming also serves an important social function: it is a sign of reassurance, submission, and what we would call friendship. Primate mothers, for example, spend a great deal of time grooming their young. Subordinate animals often groom superiors as a sign of appeasement or submission. In short, grooming is an important cohesive force in the social bond that holds the primate group together.

Interpersonal relations are quite relaxed among chimpanzees. Although a dominance hierarchy does exist, it is not as rigid as that of the savanna baboons. Apparently, the chimps living in the protection of the forest are not as exposed to danger as are the baboons living in the open. Hence, the apes do not require a tight defensive social organization. Long friendships are not uncommon among chimpanzees, and close friends will sometimes come to one another's aid in time of need. In sexual relations, these primates are, to human eyes at least, quite casual. An estrous female, for example, will mate with all the males who approach her, one after the other.

As with baboons, the environment is a factor in the social structure of chimpanzee troops. Savanna chimpanzees, for example, are organized more rigidly than Goodall's forest-dwellers and tend to be more aggressive. Studies by A. Kortlandt[19] emphasize this point. In one experiment, this investigator placed a stuffed leopard in a clearing. The dummy was mounted on a trolley and had realistic looking glass eyes, a mouth that opened and closed, and a head that turned. When confronted with this lifelike predator, the forest chimpanzees tended to flee, typically by scurrying up the nearest tree. But their savanna-dwelling counterparts behaved quite differently: They flailed at the phony leopard with sticks, clubbed it, and threw objects at it. Again, many investigators interpret this behavior as demonstration of the hypothesis that primate behavior is flexible and varied, that it is modified by the environment and is not entirely preconditioned by heredity. From such studies, Kortlandt concluded that the use of weapons by our early ancestors originated as a result of the demands of open-country living.

18. Schaller, *The Year of the Gorilla,* and "The Behavior of the Mountain Gorilla."

19. A. Kortlandt, "Experimentation with Chimpanzees in the Wild," in *Neue Ergebnisse der Primatologie,* ed. D. Starck, R. Schneider, and H.-J. Kuhn (Stuttgart, Germany: Fischer, 1967), pp. 208–224.

PROTOCULTURE OF THE CHIMPAN-ZEES. Chimpanzees and some other nonhuman primates possess a *protoculture* —a simple set of learned behavior patterns that are passed down through the generations. As we saw, chimpanzees perform rain dances. They also may make and use tools—leaf sponges to sop up drinking water, leaves to clean themselves, sticks and rocks to hurl at enemies, and sleeping nests. One of the more interesting of the chimpanzee tools is the *termite fishing stick*—a grass stalk or twig, stripped of its leaves and shortened when necessary to fit into a termite nest. The ape places this tool into a hole in the nest, withdraws it, and licks off the protein-rich termites clinging to the twig. An animal will continue this "termite fishing" for hours, until its appetite is sated. The important point about chimpanzee tool use is that it is not innate, stereotyped behavior like the gorilla's chest-beating display. Rather, it is learned and passed on to other animals. As such, it qualifies as a *protocultural practice.*

Another protocultural element of chimpanzee society is the cooperative hunting of other animals, such as the colobus monkey hunt described at the beginning of the chapter. After a successful hunt, the apes may congregate in *sharing clusters,* in which they share and eat the fruits of the kill.[20] Apart from humans, chimpanzees and baboons are the only primates who have been seen sharing meat.

The discovery that chimpanzees use tools and cooperatively hunt and share food is extremely important for students of human evolution. As we shall see in Chapter 5, these practices are found among our early ancestors and are frequently part of a set of diagnostic markers used by anthropologists to separate species belonging to the human line from those of the nonhuman line.

Chimpanzees and gorillas have also been taught by humans to communicate symbolically. In 1966, for example, Allen and Beatrice Gardner raised a chimpanzee in their home and taught the animal to communicate with them in the American Sign Language. The chimpanzee, named Washoe, eventually developed a vocabulary of 150 different signs. This experiment and others are fully discussed in Chapter 15.

In summary, this chapter has attempted to show that all members of the primate order, including humans, share a large number of characteristics that set them apart from the rest of the animal kingdom. It has tried to demonstrate that the study of primate behavior is relevant to the study of our own behavior because certain non-human primates, particularly some great apes, resemble us in feeding, sexual activity, intelligence, aggression, and even murder.

At the same time, it must be pointed out that there is no simple conclusion regarding the ways humans differ from their fellow primates. In the words of Alison Jolly, humans "are not just oversexed apes or killer apes or grammatical apes."[21] The one common denominator,

20. G. Teleki, "The Omniverous Chimpanzee," *Scientific American* 288 (January 1973) : 32–42.

21. Alison Jolly, *The Evolution of Primate Behavior* (New York: Macmillan, 1972), p. viii.

however, appears to be that all primates are social beings. For example, virtually every facet of human behavior, from eating to sexual relations to reading textbooks, depends on the kind of society we live in and the support it gives us. As we shall see, this theme is woven throughout the sections of this text that deal with cultural anthropology. Our next task in this physical anthropology section is to see how all organisms—including human and nonhuman primates—evolved to their present status.

Summary

1. Taxonomy provides the rules for classifying organisms and for indicating their relationships to one another in terms of body structure, and evolutionary development.
2. As a result of adaptation to an arboreal environment, primates developed a series of traits involving the sense organs and brain, limb and locomotor structures, and reproductive system. Among these are a relatively large, complex brain, prehensile digits, a clavicle, a reproductive system designed for single rather than multiple fetuses, and a relatively long period of maturation.
3. The prosimians, which include the lemur, loris, and tarsier, are the least evolved of the primates. They exhibit numerous specializations in locomotion, body type and size, and other features.
4. New World monkeys are entirely arboreal, with little sexual dimorphism; they show a great variety of body forms and locomotor patterns. Old World monkeys live in many varied habitats and have marked sexual dimorphism. In form and patterns of locomotion,

they are less varied than the American monkeys.
5. Trends in the evolution of the apes include increasingly complex brains, a tendency toward erect posture, wide variation in size, and extended period of infant dependency.
6. As an adaptation to their open-country environment, savanna baboons have developed a tight social organization, including a rigid dominance hierarchy, a high level of controlled intragroup aggression, and pronounced sexual dimorphism. The fact that forest-dwelling baboons do not have the same kind of social organization suggests that primate social structure is environment-specific rather than species-specific.
7. Chimpanzees possess a protoculture which includes tool manufacture and use, cooperative hunting, food-sharing, and symbolic communication.

Review Questions

1. What is taxonomy and why is it important to the study of primates and other organisms?
2. As a result of their arboreal adaptation, primates developed a number of interrelated traits. In your own words, describe any two of these traits and their relationships to one another.
3. List some of the ways in which Old World monkeys differ from New World monkeys.
4. What is the relationship between the social organization of the savanna baboon and its environment?
5. What is protoculture? Give an example. Why is it significant for studies of human evolution?

Suggested Readings

Jay, Phyllis C., ed. *Primates: Studies in Adaptation and Variability*. New York: Holt, Rinehart and Winston, 1968.

An excellent collection of nineteen articles by leading primatologists on aspects of various primates, including learning, communication, territoriality, tool use, aggression, and social organization.

Jolly, Alison. *The Evolution of Primate Behavior*. New York: Macmillan, 1972.

A comprehensive look at virtually all aspects of the primates, with sections devoted to taxonomy, ecological adaptation, social life, and intelligence.

Kummer, Hans. *Primate Societies: Group Techniques of Ecological Adaptation*. Chicago: Aldine Publishing, 1971.

An examination of the effect of the environment and other factors on primate social behavior and the ways in which different terrestrial monkeys adapt to their surroundings.

Napier, J. R., and Napier, P. H. *A Handbook of Living Primates*. New York: Academic Press, 1967.

A highly regarded study of the primate order, genus by genus, by two leading authorities on the subject.

van Lawick-Goodall, Jane. *In the Shadow of Man*. New York: Dell Publishing, 1971.

An engaging, informative account of the author's study of the chimpanzees at the Gombe Stream Reserve in Tanzania. The book conveys much of the flavor of what it is like to live among wild primates on a day-to-day basis.

Chapter 4

Organic Evolution

CHARLES DARWIN AT THE GALÁPAGOS ISLANDS

In September of 1835 the *Beagle* reached the Galápagos Archipelago 600 miles off the coast of South America and directly upon the Equator. These burnt-out volcanic chimneys, parched and blackened as an iron foundry, made a profound impression upon Darwin. The sequence of his travels had been such that his arrival could not have been better timed to impress upon his mind a series of facts, both geological and biological, which were necessary to the formulation of his theories. . . .

What Darwin has to say in his autobiography will gain in emphasis if we first place ourselves under the conditions encountered by the young naturalist in 1835 and try, as nearly as we can, to see the Galápagos fauna as he first saw it. He came to the islands already impressed by the similarity of the extinct armored glyptodonts to their living relative, the armadillo. He had seen the slow variation in the form of related species as one moved along the great distances of the South American coasts, or passed from one side of the great Andean mountain barrier to the other. He had obtained an impression of creatures, both from times remote and from the diverse conditions of the present, showing surprisingly similar types of

Source: Loren Eiseley, *Darwin's Century: Evolution and the Men Who Discovered It* (Garden City, N.Y.: Doubleday & Company, Anchor Books, 1961), pp. 167–168, 171– 173.

structure—surprising, that is, if one had to assume the orthodox view that they were all totally distinct creations and in that sense unrelated to each other. He had stared at a penguin's wing and had perceived that by certain modifications a wing could be made to beat its way through either water or air. Was it logical to suppose that all these clever adaptations to circumstance had been plucked out of a vacuum? Were not these remarkable structures built on what was basically the same plan? And could not this plan be, perhaps, pulled this way or that way, distorted, remolded, made to fit the animal to some difficult environment? But if so, what influence was at work? Did life in some manner respond to the environment? Did the climate, the surroundings of an animal, in some manner impinge upon his protoplasm and slowly draw these modifications of structure out of him? It seemed fantastic. How could climate, about which people talked so glibly, adapt a woodpecker for climbing trees or a hummingbird to probe into a flower? . . .

In this strange little isolated world Darwin set immediately to work collecting all the animals, plants, insects, and reptiles he could locate. He visited several of the islands and collected upon all of them. In this work he made one serious mistake: he did not, until late in his visit, attempt to keep similar species from individual islands separately labeled in his collections.

This situation quite clearly came about because Darwin—although impressed from his South American experience with the evidence pointing toward plant and animal evolution—had not as yet fully grasped the possibility of dissimilar paths of development being taken by related organisms in close proximity on nearby islets. Darwin was, in other words, still seeking for the key to evolution in the exterior environment, in climate, in the natural surroundings of a given area. He had not expected to observe, in this score of islands clustered together and containing less than 2,800 square miles all told, much in the way of regional distinctions. That the fauna might differ from that of the neighboring continent was to be expected, but scarcely this strange divergence over little patches of sea in a totally similar climate.

Slowly, as Darwin talked with the local inhabitants, a different and strange impression grew upon him—an impression destined to be confirmed and heightened after his return home, when the intensive examination of his specimens was to begin. In one of his notebooks of 1835 he dwells on the fact that the Spaniards could distinguish from which island the huge tortoises had been brought, and he similarly notes, "Islands in sight of each other . . . tenanted by . . . birds but slightly differing in structure." From this time on, the full force of his wide-ranging mind is turned upon the archipelago. Such facts as these, he grows powerfully aware, "would undermine the stability of species."

By the time that the first edition of the *Journal of Researches* was published, Darwin, when he came to the subject of the Galápagos, was willing to throw out several evolutionary hints. "There is a rat," he records, "which Mr. Waterhouse believes is probably distinct from the English kind; but I cannot help suspecting that it is only the same altered by the peculiar conditions of its new country." The finches in particular fascinated him. They differed remarkably in the structure of their beaks. Some had small beaks like warblers, some had thick, massive beaks. In the end, Darwin wrote regretfully of his many species of finches that although he suspected certain of the distinct types were confined to separate islands, he "was not aware of these facts till my collection was nearly completed." *"It never occurred to me,"* he explained, *"that the productions of islands only a few miles apart, and places under the same physical conditions would be dissimilar.* I therefore did not attempt to make a series of specimens from the separate islands."

This statement is extremely revelatory. As we have previously intimated, Darwin had, up to this point, been looking at variation largely over the great vertical distance of past time or horizontally over wide geographic areas. Under such circumstances one was apt to invoke climatic change as the primary mechanism involved in evolution. Here, in the Galápagos, Darwin was brought up short by a new series of facts: variation in form under isolation with the physical environment remaining precisely the same. As Darwin himself was later to observe, "One might really fancy that from an original paucity of birds in this archipelago one species had been taken and modified for different ends." Darwin at last was face to face with the greatest of the evolutionary mysteries. If life varied on the individual islands of an archipelago subjected to the same climatic conditions, what determined this variation?[1]

• • • • • • • •

Organic Evolution

During the nineteenth century, the prevailing view of life in the Western world was that all organisms had been created by God at the same instant and remained changeless for all time.

The primates discussed in Chapter 3 reached their present state of development through the process of *organic evolution*—which, for the moment, can be defined as the process whereby characteristics of a group of organisms change over time. Starting with the work of the British naturalists Charles Darwin (1809–1882) —the subject of the capsule study—and Alfred Wallace (1823–1913), this chapter will examine how the study of evolution began, took root, and became refined. We will also look at the mechanisms of evolution, including the basis of heredity, the way organisms change, and the forces that advance and retard this change.

1. Loren Eiseley, *Darwin's Century: Evolution and the Men Who Discovered It* (Garden City, N.Y.: Doubleday, Anchor Books, 1961), pp. 167–168, 171–173.

Chapter Four

An Outline of Evolutionary Theory

The accomplishment of Darwin and Wallace was to develop a theory of organic evolution that explained how plants and animals evolve. As Richard Leakey and Roger Lewin have put it:

> *What Darwin had accomplished was to demonstrate how, through an exceedingly gradual (passive) adaptation to the environment and through changes from generation to generation, a species may diversify or simply become better attuned to its world, producing, ultimately, a creature which is different in form from its ancestor.*[2]

During the time of Darwin and Wallace, the prevailing view of Western scholars was that the earth and all living things had been created by God 6,000 years before. This school of thought held that every kind of plant and animal was created fixed and immutable for all time. Even human beings were not exempt from this Divine act: The first man and woman arrived on the scene, full-blown, in the form of Adam and Eve. Indeed, some 200 years before Darwin, the English Bishop James Ussher (1581–1656) worked out the time of the Creation down to the very hour. God made the earth, he said, precisely at 9 A.M. on October 23, 4004 B.C.

During the eighteenth and nineteenth centuries, a number of thinkers supplied ideas which helped Darwin and Wallace devise a theory that would contradict the

---

2. Richard E. Leakey and Roger Lewin, *Origins* (New York: E. P. Dutton, 1977), p. 30.

above beliefs. One of the first names that figures in the history of evolutionary theory of this time is one we met in Chapter 3—Carolus Linnaeus (1707–1778). This Swedish botanist classified all known plants and animals into categories that ranged from the least inclusive to the most inclusive. Although Linnaeus agreed with the idea that species were fixed, he contributed to evolutionary thought by giving Darwin and Wallace a classificatory device that enabled them to organize all of their observations concerning evolutionary change in organisms.

Other important pieces of information came from the English social philosopher Thomas Malthus (1766–1834). Malthus placed reproduction at the top of a chain of events that would always result in the production of more offspring than food available to feed them. That is, the food supply of a given group of organisms would remain relatively constant, while the numbers of these organisms would swell dramatically. Malthus envisioned a constant, unrelenting struggle, arguing that the human race would overrun the earth if not held in check by war, famine, and disease. Darwin later restated this same idea somewhat differently, noting that "more offspring would always be born than would survive." He noted further that even considering the tremendous reproductive force, there always seemed to be a balance due to the death of large numbers of individuals in every generation.

Another contribution came from the English geologist Charles Lyell (1798–1875). Lyell advanced the theory of *uniformitarianism*, which holds that the same physical forces that shape and change today's earth—wind, water, earthquakes, and the like—also altered the ancient earth. Moreover, these forces would require extraordinarily long periods of time to do their job and to produce the layers of earth that had been documented by many investigators. This meant that the age of the earth was far older than the Biblical 6,000 years—an idea that was absolutely necessary if an evolutionary theory of slow, gradual organic change was to be accepted by scholars.

The next character in the drama of evolutionary history was the Frenchman Chevalier de Lamarck (1744–1829). This naturalist proposed an evolutionary theory that fully explained how organisms evolved and diversified. Lamarck's achievement was to offer a mechanism that explained how evolution proceeds. As Darwin and Wallace would state later, Lamarck proposed that organisms constantly interacted with their environment. As the environment changed, these organisms changed anatomically and behaviorally in order to survive. A modern investigator would say that the organisms *adapted* to their surroundings, just as the baboons and chimpanzees discussed in Chapter 3 did. During the course of their adaptation, said Lamarck, certain physical structures changed—becoming larger, longer, or stronger—the more frequently they were used. Conversely, structures that were not being used in adaptation were reduced. All these acquired changes were inherited by individuals of the next generation.

Today, most scholars believe that an organism does not inherit characteristics acquired by its parents during the course of their lives. A weight lifter's son, for example, will not be born with bulging muscles. But Lamarck's real contribution to evolutionary theory was his proposal that plants and animals do change over time and some natural mechanism is responsible for this change. It is this mechanism that Darwin was on the threshold of discovering in the capsule study.

Darwin's Theory of Evolution

Charles Darwin synthesized many of these ideas discussed in the preceding section into a theory of evolution that is accepted by most modern investigators. His other important contribution was to provide a mechanism that would plausibly explain how evolution proceeded. But he was not alone in this momentous achievement. Darwin is thought to have developed his theory some time around 1838, soon after he returned from the trip described in the capsule study. But he did not publish it. During the next twenty years, he collected the data that he would need to support his hypothesis.

In 1858, he was shocked when he received in the mail a short article by Alfred Wallace, a fellow naturalist who at the time was studying in Malaysia. The article, entitled "On the Tendency of Varieties to Depart Indefinitely from the Original Type," summarized the theory that Darwin had spent twenty years of his life refining. Darwin proposed to Wallace that they combine their efforts, each reading his paper before the Royal Society so that both would receive credit for the discovery. Wallace agreed, and the papers were presented in 1858. One year later, Darwin published the fruits of his research in a book entitled *On the Origin of Species by Natural Selection.*

This work denied the notion that every species of plant and animal appeared on the earth all at once by force of Divine

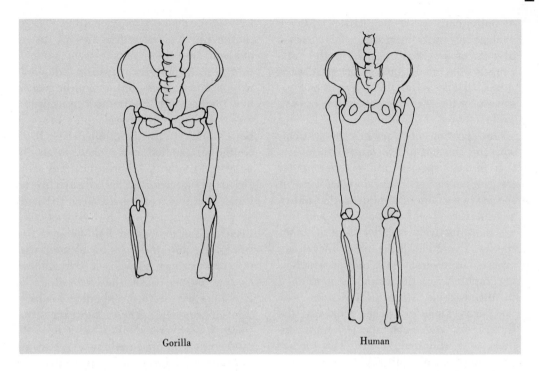

Gorilla   Human

Figure 4–1   *Darwin's theory of evolution was supported by anatomical studies. The similarities between the pelvises of gorillas and humans hinted that the two were related through a common ancestor.*

Creation. Instead, Darwin argued, all organisms are related to one another because they evolved over billions of years from the same ancestor, and they differ from one another today because they have separated from that ancestor as they adapted to different environments.

THE THEORY OF NATURAL SELECTION. Darwin observed that individual organisms have the potential to produce more offspring than can necessarily survive. This leads to competition for food, living space, and other resources, and the struggle tends to favor the fittest individuals. In this case, "fitness" refers solely to reproductive success: those offspring within a species that reproduce the greatest number of viable offspring are the fit. These organisms are those that have adapted most successfully to their environment.

Darwin also noted that individual organisms vary in physical characteristics that seem related to their success or failure in the struggle for survival. From these observations he deduced that individuals who possess characteristics or traits that better adapt them to their environment are more likely to survive and increase at the expense of less favored individuals. Very gradually the proportion of individuals in the population with advantageous traits increases. This process of *natural selection* results, in the long run, in the evolution of better-adapted forms. Hence Darwin's hypothesis is known as the *theory of evolution by natural selection.*

One portion of Darwin's book deals with the concept of *speciation*, the evolution of one species into another under the influence of natural selection. A *species* is a group of organisms that naturally interbreed with one another and that are reproductively isolated from all other species. Evolution at the species level can proceed in several ways, one of which is geographical isolation, which is mentioned in the capsule study. There, we saw that many kinds of finches inhabited the Galápagos, and each species was confined to a different island. The finches had adapted to different environments, each group of birds becoming so different in behavior and structure (particularly the beaks) that they could not interbreed. Thus, these different groups of finches are said to belong to separate species.

Environmental change is another important factor in evolution. If a forest were to be transformed into a grassy plain as a result of climatic changes, for example, the forest-dwelling creatures would be pressured into making behavioral modifications if they were to survive. As we shall see in Chapters 5 through 7, environmental change has been a key variable in the evolution of our own ancestors.

Natural Selection in Action

It is difficult to see the process of natural selection at work because it usually takes place slowly over numerous generations, by means of subtle, imperceptible changes in the physical characteristics of an organism. But there is a classic example that reveals how an organism adapts in response to changes in the environment— how the best-fitted individuals are selected to survive and the least-adapted are winnowed out. The British biologist H. B. D. Kettlewell studied color changes in the peppered moth in Manchester, England.[3] He noted that prior to the Industrial Revolution, the moth had a light-colored body and wings, peppered with dark spots, and lived on the lichens of light-colored tree trunks. Because the creature blended with its surroundings so well, it was difficult to spot by the birds that preyed on it. But there were also dark-bodied moths in this environment. These, however, were small in number (about 1 percent of the total number of peppered moths). Because their dark bodies stood out against the light color of the trees, many were eaten by the predatory birds. In evolutionary terms, the birds acted as the selective agent that eliminated those moths that were not well adapted to the environment.

With the coming of the Industrial Revolution, however, this situation was reversed. Soot from the factories settled on the trees, making them darker. As a result, the light moths, which now stood out, were taken by the birds in greater numbers than their dark counterparts. In short, selective pressure against the dark individuals was relaxed at the same time that it was tightened against the light-

---

3. H. B. D. Kettlewell, "The Phenomenon of Industrial Melanism in Lepidoptera," *Annual Review of Entymology* 6 (1961): 245–262.

The dark-colored moth shown here successfully adapted to environmental changes.

complex and uniquely human adaptive response to our environment—culture.

Darwin's Dilemma

The theory of evolution by natural selection had great impact on nineteenth-century thought because it offered a convincing, scientific explanation for the evolutionary development of life on earth. Moreover, it explained the diversity of life—how organisms were related to one another and how they differed from one another, both because of evolution. But powerful as it was, the theory had one loophole that Darwin himself could not close. What was not clear was how new variations arose and how they were inherited. In *On the Origin of Species*, Darwin wrote:

> *The laws governing inheritance are for the most part unknown. No one can say why the same peculiarity in different individuals of the same species, or in different species, is sometimes inherited and sometimes not so; why the child often reverts in certain characters to its grandfather or grandmother or more remote ancestors.*[4]

In the end, Darwin fell back on the Lamarckian fallacy of the inheritance of acquired characteristics. Darwin died in 1882, unaware that the answer to his problem had been worked out in detail sixteen years earlier by an obscure Austrian monk named Gregor Mendel.

colored animals. Consequently, the fitness —the reproductive success—of the darker moths rose while that of the light ones fell. By the turn of the century, the dark variety had increased to the point where they comprised about 99 percent of the moth population.

Behavioral adaptations can also result from environmental changes and pressures. In Chapter 3, we saw how the social behavior of baboons is an important part of their survival mechanism. The social units of these monkeys are tightly organized and arranged in dominance hierarchies. Living in such groups affords the baboons advantages in food-getting and protection against predators that living alone cannot. Humans also live in groups for protection, subsistence, and companionship. But we have developed a

4. Charles Darwin, *On the Origin of Species* (1859; reprint ed., New York: Random House, Modern Library, 1936), p. 19.

The Mechanisms of Heredity

Mendel (1822–1888) was the first to predict mathematically the inheritance of certain traits and the way they were transmitted from parent to offspring. Mendel's research went unheeded by the scientific community for thirty-five years. Then, in 1903, his findings were discovered by three scientists working independently. With this find, the science of heredity took a great leap forward. The development of powerful microscopes enabled researchers to peer deeper into the cell where the hereditary materials were located. Around the middle of the present century, workers were able to unravel the very molecular structure of these materials.

Mendel and Heredity

Mendel performed a series of systematic and meticulous experiments with the pea plant over a two-year period. He studied how seven clearly identifiable characteristics of the pea plant were passed on from one generation to the next. Among the characteristics were the color of the peas (green or yellow), the form of the ripe seeds (wrinkled or smooth), and the stem length (tall or dwarf). In one experiment, for example, he transferred pollen from a plant having smooth seeds to one having wrinkled seeds. When Mendel opened the pods of the hybrid offspring, he saw that the seeds were all smooth.

Had the characteristics that governed the wrinkled coats vanished? Mendel wondered. To find out, he allowed the hybrids to pollinate themselves, as pea plants normally do. Examining the offspring of this self-pollination, he found that the wrinkled seeds of the grandparents had reappeared. When he counted the offspring, Mendel discovered that out of a total of 7,324 peas, 5,474 were smooth and 1,850 were wrinkled—an approximate ratio of three to one. The same was true for the other traits he tested. In the experiment on stem length, for example, approximately three-fourths of the hybrid offspring plants had tall stems and one-fourth had dwarf stems.

In crossing each of the seven characteristics, one at a time, one trait seemed to prevail over, or dominate, the other. The smooth seed dominated the wrinkled one, for instance. This Mendel called the *dominant trait*. It is normally indicated by a capital letter (*S* for smooth, *T* for tall, and so on). The trait that appeared to be lost in one generation, only to show up in a succeeding one, he called *recessive*. This is typically labeled with a small letter (*s* for not smooth, *t* for not tall, for example).

Furthermore, Mendel concluded that smoothness, tallness, and all the other traits were somehow locked into the plant's hereditary machinery. The hereditary units that determine the characteristics of each plant, he said, are found in pairs, and the offspring receives one hereditary unit for each trait from each parent. When the plants were bred, it was the union of the hereditary units that determined the outward physical appearance of the offspring.

Today, Mendel's hereditary units are known as *genes,* and the science that studies gene structure and function is called *genetics.* Each of a pair of genes that govern any given trait is known as an *allele.* If both alleles of a gene pair for any particular trait are the same—be they dominant or recessive—the individual is said to be *homozygous* for that trait. Conversely, if the alleles of a gene pair are different, the individual is *heterozygous* for the trait.

The genetic makeup of an organism is called its *genotype* and its observable characteristics, its *phenotype*. To see what these terms mean, let us examine Figure 4–2. The three round offspring of the second generation of peas have the same phenotype—that is, in appearance all the seeds are smooth. But the genotype of the pea to the far left is different from that of the two peas to its right, in that it has genes only for the smooth trait. The two other smooth peas, by contrast, are heterozygotes, having inherited both the smooth and wrinkled traits. The pea to the far right, by contrast, is different from the other three, both in phenotype (it is wrinkled in appearance) and in genotype (it has inherited only genes for the wrinkled trait).

Figure 4–2   *A simple Mendelian cross between round and wrinkled peas.*

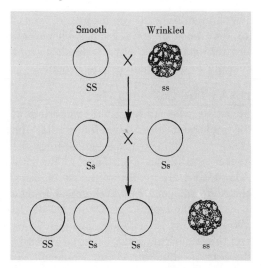

It is important to point out that natural selection acts on phenotypes. But, as a result of differential reproductive success over time (that is, only the fittest phenotypes survive to reproduce), genotypes change. In the case of the moths after the arrival of industrialism, for example, natural selection winnowed out the light-colored phenotypes. Because many more dark-colored animals than light-colored ones were contributing genes to the succeeding generation, the genotypes, too, changed.

Gene Action

Mendel worked without a microscope and had no way of directly observing the mechanism that governed the transmission of genes. But later studies revealed that the genes are located on threadlike structures in the cell nucleus known as *chromosomes*—so called because they are visible under the microscope when stained with dye. Indeed, the word comes from the Greek *chroma*, "color," and *some*, "body." Chromosomes are found in pairs and different organisms have their own characteristic number of pairs of chromosomes. Each body cell of Mendel's pea plant, for instance, has seven pairs of chromosomes, and each body cell of humans carries 23 pairs. Chromosomes can contain hundreds of thousands of genes, arranged in a definite sequence along their length.

How are the chromosomes, and the alleles they contain, transmitted? The answer is found in the way cells behave during reproduction. When most human body cells reproduce, each of the 46 chromosomes divides in two, then migrates to the opposite end of the cell. A cell wall appears between the two groups of chromosomes, pinches off, and two

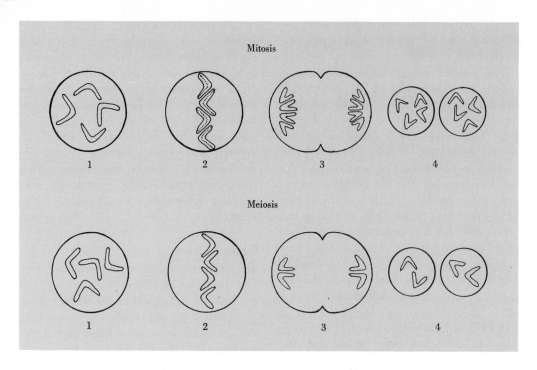

Figure 4–3   *Mitosis and meiosis are different forms of cellular reproduction. Mitosis occurs in body cells (those that make up the arm, eye, or liver, for example). Meiosis occurs in sex cells (the sperm and egg).*

cells, each containing 46 chromosomes, are formed. This kind of cellular reproduction is called *mitosis* (see Figure 4–3).

Reproduction is quite different for sex cells—the egg and the sperm. In this process, one member of each chromosome pair migrates to the opposite end of the cell. Consequently, when the cell appears and pinches off the two chromosomal groups to form two new cells, there are only 23 chromosomes in each cell. This division is called *meiosis*. When a human zygote, or embryo, is created after a sperm cell penetrates and fertilizes an egg cell, it receives 23 chromosomes from each sex cell—or a total of 46. In this way, the

new human inherits thousands of genes for thousands of traits from each parent, and the chain of life that stretches from ancestor to descendant is lengthened.

DNA: The Code of Life

Scientists who study genetic materials at the molecular level have found that the genes of all organisms—including the finches and turtles mentioned in the capsule study—are really segments of long, chainlike molecules of a chemical known as *deoxyribonucleic acid,* or *DNA.* In 1954, the British chemist Francis Crick and the American biologist James Watson discovered that the DNA molecule is shaped like a spiral staircase, or double helix. The twin helices are connected by steps in the form of chemical bases known as adenine (A), guanine (G), cytosine (C), and thymine (T). A is always paired with T, and G with C (Figure 4–4).

The strict arrangement of these four bases serves as a code, or set of instructions, carrying the genetic message of DNA. The information contained in the genetic message governs the manufacture of proteins, complex molecules that form the structure and maintain all organisms. Because the DNA molecules are located in the nucleus, or central portion of the cell, and the proteins are assembled in a different region (known as the cytoplasm), another chemical must enter the picture. This substance, known as *ribonucleic acid* (*RNA*), serves as a messenger carrying the code to the cytoplasm. If the code for the bases that the messenger RNA receives from the DNA molecule are arranged one way, a certain protein will be produced. The arrangement T–A–G, for example, may produce the protein responsible for hair color. Another arrangement—say, A–T–G—might produce the protein for hair texture. Thus, a gene can now be defined as a segment of the DNA molecule which carries a set of instructions for the manufacture of proteins that govern inherited traits.

How many different patterns are possible for these four bases? According to George Beadle and Muriel Beadle,

> . . . if one could transcribe into written form all the instructions for making a man that are contained in his genes, and were to publish the "recipe" in as many 500-page books as were necessary to do the job, one would end up with close to a thousand volumes.[5]

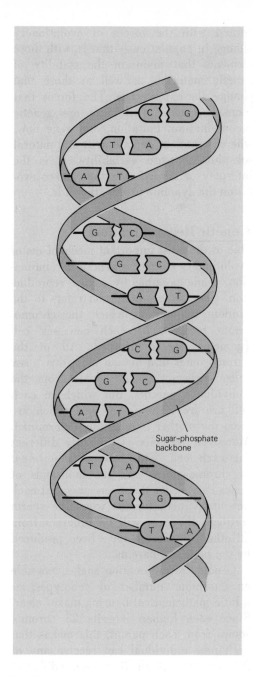

Figure 4–4   *The spiral structure of the DNA molecule with chemical bases.*

Sugar–phosphate backbone

Organic Evolution

How is the genetic code contained in the DNA molecule passed on to new cells during the process of cell reproduction? The answer is that the DNA molecule has the capability of reproducing itself, usually making an exact replica, so that the new cells will resemble the original in every detail. In this way, the same genetic material is typically passed on from the cells of the parent to those of the offspring, guaranteeing the continuity of life.

Evolutionary Change in Populations

The replication of the DNA molecule assures that genes are transmitted from one individual to the next. But physical anthropologists are more concerned with the way evolution affects groups of people rather than the individual. Although every person changes with time—a man aged sixty-five is obviously not the same person he was at sixteen—this is not evolution. Rather, evolution consists in behavioral and structural changes, over generations, in groups of organisms known as populations.

A *population* consists of a group of organisms within a species that breed mostly among themselves and that reproduce viable offspring. All of the genes and alleles of a given population—its collective genotype, so to speak—constitute its *gene pool*. *Population genetics*, then, is the study of the way gene pools change from one generation to another. It is con-

5. George Beadle and Muriel Beadle, *The Language of Life* (Garden City, N.Y.: Doubleday, 1967), p. 122.

cerned with the forces of evolutionary change in populations—that is, with those elements that maintain the stability of genetic materials as well as those that change these materials. The forces that increase genetic variability are genetic recombination, mutation, and gene flow, whereas random genetic drift and natural selection decrease variability. It is the interplay of these forces that makes evolution the dynamic process that it is.

Genetic Recombination

One of the most important mechanisms of evolutionary change is genetic recombination, made possible by sexual reproduction. *Genetic recombination* refers to the random manner in which the chromosomes received by each new sex cell (gamete) are distributed. All of the chromosomes in a human individual's sex cells (eggs or sperm) come from the individual's parents. But which in each cell are from the father and which are from the mother is randomly determined. Moreover, the mix is probably different for each cell. This *random assortment* of chromosomes—and the thousands of genes carried by them—assures that each new individual, formed when the sperm fertilizes the egg, will be different from all others that could have been produced by the same two parents.

Genetic recombination makes possible an enormous number of genotypes, as a little mathematical figuring makes clear. Since each human inherits 23 chromosomes from each parent, this means that each new individual can receive any of 2^{23}—or more than 8 million—different combinations. This genetic variety is then acted upon by natural selection to produce evolutionary changes. Genetic recombination shuffles the pack of genes, but introduces no new genes into the gene pool of the population. The only source of new genes is mutation.

Mutation

A *mutation* is a random alteration of the molecular structure of the DNA molecule, producing a new gene and possibly a new effect on the phenotype. A mutation arises, for example, when one base of the DNA molecule is substituted for another, or is deleted, or gets out of sequence. Suppose the base order that normally produces a certain protein is G–A–T, for instance. If this order were changed to A–G–T, an abnormal protein would be produced. A more concrete example is seen in the genetic disorder known as phenylketonuria (PKU). An alteration of a single base that makes up the DNA molecule will produce a protein that causes this form of severe brain damage (and possibly death) in children.

How often do such mutant genes appear in humans? Mutation rates vary. For instance, the gene responsible for albinism (a condition that results in a deficiency of skin pigmentation) appears in five out of every 1 million human sex cells. The mutant gene that causes a certain form of muscular dystrophy appears in 100 out of every 1 million sex cells. All told, there are nearly 3,000 known diseases caused by mutations.

A mutation is produced in a number of ways. It can arise spontaneously, as when something goes amiss in the genetic code. Or it can be induced by environmental agents. *Induced mutations,* as geneticist Hermann Muller found, can be produced by exposure to radiation such as that produced by X-rays or atomic particles. Some

chemicals found in food, pesticides, and insecticides, as well as in waste substances from certain manufacturing processes, have been found to produce mutant genes in bacteria.

The effects of mutations on the phenotype of an organism vary. If the mutant gene is recessive, for example, the phenotype may not be affected at all. Some mutations, however, can lower the fitness of the individual and even cause death. If the mutant gene controls a characteristic that is vital to life—the way the blood is made, for example—the organism will die immediately. But if it controls some other trait such as the proportion of the limbs so that an achondroplastic dwarf (who is characterized by normal-sized head and trunk contrasting with short arms and legs) is produced, the organism "dies" in a more subtle manner. This type of organism is more susceptible to certain diseases, is less fertile, and produces fewer offspring. In time, its genes vanish from the earth.[6] Thus, many achondroplastic dwarfs have a low rate of reproduction. In addition, they may not marry and reproduce, partly because they do not want children who may inherit the defect, partly because it is difficult for them to find a partner.[7]

Those few mutant genes that do receive phenotypic expression and prove adaptive will be selected for and will be dispersed throughout a given population, changing its genetic makeup. Mutants enable cer-

6. Beadle and Beadle, *The Language of Life,* p. 124.

7. Theodosius Dobzhansky, *Mankind Evolving: The Evolution of the Human Species* (New York: Bantam Books, 1962).

tain individuals to survive and reproduce in the event of a drastic environmental change—as happened in the case of the moths.

The selective value of a mutant gene thus depends upon factors in the internal (genetic) and external environment. In the *Drosophila*, or fruit fly, many mutant genes are superior to normal alleles under high temperature conditions, but inferior at low temperatures. As Ernst Mayr observes, a gene may add to viability in one environment but prove lethal in another.[8]

Gene flow

Another factor that provides variation for evolutionary change is *gene flow*, the situation in which individuals of one population of a species mate with those of another, introducing new alleles into the gene pool. Gene flow occurs when populations normally isolated by geographical boundaries or cultural practices exchange genes. This phenomenon was undoubtedly one of the major factors that shaped human evolution. Our earliest ancestors probably traveled in small isolated bands, hunting and gathering food. When these bands met, they possibly interbred and exchanged genes, transforming the gene pool of each group and endowing each with greater genetic variability upon which natural selection could act.

A good example of gene flow between two different populations can be seen in the United States, which contains numerous different populations, including more than 20 million blacks. Many of these

have African genes. It has been estimated that the modern American black carries an average of 75 percent African genes and 25 percent white genes. This is largely the result of gene flow between black and white populations during the days of slavery, when many black females were forced to sleep with their white masters.

What will be the future effects on the phenotypes of both populations if this gene flow continues? Anthropologist Joseph Birdsell predicts that such interpopulational mergers will affect skin color and hair form of both populations:

> *Brunette complexions will become commoner and very fair ones rare. Honey-toned skin color will appear more frequently. In general, hair form will show more waviness than it does today, but tight spiral curls will be unusual. In a sense, the extreme differences of form and pigment which exist in parental populations will disappear as the two different racial codes are blended.*[9]

Random Genetic Drift

In some small populations, there is an accidental, or random, gain or loss of genes in the gene pool. The evolutionary importance of such fluctuation depends on whether or not the change renders the population more fit, as well as on the size of the population and the degree to which it is isolated from other gene pools.

As a simplified example of genetic drift, imagine a tribe of 100 hunter-

8. Ernst Mayr, *Populations, Species, and Evolution* (Cambridge, Mass.: Harvard University Press, Belknap Press, 1970).

9. Joseph B. Birdsell, *Human Evolution: An Introduction to the New Physical Anthropology*, 2nd ed. (Chicago: Rand McNally, 1975), p. 417.

gatherers. Imagine further that fifteen of these people—who happen to have no offspring—have the same kind of curly hair that is inherited only in the dominant condition. In other words, since the gene is dominant, it will be expressed only in those individuals who carry it. Therefore, only these fifteen people will have the gene. The hair of the other members of the tribe, by contrast, is straight. One day, the fifteen curly-haired individuals go off on a hunting expedition and all are killed by a rockslide. This means that the genes for curly hair have been accidentally removed from this small population by a random act of nature. The loss of the men as hunters will probably have some effect on the fitness of this population, and they may have had a number of other important genes necessary for the survival of the group. But it is doubtful that the loss of all the genes for curly hair will affect the group's fitness.

Genetic drift undoubtedly has played a major role in human evolution, at least until recent times. Because human groups have been small for most of our evolutionary history, genetic drift has caused drastic, short-term changes in the features of such groups. In Chapter 7, for example, we shall see that Neandertal hunting-gathering groups consisted of only thirty-five to forty individuals. A particularly bad winter, an avalanche, or a sudden stampede by mammoth conceivably could have removed ten or fifteen of these individuals from the population. A small population that loses 25 to 37 percent of its members would undeniably be less fit for survival.

Natural Selection

While the sources of genetic variety discussed above change the frequencies in the gene pool of a population, they do nothing to further evolutionary change. This is the task of natural selection, which screens out the maladaptive genes and increases the proportions of the adaptive ones by applying selective pressures on the phenotypes of the population. The interplay of natural selection and mutation comprises the two major driving forces of evolution. Although natural selection is itself an evolutionary force, it also acts on the results of all other sources of variability, selecting and rejecting behavioral and structural traits according to the organism's ability to adapt to its environment. Natural selection occurs in all populations, in all environments, at all times.

Earlier in the chapter we learned how natural selection worked to rapidly increase the frequency of certain genes in a moth population. An even more dramatic example is seen in certain kinds of bacteria that have become resistant to penicillin. As was the case with the moths, the genes that render certain bacteria resistant to this antibiotic were present in the bacteria population. These penicillin-resistant individuals continued to reproduce while their nonresistant counterparts were being eliminated by the penicillin. As a result, their numbers swelled until they soon were the most numerous genotypes in bacteria populations that had been subject to penicillin. Scientists were then required to develop new antibiotics to combat these strains of bacteria.

Evolution and Culture

Cultural and social practices can override the effects of natural selection by allowing certain harmful genes to survive down the generations. Those suffering from certain serious inherited diseases—phenyl-ketonuria, or PKU, hemophilia, certain kinds of anemia, and other diseases—are protected by modern medicine. It is now standard practice in the United States to test all newborn infants for PKU. If the test is positive, the disease can be corrected by restricting foods containing a certain substance, known as phenylalanine, from the infant's diet. In this way, some individuals affected with harmful genes may survive. They may also reproduce and pass on their defective genes to future generations. In other words, cultural practices often interfere with the process of natural selection and the survival of the fittest. As Dobzhansky notes, "The more hereditary diseases are 'cured' the more of them will be there to be cured in the succeeding generation. . . ."[10]

By the same token, many investigators believe that selection also acts on human cultural and social practices to increase fitness. Natural selection is thought to have been instrumental in pressuring our early ancestors to depend more on social adaptations for survival—the formation of groups for hunting food and defense against predators, and the use of tools, for example—than on physical adaptations. So it appears that cultural behavior has been both a cause and an effect in the evolution of humankind. In short, there is a systematic relationship between culture and evolutionary forces, in that changes produced by one affect the changes produced by the other, and vice versa. But this is another story which will be related in the chapters that follow.

10. Dobzhansky, *Mankind Evolving*, p. 309.

Summary

1. Building on the work of others, notably Linnaeus, Malthus, Lyell, and Lamarck, Charles Darwin devised the theory of evolution by natural selection.

2. Darwin's theory of natural selection states that individuals of a species who are best adapted to the environment by virtue of their physical makeup will reproduce more offspring than those less fit to survive and pass on their genes.

3. Natural selection typically acts very slowly over numerous generations, making subtle changes in the physical characteristics of an organism. At times, however, it can bring about organic changes rather quickly. The color change in the peppered moth in England is an example of selection at work.

4. Mendel was the first to predict mathematically the inheritance of certain traits and the way they were transmitted from parent to offspring. He found that some characteristics (the dominant ones) prevail over certain others (the recessive traits), and that hereditary units that determine the traits of an organism are found in pairs. According to Mendel, the offspring receive one discrete hereditary unit related to each trait from each parent.

5. Biochemical studies have shown that a gene is a segment of the DNA molecule which carries a set of instructions for the manufacture of proteins that govern inherited traits.

6. A mutation is a change in the genetic code of the DNA molecule. It can arise spontaneously, or it can be induced by environmental agents.

7. Population genetics is the study of the way gene pools change from one generation to another.

8. Gene pools change and evolution proceeds because of the interaction of the sources of genetic variability—mutation, gene flow, gene drift, and natural selection.

9. Cultural behavior can negate or reduce the

effects of natural selection by allowing certain harmful genes to remain in the gene pool. At the same time, selection also acts on cultural behavior to increase fitness.

Review Questions

1. Why were Lyell and Malthus important to Darwin's theory of natural selection?

2. In your own words, explain Darwin's theory of natural selection and give an example.

3. What was Mendel's chief contribution to evolutionary science? How did his findings help to refine Darwin's theory?

4. What is a mutation? How do mutations occur?

5. Name four sources of genetic variability. Give an example of a source that leads to change and one that retards it.

6. In this chapter, it was stated that culture can be both a cause and an effect of the force of natural selection in human development. Explain this statement and give an example.

Suggested Readings

Beadle, George, and Beadle, Muriel. *The Language of Life: An Introduction to the Science of Genetics*. Garden City, N.Y.: Doubleday, 1967.
One of the clearest, most readable introductions to genetics, written by a man who received the Nobel Prize for physiology and medicine, and his wife. Includes a section on DNA and the manufacture of proteins.

Darwin, Charles. *On the Origin of Species*. 1859. Reprint. New York: Random House, Modern Library, 1936.
Darwin's own captivating exposition of his theory of natural selection.

Eiseley, Loren. *Darwin's Century: Evolution and the Men Who Discovered It*. Garden City, N.Y.: Doubleday, Anchor Books, 1961.
A superbly related history of evolutionary thought from its fifteenth-century beginnings to Darwin, by a master writer and highly respected anthropologist.

Lawrence, Jerome, and Lee, Robert E. *Inherit the Wind*. New York: Random House, 1955.
A play about the dramatic confrontation between evolutionists and fundamentalists. Based on the infamous Scopes "monkey trial" that took place in Tennessee in July 1925, the drama focuses on the courtroom battle between two of the most eloquent lawyers of the time—Clarence Darrow and William Jennings Bryan.

Watson, James D. *The Double Helix*. New York: Atheneum, 1968.
A candid, irreverent behind-the-scenes look at the way modern science is done, by the American half of the team that won the Nobel Prize for unlocking the structure of DNA.

Chapter 5

Evolution of Apes & Hominids

EARLY HOMINIDS ON AN AFRICAN SAVANNA

If an observer could be transported back through time and climb a tree in the area where the Koobi Fora Formation [in East Africa] was accumulating—what would he see?

As the upper branches are reached, the climber would find himself in a ribbon of woodland winding out through open areas. A kilometer or so away to the west would be seen the swampy shores of the lake, teeming with birds, basking crocodiles, and *Euthecodons.* Here and there are schools of hippos. Looking east, in the distance some ten or twelve kilometers away lie low, rolling hills covered with savanna vegetation. From the hills, fingers of trees and bush extend fanwise out into the deltaic plains. These would include groves of large *Acacia, Celtis,* and *Ficus* trees along the watercourses, fringed by shrubs and bushes. Troops of colobus move in the tree tops, while lower down are some mangabees. Scattered through the bush, the observer might see small groups of waterbuck, impala, and kudu,

Source: Glynn Ll. Isaac, "The Activities of Early African Hominids: A Review of Archaeological Evidence from the Time Span Two and a Half to One Million Years Ago," in *Human Origins: Louis Leakey and the East African Evidence,* ed. Glynn Ll. Isaac and Elizabeth R. McCown (Menlo Park, Calif.: W. A. Benjamin, Inc., 1976), pp. 483–485. Copyright 1976 by W. A. Benjamin, Inc. Reprinted by permission.

while out in the open areas beyond, would be herds of alcelaphine antelope and some gazelle *(Megalotragus* and *Antidorcas).* Among the undergrowth little groups of *Mesochoerus* pigs rootle, munching herbiage.

Peering down through the branches of the tree, the climber would see below the clean sandy bed of a watercourse, dry here, but with a tidemark of grass and twigs caught in the fringing bushes and showing the passage of seasonal floods. Some distance away down the channel is a small residual pool.

Looking out beyond the bushes can be seen large open flood-plains, covered with grasses and rushes, partly dry at those seasons of the year when the lake is low and when the river is not in spate. Far across the plains, a group of four or five men approach; although they are too far off for the perception of detail, the observer feels confident that they are men because they are striding along, fully upright, and in their hands they carry staves.

To continue the reconstruction in a more purely imaginative vein: as the men approach, the observer becomes aware of other primates below him. A group of creatures has been reclining on the sand in the shade of a tree while some youngsters play around them. As the men approach, these creatures rise and it becomes apparent that they too are bipedal. They seem to be female, and they whoop excitedly as some of the young run out to meet the arriving party, which can now be seen to consist mainly of males. The two groups come together in the shade of the tree, and there is excited calling, gesturing and greeting contacts. Now the observer can see them better, perhaps he begins to wonder about calling them men; they are upright and formed like men, but they are rather small, and when in groups they do not seem to engage in articulate speech. There are a wealth of vocal and gestural signals in their interaction, but no sustained sequential sound patterns.

The object being carried is the carcass of an impala and the group congregates around this in high excitement; there is some pushing and shoving and flashes of temper and threat. Then one of the largest males takes two objects from a heap at the foot of the tree. There are sharp clacking sounds as he squats down and bangs these together repeatedly. The other creatures scramble round picking up the small sharp chips that have been detached from the stones. When there is a small scatter of flakes on the ground at his feet, the stone worker drops the two chunks, sorts through the fragments and selects two or three pieces. Turning back to the carcass, this leading male starts to make incisions. First the belly is slit open and the entrails pulled out; the guts are set on one side, but there is excited squabbling over the liver, lungs, and kidneys; these are torn apart, some individuals grab pieces and run to the periphery of the group. Then the creatures return to the carcass; one male severs skin, muscle and sinew so as to disengage them from the trunk, while some others pull at limbs. Each adult male finishes up with a segment of the carcass and withdraws to a corner of the clearing, with one or two females and juveniles congregating around him. They sit chewing and cutting at the meat, with morsels changing hands at intervals. Two adolescent males sit at the periphery with a part of the intestines. They squeeze out the dung chew at the entrails. One of the males gets up, stretches his arms, scratches under his arm pits and then sits down. He leans against the tree, gives a loud belch and pats his belly . . . .[1]

● ● ● ● ● ● ● ●

This scenario, depicted by archeologist Glynn Isaac, is set in the savanna of East Africa, some 2.5 million years B.P. (before the present). The humanlike creatures who share in the game the hunters have just brought home are australopithecines, who were *hominids*—members of the human family, including modern humans and their immediate ancestors. The australopithecines are an important link in the chain of human evolution that begins with a tiny squirrel-like creature and continues to modern humans.

1. Glynn Ll. Isaac, "The Activities of Early African Hominids: A Review of Archaeological Evidence from the Time Span Two and a Half to One Million Years Ago," in *Human Origins: Louis Leakey and the East African Evidence*, ed. Glynn Ll. Isaac and Elizabeth R. McCown (Menlo Park, Calif.: W. A. Benjamin, 1976), pp. 483–485.

This chapter will examine how the forces of evolution discussed in Chapter 4 shaped the course of human development. It will describe what our early ancestors were like, how they were similar to us, how they were different, where they fit in the story of human development, and how the human family arrived at its present stage of evolution. Much of the story of human evolution is told by the remains of our ancestors. These relics are of two varieties: skeletal remains, largely in the form of bones, and cultural remains, chiefly in the form of stones that have been shaped into tools.

Fossils

Investigators have been able to reconstruct past life forms by examining *fossils* —the mineralized remains or impressions of ancient organisms that have been preserved, usually in earth materials.

Fossils are preserved in the earth's crust or other materials. The dry climate of the Near East, the location of the archeological dig shown here, preserves the remains of human activity.

The Process of Fossilization

When an animal dies, some of its hard parts—bones and teeth, for example—may be preserved in the earth's crust or in other materials. The actual process that preserves a jaw bone or skull fragment is not well understood. But most investigators believe that soon after an organism dies (putrification) and is buried in mud or volcanic materials, minerals from these sediments enter the organism's hard parts and replace them (petrification). These mineralized remains are then known as fossils.

Fossilization is a relatively rare oc-currence. Whether an animal becomes fossilized depends largely on the environment in which it dies. When a marine organism dies, for instance, its body may end up on the sea floor, where it is buried by soft silt and mud. On land, fossilization is less common, because predators and geological forces, such as wind, water, and earth movements, tend to scatter the remains.

What Fossils Tell Us

After investigators discover a fossil, they painstakingly remove it from the material in which it is embedded. They examine it for clues that will tell them how the ancient animal, which may now be extinct, lived, and how old it was when it died. The size and shape of the bone, for example, may hint at the size of the animal, and possibly even its sex. The impressions left by muscles on some bones can help determine the size of the muscles and how they functioned. This information may reveal whether the creature walked upright or on all fours.

Similarly, the inner surface of the skull will be marked by an impression of the animal's brain. A mold may be made of the inner surface, and this *endocranial cast* can tell much about the brain's size, shape, and blood vessels. Jaws and teeth, too, tell interesting stories. The number, shape, size, and arrangement of the teeth (the *dentition*) are helpful in revealing the nature of an organism's diet—whether it was a herbivore (plant-eater), carnivore (meat-eater), or omnivore (plant- and meat-eater). The examination of teeth also reveals a specimen's age and its place in primate evolution—that is, whether it was an ape or a member of the human family.

By coordinating all this information, the anthropologist can determine the fossil's taxonomic status—whether it belongs to a known genus or species or is an entirely new entity. Having done this, the next step is to ascertain how the specimen is related to other organisms. This is a particularly difficult undertaking and numerous errors have been made at this stage of analysis. As we shall see, there is a good deal of controversy over whether certain fossils belong to the line leading to humans. There is also considerable debate over the place in evolution of certain human specimens.

Developing a Chronology

Fossils can also tell the investigator approximately when the organism lived. A number of dating methods can be used to determine the age of the specimen. These fall into either of two categories. *Relative dating techniques* help an investigator estimate the age of a fossil or earth deposit in relation to other fossils or deposits. *Absolute* or *chronometric dating techniques,* by contrast, provide the researcher with the age of the fossil or geological deposit in actual years.

RELATIVE DATING TECHNIQUES. One relative technique is based on *stratigraphy,* which is the study of the arrangement of earth strata, or layers. The stratigraphic technique depends on the *principle of superposition.* This assumes that strata of earth materials are laid down, one atop the other, so that the oldest are on the bottom and the youngest on top— provided that the deposits have not been disturbed by geological or human forces. It follows from this principle that the fossils found at the lower layers were deposited first, and therefore are older than those lying above them. This technique enables the investigator to arrange the fossils found in a given cross-section of earth in a sequence, from youngest to oldest. It is important to remember, however, that the earth strata are not always stable, because geologic processes, such as earthquakes, are constantly at work changing the order of the layers.

Analysis of certain chemicals in fossils can also reveal whether two fossils were contemporaneous. Over time, for example, bones and teeth absorb fluorine and uranium from groundwater. The fossils also lose nitrogen as they age. By calculating the quantities of these materials in specimens found at the same site, the investigator can arrange them in a chronological sequence. This technique is known as the F-U-N test.

ABSOLUTE (CHRONOMETRIC) DATING TECHNIQUES. To get the chronological age of a fossil, the anthropologist must turn to one of the several absolute dating techniques available. One such technique, known as *radiocarbon dating*, measures the amount of carbon-14 (C^{14}) —which is an isotope, or variant form, of carbon—that remains in organic material. While they are alive, all organisms accumulate quantities of C^{14} in their bodies through their food. When they die, this build-up stops, and the C^{14} steadily decays to an isotope of nitrogen, known as nitrogen-14 (N^{14}). The carbon changes to nitrogen at a known rate—every 5,730 years, one-half of the atoms of C^{14} have changed to N^{14}. This kind of decay rate is known as the *half-life* of an element. By measuring the amount of C^{14} left in a fossil, then comparing this figure with the carbon's half-life, the investigator can determine how many years have passed since the organism died.

However, only a tiny amount of carbon-14 remains in a fossil after 70,000 years —a quantity too small to measure. Therefore, the age of a specimen older than 70,000 years cannot be determined by this method. Instead, investigators can use another radiometric method, known as *potassium–argon (K–A) dating*. This technique has been employed to date the age of the earth itself and is the basis for Figure 5–1. Potassium–argon dating is similar to the C^{14} method: the atoms of an isotope of potassium (K^{40}), with a half-life of 1.3 billion years, decay into the atoms of an isotope of argon gas (Ar^{40}). The K–A method differs from radiocarbon dating in that it dates the volcanic rock in which fossils are found, rather than the fossils themselves. Moreover, it cannot date rocks that are younger than 500,000 years old. This is unfortunate for students of human evolution because many of our ancestors lived between 70,000 years ago (the upper limit for radiocarbon dating) and 500,000 years ago (the lower limit for the K–A technique).

Most recently, another absolute dating technique, which also dates earth materials in which fossils have been deposited, has been used with some success. Known as *fission-track dating*, this method can help determine the age of a variety of materials, including obsidian (a volcanic glass), crystal, and minerals that contain the variety of uranium known as uranium-238 (U-238). As the uranium atoms fission, or spontaneously divide, they leave scars which can be chemically treated and detected under the microscope. Since U-238 decays at a known rate, investigators have only to compare the number of fission scars with the amount of uranium remaining in the sample to calculate its age. The fission-track method is reliable for dating samples from 20 years to 5 billion years in age. Often the fission-track technique and the K–A technique are used together, the one serving to verify the date obtained by the other.

Both relative and absolute dating have enabled investigators to arrange all known fossils in a time sequence relative to one another. This arrangement, known as the *fossil record*, shows the course of evolution for each species.

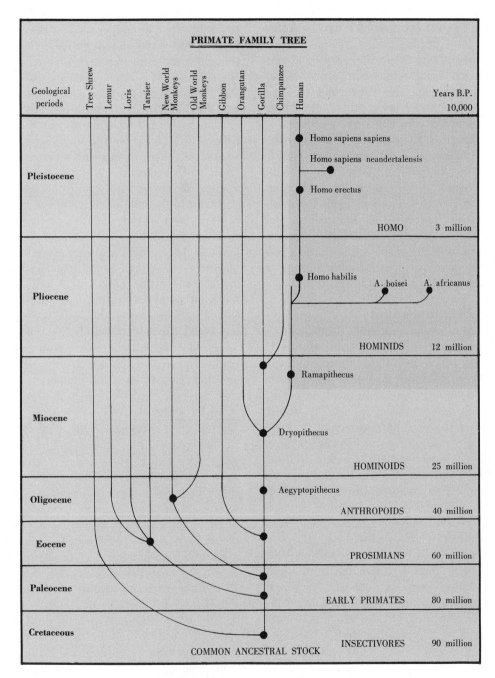

Figure 5–1   *One reconstruction of the primate family tree. Darker area shows Richard Leakey's theory of the course of human evolution, from Ramapithecus to modern humans.*

Evolution of Apes and Hominids

The Fossil Record of Early Apes

The fossils that relate the story of human evolution from nonhuman primates are woefully incomplete. They consist of numerous teeth and jaws, skulls, long bones (those of the arm and leg), fragments of vertebra and, in some cases, nearly complete skeletons. There are many gaps in the record, too—long stretches of time from which we have no primate remains. The first traces of our primate forebears have been unearthed on four continents: Africa, Europe, Asia, and North America. Such a wide geographic distribution is a reflection of a successful adaptation to a number of diverse environments.

The Oligocene Apes

The first really important primate fossil finds were made in the Fayum region in Egypt, which lies sixty miles southwest of Cairo. Today, this area is a desert region, but 28 to 26 million years B.P., during the Oligocene epoch, it was a tropical forest containing rivers. A number of primates lived in the area. One of these was a member of the genus *Apidium* (named after *Apis,* the sacred bull of Egypt). This creature, which had a short face and a body the size of a squirrel monkey, had the same number and kind of teeth as New World monkeys. However, paleontologist Elwyn Simons believes that it may be related to the line from which Old World monkeys evolved.[2] Its thirty-six teeth were arranged according to the *dental formula* 2:1:3:3—which is a shorthand way of indicating that it possessed

two incisors, one canine tooth, three premolars, and three molars on each side of the upper and lower jaw (see Figure 5–6). By contrast, the dental formula of the Old World monkeys, apes, and humans is 2:1:2:3, for a total of thirty-two teeth.

The largest and most significant Fayum primate was *Aegyptopithecus* (*Aegypto* is Greek for "Egypt," and *pithecus* means "ape"). This creature is the first known ape and is important because the apes—particularly the chimpanzee and the gorilla—are more closely related to humans than are the monkeys. No smaller than a gibbon, *Aegyptopithecus* was probably a quadruped and had teeth like those of modern apes—the canines were large and the front premolars rather long. Like the Old World monkeys, apes, and humans, its dental formula was 2:1:2:3. Simons thinks that *Aegyptopithecus* was the generalized primate from which evolved the line that leads to apes and humans.[3]

The Miocene Apes

During the Miocene epoch (25 to 12 million years B.P.), Africa looked much as it does today, with forests and open savannas. But southern Europe was very different from today: its dry climate fostered the spread of savannas. In the forests of these regions, and in similar environments in Asia, ranged various species of a genus of apes known as *Dryopithecus* (oak ape). This creature flourished a full 20 million years and its only remains consist of jaws and teeth.

The dryopithecines, which probably sprang from *Aegyptopithecus,* are thought to be ancestors of modern apes and humans. Thus, Simons believes that one

2. Elwyn L. Simons, "The Earliest Apes," *Scientific American* 217 (1967): 28–35.

3. Simons, "The Earliest Apes," p. 33.

dryopithecine species gave rise to the modern gorilla, another to today's chimpanzee, and a third to later *hominids* (members of the human family) who were ancestors of humans.[4] Anthropologist David Pilbeam summarizes the features of dryopithecines as follows:

> *They were probably medium-sized arboreal apes (weighing 30 to 50 pounds), with fore- and hindlimbs of approximately equal length, relatively short stout trunks, broad shallow thoraxes, and shoulder girdles adapted to suspensory posturing and arm swinging. They may well have been knuckle-walkers, at least incipiently so. They are likely to have been frugivorous [fruit-eating] forms and probably had a social organization not unlike that of the chimpanzee in which the social group was subdivided for purposes of foraging into subgroups.*[5]

The Hominids

Between 15 and 10 million years B.P., *Dryopithecus* appears to have given rise to a number of other primate genera. One of them was *Ramapithecus*. This creature lived in Africa, Asia, and Europe. Because its remains are somewhat fragmentary, many anthropologists have reserved their opinion of the status of this animal in human evolution. However, this text agrees with the conclusion of Yale University's Elwyn Simons—a leading primate paleontologist—whose studies show that *Ramapithecus* was "a very early hominid."[6] Moreover, this prehuman probably gave rise to another extinct prehuman genus called *Australopithecus*, and ultimately to the first humans.

Ramapithecus

The first correctly identified fossil of *Ramapithecus* (or "ape of Rama," hero of an Indian folk epic) consisted of an upper jaw and was found in the Siwalik hills of India in 1932.[7] Later finds from Africa, Asia, and Europe—also jaws and teeth—have enabled anthropologists to piece together this hominid's lifestyle and place in human evolution. Remains show that *Ramapithecus* had thick jaws, small incisors and canine teeth, and large, flat molars with heavy enamel. The canines did not project or overlap as in apes. Moreover, the dental arch (the arch formed by the row of teeth) was rounded as in humans, rather than U-shaped as in chimpanzees and gorillas. The lower jaw was buttressed with bone to protect it against the stresses of heavy chewing, which was mainly from side to side, much as a cow or horse chews.

What is the importance of these findings? For one thing, they show that *Ramapithecus* had adapted to a way of life that was quite different from that of the forest-dwelling *Dryopithecus*, whose diet consisted chiefly of soft fruits. According to Simons, the reason for this dietary shift was a change in the environment: the Eurasian forests of the late

---

4. Elwyn L. Simons, "Ramapithecus," *Scientific American* 236 (1977): 28–35.

5. David Pilbeam, *The Ascent of Man: An Introduction to Human Evolution* (New York: Macmillan, 1972), p. 48.

6. Simons, "Ramapithecus."

7. Simons, "Ramapithecus," p. 28.

Miocene times were not like those of tropical regions which provided fruit all year long. This scarcity of food pressured the Eurasian *Ramapithecus* to forage on the ground and along the margins of forests for small, tough foods such as nuts, seeds, and roots. Thus, says Simons, *Ramapithecus* was the first hominoid (the larger branch of the human family tree that includes apes) to come down from the trees and live mostly on the ground. It was perhaps with *Ramapithecus*, then, that the apes began evolving into members of the human family. The diet acted as a selective agent that favored the survival of the individuals with robust jaws and thick tooth enamel. Many of these dental features foreshadow those possessed by later extinct near-humans, the australopithecines.

The conclusions of Simons are based on a theory proposed by Clifford Jolly.[8] In the past, it was thought that the reduction in the size of the canine teeth in early hominids was due to the fact that these creatures were using tools—stone, bone, and wooden implements—to process food, to ward off predators, and to clean and scrape animal hides, among other things. As we saw in Chapter 3, the canine teeth of most modern ground-dwelling nonhuman primates are quite long, sharp, and deadly looking. They are a means of defense against predators and are flashed to intimidate others members of the primate troop. The daggerlike teeth also enable the animal to tear into tough foods. Without these teeth, the old theory goes,

a hominid on the ground would be defenseless unless it was using some kind of tools as weapons, such as clubs or stones.

For this reason, many investigators concluded that the mechanism that compensated for the reduction of the canines was the use of tools. But Jolly believes that the decreased size of the canines was not the chief determinant of tool use. Rather, the teeth grew smaller as a result of the animal's diet. The long projecting teeth would get in the way when the individual ground its tough, pulpy food with the side-to-side rocking of its jaws. Thus, selective pressures acted to reduce the canines. At the same time, the hands and fingers became more dextrous, developing the precision grip necessary to pick up these small foods. This latter trait would be important for the hominid descendants of the animal because it would increase their manual dexterity, predisposing them to manufacture and use tools.

Patterns in Hominid Evolution

During the late Miocene–early Pliocene period (16 to 12 million years B.P.), the tropical rain forests of Africa were replaced by savannas and scattered woodlands. Some primates left the forests and began exploiting the resources of the grasslands. As a result of adaptations to the new environment, the ground-dwelling hominids developed a series of biological and cultural traits that brought them closer to human status.

These characteristics did not appear full-blown and at the same time in these populations. Rather, the traits evolved at different rates in response to different intensities of certain selective pressures. This process is known as *mosaic evolution*. Moreover, the traits probably interacted

8. Clifford Jolly, "The Seed-eaters: A New Model of Hominid Differentiation Based on a Baboon Analogy," *Man* 5 (1970): 5–24.

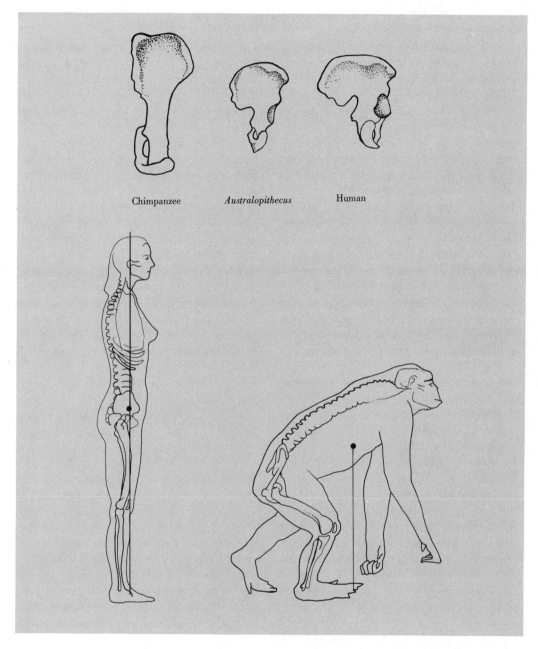

Chimpanzee   *Australopithecus*   Human

Figure 5–2   *Bipedalism was a crucial development in human evolution. Top figure shows that pelvises of* Australopithecus *and human are quite similar. Bottom figure shows how pelvises of human and chimpanzee articulate with rest of skeleton. Lines indicate centers of gravity.*

Evolution of Apes and Hominids

in a systematic fashion, each reinforcing and being reinforced by the others. Some of the characteristics helped shape the evolution of the australopithecines whom we met at the beginning of the chapter.

One characteristic was erect bipedal posture. Walking erect on two feet requires complex control by the central nervous system and a large number of bendings and extensions of many joints, along with the rotation and tilting of the pelvis.[9] Moreover, quadrupedal locomotion is a very efficient means of getting about. Therefore, the reasons why our early hominid ancestors changed to bipedalism must have been important enough to convey some selective advantage on them. One possible contributing factor may have been the fact that bipedal walking is most efficient for covering long distances of relatively flat terrain—such as between clusters of trees on a savanna.

The reason for bipedalism, however, was undoubtedly the result of a number of interacting factors. Perhaps the reduction in the size of the canines had something to do with it. Hominids on the savanna without these teeth may have had to resort to other weapons—brandishing branches, or hurling sticks and stones at predators, for example. Chimpanzees in the savanna have been seen doing exactly these things. And they do them from a standing position, making the animals appear all the larger. In an environment where threatening displays are as important as actions, early hominids might well have developed such protective strategies. Finally, an erect posture might have been an adaptation to the savannas when the grass grew quite high: it enabled

the hominid to see over the grass and detect predators and prey.

Freeing the hands could have led to another significant development in human evolution, namely the manufacture and use of tools. The first time one of our early ancestors picked up a piece of flint, bone, or wood and shaped it into a tool marked a major event in human evolution. The manufacture and use of tools reflect the fact that our predecessors possessed culture. Tools also show that the users were active agents in adapting to their surroundings. Rather than being passively shaped by the environment, as is the case with other primates, our tool-making ancestors began to exercise some control over it. Moreover, tools also contain clues to ancient lifeways: by studying these implements—particularly their mode of manufacture and use—the investigator is able to piece together the ways in which these long-dead people eked out their living. Thus, tools can reveal ancient living habits.

Although *Ramapithecus* and the early hominids, who lacked large defensive canine teeth, may have been using wooden tools—which would not have been preserved—there is little evidence that they made and used stone tools. The use of tools would have led to bigger and more complex brains because tool manufacture and use require hand–eye–brain coordination. Thus, certain parts of the hominid brain, the hand (dexterity), and tool use probably evolved at about the same rate. Tools improved subsistence, so they were selective agents that pressured the evolution of the brain and the hand. In this way, culture, as suggested by tools, became a factor in the hominid's way of adapting to the environment. As we saw in Chapter 3, other species have been ob-

9. Pilbeam, *The Ascent of Man*, p. 64.

served using tools, but humans are the only forms that use tools to make other tools according to certain preconceived patterns. Tool-making also presupposes the ability of the individual to anticipate future circumstances that might call for a particular implement.

Another characteristic was hunting-scavenging, which added meat to a diet that previously had included only plant foods. Besides adding high-quality protein to the hominid's menu, meat-eating would also have affected dentition: the teeth, no longer needing to be large for processing tough plant food, would have grown smaller. The reduction in the size of the teeth and jaw would have affected the geometry of the face and head (see Figure 5–6). These, in turn, could have influenced the enlargement of the brain case and, possibly, the brain itself.

How do the brains of various primates compare in size and complexity? Investigators denote brain size by *cranial capacity*—the amount of space taken up in the cranium by the brain. This space is measured in cubic centimeters (cc). The cranial capacity of the modern chimpanzee is about 400 cc, whereas that of the gorilla is more than 500 cc. The brains of modern adult humans range anywhere from 900 to 2,200 cc, with an average of about 1,450 cc. But normally functioning brains that measure below 1,000 and above 2,000 cc are not at all rare. The brains of writers Jonathan Swift and Ivan Turgenev, for example, took up more than 2,000 cc of space, whereas that of Anatole France filled barely 1,000 cc. Thus, the size of the brain is not as important as the way the neurological parts are organized.[10]

The neurons, or brain cells, of the human cerebral cortex are larger and more complex than those of apes. The frontal lobe of the cerebral cortex is also much larger. This area is involved with the inhibition of drives, enabling humans to concentrate on long-term goals. Many of the activities important to the course of human evolution would not be possible without the development of the frontal lobe. These activities include planning a hunting expedition; suppressing the drive to devour one's food on the spot rather than sharing it with others; and putting in years of study to become a doctor or a lawyer. The size of the parietal area (at the roof of the brain) has also increased enormously in humans. This area coordinates information stored and processed by other association areas of the brain, including data from different sensory channels, such as those concerned with hearing and speech.[11]

Finally, bipedalism, tool use, hunting-scavenging, and increased brain size and complexity were probably influential in the formation of early social groups. Cooperative hunting, food sharing, and defensive cooperative behavior against predators could have led to greater social cohesion. Vegetarians typically do not share food, but some meat-eating animals do. As we saw in Chapter 3, for example, baboons and chimpanzees have been seen hunting cooperatively and sharing meat with others of the troop. Also, the African wild dog brings food back to others who have not taken part in the hunt. It is possible that the same practice was fol-

10. Ralph L. Holloway, "The Casts of Fossil Hominid Brains," *Scientific American* 231, no. 1 (July 1974): 106–115.

11. Pilbeam, *The Ascent of Man*, p. 77.

lowed by our early hominid ancestors.[12] Like the dogs, the hominids would have operated out of some sort of "base camp" where other members gathered vegetable foods and cared for the young, the aged, and the sick and wounded while the hunters stalked game.

Such a *division of labor* by sex and age is another important uniquely human trait: the abler men probably hunted (birds, fish, and mammals, for example), while the women, children, and old men gathered plant and small animal food (amphibians, small reptiles, and insects, for example) near the home base. This arrangement would have the added adaptive advantage of increasing the variety of the foods shared by the group.[13] The australopithecines described in the capsule study had a base camp. The base camp is not seen among modern apes who move from place to place each day. The old and the sick of these species are left behind at the mercy of predators.

Australopithecus: The Southern Ape

The next important fossil in the pageant of human evolution is *Australopithecus*, or the southern ape. These hominids were depicted at the beginning of the chapter. *Australopithecus* is thought by many investigators to have appeared about 5 or 6 million years ago. There is a good deal of controversy about the course of its sub-

sequent evolution. Most investigators believe that some *Australopithecus* groups evolved into the first true humans, whereas others became extinct.

The first *Australopithecus* fossil was discovered at Taung in South Africa in 1924. At this time, Raymond Dart uncovered the skull of a child which was clearly more than ape. For example, the skull was quite large, larger than that of other nonhuman primates. The incisor and canine teeth were relatively small, resembling the teeth of humans. And the overall shape of the face was definitely hominidlike. Dart christened his find *Australopithecus africanus*, which means "southern ape of Africa."

In the next few decades, hundreds more

Skull of Australopithecus africanus *reveals characteristics of both apes and humans.*

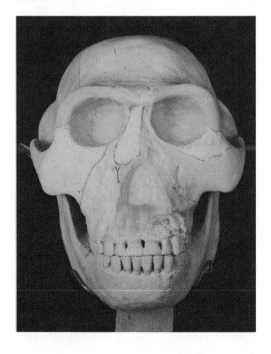

12. Richard E. Leakey and Roger Lewin, *Origins* (New York: E. P. Dutton, 1977), p. 76.

13. Glynn Isaac, "The Food-sharing Behavior of Protohuman Hominids," *Scientific American* 238, no. 4 (April 1978): 90–108.

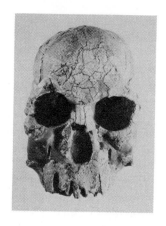

Two views of the skull of KNM-ER 1470 showing gaps filled in with plastic. This 2.5-million-year-old fossil has modern human features, including thinner bones and less protruding eyebrow ridges.

specimens were unearthed, including leg and arm bones, parts of a pelvis, and more crania (skulls) and mandibles (lower jaws). From these remains, investigators have determined that *Australopithecus* was definitely a biped. The finds have also led to a confusing picture of the course of hominid, and ultimately, human evolution. Some investigators have pieced together the bones and concluded that there were two species of *Australopithecus*—a small-bodied, small-toothed, somewhat primitive omnivore called *Australopithecus africanus*, and a large-bodied, large-toothed, more evolved vegetarian found in South Africa and called *Australopithecus robustus*. Some researchers believe that a third species, *A. (Australopithecus) boisei*, existed. This was a large, relatively evolved vegetarian that inhabited East Africa. Most anthropologists believe that both *A. robustus* and *A. boisei* sprang from *A. africanus*, and that *A. africanus* ultimately gave rise to *Homo*.

To complicate matters further, another form, believed by many to be the first true human, is thought to have coexisted with these near-humans some 1.75 million years ago. The fragmentary remains of this specimen were found in 1961 in Tanzania's fossil-rich Olduvai Gorge by Louis Leakey. Based on the size and shape of the incomplete brain case (the part of the skull that houses the brain), Leakey called his find *Homo habilis*, or "handy human." Eleven years later, Leakey's son, Richard, discovered at Lake Turkana in northern Kenya what he thinks is an ancestor of *Homo habilis*.[14] This specimen, known only as *KNM-ER 1470*, after its catalog number at the Kenya National Museum, consists of a nearly complete skull. The younger Leakey believes that KNM-ER 1470 was an early example of

14. Richard E. Leakey, "Evidence for an Advanced Plio-Pleistocene Hominid from East Rudolf, Kenya," *Nature* 242 (1973): 447–450.

Homo habilis who lived 2.5 million years ago. Its cranial capacity was about 800 cc, which is more than half the cranial capacity of the average modern human.

What bearing do all these finds have on human evolution? For one thing, they show that the picture of human evolution may be changing. Many anthropologists believe that humans evolved in a single lineage, from *Australopithecus africanus* to a later form that lived about 500,000 years ago, *Homo erectus* (upright man), through Neandertal man, to modern humans. *Australopithecus boisei* and *Australopithecus robustus*, they believe, became extinct. Now, the finds by the Leakeys and others at Olduvai and Lake Turkana have caused some investigators to question this picture. The new view shows that humans may be much older than previously thought.

Thus, speculate Richard Leakey and Roger Lewin, sometime around 6 million years ago, the *Ramapithecus* line split into three branches (shaded area in Figure 5–1). Some ramapithecines themselves continued until about 3 or 4 million years ago, then died out. One offshoot of the ramapithecine stock was *A. africanus*, which became extinct about 2.5 million years ago. The other *Australopithecus* species—*A. boisei*—died out about 1 million years ago. A third branch was *Homo habilis*, from whom evolved *Homo erectus*. From this species *Homo sapiens* originated about 250,000 years ago. According to Leakey and Lewin, then, the australopithecines are not our ancestors. Rather, they are our ancient cousins.

But the picture drawn by these two investigators is disputed by many anthropologists. As indicated earlier, some be-

Figure 5–3   *Two alternate schemes showing place of* Australopithecus *in human evolution. Compare these with theory of Richard Leakey, shown in darker area of Figure 5–1.*

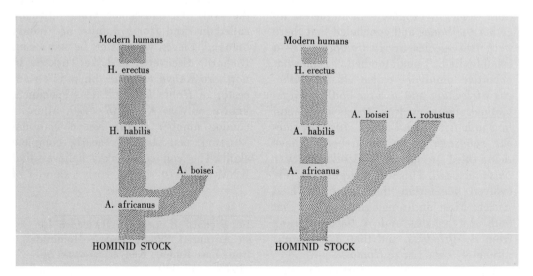

lieve that the line leading to modern *Homo* includes *A. africanus*. Others think that *H. habilis* was really a species of *Australopithecus* and that it descended from *A. africanus*. And recent finds, dating *Homo erectus* at 1.7 million years, indicate that *H. (Homo) erectus* and *Australopithecus* were contemporaries. Two conflicting theories on the position of *Australopithecus* relative to modern humans are shown in Figure 5–3. Compare these with the darker area in Figure 5–1.

The Australopithecine Pattern

Now that we have some idea about their position in our family tree, we can take a closer look at the biological and behavioral characteristics of the australopithecines, as represented by the most primitive of the genus, *Australopithecus africanus*. First, *A. africanus* lived on the ground of the African savanna where an arid seasonal climate prevailed at the time. Its cranial capacity ranged between 420 and 585 cc—which is relatively large considering that the body weight was only 50–70 pounds. Ralph Holloway has studied the endocranial casts of *A. africanus* and *Homo habilis* and found that the neurological organization of the brains of both was definitely hominid. The frontal lobes, for example, were larger and more convoluted than those of ape brains of the same size. The parietal and temporal lobes were also enlarged. The temporal lobes are involved with storing visual and auditory data and in performing activities that must be executed in a definite sequence.[15]

---

15. Holloway, "The Casts of Fossil Hominid Brains."

The teeth and jaws of an australopithecine, while big, are more hominidlike than apelike. The premolars and molars of *A. africanus*, for example, are quite large, whereas the incisors and canines are relatively small. The shape of the jaw indicates that the muscles that operated it were powerful, a finding that points to the possibility that this species used its teeth to grind and pulverize its food, much as vegetarians do, rather than slicing it, as meat-eaters do.

Australopithecus was undoubtedly a *habitual biped*, like modern humans, rather than an *occasional biped*, like chimpanzees and gorillas. This conclusion has been reached by examining the foramen magnum, mentioned above, certain parts of the spine (which is curved in humans rather than straight as in our closest primate relatives), and the pelvis (Figure 5–2).

The fact that its canine teeth were small and that *A. africanus* walked upright, freeing the hands, raises the question of whether it made and used tools. As of now, there is no solid archeological evidence that the species was a tool-maker. But given their relatively large brains, small canine teeth, bipedal locomotion—and assuming that they were at least as intelligent and as curious as a modern chimpanzee that does make and use tools—one may speculate that *A. africanus* probably did use wooden clubs, pounders, and stone and bone cutting implements.

But the tool-making ability of the more evolved *Australopithecus*, particularly *A. boisei*, is another story. Stone tools were found at Olduvai Gorge, in association with a skull of *A. boisei*, prompting some investigators to conclude that this australopith made the tools. But some anthropologists, notably the Leakeys and others,

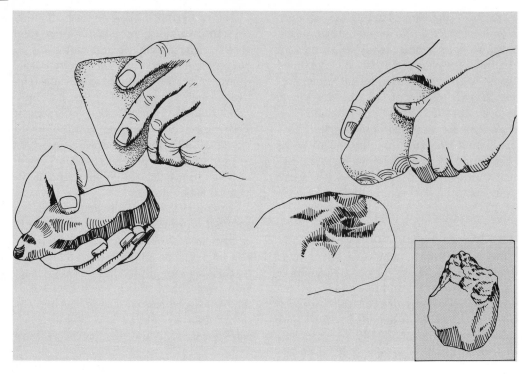

Figure 5–4 *Chopper tools, used by early hominids for cutting meat, crushing seeds, and other purposes, were made by direct percussion. In darker area is a chopper manufactured by this process.*

believe that the first tool-maker was *Homo habilis*, the contemporary of the australopithecines.

At any rate, the stone tools found at Olduvai and other African sites such as Koobi Fora comprise, appropriately enough, the Oldowan culture. The tools were made between 2 and 3 million years ago.[16] The earliest method of stone tool manufacture seems to have been simply striking one stone against another to obtain a cutting edge. The most common type of Oldowan tool is the *chopper*, made by removing several flakes to form a sharp cutting edge (Figure 5–4). Choppers were general-purpose tools that could have been used for a variety of tasks: crushing seeds, cutting meat, hides, or wood, and so on. The hunter depicted in the capsule study, for example, may have been using a chopper to skin the impala. Scrapers, basically choppers with a steep cutting edge, were probably used to scrape bone and hides and to shave wood.[17] Crude as

16. Isaac, "The Food-sharing Behavior of Protohuman Hominids," p. 95.

17. Mary D. Leakey, "A Review of the Oldowan Culture from Olduvai Gorge, Tanzania," *Nature*, April 30, 1966, pp. 462–466.

they seem to us today, these tools represented an enormous advance in human cultural evolution.

In several sites in east and south Africa, chopping tools are found in association with what appear to be the butchered remains of game animals (chiefly mammals such as giraffes, horses, and a few primates). Further, the way the bones have been broken follows patterns which indicate that the people had consistent butchering techniques. It has been inferred from some of the material that some hominid groups—consisting either of advanced australopithecines or *Homo habilis*—may have scavenged from the kills of some predators, rather than actually hunting the animals. At any rate, the evidence is that the groups were fairly successful hunter-scavengers, but that they probably subsisted more on vegetable foods than on meat.

Even more important—if these prehuman or human groups hunted—is the probability that their social organization was to some extent shaped by this practice. Since their technology was crude, hunting techniques probably called for a collective effort similar to that seen in modern hunting societies. The practice of surrounding game, stalking herds, or chasing them into water or over cliffs requires cooperative and coordinated efforts—all of which foster group cohesion. Like modern hunter-gatherers, these early groups may have had base camps to which they returned and where they shared the fruits of the hunt. Indeed, archeologist Glynn Isaac has uncovered evidence suggesting that these early prehumans or humans "carried animal bones (and meat) around and concentrated this portable food supply at certain places."[18] The base camp food-sharing complex also suggests a division

of labor: some individuals, probably the ablest males, went out to hunt, while other individuals, probably females and older males, stayed behind to gather plant foods and tend for the sick and the young. Indeed, Isaac suggests that food-sharing was the central element of a new complex of adaptations that included hunting/scavenging, gathering, and carrying.[19] Exactly this situation was depicted in the introductory capsule study.

The small, mobile hunting groups of this period may have found it beneficial to assemble in larger bands during times when game and vegetation were plentiful and to disperse into smaller bands during times of scarcity, thus avoiding a strain upon the available resources and possibly destructive competition. Richard MacNeish found this to be true for early hunter-gatherer populations in Mexico.[20]

Homo

The next principal character in the story of human evolution is *Homo erectus* (upright human). The earliest remains of *H. erectus* have been unearthed in China and date back 1.7 million years. At Yuanmou, a town in the southern Chinese province of Hunnan, for example, were found some teeth in association with chopper tools, burned bones and charcoal, and a

18. Isaac, "The Food-sharing Behavior of Protohuman Hominids," p. 100.

19. Isaac, "The Food-sharing Behavior of Protohuman Hominids," p. 102.

20. Richard S. MacNeish, "Ancient Mesoamerican Civilization," *Science* 143 (1964) : 531–537.

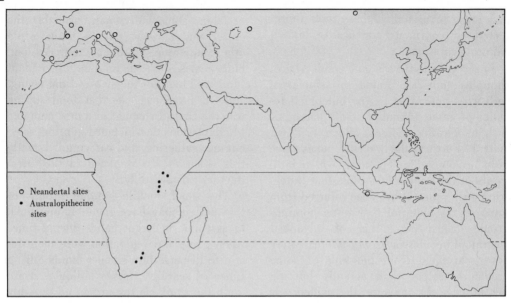

Figure 5–5 *The distribution of known* Australopithecus *and Neandertal sites. No* Australopithecus *remains have been found outside Africa, whereas Neandertals adapted to a wide variety of environments.*

variety of fossil mammals. Among the latter were horse gazelle, rhinoceros, elephant, and cattle. Certain aspects of the teeth of "Yuanmou man" resembled those of *Australopithecus*.[21]

Remains of the African variety of this fossil species are about 1.5 million years old. Because *Ramapithecus* lived in Europe, it is possible that *H. erectus* also inhabited that continent as early as 1.7 million years B.P. *H. erectus* appears to have evolved into *Homo sapiens*, and the earliest known traces of this species are about 250,000 years old.

21. Walter Sullivan, "Human Teeth in China Dated at 1.7 Million Years," *New York Times*, February 6, 1978, p. B5.

Homo erectus

With *Homo erectus*, the evolutionary forces that molded the physical characteristics of the hominid line become less important than cultural forces. *H. erectus* groups conquered their environments with better tools, cooperative hunting of large animals, the manufacture of clothing and shelter and, most important, fire. The domestication of fire made living in dark caves possible and extended the range of the human habitat to areas other than the tropics. It provided light at night, thus enabling the early humans to continue routine daily tasks after sunset. Fire also afforded protection from animals and allowed its users to cook food. Cooking killed harmful bacteria and made meats and other foods more digestible, thus increasing the human life span.

The physical characteristics of *H. erectus* included a larger, more complex brain (775 to 1300 cc) with a cranium shaped like a dome, a protruding brow ridge and jaw, and smaller teeth that approached those of modern humans in size (Figure 5–6). These features have been interpreted to mean that *H. erectus* was using tools routinely to process food and hence no longer required the large molars of its *H. habilis* predecessors. Limb bones and other remains show that *H. erectus* walked upright, much like their modern descendants.

Evidence of the kind of shelters used by European *H. erectus* was discovered by Henry de Lumley at Nice, France, at a place called Terra Amata (beloved earth).[22] He found that huts, the earliest known architecture, were made by nomadic hunter-gatherers some 300,000 years ago. The huts were oval in shape, and ranged from 26 to 49 feet long, and from 13 to 20 feet wide. They were made of wooden stakes, probably covered with foliage or hides, and contained hearths. Bones of deer, boar, elephant, and other animals were found, as were a quantity of ocher, a coloring substance later used

22. Henry de Lumley, "A Paleolithic Camp at Nice," *Scientific American* 220, no. 5 (May 1969) : 42–50.

Figure 5–6　*Comparison of skulls and teeth of four primates. The evolutionary trend is toward a larger braincase with higher average cranial capacity and smaller face, jaws, and teeth.*

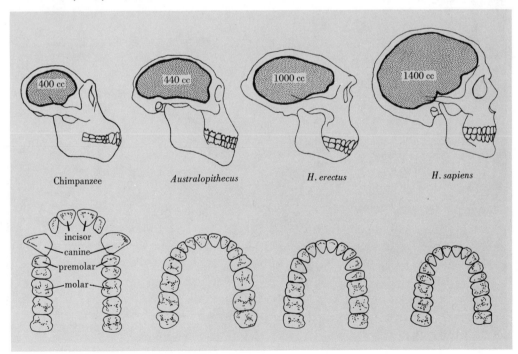

for painting, body decoration, and burial rites.

An implement of Western *H. erectus* populations was the *Acheulean hand axe* —a 4- to 8-inch-long, almond-shaped stone with a point at one end, a thick butt at the other, and sharp edges. Since the hand axe had two cutting edges, it is known as a *biface*. A tool with a single cutting edge, by contrast, is called a *uniface*. This tool was used for a variety of purposes, from digging roots from the ground to skinning and butchering animals. The hand axe, and other tools of *H. erectus*, were quite standardized and required considerable skill in their manufacture. Indeed, many appeared in different patterns, a sign of technological advance. The hand axe was made by removing the end of the *flint core*, or *nodule*, with a hammerstone. This left a level area at the top of the core called the *striking platform*, from which flakes of desired size could be removed.

Skull of the Chinese variety of Homo erectus. *Western* H. erectus *groups made domestic fires, lived in huts, and probably conducted large, organized hunts of rhinoceroses, elephants, and horses.*

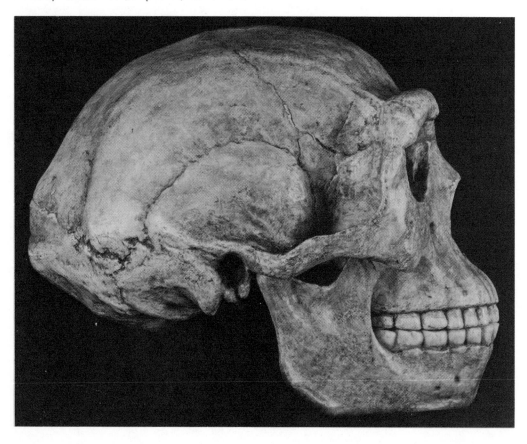

H. erectus apparently arranged relatively large, well-organized hunting expeditions, evidence for which is seen at Torralba and Ambrona in Spain. At Torralba, for instance, F. Clark Howell found the bones of rhinoceros, red deer, elephants, and horses.[23] There are signs that grass had been set afire to direct the stampede of the animals into a swamp where they could easily be dispatched. An expedition of this size would probably have required the efforts of several hunting bands who had established relations with one another and who undoubtedly exchanged men and women in what we would call marriage. Such an arrangement is in evidence among hunter-gatherers of today. The exchanges may have been the beginning of networks that were to form the basis of the social organization of later human populations.[24]

Homo sapiens

The evolution of *Homo erectus* to *Homo sapiens* continued the trends seen in earlier populations: the brain grew larger and more complex and the molar teeth grew smaller. Because evolution is a continuous process and there are many fossils of human populations that succeeded *H. erectus*, it is more difficult to distinguish *H. erectus* from their early *H. sapiens* descendants than to distinguish *H. erectus* from the australopithecines. Investigators have found fossils of individuals who lived around 250,000 years B.P. in Swanscombe, England, and Steinheim, Germany. At first, it was difficult to place the remains in the human family tree. Today, however, these humans are considered transitional between *H. erectus* and *H. sapiens*, chiefly because the structure of the skull resembles that of *H. erectus*, but the brain is closer in size to that of *H. sapiens*.

The next fossil forms in our ancestral line are also members of the species *Homo sapiens neandertalensis*. The skulls of the Neandertal people show an average cranial capacity of 1470 cc. These forms were present in Africa, western Europe, central and southern Europe, the Middle East, and Asia from about 110,000 to 35,000 B.P. (Figure 5–5). The Neandertals apparently came in two varieties: a stocky, rugged type found mostly in western Europe and known as the Classic Neandertal, and a more graceful, almost modern variety, found in the Middle East and in Mediterranean climes and known as Generalized Neandertal. The proper taxonomic designation of both forms is *Homo sapiens neandertalensis* because they are considered to be subspecies of *H. sapiens*. Modern humans also represent a subspecies of *H. sapiens* and are called *Homo sapiens sapiens*.

The Classic Neandertals were short in stature, and had elongated skulls with cranial capacities ranging up to 1800 cc —well in excess of many modern humans. The robust features—heavily boned faces with thick brow ridges, stocky body with short legs and arms—are believed to be adaptations to the glacial environment in which they lived.

23. F. Clark Howell, "Observations on the Earlier Phases of the European Lower Paleolithic (Torralba-Ambrona)," *American Anthropologist* (Special Publication: *Recent Studies in Paleoanthropology*), April 1966.

24. Sally Binford, "Early Upper Pleistocene Adaptations in the Levant," *American Anthropologist* 70 (1968) : 705–712.

An anthropologist's idea of what early humans may have looked like. Shown are reconstructed skulls of, from left, H. erectus, H. sapiens neandertalensis, *and* H. sapiens sapiens.

Because there is such a wide range of variation among the Generalized Neandertals that lived in the Near East and elsewhere, it is difficult to make valid generalizations about them. At Mugharet et-Tabūn and Mugharet es-Skhūl in Israel, for example, have been found specimens which date back 60,000 to 40,000 B.P. The two individuals found at Tabūn appear to be intermediate in physical features between Neandertals and modern humans. And the ten fossils found at Skhūl "include specimens that are as modern as some of the earliest undoubted *Homo sapiens sapiens* from Europe, even though the Skhūl hominids are geologically older."[25]

One theory holds that the generalized Neandertals eventually evolved into *Homo sapiens sapiens,* sometime around 40,000 to 35,000 B.P. Classic Neandertals became extinct because they were isolated from other human groups by the glaciers. An alternate theory holds that the rugged types interbred with, and were absorbed into, *Homo sapiens sapiens* groups who entered Europe from elsewhere, possibly the Middle East, at the end of the glaciation.[26]

The remains of modern humans were found at Cro-Magnon, a cave near Dordogne, France, in 1868. These individuals had rather high foreheads, reflecting larg-

---

25. Pilbeam, *The Ascent of Man,* p. 184.

26. John Buettner-Janusch, *Origins of Man* (New York: John Wiley, 1966).

er frontal lobes. The face was flatter and more modern in appearance than that of the Neandertals, in that it exhibited a small jaw with a real chin.

Thus it is clear that 40,000 years ago, the human species was well on its way to becoming the dominant life form on the planet. Evidence of the cultural advances made by the Cro-Magnons—and by the Neandertals as well—is discussed in Chapter 7.

Summary

1. Fossils are the remains or impressions of ancient organisms preserved typically in earth materials. The study of fossils can reveal many things about ancient life forms, including when they existed, their diet, size, means of locomotion, brain size, and evolutionary relationships.

2. The age of a fossil can be determined by relative and absolute dating techniques. Stratigraphy and analyses of certain chemicals can reveal the relative age of a specimen, whereas radiocarbon and potassium–argon dating fix absolute age.

3. The earliest known apes, unearthed from the Fayum region of Egypt, include specimens belonging to the genus *Apidium*, as well as *Aegyptopithecus*. The dryopithecines of the Miocene epoch are thought to be ancestral to modern apes and humans.

4. Ramapithecus, thought by many to be the first hominid, existed some 15 to 10 million years B.P. It foraged on the ground along the margins of forests for seeds, nuts, and roots. Unlike other savanna-dwelling primates, its teeth were small—a development due largely to diet.

5. A number of biological and behavioral factors interacted systematically to help shape hominid evolution. These factors included erect bipedal posture, use of tools, meat-hunting and meat-eating, and increased cranial capacity.

6. *Australopithecus* is the first generally accepted member of the human family. This biped, which may have come in three varieties, is thought to have coexisted with *Homo habilis*, from whom *Homo erectus* and ultimately, modern humans may be derived.

7. Early humans used crude chopper tools manufactured by percussion. They were probably hunter-scavengers, a lifestyle which shaped their social organization.

8. The tool culture of later human populations is known as the Acheulean industry; one implement was the Acheulean hand axe.

9. With the appearance of *Homo erectus*, the tempo of human evolution picked up considerably. These populations engaged in cooperative hunting of large animals, made clothing and shelters, and used fire to extend their range into Asia and Europe.

10. The first generally accepted *Homo sapiens* was the Neandertal, who lived in many environments, including Europe, Africa, China, and the Near East. Some time around 30,000 to 40,000 years ago, the first modern humans (*Homo sapiens sapiens*) appeared in western Europe. At about the same time, the European Neandertals appear to have died out.

Review Questions

1. What is a fossil? What are some of the important things fossils tell us about ancient organisms?

2. Describe radiocarbon dating. How does it differ from the potassium–argon technique?

3. What is the importance of *Ramapithecus* to human evolution?

4. List three trends in hominid evolution and describe how they are interrelated.

5. Beginning with *Dryopithecus*, draw the family tree of the human family that ends with modern humans.

6. Describe some of the cultural achievements of *Homo erectus*.

A highly respected book on the fossil evidence of hominid evolution, discussed in terms of geographical areas. Includes an important chapter on hominid adaptations, with many illuminating drawings.

Simons, Elwyn L. *Primate Evolution*. New. York: Macmillan, 1972.

A comprehensive view of fossil primates, from the beginnings to *Ramapithecus*, by the leading paleontologist in this field.

Suggested Readings

Birdsell, J. B. *Human Evolution: An Introduction to the New Physical Anthropology*. 2nd ed. Chicago: Rand McNally College Publishing, 1975.

One of the best introductory physical anthropology texts available today, this book has four chapters devoted to the physical evidence for human evolution. Highly recommended for advanced students.

Clark, J. D. *The Prehistory of Africa*. New York: Praeger Publishers, 1970.

A specialist in African archeology describes and interprets the evidence for human evolution on that continent.

Leakey, Richard E., and Lewin, Roger. *Origins*. New York: E. P. Dutton, 1977.

An engrossing account of human evolution with chapters on nonhuman primate behavior; intelligence and language; and aggression, sex, and human nature.

Pfeiffer, J. F. *The Emergence of Man*. 2nd ed. New York: Harper and Row, 1972.

One of the most colorfully written accounts of human evolution, with chapters on experimental archeology, the importance of big-game hunting, the evolution of language, the human infant, and primate behavior.

Pilbeam, David. *The Ascent of Man*. New York: Macmillan, 1972.

Human Variation

UNESCO "STATEMENT ON RACE AND RACIAL PREJUDICE"

1. "All men are born free and equal both in dignity and in rights." This universally proclaimed democratic principle stands in jeopardy wherever political, economic, social and cultural inequalities affect human group relations. A particularly striking obstacle to the recognition of equal dignity for all is racism. Racism continues to haunt the world. As a major social phenomenon it requires the attention of all students of the sciences of man.

2. Racism stultifies the development of those who suffer from it, perverts those who apply it, divides nations within themselves, aggravates international conflict and threatens world peace.

3. The conference of experts meeting in Paris in September 1967 agreed that racist doctrines lack any scientific basis whatsoever. It reaffirmed the propositions adopted by the international meeting held in Moscow in 1964 which was called to re-examine the biological aspects of the statements on race and racial differences issued in 1950 and 1951. In particular, it draws attention to the following points:

    a] All men living today belong to the same species and descend from the same stock.

Source: Abridged from United Nations Educational, Scientific, and Cultural Organization (UNESCO), "Statement on Race and Racial Prejudice," *International Social Service Journal* 20, no. 1 (1968) : 93–97. Reprinted by permission of UNESCO. © UNESCO 1968.

b] The division of the human species into "races" is partly conventional and partly arbitrary and does not imply any hierarchy whatsoever. Many anthropologists stress the importance of human variations, but believe that "racial" divisions have limited scientific interest and may even carry the risk of inviting abusive generalization.

c] Current biological knowledge does not permit us to impute cultural achievements to differences in genetic potential. Differences in the achievements of different peoples should be attributed solely to their cultural history. The peoples of the world today appear to possess equal biological potentialities for attaining any level of civilization.

Racism grossly falsifies the knowledge of human biology.

4. The human problems arising from so-called "race" relations are social in origin rather than biological. A basic problem is racism, namely, anti-social beliefs and acts which are based on the fallacy that discriminatory intergroup relations are justifiable on biological grounds.

5. Groups commonly evaluate their characteristics in comparison with others. Racism falsely claims that there is a scientific basis for arranging groups hierarchically in terms of psychological and cultural characteristics that are immutable and innate. In this way it seeks to make existing differences appear inviolable as a means of permanently maintaining current relations between groups.

6. Faced with the exposure of the falsity of its biological doctrines, racism finds ever new stratagems for justifying the inequality of groups. It points to the fact that groups do not intermarry, a fact which follows, in part, from the divisions created by racism. It uses this fact to argue the thesis that this absence of intermarriage derives from differences of a biological order. Whenever it fails in its attempts to prove that the source of group differences lies in the biological field, it falls back upon justifications in terms of divine purpose, cultural differences, disparity of educational standards or some other doctrine which would serve to mask its continued racist beliefs. Thus, many of the problems which racism presents in the world today do not arise merely from its open manifestations, but from the activities of those who discriminate on racial grounds but are unwilling to acknowledge it. . . .

11. The committee of experts agreed on the following conclusions about the social causes of race prejudice:

a] Social and economic causes of racial prejudice are particularly observed in settled societies wherein are found conditions of great disparity of power and property, in certain urban areas where there have emerged ghettos in which individuals are deprived of equal access to employment, housing, political participation, education, and the administration of justice, and in many societies where social and economic tasks which are deemed to be contrary to the ethics or beneath the dignity of its members are assigned to a group of different origins who are derided, blamed, and punished for taking on these tasks.

b] Individuals with certain personality troubles may be particularly inclined to adopt and manifest racial prejudices. Small groups, associations, and social movements of a certain kind sometimes preserve and transmit racial prejudices. The foundations of the prejudices lie, however, in the economic and social system of a society.

c] Racism tends to be cumulative. Discrimination deprives a group of equal treatment and presents that group as a problem. The group then tends to be blamed for its own condition, leading to further elaboration of racist theory. . . .

18. Ethnic groups which represent the object of some form of discrimination are sometimes accepted and tolerated by dominating groups at the cost of their having to abandon completely their cultural identity. It should be stressed that the effort of these ethnic groups to preserve their cultural values should be encouraged. They will thus be better able to contribute to the enrichment of the total culture of humanity.

19. Racial prejudices and discrimination in the world today arise from historical and social phenomena and falsely claim the sanction of science. It is, therefore, the responsibility of all biological and social scientists, philosophers, and others working in related disciplines, to ensure that the results of their research are not misused by those who wish to propagate racial prejudice and encourage discrimination.

This statement was unanimously adopted at the conclusion of a meeting of experts on race and racial prejudice which was held at Unesco House, Paris, from 18 to 26 September 1967.[1]

● ● ● ● ● ● ● ●

Chapter 4 emphasized the importance of genetic variation for evolution: natural selection acts upon variation to produce evolutionary change. In Chapter 5, we saw that the human species had been established as the dominant life form on the planet and had adapted to a wide range of environments in both the Old and New Worlds. This adaptation to selective forces (climate, altitude, and exposure to solar radiation, for example) produced variation among our species. The evolutionary forces of mutation, genetic drift, and gene flow also contributed to these changes. Because of the actions of such forces on the human gene pool, the widespread species became *polytypic* —that is, the species came to be composed of numerous different breeding populations.

What are some of the ways these populations differ? Obvious variations include skin, eye and hair color, body build, and height. Not so obvious are differences in susceptibility to certain diseases, in blood chemistry, and a host of other biochemical variations. The ultimate goal of physical anthropology is to define the genetic, evolutionary, and adaptive significance of these and all other varying traits.

Thus, in this chapter, we will see how investigators have attempted to clarify the evolutionary meaning of human differences. We will examine exactly how certain variations are produced largely as a result of adaptations to different environ-

ments. Some of the implications of these adaptations for human behavior will also be discussed, as will the usefulness of describing human variation by the term "race"—which is the subject of the capsule study.

The Adaptive Basis of Human Variation

In Chapter 4, we noted that a species adapts to its environment through evolution. In reality, a particular species may occupy several environments, so that it is subject to varying natural selective forces. Thus, the differences in the expression, or even presence, of a trait from one breeding population of a species to the next represent a kind of evolutionary "fine tuning." That is, the species as a whole exhibits adaptive traits that differentiate it from other species. But the different breeding populations that comprise the species are marked by further adaptations to selective forces that prevail in their various environments. What follows is a discussion of two such forces, together with a few examples of the ways different human breeding populations have adapted to these forces. The selective agents to be considered are climatic stress and disease.

Climatic Forces and Human Adaptation

The first force—climatic selection—may be subdivided into three chief components: temperature, solar radiation, and oxygen pressure.

TEMPERATURE. Research has revealed that human populations living in different climates have adapted to such differences

---

1. Abridged from United Nations Educational, Scientific, and Cultural Organization (UNESCO), "Statement on Race and Racial Prejudice," *International Social Service Journal* 20, no. 1 (1968): 93–97.

through body form. It has been found that heat loss from the human body in different climates is controlled largely by differences in the ratio of body surface area to body mass. Thus, *Bergmann's rule* states that breeding populations within a bird or mammal species will be distributed throughout the geographic range so that groups with larger body sizes live in colder regions and those with smaller bodies inhabit warmer regions. Since a sphere is the geometric shape that affords minimum surface area proportional to mass (volume), a stocky physique would enable the individual to lose less vital body heat to the environment (see Figure 6–1). Accordingly, one would predict that among humans, Eskimos should be heavily built. Conversely, individuals in hot climates must shed heat to maintain optimal internal temperatures. Thus, a linear body would be predicted for such populations as Nilotic Negroes in equatorial Africa.

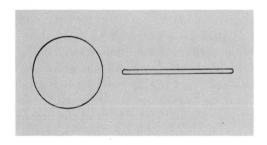

Figure 6–1   *The sphere and the cylinder have the same surface area but different volumes.*

A companion principle, *Allen's rule,* states that the limbs and other exposed appendages will be shorter and thicker in cold-stressed populations (such as the Eskimos). This constitutes an adaptation

against heat loss from exposed bodily structures, thus preventing frostbite. Again, heat-adapted individuals (such as the Nilotic tribes) would tend to possess longer fingers, arms, legs, and toes so that heat may be more easily radiated to the environment. The exceptions to the above generalizations are usually attributable to *migration* and *cultural adaptation* (the use of special clothing or shelter, for example). Moreover, such rules should be expected to apply only in populations that have lived in their environments for long periods, so that selection has had sufficient time to forge the adaptation.

SOLAR RADIATION. Skin color is considered by many people to be the most important marker of racial difference. Often, individuals treat others differently solely on this basis. As we saw, the UNESCO statement considers this wrong. At the same time, we cannot deny that there exists a wide range of skin color among the people of the world. We do not fully understand why some people have light skin while others have very dark or yellowish skin. Biologists have noted the same phenomenon among species of lower animals. Indeed, *Gloger's rule* states that breeding populations of bird and mammal species that inhabit the warm areas of a geographic range are darker (in feathers, fur, or skin) than populations that live in cooler regions of the range. Several theories have been proposed to explain these variations.

The first begins with the observation that dark skin color is influenced by the presence of the pigment melanin. The more melanin, the darker the skin. When skin is heavily pigmented or dark-colored, it contains a great deal of melanin, which protects the sensitive inner skin layers from the sun's damaging ultraviolet rays. Therefore, dark-skinned people, especially those living in tropical regions, are afforded protection from excess ultraviolet radiation, sunburn, and possible skin cancer. Light-skinned people living in sunny, tropical areas are clearly at a disadvantage.

A second theory turns on the role played by ultraviolet radiation in synthesizing vitamin D. This substance is important for the growth of bone and connective tissue. Deficiency of vitamin D can result in the crippling bone disease known as rickets. Too much vitamin D, however, can cause illness with symptoms including nausea, weakness, and loss of appetite. In less sunny, northern climates, a light skin probably maximizes ultraviolet penetration, insuring production of a sufficient amount of vitamin D. In tropical climates, dark skin, on the other hand, minimizes penetration and probably prevents a sickening overdose of ultraviolet rays. Thus, natural selection has favored light-skinned people in cloudy northern areas and dark-skinned people in tropical climates.[2]

THE EFFECTS OF ALTITUDE. Some who have traveled to the Colorado Rocky Mountains or the Peruvian Andes—or climbed a particularly high mountain—may have noticed the effects of such environments on the body. The traveler is forced to take more breaths. The heart beats faster and walking and climbing even a short flight of stairs become stressful, causing one to tire easily. This condition is known as *hypoxia* (low oxygen). It affects most people who visit altitudes of greater than one mile above sea level. At such heights, the partial pressure of the oxygen—the barometric pressure—is less than at lower altitudes.

But millions of people live normal lives at altitudes greater than one or two miles above sea level. The Sherpas in Nepal and the Bolivians and Peruvians of the Andes are a few examples. How is it that these individuals do not experience hypoxia? The answer is that they have adapted, both anatomically and physiologically, to the conditions of low barometric pressure. The inhabitants of such places, for example, have responded by making more red blood cells, thus increasing their blood volume. This, in turn, increases the amount of the blood's hemoglobin, the respiratory pigment that carries oxygen throughout the body. This explains the observation that visitors to high altitudes adjust to such altitudes by an increase in their usual red blood cell count after a week or so.

High-altitude natives also have a reduced rate of respiration, thus cutting down their need for oxygen. Moreover, they take in more air with each breath. These characteristics are reflected in an increase in chest size. For example, people living in the Andes are barrel-chested, having much larger lungs than natives of lower altitudes.[3]

Adaptations to Disease

While temperature, solar radiation, and altitude represent long-standing selection

2. W. F. Loomis, "Skin Pigment Regulation and Vitamin D Synthesis," *Science* 157 (1967) : 501–506.

3. Stanley J. Hock, "The Physiology of High Altitude," *Scientific American* 222 (February 1970) : 52–67.

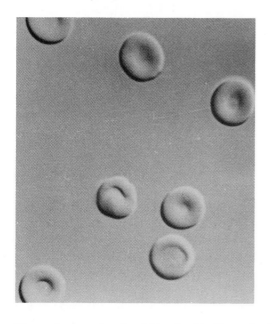 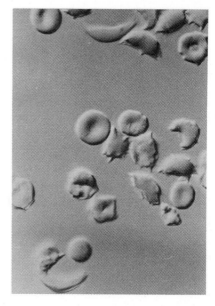

Photomicrographs of red blood cells. Normal cells are shown at left, sickle cells at right. The diseased cells clog blood vessels, preventing normal oxygen-carrying blood cells from passing.

forces that have molded human variations throughout our history, other agents have also been at work. Infectious diseases, for example, have presented a different kind of problem to human variation. To a great extent, the growth of the human population, its movements, and its techniques for obtaining food from the environment have subjected the species to new forms of selection.

With the domestication of plants and animals (discussed in Chapter 8), human populations established permanent settlements. Increases in the density of populations over the past 10,000 years followed the production of food surpluses. Such dense sedentary populations were one of the factors that opened the door to the spread of infectious diseases. For example, the plagues that ravaged large European population centers between the thirteenth and sixteenth centuries were at least partly due to cultural factors such as lack of sanitation measures and overcrowding.[4] The result has been selection favoring populations possessing genetic resistance to a variety of infectious diseases.

SICKLE-CELL ANEMIA AND MALARIA. A classic example of this phenomenon is seen in the disease known as sickle-cell anemia (sicklemia). The carriers of this condition have a selective advantage over noncarriers in certain malaria-infested environments.

4. William L. Langer, "The Black Death," *Scientific American* 210 (February 1964): 114–121.

Human Variation

In this disease, a recessive gene produces abnormal hemoglobin that changes the shape of the red blood cells. These are the cells that transport oxygen throughout the body during respiration. In sicklemia, the ordinarily round or oval shape of the red blood cell is twisted into a sickle shape. These deformed cells clog the skin capillaries, preventing other oxygen-carrying blood cells from passing. As a result, the victim experiences difficulty in breathing, chest and abdominal pains, dizziness, vomiting, and other symptoms, and sometimes death.

Sickle-cell anemia is an inherited condition that occurs in Africa, certain Mediterranean countries, and India. But it can also arise in other areas as a result of mutation. In the United States, many blacks of African descent carry the sickle-cell gene. It can be inherited in either of two forms: homozygotes (*ss*) receive a recessive sickle-cell gene from each parent and experience most of the symptoms of the condition. These individuals actually have sicklemia, and few of them reach adulthood. Heterozygotes (*As*) receive a dominant allele for normal hemoglobin (*A*) from one parent, and a recessive allele for the sickle-cell condition (*s*) from the other parent. The heterozygotes are merely carriers of the trait—that is, they are unaffected by the disease, or are only slightly affected, because the dominant allele masks the effects of the deleterious recessive allele. Thus, having the gene is not the same as having the disease.

The gene is carried in the heterozygous condition by as many as 40 percent of certain populations living in central Africa. This high proportion prompted investigators to ask why the harmful gene had not been weeded out by natural selection. The puzzle was finally solved when research revealed that the gene was beneficial to heterozygotes in certain environments. In those areas where a certain kind of malaria is prevalent, the gene prevents the malaria parasites from multiplying in the blood cells of the heterozygote. Thus, the sickle-cell disease protects its victims from malaria. On the other hand, individuals who are homozygous for normal hemoglobin (*AA*) are unaffected by anemia, but have no defense against the malaria infection, and so are less fit than their heterozygous counterparts.

Similarly, the recessive homozygotes (*ss*), who are the least fit of all, are protected from malaria but die at an early age of anemia because they lack even normal hemoglobin. In this example, natural selection works against both of the homozygotes. But it favors the heterozygotes, who are most likely to survive and reproduce. The two selective agents—malaria and anemia—together balance the frequencies of both genes in the population.[5]

The importance of the environment for this disease is highlighted by the fact that natural selection gradually filters out the recessive allele from those who leave malaria-infested areas. This results because the gene is not adaptive to the new environment and no longer confers fitness on those who carry it. It has been estimated, for instance, that more than 20 percent of the African slaves first brought to the United States carried the sickle-cell gene. Today, because of the pressure of selection, fewer than 10 percent of their descendants are marked by the trait.

---

5. Anthony C. Allison, "Sickle Cells and Evolution," *Scientific American* 195 (August 1956) : 87–94.

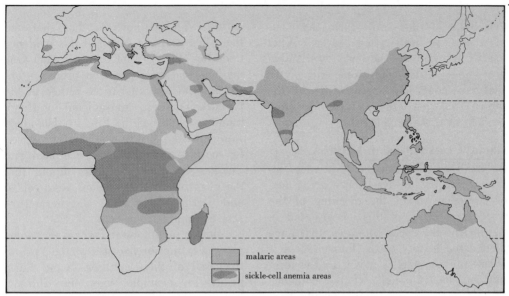

Figure 6–2   *Map showing distribution of malaria and the gene for sickle-cell anemia. Both are found in virtually the same regions, indicating that the sickle-cell gene is an adaptation to malaria.*

Eventually, the frequency of the recessive gene in the United States will approach zero. But it will never be eliminated entirely as long as it is carried in the heterozygote condition, in which it is somewhat sheltered from the effects of selection.

The significance of adaptive responses to climate, disease, and other selective agents is that they underlie human variation. Very likely, only a fraction of the ways in which the species varies has been uncovered. And most of the adaptive variations known are not well understood. In addition, there are so-called *neutral traits*—such as thick or thin lips, blue or brown eyes, red or brown hair—that do not seem to affect the fitness of their carriers, one way or the other. This seems to be true no matter what the environment

of the carriers. For this reason, most investigators believe that these traits were not shaped by the forces of natural selection. Instead, they probably arose as a result of gene flow or random genetic drift.

Human Variation and Race

It has been emphasized that some important physical variations between different human breeding populations are the results of adaptation to different environments. But anthropologists have not always believed this. Many investigators have employed certain phenotypical variations—physique, skin color, and hair form, for example—to classify the varieties of humankind. Indeed, some modern investigators still follow this practice. The variations in such traits form the basis of what have been called "races." What exactly is meant by the term *race?* What are some of the confusions and myths that have come to be associated with the term? And what is its usefulness in modern physical anthropology?

Racial Confusions and Myths

As the UNESCO statement on race implies, there has always been a great deal of confusion about the meaning of the word *race.* Much of this has resulted in the racism and racial prejudice that have blotted the history of the human species. What, for example, is meant by the term *human race?* In light of the evidence presented above regarding the adaptiveness of different human populations to different forces in the environment, does the term have any real meaning? Equally meaningless is the term proposed by Hitler's racial propagandists, the Aryan race. The word "Aryan" refers to individuals who speak any of the Indo-Aryan family of languages. These include Bengali, Hindi, Urdu, and other languages of those living in such countries as India, Pakistan, and Nepal.

The Aryan race, according to the Nazis, was supposed to be superior to the "Jewish race." In reality, however, Judaism is a religion, and Jews are not biologically different from other human groups. Moreover, individuals from many groups, including blacks, Chinese, and Indians, can be Jews. Race is also confused with nationality by many individuals. The Italians and French, for example, are not distinct races. Rather, these labels refer to people of many human groups who share the same culture and language.

Such confusion has also been associated with various myths about race. Sci-entific evidence, however, has shattered these false notions. Much of this evidence underlies the UNESCO statement. One myth is that miscegenation produces offspring who are inferior to either of the parents. This was contradicted by Harry Shapiro's study of the Pitcairn Islanders, who consisted of a hybrid stock produced by matings between European men and Polynesian women. Shapiro found that the offspring of these unions were robust and fertile rather than degenerate, as racists would have us believe.[6]

Another myth long in favor is that some races are inferior because of the "primitiveness" of their cultures. Some Europeans, for example, view the Chinese, Indians, Africans, and South Americans as belonging to primitive races. But anthropologists have found that advanced civilizations were blooming among such peoples long before Europe left the Dark Ages. We shall see in Chapter 9, for example, that the Shang dynasty flourished in China, the Harappan civilization in India, and the Mayan culture in Mesoamerica—all hundreds of years before civilizations of equivalent sophistication appeared in Europe.

Racists have also been responsible for the myth that blood differences exist between blacks and whites. Such terms as "Negro blood" and "mixed blood" are artifacts of this idea. To be sure, physical anthropologists have found that different types of blood types do exist among different human populations. But there appears to be no relationship between the color of one's skin and the type of blood

---

6. Harry L. Shapiro, *The Heritage of the Bounty* (Garden City, N.Y.: Doubleday, 1962).

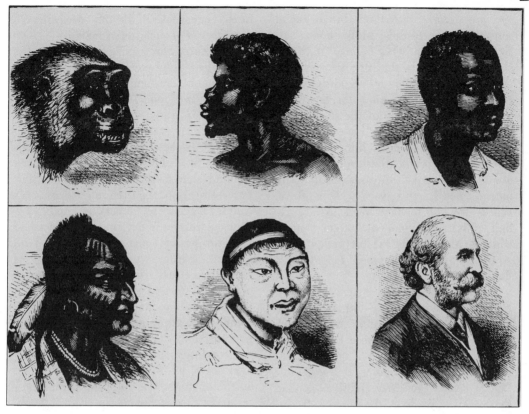

Figure 6–3   *Early evolutionists attempted to group all humans into developmental stages. In the scheme shown here, the Caucasian was considered the most advanced of the five races.*

that flows through his veins. Thus, a white person who receives a blood transfusion from a black of the same blood type may be saved from death. But a white person who receives a transfusion from another white may die if the donor's blood is not compatible.

Finally, many whites have long believed the myth that black people are closer to apes in anatomical traits than members of other of the so-called races. The truth of the matter is, however, that no one race is more like the ape than any

other. Nor is any one race less apelike than others. All members of the human species have apelike characteristics because, as we saw in Chapter 5—and as the UNESCO statement makes clear—humans and apes are descended from a common ancestor.

Defining the Race Concept

Not surprisingly, the above-mentioned confusions and myths have affected the meaning of the term *race*. For many individuals, the members of the human species are divided into three broad racial categories: Caucasoids, Mongoloids, and Negroids. People who believe in these classifications state that one race is separated from the others by certain physical characteristics. Thus, skin color, hair form and texture, the shape of the eyes, nose, and lips, and other traits have been used to classify an individual into one of the three broad groups. Caucasoids, for example, are thought to possess white skin, narrow noses, and varied hair form. Blacks are said to have black skin, curly hair, thick lips, and a flattened nose, whereas Mongoloids exhibit yellow skin, straight hair, and flattened face with a flattened nose.

But how accurate are such classifications? Considering only skin, it is apparent that the differences within each racial category exceed those between the categories. The skin of a Kalahari Bushman of Africa, for instance, may resemble that of a native of New Delhi more than that of an individual who supposedly belongs to the same race, such as a Nilotic Sudanese.

THE TYPOLOGICAL APPROACH.

This popular belief about distinct racial categories is the result of early studies that attempted to devise racial *typologies*. This thinking, which prevailed in anthropology early in this century, held that certain individuals were "ideal" representatives of a population. These individuals constituted a *type*. The typological classification of races represents an attempt to objectively characterize the "ideal type," or the perfect example of the outstanding features of the entire population. Thus, a "typological race" would be a collection of individuals who share certain arbitrarily designated features, irrespective of the geographical distribution of such individuals.

How many races exist according to the typological approach? The answer depends upon the number of traits selected and measured, and the methods of measurement or study of such traits. Or, as the UNESCO statement observes, the division of human species into such groups is partly arbitrary. As an example, if one selected skin coloration as the sole trait in classification, then the number of races could vary widely, depending upon how skin coloration is determined. One could have three races consisting of light, dark, and intermediate types, or hundreds of races if an equally large arbitrary number of shades were designated. However, if one added a second trait—such as eye color—then groupings would become compounded because individuals might meet the conditions for group membership on skin color, but not eye color, and so on. In this manner, the addition of more criteria for race membership—hair texture, shape of nose and lips, for example—would increase the number of races.

Most typologies can lead to absurdly large numbers of races even when only a few characteristics are employed. This, as well as the fact that most investigators tend to choose their own characteristics, tends to negate the value of the typological approach. Moreover, for any typological classification it will be practically impossible to find any individuals who are "perfect" members. As implied above, even a small number of characteristics, when measured with great refinement, can exclude virtually anyone from membership in short order.

THE POPULATIONIST APPROACH.

In recent years, many physical anthropologists have focused on the idea of the breeding population as the racial marker. Thus, Stanley Garn, the chief spokesman for this *populationist* school of thought, believes that a race is a breeding population largely isolated reproductively from other breeding populations.[7] Such populations are sometimes called *demes*.

Races, or racial boundaries, say Garn and the populationists, depend upon the degree of geographical separation between breeding populations. The boundaries between various demes are marked by groups of measurable physical traits. These, in turn, reflect the genetic makeup of each population.

Working from this idea, Garn delineates several ways of grouping races. First are the *local races*, which are true breeding populations in the above sense. They are isolated reproductively from one another and their phenotypes are different. Garn finds thirty-two examples of such races. Examples include certain groups of American Indians, such as the Navajo, Hopi, and Cherokee.

On a broader scale, several local races may be grouped into a *geographical race,* which is isolated from other similar groups by a major geographic boundary such as a continent, a body of water, or a desert. Garn's nine geographical races are:

1. European (people of Europe, North Africa, and the Middle East)
2. Asian (people of China, Japan, Siberia, Mongolia, Southeast Asia, and Indonesia)
3. Indian (people of India)

4. American (aboriginal people of North and South America)
5. African (people of Africa south of the Sahara Desert)
6. Micronesian (people of the islands of the western Pacific, from Guam to the Marshall Islands)
7. Melanesian (people of the western Pacific islands, south of Micronesia)
8. Polynesian (people of the islands of the eastern Pacific, from Hawaii to New Zealand)
9. Australian (aboriginal people of Australia)

The central idea behind such a classification is that individuals are assigned to races by breeding habits—that is, according to whom they share their genes with. Many anthropologists believe that the populationist approach offers great promise to studies of human variation because it focuses on the basic evolutionary unit, the deme. By studying how this isolated reproductive unit adapts to selective pressures, physical anthropologists can learn how it changes over time. Such information would advance our knowledge of human variation in that it would help unravel the genetic, evolutionary, and adaptive bases of all human traits.

The Race Concept: Present Status

In the extensive discussion of the term *race*—its meaning in various contexts, its social and emotional connotations—it has become clear that real and measurable differences exist among all humans. These variations may be classified according to many schemes for a variety of purposes. What is not clear, however, is the "meaning" of all these differences in physical and behavioral terms.

Most investigators agree that there should be some way to talk about differ-

---

7. Stanley Garn, *Human Races,* 3rd ed. (Springfield, Ill.: Charles C Thomas, 1971).

we are bound to unloose an avalanche of contexts—some valid, some inhumane—with which we must deal. As we have seen, the goal of physical anthropologists is to clarify the evolutionary meaning of human differences, not to deny their existence. As the UNESCO statement indicates, the task is not complete. Denying the term *race* will not banish the misunderstanding it represents.

Most investigators agree that the word *race* corresponds to no identifiable bio-

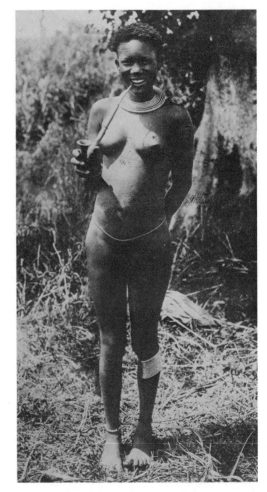

ences without the social nuances that always seem to arise, clouding the issues. Some have suggested substituting the term *subspecies* for race. A *subspecies* is a subdivision of a species that differs from other similar groups, usually in certain observable features.[8] But throwing away the term *race* in favor of a less socially loaded one, such as *subspecies*, has had little effect. Instead of delineating units for study, switching to other terms seems to compound the problems—quite aside from having no effect on the public.

Years ago, the linguist Edward Sapir and the anthropologist Benjamin Whorf stated that "when we think, we think in language." Thus, when we think "race"

8. Ernest Mayr, *Animal Species and Evolution* (Cambridge, Mass.: Harvard University Press, Belknap Press, 1963), p. 348.

Chapter Six

logical reality. In fact, however, the term corresponds to many realities, some meaningful ones in scientific texts, some which evoke feelings of *xenophobia* (fear of foreigners), ethnocentrism, and hatred. Humans will learn to put the term *race* in proper evolutionary perspective only as they come to appreciate their differences. And they will see these differences as strengths because natural selection acts on them to bring about evolutionary change.

Shown here are examples of five of Garn's nine geographical races. On facing page are an Asian and an African. On this page, clockwise from upper right, are a Polynesian, an American, and an Australian.

Human Variation and Behavior

American Indians are violent and self-destructive. Blacks have rhythm and are good singers and dancers. The Chinese are better than almost any other race at mathematics. Americans are practical people who can improvise solutions to emergency situations. Each of these widely held stereotypes associates some special kind of behavior with a certain race. Such behavior, say those who believe these statements, is a racial characteristic, locked into the genes of every member of the race.

Other individuals, however, say that these traits are the result of the cultural environment and are not inherited. Thus, the Chinese ability in mathematics springs from the pictographic nature of the Chinese language, which approaches mathematics in its symbolism. Which side is correct? Is behavior due to inheritance or to environment, in the form of culture?

One of the great advances made in recent years has been the realization that to ask whether behavior is due to genetics or to environment is a trifle foolish. The correct question should be, "How much of behavior is determined by genes and how much by environment?" It has been known for some time that environmental circumstances of all sorts influence gene expression. Thus, to talk about the relationships between race and behavior sensibly, we must talk about the relationship between gene-regulated phenomena and the environmental influences that modify their expression. Specifically, we must note that humans exist in two environments at all times. First is the physical environment, which includes climatic stresses, toxic substances, perhaps even dangerous animals or traffic. Second is the cultural environment, which includes explanations for all these things, and values related to everything—from the physical environment and its threats to economics and ideas about other human groups.

The inseparability of these two environments presents the principal difficulty for the student of human variation. It is difficult to establish a clear understanding of how each of these environments interacts and to what extent each affects the individual. A current issue may help to put the problem into focus. This is the issue of intelligence, which has long been at the center of the heredity–environment controversy.

The Jensen Controversy

The psychologist Arthur Jensen has claimed that his studies of identical twins show that a person's environment has only a limited effect upon his or her intelligence as measured by an IQ test. Jensen analyzed intelligence studies on identical twins that had been conducted in England, Denmark, and the United States. He found that there is about a 15-point difference between the IQ test scores of American black and white children. He feels that as much as 80 percent of this gap may be due to heredity and, therefore, cannot be modified through environmental changes.[9] These findings were widely publicized and served to reinforce some people's prejudices and segregationist tendencies.

As one might expect, Jensen's position created an uproar among scientists and laypersons alike. One primary objection to Jensen's study was his use of standard IQ tests to measure intelligence. Critics pointed out that the IQ tests had been developed in the context of a largely white, middle-class culture that was very different from the culture of the black

---

9. Arthur Jensen, "How Much Can We Boost IQ and Scholastic Achievement?" *Harvard Educational Review* 29 (1969): 1–123.

children being tested. Black children also tended to be unfamiliar with formal classroom test situations. They may have felt intimidated by an examiner of another race, and may have lacked interest and motivation in the test procedure.[10]

The most important point to bear in mind is that many studies done after Jensen's original results were published have shown that large changes in IQ scores can be produced by altering the environment of black children. Removal of various environmental handicaps has resulted in the upward modifications of 15 to 30 points in average IQ scores. By merely retesting the children in an environment in which they felt comfortable, Jensen himself noticed that 8- to 10-point gains were common.[11] Even larger gains in IQ have been reported when the subjects were moved from severely deprived home environments to more "normal" ones. J. M. Hunt has shown that an astounding 35-point increase can often occur when children are transferred from orphanages to good foster homes.[12]

Even studies conducted prior to that of Jensen show that environment is an important variable in intelligence. During the 1930s, for example, Otto Klineberg

found that American blacks from Northern cities scored higher on IQ tests than did blacks from Southern cities.[13] Many investigators concluded from these results that the Northern cities—particularly the larger ones—had better schools and more varied and stimulating environments than their Southern counterparts. Later studies revealed that Northern blacks achieved higher scores than Southern whites.

In recent years, it has become increasingly clear that economic and nutritional variables must be considered in any attempt to assess intelligence. Often, individuals of low economic status simply do not know about nutrition, or are unable to secure nourishing food. The absence or deficiency of protein in the diet of an infant or young child is now known to affect brain development. Such imperfect development is irreversible. It inevitably causes the child to fall short of whatever genetically based intellectual potential he or she may have had.[14]

Even when nutritional aspects are acceptable, however, other environmental factors can thwart achievement. Several anthropologists have noted that some parents of minority-group children do not reinforce educational values that the children learn at school. Such a climate can hardly be expected to foster academic accomplishment—the sort of accomplishment measured in most standard, culture-

10. I. Katz, T. Heuchy, and H. Allen, "Effects of Race of Tester, Approval, Disapproval and Need on Negro Children's Learning," *Journal of Personality and Social Research* 8 (1968): 38–42.

11. Jensen, "How Much Can We Boost IQ and Scholastic Achievement," p. 100.

12. J. M. Hunt, "Has Compensatory Education Failed? Has It Been Attempted?" *Harvard Educational Review* 39 (1963): 278–300.

13. Otto Klineberg, *Negro Intelligence and Selective Migration* (New York: Columbia University Press, 1935).

14. Walter F. Bodmer and Luigi Luca Cavalli-Sforza, "Intelligence and Race," *Scientific American* 223 (October 1970): 19–29.

bound tests of intelligence. Most devastating to the development of intelligence potential is the combined interaction of early nutritional deprivation, lack of reinforcement of learning, and a backdrop of economic hopelessness that often encourages departure from the school environment prematurely.

Clearly, no valid comparisons can be made between the intelligence of black and white individuals until all people live in comfortable environments with equal opportunities to develop their potentials. When this happens, evidence indicates that no racial differences in IQ are likely to exist. Perhaps this has been best summed up by the UNESCO statement on race and racial prejudice, part of which was reprinted at the beginning of the chapter:

> *Current biological knowledge does not permit us to impute cultural achievements to differences in genetic potential. Differences in the achievements of different peoples should be attributed solely to their cultural history. The peoples of the world today appear to possess equal biological potential for attaining any level of civilization.*[15]

2. Natural selective forces operate on the human species, pressuring different populations to adapt to these forces. Thus, various breeding populations have made special adaptations to climatic stress (temperature, oxygen pressure, and solar radiation) and disease (sickle-cell anemia and the plague). Such selective forces underlie human variation.

3. The term *race* has engendered much confusion about human physical differences. Individuals have confused race with language, religion, and nationality. Adding to these false ideas are the large number of racial myths that have arisen during the course of human history.

4. Attempts to define the term *race* as a scientific concept have given rise to various approaches to this subject. The typological approach to human variation holds that there exist certain individuals who are ideal representatives, or types, of a population. The populationist approach centers on reproductively isolated breeding populations, or demes. This approach has yielded several ways of grouping races, including local races and geographical races.

5. Behavior determined by genes and behavior determined by the environment are virtually impossible to separate. The issue of genes and intelligence has generated a host of inaccuracies and half-truths which have fed the fires of racial discrimination.

Summary

1. Human variation is the result of evolutionary adaptations to selective forces operating in different environments over hundreds of thousands of years.

---

15. UNESCO, "Statement on Race and Racial Prejudice."

Review Questions

1. Human variation results from the adaptation of populations to different environments. Which of the evolutionary forces is most important in bringing about this variation? Why?

2. Explain in detail one example of human adaptation to some aspect of the physical environment.

3. Compare and contrast the central points of the typological and populationist approaches to human variation.

4. Arthur Jensen holds that there is a relationship between one's genes and his or her intelligence. Explain Jensen's position and describe two studies that offer evidence that refutes Jensen.

emphasize genetic bases of human adaptation, as well as the interaction of biological and cultural factors in human variation.

Mead, Margaret, et al., eds. *Science and the Concept of Race.* New York: Columbia University Press, 1968.

A collection of essays on race by anthropologists, biologists, medical scientists, and psychologists. This book is the outcome of a 1966 symposium of the American Association for the Advancement of Science.

Suggested Readings

Alland, A. *Human Diversity.* Garden City, N.Y.: Doubleday, Anchor Press, 1973.
A readable discussion of human variation that focuses on race as a social rather than a biological reality.

Garn, Stanley M. *Human Races.* 3rd ed. Springfield, Ill.: Charles C Thomas, 1971.
An authoritative treatment of human variation that delves into biological and social aspects of the subject, including the controversy over race and intelligence.

Katz, Solomon, ed. *Biological Anthropology.* San Francisco: W. H. Freeman, 1975.
Forty-one *Scientific American* offprints by prominent physical anthropologists, biologists, and geneticists. Subjects range from studies of primates, fossil humans, and language, to the genetic code and the effects of disease and other environmental variables on human adaptation and variation.

Laughlin, W. S., and Osborne, R. H., eds. *Human Variation and Origins.* San Francisco: W. H. Freeman, 1967.
Another excellent collection of *Scientific American* offprints. The twenty-seven articles

PART THREE

In the preceding section, organic evolution was defined as a change in the form and behavior of organisms as they adapt to environmental conditions over time. The cultures of humankind also adapt to their environment and change through evolution. The discipline that studies past cultures and their evolution is archeology, the subject of this section of the text. Archeology is the scientific study of the nature and cultural behavior of humans, including the evolution of such behavior, by means of the analysis of the material remains of their past activities. Archeology is sometimes called paleoanthropology because it attempts to unravel the ancient behavior patterns that produced material remains. (The methodology used by archeologists to bring ancient cultures back to life is discussed in Appendix A.)

Both anthropologists and archeologists want to know how and why human cultures adapt to environments and change. These adaptations have been both biological and cultural. Over the years, a number of dramatic breakthroughs in cultural evolution have become the subject of intense archeological scrutiny. How and why, for example, were our early ancestors pressured into developing the basic elements of culture, including different traditions of tool-making, clothing, shelter, the division of labor, and social organization? These subjects are discussed in Chapter 7. A second area of interest focuses on the processes by which certain groups settled down and began producing their own food—the subject of Chapter 8. Third, what forces pressured small farming villages to make the next big adaptation—to expand into cities and states? This important cultural adaptation is discussed in Chapter 9.

Those who study cultural evolution and human history customarily divide the story of our development into two general periods: prehistory and history. Prehistory, in turn, is divided into three great cultural epochs: the Paleolithic (Old Stone) Age, which stretched from 5 million to 14,000 years B.P.; the Mesolithic (Middle Stone) Age, which lasted from 14,000 to 10,000 B.P., and the Neolithic (New Stone) Age, which extended from 10,000 to 5,000 B.P. The cultural adaptations of the Paleolithic period are discussed in Chapter 7, whereas those of the Mesolithic and Neolithic are covered in Chapters 8 and 9. The beginning of the historical period is generally set at around 5,000 B.P., when the first written records appeared.

In seeking to explain how cultures evolved over these periods, archeologists focus on three main aspects of human culture: technology, ecology, and social organizations. *Technology* includes all those things, such as tools and fire, that a human group employs to extract food or energy from its habitat. Chapter 7, for example, will examine the ways in which the early

Evolution
of Culture

hunters and gatherers of the Middle and Upper Paleolithic periods manufactured and improved tools as they adapted to different environments. Among the stone tools of these periods were handaxes, knives, boring implements, and scrapers. Later, the bow and arrow and the spear thrower increased enormously the amount of energy that each person in a given culture could squeeze from the environment.

Ecology is a term discussed in the last section of the text; it is in favor among many modern people who are concerned about the ways humans are treating their habitat. Ecology refers to the relationships of organisms to their environments. Cultural ecology studies the ways that different human groups interact with their environment to survive, to change—or not to survive as groups. In studying ecology, archeologists ask how effectively a culture exploits the resources of its habitat, and how the habitat influences the behavior patterns of the individuals in that particular culture. Thus, Chapter 8 will analyze how some hunter-gatherer groups exploited a wide range—or "broad spectrum"—of resources in their habitats. It was such an adaptation that paved the way for one of the most monumental events in human history—the domestication of plants and animals.

Finally there is *social organization*. Archeologists are interested in the effects of technology and ecology on human social organization. How, for example, does a new adaptation such as farming or the rise of a city affect social relations? In Chapter 8, we shall see how the domestication of plants and animals increased food supply, which led to an increase in population. High population density, in turn, resulted in the division of society into classes. The lower classes usually included farmers and serfs, and the upper classes included those who had some kind of economic, political, or religious control over those below them. For example, among the upper classes were priests, who, sanctioned by the religious beliefs of the society, were probably the managers of early farming villages. Thus, religion apparently became a means for controlling the internal dynamics of the first farming communities.

A culture, then, is viewed by archeologists as an organized community that exploits its environment for basic resources. As Chapters 8 and 9 make clear, each society extracts energy from its environment with differing degrees of efficiency, depending on its technology, social organization, and ideology (ideas about the nature of reality). Changes in any of these three elements can be related to modifications in a group's habitat, to an increase (or decrease) in the efficiency with which the culture exploits its stable environment, or to a combination of both.

Chapter
7

Prehistory & Culture

High in the Zagros Mountains of Iraq, some 250 miles north of Baghdad, is a hollow in the rock known as Shanidar Cave. A geologist would find nothing extraordinary about this cave. It is large, to be sure, large enough to house four tennis courts, and its highest point rises 45 feet above the floor. But to the student of human evolution, Shanidar is one of the most exciting finds in recent history. It was here that archeologist Ralph Solecki unearthed a number of Neandertal skeletons. Two of these specimens—designated by Solecki as Shanidar IV and VI— had been buried with flowers. This find indicates that culture, in the form of altruistic concern for a fallen kinsman and a belief in a life hereafter, had become a moving force in human evolution. In the passage below, Solecki describes his discoveries at Shanidar and their importance.

NEANDERTALS: THE FIRST FLOWER PEOPLE

Reflecting on the events of the season thus far, we thought it might be better if I did not make any more cuts in Layer D, the Neandertal-containing layer. Admittedly, one of our field objectives was to recover the rest of Shanidar II. The others were dividends. In any

Source: From *Shanidar: The First Flower People*, by Ralph S. Solecki. Copyright © 1971 by Ralph S. Solecki. Reprinted by permission of Alfred A. Knopf, Inc. and the author.

case, in order to use the remainder of our time in the season advantageously and yet not get into any new complications with fresh Neandertal skeletons, I followed a plan which I had outlined in my mind long ago. This was to extend the northern end of our trench toward the rear wall of the cave. In this way, we would see if there was anything of note at the wall. I remembered that some of the best occupational traces were to be found at the wall of occupied caves. Furthermore, the present Kurdish occupants ranged their little huts around the wall of the interior of the cave, and presumably the prehistoric peoples before them did the same. With this thought in mind, we began work. We outlined an area 26 feet by 26 feet and had barely started to excavate when our "green thumb" for human skeletal remains turned up something more. In the proto-Neolithic layer, at about 3 feet deep, we uncovered 28 human skeletons, a whole graveyard of them. We ended the season two weeks later on an almost frantic note, working from morning until night on these new skeletal remains.

I took routine soil samples from around and within the area of [the site of] Shanidar IV and [the] adjacent [site of] Shanidar VI, as well as some samples of soils from outside the area of the skeletal remains. There seemed to be no point in taking these samples of soils, but I recalled my work on an Indian mound in the Ohio Valley, and the dividends obtained from soil studies. Actually we would not know until eight years later that the soils I had collected for analysis would produce significant, if not startling, results.

By then I had submitted these soil samples to Mme Arlette Leroi-Gourhan, of Paris, our palaeobotanist, for pollen analysis. She had been doing this work for the Shanidar expedition for several years. She examined the six soil samples I had taken from around Shanidar IV and VI and the immediately adjacent area. Several of the prepared slides under the microscope showed not only the usual kinds of pollen from trees or grasses, but also from flowers. She hastened to write me, asking for a diagram of the positions of the soil samples relative to the skeletons. Additional study confirmed the first suspicions that Shanidar IV was buried with flowers. Here were the first "Flower People," a discovery wholly unprecedented in archaeology, as well as unexpected. Many thousands of burials had been unearthed since prehistoric archaeologists began to pursue their profession scientifically over a hundred years ago, but nothing like this had even been suspected. The wider applications of palynology, or pollen analysis, to prehistory have been known for at least forty years. Pollen studies had been made in all kinds of soils, but for some reason flowers had not been found around skeletons until this association was found with Shanidar IV. The simplest explanation appears to be that no one had ever thought of looking for pollens in graves.

Mme Leroi-Gourhan estimated that this individual was laid to rest sometime between late May and early July, taking into account the climatic differences because the burial took place in the Last Ice Age. She found under her microscope pollen and flower fragments from at least eight species of flowers. These flowers represented mainly small, brightly colored wild flowers. She recognized relatives of the grape hyacinth, bachelor's button, hollyhock, and a yellow-flowering groundsel. Mme Leroi-Gourhan thinks that the flowers were probably woven into the branches of a pinelike shrub, evidence of which was also found in the soils. . . .

From archaeological findings elsewhere we already know that Neandertal man seems to have had a spiritual concept, since he evidently practiced funerary rites over his dead. But the occurrence of flowers with Neandertal burials raises the question, Where else in prehistory is there any parallel? Searching through the literature on Stone Age cultures yields nothing, with the apparent exception of an image scratched in bone, which is interpreted by Marshack as a flower in bloom. None of the voluminous books on cave art sheds any light on the matter. The depictions in caves are concerned mainly with the food animals. On the economic uses of plants in prehistory there is a growing wealth of information, but on flowers there is silence. With the finding of flowers in association with Neandertals, we are brought suddenly to the realization that the universality of mankind and the love of beauty go beyond the boundary of our own species. No longer can we deny the early men the full range of human feelings and experience.[1]

●　●　●　●　●　●　●　●

When we left the Neandertals in Chapter 5, we saw that there was some dispute about their place in the human family tree. But as Ralph Solecki indicates in the passage above, these Stone Age hun-

ter-gatherers were quite human. Indeed, it is with the Neandertals that the pace of human evolution accelerates greatly because cultural factors, rather than only biological ones, begin to play an increasingly important role in their development. New tools and new cultural practices appear with these people. And those who came after them in Upper Paleolithic times—the Cro-Magnons of Chapter 5—

1. Ralph S. Solecki, *Shanidar: The First Flower People* (New York: Alfred A. Knopf, 1971), pp. 244–247, 250.

were responsible for even greater changes in technology, art, religion, and probably social organization. In fact, the passing of the Upper Paleolithic marks the end of the Old Stone Age.

This chapter, which actually is a continuation of Chapter 5, will examine the evidence for the cultural remains of the Neandertals and their Upper Paleolithic successors. We will look at the ways tools, housing, clothing, art, religion, and other aspects of human social organization evolved during these important periods. The focus of the discussion will be on the cultural relics unearthed in eastern and western Europe and Russia, largely because these areas have been extensively studied. Developments in the Americas will also be briefly considered.

Neandertal Culture

Far from being the hulking, dim-witted, brutish "cave man"—the stereotype usually associated with this fossil human subspecies—the Neandertal, in fact, possessed a relatively evolved culture. First discovered by archeologists in the Neander Valley near Düsseldorf, Germany, these early people had successfully adapted to a wide range of environments, including the frigid areas of eastern and western Europe, the balmy Mediterranean regions of Europe and the Near East, and the jungles of tropical Africa. The Neandertals lived both in caves and in open campsites, in small hunting-gathering bands of from ten to forty individuals. Although some groups were nomadic, following the changing seasons in the quest for food, others may have been sedentary, inhabiting some sites year-round.

The Neandertals knew much about plants and animals, and they were successful big-game hunters as well. They were familiar with the properties of different kinds of stone, using a wide variety of stone tools to exploit and control the environment. They were mystics who believed in supernatural forces. They also cared for their injured and their sick. In short, they possessed many of the hallmarks of modern human populations.

Since Europe has been most extensively studied with regard to recent cultural and human evolution, it should not be surprising that we know more about the paleo (ancient) environment of this continent than of any other.

Neandertal populations occupied the forest tundra and cold steppe zones of Middle Paleolithic Europe (about 60,000 B.P.). Although the climate to the south was considerably warmer and consisted of temperate woodlands, this area was not so densely populated. Why should this be so? For one reason, the Neandertals, like *Homo erectus* before them, had domesticated fire, which enabled them to survive the coldest winters. For another, they also wore skin clothing. The most important reason, however, had to do with the large mammals upon whom the Middle Paleolithic hunters depended for subsistence: these herd-dwelling herbivores (elk, bison, and horse, for example) were adapted to the cold climate of the time. As a result, the Neandertals adapted to this important source of food, hides, and bones.

Neandertal Technology

The earliest Neandertals may have lived in Europe, Africa, and Asia 100,000 years before the present (B.P.). But the period during which they were most numerous and successful—as revealed by the wealth of skeletal and cultural remains—was be-

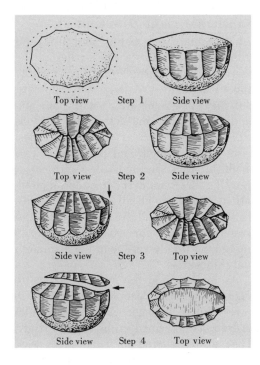

Top view   Step 1   Side view

Top view   Step 2   Side view

Side view   Step 3   Top view

Side view   Step 4   Top view

Figure 7–1 *Steps in Levallois method. Step 1, edges of nucleus are trimmed. Step 2, top surface is trimmed. Step 3, striking platform is made. Step 4, flake removed from nucleus.*

tween 85,000 and 35,000 B.P. in western Europe. As stated previously, most of our knowledge of the culture of Neandertals, as well as of those who came after them, is derived from western European sites, because these have been studied more thoroughly.

The cultural remains of European Neandertals are given the name *Mousterian*, after the village of Le Moustier in southwestern France, the site of an early find. The chief cultural relics of these people are stone and bone tools—tools to hunt animals, to prepare food, to tailor hide

skins into clothing, to make tents, and so forth. As we saw in Chapter 5, the anthropologist analyzes tools to work out the ways in which our early ancestors adapted to the environment. In short, tools help illuminate ancient living habits.

The Neandertals were skilled flint-knappers (tool-makers) who knew a good deal about the properties of stone. One tool of their western *Homo erectus* predecessors of 500,000 B.P. was the *Acheulean hand axe*, the manufacture of which is described in Chapter 5.

Later, tool-makers of about 200,000 years B.P. improved on this method with one known as the *Levallois technique* (Figure 7–1). With this technique the flint core was carefully finished by removing small flakes from the sides and top and finishing a striking platform. The tool-maker then gave the platform a sharp tap with a hammerstone and detached a flake. The advantage of this technique is that it enabled the flint-knapper to remove flakes of predetermined size and form which, in turn, could themselves serve as tools.

The Neandertal tool-makers improved on the basic Levallois technique by getting not two or three flake tools from a single core, but as many flakes as possible. These flakes were, in turn, retouched and used as tools.[2] Besides the hand axe, the Neandertals had used a variety of other tools. Archeologists have divided these implements into *tool kits*—assemblages of tools used for different purposes. Not surprisingly, the people of the Middle Paleolithic continued using some of the tools

2. Jacques Bordaz, *Tools of the Old and New Stone Age* (Garden City, N.Y.: Natural History Press, 1970).

devised by their predecessors, including the implements discussed in Chapter 5. But the Neandertals greatly improved on these basic implements. Moreover, Neandertal tools were more numerous and varied.

One Neandertal tool kit, for example, consisted of boring and engraving tools with sharp points, probably used to make holes in animal hides, and in wooden handles for axes. Another kit included spear points and scrapers, the one for killing animals, the other for scraping the hides clean. A third tool kit contained knives for cutting wood and other similar materials, and flakes—sharp, bladelike implements used to work with softer material such as meat. Fourth were more scrapers, flakes, and tools known as *denticulates*—notched stones that were probably used to shape wooden pieces, to put points on wooden spears, for example. Finally, there were pointed implements—those like spearheads used for killing game.[3]

Archeologist Sally Binford believes that the existence of different tool kits reflects the fact that the tools were used for different activities at different places and different times by the same group of culturally related people. Thus, there are different Mousterian kits for the same reason that a modern plumber's tool kit is different from that of a television repair person—because the two are used for different tasks.

---

3. Sally R. Binford, "Variability and Change in Near Eastern Mousterian of Levallois Facies," in *New Perspectives in Archeology*, ed. Lewis R. Binford and Sally R. Binford (Chicago: Aldine Publishing, 1968).

Subsistence and Housing

What animals were hunted and processed with the tools? As we saw earlier in the chapter, the Neandertals successfully hunted a number of large herd animals. But they also went after small game, including rabbits, muskrats, and various kinds of fowl, such as duck and cranes. Fish, such as perch and pike, as well as shellfish, crabs, and mollusks, were eaten, too. Of course, not every Neandertal population exploited all of these resources. Those in the glacial areas of eastern and western Europe, for example, primarily hunted the woolly variety of the mammoth and rhinoceros.

As for housing, the evidence seems to suggest that these people lived mostly in caves and rock shelters such as Shanidar in Iraq, as described in the capsule study. They also sheltered in tents which were pitched both inside the caves and on the open ground. Thus, at Combe-Grenal, a site some 300 miles southwest of Paris rich in Neandertal remains, was found a *postmold*—a small cavity in the earth made by a pointed stake, a hole a tent peg might make. Since this was located near the mouth of the cave, the French archeologist François Bordes speculates that the ancient people probably used pegs to anchor animal skins or branches or other material to the ground at the cave opening, as protection against the biting winds and driving snows of the glacial era.[4]

Religion

As we have seen at Shanidar, there is strong evidence that the Neandertals con-

---

4. François Bordes, *A Tale of Two Caves* (New York: Harper and Row, 1972).

ducted religious rituals. Similarly, at Le Moustier, investigators discovered an interesting burial which suggests that the people believed in a life in the hereafter. They found the remains of a young boy placed in a trench lying on his right side. He seems to have been placed in the sleeping position—his head was resting on his right forearm and his knees were drawn up. A pile of flints served as a stone pillow and a stone axe was placed in his left hand. Cattle bones, some of which were charred, were scattered around the body.[5]

Other finds support the idea that Neandertal people practiced religion and were concerned with supernatural questions. Near Monte Circeo in Italy, there is a cave containing a circle of stones, in the center of which was found a human skull with a hole bored in it. At another cave in the Uzbek Mountains of Central Asia, there is evidence that the ibex (wild goat) played a part in a Neandertal ritual, much as it does among those who inhabit this region today. Six pairs of ibex antlers were placed around the head of a young boy buried in a cave.[6]

Archeologists also have unearthed evidence suggesting that the cave bear may have been a central figure in Neandertal religious belief. At Drachenlock, Switzerland, for example, several cave-bear skulls were discovered in a trunklike container of stone. Anthropologist Clark Howell[7]

suggests that perhaps they were hunting trophies. Or were they part of a religious ritual? At the same site is the skull of a young bear, its cheek pierced by the leg bone of an even younger bear. The skull sits on the bones of other bears. Was magic intended, or an invocation of the supernatural? One of the more interesting sites that supports the idea of a cave-bear cult is in eastern Austria. Here, in a square burial chamber, were seven bear skulls, all facing the mouth of the cave.

What does all this mean, these elaborate burials and the carefully placed cave-bear remains? For one thing, they represent the first purposeful disposal of the dead among our prehistoric ancestors. For another, the findings strongly suggest that the Neandertals were true humans who possessed, as Ralph Solecki observed in the capsule study, "the full range of human feelings and experience."[8]

Upper Paleolithic Culture: Homo sapiens sapiens

The culture of the Neandertals was outstripped in virtually every respect by the populations who came after them in western Europe about 40,000 years ago. These people are sometimes referred to as Cro-Magnons, after the rock shelter at Les Eyzies in France, where their first fossils were found.

The Cro-Magnons are the first true representatives of *Homo sapiens sapiens*, or modern humans—that is, in cranial capacity and skeletal features, they were virtually identical to contemporary humans. In technology, in hunting tech-

5. John Pfeiffer, *The Emergence of Man*, 2nd ed. (New York: Harper and Row, 1972).

6. Pfeiffer, *The Emergence of Man*.

7. F. Clark Howell, *Early Man* (New York: Time-Life Books, 1965).

8. Solecki, *Shanidar*, p. 250.

niques, in artistic expression, and possibly in social organization, they were like no creatures who had walked the earth before them. Beginning with these folk, the tempo of cultural evolution accelerates at a rapid rate.

Like their Neandertal predecessors, the Upper Paleolithic populations of Europe had adapted to hunting the large herd animals of the tundra and cool steppe.[9] Bison, mammoth, wild horses, and reindeer inhabited the steppe and tundra regions, whereas ibex (wild goats), oxen, and fallow deer lived in the forests of southwestern Europe.[10]

New Tools and Tool-Making Techniques

Although the Upper Paleolithic people continued to use Neandertal tools and tool-making techniques, they made notable improvements on many of them. These people also were using a greater number of different types of tools. Investigators have been able to distinguish some 100 different tools, as compared to about seventy for the Neandertals. The principal characteristic of the later technology is the increase in the use of stone blades— long, thin flakes with parallel sides.

Blades were produced by a new method known as *indirect percussion* (Figure 7–2). An intermediate tool, called a *punch*, usually made of bone, wood, or antler, was placed against the striking platform (a prepared area) of the flint

core and then struck with a hammerstone. This technique enabled the craftsman to direct the force of the blow at a small point on the striking platform. In this way, the blades were produced with more precision and in a wider variety of forms, and a great deal more cutting edge per pound of flint was made available to the flint-knapper than with older techniques. It has been estimated, for example, that the most primitive stone-making methods —that is, those used to make the Oldowan choppers discussed in Chapter 5—yielded about 2 inches of cutting edge for each pound of flint. Later flint-knappers, working in Acheulean hand axe tradition, were able to get about 7 inches of edge per pound of flint. Their Upper Paleolithic descendants could obtain 120 to 480 inches of working edge from the same amount of flint—an important technological advance.[11]

The most common new blade tools of the period were the backed blade, the end-scraper, and the burin. *Backed blades* had one cutting edge and one edge that was purposely blunted to serve as a handle of sorts. The backed edge enabled the tool user to grasp the blade with the whole hand, thus being able to put more muscle behind the cutting or scraping action. *End-scrapers* were blades with one blunted end, probably used for scraping hides or hollowing out wood or bone. Finally, the *burin* was a type of chisel with which the artisan worked bone, antler, wood, and ivory to fashion awls, needles, spears, and harpoon points with tangs (projecting prongs). With the burin, hu-

9. James J. Hester, *Introduction to Archeology* (New York: Holt, Rinehart and Winston, 1976).

10. K. Butzer, *Environment and Archaeology*, 2nd ed. (Chicago: Aldine-Atherton, 1971).

11. Frank E. Poirier, *Fossil Man: An Evolutionary Journey* (St. Louis, Mo.: C. V. Mosby, 1973).

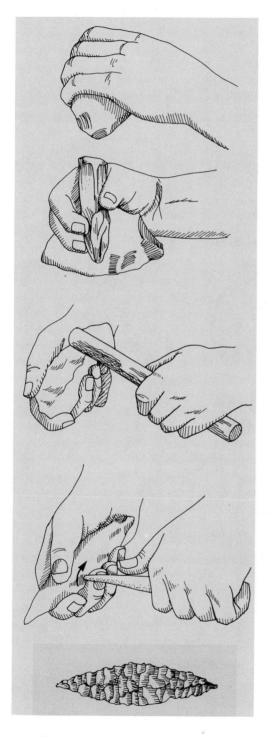

mans invented one of the first tools with the sole function of making other tools. This, of course, is the purpose of machine tools today.[12] (See Figure 7–3.)

This period also witnessed the appearance of the *multiple tool*, blades that have a tool for one purpose at one end and a tool for a different purpose at the opposite end. There is also evidence that these people, like the Neandertals, increased the efficiency of their tools by *hafting* (fastening) them to wood, bone, or ivory handles, thus amplifying the muscle power of the user.

Among the most distinctive and elegant tools of the period were the so-called *Solutrean laurel leaves,* which probably served as projectile points and knives. These large, thin, triangular points (4 or 5 inches long) were probably manufactured by a precision technique known as *pressure flaking* (Figure 7–2). In this method, one edge of the core was wrapped in leather or some other protective material and held in one hand. A flaking tool, such as a piece of antler, was then held by the other hand to chip small flakes from the core.

Other articles, such as large-eyed ivory needles and bone and ivory belt fixtures,

---

12. Bordaz, *Tools of the Old and New Stone Age.*

Figure 7–2   *Three tool-making techniques of Upper Paleolithic people. From top are indirect percussion, baton technique, and pressure flaking. Solutrean laurel leaf in darker area was produced by pressure flaking method.*

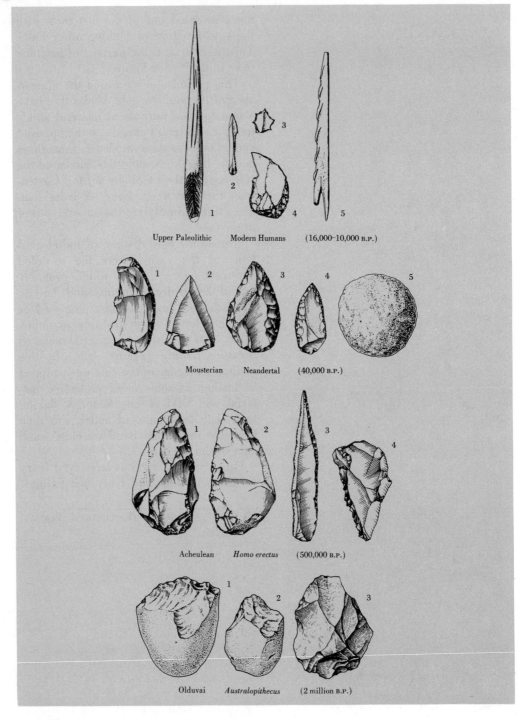

Upper Paleolithic   Modern Humans   (16,000–10,000 B.P.)

Mousterian   Neandertal   (40,000 B.P.)

Acheulean   *Homo erectus*   (500,000 B.P.)

Olduvai   *Australopithecus*   (2 million B.P.)

indicate that the people wore clothes cut and sewn to fit the body. Barbed points, harpoons, and ivory fish hooks tell us that the Cro-Magnon people engaged in fishing. Big-game hunting was still a major activity, as indicated by spears, javelins, harpoons, and *bolas*—stones bound together with leather thongs which were thrown at the legs of running animals to trip them. (There is evidence that the Neandertals also used the bola.) Another advance was the *spear thrower*, usually now identified by its Aztec name of *atlatl*. The spear thrower consisted of a grooved piece of wood a little more than a foot in length, with a notch or hook at one end to hold the spear. By snapping the atlatl from the shoulder the way a javelin thrower hurls a javelin, the hunter could launch the spear with greater velocity than if he threw the weapon by hand.

Reindeer were the most hunted game in western Europe. Not only did the meat provide food energy, but the bones and horns were used for tools and other implements, the hides for clothing and shelter, the sinews for sewing thread, and even the teeth served as ornaments. The woolly mammoth and rhinoceros were

Figure 7–3   *The evolution of stone tools, from Olduvai to Upper Paleolithic tool cultures. The three Olduvai tools are choppers. Acheulean tools are hand axes (1, 2), backed blade (3), and denticulate (4). Mousterian tools are knife (1), Levallois point (2), scraper (3), Mousterian point (4), and bola (5). Upper Paleolithic tools are bone point (1), Magdalenian shouldered point (2), multiple borer (3), parrot-beak burin (4), and harpoon (5).*

hunted by eastern Europeans and Russians.

Housing

In eastern Europe and Russia, Upper Paleolithic poeples lived on open ground in tents, sometimes in relatively large settlements (Figure 7–4). Archeologists have come to this conclusion from the bones of mammoths they have found, placed in oval outlines in conjunction with hearths and postholes at a great many sites in the Ukraine.[13] At Pushkari, for example, Russian investigators found a shallow depression roughly 40 feet long and 5 feet wide. The depression was divided in half lengthwise, and three evenly spaced hearths ran down its center. Surrounding each hearth were a number of small pits which may have been for storage. On the floor of the depression were stone artifacts, broken animal bones, and small quantities of *ocher,* a red powder used for body decoration, painting, and other coloring purposes. Also found were mammoth tusks which probably were used to hold down the edges of a tentlike structure. Russian archeologists believe that a tent stood on this spot; it was divided into three parts, each of which contained a hearth for heat and cooking. Thus, three families probably shared the structure.

There are other Russian sites, such as Avdeevo and Kostienki, that contain even larger settlements. The oval at Avdeevo, for example, covers 500 square meters with many artifacts and bones. Fifteen large pits, in which, it is believed, the people slept, lie at the site. Other pits are

13. Richard G. Klein, *Ice-Age Hunters of the Ukraine* (Chicago: University of Chicago Press, 1973).

Figure 7–4   *Reconstruction of Upper Paleolithic housing in eastern Europe. Tents were made of animal hides placed over wooden supports and weighted down with animal bones, notably mammoth tusks.*

thought to have served as storage areas, and still others, as work areas. Researchers do not mention how many people lived in these "tent cities," but Dolní Věstonice, a site in Czechoslovakia, which included four hearths and tentlike structures, is thought to have been inhabited by 100 people all year round.

Upper Paleolithic Art

Nowhere is the superiority of Upper Paleolithic culture more in evidence than in its art, some of which equals works created in more recent historical times. Upper Paleolithic art, consisting of paintings, sculptures, and engravings, has been found mostly in France in the Vézère and Dordogne Valleys of the Périgord region and in the Cantabrian Mountains of Spain.

At the famous Lascaux cave in the Les Eyzies region of France, for example (see Chapter 16), are some of the finest paintings of this era.[14] Along an upper wall is a frieze of animals. Four bulls, outlined in black, immediately catch the eye. Two of these beasts—separated by five red stags—directly face one another. One of the bulls measures 18 feet in length—the longest Upper Paleolithic painting known to scholars. A red horse, six black ones, three cows, and other animals complete this frieze. Below it are two caves, one

14. Peter J. Ucko and Andrée Rosenfeld, *Paleolithic Cave Art* (New York: McGraw-Hill, World University Library, 1973).

of which holds forty paintings. The other, a bit difficult to negotiate, includes a pit known as "The Shaft of the Dead Man." On a ledge in this chamber are painted a buffalo which has been speared through its hindparts, a stick figure of a human being with a bird's head, a bird perched atop a pole, and a rhinoceros.[15]

In some caves, such as Altamira in Spain, the prehistoric artist took advantage of the natural rock shape of the cave. On the ceiling of Altamira are bison,

---

15. Pfeiffer, *The Emergence of Man.*

One of a large group of paintings found on the walls and ceiling of a cave near Altamira, Spain. Archeologists think such animal art may have played a role in the religious life of its creators.

Prehistory and Culture

painted on the natural contours of the rock, which gives these animals a startling three-dimensional, sculptural reality. Other caves contain depictions of different animals, largely in profile. Among the most common of these beasts are oxen, horses, deer, reindeer, bison, mammoth, and the woolly rhinoceros. Lions, bears, fish, and a rare bird or two are also shown.

Most of these figures are painted in colors obtained from natural pigments— in bold blacks, yellows, browns, reds, and red-browns. They were mixed with fats from animals to make a paste, and applied with moss or with brushes, probably made from human or animal hair.

There are few who would deny that the polychrome cave paintings of these times are truly breathtaking in splendor. Yet, there is something strange about them, something that requires explanation: the painters appear to have been obsessed with animals. It is this situation that has prompted a flurry of theories about the reasons behind this "animal art." All of the explanations hinge on the hypothesis that the paintings and other art played a major role in the spiritual and religious life of the people. See Chapter 16 for several explanations of Paleolithic cave paintings.

Statues of bone and ivory, on the other hand, are almost invariably of women, whose ample proportions rival anything ever painted by Rubens. The ancient artists endowed these voluptuous sculptures with large breasts, buttocks, and bellies. Because the sexual features are so dramatically accentuated in these *Venuses*, as they are called, many investigators have suggested that they probably represent fertility goddesses, or the archetypal mother figure.

This part-human, part-animal figure from Les Trois Frères, France, is known as "The Sorcerer."

In addition to their art, one investigator has found evidence that these people had some sort of notational system by which they kept track of the waxing and waning of the moon. Alexander Marshack has examined numerous previously unexplained markings on certain bone and stone implements and found what he interprets as a lunar calendar that shows the path of the moon over a six-month period.[16]

The Cultural Diversity of Homo sapiens sapiens

Although we have been speaking of the people of the Upper Paleolithic period as

16. Alexander Marshack, *The Roots of Civilization* (New York: McGraw-Hill, 1972).

if they shared one homogeneous culture, this is not entirely accurate. Archeologists have been able to discern a number of distinct cultural traditions among *Homo sapiens sapiens* populations. Each of these traditions prevailed at different times in different parts of Europe. Chief among these are the Aurignacian, Gravettian, Solutrean, and Magdalenian traditions. Moreover, there were differences between these cultural traditions and those of Upper Paleolithic populations in other parts of the Old World. Such cultural diversity would be expected, based on the known variations among different societies today.

AURIGNACIAN. The people of the Aurignacian culture lived in western Europe between 28,000 and 22,000 years ago.[17] Since the tools of these people are noticeably different from those of the preceding cultures in the area, archeologists believe that the Aurignacians may have migrated to Europe, possibly from the Middle East or Southwest Asia. Aurignacian tool collections feature bone projectile points, flat blades, burins, and small bladelets. The people lived in caves and shelters in large groups. They were among the first cave artists, producing crude, stylized line drawings of animals.

GRAVETTIAN. The Gravettians inhabited central and eastern Europe from 27,000 to 17,000 years B.P. Their most distinctive tool was the La Gravette point, a small tool with a blunted back that may have been hafted to wood, bone, or ivory handles.[18] The Gravettians lived on the steppes of Asia in tents and specialized in hunting mammoth and other large herd animals. They also produced beautifully crafted stone and ivory Venuses. Gravettian hunters were apparently given elaborate funerals. Some have been found garbed in headdresses and girdles of snail shells, bracelets, and necklaces of ivory.[19]

SOLUTREAN. The Solutreans, who inhabited western Europe at roughly the same time as the Gravettians (21,000 to 17,000 B.P.), are best known for their exquisite laurel leaf blades. Indeed, some of these tools are so thin that archeologists have concluded that they were intended as works of art. Late Solutrean populations made points with shoulders, probably for hafting.[20]

MAGDALENIAN. The Magdalenians, who lived in western Europe between 17,000 and 10,000 years ago, carried cave art to its highest form. They were actually the Cro-Magnons referred to earlier. They are also distinguished by the marked use of bone and antler for weapons and for items of personal adornment. The harpoon and atlatl were developed by these innovative people, as were tiny narrow blades —called *microliths*—that are the forerunners of those produced by more advanced later cultures.

---

17. Grahame Clark, *World Prehistory: An Outline* (London: Cambridge University Press, 1967).

18. Hester, *Introduction to Archeology.*

19. Clark, *World Prehistory*, pp. 57–58.

20. Hester, *Introduction to Archeology,* p. 167.

Early Cultures in the Americas

The peopling of the New World carried on the expansion into new habitats begun by earlier hominid populations. It is now virtually certain that the earliest inhabitants of the New World crossed the Bering Strait on foot from Asia into Alaska. Based on studies of tools and other artifacts, many archeologists have concluded that the first Americans were descendants of the hunter-gatherers who peopled Siberia during the Upper Paleolithic. There is a great deal of controversy about when the first crossing occurred. The earliest pioneers could have made the trek during the Wisconsin Ice Age and before. At certain times during this period, a wide, grassy plain linked the two continents, because the sea level was considerably lowered when vast ice sheets locked up immense quantities of sea water. On this plain lived steppe and tundra animals, such as mammoth, reindeer, bison, and musk oxen.

A few investigators believe that the Paleolithic hunters followed the herds of tundra herbivores across this land bridge sometime before 500,000 years ago. At the Calico Hills site near Yerma, California, for example, Louis Leakey and his associates claim to have found scrapers, flakes, and other crude implements which have been dated between 500,000 and 50,000 B.P.[21] But some archeologists do not agree with these dates. Others do not think that the objects found are actually tools fashioned by the human hand.

The evidence for early occupation of the New World is a bit stronger in Central and South America. At a site near Puebla, Mexico, for instance, archeologists have found artifacts which have been dated as early as 24,000 B.P.[22] Near Ayacucho, Peru, archeologist Richard MacNeish claims to have found stone tools that show that people lived in this region 22,000 years ago.[23] Since Ayacucho lies between present-day Lima and Cuzco, it must have taken the early hunters considerable time to reach this area. Therefore, the first people must have entered the New World long before 24,000 B.P. Most of the evidence for early humans in the New World, however, dates to only 12,000 years ago. The people who lived at this time are known as *Paleo-Indians*. They were big-game hunters, and their cultures included the Llano, Folsom, and Plano traditions.

Paleo-Indians of North America

When the first human immigrants entered the New World, the environment of North America was quite different from that of today. For one thing, the Northwest and northern Great Plains regions were colder than today, with an average annual temperature below the freezing point. Spruce trees and grasslands prevailed throughout the Great Lakes and Great Plains regions, whereas the Midwest was marked by for-

21. Louis Leakey, R. de E. Simpson, and T. Clements, "Man in America: The Calico Mountains Excavations," in *Britannica Year Book of Science and the Future* (London: Encyclopedia Britannica, 1970), pp. 65–79.

22. C. Irwin-Williams, "Archeological Evidence on Early Man in Mexico," *Contributions in Anthropology* 1 (1968): 39–41.

23. Richard S. MacNeish, "Early Man in the Andes," *Scientific American* 224 (April 1971): 36.

A Folsom projectile point, showing fluting, made by Paleo-Indians about 11,000 B.P.

est grasslands. The Southwest, which now has an arid climate, had a moist climate, with grassy savannas and wooded valleys cut by streams. Large lakes dotted much of the western part of the country. The animals of these regions included mammoth, mastadon, bison, reindeer, and antelope.

Three distinct Paleo-Indian cultures have been identified largely on the basis of artifacts used to hunt the herd animals to which they were adapted. The first of these is the *Llano tradition*, sometimes called the *Clovis tradition*. These people, who are named after the *Llano Estacado*, or Staked Plain, of the American Southwest, hunted mostly mammoth beginning around 11,500 years ago. They were quite widespread and ranged across North America from coast to coast, as far north as Alaska and as far south as Mexico.[24] The distinguishing artifact of these hunters was the *Clovis point*—a projectile point with fluting, or a channel, that extended from the concave base up to half the length of the point.

Next were the hunters of the *Folsom tradition*. Overlapping in time with the Llano folk, these people existed 11,000 to 9,000 years ago in the American West and Southwest and hunted the now-extinct big-horned bison. The tradition is named after the Folsom site in New Mexico, and its most distinctive characteristic is the *Folsom point*. Smaller and more delicate than the Clovis point, this artifact has flutings on both sides that extended nearly the entire length of the blade.

Finally, there was the *Plano tradition*, which flourished on the American High Plains from about 9,000 to 8,000 years ago. Plano points were not fluted, but were characterized by superb pressure flaking, and some had a ridge running down the center of the blade.

The Day of the Hunters

Save for the fact that the Paleo-Indians had successfully adapted to the large herds of the herbivores for food and other basic subsistence needs, we know little about other aspects of their cultures. The details of their settlement patterns, social

24. C. Vance Haynes, "Elephant Hunting in North America," in *Early Man in America*, ed. Richard MacNeish (San Francisco: W. H. Freeman, 1973).

organization, religious beliefs, modes of dress, and so on can only be inferred from the remains they left behind.

One thing, however, is certain: if nothing else, they were first-rate hunters. The chief prey of the Clovis hunters was the American elephant, or mammoth, which vanished from the American continent about 10,000 years ago. The later Folsom hunters went after the big-horned bison, which had horns 6 feet in length and were much larger than modern bison.

Archeologist C. Vance Haynes[25] has studied the sites of the Llano-Folsom peoples and found that they fall into two categories. A *campsite*, where the Paleo-Indians bivouacked for an indefinite period, is marked by fluted points and a wide variety of flint tools. It was typically located on high ground, such as a ridge overlooking the floodplain of a river or creek. A *kill site*, where the people killed and butchered the mammoth, usually contains animal bones, fluted points, and some flint tools used for butchering purposes. Kill sites were located near lakes that attracted the large herbivores.

By analyzing kill sites, Haynes has been able to piece together some of the hunting techniques of the Clovis people. One favorite tactic appears to have been the stampede, in which the hunters frightened the beasts over the edge of a bluff. Next, the Paleo-Indians bombarded the wounded animals with boulders, then waded into the dying beasts to administer the *coup de grace* with spear thrusts.

In some cases, the hunters were apparently clever enough to cut the herd—that is, to separate the young and less formidable animals from the more dangerous, larger ones. The young were then easily dispatched.

The hunting techniques of the later Folsom and Plano cultures have been described by archeologist Joe Ben Wheat.[26] Because the mammoth had become extinct by Folsom times, the favorite prey of the Folsom-Plano hunters was the bison. This beast was the primary source of sustenance for the peoples who lived on the Great Plains—both in historic and late prehistoric times. As Wheat observes:

> Its meat, fat and bone marrow provided them with food; its hide furnished them with shelter and clothing; its brain was used to tan the hide; its horns were fashioned into containers. There was scarcely a part of the animal that was not utilized in some way.[27]

Wheat has studied the bones of bison found at a kill site in southeastern Colorado and has reconstructed the events that occurred there one day some 8,500 years ago. At the bottom of an *arroyo*, or canyon, were the remains of nearly 200 buffaloes. The animals had apparently been stampeded into this death trap by a party of Paleo-Indian hunters.

The hunters knew that a herd of bison tends to group together and stampede when frightened. One group of hunters stationed themselves downwind and north

---

25. Haynes, "Elephant Hunting in North America."

26. Joe Ben Wheat, "A Paleo-Indian Bison Kill," in *Early Man in America*, ed. Richard MacNeish (San Francisco: W. H. Freeman, 1973).

27. Wheat, "A Paleo-Indian Bison Kill," p. 80.

of the herd to avoid detection by the beasts, who have a keen sense of smell. The hunters then frightened the animals to run in a southerly direction, probably by shouting, clapping their hands, and making other loud noises. Two other groups of hunters stationed themselves on either side of the herd to prevent the bison from escaping eastward or westward. In this way, the three groups guided the animals toward the *arroyo*, over which they plunged. Some died immediately, others were seriously injured. Thus, the hunters slaughtered nearly 200 animals in the brief space of a few minutes. Wheat estimates that such a kill would have provided the people with nearly 57,000 pounds of meat—enough to feed 150 people for about twenty-three days.

Although mammoth and bison were the mainstays of the Paleo-Indians' subsistence, this does not mean that they did not engage in extensive food-gathering as well. Plant foods, and undoubtedly fish and shellfish taken from the many lakes that dotted the area, were also part of their diet. At many Plano sites in the West and Midwest, for example, were found grinding stones, similar to those used by later advanced cultures for processing grains and other vegetable matter.

From the large number of hunters involved in the undertaking described by Wheat, archeologists have concluded that social organization must have advanced beyond the simple hunting band consisting of twenty-five to forty individuals. Perhaps by this time, larger social groups such as multiband hunting parties may have been an important form of social organization. These groups came together when the bison were in substantial herds and dispersed when the bison did.

From the Neandertals of Shanidar Cave to the big-game hunters of North America has been a long journey covering many eons and miles. It is at this point that the Old Stone Age ends and the next outstanding event in human cultural evolution—the domestication of plants and animals—begins.

Paleo-Indians stampeding a herd of bison toward the edge of a cliff.

Summary

1. The Neandertals, who had adapted to a wide range of environments, were knowledgeable about plants and animals, as well as being successful big-game hunters, and believers in an afterlife. Their cultural remains, chiefly in the form of stone tools, are referred to as Mousterian.

2. The Neandertals improved the techniques of earlier tool-makers by perfecting the Levallois technique. The Neandertals lived in caves and in the open, sometimes using tents of ani-

mal hides or foliage.

3. Neandertal ritual may have centered on the cave bear. Because of their religious practices, these populations are thought to have probably possessed the full range of human feelings and experience.

4. The first modern humans (*Homo sapiens sapiens*) appeared in western Europe during Upper Paleolithic times. These hunter-gatherers made many advances in tool manufacture. Two new techniques were indirect percussion and pressure flaking. These people used multiple tools, spear-throwers, and harpoons.

5. Upper Paleolithic people in eastern Europe lived in the open in tents, sometimes in relatively large settlements. The primary unit of social organization at this time—the band—may have been replaced by the multiband group.

6. The most remarkable remains left by Cro-Magnon people of southwestern Europe are their polychromatic cave art, which centered on animals.

7. The Upper Paleolithic witnessed great cultural diversity among different populations of *Homo sapiens sapiens* as these populations spread to virtually all parts of the known world. The Aurignacian, Gravettian, and Solutrean cultures in Europe, for example, differed from one another and from other cultures in Africa. In the New World, different groups of big-game hunters had adapted to the environments of the North American High Plains as well as of the West and Southwest.

Review Questions

1. How did the Neandertals improve the Acheulean hand axe?

2. List five types of tools used by Neandertals.

3. Archeologists have found evidence suggesting that the Neandertals were religious people. Give three examples of such evidence.

4. Why were the tool-making techniques of the Upper Paleolithic people so superior to those of their predecessors? Name four important Upper Paleolithic innovations in tools.

5. Archeologists believe that Upper Paleolithic hunters in middle and eastern Europe lived in large groups in tents. What proof is there of this?

Suggested Readings

Bordaz, Jacques. *Tools of the Old and New Stone Age.* Garden City, N.Y.: Natural History Press, 1970.
A good summary of the tools and tool-making techniques of ancient humans. This paperback contains photos and diagrams that show the tool-making process step by step.

Deetz, James. *Invitation to Archeology.* Garden City, N.Y.: Doubleday, 1967.
A brief paperback that explains in a lucid, engaging manner what archeology is all about, both from practical and theoretical perspectives.

Leone, Mark, ed. *Contemporary Archeology.* Carbondale, Ill.: Southern Illinois University Press, 1972.
A modern reader containing articles by leading archeologists on all aspects of archeological theory and practice. Highly recommended for advanced students.

Ucko, Peter, and Rosenfeld, Andrée. *Paleolithic Cave Art.* New York: McGraw-Hill, World University Library, 1973.
An inexpensive paperback that contains one of the best summaries of the many theories that explain cave art. Includes many full-color photos.

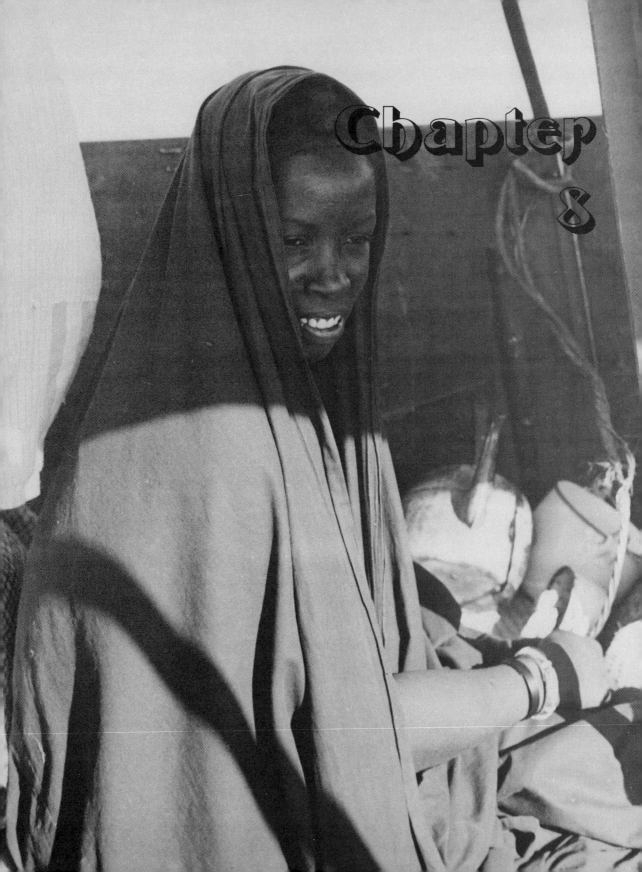

Chapter 8

The Effects of Domestication

EARLY FARMERS OF THE DEH LURAN PLAIN

The Bus Mordeh Phase (9500 to 8750 B.P.)

Nine thousand years ago, much of the surface of the Deh Luran plain [in modern Iran and Iraq] was an undulating expanse of sandy loam and reddish clays. . . . The center of the plain, a seasonally-inundated natural depression today, may at that time have been a semi-permanent slough bordered with sea club-rush, sedge, and feather grass. The villagers of the Bus Mordeh phase settled in the southeastern part of the plain, in a sandier and better-drained area. . . .

Out of a natural red clay deposit in the floor of the plain, the Bus Mordeh group cut slabs averaging 15 by 25 by 10 cm., which they used as unfired "bricks" in the construction of small houses or huts. The rooms they constructed were often no more than 2 by 2.5 meters, with walls 25 to 40 cm. thick and doorways a meter-and-a-half wide. As yet there are no certain indications—such as floor features and other architectural details—that prove these structures were dwellings rather than storage rooms. Size is not the critical factor here,

---

Source: Adapted from Frank Hole, Kent V. Flannery, and James A. Neely, "Prehistory and Human Ecology of the Deh Luran Plain," *Memoirs of the Museum of Anthropology, University of Michigan*, no. 1 (1969) : 342–345. Reprinted by permission of the Museum of Anthropology, University of Michigan, Ann Arbor, and the authors.

for many prehistoric dwellings in the Southwestern United States are no more than 1.5 meters on a side.

The floors were of stamped mud or clay. No plaster of any kind is yet known from this period, but there is a suggestion of simple . . . matting which may have been used as a floor covering or in roof construction (based on the way roofs are made in the area today). The clay-slab brick architecture is unlike anything known from the Zagros Mountains at this time. . . . This suggests that it is a type of architecture native to the lowland steppe, where building materials other than mud or clay have always been scarce.

The subsistence pattern of the Bus Mordeh phase also shows a relative independence from the Zagros Mountains. The tens of thousands of carbonized seeds and broken animal bones left behind by these people show a high degree of orientation to the steppe environment. Nine-tenths of the seeds found in Bus Mordeh levels were from annual legumes and wild grasses native to northern Khuzistan [in modern southwestern Iran]. They systematically and intensively collected the seeds of medic or wild alfalfa, spiny milk vetch, *Trigonella* (a small plant of the pea family), canary grass, oat grass, and goosefoot, and ate the fruit of the wild caper. Since some of these plants have seeds no larger than clover seed, the amount of work involved in these harvests—which had to take place some time after the peak growing season in March—must have been considerable.

In addition, the Bus Mordeh folk planted emmer wheat and two-row hulled barley, two annual grasses which are not native to [the region]. Although constituting less than a tenth of the carbonized seeds left by these people, wheat and barley have significantly larger grains than most of the wild plants mentioned above, and were probably two of the preferred foods. They underscore the fact that the Bus Mordeh development, for all its peculiar architecture and its steppe collecting pattern, was not unrelated to developments in the highlands of the Near East, where the wild ancestors of wheat and barley are at home. . . .

Carbonized seeds of club-rush *Scirpus* included with the grains indicate that the fields must have been very near the margins of our postulated marsh or slough. The cultivated cereals were harvested with flint sickles, roasted to render the glumes [husks] brittle, and then "threshed" by grinding with flat-topped or saddle-shaped grinding slabs of pitted limestone, a few of which were found in the rooms of this phase. "Groats," or coarsely-ground grits of wheat and barley, were recovered in some quantity.

Apart from their seed-gathering and wheat-harvesting in the late winter and spring, the people of the Bus Mordeh phase were herdsmen. A major aspect of their subsistence was the herding of goat, an animal not occurring normally on the plain (although wild goats inhabit the cliffs of the Kuh-i-Siah and Jebel Hamrin, not far away). North Khuzistan is excellent winter grazing land, a fact which may have had a great deal to do with the beginnings of food production there.

Most of the goats eaten during the Bus Mordeh phase were young; only a third of the flock reached the age of three years, and there were virtually no elderly goats represented in the bone remains. Judging by the discarded horn cores, mostly young males were eaten, presumably to conserve the females for breeding. Numbers of small, lightly-baked figurines resembling goats suggest that "magical" means may also have been resorted to in an effort to increase the herds. . . . [T]he age-ratio of the herd differed strikingly from that of a wild goat population, not merely in terms of yearlings, but also in terms of the survivorship of two-year-olds, three-year-olds, and so on.

The Bus Mordeh villagers also herded sheep, but in much smaller numbers. One sheep skull from a basal Bus Mordeh phase house floor is hornless, indicating that sheep had been domestic for some time prior to the Bus Mordeh period. Our evidence tentatively suggests that horn loss by female sheep was one of the first osteological changes to follow domestication, and that male sheep underwent a change in horn core cross-section at a later date. There is no evidence that male sheep ever lost their horns at any time in our sequence. It is difficult to estimate the relative proportions of sheep to goat in the Bus Mordeh phase herds, but goats were certainly more than ten times as numerous. This would seem to be typical of the Southern Zagros. . . .

Hunting and fishing constituted the fourth major component of Bus Mordeh subsistence. The common ungulate [hooved animal] of the Khuzistan steppe is the Persian gazelle, which was brought down by the villagers in tremendous numbers. Onager, wild ox, and wild boar were also taken; small mammals, like the red fox, were a very small part of the diet. In particular, the Bus Mordeh phase stands out in the Deh Luran sequence for its use of aquatic resources like carp, catfish, mussel, and water turtle. Seasonal waterfowl, which visit the Deh Luran region between November and March, were also eaten, and, along with the harvested wild legumes, indicate the real importance of the winter resources of northern Khuzistan. On the basis of plants and animals recovered, we could not prove beyond a shadow of doubt that the Bus Mordeh folk were in the Deh Luran plain during the hot, dry summer months.

The flint tools manufactured by the Bus Mordeh villagers were varied and abundant, but for the most part it is impossible to separate those designed to deal with hunting and those designed to deal with domestic animals. . . .

From narrow, bullet-shaped cores, the Bus Mordeh people struck tens of thousands of flint blades, some of them only a few millimeters wide. A relatively small percentage of these were turned into other tools by means of bone pressure-flakers. Flint nodules from the bed of the Dawairij River served as raw material for the flint-knappers, and waste flakes were strewn through the rooms we found. About one per cent of the chipped stone was obsidian, identified . . . as native to the Lake Van region of eastern Turkey [which is about 300 miles away].

Other tools used by the Bus Mordeh villagers for dealing directly with problems of subsistence included pounders made from flint nodules or chunky, only partially-used flint cores; small abraders made from gritty slabs of sandstone; small "picks" of chipped flint; and bone awls made from the metapodials [lower leg bones] of goat or gazelle. The only evidence of containers so far recovered from this phase are three fragments of bowls ground from soft stone. Baskets may have been present, but our limited exposure did not reveal any evidence beyond the weaving of simple reed or club-rush mats. Compared with the phases which were to follow, the Bus Mordeh tool assemblage is lacking in variety, especially in the category of ground stone and heavy chipped-stone tools. . . .

The relative scarcity of summer-season products in the refuse, plus the abundance of goats, suggests that the Bus Mordeh people may have been at least partially transhumant [that is, they combined pastoralism with farming]. Within a few days' travel from Deh Luran are mountain valleys like that of the Saimarreh River, which even today serve as summer pasture for Khuzistan herders. Transhumance would have been one mechanism for preventing total isolation of the Deh Luran villagers from happenings in the uplands, and it would have given them the opportunity to exchange new products or ideas with their neighbors. And yet, beyond the few items mentioned above, there is little tangible evidence to show an awareness, on the part of the Bus Mordeh folk, of the world beyond the plains of Khuzistan.[1]

• • • • • • • •

It is small wonder that the shift to dependence on domesticated plants and animals has been treated as a revolutionary development in human history. The way of life that had persisted for more than 99 percent of human history—food hunting and gathering—was in some parts of the world radically transformed by a new subsistence based on farming and animal husbandry. This new era is known as the *Neolithic* (new Stone) *Age.* As a result of this revolution, small communities of hunters and gatherers, such as the one discussed in the capsule study, were transformed into permanent settlements. Some, like the Bus Mordeh people, became full-time *horticulturists*—that is, they cultivated crops using simple implements such as hoes and sticks, rather than plows and fertilizers as *agriculturalists* do. (The emergence of agriculture could not take place until suitable animals—horses or oxen, for example—to pull the plow could be domesticated.) Other groups continued their hunting and gathering ways of life or became extinct.[2]

The earliest permanent settlements appeared in the Near East around 10,000 B.P., in Southeast Asia around 11,000–9200 B.P., and in central Africa by 6000 B.P. In the New World, evidence for the first domesticated plants dates back to about 7000 B.P. in Mesoamerica and 7600 B.P. in Peru. Sparse populations became substantial; simple technologies gradually became complex, as stone knives and grass baskets were replaced by less movable property, storage facilities, pottery, and masonry. Social systems were also transformed. People living in permanent villages required a lifestyle quite different from that of nomadic hunter-gatherers. The rate of culture change was enormously accelerated by the technological and sociological challenges of a new way of life.

One of the most fascinating problems in archeology is to answer, from the fragmentary data available, the following questions: Why did certain groups give up hunting and gathering for the risks of a new way of life based on plant and animal domestication? Were the pressures and circumstances underlying this change in food-getting the same everywhere—in the Near East, Mesoamerica, Southeast Asia, China, and Peru?

The Mesolithic Age

When the glaciers of the last great Ice Age retreated around 15,000 B.P. in parts of Europe, the environment changed dramatically. As the ice melted, the oceans rose and moved inland to form numerous islands, inlets, bays, and swamps. Moreover, the tundras were replaced by dense woodlands. These environmental changes may have been partly responsible for the extinction of the large herbivores upon which hunter-gatherers depended for their livelihood. In addition, the paleohunters discussed in Chapter 7 may also have speeded up these mass extinctions by killing off enormous numbers of the big-game

1. Adapted from Frank Hole, Kent V. Flannery, and James A. Neely, "Prehistory and Human Ecology of the Deh Luran Plain," *Memoirs of the Museum of Anthropology, University of Michigan,* no. 1 (1969): 342–345.

2. Howard Winters, Introduction to *Indian Knoll,* by William S. Webb (Knoxville: University of Tennessee Press, 1974).

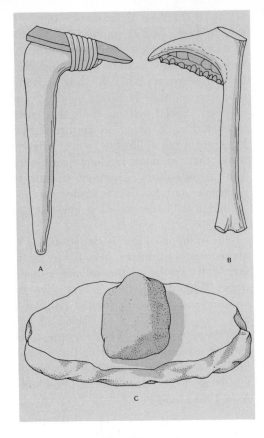

Figure 8-1   *Mesolithic tools used in food production. Shown are digging tool (a), microlith sickle (b), and grain-grinding tools (c).*

animals. More modern animals, such as the deer and elk, took the places of the extinct plant-eaters. As a result, the human groups of the time were pressured into developing new tools and technological systems to exploit these new fauna. The bow and arrow, for example, was invented to bring down game in the woods. Similarly, nets for snaring birds, fish, rabbits, and other creatures appeared. Dugout canoes for penetrating swamps and for fishing also

arrived on the scene. So did *microliths* (microblades), small stone blades which enabled the people to create composite tools, such as sickles, harpoons, axes, and adzes, and swords, to more effectively exploit the environment (Figure 8-1).

In addition, the people of the time were forced to turn to foods that had been previously ignored—snails, turtles, shellfish, fish, and wild grass seeds and nuts. Such a "broad-spectrum" subsistence base is viewed by many as *preadaptation* to an economy based on the domestication of plants and animals. (A preadaptation is a biological structure, behavior pattern, or artifact that appears at one period but that has greater adaptive value at a later time.) The period during which these important changes took place is known as the *Mesolithic* (middle Stone) *Age*.

Mesolithic Culture

About 11,000 years ago, two cultures—the Natufian and the Karim Shahirian cultures—developed in the Near East. These people used food-growing implements such as sickle-blades, grinding stones, and polished stone axes called *celts*. The sickle blades were microliths which were fitted into slots on wooden or bone handles and cemented with gum or asphalt. Some of the grinding stones found with the remains of the two cultures could have been used for crushing grain and seeds into flour, but they probably were employed to make pigments and to process meat. It is probable that the Natufian and Karim Shahirian cultures possessed preagricultural, harvesting economies. That is, people harvested wild grain as part of the broad spectrum of food resources being exploited. Archeologists have shown that wild wheat still grows thick enough in the Near East for a single individual, using only a flint-bladed sickle, to harvest enough grain in three weeks to last a family of four for a whole year.[3]

The members of the two societies were even able to establish permanent villages similar to that of the Bus Mordeh settlement. At Ain Mallaha, a Natufian site in the Jordan Valley, are stone foundations of round houses with plastered pits for storing crops. At Zawi Chemi Shanidar (a Karim Shahirian site), there is evidence for preagricultural grain-cutting, roasting, and storage, as well as the presence of domesticated sheep, by 10,900 B.P.[4] At Tell Mureybat in Syria were found clay-walled houses, grinding stones, pits for roasting grain, and eighteen different types of wild seeds, including wild wheat and barley.

It is probable that the settled villages based on wild grain collecting were a preadaptation to intentional cultivation and domestication. In the villages, garbage thrown outside the houses and into refuse areas provided ideal growing conditions for grain seeds. Humans then could have appreciated this accessible source of food and deliberately planted the grain seeds the next season. It has been suggested that these experiments would have been the work of women because in most existing preliterate societies, gathering plants and preparing them for eating is women's

work. For the same reason, experiments with animals presumably would have been the work of men. Fields immediately adjacent to villages would have attracted animals which virtually would have had to be exterminated or brought under control to insure the safety of the grain. In order not to lose valuable meat provided by the animals, the second alternative was tried. In this way, it is believed, the sheep and goats indigenous to the area were domesticated.

How do archeologists know when they have uncovered the remains of domesticated plants and animals, rather than wild ones? The signs are quite unmistakable. Wild grains, such as barley and wheat, have a dry, brittle *rachis* (the part of the stalk which holds the seeds). Such a structure is an adaptive mechanism for seed dispersal in the wild plants: the fragile rachis breaks open and the seeds scatter at the slightest stimulus, as when struck by a gust of wind or a twig.

But a plant with a fragile rachis would be quite disadvantageous for the early harvesters because they could unintentionally scatter the seeds with a slight blow of a sickle, so diminishing their harvest. The first farmers, therefore, unconsciously selected for plants with a tough rachis so the seeds would stay on the plant long enough to allow harvesting. In the beginning, the farmers took only those variants of the plants that had tough rachis. They then planted the seeds and these plants eventually predominated over the wild variety. In this way, humans replaced natural environmental forces as selective agents which pressured the plants into changing. Other genetic changes in the wild plants were also brought about by the farmers. Wild barley having only two fertile rows of kernels, for example,

3. Jack R. Harlan and D. Zohary, "Distribution of Wild Wheats and Barley," *Science* 153 (1966): 1074–1080.

4. Karl W. Butzer, "Agricultural Origins in the Near East as a Geographical Problem," in *Prehistoric Agriculture*, ed. Stuart Struever (Garden City, N.Y.: Natural History Press, 1971), pp. 209–235.

The Effects of Domestication

This reproduction of an Egyptian wall painting from about 1600 B.P. shows steps in harvesting, transporting, and storing grain. Food production first occurred in the Near East around 10,000 B.P.

was transformed into barley having six rows.

The early domesticators also exerted selection pressures that produced genetic changes in wild sheep. Wild sheep have relatively little wool. Indeed, their coats are better described as hairy. Because humans are interested in wool for clothing, they selected only those sheep having woolly coats. Humans even brought about genetic variations that appear to have been nonadaptive in that such variations do not contribute to the animals' survival in the wild state. The horns of wild goats in the Near East are curved like a saber, whereas those of the domesticated variety exhibit a corkscrew twist. Finally, as we saw in the capsule study, the remains of wild and domestic sheep and goats show different age and sex ratios. At Bus Mordeh, the proportion of immature to mature sheep was higher than that for wild sheep. The reason for this appears to be that the younger sheep were being eaten, whereas the older animals were kept for breeding purposes. The large number of young sheep bones at the site reflects the fact that it was they that were regularly and systematically being slaughtered and eaten rather than the older animals. At another village, there were more remains of butchered young males, relative to females—apparently a reflection of the fact that the females were saved for breeding and for milk production.[5]

Why Did Food Production Occur?

During the Neolithic Age, different plants

5. Kent V. Flannery, "The Ecology of Early Food Production in Mesopotamia," in *Contemporary Archaeology*, ed. Mark P. Leone (Carbondale, Ill.: Southern Illinois University Press, 1972).

were domesticated in different parts of the world. Thus, wheat and barley were grown in the Near East, while corn and beans were cultivated in the New World. Rice was the principal crop of Southeast Asia, millet, of China. The domestication of animals never became as important in Mesoamerica and Peru as it was in Mesopotamia. Large animals that could easily be domesticated were just not naturally present in the New World, with the exception of the llama and the alpaca. But a number of animals were domesticated for food in America. Examples include ducks, turkeys, bees, guinea pigs, and dogs. The indigenous plants and animals of an area obviously have a great deal to do with what is eventually cultivated or domesticated, but their presence does not tell us why the first hunter-gatherers planted the first seeds.

A number of theories have been proposed to explain just how this momentous event occurred. One such hypothesis, accepted by a large number of anthropologists, is a synthesis of two theories proposed by archeologists Lewis Binford[6] and Kent Flannery.[7, 8] This composite theory

hinges on the idea that growing populations placed pressures on individuals in certain areas to develop new food-getting strategies.

The Binford–Flannery Hypothesis

According to Binford and Flannery, the impetus for seeking new food supplies must come from changes in population or in the environment. Binford argues that post-Pleistocene climatic changes created new coastal environments that would have been very productive for groups who combined fishing with foraging as a way of making a living. Binford calls such areas *optimum zones*. This situation would have been rich enough to support even large, sedentary populations.[9] Expanding populations in these coastal areas would move into the adjacent "marginal" areas where less sedentary people were living in balance with their habitat. This area of contact (what Binford calls the *tension zone*) would be a likely area for the development of more effective means of food production.

Flannery points out, for example, that optimum and tension zones were present in the Near East where the earliest farming appeared. Indeed, the Near East is a mosaic of habitats representative of this theory: there is the fertile alluvial plain of Mesopotamia, the steppeland of Assyria, a high woodland belt of oak and pistachio trees, and the high central plateau of Iran (see Figure 8-2). In the hilly flanks of the woodland belts (where the Bus Mordeh village was located) grew

6. Lewis R. Binford, "Post-Pleistocene Adaptations," in *New Perspectives in Archeology*, ed. Lewis R. Binford and Sally R. Binford (Chicago: Aldine Publishing, 1968), pp. 313–341.

7. Kent V. Flannery, "Archeological Systems Theory and Early Meso-America," in *Anthropological Archeology in the Americas*, ed. Betty J. Meggers (Washington, D.C.: Anthropological Society of Washington, 1968), pp. 67–87.

8. Kent V. Flannery, "The Origins of Agriculture," *Annual Review of Anthropology* 2 (1973): 271–310.

9. Michael E. Moseley, *The Maritime Foundations of Andean Civilization* (Menlo Park, Calif.: Cummings Publishing, 1975).

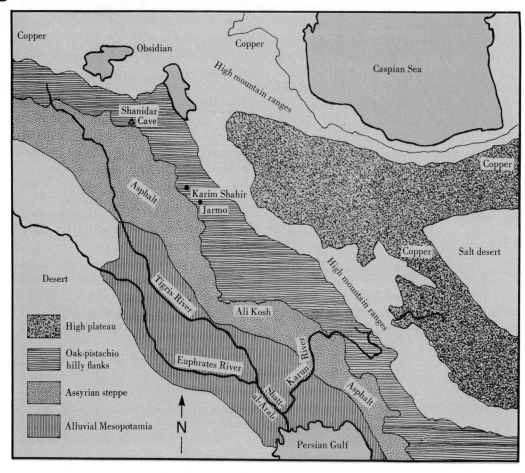

Figure 8–2   *Map of Greater Mesopotamia, showing ecological zones,
mineral resources, and some archeological sites. The hilly flanks of the oak-
pistachio belt, rich in plant and animal resources, are thought to have been
an optimum zone. Rugged Assyrian steppe may have been a marginal
tension zone where domestication first occurred.*

abundant wild stands of wheat, barley, and other plants. These zones also contained wild sheep, goats, oxen, pigs, and gazelles. The density of the human populations in this optimum area was quite high. Even before the emergence of agriculture, these people lived in villages. They appear to have relied on a mixed strategy of harvesting wild cereals such as wheat, barley, and rye grass; nuts, such as pistachios, walnuts, almonds, and acorns; and legumes. They also hunted wild sheep and goats, and collected a variety of smaller animals such as fish, turtles, snails, mussels, and crabs.

As the population in this optimum zone

increased, individuals began emigrating into adjoining marginal (tension) zones —into the Assyrian steppelands, for example. Faced with starvation, says Flannery, these colonies began domesticating the plants and animals in the marginal area, plants and animals with which they were already familiar.

But as Flannery himself admits, this theory is very speculative and still remains to be proven. Indeed, it even contains a serious loophole: some archeological data have shown population decreases in optimum areas and striking increases in marginal areas. Finally, Flannery observes that we may never know why domestication began in the Near East. All we know is that it was initiated at the end of a long, cool, dry period by partly sedentary people with a high population density who had recently adopted a broad-spectrum subsistence base. Moreover, the region where these people lived was one of great environmental diversity.[10]

The Neolithic Revolution in the Old World

It was originally assumed that plant and animal domestication was achieved only once. The complexities of the discoveries seemed too great to have been duplicated. Thus, most investigators thought domestication must have diffused from its origin to other parts of the world. The center where domestication began and spread, said these investigators, was the Fertile Crescent in Mesopotamia. To be sure, the Near East may have been the earliest area of domestication. But current evidence reveals that it was certainly not the only one. Domestication also appeared independently in Southeast Asia and China.

A Neolithic Community in Turkey

One of the earliest farming communities in the Near East was Çatal Hüyük in southern Turkey (8500–7600 B.P.). This settlement had a substantial population and was sedentary enough to support all sorts of technological innovations. Çatal Hüyük covered thirty-two acres. The crops raised were barley, wheat, lentils, and peas; sheep and cattle were herded. People lived in plastered, mud-brick interconnected houses which were laid out around courtyards. Walls were decorated with paintings depicting animals and hunters holding bows. The inhabitants wove cloth and made symbolic sculpture, jewelry, cosmetics, and pottery.

There is also evidence of trade: shells were imported from the Mediterranean region, and obsidian (a black, volcanic glass used for making cutting tools and mirrors) and marble came from western Turkey. Evidence of the importance of religion in the lives of the inhabitants is seen in the numerous shrines and sanctuaries found at the site. The shrines contained stylized heads of goats and other animals, as well as representations of women's breasts. Many shrines also had sophisticated paintings depicting scenes of human life and death. On the east wall of one sanctuary, for example, are paintings showing vultures attacking headless human corpses.[11]

---

10. Flannery, "The Origins of Agriculture," p. 283.

11. James Mellaart, "A Neolithic City in Turkey," *Scientific American* 210 (April 1964) : 94–104.

Southeast Asia

Because the Near East was for so long considered the origin of all civilization, research in other areas was badly neglected. But now we are absolutely certain that plant and animal domestication were developed independently in other parts of the world. At Spirit Cave in Thailand, for example, are deposits dating back to 11,000 B.P. which include nuts, bottle gourds, water chestnuts, cucumbers, black pepper, taro, yams, and a possible bean.[12] Root crops also have been reported at this site.[13] Conspicuously absent from this early site is rice. But imprints of cultivated rice grains and husks have been identified in pottery fragments from Non Nok Tha in central Thailand, a site that dates to 6000 B.P. Rice was presumably mixed with the clay to give it strength and would have had to be domesticated some time before Non Nok Tha was founded. Archeologist Chang Kwang-Chih[14] has speculated that rice was originally cultivated in Southeast Asia, where it grew as a weed in yam and taro gardens—another example of humans taking advantage of the disturbance their own activities have created. But there is, as yet, no proof for Chang's speculations.

China

Early cultivation in China provides convincing evidence that the Neolithic Revolution need not have taken place in an arid environment. In the Hwang-Ho river valley, the fertile soil could be cultivated with a simple digging stick—which was usually a sturdy tree branch sharpened to a point and measuring 4 or 5 feet in length. Here, the first domesticated plant was millet, a course, hardy grain. Bushels of foxtail millet seeds stored in pits, weeding knives, hoes, and spades have been found at sites dating back to 6000 B.P. Animal remains also show that dogs, pigs, goats, cattle, and sheep were domesticated. A sixth-millennium B.P. village, Pan-p'o-ts'-un, had round and oblong semisubterranean houses with thatched roofs.[15] The houses were arranged around a central plaza which contained a large communal structure. Six kilns found on the outskirts of the settlement indicate that ceramic manufacture was important to the people. Most pottery found at the site was coarse, but some, especially that found in burial contexts, was finer and decoratively painted. The inhabitants of Pan-p'o-ts'un subsisted on cultivated millet and wild deer.

The Spread of the Neolithic

The advantages of plant and animal domestication spread rapidly from wherever they were first developed. It is possible that cultivation was also developed quite early in India, but convincing evidence of this is yet to be produced. New discoveries

12. Chester F. Gorman, "Hoabinhian: A Pebble-Tool Complex with Early Plant Associations in Southeast Asia," *Science* 163 (1969): 671–673.

13. William Soheim, "Relics from 2 Diggings Indicate Thais Were the First Agrarians," *New York Times*, January 12, 1970, p. 35.

14. Chang Kwang-Chih, "The Beginnings of Agriculture in the Far East," *Antiquity* 44 (1970): 175–185.

15. Chang Kwang-Chih, *The Archaeology of Ancient China* (New Haven, Conn.: Yale University Press, 1963).

in the next few years, however, undoubtedly will amplify our understanding of the Neolithic in India and elsewhere.

Ruth Tringham[16] believes it highly unlikely, for example, that cereal cultivation developed independently in southeast Europe, since there is little continuity between the new farming cultures that appeared after 8000 or 9000 B.P. and earlier European tools and technology. When introduced, farming transformed the local economy and brought with it various technological innovations. Greece and the Balkans also received Neolithic ideas from the Near East, and by 7000 B.P. Neolithic advances had diffused up and down the Danube into the Hungarian Plain. It was ideas more than specific crops that diffused: hunter-gatherers adapted their own local conditions to the concepts of domesticating their indigenous plants and animals, settling down, building houses, making pots, weaving textiles for clothing, engaging in long-distance trade, and so on.

The Neolithic in the New World

One of the most exciting discoveries in New World archeology has been that the basis for civilization did not diffuse from the Old World. Plants indigenous to the New World were brought under human control in a process as gradual as that which occurred in the Old World. What is exciting is that New World peoples had the capacity for domesticating plants and

that the process can be compared with that in the Old World. Such a comparison may help us reach a real understanding of how this significant occurrence in human history came about.

Mexico

Since it was known that corn supported the major early New World civilizations, the search for its wild ancestors and early cultivated forms has been a major effort in American archeology. In 1953, samples of earth from the lake beds under Mexico City produced corn pollen estimated to be about 80,000 years old. Based partly on this find, paleoethnobotanist Paul Mangelsdorf concluded that the wild progenitor of corn was corn itself—probably a popcorn with its kernels encased in pods.[17] Herbert Dick, in New Mexico, and Richard MacNeish, in Tamaulipas (a state in the far north of Mexico), found small corn cobs that were 4,000 to 5,000 years old and that were clearly of a domesticated variety.[18] Excited by this discovery, MacNeish began looking for an even older form of corn and began to trace the process that led to the domestication of the wild corn. He went south to the Tehuacán Valley, where he investigated a number of caves. One of these, the Coxcatlan Cave, dated back to 12,000 B.P. Combining evidence from Coxcatlan with that found at

16. Ruth Tringham, *Hunters, Fishers and Farmers of Eastern Europe: 6000–3000* B.C. (London: Hutchinson University Library, 1971).

17. Richard S. MacNeish, "The Origins of New World Civilization," in *New World Archaeology*, ed. Ezra B. W. Ziebrow, Margaret C. Fritz, and John M. Fritz (San Francisco: W. H. Freeman, 1974), pp. 155–163.

18. MacNeish, "The Origins of New World Civilization."

other sites—including Purron Cave—MacNeish could archeologically trace 12,000 years of prehistory. The oldest corn found in the caves dates from 7,000 years ago. To be sure, the cobs are tiny (no bigger than the filter tip of a cigarette), and may have been only partly domesticated. But they are, according to Mangelsdorf, "the original parent from which modern corn is descended."[19]

The Tehuacán Valley is not necessarily the first place corn was cultivated in the

---

19. MacNeish, "The Origins of New World Civilization."

Pottery for storing, carrying, and cooking water, grain, and other foodstuffs is typically found among sedentary domesticators. Shown here is a Hopi potter at work.

New World. But MacNeish's work is important in that it provides an unprecedented cultural sequence from 12,000 years ago—when a few people wandered the valley from season to season in search of jack rabbits, rats, birds, turtles, and other small animals as well as a broad spectrum of plant resources—up to 2200 B.P., when the valley boasted large irrigation projects and monumental hilltop religious centers surrounded by villages. Thus, thanks to MacNeish's efforts, we now know that horticulture was invented in Mexico.

Peru

In Peru, corn was probably introduced from the north, but several varieties of bean had been cultivated even before the earliest beans in Mexico. Other crops indigenous to Peru became important—white potato, chile peppers, tubers, manioc, and a grain called quinoa adapted to the high altitudes of the region. Large populations were supported by marine resources on the coast which may at first have held up the cultivation process. But later, these same coastal populations expanded inward, placing a serious drain on resources. This situation created a tension zone which probably stimulated the cultivation process. Substantial sedentary populations were more prevalent in Peru before domestication than in Mexico, where population growth and village life followed the invention of horticulture. The significance of Peru, however, lies in the fact that it was the only place in the New World where there is evidence that animal domestication was practiced on a large scale. The llama was domesticated (as a pack animal) by 7500 B.P. and the alpaca (domesticated mostly for wool) somewhat later.

The Spread Northward

There is some question whether cultivation was achieved in North America before the diffusion of ideas from the south. Beans, corn, and squash were probably introduced from Mexico by around 500 B.P., but local plants may have been cultivated in both the Southwest and Midwest. In our ethnocentric search for the plants that we consider staples, we have tended to ignore other perfectly nutritious possibilities such as amaranth, common chenopods, iva, and sunflowers.

The New World Neolithic, like that in the Old World, supported large sedentary populations and large villages, and required technological innovations and social institutions previously unknown. As in the Old World, the results were revolutionary, but the process was gradual. Indeed, villages came to the New World much later after the advent of plant domestication. We must now consider what those results were in both areas.

Social Implications of Settling Down

When human beings took control of food production, the world became a different place for them. Hunter-gatherers do not own territory. Most take from the land only what they need to survive. Cultivators, on the other hand, invest their own labors in many crops. They come to see the land and its produce as their own. In their eyes, the world's land is divided up and owned by humans, and its products belong to the individuals whose efforts have brought them to fruition. This transformation has enormous implications for human life.

The Effects of Domestication

The Management of Water

The earliest efforts at cultivation, wherever they took place in the world, were in areas with adequate natural precipitation to water the crops. Increased food production, however, and the settling down into permanent villages, led to population expansion. This, in turn, put pressure on farmers to expand their fields into areas where water was not readily available. People became obsessed with water and devised various ways to bring it into their fields from natural rivers and springs.[20] In Egypt and elsewhere, river floodplains were exploited when the overflow could be predicted. In the Valley of Oaxaca, in Mexico, *pot irrigation* was practiced: shallow wells were dug right in the field and water was drawn directly from them by hand to water each individual corn plant.

But most common, and most complicated in terms of its social implications, was a system using large *canals*. In some places, canals were simply shallow channels scratched on the earth, but in other locales—certainly in the Near East, and probably in the Valley of Mexico—they were complex systems of ditches requiring major investment in terms of construction, maintenance, and management. In fact, it has been suggested by Karl Wittfogel[21] that the managerial requirements

Plant and animal domesticators, such as this shepherd, have a vested interest in the land.

of large irrigation systems are the foundation for the growth of civilization. Wherever present, canals certainly created differential access to resources. People who could irrigate their fields more effectively could produce more and better crops. Those who could not were at a clear disadvantage. In some cases, control of water made the growth of permanent settlements an absolute necessity.

Impact on Social Institutions

Villages based on horticulture were widespread by 10,000 B.P. in the Near East, by 6000 B.P. in China and Europe, by 4500 B.P. in the Andes, and by 3500 B.P. in Mexico and the American Southwest. The villages became different sorts of communities from those formed by hunter-gatherers. Settled villagers are less communal than nomadic hunter-gatherers.

20. Richard A. Watson and Patty Jo Watson, "The Domestication of Plants and Animals," in *Prehistoric Agriculture,* ed. Stuart Struever (Garden City, N.Y.: Natural History Press, 1971).

21. Karl Wittfogel, *Oriental Despotism: A Comparative Study of Total Power* (New Haven, Conn.: Yale University Press, 1957).

Hunter-gatherer society is organized around the *band*—a small group (usually less than 100) of men, women, and children who are related through kinship or marriage. Each adult member of the band acquires food, the women typically gathering plants and small animals and the men obtaining meat by hunting larger animals.

For sedentarists, by contrast, the family is the basic production unit, and its efforts are usually shared only among its members. In villages, family interests are not the same as community-wide interests, as in hunting and gathering bands. Some families, for example, may have better land or just better watered land than others. Families not only may have qualitatively different productive resources, but they may also invest more or less effort in production. They may build elaborate houses and accumulate furniture and other material possessions, all of which are impractical for nomadic or even seminomadic hunter-gatherers. Children also become more valuable to sedentary communities since they contribute to the economy at an early age by performing such tasks as weeding and caring for animals. For nomadic hunters, by contrast, children are burdensome because they must be carried when young and are not economically helpful for years. Indeed, the contribution of children to the subsistence base of horticulturists may be one of the reasons for the population explosion after sedentarism occurred.

Another difference between sedentarists and hunter-gatherers is that the *tribe*—composed of numerous families or generations of individuals together with their dependents—replaces the band as the political unit of sedentary society. Tribal organization has the advantage of being able to extend beyond local communities to large political groupings. These groups become important for purposes of defense, trade, and subsistence. When a village has to move, for example, it may need allies on whom it can depend in the transitional period.

There is greater likelihood that conflicts will arise when larger groups of people settle down together. Conflicts between communities are also more likely because vested interests in territory have been established. Therefore, mechanisms for settling such disputes must be developed. Even the building of houses in places where space was circumscribed in any way could become an issue. Clearly, political organization at all levels is more necessary in settled communities than in groups that are more informally and impermanently structured.

Other changes involved religion. As we saw in Chapter 7, the hunter-gatherers of the Upper Paleolithic were greatly concerned with animal spirits because animals played a major role in subsistence. With the rise of domestication, however, the emphasis shifted to a concern with fertility and control of the weather for a good crop year. At Çatal Hüyük, for example, the supreme deity was the Great Goddess, whose ample proportions had led investigators to conclude that she was a fertility symbol. Moreover, statues and other art forms show the female deities either as two goddesses or as twins. As James Mellaart notes, the idea behind duplication was to insure the propagation of crops, farm animals, and even humans themselves.[22]

---

22. Mellaart, "A Neolithic City in Turkey."

The Effects of Domestication

Trade

Soon after horticultural communities developed, extensive trade networks were established to assure the flow of needed resources from distant areas. These networks aided in the dispersal of ideas, raw materials, and finished products. When varied environmental zones are in close proximity to one another—as in Mexico, the Near East, and the Central Andes—the exchange of products is inevitable. As we saw among the Bus Mordeh villagers, exotic raw materials were carried over hundreds of miles. In the New World, copper circulated from New York to Kansas, from Michigan to Florida. Clay seals, figurines, and ornamental shells made their way to southeast Europe from the Near East. Metallurgy, masonry, and advances in transportation, farming, and housing—all that food production indirectly made possible—spread rapidly.

Thus, controlling food production led humans to appreciate all the other kinds of control they could have and how they could "modify the physical environment at will to serve their own purposes."[23] The Neolithic Age, then, was the beginning of human control over a complex technology. It prepared the way for the next great development in human history—the urban revolution and the beginnings of civilization.

Summary

1. At the close of the Pleistocene, environmental changes pressured advanced hunter-gatherers into developing new tools and food-getting strategies. The resulting "broad-spectrum" subsistence base is thought to have been a pre-adaptation to an economy based on the domestication of plants and animals.

2. Mesolithic foragers consciously manipulated the plants and animals in their environments. When some of these groups became horticulturists, the Neolithic Age was born.

3. Archeologists can recognize the remains of domesticated grains, such as wheat and barley, by examining the rachis of the plants. The remains of domesticated goats and sheep can also be differentiated from those of their wild counterparts by the shape of the horns and by differences in age and sex ratios.

4. The Binford–Flannery theory states that population pressure on marginal environmental zones was the primary factor behind the rise of plant and animal domestication.

5. Present evidence indicates that plant and animal domestication first appeared in the Near East (10,000 B.P.), as well as in Southeast Asia (8800 B.P.) and China (6000 B.P.). It arose in the New World around 7000 B.P.

6. One aspect of social organization to be influenced by the Neolithic Age was the family. Among sedentary villagers, the family, rather than the band, became the basic unit of production and consumption. Children, too, became important because they could contribute to the subsistence base of the village. Sedentarism also had significant effects on religion, trade, and political organization.

Review Questions

1. What is meant by the term "broad-spectrum subsistence base"? Why was it important among certain human groups during the Mesolithic Age?

23. Watson and Watson, "The Domestication of Plants and Animals," p. 10.

2. Explain how an archeologist determines whether such plants as wheat and barley have been domesticated.
3. What are the chief elements of the Binford–Flannery theory of the beginnings of domestication? What are its limitations?
4. How did the coming of horticulture affect religious beliefs and practices?
5. Why would the creation of trade networks be important for early settled communities?
6. Why is the Neolithic Age such an important period in human history?

Garden City, N.Y.: Natural History Press, 1971.
A valuable collection of readings by many authorities on the rise of food production in many parts of the world.

Ucko, P. J., and Dimbleby, G. W., eds. *The Domestication and Exploitation of Plants and Animals*. Chicago: Aldine Publishing, 1971.
An important anthology of articles by anthropologists and biologists on many aspects of domestication, including its origin and spread.

Suggested Readings

Clark, Grahame. *World Prehistory: An Outline*. Cambridge: Cambridge University Press, 1967.
A comprehensive discussion of all aspects of prehistory, in both the Old and New Worlds.

Flannery, Kent. "The Origins of Agriculture." *Annual Review of Anthropology* 2 (1973): 271–310.
A clearly written, but somewhat technical, examination of the factors that must be considered in any theory that purports to explain the beginnings of domestication. Flannery, perhaps the foremost American archeologist, looks at the processes behind the rise of food production in the Near East, Mesoamerica, Peru, and Southeast Asia.

Sanders, W. T., and Price, B. J. *Mesoamerica: The Evolution of a Civilization*. New York: Random House, 1968.
An interesting study of the rise of farming and civilization in Mesoamerica from the point of view of cultural ecology.

Struever, Stuart, ed. *Prehistoric Agriculture*.

Chapter 9

The Origin of Cities

THE HARAPPAN CIVILIZATION OF INDIA

As a result of more than thirty years of excavations at these sites [which were part of the civilization of Harappa, one of the earliest cities that flourished in India between 4500 and 3500 B.P.], there is a great body of evidence relating to the life of the civilization which produced them. . . . Here we shall summarize the main outlines which present themselves to the observer. Our overwhelming impression is of cultural uniformity, both throughout the several centuries during which the Harappan civilization flourished, and over the vast area it occupied. This uniformity is nowhere clearer than in the town-planning. The basic layout of the larger settlements, whether cities or towns, shows a regular orientation, with a high citadel on the west dominating the lower town. Probably the latter was originally more or less square. Equally careful was the oriented grid of streets which intersected the blocks of dwellings. . . . A similar uniformity is found throughout the Harappan structures. There is a remarkable standardization of brick sizes, both of burnt- and mud-bricks, and this too is in basic contrast to that of the pre-Harappan period. The skill of the bricklayers is particularly clear in the great public buildings of the citadel complexes, for example in

Source: Adapted from Bridget Allchin and Raymond Allchin, *The Birth of Indian Civilization* (London: Penguin Books Ltd., Pelican Original, 1968), chap. 6, pp. 131–138. Copyright © 1968 by Bridget and Raymond Allchin. Reprinted by permission of Penguin Books Ltd.

the great bath at Mohenjo-daro, and in the granaries at both cities. On the other hand one cannot but be struck by the monotonous regularity of the plain undecorated brickwork of the acres of uniform houses of the lower town at Mohenjo-daro. Another feature of the towns that calls for attention is the care expended on domestic bathrooms and latrines, and on the chutes which linked them to brick drains running down the streets. At intervals the drains were connected with soakage pits or stumps, and their maintenance implies some sort of highly effective municipal authority.

The mainstays of life must have been extraordinarily like those of recent centuries in the Indus valley. Wheat and barley were the main crops; leguminous plants, field peas and dates were other items of diet. Sessamum and mustard were used, presumably for oil. . . . Among domestic animals were sheep, goats and cattle, and the domestic fowl was also kept. It is not clear whether bones of pig and buffalo indicate the presence of domesticated stock, or only that these animals were hunted for food. Several varieties of deer were certainly hunted. The discovery of fragments of woven cotton is of great interest, attesting the antiquity of an industry for which in later times India has been particularly famous.

A similar uniformity of culture can be observed in the technology of the Harappans: indeed it is as strong as in the town-planning, and so marked that it is possible to typify each craft with a single set of examples drawn from one site alone. It is not yet established whether this uniformity was achieved by the centralization of production, linked with efficiency of distribution, or whether by other factors, but in either case it calls for special study. A standard range of tools of copper and bronze is recorded at site after site. Many among them set the pattern for later Indian types for centuries to come. The majority exhibit what Piggott called "competent dullness," a simplicity of design and manufacture linked with adequate, but not great functional efficiency. The range of bronze and copper vessels is technically more worthy of remark. There is little doubt that such special objects as the cast bronze figures of people or animals, or the little model carts (of which nearly identical examples come from sites as far apart as Harappa and Chanhu-daro) were the products of specialists' workshops in one or other of the cities. In spite of the commonness of metals, stone was not abandoned, and chert blades were prepared from cores which in turn had probably been exported from such great factories as that at Sukkur (Sakhar). . . .

Other categories of information are less easily obtained by excavation, but include aspects of life and culture which are essential if a full and balanced picture is to be obtained: thus from variations of house sizes, and from localization of groups of "barracks," some

Chapter   Nine

scholars have inferred class differences even amounting to slavery. The same evidence has been used to suggest the presence of a "caste" structure like that of later times. Again the presence of great granaries on the citadel mounds and of the "citadels" themselves, have suggested, partly by analogy with Middle Eastern cities, the presence of priest-kings or at least of a priestly oligarchy who controlled the economy, civil government and religious life of the state. The intellectual mechanism of this government and the striking degree of control implicit in it are also very worthy subjects of research.

The language of the Harappans is at present still unknown, and must remain so until the Harappan script is read. . . . Numerous attempts have been—and are still being—made, but none so far can inspire much confidence. In recent years the most significant advance has been the certain proof, offered by B. B. Lal, that the script was written from right to left. The shortness of the inscriptions, nearly all on seals or amulet tablets, further renders decipherment difficult. The uniformity of weights and measures is another indication of the efficiency of state control throughout a large area. . . .

The information that has been gathered on such topics as the economy, social system, government or religion, was largely the product of chance finds in the earlier excavations. It is to be hoped that as archaeological research in India and Pakistan advances further excavations may be conducted with the aim of answering specific questions and elucidating specific problems.[1]

● ● ● ● ● ● ● ●

The Harappan civilization described above was one of the first to develop in the Indus Valley of India. The origin of cities, the emergence of the state, and the birth of civilization are all aspects of the same great transformation in human history.

This transformation was based largely on the events discussed in Chapter 8: the domestication of plants and animals led to a population explosion, which in turn led to intensification of agriculture and food surplus. It goes without saying that the early states had to be located in areas where prime agricultural conditions prevailed—that is, where fertile soil and abundant water were present. However, not all agricultural settlements developed into civilizations. Nor were all societies at the state level civilizations.

1. Adapted from Bridget Allchin and Raymond Allchin, *The Birth of Indian Civilization* (London: Penguin Books Ltd., Pelican Original, 1968), chap. 6, pp. 131–138.

One of the most interesting aspects of the early civilizations is the fact that they emerged fairly rapidly after the appearance of the first farming villages. In the Near East, some early Neolithic villages had been transformed into cities by about 5500 B.P. As the capsule study indicates, the first civilization arose in India one thousand years later. In China, the earliest cities appeared around 3500 B.P. Civilization did not come to the New World until much later than in the Near East: the first Mexican and Peruvian states appeared around two thousand years ago.

The terms *city, civilization,* and *state* have been treated similarly by many authors. But it is not entirely accurate to do so. Thus, a city is defined by dense populations—people live close to one another and depend on others for a variety of goods and services. In an urban society, people no longer live in self-sufficient family units, as they did in Neolithic times. The city is a society of specialists, only some of whom still engage in food production. Others practice crafts, build buildings, clean the streets, make laws, interpret the stars, and write history books.

The state, by contrast, is a form of sociopolitical organization. In an urban society, social control is maintained by the state. It is the political form appropriate to societies with numerous composite groups, social classes, and associations. The state brings together under common rule many different kinds of people. There is no single definition of a state that all investigators would agree on. But most would concur that a state must have definite social classes; a monopoly on physical force which is used to maintain social control; and a number of governmental branches, typically employing numerous people (police, army, or militia) who exercise authority that is impersonal. This form of sociopolitical organization, then, is quite different from that in tribal and other societies in which orderly social relationships derive from the obligations that individuals have to one another typically because they are related by blood or marriage. The political organization of the state and the tribal society are fully discussed in Chapter 12.

Civilization is a process (the very word means "city making"). This process is related to population size and density, the development of social stratification (that is, status based on one's social class), and the strength of the ruling polity. In addition, civilization involves a change in the nature of trade, the size and role of markets, and many technological and intellectual advances[2]—all of which result in a complexity of social relationships in the economic sphere. Civilization is a process that has been set into motion more than once in world history, at various times, and now it virtually encompasses the entire world.

What, exactly, are the identifying characteristics of a civilization? What sets off such a complex social organization from a simpler one, such as a Neolithic farming community? Over the years, investigators have compiled a list of traits that distinguish a civilization. It is marked, for example, by a centralized political system, social stratification, occupational speciali-

---

2. Jeremy Sabloff and C. C. Lamberg-Karlovsky, eds., *The Rise and Fall of Civilization: Modern Archaeological Approaches to Current Cultures* (Menlo Park, Calif.: Cummings Publishing, 1974), p. 2.

Figure 9-1   **Comparative Hallmarks of Civilization and Neolithic Community**

CIVILIZATION	NEOLITHIC COMMUNITY
1. State: centralized political system. Privileged ruling class backed up by force. People taxed and drafted for work and war.	No formal government (marriage and family ties). No force.
2. Social stratification: social classes.	Egalitarian.
3. Occupational specialization.	No full-time specialists.
4. Cities: urbanization. (Not all civilizations had cities—for example, Old Kingdom settlements in Egypt.)	Small communities: villages.
5. Monumental public works: temples, palaces, tombs, irrigation systems, storehouses.	Absence of such structures.
6. Art: A sophisticated or elaborate style.	Usually at level of crafts.
7. Writing and development of mathematics and science, especially astronomy. (Not all civilizations had writing—for example, the Aztecs and Incas.)	Preliterate.
8. Relationships: impersonal, determined by class, status, rank, etc.	Relationships personal, based on marriage and family ties.
9. Long-distance trade routes.	Small-scale trading.

zation, urbanization, monumental public works, and other characteristics. The complete list—and a comparative list of the traits which mark a Neolithic community—is shown in Figure 9–1.

A number of other developments were also associated with the appearance of civilization. Metallurgy, for example, became important. Copper was combined first with arsenic, then with tin, to manufacture tools and weapons superior to stone and bone. Indeed, because of this development, the period of the first states is known as the Bronze Age.

Other characteristics include the waging of war and the standing army (with the possible exception of the states in the Indus Valley). The position of women fell in that they became the legal wards of their fathers, brothers, and husbands. In a related development, many freedoms were relinquished by the common folk. Indeed, for the past five or six thousand years, fully 90 percent of all the people who ever lived were peasants or members of some servile caste or class.

Early Civilizations

Before the anthropological publications of the British historian V. Gordon Childe in the 1940s, most historians proclaimed the

Fertile Crescent of Mesopotamia to have been the cradle of civilization. Agriculture, urbanism, writing, science, indeed all the great human accomplishments were thought to have had their roots in Mesopotamia. Just as investigators believed agriculture could have been invented only once, they believed civilization far too complex to have been invented more than once. Unlike agriculture, however, civilization was not invented many times. It seems to have happened in six places, most of which were in river valleys: Mesopotamia and southwest Iran, Egypt, the Indus River Valley in India, north China, Mesoamerica, and Peru (Figure 9–2).

These six places were the first states. Anthropologists are interested in the process that led to the formation of these states and how they are alike. Archeologists are interested in knowing more about each of the six places so that they can document the broader anthropological ques-

Figure 9–2   *Location of the first six civilizations in the Old and New Worlds. First states appeared about 5500* B.P. *in Old World (Near East) and about 2000* B.P. *in New World.*

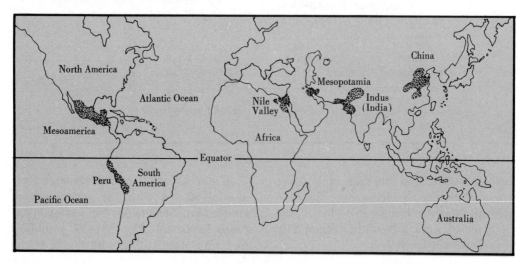

Monumental public works are one characteristic of civilization. Shown here is part of the ruins of Persepolis, capital of the Persian Empire from 728 to 530 B.P.

tions—how people lived, their subsistence base, sociopolitical organization, and so on. As it stands, the data are very uneven. Mesopotamia and Egypt are perhaps the best known and have long been included in the study of ancient history. Mesoamerica has been studied intensively for years, but only now are anthropologists beginning to make sense of these civilizations. Our knowledge of India and China is good but limited, and that of Peru is improving all the time.

There are problems in the reconstruction of early civilizations. By definition we are dealing with large societies, and therefore need large samples to encompass the life and perspective of the inhabitants.

Archeologists in the early days were more interested in the rare achievements of early peoples than in the reconstruction of whole social systems. Early work in the field emphasized monumental public works, both because of their awe-inspiring size and workmanship (the Pyramids of Egypt, for example) and because they were the most likely places to find caches of art objects and treasures. We now realize that in order to answer questions about the decisions of these larger populations to settle down, to govern themselves, and then to move on to great technological developments, we have to know more than how many temples or pyramids they built. We have to know who built them, where

The Origin of Cities

they lived and were buried, who used these public works, and how all these people were fed. Finding data by digging for all of this is an impossibility. Digging up even a representative sample is a Herculean task, and the interpretation of mute material remains not nearly so easy as one would wish.

In the capsule study, we got a glimpse of what early civilization in the Indus Valley was like. Now we will examine the early civilizations that appeared in three other areas of the world—Sumer, Middle America, and China.

Sumer

Sumer was the lower half of Mesopotamia, the area that makes up modern Iraq from north of Baghdad to the Persian Gulf. It was a flat, river-made land with no natural minerals, almost no stone and no timber except the huge reeds that grew along the river. In this unlikely environment one of the earliest civilizations became established. Between 10,000 and 5000 B.P. a people consisting of self-sufficient bands of nomadic hunters and gatherers changed into politically integrated city dwellers.[3] Samuel N. Kramer, the leading Sumerian scholar, emphasizes that even the earliest settlers practiced irrigation.[4] Irrigation

---

3. Frank Hole, "Investigating the Origins of Mesopotamian Civilization," in *The Rise and Fall of Civilization: Modern Archaeological Approaches to Current Cultures,* ed. Jeremy Sabloff and C. C. Lamberg-Karlovsky (Menlo Park, Calif.: Cummings Publishing, 1974), pp. 269–281.

---

4. Samuel N. Kramer, *The Sumerians: Their History, Culture, and Character* (Chicago: University of Chicago Press, 1963).

was essential to the success of the barley and wheat crops that were their principal food. To make up for the lack of minerals and stone, the people had learned to bake the river clay into pots, plates, and jars, and to braid the river reeds into mats that could be used with plaster for construction. They invented the potter's wheel, the wagon wheel, the plow, the sailboat, the arch, vault, and dome. They learned to cast copper and bronze, to rivet, braze, and solder, to sculpt in stone, inlay, and engrave, and to write on clay tablets.

Sumerian communities were city-states, each consisting of a large and usually walled city surrounded by suburban villages and hamlets. The wall, probably for protection against invaders, is a common element of early cities. In later times, many early European cities originated as fortified places (burgs). Most famous among the Sumerian city-states are Eridu, Ur, Uqair, Tello, Uruk, and Susa. Each city was dominated by a high, main temple situated on an elevated terrace. The form of these temples gradually developed into what is known as a *ziggurat*, a massive tower with stages.

The Sumerian civilization possessed many of the trappings of our own. For example, it had a legal system with definite laws, a bureaucracy to keep the wheels of state running smoothly, an army, a sewer system, and even a farmer's almanac of sorts. Like the Harappans, the Sumerians had developed a system of writing, largely to keep track of mundane administrative and business affairs. In its *cuneiform* (wedge-shaped) script, for example, were recorded such weighty matters as how many pounds of grain were harvested, how many fields were planted and with what crops, and how many barrels of oil were stored in the temple ware-house. In the early days of Sumer, says Kramer, political power lay in the hands of free citizens who were organized into two legislative bodies, an upper house of "elders" and a lower, of "men."[5] Later, as military pressures became greater, leaders were appointed and eventually families inherited positions of power.

As in the Harappan civilization, social stratification is in evidence. The population was divided into four strata, or classes: nobles who owned great estates; commoners who, as members of families, worked much more modest plots of land; clients who were either well-to-do dependents of the temple, regular temple personnel, or dependents of the nobility; and slaves, most of whom were prisoners of war.

The Sumerians were good business people. Because communities were large and resources scarce, the importance of trade cannot be overemphasized.[6] Some system of distribution of goods and services had to be devised. Moreover, the massive irrigation works—one of the crowning achievements of Sumerian civilization—had to be centrally controlled and systems of defense organized by the state. Thus, the self-sufficiency of the original hunter-gatherers was exchanged for a political system featuring interdependence and its regulatory mechanisms. The new system encouraged occupational specialization and led to a higher standard of living and to the great achievements of civilization that otherwise would have been impossible.

Mesoamerica

In Mesoamerica, the first states developed in two areas, the highland valley of Mexico, the Yucatán Peninsula of Mexico, and the lowland Petén region of Guatemala. Whether one stimulated the growth of the other is still unknown, although different scholars entertain different theories on the subject.[7]

THE VALLEY OF MEXICO. Archeologist William T. Sanders[8] argues that the rise of civilization in the valley of Mexico was related to the fact that there were many different environmental zones containing different resources and occupied by many different communities. Therefore, as different groups came into control of different areas, they had to interact with each other in order to gain access to the various raw materials. An imposing city grew up in the Teotihuacán Valley between 2300 and 1300 B.P., not far from the site of the later Aztec city, Tenochtitlan. Teotihuacán (which means "Place of the Gods") flourished in an area that had been only sparsely populated from 3000 B.P. onward. Sanders believes that the adoption of irrigation led to substantial

5. Kramer, *The Sumerians.*

6. Hole, "Investigating the Origins of Mesopotamian Civilization."

7. William T. Sanders and Barbara J. Price, *Mesoamerica: The Evolution of a Civilization* (New York: Random House, 1968).

8. William T. Sanders, "Hydraulic Agriculture, Environmental Symbiosis, and the Evolution of States in Central Mexico," in *The Rise and Fall of Civilization: Modern Archaeological Approaches to Current Cultures*, ed. Jeremy Sabloff and C. C. Lamberg-Karlovsky (Menlo Park, Calif.: Cummings Publishing, 1974), pp. 119–133.

Pyramid of the Sun at Teotihuacán, about 25 miles north of modern Mexico City. This 200-foot-high structure, built of adobe and earth and faced with stone, was probably used for politico-religious purposes.

population growth and the possibility for permanent settlement.

Because of its orderly pattern, Teotihuacán was probably laid out by architects. In its classic period, it had an estimated population of between 85,000 and 200,000.[9] The city eventually covered 8 square miles, an area larger than that of Classical Rome. At its center were two great streets that were lined with public and politicoreligious buildings. At the northern end of the 3-mile-long north/south concourse (the Street of the Dead) stood the Pyramid of the Moon. On the eastern side was the enormously imposing Pyramid of the Sun—some 200 feet in height and 1,400 square feet in area at its base. This monumental structure was built of sun-dried bricks (adobe) and earth and was faced with stone. At the intersection of the two streets stood two complexes, on one side the gaily painted Temple of Quetzacoatl, which included a pyramid decorated with elaborate sculp-

9. Gordon R. Willey, "Pre-Columbian Urbanism: The Central Mexican Highlands and the Lowland Maya," in *The Rise and Fall of Civilization: Modern Archaeological Approaches to Current Cultures,* ed. Jeremy Sabloff and C. C. Lamberg-Karlovsky (Menlo Park, Calif.: Cummings Publishing, 1974), pp. 134–144.

ture (large stone serpent heads and wide-eyed human faces), and a mammoth rectangular enclosure thought to be the principal palace of the city. On the other side was another enclosure, the Great Compound, which probably served as the city's central marketplace.

All around the Pyramid complex were buildings that may have served as palaces where the city's priests and elite dwelled. The walls of some of these buildings attest to the luxury of the place: brightly painted frescoes depict priests, animals, and gods moving in grand processions. The rain god Tlaloc is often shown dispersing his largess in the form of water.

Beyond the main streets were thousands of apartment buildings. As at the Harappan sites, these were laid out in a grid pattern. They were one-story structures with several apartments surrounding interior courtyards. Well-defined concentrations of surface remains suggest that craft groups such as potters and workers in stone and obsidian lived together in neighborhoods.[10] There seem also to have been ethnic neighborhoods, the western part of the city having been occupied by people from Oaxaca.

Because there are no written records for Teotihuacán as there are for Sumer, we know less about the details of the government and the characteristics of the population. There certainly were specialized craftsmen, traders, politicians, and priests. Some people had more power than others, regulated irrigation systems, and managed military campaigns.

We do know that long-distance trade was important, because items not native to the area (bird feathers and cotton, for example) were discovered ·in graves. Moreover, the influence of the city on other parts of Middle America was great. Other cities, for example, imitated its architecture and venerated the same deities. Obsidian, which apparently was sought after by other cities the way oil is today, was one of Teotihuacán's principal exports. It goes without saying that state organization was a necessity for a place of the proportions of Teotihuacán, with all its craft specialization and class stratification.

THE MAYA.   The Mayan cities of the Petén were smaller than Teotihuacán, but not necessarily any less differentiated, nor less organized. Tikal, the best-known of the major Mayan centers, probably had a population of 10,000 in its central "downtown" area and another 15,000 to 30,000 within its political and economic sphere.[11] Whereas the city of Teotihuacán dominated highland Mexico, the Mayan area had cities every 10 or 20 miles. They included central areas with monumental architecture, the outstanding feature of which was a very steep, tiered pyramid with a flat top which held a two-roomed temple decorated with an elaborate, painted roof comb.

They also included residences scattered about the center in a disorganized manner, in contrast to the tight grid of

10. René Millon, "Teotihuacán," in *New World Archaeology: Theoretical and Cultural Transformations*, ed. Ezra B. W. Zubrow, Margaret C. Fritz, and John M. Fritz (San Francisco: W. H. Freeman, 1974), pp. 115–125.

11. T. Patrick Culbert, *The Lost Civilization: The Story of the Classic Maya* (New York: Harper and Row, 1974).

Teotihuacán. Some of these residences, which belonged to peasant farmers, were tidy and well built, presenting a semirural appearance. Gardens and groves of trees grew between the houses, which were well spaced. Indeed, the Mayan working class was relatively prosperous.[12]

12. Culbert, *The Lost Civilization*, pp. 64–65.

Temple I at Mayan site of Tikal. Words spoken in a normal voice by a person standing in doorway beneath the roof comb can be heard throughout the plaza below—a tribute to Mayan acoustical engineering.

The Mayan centers were based on slash-and-burn agriculture, an intensive technique that could support large populations for a short time, but not indefinitely because of the nature of land use. (In slash-and-burn agriculture, land must be allowed to lie fallow after it has been cultivated for some period of time.) The Mayan area is also lacking in such essential natural resources as salt and hard stone, which had to be obtained through trade. What did the Maya offer in return for these necessities? Recently it has been suggested that they developed a complex sociopolitical organization to manage a consistent procurement, importation, and distribution of nonlocal goods used in every household.[13] In other words, they specialized in the techniques of exchange and distribution in return for the products other peoples had to offer. In addition, they invested their skills and resources in the creation of cultural centers where more provincial peoples might worship the gods and learn the arts. Indeed, because of their cultural interests, the Maya have been likened to the Classical Greeks.

The Maya had a writing system, and as more and more of their stone tablets, which are known as *stelae*, are interpreted, the details of their social organization become clearer. There were the great lords and priests at the top of the social pyramid, the common laborers at the bottom,

and it has recently been proposed that there was a reasonably prosperous group of professionals and artisans in the middle.[14] Murals show subservient individuals who may have been slaves, probably captives of war. These wall paintings also show Mayan battles and ceremonies.

As in India, Sumer, and the valley of Mexico, the Maya had developed the arts. Their sculpture, jade carvings, and ceramics are celebrated. They wrote their books on paper of bark, and they were using the arithmetical zero even before Europeans. Most impressive was their complex calendrical system—a testament to their skill as astronomers—that combined the ritual and the lunar year cycles. Many of the *stelae* record important dates —succession of one leader over another, for instance—in these cycles. Mayan civilization endured for about 700 years, until around 1100 B.P., when it collapsed.

China

Like the Harappans and the Maya, the early Chinese also recorded events of state with a system of writing. They wrote with brush and ink on scraps of bamboo and wood and bound them together into books. They also recorded acts of divination by incising on the shoulder blades of animals and on turtle shells. Signs of possession and offerings were cast onto bronze vessels.[15] The earliest civilization in China is believed to be the Shang dynasty, which spanned 2050 to 1300 B.P. Honan is the best-known Shang area, but very recent

13. William L. Rathje, "The Origin and Development of Lowland Classic Mayan Civilization," in *The Rise and Fall of Civilization: Modern Archaeological Approaches to Current Cultures*, ed. Jeremy Sabloff and C. C. Lamberg-Karlovsky (Menlo Park, Calif.: Cummings Publishing, 1974), pp. 84–94.

14. Culbert, *The Lost Civilization*, pp. 65–67.

15. Kwang-chih Chang, *The Archaeology of Ancient China* (New Haven, Conn.: Yale University Press, 1977).

archeology has shown the presence of Shang civilization in Shantung, Kiangsu, and Hupei.

According to archeologist Kwang-chih Chang, the foremost feature of Shang sites is that of individual villages organized into economic, administrative, and religious networks. There was a political and ceremonial center where the royal family and nobles lived. Immediately outside this nucleus were industrial quarters, and beyond were the farming villages. One Shang city, Cheng-chou, is notable in that, like early cities in other areas, it was surrounded by a wall. The 30-foot structure enclosed a rectangular area of a little more than 2 square miles. Goods circulated among the villages, with the administrative center, as in the Mayan area, serving as the center for redistribution. Chang does not think that these complexes of villages around a center reached the population levels of Teotihuacán or of the cities of Mesopotamia.[16] He does believe, however, that the Shang capital sites served all the essential functions of a city.

The Shang capitals of Cheng-chou and An-yang were seats of a powerful centralized government that controlled a number of settlements scattered over a part of north China. The population was made up of three groups: an aristocracy; artisans, craftsmen, and warriors; and farmers. At the capitals, and perhaps at a few other sites, artifacts and architecture have been uncovered by archeologists that represent the aristocratic stratum of the population. Not surprisingly, the houses of the rich were different from those of the poor. The wealthy lived in rectangular structures with stamped earth floors. The more elaborate houses boasted stone pillar foundations with stone sculptures supporting the bases. Tombs of gigantic dimensions show evidence of human sacrifice and animal offerings, including, in some, an entire horse-drawn chariot. At one burial site were discovered bodies that perhaps had been buried alive. Their hands were tied and the heads or parts of the limbs had been severed from some. "These burials," writes Chang, "indicate most vividly a stratified society in which members of a lower class were sometimes victims, perhaps for religious ceremonies."[17]

Ceremonial pottery and bronze vessels are distinguished from the wares of the common people. Horse and chariot fittings, prepared and inscribed oracle bones, jade and bronze weapons, and exquisite jade hairpins are all associated with the upper class. This aristocracy presumably administered the central city and appointed lords to oversee the outlying settlements. Members of the aristocracy sponsored and organized warfare and frequent raids. They also controlled and managed the goods.

The craftsmen lived in simpler semisubterranean quarters outside the center. Two-room houses were uncovered at An-yang that seem to be associated with a bronze technology. Chang suggests that handicrafts may have been produced by groups of related individuals and that the two-room structures, which usually were found in clusters, probably belonged to extended families, all of whom practiced the same craft. It is believed that the artisans—workers in bronze, bone, and

---

16. Chang, *The Archaeology of Ancient China*, p. 282.

17. Chang, *The Archaeology of Ancient China*, p. 284.

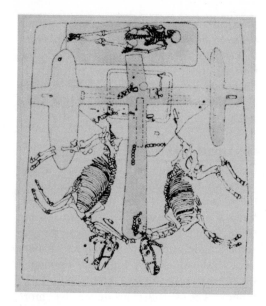

Figure 9–3   *Drawing of royal Shang tomb, with chariot and remains of horses and driver.*

jade—were directly supervised by members of the upper classes. At An-yang, the commoners were buried where they lived, with the result that living and burial remains are often mixed. The royalty, by contrast, had their own cemetery which, together with the royal palace, was controlled by the ruling class.

The farmers lived still farther away from the center and depended on the old stone technology rather than on the bronze of the upper class. The farming of millet, rice, and wheat was supplemented by hunting and fishing. Irrigation was probably employed, although the water ditches discovered at An-yang and Chung-chou have not been clearly shown to be used for irrigation.[18] The Shang, like the

---

18. Chang, *The Archaeology of Ancient China*, p. 289.

Harappans, Sumerians, and Mesoamericans, had an organized state that provided the political and economic integration of many different groups of people into one society. Whether or not the Shang used irrigation to grow food for themselves, they did manage the exchange of food for the goods and services produced by their specialists.

The Character of Civilization

We have seen in the capsule study, and in other examples of early cities, that civilization had a profound effect on all aspects of human existence. Indeed, this event is so crucial that it has been called the second greatest revolution in human history (the first being the domestication of plants and animals, discussed in Chapter 8). The change from a simple Neolithic community to a complex city involved a number of factors. Among the most important of these were population density, class stratification, occupational specialization, and long-distance trade.

Population Density

The emergence of civilization clearly is associated with the management of larger populations. As we learn more of China and the Mayan area, however, it seems that it is not necessary for people to live in densely populated areas such as cities, as we know them, for the political organization of the state to manage and control their affairs. The function of early cities seems to have been, in all cases, administrative and probably concerned with economic distribution, but only in some cases were these cities densely settled. Teotihuacán, with its 4,000 apartment buildings and a population numbering in the hundreds of thousands, conforms to modern expectations of a city, but Tikal administered to an equally diverse population although the people did not live in such close quarters.

Class Stratification

What appears to be as significant as numbers of people is their diversity. In all centers of new state formation, social classes had emerged out of egalitarian society. In an egalitarian society, every member of the population lives essentially in the same way and makes a living in the same fashion. Almost every member of the Nuer of East Africa, for instance, keeps cattle. Moreover, virtually all members of such societies are more or less equal in standing. With the coming of civilization and social stratification (the emergence of social classes), individuals no longer had access to the same resources. As we saw in Harappan civilization and elsewhere, society was stratified into different classes. Among the Sumerians, for example, were nobles, commoners, clients, and slaves.

One of the earliest sources of social stratification was undoubtedly the water used for irrigation. The control of irrigation water for increased agricultural production served to enrich those who had the power to determine what happened to the water: those landowners with an assured water supply could count on a rich harvest. Thus, the emergence of class stratification is most accurately seen as a consequence of ownership of private property: investment in private property caused inequities between owners and workers. The interests of different groups of people diverged. Order was no longer kept only by collective consent as political leaders backed up their authority with physical force. In this way, some people came to have power over others. In order to keep the peace, the political organization of the society became qualitatively different; order was imposed by a ruling class, by means of soldiers, police, or a militia.

Occupational Specialization

Class stratification created certain advantages for the members of society. One of these was that, unlike the Nuer, everybody did not have to do the same thing for a living. Of course, the activities of some people were more valuable to society than those of others, but each depended to a greater or lesser extent on all the others. The surplus produced by more intensive agricultural techniques enabled some people to give up food production and to specialize in other activities.

The freeing of part of the population from subsistence pursuits allowed their energy to be channeled in ways not permitted by egalitarian society. People could work at art or science or religion or government full time. Some became carpenters, some architects, some politicians, some their servants; some learned crafts such as ceramics, tool manufacture, or sculpting; others traded, fought wars, and created technological innovations. These specialized efforts, however, had to be coordinated. People depended on each other's efforts. The farmers provided the food, but they no longer were self-sufficient. They depended on the products of the craftsmen, just as the craftsmen needed the farmers' food. These exchanges had to be worked out and were undoubtedly one of the important reasons for the rise of more complex political institutions than had existed previously.

It is clear that a socially stratified,

occupationally specialized population, no matter what its size, needs the direction provided by specialized leadership not required by an egalitarian society. To be sure, some egalitarian societies, with populations numbering in the tens of thousands (such as, for example, the Nuer), have managed without a central authority. But as we have seen, there are few, if any, specialists in such a society. In short, when there are differences of stratification and specialization among people, there is need for direction and control.

Long-Distance Trade

The management of long-distance trade was one of the basic functions of early states. Indeed, some investigators believe that such trade was the force behind the birth of early civilizations. As discussed above, Sumer and the Mayan Petén were lacking in certain very basic resources. These had to be procured and, most important, distributed. The organization of this process undoubtedly formed the basis for political control in a number of cases.

It is organization that lies at the base of the state as an institution. Although monumental public works are cited as a characteristic of the presence of civilization, such efforts were possible only because there was a sociopolitical organization, the state, capable of bringing together a large labor force and of directing such projects. Similarly, long-distance trading requires organization and direction. Archeologist T. Patrick Culbert has suggested that the managed economy— that is, an economy directed by a special group of individuals with political authority—is one good way to increase production.[19] But Culbert does not explain why

---

19. Culbert, *The Lost Civilization*, p. 20.

some groups chose to maximize production and developed the means to do so, and others did not. The "management" hypothesis helps to explain the civilizing process but does not provide a triggering mechanism that gets civilization underway.

Why Civilizations Emerge

We have seen that civilizations are marked by a number of characteristics. We have also examined four early civilizations in some detail. As in theories of food production described in the preceding chapter, there is still one unanswered question about the early civilizations: Why did they emerge? In other words, what were the factors that pressured Neolithic farming communities to evolve into cities? A number of theories have been advanced to explain this momentous event in human history.

Theories of Civilization

As noted at the beginning of this chapter, in most cases, the production of an agricultural surplus is usually the first step toward civilization. The surplus makes possible an expanded population. There is no innate tendency, however, for a population to produce a surplus, or even to increase its numbers. Many societies could raise more food and thus support larger numbers, but their members do not choose to do so. However, in some areas of the world, societies did expand their agricultural production and the surplus did lead to considerable population growth. All of the theories that deal with the emergence of the first states imply the need for organization: the necessity of organizing a large population for a collective purpose. Three such theories focus on environmental circumscription, environmental diversity, and the need to manage large irrigation projects.

ENVIRONMENTAL CIRCUMSCRIPTION. Anthropologist Robert Carneiro bases his theory on the idea that most civilizations began in regions containing relatively small, agriculturally fertile areas surrounded, or circumscribed, by areas that were totally infertile or only marginally so.[20] We saw in Chapter 8 how such a situation prevailed in the Near East: a relatively fertile plain was bordered on one side by an alluvial desert and on the other by the Zagros Mountains. According to Carneiro, population grew rapidly in the productive area because food was plentiful. When these farmers exploited this limited area to the fullest and when the land could no longer support its burgeoning population, competition broke out over the limited resources and warfare ensued. Large organized bodies emerged to summon up and guide the armies. Eventually, the conquering armies became the leaders of the new society, using their organizational skills to keep the peace, govern the conquered, and distribute the resources over which the conflict had erupted in the first place. The losers became the lower class. Thus, a stratified society with a management class emerged out of conquest, and the conquest was a result of economic competition and population pressure.

ENVIRONMENTAL DIVERSITY. Kent

Flannery presents a similar theory, in that he envisions stratified societies developing in situations where the land available for agriculture varies in its productiveness.[21] The good land was occupied first, followed by an expansion of the population. Then the less productive land had to be put into use. The people who were in possession of the good land were obviously at an advantage and seized the opportunity to establish themselves as an elite at the expense of their poorer compatriots. In Flannery's view, the basis for stratification is again competition over limited resources.

HYDRAULIC HYPOTHESIS. Karl Wittfogel claims that the early states developed in arid areas.[22] In these regions, large irrigation projects, such as canals, had to be constructed to distribute the scarce water resources. The management of these works—which included building, maintaining, cleaning, and repairing them—called for a highly organized class of administrators. By controlling the water, these managers also had in their hands an effective means of controlling others in that they could easily deprive uncooperative farmers of water. From this core of petty despots with managerial skills,

20. Robert Carneiro, "A Theory of the Origin of the State," *Science* 169 (1970) : 733–738.

21. Kent Flannery, "The Cultural Evolution of Civilization," *Annual Review of Ecology and Systematics* 3 (1972) : 399–426.

22. Karl Wittfogel, "Developmental Aspects of Hydraulic Societies," in *Irrigation Civilizations: A Comparative Study*, ed. Julian H. Steward, Social Science Monographs of the Pan American Union (Washington, D.C.: Pan American Union, 1960).

says Wittfogel, the first states arose.

But none of these theories is completely adequate because none fits every case. As a matter of fact, a state even emerged in one nonagricultural situation. Anthropologist Michael Mosely has argued that the coastal peoples of Peru had, between 5000 B.P. and 3000 B.P., evolved the complex social institutions associated with civilization based, not on an agricultural economy, but on a maritime one.[23] Their shellfish resources were rich enough to produce a surplus. This resource supported a large, settled population, not all of whom had to engage in food production. Culbert's "management hypothesis" would fit this case, since he identifies the origins of civilization with the economics of a surplus and the politics of the state political organization and its management of production and diversity. The elusive matter yet to be explained satisfactorily is why some peoples began intensive agriculture, or even collecting, and others did not.

It is obvious that although each of the first states described in this chapter had its own distinctive character, each did share a number of factors. These factors still mark the large cities of today. A visitor to modern Paris, for example, will be struck by the ways in which it differs from New York, London, or Moscow. At the same time, the hypothetical visitor would note that the four cities have high population densities, and are socially and economically diverse. These three patterns in the cultural evolution of humankind

23. Michael Mosely, *The Maritime Foundations of Andean Civilization* (Menlo Park, Calif.: Cummings Publishing, 1975).

appear to be continuing. Whether they will be characteristic of cities of the future, however, is another question. Given the speed at which our cultural institutions are evolving, it is possible that future urban areas will be entirely different, both from those of 5,000 years ago and from the giant metropolises of today.

Summary

1. The state differs from traditional tribal society in that in the former, authority issues from a central office, is asserted impersonally, and is backed up by force. In the latter, by contrast, orderly social relationships derive from obligations one has to his or her relatives.
2. The first civilizations arose in six places in both the Old and New Worlds. These six places —Mesopotamia, Egypt, the Indus Valley, northern China, Mesoamerica, and Peru—were the first states.
3. In the lower half of Mesopotamia, nomadic hunters and gatherers organized the Sumerian civilization between 10,000 and 5000 B.P. Sumerian communities were city-states, each consisting of a large walled city surrounded by villages and hamlets. The new system of social organization led to occupational specialization, a higher standard of living, and the development of writing, mathematics, and astronomy.
4. In Mesoamerica, the first states grew in the valley of Mexico and the Yucatán Peninsula. In Mexico, Teotihuacán flourished between 2300 and 1300 B.P.; at its peak, it had between 85,000 and 200,000 inhabitants and covered 8 square miles. In Guatemala, the Mayan city of Tikal had a population of 15,000 to 20,000. The Mayans also had a system of writing and a complex calendar.

5. The first Chinese civilization also boasted a writing system. The earliest civilization in China is thought to have been the Shang dynasty, which spanned 2050 to 1300 B.P. Individual Shang cities were organized into economic, administrative, and religious networks. Outside the political and ceremonial center were industrial quarters, and beyond these were farming villages. Examples of Shang capitals include Cheng-chou and An-yang.

6. The characteristics of civilization include monumental public works, the development of writing, mathematics, and exact science, long-distance trade, stratified society, full-time occupational specialization, and the emergence of the state as the chief means of political organization to exact taxes, draft labor, and enforce the edicts of the central government.

7. Various theories have been advanced to account for the emergence of civilization. Among these are environmental circumscription, the presence of diverse environments, and the appearance of huge irrigation projects. All of these imply that the early states required organized administration that only a centralized government could provide.

Review Questions

1. What is the difference, from a political point of view, between a state and a tribal society?

2. Compare and contrast the civilizations that arose in Sumer and the valley of Mexico in terms of size, and political, social, and economic organization.

3. List any five of the characteristics of civilization, and give their counterparts in Neolithic communities.

4. The emergence of civilization did away with egalitarian society. Explain the meaning of this statement.

5. In your own words, explain any one of the theories that have been advanced to account for the emergence of the first states.

Suggested Readings

Adams, Robert McC. *The Evolution of Urban Society: Early Mesopotamia and Prehispanic Mexico.* Chicago: Aldine Publishing, 1966.

A fascinating study by an outstanding student of early civilizations, this book compares the first states as they developed in the Old and New Worlds, and finds numerous political, social, ecological, and economic parallels. Adams's point is that civilizations in both areas arose as the result of the same processes.

Chang Kwang-chih. *The Archaeology of Ancient China.* New Haven, Conn.: Yale University Press, 1977.

A comprehensive treatment of the prehistory of this ancient civilization by the leading archeologist in this area.

Culbert, T. P. *The Lost Civilization: The Story of the Classic Maya.* New York: Harper and Row, 1974.

A solid discussion of the classic Mayas, from their beginnings to their collapse, with some interesting hypotheses about the reasons for their fall.

Sabloff, Jeremy, and Lamberg-Karlovsky, C. C., eds. *The Rise and Fall of Civilization: Modern Archaeological Approaches to Current Cultures.* Menlo Park, Calif.: Cummings Publishing, 1974.

A collection of articles by leading anthropologists that deal with the causes of the emergence and decline of civilizations.

PART FOUR

Through the course of their social development, human groups have adapted to a variety of environments, adopting different resources and ways of living in order to survive. People have done more than just "fit in," however. Their history shows that they have been creative, instituting new adaptations, new technologies, and more complex social organizations. From their simple beginnings, human beings have been able to think of new ways of living, changing and expanding their groups over the surface of the earth. We have seen this creative capacity at work in the preceding chapters.

Each development in technology has meant that people have been able not only to control more and more of the environment around them, but often to change it as well. The early hunters who burned the forests of Australia may have changed those areas forever. Since the development of irrigation, people have continued to alter the environment, diverting and damming rivers or fertilizing soils. As the scope of human activities expanded, people have been able to live freer of fear of natural disaster. Clearly, we have not "mastered nature," but the humans of today have seen the creation of resources that our grandparents could not even have imagined.

The expanding use of natural resources has also meant more complex social organization. An example may help us explain why this should be so. During the Middle Ages, the energy for heating and early manufacturing in Europe was derived from wood. As European societies developed better tools and agriculture, trade and population increased. This growth put great demands on the forests. By Elizabethan times, England had an energy crisis in the form of a wood shortage, which threatened to slow shipbuilding, iron working, and other manufacturing. There were threats of layoffs, and wood prices soared.

During the inflationary spiral, Europeans turned to a bad-smelling, smoky mineral which no one wanted to use. This mineral required people to dig for it, and to pump the water that rushed into tunnels as a result of the digging. Moreover, it had to be shipped from its locations throughout Britain because it was not found as commonly as wood. Further, it demanded the research and development of an entirely new manufacturing technology.

As you may have guessed, this mineral was coal, and it formed the basis for the Industrial Revolution. Rather than reducing the work force, the new resource demanded even more labor: miners and excavators; the development of rail and ship transportation; scientists to develop the new ovens; and techniques to vent the damaging coal gases.

And of course, there were also the marketers, managers, and distributors. Nor were these the

Social Adaptation

only effects: lime dried in coal-heated ovens created fertilizers which increased agricultural yields from five- to tenfold. The outcome of the process in England, as in the Agricultural Revolution, was more people tied together in ever expanding relationships.

More and more, people have had to deal not with "nature" but with other people to meet their needs. We go to schools rather than learning "on the job." We buy our food rather than producing or gathering it ourselves. Even though "nature" is still a resource for modern societies, many more people are now able to live and work in ways that have nothing to do with producing food. In a way, culture has become a kind of environment in itself.

Anthropologists have learned much about societies by studying how they have changed. They also learn how human groups survive by examining the interplay among societies and their environments, among individuals in groups, and among different cultural groups. Every society is a structured group of people organized around a technology, using some aspect of its environment to survive. Because this relationship is so basic, anthropologists classify societies in terms of their ecology, their relationship to their environment. Thus, we can talk about groups that simply gather their food, compared to those who raise food. Food raisers can be compared, too, dividing those who use simple tools from those who use irrigation or more complex technologies.

In the chapters that follow we will look at cultural ecology. We will also examine other aspects of the organization of human groups, since that organization is a vital part of survival and adaptation. All societies divide the work to be done; all have rules regulating relationships within the society, and rules for acceptable behavior. Land, water, and other resources usually have to be regulated, which leads us to a consideration of authority. Who has the power in a group? How are decisions made and conflicts resolved? We will also examine trade, markets, and other kinds of exchanges that tie human groups together and help them to survive. Most societies exchange some things with others in some form of trade. This may be of central importance to a society—just as English coal was to much of Europe. Think, for example, how vital oil is to modern industrial nations and how it affects the international political situation, to say nothing of the world economy.

The ways in which these relationships are structured—relations of power, exchange, and production—reveal much of the nature of human cultural groups, and form much of the substance of anthropology. As you read these chapters, you might consider what it means as different cultures and societies are more tightly bound through international trade, technology, and communications. What kinds of innovations and problems would you expect?

Chapter 10

Cultural Ecology

THE NETSILIK ESKIMOS

NATIVE NAME: Netsilingmiut
POPULATION: 259 (150 male, 109 female)
ENVIRONMENT: 30,000 square miles northwest of Hudson's Bay, Canada; barren, rocky coast and tundra habitat with severe Arctic climate
FIELDWORK: Data on the Netsilik Eskimos were collected in the field in 1960 from elderly informants as part of a general reconstruction of traditional Netsilik culture.
ETHNOGRAPHIC PRESENT: Approximately 1910–1930

The Netsilik Eskimos inhabit a vast area over 300 miles in length and over 100 miles in depth north and west of Hudson Bay. The region is barren, covered with innumerable rocky hills, lakes, sea inlets, and vast stretches of flat tundra. The climate is arctic, characterized by extremely cold winters and short cool summers. The local tundra bears no trees and its vegetation consists of creeping shrubs, tufted grasslike plants, lichens, and mosses. When traveling through this cold desert in 1923, Knud Rasmussen counted 259

Source: Adapted from Asen Balikci, "The Netsilik Eskimos: Adaptive Processes," in *Man the Hunter*, ed. Richard B. Lee and Irven DeVore (Chicago: Aldine Publishing, 1968), pp. 78–82. Copyright © 1968 by the Wenner-Gren Foundation for Anthropological Research, Inc. Reprinted by permission of Aldine Publishing Company.

Eskimos of whom 150 were males and only 109 females. They lived a nearly traditional life, having had only minimal contact with Europeans up to that time and having obtained guns only a few years before. The Netsilingmiut ["people who hunt the seal"] hunted the caribou, the musk-ox, and the seal, they fished the salmon trout and, with the exception of some berry picking in August, did no gathering. . . . What were the adaptive processes and survival strategies utilized by the Netsilik Eskimos in this extremely harsh environment? It is assumed here that adaptation can be analyzed at three distinct levels: (1) the technological, (2) the ecological, and (3) the demographic.

TECHNOLOGICAL ADAPTATION

Netsilik technology consists of four major complexes, on the basis of the raw materials utilized: the snow-ice complex (snowhouses, ice-houses, ice-caches, etc.), the skin complex (clothing, kayaks, sledges, tents, etc.), the bone complex (tools and weapons), and the stone complex (cooking utensils). Netsilik technology is thus adaptive in two ways: first, through the ingenious manufacture of a large number of specialized artifacts from a small number of locally available raw materials; and second, in reference to the adaptive features of the finished artifacts related to specific environmental conditions. It is primarily these forms of easily visible technological adaptation that drew the admiration of ethnographers.

ECOLOGICAL ADAPTATION

Order and Predictability in the Annual Round

Among the four ecological processes of adaptation to be considered is the predictability and order implicit in the annual migration circuit. . . . In winter, after the caribou had left the country, the Netsilingmiut had to rely almost exclusively on the seal for survival. Since the seal keeps open a large number of breathing holes, it was advantageous to have numerous hunters, with harpoons in hand, to control an equal number of holes. Large hunting parties had maximal chances for a speedy catch. Hence the rationale for extended igloo communities consisting of over sixty people and comprising several distantly related extended families. Winter was the season of intense social life, spectacular shamanizing and other ceremonial activity. . . .

Early in June when the seals came lying on the ice, the large winter camp broke up into smaller social units having usually an extended family as a core. Tents were set up on the shore and group sealing continued at the large breathing holes. In July, the restricted groups moved inland, fishing with the fishing harpoon and occasionally hunting caribou with the bow and arrow. After the first week of August, the stone weirs [fences or dams] were built across rivers and the salmon trout running upstream were caught in large amounts with leisters. At the end of August began the vitally important caribou hunts from kayaks at the caribou crossing place. This was a collaborative activity involving a division of tasks between beaters and spearers. Early in October the restricted groups moved camp to some larger river and fished salmon trout with leisters [spears] through the thin river ice. As winter came on the larger groups re-formed for sealing through the breathing holes.

During spring, summer, and autumn the restricted social units were isolated in the tundra and social life was markedly less intense. . . . There is thus a clear correlation between the movements of society and the known distribution of game. . . . It clearly indicates an adaptive pattern, the migrating groups taking advantage of particular game concentrations through the different seasons.

Alternatives and Substitutions in Subsistence Strategy

The endless search for alternatives, the practices of substitution and *ad hoc* inventiveness constitute another class of adaptive strategies. Each seasonal hunt knows of some alternative. If the fall caribou hunts with spears from kayaks failed, the bow and arrow was used. In winter, musk-ox hunting could be substituted for sealing. In summer, if fishing with the leister was unrewarding, the fishing harpoon or the sleeping hooks were employed. There always seems to have been a way out of a difficult situation. The alert hunter had to take advantage of any changes in game availability and specific local conditions such as wind direction and topography and adapt his hunting strategy with ingenuity. In hunting, no conditions are static and quick *ad hoc* decisions were necessary.

Flexibility of Group Structure

Constantly changing opportunities and pressures favored flexibility in residence and determined temporary fission of co-residential groups. At all seasons the co-residential groups functioned as production and distribution units, yet in various stress situations the community would split, separating extended families. Or a nuclear family would go on extensive fishing or trading trips. Or two brothers would hunt temporarily in different areas and thus maximize game returns, the possible failure of the first being compensated for by the success of the second. Later the original group would reassemble. . .

Sharing

Delayed consumption involving elaborate caching techniques [hiding and storing of food] and various sharing patterns equalized food distribution both through time and within the community. Sharing patterns ranged from informal gift giving and occasional or regular commensality [sharing of meals] to rigidly structured, community-wide division of seal meat. . . . An unlucky hunter was always certain by right to obtain a portion of the daily catch secured by any one of his partners. . . . Clearly such a system is adaptive. Camp fellows share together or starve together.

The adaptive processes described here can be best understood in relation to the almost continuous ecological pressure to which the Netsilik were subjected. Traveling and moving camps was a very arduous task. Lack of dog feed severely limited the keeping of dogs to only one or two per family. The heavy sledges had to be pulled or pushed by both men and women. Only very small children were allowed to sit on the sledge. Old people had to drag themselves behind, and were often left behind to sleep on the ice if they had not caught up with the others. Seal hunting involved a motionless watch on the flat ice under intense cold maintained for many hours. In order to build the stone weir, the stones had to be carried in the ice-cold water for several days. Beating the fast-running caribou over great distances in the tundra was an exhausting task. Stalking the caribou with the bow and arrow also involved endless pursuits across the tundra, the hunters lying on the wet grass and trying to approach the game while hiding behind tufts of moss. The nomadism of the hunting life in this extremely rigorous climate imposed a constant strain on the humans. Hunting was a never-ceasing pursuit, the game had to be brought to camp at all cost, and the hunter had to stay out until a successful kill: "The man that is wise never lolls about idle when the weather is good; he can never know when bad days may eat up his meat caches and drive him and his family into starvation." . . . At a camp of Kugguppamiut, Rasmussen observed that for the whole of the winter twelve hunters caught about 150 seals: "this may well be said to have been dearly bought food."

DEMOGRAPHIC ADAPTATION

Such continuous pressures and hardships necessitated internal, demographic [population] controls. The most rigorous was female infanticide. . . . On King William Island, Rasmussen counted 38 girls killed out of 96 births, in a genealogical sample of eighteen marriages. He concluded: "Despite the high birth rate the tribe is moving towards extinction if girl children are to be constantly suppressed.". . . The Netsilingmiut considered life as harsh and short, and girls were thought to be less productive than boys who were the future hunters. An informant said to Rasmussen, "Parents often consider that they cannot afford to waste several years nursing a girl. We get old so quickly and so we must be quick and get a son." . . . In the same context, a Pelly Bay Eskimo pointed to his dog team and added, "Bitches simply don't pull as hard as the dogs do." This high rate of female infanticide generated the sex imbalance noted by Rasmussen and resulted in great difficulties in finding a wife. So anxious were the parents to secure future wives for their little boys that they betrothed them to any one of their female cousins. . . . Cousins, both cross and parallel, were preferred because the parents of the promised couple were closely related, trusted each other, and kept their word; their children thus had maximal chances to become husband and wife. Furthermore, suicide in crisis situations, invalidicide and senilicide were additional responses to harsh pressures. . . . We may consider these forms of demographic controls as adaptive, in the sense that unproductive members of society were eliminated, the size of the family adjusted to the capacity of the provider, and the survival chances of future hunters were maximized.[1]

● ● ● ● ● ● ● ●

Members of all societies, even those people in very complex ones, interact with the environment to "make a living," but they do so in different ways. *Cultural ecology* is the study of the ways in which different human groups interact with their environment to survive, to change—or *not* to survive as groups. The process of interaction between human groups and their environment is called *adaptation*. Adaptation is a two-way process: a group may

1. From Asen Balikci, "The Netsilik Eskimos: Adaptive Processes," in *Man the Hunter*, ed. Richard B. Lee and Irven DeVore (Chicago: Aldine Publishing, 1968), pp. 78–82.

change its strategies or tools in order to make better use of a particular environment, it may use new elements in that environment, or it may move into a different environment altogether. On the other hand, groups may interact with the environment to change it. Thus, cultural ecologists study the effect that human groups have on their environment as well as the way in which groups adapt to an environment.

Because the environment poses the problems with which human groups have to deal in order to survive, we find the thread of adaptation running through much of the fabric of human history. Because human life is social—dependent on relations with the other people in a group—cultural ecologists take the social group as a whole as the *unit of adaptation*. This may be a small group, as in the case of the Eskimos, or it may be a large and developed society such as the Kpelle, whom we will discuss later on in this chapter.

Adaptation and Cultural Ecology

Cultural ecology is a part of the larger subdiscipline of cultural anthropology, but some of its basic ideas are drawn from the life sciences rather than from the traditional social sciences. Since the late nineteenth century, biologists have been concerned with how each species adapts to the environment and how each relates to other groups in the environment. However, when a social scientist investigates these same questions with respect to human populations and human culture, the study is called cultural ecology. The cultural ecologist is often concerned with the same basic information as any other cultural anthropologist: agricultural and hunting tech-

niques, kinship groupings, patterns of settlement, puberty rites, and child-rearing techniques, for example. But the cultural ecologist asks other kinds of questions as well: How do the cultural forms help a society adapt to the quality and availability of natural resources in the environment? How does the society interact with other human groups? The ecologist might also ask whether these cultural forms hinder the society from using or developing resources, or make it difficult for the people of a group to make changes in their way of life without great suffering.[2] These last questions are more and more important as the last small-scale, closed societies come into contact with the industrialized nations.

The Rise of Cultural Ecology

The easy equation of climate with personality and culture has been a popular means of explaining human behavior for a long time, long before anthropologists began to explore just what that relationship might be. For example, the Greek philosopher Aristotle, some centuries before Christ, wrote that the inhabitants of the colder northern countries were "braver, but deficient in thought and technology." As a result, these northerners were not easily conquered by outsiders, but by the same token they were "wanting in political organization and unable to rule their neighbors." President John F. Kennedy described Washington, D.C. as a "city of Southern efficiency and Northern charm," making a joke out of our popular stereo-

---

2. John Adair and Evon Vogt, "Navajo and Zuñi Veterans: A Study of Contrasting Modes of Culture Change," *American Anthropologist* 51 (October–December 1949) : 547–560.

types. Many people are still likely to equate the northern climates with "cool," "efficient" management and the warmer climates with laziness and disorganization.

This simplistic *environmental determinism* has been very appealing—and not only to those looking for an intellectual shortcut. The idea of a direct, causal relationship between environment and culture is found in the work of many important ethnologists at the turn of the last century. Typically, the anthropologists of that period thought that nonliterate, small-scale societies represented lower, primitive forms of human society. As followers of Darwin, they believed that not only the species developed from the simple to the complex, but cultures progressed according to the same pattern. They adduced from European and Latin mythology, and from scanty ethnographic evidence, that "simple" (nonliterate, small-scale) societies would evolve into something like the industrialized societies of Western Europe. Since "primitive" societies were found in such climatically exotic areas as Borneo, Central Africa, and the Caribbean, it followed that the climates of these areas were not favorable for progress.

The hypotheses of the early evolutionists were, of course, toppled by the anthropological studies of the twentieth century. We know now that there have been highly developed civilizations in such places as Mexico, Peru, Cambodia, and Western Africa, the regions that were once described as "unfavorable for civilization." We also know that the relationship between environment and culture is a very complex one, even in the simplest cases.

ENVIRONMENTAL POSSIBILISM.

Many modern anthropologists now view all cultures as adaptive schemes, systems that provide human cultural groups with varying amounts of energy—that require more or less effort on the part of the groups. When anthropologists abandoned the attempt to find simple, one-to-one explanations for the relationship between humans and their environments, they turned to a position that might be called *environmental possibilism*.[3] In other words, they argue that while the environment does not actually determine what a human group does to survive, it does pose limiting conditions, or conditions for possible growth. On the other hand, they recognize that what must be examined is the technology and the social groupings that are the means by which cultural groups actually exploit the environment. Within those limits, there are alternatives in the forms of cultural adaptation.

The Netsilik Eskimos described in the capsule ethnography are a good example. To cope with the hardships of the Arctic environment, the Netsilik had to adapt in certain specific ways: they had to hunt large game, because vegetable and other foods were scarce at best; and they had to hunt well, because opportunities for a kill were not frequent. They needed to develop hunting and traveling techniques suited to the freezing cold of most of the year. For materials they were forced to use the few raw materials available: stone, bone, skin, ice, and snow. In other areas of life, however, the Netsilik had more freedom to choose what they would do. In their social organization, their arts, in how they related to others by sharing food, shelter, and companionship, their choices were not so completely determined by the environment.

---

3. Franz Boas, *Race, Language and Culture* (New York: Free Press, 1966), pp. 281–294.

These grass houses come from widely differing cultures. The long low houses are Hawaiian; the sharply pointed conical houses are built by the people of Bobo Dioulasso in Upper Volta; and the rounded cone belongs to Peruvian peasants. But the similarities, based on similarity of climate and available building materials, are as striking as the differences.

Even under the harsh Arctic conditions, a great deal of Netsilik culture can be explained by choices the Netsilik made.

In the present period, groups like the Netsilik can choose to adopt new technologies which enable them to survive more effectively in the same environment—such as the rifle and the snowmobile. These new technologies, however, are part of a whole network of social relationships, and also may make unexpected changes in the ecology of the group, the most dramatic being, for example, the rapid depletion of the traditional food supply. Different cultural alternatives carry different effects with them. Environmental possibilism suggests

Chapter Ten

to us that when we know only about the environment, there is no sure way to predict which adaptive alternatives a group will choose.

Culture as Environment

How is culture related to the environment? Part of the answer, as suggested by recent anthropologists, is to see culture as a kind of environment, one made by humans. Some social scientists have thought of it as "artificial," or somehow less "natural" than the environments of other species. This is a point to consider further. All species, human and nonhuman, survive by exploiting some sector of the environment. They also play a part in the forming of that environment. For example, many plant species depend on the activities of some insects in order to survive. Other insects, and some grass-eating animals, may cause important defoliation (damage to the grass cover and vegetation). All the cultural forms and resources used by humans are, of course, derived from the environment, just as are those used by other species; so they must be "natural" in some way. What distinguishes the activity of humans

from other species is that the human interaction with nature is buffered, or mediated, by culture and social organization.

Unlike most other species, humans do not have to rely on biological mutations to change the way they use resources. People can deliberately change their behavior to meet new situations or to make better use of present ones. Of course, cultures are not changed easily. We know that people usually are not willing to change the way they

Cultural Ecology

live, especially if they feel that they are living well. But if there is a change in the environment, or competition from another group, then the traditional beliefs and activities may not work as well as before in the opinions of the people involved. At that point, people may consider alternative activities and explanations for their situation.

Because people rely on their culture as a means of survival, the culture becomes the environment, in a way, for the members of a group. The culture acts as an arena where people are born and grow, where they cope with problems and live out their lives. So, although cultures are constructed to deal with the environment in the course of day-to-day life, most people find themselves faced with demands and problems which are social in nature, such as how to get good medical advice, how to find a job, or even how to keep from offending your mother-in-law.

Variability of Adaptations

Although cultures are not easily changed, they must be adapted to variations in climate and geography—and to the changes that people make in the environment, as well. Some areas of the world, such as the arid areas where the Bushmen of Africa or the aborigines of Australia live, permit only a shifting way of life for a small group. With a limited technology, many of the activities of these peoples are involved solely with food-getting. Other areas of the world are easier to work in because of better climate and soil conditions. In these areas, even peoples with limited technology can gather more food, and some plant gardens to produce their food supply. High altitudes can also play a role in cultural adaptation, since many plants do not grow in high places and there is a short growing season. It is not accidental that people who

live off flocks of animals, *pastoralists*, often live in mountainous areas where other ways of living are not successful. Thus, the climate and land forms of an area pose problems to which the people of the area adapt in a variety of ways. How people actually deal with problems of the environment depends at least in part on the technology available to them.

Some of the environmental problems people face are actually created by humans in the process of food-getting. Anthropologists now believe, for example, that the practice of the North American Plains Indians of setting fires to the prairies (to drive and trap game) also drove back the forests in North America.[4] It appears that the Australian Bushmen had a similar practice, with similar results: the reduction of the rain forests of northeastern Australia.[5] Some anthropologists believe that the Bushmen killed off the Pleistocene kangaroo; the bison became extinct west of the Rockies by 1830, because of the hunting activities of the Indians there. More and more, researchers are exploring the cumulative effects of human activity on the environment.

New cultural forms have developed through human history which include the development of new technologies for a greater mastery of the environment. Long before the beginnings of village farming

4. O. C. Stewart, "Fire as the First Great Force Employed by Man," in *Man's Role in Changing the Face of the Earth*, ed. W. L. Thomas, Jr. (Chicago: University of Chicago Press, 1971).

5. L. R. Hiatt, "Ownership and Use of Land among the Australian Aborigines," in *Man the Hunter*, ed. Richard Lee and Irven DeVore (Chicago: Aldine Publishing, 1968).

lenges from the environment. Their different strategies for survival form the basis for the rest of this chapter.

Culture-Subsistence Types

In order to survive, humans have interacted with their environment to obtain food, tools, and shelter. Because food-getting plays a central role in the activities of humans, anthropologists have classified different human groups as *culture-subsistence types*. Each type is an adaptive strategy, a pattern of "doing business" with certain kinds of tools in order to survive. That is, the cultural types refer to patterns of technology and the way social groups are organized to interact with the environment. Cultural ecologists emphasize the relation between a group's technology and the environment in which the technology functions. These techniques and work patterns, often referred to simply as the modes of production, play a large part in shaping social relations, determining the size of the

One of these scenes is from Bolivia, the other from Nigeria: the life of a herdsman is much the same in the two cultures.

some ten thousand years ago, people found different strategies for dealing with the environment—and for dealing with the changes people have made in that environment. Today, for the remaining nonliterate societies, there is the decision whether or not to adopt new technologies for dealing with their environment. This is a decision that brings many changes, some unexpected. For the industrialized nations, there is the necessity to deal with the changes humans have made: the "ecology crisis." Human beings have always faced chal-

group, certain aspects of religion, art, and myth, and many other aspects of culture.

The principal culture-subsistence types are the hunter-gatherer, horticultural, pastoral, agricultural, and industrial; we will discuss all but the last of these. The anthropologist's interest in the industrial type of adaptation is limited, by and large, to the impact and consequences of industrial society on small-scale cultures. Some of these implications will be discussed in Chapters 11, 18, and 20. As we compare these different cultural types, several points will become clearer.

First, there are variations in the efficiency with which humans utilize the environment. That is, some ways of getting food require a large proportion of all the energy that a group produces. Other ways of food-getting produce more food, so that energy is left over, or free for other purposes. A given type of food provides its users with a certain amount of energy, which can be measured. Measured against the energy they provide, some food sources require or yield much more energy than others. Some groups must work all day to produce their food; others can produce much more in the same or less time. The difference in efficiency depends primarily on the development and the reliability of the group's food-getting technology. Studies by Marvin Harris and others show that cultures varied in food-getting efficiency from 9 on Harris's scale for the African Bushmen to 210 for the American farmer.[6]

Second, the more efficient cultures are more complex. The efficient culture is likely to use more—and more complex—technology. This requires more people in different activities. Because they have more sophisticated technology, these groups have a greater range of adaptive strategies. The relationship of the individuals to the natural environment is less direct; many people may not interact with it directly at all. At the same time, the relations among different cultural institutions become more complex as well.

Third, in almost every part of the world there is more than one alternative strategy for utilizing the environment, although strategies, such as those of fertilizer and machine agriculture, may be more efficient in terms of energy input to yield than others. Alternatives have generally developed over a long period of time, but not all societies have used each strategy. Rather, strategies have diffused by means of contact between groups, just as they are diffusing today.

Finally, there is no set evolutionary sequence for stages in food-getting, nor does every environment lend itself to every food-getting strategy. A technologically more efficient culture may mean a better adaptation to the environment. It does not, however, imply that the quality of life for the individual is superior. Loving relationships, the greatest possibility for fulfilling human potential, a stable, predictable social environment, and other cultural goals can be met as well—if not better—in a small-scale society as in a large, complex one. Who is to say that the life of a Zuñi or a Jívaro is any less rich or less rewarding than that of a corporation executive?

---

6. Marvin Harris, *Culture, Man and Nature* (New York: Thomas Y. Crowell, 1971), pp. 200–216.

Hunting-Gathering

For the many thousands of years before the development of agriculture 10,000 years ago, humans gathered wild plants to survive and fished and hunted the animals in their habitats. Survival of *Homo sapiens* depended on the ability of each of the small groups that lived widely scattered over most areas of the world to feed themselves. They lived in all kinds of environments, some being very abundant. Today, only a few groups live by hunting and gathering, and these live in marginal areas which agriculturalists do not exploit. Human groups that depend on naturally occurring animal and plant food sources, without any attempt to manipulate or replace such sources, are called *hunter-gatherers*. Those who rely almost exclusively on plant food are called *foragers*. Such groups, often organized into *bands*, or small groups of related families, have been the traditional subject of ethnological studies.

Among the Netsilik Eskimos, it is easy to see how the environment imposes demands and choices for survival on the human group. "Netsilik" is an adaptation of the Eskimo *Netsilingmiut*, "people who hunt the seal," and most of the striking features of Netsilik life, such as their seasonal migrations, their skill at hunting, and their willingness to share resources within the group, relate directly to environmental pressure. The Netsilik represented the hunting society in an almost pure form, but few human groups rely so completely on animal species for their food. Most groups of this type survive by some hunting (engaged in by the men), which generally supplements a diet of plant products gathered by the women, who may make the major contribution to the caloric intake of the group. The Bushmen are an example of this type of adaptation. In foraging groups, on the other hand, both men and women gather roots, berries, nuts, and even insects which

the group may depend on. The Shoshones of the Great Basin in the American West are an example of a foraging group.[7]

In her study of the !Kung Bushmen of the Kalahari Desert, Lorna Marshall found that hunting provided valuable protein, but roots and other food gathered by the group provided most of their diet.[8] This is true for those few other groups which rely on hunting and gathering today, such as the Tasaday of the Philippines or the Ngatatjara of Western Australia. Marshall's study of the !Kung indicated that surprisingly little effort is necessary for the group to maintain itself: men and women spent no more than three days a week in getting food. In most cases, however, the work of subsistence is much more difficult. The ways of life of these diverse groups have certain features in common. These features reflect their general level of technology and the environments in which they live.

TECHNOLOGY. One important factor affecting subsistence is the level of technology. Hunting-gathering societies are defined by the limited technology they have

---

7. Julian H. Steward, *Basin Plateau Aboriginal Socio-Political Groups*, Bureau of American Ethnology Bulletin no. 120 (Washington, D.C.: Smithsonian Institution, 1938), pp. 21–32.

---

8. Lorna Marshall, "The !Kung Bushmen of the Kalahari Desert," in *Peoples of Africa*, ed. James L. Gibbs, Jr. (New York: Holt, Rinehart and Winston, 1965).

Because of the difference in climate, these two hunting groups (Eskimos and Australian aborigines) are dressed very differently, but the technology of these hunting cultures shows striking parallels.

available to exploit the environment. These groups make their living by using the raw materials that are at hand. Raw materials such as stone, wood, or skins are used to produce weapons, tools, storage containers, shelters, and other possessions.

Not surprisingly, the "tool kits" of hunter-gatherers are few. The !Kung, for example, carry with them a bow and arrows for men, a digging stick for women, carried in leather bags called *kaross*. Tools and shelters can be made on the spot. The clothing of the Shoshones of the Great Basin was of bark and they wore very little: an apron for women and a type of loin cloth for men, and sandals or pitch smeared on the feet. They made temporary shelters with brush, since they moved frequently. Food, consisting largely of wild seeds, was winnowed and stored and carried in baskets. Indeed, most of their material goods could come under the heading of basketry, even the women's hats.

Among the Sirionó of Bolivia, material possessions reach what might be a record low. Simple baskets and clay pots are made and used; simple hunting and collecting tools are made, as are hammocks. The Sirionó must carry fire with them, because they cannot make it. They have little else. Other gatherers such as the Ituri Pygmies trade with neighbors of more advanced technology for steel blades, axes, and knives. However, their material possessions remain simple.

Because these groups rely on what they can make or gather directly from the environment, they are forced to move frequently to take advantage of available food sources. Since they carry with them what they use, possessions are kept to a minimum as they travel with the seasons or in search for new food sources.

POPULATION AND DEMOGRAPHY. Hunter-gatherers generally live in small

groups because the number of people in an area is limited by the natural resources of the area and the group's technology. The important feature to consider is the technology available to a people to cope with a particular environment. In the case of the Netsilik, there was a direct relationship, for example, between the number of seals in an area, as indicated by the number of breathing holes in the ice, and the size, structure, and movement of human groups. The Netsilik came together in large numbers when resources were abundant and many hands were needed for subsistence activities. Later, when large game became scarce, smaller groups formed and went their separate ways. Studies of the Nye Nye, another tribe of the Kalahari, indicate that their seasonal migrations are likewise based on predictable changes in the natural resource base—water and game. Thus, in hunter-gatherer groups the upper limit of the population will be determined by the food and water available in an area. In addition, seasonal and other variations in the food supply will result in changes in the structure of hunting and gathering groups, to maximize the chances for survival.

These processes of coming together and splitting up of groups are called *fusion* and *fission*. Generally, fissioning is a characteristic of societies of low levels of technology because each small group is relatively self-sufficient and can assume for itself all the functions of the larger group. Many hunting-gathering groups, such as the Ituri Pygmies and the Cheyenne of the Great Plains, show patterns of fusion and fission. The Cheyenne and other Plains Indians would split into bands of related families for the harsh winters, when food was scarce. In spring and summer, the bands would come together as a tribe when the buffalo formed into great herds. Then they could hunt cooperatively and have sufficient food to stay together and put on their great tribal ceremonies.[9]

SOCIAL RELATIONS. Hunter-gatherer groups are relatively uncomplicated in structure. They are based, usually, on monogamous families, with a division of labor between husband and wife, man and woman. Food is shared between the spouses, both of whom make food contributions to the family. In addition, food is shared within the group, which is usually made up of several related families—for instance, several brothers and their families, and an aged parent or two. The exchange of support, protection, and food is called *reciprocation*. Families within the group exchange food, protect one another, and help in sharing the responsibilities of child care. This sort of systematic interdependence between members of related families is part of *kinship*. (See Chapter 13 for a full discussion of kinship ties.) Kinship, with its ties of responsibilities and privileges, is the main form of social ordering in hunting and gathering groups.

Leadership in these groups is generally situational. That is, an individual who has superior skill at a particular task, such as butchering, divining, stalking large game, or preparing food, assumes leadership for the duration of that task. As other phases of an activity are carried out, other leaders may emerge. No permanent leader has the authority over the group in all situations. Thus, hunter-gatherer groups are usually described as *egalitarian* in their institutions. Egalitarianism also extends

9. E. Adamson Hoebel, *The Cheyennes: Indians of the Great Plains* (New York: Holt, Rinehart and Winston, 1960).

across sex lines in gathering groups. Women do a great deal, if not most, of the food-getting, and make a major contribution to group survival. Probably as a result, there tends to be more social equality in these groups. The position of women in more complex societies is determined in a somewhat different way, as we will see, since they may play a less direct role in food production in other forms of cultural adaptation.

Horticulture

Horticulture, literally "hoe culture," refers to farming carried out with simple tools and techniques. The crops cultivated may include such root crops as manioc, taro, and yams, as well as greens, rice, maize, palms, and other tree foods. Usually only small amounts of land are worked at one time, using hand tools. Plows, draft animals, and irrigation systems are lacking. A common form of horticulture is *swidden* or *slash-and-burn* subsistence. To start a new garden, a new or fallow area is cut down, or the existing trees are killed by girdling them (cutting around the bark so that the tree dies). The trees and vegetation are then burned, after which the land is planted and tended with hoes or digging sticks. Such fields are worked for only a few seasons, and then left for a period of time, which may range from about five to fifty years.

The human population has lived for most of its history in small groups which were well distributed over the earth at the end of the Pleistocene Age.[10] At around this time, some 10,000 to 12,000 years ago, the climate began to change. The ice

---

10. Edward S. Deevey, Jr., "The Human Population," *Scientific American* 203, no. 3 (September 1960) : 194–204.

sheets that had covered large areas of the earth and had controlled the climate of much of what is now Europe and the Soviet Union were melting away, causing the seas to rise and flood what had been rich areas. As the ice receded, the large Pleistocene mammals, such as the mammoth tiger and wooly rhinoceros, became scarce and died out. Barren plains and grasslands gave way to dense forests where different hunting techniques were required. The human population of that period, which had been growing slowly, but still growing, faced a different sort of "ecology crisis." Some of the human groups of that time probably followed the retreat of the cold-climate game animals into new regions. Others probably began to forage in different ways.

Around 8000 B.C., in at least several areas of the world—in the Near East, the Tehuacán Valley of Mexico, and in Southeast Asia—people began to plant certain food which had been in their environments, discovering that they could control the vegetation they depended on by planting seeds. In the Middle East, people apparently collected certain grains, mainly wheat and barley, especially those varieties that did not lose their seeds to the winds. These plants, which might have died out if left alone, were those cultivated in the area above the Fertile Crescent—because they were more appropriate for human collection. In this way, some domesticated species were created by human use.

During the same period, however, hunting and gathering activities continued to be important sources of food. Of course, all of these early horticulturists were not alike, any more than they are today. Nor can we know how similar modern horticulturists are to those of the past. Some of

These South American farmers still do most of their agricultural work with hand tools.

the early groups gave rise to great civilizations, whereas others had different histories. At best we can compare tools and the size of the settlements of both.

TECHNOLOGY AND POPULATION. Human groups that practice horticulture have greater control over their food supply than those who only hunt and gather. It might seem that there is more variation in the yields of horticulturists because of changes in weather, but these farmers can produce more food than can the gatherers. And gatherers, too, are always at the mercy of the weather. Horticultural groups are less mobile as well. They can support greater numbers of people at greater densities of population. This creates the potential for new forms of social organization and a new perspective on the individual man or woman's relation to the environment.

Compared to that of modern agriculture, horticultural production is low. In addition, it has its own effects on the environment. We have already seen that the practice by some hunters and gatherers of burning the brush and grasses where they live has had the effect of driving back the forests in North America and Australia. Slash-and-burn horticulture for a time exhausts the fertility of the soil in the plots that are cleared in this way.[11] This forces many horticulturists to move their settlements to new areas. Some anthropologists also suggest that horticulturists move their plots because it is more difficult to clear the growth of weeds from a plot than it is to clear a new one. In any case, these plots change the character of the growth in the areas worked.

Differences among Horticulturists

As with gatherers, because of their limited technological mastery of the environment, the level of living of horticulturists is greatly affected by variations in the environment. Since they cannot break hard soil, irrigate in times of drought, or fertilize their plots, horticulturists vary a good deal in the amounts of food they can produce. Depending on the growing potential of the natural environment, a horticultural group may produce barely enough to survive, or it may generate a surplus. Anthropologists distinguish between two types of horticultural societies: those societies termed *subsistence*, as, for example, the Jívaro, and *surplus* horticultural groups,

such as the Kpelle. The Jívaro raise just enough to meet their own needs; the Kpelle are able to create a surplus. Both are discussed below.

The Jívaro (see capsule ethnography, Chapter 13) are a horticultural group of about 8,000, living in small village groups in the rain forests on the eastern slopes of the Andes.[12] They depend on crops which they grow in plots cleared by the slash-and-burn method. Undergrowth is cut away; trees are girdled and felled. When dry, the plot is burned. Men clear the garden, but women do the cultivation. The Jívaro depend primarily on manioc tubers that are made into flour and beer. The ground is worked with digging sticks and used for a short time until the soil is exhausted. Then the group must move plots and village to a new site. Hunting and fishing are the work of men and form an important part of the food supply. Monkeys and birds are hunted with blowguns and darts; fish may be poisoned in pools. Today, the Jívaro trade with neighbors for machetes, axes, and guns, but continue to live in a relatively self-sufficient fashion.

The Jívaro live in long houses, each about 75 feet long and 40 feet wide, with parallel sides and rounded ends.[13] In each house there is a family group of men, all of whom are related to each other through male relatives, and their families. Each

11. Robert Carneiro, "Slash and Burn Cultivation among the Kuikuru and Its Implications for Cultural Development in the Amazon Basin," in *Man in Adaptation: The Cultural Present*, ed. Yehudi Cohen (Chicago: Aldine Publishing, 1968), pp. 131–145.

12. Michael J. Harner, *The Jívaro* (Garden City, N.Y.: Doubleday, Anchor Books, 1973).

13. M. W. Stirling, *Historical and Ethnographical Materials on the Jívaro Indians*, Bureau of American Ethnology Bulletin no. 117 (Washington, D.C.: Smithsonian Institution, 1938), p. 38.

house is an independent unit, subservient to no one. The houses are made of laths of palm or bamboo, tied to a frame, with a thatched roof. The doors at each end are of heavy planks, and can be barred from inside. The houses are divided inside, half for men and half for women, with each man having a sleeping platform on one side and each woman on the other. There are no other family divisions in the house and no other forms of social organization beyond the household. Occasionally, in times of war, five or six households become allies under a common war leader, but there are few other social distinctions or organizations.

The Kpelle are another horticultural society, of about 86,000 people.[14] Their level of living and organization is quite different from that of the Jívaro, although their tools are similar. They live in areas of bush country and forest in central and western Liberia. The Kpelle raise rice for subsistence and for sale. Manioc is also raised. Men and women together clear the growth from the land and burn it, using the ashes as fertilizer. Women do a great deal of the farming, and may have rice fields of their own. They also grow other crops such as vegetables and peanuts for cash. There is little hunting, although the women do a little fishing. Few Kpelle keep livestock. It is a wealthy man who has cattle or numbers of goats or sheep.

Kpelle agriculture is so productive that many individuals have part-time specialties in addition to farming. Men may be medicine men or blacksmiths. Some cut timber or make clothing. A few operate small shops or cafes. The Kpelle generally dislike working in mines or on the rubber plantations, although a few do so. Women may become midwives, and many engage in small-scale trade of garden crops or prepared foods. The blacksmith is a man of high status, making tools and implements for the important secret societies. The Kpelle use many resources: iron, clay, wood, and raffia. They make baskets, furniture, musical instruments, cloth (for which they grow the cotton), jewelry, and ceremonial items.

Unlike the Jívaro or the gathering groups, the Kpelle are organized into towns, divided into *quarters* which are social entities and which are said to belong to a "family," although it is a loose grouping at best. The quarter "owns" the land and distributes it to members of the "family." It is also the unit of tax collection and labor recruitment. Above the officials of the quarters are those of the districts, with the *paramount chief* above them. There are several paramount chiefs, all of equal status, each heading an administrative district in the provinces of Liberia. The paramount chiefs are now salaried officials of the government as well. Political authority is reinforced by the tribal fraternities, the Poro for men and the Sande for women, which include all individuals and exercise considerable authority over them. There are other societies as well, with different functions.

Unlike gatherers of the Jívaro, the Kpelle consider the polygynous family—the man with many wives—as the ideal type. Because women are important sources of wealth in produce and in children, as well as in their lovers, from whom the husband can collect regular adultery fees as a source of income, the acquisition of wives is an important way to amass

14. James L. Gibbs, Jr., ed., *Peoples of Africa* (New York: Holt, Rinehart and Winston, 1965), pp. 197–240.

wealth and prestige. Forms of marriage vary. A man may secure rights over a woman with bridewealth or by working for the bride's father. A poor man may offer himself as a client to a rich man in order to acquire sexual rights to a woman, since the man of many wives allows a man to live with one wife. The client, in turn, works for the husband, who has rights over any children born. Women may live with men without marriage for a trial period. Divorce is relatively common, and women find it easy to make other marriages, since a hard-working woman is an asset.

Although women are given no formal authority in the system of administration and courts, their importance is underscored in that the woman keeps the key to the granary and distributes the rice; the women's society shares ritual authority with that of the men, alternating the periods of ritual control. There are differentiations among families of wealth, well-being, and status. Differences are not based on birth or family distinctions, but on how well a man manages his marriages and client relationships through his wives.

SOCIAL FORMS. As we have seen, the levels of living of horticulturists may vary a good deal. With the production of surplus food, the control or disposition of the surplus may be translated into social power or authority and prestige. The result is that the first forms of social divisions by prestige appear in horticultural groups. Horticulturists who produce a surplus may develop crops specifically for trade. A trade network may eventually fall under the control of individuals who manipulate surplus into permanent rank and power for themselves and their kinsmen.

In areas where the accumulation of surplus is difficult for environmental reasons, there may be high competition for resources. Therefore, some groups of subsistence horticulturists tend to organize in social units that are based on kin groups. These are often dominated by men, who see their main role to be the defense of their existing territory, as well as the acquisition of more desirable territory for planting and growing. With groups in more lush environments, such as that of the Kpelle, the abundance of land and ease of production usually foster more cooperative planting and harvesting strategies. Among the Kpelle, this takes the form of the voluntary work groups, formed by both men and women, friends and family, who exchange labor on each other's lands.

The simplest forms of village organization are found in horticultural groups. They have a more fixed relation to the land than do foragers, but they rarely have a developed concept of private land ownership. Most commonly, land and crops are regarded as belonging to the group—the family, village, or some other kind of enlarged kin group. As with the Kpelle, or the people of Truk, land is granted to an individual to use, but it is not granted outright.

The personal property of most horticulturists is modest by our standards, although it is clear that the property of a Kpelle farmer would outstrip that of a Jívaro. Generally, the individual in a horticultural society has more material possessions which are thought to be his personal property than a person from a hunting-gathering group. Even so, there are clear limitations on the right to exclusive ownership. A Trukese, for example, is expected to share digging sticks, hoes, canoes, or nets with any closely related person who needs them, although the owner has first claim to their use. A similar reciprocal borrowing right is found in most horticultural groups, in which there is a high degree of interdependence and in which most people are engaged in similar or identical subsistence work.

As we have seen from the populations of the Kpelle, horticulture may support much larger numbers of individuals than hunting and gathering. The numbers are related to the productivity of the environment, although there are other considerations as well, such as fluctuations in growing conditions.

SURPLUS. Anthropologists have puzzled for some years over why some societies can produce a surplus and do not do so,[15] and why some groups who do produce surplus food do not develop more complex forms of social organization. Some researchers suggest that an important consideration is whether or not a society feels it is necessary to produce more than it needs for immediate use. One anthropologist argues that in the case of the Kuikuru, there was no compelling reason for them to grow more than they used, so they did not.[16] Robert M. Adams and other archeologists point out that evidence seems to indicate that the priests of Mesopotamia were able to command the production of the workers in order to produce a surplus, and used it for such social projects as irrigation systems.[17] Anthropologists also theorize that a people may produce a surplus if there are opportunities for exchanges or trade with other groups in order to obtain items of value they could not produce themselves.[18] Trade might also encourage the rise of leaders to organize the exchanges. And finally, some researchers have suggested that cultures may not develop a surplus unless they have to—that is, unless there are either shortages or an increase in population pressure on traditional resources. Or a group may be forced to produce a surplus by political or military pressures from other groups.

Pastoralism

In marginal environments—that is, in places with a low potential for food production—*pastoralism*, or nomadic herding, may be adopted as an alternative to horticulture. Pastoralists are basically dependent on large herds of domesticated or semidomesticated grazing animals, usually cattle, sheep, goats, or—among the Lapps of northern Scandinavia—reindeer. To raise and maintain large herds of animals, little is needed in terms of resources beyond suitable pasture and a predictable water supply. Pastoral societies are therefore able to survive in the dry and inhos-

15. Harris, *Culture, Man and Nature.*

16. Carneiro, "Slash and Burn Cultivation among the Kuikuru and Its Implications for Cultural Development in the Amazon Basin."

17. Robert M. Adams, *The Evolution of Urban Society* (Chicago: Aldine Publishing, 1966). See also Robert M. Adams, "The Origins of Agriculture," in *Horizons of Anthropology*, ed. Sol. Tax (Chicago: Aldine Publishing, 1964).

18. Ester Boserup, *The Conditions for Agricultural Growth* (Chicago: Aldine Publishing, 1965).

The Tuareg are nomadic herdsmen who move their sheep, goats, and camels across the Sahara Desert in regular annual migrations.

pitable areas that other peoples would not consider desirable: the steppes of Asia, the tundras of northern Europe, the dry plains of East Africa, or the semideserts of the Middle East.

The pastoral way of life requires almost constant movement, since good pasture land is exhausted even more rapidly than horticultural land. For this reason, pastoralists do not seem to be able to accumulate much surplus in forms that would enable them to settle in an area or increase their numbers. Unlike horticulture, pastoralism is always a subsistence lifestyle, requiring a constant shifting of pastures and a continual struggle to maintain a pre-carious existence. The aBrog Pa, nomadic pastoralists of the Tibetan plateau, for example, must travel many hundreds of miles each year to find adequate pastures for their yak and other livestock, contending with extremes of heat and cold at altitudes of more than 12,000 feet. Despite their efforts, by the end of every winter the herds are usually at the brink of starvation and vulnerable to destruction by a spring blizzard.[19]

19. Robert B. Ekvall, *Fields on the Hoof* (New York: Holt, Rinehart and Winston, 1968).

The problem of scarce resources often fosters competition among neighboring groups of pastoralists, and a readiness—even an eagerness—for combat. The Bedouins, camel pastoralists of the Arabian desert, were well known for their fierceness in fighting and for the blood feuds and raids that often took place between neighboring groups.[20] The Sarakatsani, pastoralists of northern Greece, also raid one another frequently.

In the division of labor by sex, fighting, like hunting, is usually a male task. For this reason, social organization in pastoral societies, and in many horticultural societies as well, tends to center around male-dominated family groups. Among the aBrog Pa, the *tenthold*, or extended family, is the social unit that owns and distributes property. In each tenthold, such decisions as managing the herd, distributing wealth, and planting season migrations are made by the oldest male. An extended family unit among the aBrog Pa would generally last until the death of the parents. Younger families would then break away, dividing the herd as they did so.

One generalization that may be made about pastoralists, and to some degree about horticulturists, is that these people face the problem of maintaining their rights to the land over which they migrate. They then acquire the idea of *territoriality*—securing and defending an area against use by outsiders. In the case of the pastoralists, this is a result of their dependence on a particular area and its resources. Water, good soil, and good pasture are always in high demand.

Many pastoralists now find that lands they previously moved through without restriction are occupied by farmers. Both the Fulani of Nigeria and the Sarakatsani of Greece face this problem.[21] Both have tried to work out arrangements with local farmers by exchanging grazing privileges for milk and other products of the herds. Nonetheless, pastoralists require a great deal of land for each individual the group supports: the Basseri of southern Iran, for example, require approximately one square mile of land for each individual. Such an extent of land is increasingly hard to find for grazing. Thus, it is not surprising that pastoralists are very concerned with the concepts of boundary maintenance, strong male authority over the group, control over land, and military effectiveness.

Intensive Agriculture

When humankind made the revolutionary change from foraging to producing food, a much greater control over the hazards of the natural environment was achieved. The principal difference between horticulture and agriculture lies in the use of the plough for planting. For the first time, with intensive agriculture it became possible to obtain a relatively reliable supply of food at a single location for a predictable period of time. This brought a degree of independence from seasonal variations in temperature, vegetation, and game supply. As we know, the first settlements appear with the intensive gathering and production of grains and other staple foods. Population

---

20. J. K. Campbell, *Honour, Family and Patronage* (London: Oxford Press, 1964).

21. See Derrick J. Stenning, "The Pastoral Fulani of Northern Nigeria," in *Peoples of Africa*, ed. James L. Gibbs, Jr. (New York: Holt, Rinehart and Winston, 1965).

increased dramatically thereafter, based on fishing, agricultural production, and herding. While the ecological basis in the New World was different, involving different crops and fewer animals, the results were in a similar direction: The areas developed patterns of intensive exploitation of the environment through agricultural production, involving irrigation and draft animals in the Old World, and extensive terracing, irrigation, and lake farming in the New.

For the first thousands of years when people were still dependent on horticultural production, the organization of social groups probably remained fairly simple. Food production may still have been erratic, and any growth in population probably motivated the splitting off of new groups, as well as attempts to increase food production.[22] But by 7000 B.C., settlements with villages of farmers had appeared in the Old World (by about 3400 B.C. in the New World). In the Old World, from 5000 to 3000 B.C., new forms of human organization developed that were qualitatively different from those of the horticulturists or the pastoralists.

The new intensive agricultural techniques produced substantial surpluses that were commanded by political and religious hierarchies administered by organized states. The societies were stratified—that is, marked by class differences in ownership or control of the principal productive resources. These societies were marked by a complex division of labor involving officials and religious personnel (often the same people), full-time craftsmen and artists, servants, and a great mass of laborers.

---

22. Adams, "The Origins of Agriculture."

These states often produced writing and art, some forms of law and taxation for public purposes, and religious and military establishments.

Exactly why such social developments occurred is not known, but many archeologists feel that it was the limitation of resources such as good farm land that may have led to the intensification of farming. Opportunities for trade exchanges may have brought about the rise of those who supervised the exchanges—perhaps the priests, for example. Conflicts over land may have led alliances for defense, or conquest of one group by another, who thereby could take control of the food produced by the defeated group. Conflicts over distribution of water in valleys also may have created some differentiation between those groups that could control the flow and those who lacked access to this precious resource. Whatever the cause, these complex social developments rested on a base of sophisticated agriculture, which depended on a more developed technology, such as terracing, irrigation by means of dikes and canals, and the plow and draft animals. The productivity of this kind of agriculture alone was responsible for the great increases in population.

SOCIAL ORGANIZATION. With their more sophisticated technology, intensive agricultural societies can exploit more of the environment. This capacity may motivate them to develop military organizations to expand their control over lands and other resources. Warfare, however, continues to be primarily a male activity, and probably serves to strengthen the authority of males in the societies in which it plays a significant part. The position of women is variable. To the degree that they are deprived of significant roles in the productive pro-

This dockside market in Thailand serves as a point of exchange for agricultural surplus.

cesses, women are likely to enjoy less social power than in societies where their contributions are required. Such is the common experience of many American families: the working wife commands many more prerogatives than the wife who works only in her own household.

Family groups remain important in agricultural society, but there is an increase in the power of the state, the town, or the society as a whole, at the expense of a family's control over its members. Elaborate tax systems may be imposed to distribute wealth, usually for the benefit of the ruling elite.

An example of an intensive agricultural society is that of the Pathans of the Swat valley in Pakistan.[23] The Pathans are a

23. Frederik Barth, "Ecologic Relationships of Ethnic Groups in Swat, North Pakistan," *American Anthropologist* 58 (1956).

complex group which displaced an earlier group of agriculturalists, the Kohistanis. The Pathans practice a diversified plow agriculture, planting two crops a year. They grow wheat, maize, and rice; much of their plowed land is irrigated. They manure the fields and rotate the crops. There are special beds for starting the rice. Only part of the Pathan population is actively engaged in agriculture; there are other specialists who perform services for payment.

The Pathans are organized into a complex, multicaste society. (A *caste system* is one of a hierarchy of ranked groups, each one assigned a status by birth, and all individuals of a group required to marry within the group. In India, castes are often associated with religious functions or occupations.) There is a land-owning caste which is organized into local groups of relatives descended from one man. (For a fuller discussion of descent groups, see

Chapter Ten

Chapter 13.) There are other castes and occupational groups tied to these landowners as political clients and economic serfs. An active political system is organized around the hierarchical ordering of landlords, which centers around the men's houses. Political activity apparently absorbs a good deal of local wealth, which goes into feasting and maintaining political retainers.

MARKET EXCHANGE. Agricultural production creates the conditions for a new form of economic transaction, the *market exchange*. (See Chapter 11 for a fuller discussion of the market exchange.) The requirements for a market system are surpluses of food and other goods, and some medium of exchange such as money to reckon the value of goods and services.

The market economies of agricultural societies are frequently studied by anthropologists, particularly the trade relations existing between rural peasants (agriculturalists), other peasants, and urban dwellers. If the peasants in an urban-dominated society produce a surplus, they trade food for money with which to buy manufactured items or other foodstuffs they cannot grow. While barter is possible and sometimes engaged in, peasant markets are generally dependent upon the existence of money as a medium of exchange. Labor, too, is a commodity that can be bought and sold, and the phenomenon of wage earning is more and more becoming a part of peasant and other agricultural economies.

Adaptation and Cultural Contact

Human societies have long adjusted themselves to a range of natural environments. Much of what anthropologists study today

Cultural Ecology

is the adaptation of nonindustrial cultures to the superior technology and military power of the industrialized societies. Regardless of the level of technology of the groups involved, all find themselves experiencing changes in certain directions over which they often have little control. The process is heavily weighted in one direction—toward the assimilation of these groups, mostly as poorly paid wage laborers, into the industrial economies.

One example of the adaptation of a nonindustrial society to a more powerful industrial group was the influence of Russia under Czar Peter the Great on the hunting and herding tribes of Siberia. Like the Eskimos, many Siberian tribes trapped or hunted fur-bearing animals, such as wolf, bear, and caribou, as part of their diet. Then, in the nineteenth century, the pelts of such animals became a useful commodity in Russia. The furs acquired great trade value, their demand increased, and competitive hunting of many areas depleted the game herds. At a later time a large barrel industry was founded, based upon the timber resources of Siberia. Several of the more than thirty Siberian tribes were used for labor in the logging and barrel-making industries. As a result of both of these activities of the Russians, the indigenous groups tended to be drawn from their own subsistence strategies and into a wage-labor market situation.

Similar changes were experienced by many American Indian and Eskimo tribes. If the initial boom of prosperity passed—a fall in the demand or the supply of the furs, for example—the indigenous groups were reduced to poverty, helplessness, and demoralization. For others, such as the Mundurucu of Brazil, what had begun as a part-time resource (rubber-tapping) ended as full-time work in the rubber areas, often resulting in wage labor on the rubber plantations.[24] For horticulturists such as the Tiv of Cameroun, the introduction of money and trade resulted in the raising of a cash crop and the end of self-sufficiency. The farmers had to raise and sell more in order to buy the food and other supplies they had come to depend on.[25] In large areas of Latin America and the Caribbean, horticulturists were often driven from the lands by taxes, laws, and force, onto the plantations and into the labor market.[26]

The study of cultural ecology, the adaptation of human groups to the physical and social environment, may help to teach us that it is not only the nonindustrial groups who have to learn to deal with the social forces which human beings have developed. We in the industrialized societies are only now beginning to understand our effect on the natural environment. Not only are we now being forced to solve the much larger ecological problems that we have created by our complex technology, but we still are faced with the problems of social organization seldom solved successfully by small-scale societies: to live in peace and harmony with one another in a manner in which the full potential of each human being can be fostered and realized.

24. Robert F. Murphy and Julian H. Steward, "Tappers and Trappers: Parallel Process in Acculturation," in *Man in Adaptation: The Cultural Present*, ed. Yehudi Cohen (Chicago: Aldine Publishing, 1968).

25. Paul Bohannan, "The Introduction of Money into Tribal Economy," in *Conformity and Conflict: Readings in Cultural Anthropology*, ed. James P. Spradley and David W. McCurdy (Boston: Little, Brown, 1971).

26. Eric Wolf, "Types of Latin American Peasantry: A Preliminary Discussion," in *Man in Adaptation: The Cultural Present*, ed. Yehudi Cohen (Chicago: Aldine Publishing, 1968). See also Sidney Mintz, *Worker in the Cane* (New Haven, Conn.: Yale University Press, 1958).

Summary

1. Cultural ecology is the study of the ways in which different human groups interact with their environment to survive, to change—or *not* to survive as groups.
2. The process of interaction between groups and their environment is called adaptation.
3. The physical environment of a group constitutes one part of a group's environment. The culture of a group is the other, perhaps more important, component. People rely on their culture as a means for survival; the culture becomes a part of that environment.
4. There is a great variety of adaptations by human groups, depending on climate, the land, and the limitations of the technology available in the culture. From the first villages, made possible by early farming technologies, groups have developed new strategies for survival.
5. Anthropologists have classified different human groups as culture-subsistence types.
6. Hunting-gathering cultures depend on naturally occurring animal and plant food sources. Foragers live almost exclusively on plant food. The social organization of most hunting-gathering groups consists of bands, small groups of related families. For the most part, the main caloric intake is plant food, usually gathered by the women.
7. The level of technology of hunting-gathering groups is simple, consisting of the raw materials at hand. The groups are small, although during the seasons when food is more abun-

dant, many bands may gather together for ceremonials. The processes of coming together and splitting up are called fusion and fission.

8. Horticulture refers to farming carried out with simple tools and techniques. Most horticulturists move to new sites and start new gardens from time to time. Horticultural groups have a greater control over their food supply than hunter-gatherers. Some of the horticulturists who produced a surplus were the first to have social divisions by prestige, whereas the hunting-gathering groups were egalitarian.

9. Pastoralists are basically dependent for their food on herds of domesticated grazing animals. They are nomadic, constantly moving to new pastures for their animals. Competition for land, and the need to protect their grazing rights, foster a readiness for combat among neighboring groups.

10. Intensive agriculture employs more efficient techniques, including the domestication of draft animals, irrigation, and terracing, and may produce substantial surpluses. The earliest governments, organized as states with a ruling class and military and religious establishments, were based on intensive agriculture. There was a division of labor with specialization of skills. Market exchange and, in many cases, money are characteristic of societies based on intensive agriculture.

11. Today, many anthropologists are interested in the adaptation of small-scale societies to the environments created by the great industrialized nations.

Review Questions

1. Discuss the difference between environmental determinism and environmental possibilism.
2. Hunting-gathering, horticulture, pastoralism, and intensive agriculture are four cultural subsistence types. Compare the physical environments, complexity of technology, and degree of efficiency characteristic of these strategies for obtaining food.
3. Discuss the impact of modern industrialized technology on small-scale societies.

Suggested Readings

Boserup, Ester. *The Conditions of Agricultural Growth.* Chicago: Aldine Publishing, 1965. The author presents the theory that population growth that resulted from early agriculture was a major causal factor in later agricultural development and the rise of states.

Lee, Richard B., and DeVore, I., eds. *Man the Hunter.* Chicago: Aldine Publishing, 1968. This is a comprehensive collection of papers about the ecology of hunter-gatherers today. Prehistoric groups living in apparently similar ways are also discussed, as is the role of hunting-gathering in the evolution of human cultural development.

Rappaport, Roy. *Pigs for the Ancestors.* New Haven, Conn.: Yale University Press, 1968. This study examines the interrelationships of cultural patterns (including agriculture, war, and religion) and the ecology of a horticultural group in highland New Guinea.

Struever, Stuart, ed. *Prehistoric Agriculture.* Garden City, N.Y.: Natural History Press, 1971. This collection contains papers that reflect a still-developing anthropological interest in explaining the origins and growth of agriculture. Various hypotheses are offered, including that of agriculture as one solution to an ecological or population problem.

Cultural Ecology

Chapter 11

Economic Anthropology

KULA: THE CIRCULATING EXCHANGE OF VALUABLES IN THE ARCHIPELAGOES OF EASTERN NEW GUINEA

NATIVE NAME: Kiriwina (also known as Trobriand Island, largest member of the Trobriand Island group which is part of a number of island groups participating in the *kula* trade ring)

POPULATION: approximately 10,000

ENVIRONMENT: Kiriwina is an island of 170 square miles, one of a group of islands lying 100 miles north of the eastern tip of Papua New Guinea, and north of Australia, in the South Pacific The islands are composed of coralline limestone, bordered by coral reefs; soils are very rich and most of the land on Kiriwina, except for coral outcrops and swamp areas, is under cultivation.

FIELDWORK: Data were collected by a combination of interviews and direct observation of life during the period 1914–1918.

ETHNOGRAPHIC PRESENT: 1914–1918

Source: Abridged from B. Malinowski, "Kula: The Circulating Exchange of Valuables in the Archipelagoes of Eastern New Guinea," *Man* (1920), no. 51, pp. 97–105. Reprinted by permission of the Royal Anthropological Institute of Great Britain and Ireland.

The distant and perilous trading expeditions of the South Sea islanders are a well-known feature of their tribal life. . . . All these trading systems are based upon the exchange of indispensable or highly useful utilities, such as pottery, sago, canoes, dried fish, and yams, the food being sometimes imported into islands or districts which are too small or too infertile to be self-supporting. The trading system, however, which will be described in this paper, differs in this and many other respects from the usual Oceanic forms of exchange. It is based primarily upon the circulation of two articles of high value, but of no real use. These are armshells made of the *Conus millepunctatus,* and necklets of red shell-discs, both intended for ornaments but hardly ever used, even for this purpose. These two articles travel, in a manner to be described later in detail, on a circular route which covers many miles and extends over many islands. On this circuit, the necklaces travel in the direction of the clock hands and the armshells in the opposite direction. Both articles never stop for any length of time in the hands of any owner; they constantly move, constantly meeting and being exchanged. . . .

The *Kula* looms paramount in the tribal life of all the peoples, who participate in it. . . . Some of them, living on big islands, have a very highly developed agriculture, and they harvest each year a crop amply sufficient for their needs and with a good deal to spare. . . . [Some] are, on the other hand, specialized in certain industries, notably pottery and canoe-building, and they are monopolists in intermediary trade. Thus it is evident that exchange of goods had to occur between them. The important point about it, however, is that with them, and notably according to their own ideas, the exchange of utilities is a subsidiary trade, carried on as an incident in the *Kula.*

The *Kula* has been called above "a form of trade." . . . Thus, first, the objects of exchange—the armshells and strings of shell-discs—are not "utilities" in any sense of the word; as said above, they are hardly ever used as ornaments, for which purpose they could serve. Nevertheless, they are extremely highly valued; nowadays a native will give up to £20 for a good article, and in olden days their value was an equivalent of this sum, if we take as a common measure such utilities as basketfuls of yams, pigs, and other such commodities. Secondly, the exchange, far from being casual or surreptitious, is carried on according to very definite and very complex rules. Thus it cannot be performed between members of these tribes taken at random. A firm and lifelong relationship is always established between any participant in the *Kula*, and a number of other men, some of whom belong to his own community, and others to oversea communities. Such men call one another *karayta'u* ("partner," as we shall designate them), and they are under mutual obligations to trade with each other, to offer protection, hospitality, and assistance whenever needed.

Let us imagine that we look at the whole system from one definite point, choosing the large village of Sinaketa in the Trobriand Islands. An old chief in that village would have, say, some hundred partners southwards, and about as many again in the north and east, while a young commoner would have only a few on both sides. It must be remembered that not all men in a village take part in the *Kula*, and some villages are out of it altogether.

Now another definite rule is that the armshells must always be traded to the south, and the necklets of shell-beads to the north. The word "traded" is, of course, only a rough approximation. Let us suppose that I, a Sinaketa man, am in possession of a pair of big armshells. An oversea expedition from Dobu in the d'Entrecasteaux Archipelago, arrives at my village. Blowing a conch shell, I take my armshell pair and I offer it to my overseas partner, with some such words, "This is a *vaga* (initial gift)—in due time, thou returnest to me a big *soulava* (necklace) for it!" Next year, when I visit my partner's village, he either is in possession of an *equivalent* necklace, and this he gives to me as *yotile* (restoration gift), or he has not a necklace good enough to repay my last gift. In this case he will give me a smaller necklace—avowedly not equivalent to my gift—and will give it to me as *basi* (intermediary gift). This means that the main gift has to be repaid on a future occasion and the *basi* is given in token of good faith—but it, in turn, must be repaid by me in the meantime by a gift of small armshells. The final gift, which will be given to me to clinch the whole transaction, would be then called *kudu* (equivalent gift) in contrast to *basi*.

This does not exhaust the subtleties and distinctions of *Kula* gifts. If I, an inhabitant of Sinaketa, happen to be in possession of a pair of armshells more than usually good, the fame of it spreads. It must be noted that each one of the first-class armshells and necklaces has a personal name and a history of its own, and as they all circulate around the big ring of the *Kula*, they are all well-known, and their appearance in a given district always creates a sensation. Now all my partners—whether from overseas or from within the district—compete for the favor of receiving this particular article of mine, and those who are specially keen try to obtain it by giving me *pokala* (offerings) and *kaributu* (solicitory gifts). The former (*pokala*) consists, as a rule, of pigs—especially fine bananas and yams or taro; the latter (*kaributu*) are of greater value: the valuable "ceremonial" axe blades (called *beku*) or limespoons of whale's bone are given. . . .

It must also be emphasized that all these natives, and more especially the Trobrianders, have both a word for, and a clear idea of, barter (*gimwali*), and that they are fully aware of the difference between the transactions at the *Kula* and common barter. The *Kula* involves the elements of trust and of a sort of commercial honor, as the equivalence between gift and countergift cannot be strictly enforced. As in many other native transactions, the main corrective force is supplied by the deeply engrained idea that liberality is the most important and the most honorable virtue, whereas meanness brings shame and opprobrium upon the miser. This, of course, does not completely exclude many squabbles, deep resentments and even feuds over real or imaginary grievances in the *Kula* exchange.

As said already, the armshells and shell-strings always travel in their own respective directions on the ring, and they are never, under any circumstances, traded back in the wrong direction. Also they never stop. It seems almost incredible at first, but it is the fact, nevertheless, that no one ever keeps any of the *Kula* valuables for any length of time. Indeed, in the whole of the Trobriands there are perhaps only one or two specially fine armshells and shell necklaces permanently owned as heirlooms, and these are set apart as a special class, and are once and for all out of the *Kula*. "Ownership," therefore, in *Kula* is quite a special economic relation. A man who is in the *Kula* never keeps any article for longer than, say, a year or two. Even this exposes him to the reproach of being niggardly, and certain districts have the bad reputation of being "slow" and "hard" in the *Kula*. On the other hand, each man has an enormous number of articles passing through his hands during his lifetime, of which he enjoys a temporary possession, and which he keeps in trust for a time. This possession hardly ever makes him use the articles, and he remains under the obligation soon again to hand them on to one of his partners. But the temporary ownership allows him to draw a great deal of renown, to exhibit his article, to tell how he obtained it and to plan to whom he is going to give it. And all this forms one of the favorite subjects of tribal conversation and gossip, in which the feats and the glory in *Kula* of chiefs or commoners are constantly discussed and rediscussed.

But the tradition of the *Kula* is not limited to the recounting of recent or historical exploits. There is a rich mythology of the *Kula*, in which stories are told about far-off times when mythical ancestors sailed on distant and daring expeditions. Owing to their magical knowledge—how they came to it no one knows distinctly—they were able to escape dangers, to conquer their enemies, to surmount obstacles, and by their feats they established many a precedent which is now closely followed by tribal custom. But their importance for their descendants lies mainly in the fact that they handed on their magic, and this made the *Kula* possible for the following generation. . . .

I will describe the normal and typical course of such a big overseas expedition as it takes place between the *Kula* community of Sinaketa with its surrounding villages and the Amphlett Group and Dobu districts to the south. Such an expedition would take place about once a year, but only every second or third year would it be carried out on a really big scale. On such occasions big preparations take place. . . .

After . . . the expedition is ready, many people from the neighboring villages assemble, the departing chiefs enjoin chastity to their wives and warn all the neighboring male villagers to keep off Sinaketa, and prognosticate a speedy arrival with much *vaygu'a* (valuables). They are assured that they can depart in safety as no one will visit their village surreptitiously. Indeed, during their absence, the village should be kept tabooed, and if a man is found loitering about the place, especially at night, he is likely to be punished (by sorcery, as a rule) on the chief's return.

The normal expedition . . . sails in one day with good following wind, or in several days if the wind is weak or shifting, and arrives at its first stage in the Amphletts. Some exchange is done here, as well as on the further two intermediate halts in Tewara and Sanaroa and the concomitant magic has to be performed here. There are also several mythologically famed spots in these islands: some rocks from which magic originated—how, the myths do not relate distinctly—and other rocks, formerly human beings, who traveled to their present sites from very far, and to whom the natives offer *pokala* (offerings in order to have a propitious *Kula*). . . .

But the main aim of the expedition is the district of Dobu, more especially the north-east corner of Fergusson Island, where on the flat and fertile foreshore, among groves of cocoanut, betel-palms, mangoes, and bread-fruit trees, there stretch for miles the populous settlements of Tautauna, Bwayowa, Deidei, and Begasi. . . .

Finally the party arrive, and it is the custom for the Dobuans to meet them with *soulava* (shell-disc necklaces) in their hands. The conchshells are blown and the necklaces are ceremonially offered by the Dobuans to the newcomers. Then the party go ashore, every man going to the house of his main partner. There the visitors receive gifts of food, and they again give some of their minor trade as *pari* (visitors' gifts) to the Dobuans. Then, during a several days' stay, many more *soulava* are given to the visitors. Often it is necessary for a Kiriwinian to woo his partner by gifts, solicitations, and magical rites, transparently performed, if the latter possesses a specially good and desirable article. All the transactions are carried out according to the rules set forth above.

In due time, after a year or so, the Dobuans will make their return expedition to Sinaketa, with exactly the same ceremonial, magic, and sociology. On this expedition they will receive some armshells in exchange for the necklets previously given, and others, as advance gifts towards the next *Kula* transaction.

The *Kula* trade consists of a series of such periodical overseas expeditions, which link together the various island groups, and annually bring over big quantities of *vaygu'a* and of subsidiary trade from one district to another. The trade is used and used up, but the *vaygu'a*—the armshells and necklets—go round and round the ring.[1]

● ● ● ● ● ● ● ●

In the capsule ethnography, Bronislaw Malinowski, one of the founders of modern anthropology, describes a kind of trade quite different from that to which we are accustomed. In the Trobriand *kula*, nonutilitarian but valued objects—ceremonial armshells and red shell necklaces—are produced and exchanged according to complex rules. Is this trade part of the Trobriand "economy"? Like economists, economic anthropologists have been arguing for many years about what an economy is and how it should be studied. But while economists are mostly concerned with the economy of industrial nations such as the United States or the Soviet Union, economic anthropologists study a greater diversity of societies. They have been particularly interested in the foraging or agricultural economies of small-scale societies in Africa, Asia, the Pacific, and the Americas. Because of the great diversity of economic systems they study, the problem of defining "economy" is especially difficult for anthropologists.

An economy, for most of the people reading this textbook, has something to do with money, and institutions such as banks and stores where we save or use our money. We may think of wages that we receive in return for work we do and industries that produce and sell the things we buy. We may also think of taxes, stock markets, and the GNP (Gross National Product). But from the point of view of most economic anthropologists, these features describe a special case. For example, not all societies have money as we know it—that is, "legal tender for all debts, public and private." In many societies money is not a general unit of exchange, but can be used only in certain kinds of transac-

1. From B. Malinowski, "Kula: The Circulating Exchange of Valuables in the Archipelagoes of Eastern New Guinea," *Man* (1920), no. 51, pp. 97–105. Reprinted by permission of the Royal Anthropological Institute.

tions. In some places in the Pacific, for example, a man can buy a pig with shell currency, but he cannot buy a chicken or a garden tool with it. In many societies, too, exchange is not anonymous, as it is in our society where strangers can buy and sell from each other. Instead, a seller will not sell to just anyone, but only to a person with whom he or she has a special trading relationship, and items exchanged are often "custom-made" for a particular buyer. In such societies, prices are often fixed and do not vary with supply and demand. Unlike our own society, in some societies, people may own their own tools and land, and may exchange the products they make for other products they might need, instead of selling them for cash.

But in all societies, there are written or unwritten laws concerning who has the right to own resources and tools, and the way in which labor and the products of labor are to be distributed. Specific laws vary from society to society, and economic anthropologists study these differences. In this chapter we will define *economy* as the rules in a society by which labor is organized and goods are produced and distributed. For even in a society with a subsistence economy, such as that of the Netsilik described in Chapter 10, there are rules concerning the division of labor between men and women, ownership of clothing and tools, and the distribution of food.

Resources, Ecology, and Technology

When we study an economy, we must first take account of what raw materials people have available to them, and how the resources are distributed seasonally and geographically. We must also take account of the kinds of tools, skills, and knowledge that people bring to bear in their effort to transform raw materials to fill socially determined needs. People always have many possible ways of organizing their economy in any particular natural setting. However, the features of the natural environment and of the particular technology available do not determine their economy. Furthermore, no human group lives in isolation: part of the environment is always composed of other social groups, with different customs, skills, and tools. Political relationships between groups living in the same environment often limit the alternatives open to each group even more than does the physical environment or technology. In the Kaugel Valley in the mountains of Papua, New Guinea, for example, communities working land on the valley floor near the Kaugel River can raise much-prized vegetable food and many pigs, both of which are important items in the regional exchange system.[2] Communities living on the slopes of the valley have poorer land where certain of the prized vegetables do not grow and where fewer pigs may be raised. Consequently, these groups cannot participate in regional exchange as frequently as the groups on the valley floor. Therefore, the economic fortunes of a community in the Kaugel Valley depend not only on features of the natural environment such as soil quality and erosion rates, but also on the laws people agree to, concerning who owns what land, and the military force that each group can muster to defend its claims.

2. Nancy Bowers, "Permanent Bachelorhood in the Upper Kaugel Valley of Highland New Guinea," *Oceania* 36 (1965): 27–37.

The Natural Setting of Economic Activity

The natural setting influences economic life, especially with respect to foraging, agricultural, and pastoral societies, both because of the *geographical* distribution of resources and the *seasonal* variation in their availability.

E. E. Evans-Pritchard has described the geographic environment of the Nuer, a herding and farming people of the Sudan.[3] In order to understand the Nuer's economy, we should note that their area is subject to seasonal heavy rainfall and river floods; but when the rains stop during the dry season, there may be severe drought. The Nuer's most important economic asset is cattle. Thus, in the rainy season the Nuer must migrate to the high ridges that lie above the flooded rivers, and in times of drought seek the river bottomlands where there is still water to be had for the cattle.

The work of Kent Flannery provides us with another example of the way in which the natural setting structures the timing and spacing of human economic activity.[4] Flannery is an archeologist who has studied the ancient hunting and gathering people who lived in the Tehuacán Valley in Mexico during the period 8000 to 2000 B.C. The evidence upon which he bases his account of their life comes from the fos-

silized plant and animal remains found in caves in Tehuacán which the valley's former inhabitants left behind.

Out of the hundreds of plants and animals available to the people of the valley, five were used most heavily: (1) the fruit of the maguey, available all year round; (2) the fruit of several cacti, available seasonally; (3) tree legumes, whose pods were available only during the rainy season; (4) white-tailed deer; and (5) cotton-tailed rabbits. Each of the three kinds of plants, as well as several other kinds that the Tehuacanos collected more casually, had to be harvested at a particular time of the year or a particular time during the plant's life cycle, for the people wanted to insure that next year's crop would also be sufficient for their needs. Maguey, for example, was most nutritious in the final stage of its life cycle, long after it had sent out its pollen. The fossil evidence shows that the collectors were aware of this fact, and harvested maguey at the appropriate stage of its growth. Maguey was eaten during the dry season. Cactus, on the other hand, had to be harvested quickly during the short period just before the summer rains, or else its fruit would rot. Harvesting cactus also did not endanger the next year's crop since seeds ingested by the people escape in feces to sprout that year.

The relationship between the Tehuacanos and their environment was two-way: a cycle of wet and dry seasons was imposed by nature on the human group, but the people made choices between resources available at the same time in different parts of the valley, imposing a cultural scheduling on the options naturally available to them.

When we consider the relationship between the economy of a people and their

3. E. E. Evans-Pritchard, *The Nuer* (London: Oxford University Press, 1940).

4. Kent Flannery, "Archeological Systems Theory and Early Mesoamerica," in *Anthropological Archeology in the Americas*, ed. Betty Meggars (Washington, D.C.: Anthropological Society of Washington, 1968), pp. 67–87.

The fishing boats have come in, so all the people of this coastal area in Senegal run down to the beach to get their share of the catch.

natural environment, we must also remember that people are not always limited by what is available near at hand. All people are linked with others through networks of trade, exchanging the products of their region for things from far off. For example, in the capsule ethnography, Malinowski tells us that some of the participants in the *kula* live on very small islands and cannot supply their own food needs. Instead, they exchange specialized manufactured items such as pottery and canoes for food such as yams and dried fish.

Also, natural seasons are not the only events that time people's economic activities. In parts of the world without sharply defined seasons, production varies in volume with the occurrence of feasts celebrating births, initiations, marriages, and deaths. Even in the United States and Canada, certain times of the year, such as the Christmas season, influence economic activity. White Christmas or not, retail stores turn over a great volume of sales in December.

The economic system of a people can affect their relationship to their environment, as the experience of the Tuktoyaktuk Eskimos of Canada shows us. Traditionally, the Eskimos were hunters and fishers, who made and owned their own tools, shelter and clothes, and who provided their own food and other needs. These adaptive strategies utilized the resources of their local environment. Today, according to a study by Jack Ferguson,[5] their technology includes snowmobiles, frame houses, and power boats manufactured in far-off factories, and they buy their food and clothing with cash that they obtain by selling animal skins or through wage labor. No longer self-sufficient, they have become partially integrated into Canada's national market economy.

The sociocultural and economic effects of the introduction of wage labor and Western goods were far-reaching. The introduction of paid trapping broke down the band as the primary social unit, to be replaced by the nuclear family as primary. The partnership ties that had linked Eskimo families in hunting activities were weakened. Other social changes resulted from the continuing introduction and acceptance by the Eskimos of Western trade goods, welfare and health institutions, and schools. In the area where Ferguson's fieldwork was done there was no stable way of making a living for more than a few Eskimos, so most lived on relief and from occasional trapping and hunting. Few adults had any meaningful work anymore in a land where once all had been fully employed.

Technology, Economy, and Social Change

Although other animals, such as chimps and birds, have been known to use tools, humans are the only animals who system-

atically transform the environment through the use of tools of various sorts, and who depend for their survival on this activity. Human tools include everything from the simplest digging sticks used to plant seeds or harvest roots to complex technology of modern industry and agriculture, such as blast furnaces and grain combines. A characteristic of human tools is that they are not planned and designed for usefulness alone. Even the earliest stone tools were designed for aesthetic value as well. Human tools are not just useful: they are useful in particular cultural ways.

The nature of a society's technology reflects the division of labor among the people as well as the kind of work they do. For example, among the Mbuti Pygmies of the Congo, one form of hunting was done on an individual basis with bow and arrow, but net hunting required the cooperation of the entire band, some to tend the nets and others to drive animals toward them.[6] The assembly-line technology of the modern factory requires precisely coordinated, repetitive and specialized work. The more complex the technology, the more likely it will be that the tools will be made in specialized ways and not by their users, and the less likely it will be that the users will own their own tools.

Tools may be bound up in complex ways with the social life and values of a society, as Lauriston Sharp's study of the Yir Yiront shows.[7] The Yir Yiront lived on the Cape York Peninsula on the north coast

5. Jack Ferguson, "Eskimos: A Satellite Society," in *Minority Canadians*, vol. 1, ed. J. Elliot (Toronto: Prentice-Hall of Canada, Ltd., 1971), pp. 15–28.

6. Colin Turnbull, *The Forest People* (New York: Simon and Schuster, 1961).

7. Lauriston Sharp, "Steel Axes for Stone-Age Australians," *Human Organization* 11 (1952): 17–22.

*One still goes to the market to buy cloth in Upper Volta. But one can
also buy a portable radio or a pair of sunglasses there.*

of Australia. Sharp relates that these people, in accepting steel axes as a superior adaptation replacing their customary stone axes, saw their entire social structure change. The European missionaries who introduced the steel axes about 1915 were not aware that the indigenous stone axes served not only as tools but as symbols of authority. Only men—generally old men—could own a stone axe, although they would allow women and young people to borrow the axes for cutting wood. When the missionaries gave out steel axes they gave them indiscriminately to virtually everyone, women and children included. No longer did a Yir Yiront woman have to borrow an axe from her husband or father. No longer did a young person have to make the ritual request of his elder male kinsman for the use of the stone axe. What the missionaries did not realize was that axes were symbols of masculinity and adulthood in this male-dominated society. When women and children were given their own axes, the authority of the men was undercut. In a short period of time, the social relationships long legitimated by the ownership and practices associated with stone axes disintegrated.

Other social relationships were also weakened. For example, trading partnerships had been established for many years between the Yir Yiront men and some members of neighboring tribes; the Yir Yiront exchanged sting-ray-tipped spears for stone axe heads with their neighbors to the south. When steel axes appeared, the trading ceremonies became less frequent.

Not only were political and social relationships upset by these events, but the organization of labor was also affected. In order to get an axe, the Yir Yiront often had to work for white men in a subordinate capacity, or else work under another aboriginal "leader" who was given his authority by a white.

This foreshadowed the ultimate destruction of Yir Yiront culture: the totemic system of the Yir Yiront—their entire belief system which traditionally placed great stress on the idea of continuity between the present and the mythic past—could not explain the origins of the steel axe and other European cultural items. As more and more elements of European culture found their way into the life of the Yir Yiront, there followed a point "intellectually and emotionally where the myriad new traits which can neither be explained nor any longer assimilated [into the belief system] force the aboriginal to abandon his totemic system." [8]

Yir Yiront society did not break down solely because of the new steel axes. Steel axes were only one of many changes that

8. Sharp, "Steel Axes for Stone-Age Australians."

These corn farmers near Chimbote, Peru, belong to a rural cooperative, a good way to take advantage of modern technology by pooling resources and sharing expenses.

accompanied the process by which Europeans imposed their own laws and values on native Australians, making the aborigines outsiders in their own homeland. Yet, because of the political, economic, and symbolic importance of the older stone tools, the new steel axes were an important factor that contributed to the demise of the traditional social organization.

Technological change does not affect only small-scale society. Cottrell has described the effect of the diesel locomotive on a town in the southwestern part of the United States.[9] This town was an important watering and refueling railroad center in the days of the steam locomotive. Servicing the railroad was the main industry of the town. The entire fabric of the society collapsed with dieselization of the railroad; the new trains did not even include a stop in the town, there being no necessity. The automobile, television, modern agricultural methods, even the technology of the arms race, are only a few of the major technological changes that have had repercussions throughout American society in the past fifty years (see Chapter 18).

The Allocation of Resources

The economy of any society is based on social rules that specify who owns the productive resources, how work is organized, and who has the right to dispose of the products of labor.

What is "property" and what does it mean to "own" something? This concept has different meanings in different societies, and may involve rights and obligations that are not readily apparent. For example, property may refer to tangible things such as land and tools, but it also may designate such intangible things as songs or magical and scientific formulas. Property may be owned by individuals or groups, and may be transferable, in different societies, by means of gift, sale, or inheritance, or it may not be transferable at all but may be buried with its owner when he or she dies. In the United States, land is readily transferable by sale, whereas this is not the case in many foraging and farming societies.

Property, as E. A. Hoebel pointed out, is usually thought of as a thing.[10] But in fact, this is only one aspect of property. Property is defined by social rules concerning the rights a person or group has to the use and disposition of an object. Rules about ownership are rules that identify certain people as having exclusive rights over a thing that other people do not have. Thus, rules about property define a relationship between people as much as they define a relationship between people and things. But the rights of owners over what they may do with their property is everywhere limited by the society as a whole in some way. In our society, for example, zoning laws limit the uses to which we can put our land.

Land Ownership

Land is of such importance to all people that nowhere do we find a culture that has no rules as to how it should be allocated.

9. W. F. Cottrell, "Death by Dieselization: A Case Study in the Reaction to Technological Change," *American Sociological Review* 16 (1951): 358–365.

10. E. A. Hoebel, *Anthropology: The Study of Man* (New York: McGraw-Hill, 1972).

In hunting and gathering economies, the group tends toward a common ownership of land. Common ownership of hunting territories by kin groups is commonplace; but there are often certain spots that belong to certain people or groups—for example, water holes or sacred burial grounds. However, in many cases non-owners have the right to use the land for hunting, a right that is generally freely conceded since reciprocity is essential for the survival of a hunting and gathering group. Some distinctions also may be made where gathering is important. Among the Pomo Indians of California, there were distinct property rights to land only in regard to the gathering of acorns. All Pomo could use all land for hunting.

Among herding peoples, land-ownership rules must be adapted to the requirements of seasonal migrations in search of pasturage. These migrations generally follow the same route each year. For example, among the Basseri of South Persia, grazing lands may be held by several nomadic groups in common.[11] Each group does not own the pastures it uses; it owns a unique schedule for their use. This schedule gives each group the right to use each pasture on the migration route at a particular time of the year. Pastoralists also have agreements with settled farming people about the right to graze their herds in just-harvested fields and unused land.

Among horticultural people, rules about land ownership may be quite complex. For example, on Wallis Island in the Pacific, there are three land classifications. Public

land is a central area of semidesert, uncultivated land that can be used by anyone. Village land comprises fair-to-good land allotted to individuals in plots on which they grow taro. The best land on the island is lineage land which is owned by people of common ancestry acting as a group. The leader of this group apportions the land to members of the group for cultivation.

The Nigerian Ibo classify land in four categories. Sacred land is the area encompassing and surrounding shrines devoted to various local deities. Unclaimed land is virgin forest; tribal members who wish to clear a plot of land may do so and claim it as their own. In recent years, the forest area has been cleared extensively and some villages are now holding parts of the forest as a reserve for future needs. Com-

Owning even a small plot of land makes it possible for this Ecuadorian family to raise pigs.

11. Frederic Barth, "The Land-Use Pattern of Migratory Tribes of South Persia," *Norsk Geografisk Tidsskrift*, Bind 17.

munal lands are owned by kin groups and are subdivided for use among members. Most Ibo land is private land, land that can be bought and sold, and used by those to whom the landowner gives permission. Private land can also be passed on to offspring or disposed of as the owner sees fit.

Land is not always valued for its productivity; there are other considerations. In Western Europe the configuration of cities indicates that people of higher status tended to live on the highest land. This preference may have developed as a means of protection against attack (high land is easier to defend). Today, waterfront property seems to take precedence as a symbol of wealth over other home sites.

There are also emotional and symbolic ties to land. People form an attachment to land that has been "in the family" for years. Even greater emotional attachments bind some people to sacred sites such as the cemeteries in which their ancestors are buried. In the United States there are a number of national shrines that are of great symbolic and emotional significance to its people. The Lincoln Memorial or the Arlington National Cemetery could not be bulldozed and the land converted into parking lots without provoking a great public outcry. The intangible value of land not directly related to its use for economic or monetary gain must not be overlooked.

The Division of Labor

All economies have rules concerning who is to do what sorts of work, for whom, and in what manner. Earlier we noted that the Mbuti Pygmies have two main types of hunting methods: net hunting and bow-and-arrow hunting. For each type there are clear rules specifying how the work is to be accomplished. Net hunting requires the cooperation of six or seven families—a whole camp group. The men have the job of forming their nets around a large circular area, while the women and the children are assigned the task of driving animals toward the nets. Bow-and-arrow hunting is a more individual task, and is performed only by men. But even though they may hunt alone by this method, the men do not hunt for themselves or their immediate families only. The meat they bring home is distributed to everyone in the camp.

In the preceding example, it can be seen that men and women were assigned separate yet complementary tasks. Rules concerning the *sexual division of labor* are universal in human societies: all societies define certain tasks as appropriate for men and others as appropriate for women. In most societies these separate roles are accepted as part of the natural, unchanging order of things. But anthropologists, who have studied this phenomenon in many kinds of societies, have learned that the roles are not determined by biology. They are based on social rules that vary from society to society. Among the Isthmus Zapotecs of San Juan Evangelista in Mexico, for example, women are the marketers. Their husbands do the farm work and provide many of the goods that women traders sell in the marketplace.[12] But, the New Guinea Highland Melpa people organize their labor in an opposite manner: here, women are the ones who do most of the farm work. They weed and harvest the sweet potato gardens, and they care for the household pigs. Pigs are the most im-

---

12. Beverly Chiñas, *The Isthmus Zapotecs: Women's Roles in Cultural Context* (New York: Holt, Rinehart and Winston, 1973).

In Upper Volta, as in other parts of Africa, weaving is a craft for men. Looms are set up in a special area so that the weavers can work together.

portant agricultural product of the Melpa. They are an item of wealth, and are traded for other valuables and exchanged during large ceremonial feasts. Among the Melpa, it is the men who do the exchanging and trading.[13] Similarly, in Congo tribes, men do the weaving, whereas in peasant areas of Mexico this is done by women. In most places women are assigned the task of cooking and child care; yet among the Huli of Papua New Guinea men often do

their own cooking, and Yanomamö men in Brazil often look after their children.

Are there any regularities in the sexual division of labor? Esther Boserup[14] found that in many sparsely populated regions of the world where people rely on shifting cultivation—a kind of farming where fallow periods far exceed the length of time land is under cultivation—women tend to do most of the farm work. In densely pop-

13. Marilyn Strathern, *Women in Between* (London: Seminar Press, 1972).

14. Esther Boserup, *Woman's Role in Economic Development* (New York: St. Martin's Press, 1970).

Chapter Eleven

ulated regions with plough cultivation, men, on the average, do more farm work than women do. And in the most intensive forms of agriculture, such as wet rice agriculture in Java, both men and women work an equal amount.

It has been argued that some of the cross-cultural regularities that exist in the assignment of roles to men and women are due to the physical nature of the sexes. This is not true in regard to the greater physical strength of men.[15] For example, women are often observed carrying heavy loads and doing strenuous work. However, Judith Brown [16] notes that women are usually responsible for child care, important in societies where breast-feeding provides the child with a significant amount of nourishment and may continue for the first four years of the child's life. Brown suggests that women's tasks are designed to be compatible with their child-care responsibilities. Thus, women's work usually allows them to remain close to home, is not dangerous, and is easily interrupted. This may explain why women are not more frequently hunters or soldiers.

While it may sometimes seem so from a vantage point within one society, an anthropological perspective shows us that the sexual division of labor is not "natural," nor is it unchanging; it is learned according to the rules of each society. In contemporary industrial economies, many

Colombian boys mix straw and clay to make adobe, the first step in the building of a house.

women are doing work that in the recent past had been performed only by men— such as driving trucks, ministering to a congregation, and practicing medicine. A couple may have only one or two children, or none at all, freeing women from a lifetime of child-care responsibilities. In addition, women no longer need to rely on breast-feeding their infants. Men's acceptable job possibilities are also changing; men may now be nurses or telephone operators, and some men are taking a greater share of child-rearing responsibilities. In the United States, these changes have accelerated since World War II with the entrance of large numbers of married women into the labor force. Women make

15. Michelle Rosaldo and Louise Lamphere, eds., *Women, Culture and Society* (Stanford, Calif.: Stanford University Press, 1974).

16. Judith K. Brown, "A Note on the Division of Labor by Sex," *American Anthropologist* 72 (1970): 1074.

up almost half of the work force in the United States today.

The division of labor also may be based on *age*. Among the Nyakyusa of Africa, young boys from six to eleven years of age herd the cattle belonging to the group. Since cattle represent wealth to the Nyakyusa, this is an important job for these boys, who are thus made to assume a position of responsibility early in life.

There are other criteria for the division of labor. In traditional India, work was determined by caste affiliation. *Castes* refer to endogamous (in-marrying) groups found in some highly stratified societies. Membership in a caste is determined by birth. Certain castes traditionally did certain kinds of work in India. In Indian villages, a system of rights and services linking castes together existed, called the *jajmani system*. Tillable land of the village was held in common by members of the cultivator caste. However, members of other castes also lived in the village and had a dependent relationship to the dominant cultivator caste. Some of these families belonged to the priestly, leather-working, blacksmithing, or carpentry castes. All of these groups provided services to the cultivators. In return, they were guaranteed a customary allotment of grain every year, and raw materials for their work. In addition, these specialist castes would each exchange goods and services among themselves.

In Western industrial market economies, the division of labor is very complex because *specialization of work* is developed to an even greater degree than in the *jajmani* system. In factory work, for example, a worker does not make an article from start to finish, but rather, is responsible for only a part of the whole process.

Industrial work often requires a greater degree of cooperation than is usually found in small-scale societies. The people who work together are rarely related as kin to each other as they are in nonindustrial economies.

The division of labor in small-scale societies also may be organized regionally, and may reflect the geographic distribution of resources. For example in the case of the Yir Yiront of Australia, described by Sharp, coastal people produced stingray-tipped spears and exchanged them for axe heads fashioned by the groups who lived near stone quarries far to the south.

Modes of Exchange

Integral to economic systems is the exchange of items, tangible or intangible. Earning $9.00 an hour as an electrician, giving a Christmas present, and "bumming" a cigarette from a friend are all, broadly speaking, forms of economic exchange. Karl Polanyi,[17] the late economic historian, distinguishes three basic modes of exchange: (1) reciprocal exchange, (2) redistributive exchange, and (3) market exchange. All three modes may not be present in every society, especially in small-scale societies where market exchange may not exist at all.

17. Karl Polanyi, *The Great Transformation* (New York: Rinehart, 1944).

18. Marshall Sahlins, "On the Sociology of Primitive Exchange," in *The Relevance of Models for Social Anthropology*, ed. Michael Banton (London: Tavistock, 1965).

Reciprocal Exchange

Reciprocal exchange involves the exchange of goods or services without money, and falls into three categories: (1) generalized reciprocity, (2) balanced reciprocity, and (3) negative reciprocity.[18]

Generalized reciprocity is the free giving of gifts without any conscious thought on the part of the giver of receiving something in return. However, inherent in the entire notion of reciprocity is the assumption that the giver will in time be a recipient. The distribution of meat by the !Kung Bushmen of Africa is traditionally used as an example of generalized reciprocity. The !Kung hunter who returns from a hunting expedition shares the game he brings back with his band. The first portions go to the man who made the kill and the owner of the arrow that killed the animal. The next portion goes to assistants, if any. The rest is distributed as a "gift" to the rest of the band in order of kinship to the hunter. Ideally, the !Kung hunter gives away portions of his kill without thought of being repaid. But in practice, he is kin to most other members of his band and will share in the kill of another hunter in the future. Because of the need to maintain harmony among the small band of families and to eliminate problems arising from envy over unequal distribution of wealth, the !Kung are constantly giving and receiving gifts. The person who is a giver can expect to be a receiver in due time. When examined in detail, the !Kung rules for distribution are just as "formal" as those of a Western economist.

Generalized reciprocity among the !Kung has deeper implications than simply maintaining harmony. It is a manifestation of an economic adaptation where sharing is absolutely necessary for group survival. The !Kung hunter, like most other hunters, gives meat away primarily as a form of *insurance* so that in lean times he and his family will not starve. Hunting and gathering as a means of subsisting seem to require a practice like generalized reciprocity in order to function effectively.

Balanced reciprocity is a straightforward exchange of items on a quid pro quo basis. The !Kung mentioned above, for example, trade such things as skins in return for knives with the neighboring Tswana Bantu. Balanced reciprocity is not limited to items; it can include services. On the American frontier, neighbors helped each other build houses. A newcomer to the community would receive such aid and would be expected to reciprocate when a neighbor or another newcomer needed help.

Negative reciprocity occurs when a person tries to take advantage of another in a trade relationship. This applies not only to trade relationships but in any relationship based on reciprocity. For example, among the Micmac Indians of eastern Canada, individuals who consistently take but do not give in return soon become excluded from all but the most basic forms of aid and exchange. Negative reciprocity is usually found when the trade is between members of different groups or tribes. The !Kung, for example, rarely trade among themselves but do trade with others such as the Herero and the Tswana. It is perfectly ethical from the !Kung point of view to try to cheat in such trades, and it would even be acceptable to steal outright. A point to be made here is that social rules define how unethical a person may be in dealings with others. In the !Kung society, as in other societies, cheating an outsider

*When drought and famine afflict a population, as in Niger in the early
1970s, many aspects of culture are uprooted. These refugees have
come to Toures in search of food and jobs.*

or an enemy in a trade deal may bring a
degree of prestige to a person within the
society, as well as a higher profit from the
trade.

According to Marshall Sahlins, who
has written extensively on economic exchange, a pattern can be observed in the
occurrence of reciprocal exchange systems.
Generalized reciprocity is practiced between kinsmen, balanced reciprocity is
practiced between equals who are unrelated or between distant kin, and negative
reciprocity is practiced between enemies
and strangers.

Reciprocity and Social Relations

In the capsule ethnography Bronislaw Malinowski describes the *kula* ring trade, a
system of reciprocal exchange. This example demonstrates how closely intertwined are trade relationships or the
exchange of goods with nontrade social
relationships. Malinowski lists seven categories of gifts, payments, and commercial
transactions that he found in eastern New
Guinea:

1. *Pure gifts.* This would include any
act where an individual gives an object or
renders a service without expecting or re-

ceiving any return. Such gifts have a social meaning; they strengthen social ties, such as ties between husband and wife, or between parents and children. In this matrilineal society, for example, the gifts given by a father to his son are said to be repayment for the man's relationship to the son's mother.

2. *Customary payments.* Customary payments are paid irregularly and are not a fixed amount. The most important are the annual harvest payments to a man from his wife's brothers. Malinowski feels that these were probably the strongest economic strand in the "fabric of the Trobriand social constitution." He also includes payment by vassal villages to a chief as a form of customary payment.

3. *Payment for services rendered.* The most important of these were payments to the possessor of garden magic, but there were also payments to sorcerers, canoe builders, and others. Malinowski suggests that these ceremonial payments strengthened belief in the particular knowledge of the specialists involved.

4. *Gifts that were returned in an economically equivalent form.* Examples of these would be gifts between households or between friends. It was clear to Malinowski that the Trobriand Islanders valued such gifts for their own sake.

A market in Huancayo, Peru. Ceramics and rugs made much as they were in ancient times may find their way to very different marketplaces in industrialized lands. But the principle of trade operates much the same throughout the world.

5. *Exchange of material goods for privileges, titles, and nonmaterial possessions.* These were transactions that approached "pure" trade. A major example would be the acquisition by a man of goods or privileges that were due to him by inheritance from his maternal uncle or elder brother. This, too, can be explained in terms of Trobriand values—inheritances have to be paid for.

6. *Ceremonial barter, with deferred payment.* This is the class of transaction that includes the *kula*. Malinowski describes it as consisting of "payments which are ceremonially offered, and must be received and repaid later on. The exchange is based on a permanent partnership, and the articles have to be roughly equivalent in value." [19] This type of exchange is distinct from barter; the element of *trust* is paramount.

7. *Trade, pure and simple.* Trade of this type takes place between the craft-producing communities on the islands, which manufacture wooden dishes, lime pots, armlets, etc., the fishing communities of the west, and the sailing and trading communities of the south. This is called *gimwali* trade, and is scorned by the Trobrianders because their ideal is generosity, not a haggling for greater value.

Of the seven different kinds of trade that are associated with the *kula* systems, the most attention has been focused on the ritual exchange of *soulava* (red shell necklaces) and *mwali* (white shell armbands). As we have seen, traders from one island go to another where they may have formal trade partners with whom they exchange armbands and necklaces. The trade is based on mutual trust and esteem which insure hospitality and good treatment as well as good commercial relations. Although the armbands and necklaces have no monetary value, they are prized as valuables beyond any price, are exchanged as gifts between honored partners, and are not bartered or sold.

How does a native become successful in *kula*? Malinowski lists all of the magical spells and techniques associated with the *kula*.[20] These include magic to make the hearts of their Dobuan trading partners "soft," magic to keep the food fresh, beauty magic designed to make the *kula* man appear beautiful to his trading partner, and many others. Magic is important to success at *kula*. Another major method of becoming successful is by being generous, by returning a valuable with an equivalent gift, and by not holding on to a valuable—by not being niggardly. A high-ranking member of the *kula* system may in his lifetime have several dozen trading partners with whom he exchanges armbands and necklaces; the exchange is marked by feasting, the telling of *tales*, and a general aura of goodwill.

Other trading done on a *kula* expedition, such as *gimwali* trade, involves normal market-type haggling over quantity, quality, and price. A man never engages in *gimwali* trade with his *kula* partner; this would demean both of them. He will, however, engage in *gimwali* trade with *kula* partners of other men on the expedition. Some anthropologists contend that *kula* trading of armbands and necklaces is a mere preface to "real" trading such as

---

19. Bronislaw Malinowski, *Argonauts of the Western Pacific* (London: Routledge & Kegan Paul, 1922).

20. Malinowski, *Argonauts of the Western Pacific.*

gimwali. This is doubtful. *Kula* exchange is for prestige and personal enhancement; *gimwali* and similar trade are for utilitarian purposes.

But the *kula* exchange is not only for prestige and personal enhancement. It also insures hospitality and aid from one's partners for life; reinforcement of the islands' traditions, since ritual, magic, myth, and history are all linked with the circulation of *kula* ornaments; adventure, excitement, and pleasure; wide opportunity for ownership of valuable items, if only temporarily; and above all, the maintenance and strengthening of social ties among the islanders.

Redistributive Exchange

In a *redistributive exchange system*, one person or group accumulates goods for the purpose of subsequently distributing those same goods to members of the society, including those who were the initial producers and contributors. While some form of reciprocal exchange is found everywhere, redistribution, a broader system, is usually found in societies that have a hierarchical sociopolitical system. In such a system there are rules concerning the organization of labor and the ownership of the products of labor, unlike the rules in such societies as that of the !Kung Bushmen, which are characterized by reciprocal exchange. In the kingdom of Bunyoro in Uganda, East Africa, for example, the king had the authority to grant land to his subordinate chiefs, who, in turn, gave the use of the land to their subjects. In return, everyone was required to give the king vast quantities of foodstuffs and other goods,

A floating market in modern Thailand. A network of waterways provides quick, efficient transportation of fresh produce from outlying farms directly to the urban centers.

Economic Anthropology

which the king then redistributed to the people after keeping a share for himself. The redistribution, however, was not equal; a larger proportion of the goods went to members of the royal family, to high-ranking subjects, and to those who distinguished themselves in military endeavors.[21]

More equal redistribution exchange occurs in a number of Pacific island societies also ruled by a king or chief. The Buin, for example, live on the island of Bougainville in the Solomon Islands. The Buin collect herbs, roots, and berries, and also do gardening. The main crops are taro, sago, and sugar cane. *Barter* is an important part of the economic system. The main objects of value for barter are pigs and shell money. Of these—symbols of wealth—the chief "owns" most of the pigs, but a system of redistributive exchange works to insure that everyone gets a more or less equal share of the pigs. In this society, the chief is dressed and housed in a manner somewhat better than, but essentially similar to, that of his subjects. Redistribution is usually found in hierarchical societies in which a chief or king has the responsibility for receiving and laying aside supplies of food and raw materials. However, he also has the obligation to distribute these things later on as needed.

The potlatch of the Northwest Coast Indians might also be mentioned as a well-known example of this type of exchange.[22] In the potlatch a chief accumulated a quantity of blankets and other goods and at the potlatch ceremony gave them all away.

Market Exchange

When we think of *market exchange*, we may think of a specific place where things are exchanged, such as farmers' markets or bazaars. While this is most common in non-Western economies, in our industrial economy this is not necessarily the case. Here "market" refers to a process rather than a place. The market exchange process employs a general-purpose money. The prices of goods ideally are set by the relationship between their *supply* and the *demand* for them. In a market economy such as those of the United States, Canada, and most of Europe, this exchange process is the dominant one. Almost all livelihood is derived from selling goods and services on the market and, theoretically, supply and demand influence what goods are produced and how many people are to be.employed at what sorts of jobs.

To illustrate the difference between societies with marketplaces where goods are exchanged and societies with a market-exchange economy, we may consider how exchange works among the Tolai people of New Britain.[23] Although both cash and traditional shell currency are used in Tolai marketplaces in a manner that seems roughly equivalent to the way people buy and sell goods in our economy, actually the principles on which exchanges take place are quite different. Exchange among the Tolai is personal: traders not only sell their produce to "preferred customers"

21. John Beattie, *Bunyoro: An African Kingdom* (New York: Holt, Rinehart and Winston, 1960).

22. Abraham Rosman and Paula Rubel, *Feasting with Mine Enemy* (New York: Columbia University Press, 1971).

23. Richard F. Salisbury, *Vunamami* (Berkeley: University of California Press, 1970).

Market day in rural Bolivia lets people exchange ideas and news as well as merchandise.

had a use just in case they were not sold. Production is not so highly specialized as in our society, where producers make things for sale only, not for their own use.

GENERAL-PURPOSE MONEY. The processes of the modern market economy begin to operate when long-distance trade and a high degree of labor specialization become common. Under such conditions exchange becomes less personal, and there arises a need for a *general-purpose money.* A general-purpose money is one by which the values of all other exchangeable goods in society are measured, and which is used in most exchanges. This kind of money is nonperishable, easily transportable, and divisible into convenient units (such as dollars and cents). *Special-purpose moneys,* such as the huge stone wheels of Rossel Island in the Pacific,[24] are not convenient for widespread daily use in exchanges, since they are bulky and not divided into convenient units. What is more, there are various denominations which typically do not convert into each other (as for example, ten dimes may be converted into a dollar in the United States). Each denomination has, instead, a special purpose; some are appropriately exchangeable only for certain objects such as baskets, whereas others are exchangeable only for other objects such as livestock.

With the beginnings of market economy, people also give up their ability to provide for all their needs within a personalized group of relatives; they buy what they need outside their immediate group. In order to obtain money for this purpose, a

whom they know well and can trust to reciprocate, but they have made prior arrangements to sell particular goods to the customers. In our present-day market economy, buying and selling are generally between strangers. Also, among the Tolai, the prices of goods are fixed over relatively long periods of time; they tend not to vary with changes such as inflation or short supply, as in our economy.

The money used in Tolai exchanges serves more as an accounting device than as a general medium of exchange. It symbolizes the fact that the person who gave a trader one piece of merchandise was owed another specific item in return at a later date. The system is really one of delayed barter. Finally, goods sold in Tolai marketplaces are those for which the sellers also

---

24. W. E. Armstrong, "Rossel Island Money: A Unique Monetary System," *Economic Journal* 34 (1924): 423–429.

person is in a better earning position if he or she specializes in the production of goods or services.

Specialization is thought by many economists to be a much more efficient and profitable way of producing large quantities of goods and services. It becomes a rational means of production when the goal is to maximize money income. In nonmarket economies, such as that of the Trobriand Islands or the Tolai, however, specialization may not be so desirable, since other goals, such as political status or security, motivate production.

Discussion and Debate: Formalism and Substantivism

At the beginning of this chapter, we defined the economy in a very general way as the socially agreed-upon rules by which labor is organized and goods are produced and distributed in society. Most economic anthropologists study one or another aspect of this. Some of them, called *formalist* economic anthropologists, study the economy from the point of view of the *individual actor* who must decide what work to do and what products to produce. The formalists use models derived from economic theory that were originally designed to describe and predict individual decision-making behavior as it operates in market economies. Economists, for example, assume that people make choices between *scarce means* so as to *maximize* their satisfactions. The particular means, ends, and goals of an individual are not of prime concern to the economist, who is interested primarily in the maximizing relationship among them. Despite the fact that this approach was first developed in the study of market economies, formalists believe that

it is useful in the study of nonmarket economies as well.[25] "Economizing" as a decision-making process is found everywhere, according to the formalists.

Another group of economic anthropologists, called *substantivists*, study the economy from the viewpoint of the society as a whole. They see the economy as a *social institution* which has the function of providing for the needs of members of the society. They are not concerned with predicting the decision-making behavior of individuals. Their approach, which has much in common with functionalism (discussed in Chapter 1), tries to show how the economy insures the continued survival of the society by organizing production and distribution so as to meet social needs.[26]

Formalists and substantivists disagree about whether Western economic theory, with its assumption about scarcity and maximization, is applicable to all societies. Substantivists criticize formalists for obscuring the fact that real qualitative differences exist between one economic system and another. They say that formalists are unable to explain why in one society money income is maximized, whereas in another society prestige or other intangibles are maximized. Substantivists also note that in nonindustrial societies the economy cannot be studied separately from kinship and politics, although in Western society these institutions are separate.

---

25. Harold Schneider, *Economic Man* (New York: Free Press, 1974).

---

26. George Dalton, "Economic Theory and Primitive Society," in *Economic Anthropology*, ed. E. E. LeClair and H. Schneider (New York: Holt, Rinehart and Winston, 1968).

Formalists, on the other hand, criticize the substantivists for relying on static functionalist theory, and for treating each society as a unique case. This approach will not facilitate the discovery of general laws about economic behavior, the formalists believe.

In their empirical work, however, both the formalist and substantivist economic anthropologist gathers information that is useful to each. Salisbury, for example, is a formalist, yet his description of Tolai marketplaces might be used to support the substantivist position. It is important to note that these two positions do not include all the possible theoretical positions from which to study economic exchange. A Marxist, for example, might ask which group in a society controls the means of production and to what extent economic control underlies political control. An archeologist, on the other hand, might be more interested in the details of toolmaking and the exact ways in which particular tools were used in hunting or agriculture. Economic theories, like other theoretical viewpoints, are never either right or wrong. They can be judged only according to the usefulness of the questions arising from them.

Summary

1. While Americans generally think of money when they think of the economy, not all economies employ money. However, all societies do have rules by which labor is organized, and by which goods are produced and distributed in society.
2. The natural setting—what raw materials a people have available to them—influences economic life, through the geographic distribution of resources and the seasonal variation in the availability of those resources. However, people are not limited to resources available near at hand since all people engage in trade with people living in other regions. A people's economy also has an effect on the way they use their environment.
3. Technology is related in complex ways not only to the organization of work of a society, but also to its social life and values. For example, technological change among the Yir Yiront was intimately linked to change in almost all other aspects of their lives.
4. Social rules concerning who owns productive resources, how work is organized, and how the products of work are distributed exist in all economies.
5. Property can refer to both tangible and intangible things and can be controlled by individuals or groups. Property is usually thought of as a relationship between a person and a thing, but rules concerning property also define relationships between people. since these rules identify certain people as having rights over what is to be done with a thing that other people do not have. These rights may be limited, however.
6. All cultures have rules about the allocation of land resources, though the specific rules vary from society to society. Land is everywhere valued as a productive resource, but it may also have symbolic value.
7. All cultures also have rules about the allocation of human labor, another productive resource. In all known societies, there are rules specifying a sexual division of labor, though the specific tasks assigned to men and to women vary greatly from society to society, and change with changes in economic type. Other bases for the division of labor are age and caste, as well as region. Specialization of work is most highly developed in industrial societies.
8. There are three basic modes of exchange, but not all operate in every society. They are reciprocal exchange, redistributive exchange and market exchange.
9. Reciprocal exchange can take one of three forms—generalized, balanced, and negative—

according to the closeness of the relationship between the parties involved.

10. Trade relationships and nontrade social relationships may be closely intertwined, as the example of the *kula* ring shows.

11. Redistribution may be equal, or it may be part of a hierarchical political system where high-ranking people may keep a large proportion of the products for their own use.

12. Market exchange requires a general-purpose money and a highly developed specialization of labor to operate. In market economies, almost all livelihood is derived from selling something—labor or products—and the relationship between supply and demand strongly influences the value of these things.

13. Economic anthropologists do not agree on how to study economic systems. Formalist and substantivist economic anthropologists disagree most over whether Western economic theory helps us to understand all types of economies.

Review Questions

1. Discuss the relationship between the physical environment and the economy. To what extent do you think a society's natural resources determine its kind of economy?

2. How do tools affect the organization of work? Do you think that technology has more of an effect on the way work is organized in hunting-gathering societies than in industrial societies?

3. What does it mean to "own" something? Discuss, both from the owner's and the non-owner's point of view. Give concrete examples from your own experience.

4. Discuss three examples of the division of labor. What do you think the relationship is between cooperation and specialized tasks?

Can you think of examples of cooperation without a division of labor?

5. What are the differences between reciprocal exchange, redistributive exchange, and market exchange? Give examples of each from your own experience.

Suggested Readings

Cancian, Frank. *Economics and Prestige in a Maya Community.* Palo Alto, Calif.: Stanford University Press, 1969.

A study of the interrelation between economics and religion in a modern Mexican community.

Dalton, George, ed. *Tribal and Peasant Economies: Readings in Economic Anthropology.* American Museum Sourcebook in Anthropology Q2. Garden City, N.Y.: Natural History Press, 1967.

This is a useful compendium of essays dealing with tribal economies and with market economies in peasant societies.

LeClair, Edward E., Jr., and Schneider, Harold K., eds. *Economic Anthropology: Readings in Theory and Analysis.* New York: Holt, Rinehart and Winston, 1968.

This is an excellent collection of readings in economic anthropology. The articles cover various types of economic behavior and are most useful in understanding the formalist approach to anthropological studies of economic exchange.

FIELD PROJECT
Economic Organization

I n this exercise, we will look at ecological and economic relationships in our own society. As we saw in Chapter 10, the people in all societies interact with the environment to "make a living." For all societies, too, people have socially agreed-upon rules by which resources and tools are owned, labor is organized, and goods are produced and distributed in society. Such arrangements constitute the economy of a society. The ecology and the economy of any society are closely related, since the type of economy affects the ways in which natural resources are used. The availability and location of resources, in turn, affect the economy. Our economy, for example, is heavily dependent on limited fossil fuel resources. Strip-mines in Virginia and air pollution in Los Angeles, the recording and the plastics industries, and agricultural fertilizers are all part of an integrated system involving natural resources, technology, labor, and the consumer. To consider the economy and ecology of a society, we must be aware of:

1. the resources on which people depend, where they come from, and how they are obtained.

2. the technology people use to obtain and process raw materials into useful or desired items.

3. the needs or desires of people: consumption is not just biologically determined. Needs are shaped by a people's culture and vary from society to society.

4. the organization of labor to get the job of production done.

5. the distribution of products (and such productive property as land and tools) to the people who want them.

To describe all these things for even the smallest group of hunters and gatherers is a book-length task. It requires both interviewing and observation of human activities, as well as surveying techniques drawn from biological ecology, geography, and geology. We cannot even begin to describe these things for an industrial society such as our own. In this field project, we will get only a small sense of what a study of our economy and ecology might involve.

Let us begin this exercise by looking at the requirements of people that the economic system and our resources satisfy if we are to live what we consider normal, comfortable lives. Draw on your own experience as a participant and observer of your own society. Answer the following questions in as detailed a fashion as possible:

1. *Food.* What do you usually eat for breakfast? for lunch? for snacks? Keep a record for one week, recording: where you get your food (from the store? cafeteria? friend?). How you get it (buy it? as a gift?). How and by whom it is prepared.

Look at the labels of a sample of foods you buy to determine where they were packaged or where they come from. How many come from your city? state? country?

2. *Clothing.* Make a list of your clothing, perhaps organizing it by function (work, play, party, etc.). What proportion was made by you? given to you? bought? How are your clothes cared for? With what tools? What cosmetics and jewelry do you have? Did you buy them? make them? receive them as gifts?

3. *Housing.* How many different dwellings have you lived in? Describe your current residence: its size, number of rooms, furniture and decorations, and what it is made of. How did you find it?

How do you keep it (by paying rent? by buying it? etc.)? How do you light it? heat it? Where does your water come from? How do you care for it? What tools are used in maintaining your dwelling? Do you take care of repairs yourself?

4. *Transportation.* What sort of transportation do you use? How frequently is each kind used per week? How often do you have to pay for it? If you own a vehicle, how much do you spend in upkeep per year? What reasons exist for using transportation? to get to work or school? to get food? clothes? for pleasure? visiting?

5. *Services.* What kinds of medical attention do you get regularly? Is a specialist involved? Is money given in exchange for medical services? What medical products do you need regularly? How do you get them? What are they made out of?

Do you attend religious services? Is a specialist involved? Do you pay money in exchange or support of such services?

What other services do you make use of (i.e., educational, artistic)? Do you have to pay money in order to use them?

6. *Entertainment.* What kinds of entertain-

ment do you engage in? How frequently does your entertainment involve spending money? What kinds of tools are involved? Resources?

Look over your answers to the preceding questions. As you might imagine, the number of resources you depend on—the natural products out of which your tools, dwelling, food, clothes, fuel, medical supplies, etc., are made—is vast, much greater than that of most of the people about whom you read in Chapters 10 and 11. What can you say, for example, about the geographical origins of just the food items you use? The things we use and depend upon come from all over the nation and the world, and require an elaborate network for their distribution. What proportion of the things you use in your daily life could you obtain by offering goods you have in exchange, or as gifts? How much of what you need could you make yourself? How much is made by specialists? What proportion of your needs are obtained by means of money? How much money is required to satisfy your daily needs?

Two things should be obvious by now: first, the number of resources we depend on is great and the goods come from all over the world, and second, we require money to satisfy a great deal of our daily needs. Most people in our society acquire this money by working for wages and salaries. In the second part of this field project, you will record an employment history. First record your own. Then, if possible, interview a few willing friends or acquaintances with experiences different from your own, asking them the same questions.

1. What jobs have you had since you first started earning money? List employers, job titles, and job descriptions.

2. What training or skills were involved in each job? Did these jobs involve the same skills? Was each job part of a larger process in which you were responsible for only one part of the total product? How many specialized jobs were there in the whole process?

3. How many hours per week did you work at each job? How many things did you produce or sell?

4. What were working conditions like? Describe the physical layout of the work place, the type of tools used, the danger of the work, if any, noise level, contact with other workers or supervisors, amount of break time, etc.

5. What other sources of income have you had other than jobs (loans? gifts? etc.)?

6. Have you ever been unemployed? How did you manage at that time?

Based on the information you and your classmates have collected on employment histories, what can you say about the degree of specialization of work in our society? What can you say about the degree of control people have over the production of goods and services?

Chapter 12

Social Control

TRADITIONAL GOVERNANCE AMONG THE ASHANTI OF WEST AFRICA

NATIVE NAME: Asante (also commonly known as Ashanti)

POPULATION: nearly 90,000 as of the 1960 census

ENVIRONMENT: Over 80 percent of the Asante live in the 9,417-square-mile Asante region located in central Ghana, a West African republic. From the late seventeenth century to the late nineteenth century, the region was an independent kingdom which, at the height of its power, controlled most of present-day Ghana, and parts of present-day Togo and Ivory Coast. The Asante region of Ghana is composed of a forested plateau drained by many streams in its southwestern half, and savanna in the northeast. The two zones are bisected by a scarp in which lies the crater lake Bosumtwe.

SOURCES: Data on the Asante were culled from a number of published sources, the oldest being T. E. Bowdich's *Mission to Ashantee* (London, 1819).

[With the Ashanti of West Africa] status differentiation among families is largely a political matter. The most important of all is

Source: From Elman R. Service, *Profiles in Ethnology*, rev. ed. (New York: Harper & Row, 1971), pp. 373–377. Copyright © 1958, 1963, 1971 by Elman Service. Reprinted by permission of Harper & Row, Publishers.

the royal family. Next in importance are those families whose heads are chiefs of territorial subdivisions of the kingdom. In each of the chiefdoms, a particular matrilineal lineage provides the chief, but he is chosen by the lineage from among several men who are eligible for the post.

Elections take place in the following manner. The senior female of the chiefly lineage is asked to nominate a chief from among the eligible males of the lineage. She, in turn, consults all of the elders (male and female) of the lineage, and together they make the selection. This nomination is sent to a council of elders, who represent other lineages in the town or district. They in turn present the nomination, with appropriate arguments, to an assemblage of the people. If they do not approve, the whole process is begun again to nominate a different man. The new chief is enstooled [set upon the stool that symbolizes the seat of Ashanti government] by the elders, who admonish him with the list of expectations they have of him. He, in turn, takes a solemn oath to the Earth Goddess and to his ancestors to fulfill his duties.

The chief is surrounded by a great deal of pomp and ceremony, and theoretically he has considerable despotic power, including the ability to make judgments of life or death on his subjects. When he sits upon the stool, he is sacred, as the holy intermediary between his people and the ancestors. But his power is more apparent than real. He must listen to the Council of the Elders, govern justly and bravely, and behave circumspectly. Should the Elders and public opinion turn against him, he can be impeached—destooled— and then he becomes merely another ordinary man, except that he is derided for his failure.

The chiefs of the district divisions, as well as village and sub-divisional chiefs, are elected in the same way, and each swears fealty to the one above him. The *Ashantihene* (King of all Ashanti) is chief of the division of Kumasi, the nation's capital, and is appointed in the same way as the others, but the other local chiefs are subject to him. His power, too, is circumscribed by the elders and by public opinion in his own division, and the chiefs of the other areas have a considerable constitutional check on him. As a symbol of the nation, his importance is testified to by the extraordinary deference ritually accorded to him, but the context is religious —he sits for the sacred ancestors. The land, for example, is said to belong to the king, but the phrase means actually that it belongs to the tribal ancestors whom he represents. He cannot alienate land or, in fact, indulge in any act of arbitrary power not agreed upon by the people.

The presence of aristocratic clans and the power of elders would seem to be evidence of a sort of oligarchical tendency in Ashanti political life [government by a small group of families]. But there is an additional feature of the society which in considerable measure assures a kind of democratization of the governmental process. In modern urban civilization, it tends to be the poor and the illiterate who need special machinery or organization in order to have a hearing, but in primitive life older men typically monopolize political power and young men are relatively helpless. The Ashanti have elaborated a peculiar institution called the *mmerante*, an organization of young men. At their meetings they select a representative to argue their views, and he adds his opinion at all meetings of the Council of Elders and chiefs. No action can be undertaken without consulting the representative of the young men.

The Ashanti state addresses itself to the problems of internal order by evoking religious rather than secular-legal postulates. The state is, after all, a theocracy; hence crimes are viewed as sins. Acts which are antisocial with respect to the body politic are seen as offenses against the ancestors first, and only derivatively and secondarily are they defined as harmful to the community. If the chief or king failed to punish a crime, the ancestors would be angry with the whole Ashanti people. The penalty for all crimes is death. Only the king has the power to exact this penalty. But the king also has the power to commute the sentence, which lays the way open for bribes and ransom. These are not so regulated as to be considered fines, properly speaking, but they are a considerable source of revenue to the state, which consequently welcomes quarrels and litigation. Such commutations are actually more frequent than execution.

The most abhorred crime is murder. Suicide, curiously, is considered murder, and the miscreant, though already a corpse by his own hand, is subjected to decapitation, the standard punishment for murder. In a sense a suicide is also guilty of "contempt of court," because of the rule that only the king can kill an Ashanti. Hence, he is not only decapitated but all of his property is forfeited to the king. The Ashanti feel that intent must be established in a murder trial; if the homicide is judged accidental, the murderer pays a heavy compensation to the lineage of the deceased. On the other hand, certain actions which can be interpreted as an intent or threat to kill are punished just as if an actual homicide were committed. A person judged insane would not be executed for murder because of the absence of responsible intent. And drunkenness, except for the extreme crimes of murder and cursing the king, is considered a valid defense. Several kinds of sex offenses, such as incest within either the matrilineal or patrilineal lineage, intercourse with a menstruating woman, rape of a married woman, adultery with any of the wives of a chief, are all capital crimes. Other assaults or even insults against a chief or a member of his court, or for a woman to call a man a fool, also are considered crimes punishable by death.

Cursing the king—that is, calling upon a supernatural power to cause the death of the king—is such a horrible crime that the Ashanti do not speak of it as such; they call it *blessing the king.* A man who angers another man to the point that the latter is driven to curse the king is considered also to be at fault, and he must pay a heavy indemnity. Sorcery and witchcraft are special crimes, and are not punished by decapitation but by strangling, clubbing, burning, or drowning, for a witch's blood must not be shed.

Ordinarily disputes between individuals are settled by the families or lineages concerned, but it is possible to bring disputes to a trial if one of the disputants utters a tabooed oath of a chief or of the king. The case is then tried in the court of the district chief whose oath has been used. In the end, the king's court is the sentencing court, however, for only the king can order the death penalty. In the trial, the two litigants state their cases in long orations directed to the chief and his court and the Council of the Elders. Cross-examination of the testimony can be made by anyone present, but eventually, if the proceedings do not lead to a verdict, a special witness is called, and his testimony decides the case. Strangely, there is only one witness; the two litigants do not each have their own witnesses. It is assumed by everyone that the oaths the witness must swear insure his telling the truth. The idea that he might be friendly or hostile to one of the disputants is unthinkable, even if he is a kinsman. Sometimes, particularly in cases such as witchcraft or adultery, which would have no witnesses, questions of fact are decided by ordeals. The ordeal is requested by the accused, rather than imposed by the court, and frequently takes the form of drinking poison.

The character of the judicial system emphasizes that the Ashanti concept of rectitude and good behavior favors harmony among the people. One must act always in terms of the rules made by the gods and the ancestors. Ancestor worship is fundamental to the Ashanti moral system, and lies at the base of the governmental sanctions. The link between mother and child is the relationship that is the basis of the whole network, which includes ancestors and fellow men as well.[1]

● ● ● ● ● ● ● ●

Chapter Twelve

All societies have some conceptions of what is right and proper behavior under given sets of circumstances. Obviously, the standards vary enormously from culture to culture. Among the Ashanti, as we have seen, behavior such as murder or cursing the king is forbidden because it is a transgression against the ancestral code. Marrying a sibling is frowned upon in most societies today; it was considered desirable among the rulers of Ptolemaic Egypt. Despite different attitudes toward specific behavior, all societies have developed some means of enforcing cultural norms so that impropriety can be suppressed, eliminated, or punished. In other words, every society exercises social control. It does so through the institution known as *political organization.*

In Western culture, the term "political organization" may call forth in our minds an elaborate network of elected and appointed officials; a system of making and enforcing laws; the competition for power among diverse interests through voting and pressure tactics; perhaps even such physical symbols as a flag. In another culture—that of the traditional Ashanti, say—the components are clearly different: a hierarchy of chiefs subordinate to a king; a system of punishing offenders as sinners against Ashanti religion; a kingdom unified by ancestor worship; a holy stool symbolic of royal power. In small-scale cultures, political organization might consist of nothing more than a quiet meeting of old men assembled to settle a quarrel over a stolen cow.

1. From Elman R. Service, *Profiles in Ethnology,* rev. ed. (New York: Harper & Row, 1971), pp. 373–377. Copyright © by Elman Service. Reprinted by permission of Harper & Row, Publishers.

Political organization, then, may be formal or informal. But it exists in all societies to regulate behavior that is of concern to the whole community. Political organization may be said to exist for the purpose of making and carrying out public policy (fostering social order) and resolving conflicts (discouraging social disorder). Indeed, the regulation of conflict is of the utmost importance in all societies; without mechanisms to resolve conflict, orderly social life becomes impossible. Control mechanisms develop in a variety of forms, as adaptations to actual or potential conflict. These adaptations regulate the nature of behavior by restricting or eliminating those who act in opposition to established cultural norms. When a society has a specialized system of administration and personnel concerned only with political organization, we speak of a *government.* All societies have political organizations, but not all societies have governments.

In studying political organization, anthropologists used to distinguish between "primitive" and "advanced" societies. Among "primitive" people, social control was thought to be either based on tradition or compelled by the economic need for a regulated exchange of goods and services. Only in the so-called advanced societies were people thought to be capable of ordering society through a formalized body of rules—that is, a code of law. More recently, however, anthropologists have tended to see the same basic forces at work to motivate conformity in all societies.

Types of Political Organization

Anthropologist Elman Service has classified all human political organizations into four basic types: the band, the tribe, the chiefdom, and the state.[2] In this ordering, there is a progression from the least to the most formal, from unspecialized to highly specialized, and from egalitarian to class- or caste-oriented. Although these four types are frequently seen as four stages in an evolutionary growth, this is not always the correct interpretation. For one thing, different forms of political organization may exist together in the same society. For example, some elements of tribal organization may exert a strong influence within a modern African state. And one political organization may contain elements generally characteristic of two different types. The Ifugao of the Philippines, for instance, have a large population—usually found only in chiefdoms or states—but maintain a decentralized tribal organization.

The Band

The simplest of all political organizations is the *band*, an autonomous group related by kinship. It is common among hunting and gathering peoples who live as nomads—Eskimos, the Bushmen, American Indians of the Great Basin region. Since their food supply is usually limited, a band is generally small and ranges over a fairly wide area. It may have no more than twenty members, and rarely more than a few hundred. According to many anthropologists, band organization characterized almost all human societies before the invention of agriculture some 10,000 years ago.

Within a band the concept of private ownership is practically nonexistent. Everyone shares the food that is found or caught, and individuals lay claim to only a few items such as tools, weapons, or ornaments. Democracy prevails, and political organization is quite informal. Leadership may rest in the hands of one man or several men, generally the elders of the community, but it is not inherited, nor is it maintained by force. The headman, if one exists, is often someone respected for his hunting skills, who exercises power through personal influence. Typically, decisions affecting the band are arrived at by consensus and enforced through informal social pressures.

The French anthropologist Claude Lévi-Strauss has reported that the Nambikwara of Brazil, who live in bands, do have a leader (whom he terms a chief) who takes on a number of responsibilities—choosing the itinerary for the band, arranging hunting expeditions, and supervising relations with neighboring bands. However, his authority is exercised through his prestige and his ability to inspire confidence, not through coercion. He must be generous in allocating food and the material objects of the culture, and ingenious and knowledgeable about the ways of survival in the forest.

And what are the rewards of leadership in a band? Writes Lévi-Strauss:

Around the year 1560 Montaigne met, in Rouen, three Brazilian Indians who had been brought back by some early navigator. What, he asked one of them, were the privileges of a chief ("king" was what he said) in their country? The Indian, himself a chief, said: "He's the first man to march off to war." Montaigne tells this story in his Essays and marvels at the proud definition. It was a matter, for me, of intense astonishment and admiration that I received the same reply, nearly four centuries later. The civilized

2. Elman R. Service, *Primitive Social Organization: An Evolutionary Perspective* (New York: Random House, 1962).

The men drink Coca Cola at a wedding feast in Nigeria. Marriage is an important means of forming alliances between kinship groups.

countries do not show anything like the same constancy in their political philosophy! [3]

The Tribe

The second type of political organization, the *tribe*, is in some ways not much more than an extension of the band. It is larger in size, chiefly because, as is characteristic

of agriculturalists, a more assured food supply permits greater concentration of people. Typical tribal groups are the Tiv of northern Nigeria, the Yanomamö of Venezuela, and the Navajo of the American Southwest. Though private property plays a larger role in the tribe than it does in the band, political organization is similar in its egalitarianism and its informal leadership and systems of control.

The difference between a tribe and a band is the presence within a tribe of autonomous subtribal groups. If there is an emergency—such as war—or some other

---

3. Claude Lévi-Strauss, *Tristes Tropiques* (New York: Atheneum, 1972), pp. 302–303.

situation—such as a large ceremony—that calls for united action, these groups will act together until the situation has been dealt with; then they will revert to their former autonomous existence. (An analogy in our society might be the mobilization of opinion among veterans' social clubs when Congress threatens to cut pensions; after organizing a successful nationwide pressure campaign through letters, meetings, and petitions, the individual groups throughout the country resume their normal round of local social and fraternal activities.) Within an autonomous tribal association there may be several kinds of subtribal organizations—kinship groups, societies, age-set systems, and local leaders known as "big men."

KINSHIP GROUPS.   Probably the most important association within a tribe is the *kinship group*. This is often a *clan*, a number of people who trace their descent from a common ancestor. Among the Plains Indians of North America, for example,

> *even the most remotely related, or only fictitiously related, fellow clansfolk were morally obligated to help and shield one another, and in case of intratribal murder the bereaved clan might try to punish the offender or, on the principle of collective responsibility, even a clansman of his. . . . Another general function of clans was the regulation of marriage: because fellow members of a clan were related by blood or were considered relatives, they were not permitted to marry one another.*[4]

4. Robert Lowie, *Indians of the Plains* (New York: American Museum Science Books, 1963), p. 96.

SOCIETIES.   Among tribal groups, smaller associations have been formed around a wide range of nonkinship traits. In North America alone, Indians formed *societies* devoted to the worship of supernatural beings (the kachina cults of the Southwest); to organizing shamanistic healers (the Midewiwin of the Chippewa, the False Face Society of the Iroquois); and to fighting (the seven military societies of the Cheyenne). Such organizations of warriors, which existed among many Plains tribes, had social and ceremonial functions as well as military ones. For instance, they might supervise the moving of a camp, the organization of a buffalo hunt, or the enforcement of discipline at a time of danger. Since members of the societies existed throughout Cheyenne society, they could all be mobilized whenever some outside force threatened the whole tribe.

AGE-SET SYSTEMS.   As the name suggests, an *age-set system* organizes its members not around kinship or voluntary association but according to age. In societies where these systems are common, children are initiated into them at birth or, more commonly, at puberty. A youth moves up through designated groupings until he reaches the oldest group, the elders who control the political affairs of the tribe.

In Africa, where age sets have been a common method of subtribal organization, boys might move as follows: young boys, initiates, warriors, mature men, old men, and elders. (In some cases parallel organizations existed for women.)

> *Among the Kikuyu, the age-grouping system* was *the government. Its leaders were chosen not by birth, not by election, not even by divine appointment. They arrived at their posts by*

accumulating birthdays. And as government was by "committee"—there were no formal chiefs in the Kikuyu system—every man could hope to stand at least once in the limelight and, with his fellow "committee" members, to direct tribal policy. . . . Never was a man alone in life, bereft and friendless. What if he never became an extraordinary man (which was considered not quite seemly anyhow)? He could never be entirely ordinary, either. For all men knew honor and enjoyed prestige—no man more than another—in due course and at the proper time.[5]

"BIG MEN." A fourth means of integrating groupings within a tribe is the institution of the *big man*, common in Melanesia. His authority—which may be considerable—is personal, in that he neither inherits the office nor is elected to it.

Leopold Pospisil, after studying the Kapauku confederacy of New Guinea, has outlined the characteristics and functions of the Kapauku "big man," the *tonowi* ("rich one").[6] This village headman, like political leaders in other tribes, relies more on persuasion than force; yet his leadership is real. How does he acquire it? First of all, he must be rich (in pigs, for the Kapauku economy is based on breeding and trading pigs). Second, he must be generous; this does not mean giving gifts, but lending money, often without interest.

A rich man who is not generous in this way may be reprimanded, ostracized, or even executed. Third, he must have what Pospisil calls "verbal courage"—the ability to argue forcefully and eloquently on public issues. And fourth, because of the requirements of wealth and the job itself, he must be healthy and middle-aged.

The *tonowi* has a large number of followers in those who have borrowed money from him and fear having to pay it back. In addition, he provides for a group of young boys of poor families, who live with him in exchange for serving as bodyguards and helping him in other ways. He also, of course, depends upon the loyalty of his kinsmen, for whom he can do favors and provide economic aid.

The *tonowi* has authority in a number of areas. He conducts negotiations with other villages and serves as a military leader. He mediates disputes among his own people. He initiates such projects as bridge building. And, last but not least, he determines the dates of pig markets.

The Chiefdom

Unlike the band and the tribe, where leadership is essentially informal and political units are decentralized, the *chiefdom* concentrates considerable power in one man, the chief. There is a greater population density than with the band or tribe. Instead of being egalitarian, the chiefdom is a ranked society with a definite hierarchy in which every member occupies a specific position.

Unlike the band headman and tribal leader, who often function as such only during an emergency or to handle a specific problem, the chief has permanent authority. His position may be hereditary and, frequently, after amassing considerable

---

5. Olivia Vlahos, *African Beginnings* (New York: Viking, 1967).

6. Leopold Pospisil, *The Kapauku Papuans of West New Guinea* (New York: Holt, Rinehart and Winston, 1963).

The stooling ceremony in Ghana among the Ewe-speaking people of Agave takes place annually. The great ivory stool symbolizes the social order of Agave.

wealth, he may pass his leadership on to his heir. The chief has the power to allocate resources, redistribute land, and recruit soldiers and laborers.

Chiefdoms were characteristic of many regions of Polynesia. In Tahiti, there were several paramount chiefs whose special expertise was to conduct large-scale warfare. The Hawaiians had strict gradations of rank, with a chief who claimed descent from the gods. He had the right of life and death over his subjects, and could seize their property at will.

The State

With the *state* we come to a more familiar form of political organization. Indeed, a major theme in the history of Western culture, particularly since the Middle Ages, has been the development of political organization from the decentralized units of the feudal system to the highly centralized and specialized governments that characterize industrialized nations today.

In a state, population density is great because of the practice of *intensive agriculture* (a technological adaptation superior to horticulture, characterized by plows, irrigation, fertilizers, etc.). There are strict systems of class or caste ranking and numerous diverse groups over which rule is extended. Most important, the state has a monopoly of physical force through which it exercises social control. The exercise of force is vested in various branches of government, often employing thousands of people (the police, the army, the militia, and so on), so that the authority is impersonal.

According to anthropologist Morton Fried, the political organization of the state functions to (1) maintain the economic status quo regardless of the inequities of the system, and (2) maintain social order, suppressing disorder from within and defending the state against threats from without. In order to achieve these objectives, says Fried, the state has four secondary functions: (1) It controls its population by maintaining boundaries, controlling administrative subdivisions, and determining citizenship. (2) It sets up legal codes and establishes courts and judges to interpret them. (3) It carries out court decisions through systems of law enforcement. (4) It sets up a fiscal system to pay for its own operation and to carry out state-supported projects.[7]

---

7. Morton Fried, "On the Evolution of Social Stratification and the State," in *Culture in History*, ed. S. Diamond (New York: Columbia University Press, 1960), pp. 713–731.

At the Dzawuwu *(the stooling ceremony of Agave), the chiefs pay homage to the* Awomefia, *swearing amidst war songs and mass musketry to defend and remain faithful to the ivory stool.*

How Political Organizations Operate

Whether a political organization is a band of thirty nomadic hunters in the Australian outback or a parliamentary government representing millions of people in Western Europe, it needs to exert social control over those who belong to it. Organizing people to do what they want to do is no problem: the hunters will gladly plan a feast; citizens are happy to accept a tax rebate. But how can a political organization get people to do things that they do *not* want to do: move camp, for example, or obey inconvenient parking regulations?

Force and Legitimacy

Societies impose sanctions on their members in order to shape their behavior. *Positive sanctions*—rewards for approved actions—include titles and public recognition. *Negative sanctions*—penalties for disapproved behavior—include corporal punishment and ostracism (being excluded from the group). Negative sanctions seem to have greater influence on society members than do positive sanctions. In fact, many social theorists, including anthropologists and political scientists, believe that force lies at the heart of all political systems. In the majority of societies that have been studied, the use of force appears to be the most persuasive recourse available to a political· organization that wants to remain in control of a society and enforce the compliance of its members. Physical force may range from the gentle shove of a tribal elder or a jail term, to outright execution. Almost as effective as the actual use of force is the threat of force. If people know that anyone caught crossing a well-patrolled boundary is shot on sight, there will probably be few attempts at illegal border-crossing. In order to retain authority and control, a political organization makes clear to its members what behavior will be permitted and what will be punished by force. These constraints, written or unwritten, evolve to meet changing circumstances within a society.

The concept of physical force to implement policy is most characteristic of the state level of organization. It is also found in less centralized societies, such as those of the Bedouin nomads and in other parts of the Mediterranean region where feuding is common. However, not all anthropologists would agree that physical force is essential to every political organization. Coercion of a milder sort is exercised by public opinion, a very powerful weapon for insuring conformity to cultural rules in many societies. Negative sanctions of ridicule and humiliation are widely used by the Pueblo Indians and other American groups. Traditionally, physical force is virtually never employed among the Hopi and Zuñi.

The threat of *supernatural sanctions* is powerful in a number of societies. Among the Dani of New Guinea and the Manus of the Admiralty Islands, fear of ghostly punishment keeps most members in line. *Taboos*—the setting apart of certain objects, places, or people as sacred or forbidden—are another important mechanism of social control. Taboos are usually applied to certain specific types of behavior. Thus sexual taboos (for example, ostracism of menstruating women) are part of the complex of marriage rules. Food taboos (for example, prohibitions against eating certain animals) may be part of the regulations insuring the efficacy of a shaman's cures, and thus part of a complex of religious rules.

Among most peoples there is a mixture of physical force and nonphysical forms of coercion, as well as a blend of formal and informal controls. Ashanti society is an example. The recognized king of all Ashanti, the *Ashantihene*, can order the death penalty, although his powers are circumscribed by elders and public opinion, and only certain types of crimes are punishable by execution. But, as we have seen, most disputes are settled within the family or, if necessary, in court or through ordeals.

Whatever kind of coercion a political organization uses—whether physical force or less drastic means—it will not work unless it is perceived as conforming to the recognized standards of the society. This is the principle of *legitimacy*. The Ashanti king can decree death because he has been duly chosen to hold his exalted office, which carries this power. The headman of a band can persuade its members to move camp because, respecting his hunting expertise, they are willing to accept his judgment. The government of a city can prevent the parking of cars near fire hydrants because its citizens agree that the city firemen need access to water.

Another way of understanding legitimacy is in terms of a society's expectations. People are willing to accept decisions, to obey directives, because in a sense they expect some benefit from doing so. A political organization, no matter how rudimentary, performs services for its members—keeping order, giving economic aid, providing security against enemies. If we think of our political organization as beneficial in the long run, we are willing to abide by its sanctions.

Legitimacy, clearly, is related to a society's values—to what its members perceive as just, to the goals in which they believe. For those who have no property (for example, the Bushmen), hunting prowess confers a right to lead; for those who value wealth (for example, the Kapauku), a rich man is a natural candidate for *tonowi*.

Religion plays an extremely important role in legitimizing a political organization. The Incas of Peru were among the many peoples who believed that their emperor was descended from their principal deity. In the case of the Ashanti, whose religious views define crimes as sins against Ashanti ancestors, the king, as an intermediary between the people and their forebears, must punish offenders in order to save his subjects from the wrath of the ancestors.

Ethical principles, whether or not inspired by religion, may also work to deny legitimacy to a political organization or to certain of its actions. In the United States, for instance, a significant segment of the population regarded the Vietnam War as an illegitimate exercise of the power to wage war. Many Americans showed their unwillingness to participate in that war by going to jail or fleeing the country as a protest.

Processes of Conflict Settlement

As stated earlier, the regulation of conflict is vitally important in all societies. A political organization, based on the twin factors of coercion and legitimacy, must be, to a great extent, successful in maintaining peaceful relations among its members if the society is to survive. Peaceful resolution of conflict is achieved through law; when it breaks down, violent resolution may be seen as the only solution.

The definition of law is a matter of some dispute among lawyers as well as among social scientists. To paraphrase anthropologist E. Adamson Hoebel, a *law* is a social norm whose violation beyond permissible boundaries evokes formal response by those in the society who, by common consent, have the right and privilege of determining guilt or innocence and imposing punishment on wrongdoers.[8] Enlarging on this definition, we might say that laws are culturally established standards of behavior and guides to social interaction. This behavioral road map is generally accepted by members of the society even if many of them disagree with it or deviate from parts of it. The need or desire to conform to the laws of society creates a corresponding set of obligations; these demand individual behavior that will contribute to the well-being of the society, or at least not be destructive of it.

Another fundamental point should also be made here: law is part of a political system and not separated from it, even though a distinction is sometimes made for emphasis. Law, like the political system of which it is a part, is an adaptive strategy. It arises out of, and reacts back upon, its environment, aiding and abetting the distribution of wealth and power.

There are many ways of categorizing law. The simplest method for our purposes is to divide it into formal and informal law.

Formal law (also referred to as *public* or *codified law*), which characterizes state political organizations, involves the intervention of an agency established by the government for the express purpose of resolving conflicts. Outside intervention is required when an offense has been committed against the whole society and is no longer regarded as an issue between

---

8. E. A. Hoebel, *Anthropology: The Study of Man*, 4th ed. (New York: McGraw-Hill, 1972), p. 696.

private parties. In Ashanti society, for example, it was required that the heinous offense of cursing the king be tried in a court.

Informal law (also referred to as *private, customary,* or *unwritten law*) is a system whereby an offense by one person or group against another is a matter to be settled between the conflicting parties, without intervention by the representatives of the society at large. Among the Ashanti, families or lineages tried to settle most disputes between individuals. Custom is the key element in this type of law; for the system to work, people must be well socialized in the mores of their society; that is, they must know what behavior is laudable, what is acceptable, what is frowned on, what is condemned, and what is unthinkable.

In some societies today, such as African states, where colonial regimes introduced codified law systems, these systems coexist with some features of earlier traditional systems of unwritten law. A similar situation exists in Latin America, where both Mayan and Mexican legal systems operate side by side.

In many societies there is less emphasis on determining guilt and punishment than on achieving a settlement satisfactory to all parties involved. Thus, rather than confining ourselves to distinctions between types of law, it is more helpful to think in terms of resolution of conflict. The important point to remember is that most people must agree on the procedures for resolution and how they should operate.

FORMAL SOCIAL CONTROL. Police forces, armies, courts of law, arbitration boards, and many other legal mechanisms of government are agencies common in formal systems for the purpose of resolving

In a village, Baila, Senegal, the tribal elders sit daily to settle disputes and administer village affairs.

conflicts. Let us look at one such system in Somalia. The system is organized around some 360 *dia*-paying groups. (*Dia* is an Arabic word meaning "blood compensation.") Each member of a *dia*-paying group is obligated by contract to help pay compensation for transgressions committed by members of the group. Thus, if a man kills someone from another group and the offender's *dia*-paying group agrees to pay a hundred camels to the victim's group, everyone in the slayer's group is responsible for contributing a share of the payment.

If anyone refuses to pay, compulsion is used. On instruction from the elders, young men tie the reluctant person to a tree and then slaughter, or threaten to slaughter, some of the person's livestock. Coercion ends when the individual agrees to submit to the settlement.

Formal social control may also exist in small-scale cultures. It is resorted to when an offense is regarded as having been committed against the entire society. Colin Turnbull, writing of a Pygmy band in Africa, describes an incident involving a hunter named Cephu. Failing to trap any animals himself, he had set up a net in front of the other hunters, caught the first of the animals to be driven into it by beaters, and hid meat in his hut:

> *I had never heard of this happening before, and it was obviously a serious offense. In a small and tightly knit hunting band, survival can be achieved only by the closest cooperation and by an elaborate system of reciprocal obligations which insures that everyone has some share in the day's catch.*[9]

The band met, discussed the case, heard Cephu's weak defense (a claim of unwittingness, which no one believed), and threatened to expel Cephu and his immediate kin. Cephu knew he could not survive this way.

> *He apologized profusely, reiterated that he really did not know he had set up his net in front of the others, and said that in any case he would hand over all the meat. This settled the matter, and accompanied by most of the group he returned to his little camp and brusquely ordered his wife to hand over the spoils. She had little chance to refuse, as hands were already reaching into her basket and under the leaves of the roof where she had hidden some liver in anticipation of just such a contingency. Even her cooking pot was emptied. Then each of the other huts was searched and all the meat taken. Cephu's family protested loudly and Cephu tried hard to cry, but this*

> *time it was forced and everyone laughed at him.*[10]

In societies where there are many agencies of formal law, actual control of the society is often reinforced by informal mechanisms such as gossip and peer-group pressure. People living in small communities generally have less chance to deviate from cultural norms than do people in large cities, since nonconformity is more quickly noticed and controlled in an intimate social environment. In urban areas, inhabitants find greater tolerance of deviation and more "alternate cultures" in which they may participate. Even there, however, people may live in culturally homogeneous neighborhoods where the constraints operate very much as they do in villages.[11]

In societies characterized by formal law, people may ignore its sanctions, at least in part. In the Appalachian Mountains of the United States, "moonshining" (making home-distilled liquor) has been common for decades. Making moonshine is illegal, and the federal government continues to send in revenue agents ("revenuers") to raid hidden stills and arrest those who owned them. Men, women, and children worked out an elaborate code system of birdcalls, whistles, and songs to warn of the revenuers' approach. Their methods are so effective that if the federal agents do find a still, it is generally empty and the site deserted.

INFORMAL SOCIAL CONTROL. The Eskimo song duel is an illustration of how conflicts can be resolved informally and

9. Colin Turnbull, *The Forest People* (New York: Simon and Schuster, 1962), p. 107.

10. Turnbull, *The Forest People*, pp. 107–108.

11. Jane Jacobs, *Death and Life of Great American Cities* (New York: Random House, 1961).

without recourse to physical violence. In cases where one Eskimo has done injury to another—for example, by stealing his wife—the opponents get together with their kinsmen and others of the band and settle the issue. Each man makes up songs, full of insults and derogatory remarks, designed to show how right he is and how wrong his opponent is. The singing goes on until there is a general consensus among those present as to who "wins" or "loses." The abstract issues of right and wrong have less to do with the outcome of the case than who made up the most effective songs.

In many societies, some process of arbitration involving third parties, such as elders or religious specialists, serves to help settle disputes. Among the Nuer people of the upper Nile region, a mediator known as the leopard-skin chief (so-called because of his robe) may be called in by disputants. Although his main weapon is persuasion, he uses the threat of supernatural retribution if the parties balk at reconciliation.

The role of kin is especially important in informal law systems, because frequently not only the individual but the entire kin group is involved in settling disputes. When there is a conflict, the solidarity of a kin group may be the individual's best—indeed only—means of support and defense. In some cultures, when a member of one kin group commits an offense against a member of another kin group, the offended party may attempt to resolve the situation by taking action not only against the actual offender but against his or her relatives as well. This puts an effective pressure on the kin group to bring deviants under control so as to avoid involving the entire membership. For this reason, informal law systems tend to work well in resolving conflicts with little overt physical punishment.

Even if physical force comes into play,

there may be mechanisms to confine it. Among the Tlingit Indians of the Pacific Northwest, an injury or slaying, especially of a person of rank, was customarily settled by a money payment.

> *Sometimes, . . . in cases where no blood-money settlement could be agreed upon, a chief or noble of the slayer's lineage would take it on himself to resolve the matter. He, of course, had to be of a rank as nearly as possible equivalent to that of the slain person. He donned the finest ceremonial regalia of his lineage. Then he went out of the house, dancing one of the slow, stately hereditary dances of his lineage as he approached the waiting foe. The courteous gesture on their part was to allow him the dignity of approaching to within a few yards of them before they evened matters by killing him.*[12]

WHEN LAW BREAKS DOWN: VIOLENT CONFLICT. If law, whether formal or informal, ceases to operate effectively, people may resort to violent means of resolving disagreements. Such violence ranges in scope from family feuds to tribal raids to full-scale war.

Feuding is a state of conflict between two kinship groups, usually initiated as a means of revenge and lasting a relatively long time. It may involve so many people that its dimensions seem to approach those of a civil war, but it is differentiated from the latter in that its basic intent is collective revenge, whereas the aims of civil war are to vanquish the enemy.

Among the Christian mountain peoples

---

12. Philip Drucker, *Indians of the Northwest Coast* (New York: American Museum Science Books, 1955), p. 149.

of Albania, blood feuds have a long history, although they are apparently dying out since the Communist takeover of the government. In the classic blood feud, one party would make public its intention to kill the other. The threat was usually carried out by means of an ambush: the victim was killed by stabbing or shooting. The killer, in accordance with the mountain code of honor, was required to leave a personal item beside the corpse and to see to it that the victim's family was informed of the death. To do otherwise would be considered cowardly and might result in the killer's ostracism.

Raiding is a short-term, hostile expedition with a specific goal in mind. It is usually aimed at securing livestock or other possessions and is thus fairly common among herding peoples (such as the Kikuyu of Africa, who raided for cattle) or those who value animals for hunting (such as the Plains Indians, who raided for horses). Among the Yanomamö of Venezuela, there is a chronic shortage of women because of the dual practices of female infanticide (the killing of newborn babies) and polygyny (the practice of having more than one wife). Therefore raids are conducted primarily in order to capture females.

Warfare, with armies and specialized tactics and technology, is most common among state political organizations. Its aim is usually the annexation of land and/or political domination of another people. However, the Aztecs of Mexico waged war mainly to capture prisoners, whom they then sacrificed to their gods—a practice they believed was necessary in order to perpetuate the existence of the Aztec state. Large-scale confrontations do occur among less specialized societies as well. The Dani

of New Guinea, for instance, stage formal battles with combatants in regulated battle lines and rules governing weapons, times of fighting, and so on.

Rebellion and revolution are two forms of warfare especially prevalent among state forms of political organization. In a *rebellion*, one or more opposing factions tries to overthrow the authority of the state and install its own ruler, whether a new king (or queen), president, or dictator. In a *revolution*, those who revolt deny the legitimacy of the political system itself. They wish not only to replace the present authority, but to institute a new form of rule. Thus, the French Revolution disposed not only of Louis XVI but also of the institution of monarchy itself.

Political Roles

In all human societies, individuals occupy social positions known as *statuses*; these are not necessarily associated with prestige, but simply indicate people's standing in relation to others. A status with which a person is born is known as an *ascribed status*. Such statuses include sex, racial characteristics, and family membership. A status acquired during one's lifetime—whether bum, mother of four, or Melanesian "big man"—is known as an *achieved status*. If you are born into nobility, your rank would be an ascribed status; if a monarch makes you a peer, your rank would be an achieved status.

All statuses are linked to certain patterns of behavior known as *roles*. Each role, in other words, is composed of expectations held for a given status, both by the person who occupies the status and by society at large. Thus the role for the status of judge in our society usually includes several years of education, a high income, knowledge of the law, the ability to speak well, and a dignified bearing.

In many small-scale societies, the headman is the chief political figure, "first among equals." He leads by persuasion, since he is not endowed by his people with the rights of coercion. In tribal political organization, the headman of a local group such as a clan may exercise certain coercive powers. Even in these cases, however, evidence seems to indicate that persuasion and marshaling of public opinion are still the primary tools of leadership. The headman's status, not being hereditary, is achieved rather than ascribed. In some instances, though, it is possible for a son to follow his father as headman if the son has enough personal prestige. Some groups may have several headmen at once; one may supervise hunting, while another acts as leader in trading activities.

With a chief, even more than with a headman, the observer must look beyond the status to the role. In the political organization of a chiefdom (such as existed in Polynesia), the chief had a sizable amount of authority and the legitimate coercive powers to enforce it. On the other hand, the chief in a tribal society (such as existed among the Iroquois Indians) might well be limited to relatively unimportant ceremonial activities, perhaps arising out of the religious aspect of his role. The position of chief is generally not hereditary, though in some cases the chief's son may take over the role when his father dies.

A king (or queen) inherits leadership; thus the status is ascribed. Kingship is most common among societies with a state form of political organization. Here again the analyst must examine the actual role rather than concentrating on the status.

Kings ruling European monarchies in early modern times had nearly absolute power over their subjects. Today the role is a symbolic one with little real authority. The same diminution of power has occurred in other societies, among them that of the Ashanti.

In all but the most complex state societies, kinship is important as a basis for control. Headmen, chiefs, and kings are generally constrained by the powers of kin groups, especially corporate lineages and lineage groups vested with political powers. It is probably true, as S. N. Eisenstadt contends, that "There has been too great an emphasis on the groups which perform governmental functions rather than on the functions themselves." [13] However, the importance of the principle of leadership remains, especially in complex chiefdoms and kingdoms with a system of formal law.

Functions of Political Organization

Political scientist David Easton has provided a good framework for the study of political organization.[14] It can be utilized regardless of the complexity of the society

13. S. N. Eisenstadt, "Primitive Political Systems: A Preliminary Comparative Analysis," *American Anthropologist* 61 (1959): 201.

14. David Easton, "Political Anthropology," in Bernard J. Siegel, *Biennial Review of Anthropology* (Stanford, Calif.: Stanford University Press, 1959), p. 227.

under study, and provides a useful summary for reviewing the findings of anthropologists as presented in this chapter.

According to Easton, a political organization performs five functions. The first is the *formulation of demands*. The demands people present must be collected and ordered according to priorities. This can be done by a governing group, generally some form of council, which may debate and reformulate the demands. At this point the group presents its formulations to the leader of the people, in whatever form leadership exists. Among the Yanomamö, a group of village elders may debate the demand of young bachelors for wives and then go to the headman recommending a raid. In our society, a state governor, after touring a region hit by a tornado, may ask Washington for federal disaster-area relief funds.

The second function is *legislation*. This, simply stated, is a set of procedures whereby alternative modes of action are considered, usually in the light of custom and tradition. Binding decisions can then be made. This legislative process may operate within a council of elders in a chiefdom, or within a parliament in a state. "Legislation" among the Australian aborigines is likely to be arrived at by a few old men squatting in the shade of a tree for an hour. The American system, on the other hand, is characterized by the interaction of numerous formalized agencies that can make passage of a law a tortuous affair lasting years. (States of such complexity may have methods of dispersing power, however. A New England town meeting, for example, can resolve issues of importance to the community; thus, despite state and federal regulations, local governments may have a certain amount of self-determination.)

Administration, according to Easton, is the third function of a political organization. Once rules or decisions have been made, they must be implemented and enforced. The Ashanti king, swearing obedience to the Earth Goddess, took upon himself the responsibility of carrying out his people's duties to their ancestors. Cheyenne military society members were administrators in implementing a band's chief economic activity, the buffalo hunt.

Adjudication, the fourth function of a political organization, is the means a society establishes to settle disputes over interpretation of the rules and the manner in which implementation and enforcement are to be carried out. Eskimos judging a song duel, a Nuer leopard-skin chief, and a British jury are all agents of this function in their respective societies.

In the United States, the legislative, executive, and judicial branches of the government carry out the second, third, and fourth of these functions, while all three branches share in the process of formulating demands. Rarely, generally speaking, are all these functions exercised by separate agencies. Few societies—certainly few of the small-scale groups studied by anthropologists—make formal distinctions among agencies of government. Fewer still have a system of equally balanced powers among them. In small-scale societies, and even in great empires like those of the Aztecs, Incas, and Zulus, executive, legislative, and judicial powers were vested in the same hands: those of the king and his most powerful associates.

Easton lists *support* as the fifth function of a political organization. No system of governance, however tyrannical, can long exist without the support of those being governed. Obviously, extreme force—mass imprisonment and executions—would be costly and self-defeating. Every political organization must possess legitimacy, gaining and maintaining the support of its people toward the system. The existence of legitimacy is dramatically demonstrated in a people's willingness to abide by political decisions they do not like, whether it be a Somali's giving up two camels to his *dia*-paying group or a Tlingit nobleman dancing to his death. The constitutional regime of the United States and the authoritarian regime of China both depend on support—public acceptance and compliance.

Critical questions regarding governance arise in connection with this last function: Do a few people give a great deal of support while the vast majority give only a little? Is support of the governed directed to a person or to a system? Are there elements of the population whose support is more crucial than that of others? Whatever the answers, the support of the governed legitimates the existence and operation of the governing political organization, regardless of its form.

A conclusion to this discussion lies in the concept of *contract*. There is some validity to the notion that societies maintain internal integration through a set of conscious or unconscious social contracts. By establishing customs for law and governance, people are in effect agreeing to abide by these rules within prescribed limits. Whether the agreement is formally proposed and ratified by parliamentary action or assumed by the people to be the natural order of things is irrelevant. Law, governance, authority, power relationships, and mechanisms of social control are all based upon a general consensus by people (or at least by people in control) that this is the way things should be.

Summary

1. Rules for what constitutes proper behavior vary from society to society, but all societies have some means of enforcing cultural norms. These means of social control, called political organization, may be formal and specialized or they may be informal, with no specialized political or governmental institutions. But in either case, anthropologists have found the same processes at work to control conflict and promote order.

2. Anthropologist Elman Service has classified all human political organizations into four types, in a progression from the least to the most formal, specialized, and stratified. The types are: the band, the tribe, the chiefdom, and the state.

3. Bands are usually small in population and generally found among hunting and gathering peoples. Decisions are usually arrived at by consensus and enforced by informal controls.

4. Tribes are usually larger than bands. The tribe is a common form of political organization among agricultural peoples. Tribes are often composed of autonomous subgroups, capable of acting together in specific situations, such as wars or ceremonies. Tribes are subdivided into kinship groups, military or ceremonial societies, and age-sets.

5. Whereas bands and tribes are informally organized and decentralized, chiefdoms are usually more centralized and positions of power in chiefdoms are formal and commonly inherited, reflecting an increase in social inequality over that existing in bands and tribes.

6. The state form of political organization is centralized, stratified, and has specialized political institutions. States are characterized by a monopoly of physical force by the governing group over the rest of the population, through such branches of government as the police and the army.

7. The concepts of force and legitimacy are central to any study of political organization.

8. Societies impose both positive and negative sanctions on their members to shape their behavior. Some social scientists believe that force, a negative sanction, is at the heart of all political systems. The use of physical force is most characteristic of state-level political organizations. Other negative sanctions, such as public opinion and supernatural sanctions, are commonly found in nonstate societies. All societies show a variety of sanctions, however.

9. The use or threat of force and other negative sanctions will not work unless they are considered to conform to recognized and accepted social values and goals. That is, they will not work unless they are considered to be legitimate.

10. Political organization must be, to a great extent, successful in maintaining peaceful relationships among the members of the society if the society is to survive. Peaceful resolution of conflict is achieved through law, both informal and formal, and the use of both informal and formal mechanisms of social control. When such mechanisms break down, violent means such as feuding, warfare, or revolution may be seen as the only solution to social conflict.

11. Political statuses may be achieved or ascribed, and are associated with patterns of behavior, called roles, such as that of the headman, chief, or king.

12. The functions of political organization include formulating demands, legislation, administration, adjudication, and support.

Review Questions

1. What are the important differences between bands, tribes, chiefdoms, and states? Do you think that there is a necessary relationship between large populations and centralized authority?

2. Define legitimacy. Give examples from your own experience of government policies with which you may or may not agree, but which you still consider legitimate. What would you consider not legitimate?

3. Do you think that force or the threat of it is necessary to insure peace? Discuss gossip and shaming from your own experience: Do you think they are as effective as force in controlling behavior?

4. Discuss the difference between achieved and ascribed status. Is the position of President of the United States achieved or ascribed? What about the status of "father"? Do you think that the distinction is useful?

5. What is the difference between formal and informal social control? Give examples from your own experience.

Suggested Readings

Bohannan, Paul. *Law and Warfare: Studies in the Anthropology of Conflict.* American Museum Sourcebook in Anthropology Q1. Garden City, N.Y.: Natural History Press, 1967.
This is a fine collection of articles by various anthropologists on all aspects of governance. It also can be read with reference to the case study on aggression and warfare.

Fallers, Lloyd. *Bantu Bureaucracy.* Chicago: University of Chicago Press, 1965.
This book focuses on a century of political development of a large tribal society in Uganda. It is one of the most representative works of the British school of social anthropology in its approach to African political systems.

Fried, Morton H. *The Evolution of Political Society.* New York: Random House, 1967.
This is a major theoretical treatise that

deals, from an evolutionary perspective, with the development of governance systems.

Mair, Lucy. *Primitive Government*. Baltimore: Penguin Books, 1962.
This book deals with the general subject of the governance structures in small-scale societies. It is especially useful for a study of kingship and the functions of royal families and lineages.

Schapera, I. *Government and Politics in Tribal Societies*. New York: Schocken Books, 1956.
An older book, but a very worthwhile one, that concentrates on the often elaborate systems of governance in small-scale societies, especially those in central Africa.

Social Control

FIELD PROJECT
Political Organization

As we found in Chapter 12, all societies have rules about what constitutes proper and improper behavior for particular circumstances, as well as ways of formulating, enforcing, and changing these rules. This is the political process: the way social control and power are used in a society. The political process may be formal or informal. In a formal political system, specific institutions are set up expressly for political purposes. Some examples are the United States Congress, political parties, and lobbying groups. In an informal system, there are no specialized political organizations or institutions. Instead, political action is an aspect of the activities of multipurpose organizations, short-lived coalitions of people, and interpersonal interaction. Some of these are discussed in Chapters 13 and 14. In societies with a formal political system, politics at the informal level also takes place. In this exercise, we will explore both formal and informal political action in our own society.

First we will consider the institutions in which political action is organized. Read the following questions and answer them by drawing on your own experience first. Then, select a few friends or acquaintances, preferably people with experiences different from yours, and ask them the same questions:

1. To what formal political groups do you belong (for example, your political party)?

In what way do you participate? (For example, you might participate in a political organization by voting, by helping with voter registration, by petitioning for candidates, by participating in political demonstrations, by writing, etc.)

How many members are there in each organization?

What are the criteria for membership? Is there a ceremony marking membership?

What are some of the rules? Is there a constitution, charter, or set of principles in each organization?

Do all members participate in the same way in the organization, or is there a division of labor in tasks and responsibilities? Are there events in which all members participate?

What are the goals of each organization?

2. Answer the above questions in relation to other groups to which you belong (for example, a religious organization, a sports club, a musical group, a club based on an interest in common).

3. Compare your own answers with those of your friends. Are there any differences between formal political organizations and other groups in which people participate, in terms of their *political* activities? In terms of the degree of participation of members in them? In terms of the way they are organized? (For example, do formal political groups have better-defined "offices" and "leaders" than other kinds of groups?) Do formal political organizations have better-defined goals than other kinds of organizations?

Next we will look at the organizations in which you participate from the point of view of David Easton's list of political functions (see the last section of Chapter 12 of the text). Answer the following questions, and then put these questions to a few informants. For each question, answer with reference to one informal and one formal organization—the two with which you are the most familiar. For example, you might choose to answer the questions with reference to your political party as an example of a formal organization, and a student organization to which you belong (or even your family) as an example of another kind of organization that has informal political functions. Please give specific examples of each of the following in formulating your answers, and encourage your informants to do the same:

1. Formulating demands: What sorts of demands does your organization make? Who decides what they will be?

2. Legislation: How are decisions made concerning alternate courses of action? Who decides?

3. Administration: How are decisions implemented or enforced? Who is responsible for this?

4. Adjudication: How are disputes over interpretation of the rules and over administration settled? Who is responsible?

5. Support: How are force and legitimacy used in maintaining support? Do members willingly abide by decisions even when they do not

like those decisions? What coercive measures can legitimately be taken by the organization against members who do not abide by its decisions?

Give examples, based on your experience and/or that of your friends, of an organization that lost its legitimacy and the support of its members. Over what issue or event did this happen? Was the organization destroyed or was it considerably changed as a result? How? Was it able to overcome its "crisis of legitimacy"? Describe the process. What did the members feel had gone wrong? How did they express their criticisms?

Organizations of various kinds are not the only places in which social control is exercised and public decisions are reached and implemented. For example, power relationships are also relevant to interpersonal interactions. Such factors as height, sex, age, dress, or social class of the people involved are relevant in our society, to varying degrees in different situations. Describe personal interactions from your own or your friends' experiences that illustrate the use of the following factors:

1. Sex
2. Age
3. Height (Can you separate the factor of height from the factors of age and sex?)
4. Dress
5. Social Background

Gossip and other similar mechanisms are common means of controlling behavior. Have you ever participated in or been the object of gossip? What were the circumstances? What social values had been breached by the person being gossiped about? What kinds of sanctions were informally imposed on the person being gossiped about? Did the person know he or she was being gossiped about? Did the person alter his or her behavior to conform to public opinion? Do you think that gossip is an effective form of social control?

PART FIVE

We have looked at some of the ways in which people have organized their activities to survive and to live better. We have seen how different cultures get their food, distribute resources, exchange goods, and regulate authority. But there are other kinds of human needs, too. All people need to form some sense of who they are, and where they "fit" into their world. They do this by learning from others around them, and by testing this learning in their lives. Most important, the kind of emotional support a child gets has a great deal to do with the way the child learns to feel about himself or herself. In most societies, children get this support from their families—groups of people who feel bound together by ties of "blood" (or kinship) and marriage. In Chapter 13, we will look at some of the ways in which families are important.

We usually think of a family as being made up of a married couple and their children. As we will see, many families include other people as well. The family can be extended, along lines of kinship relationships and ties of marriage, to create bigger groups. For example, a man and his sons or daughters may form a larger family by bringing in their spouses and children. Or, as among some European groups, cousins of both "sides" of the family may live close together and share food, money, and child care. In all cases, though, family groups regulate sexual relationships and care for children.

Marriages do not link only two people. They also create a bond between the families from which the marriage partners came. In this way, families can be important links in the social structure of an entire society. Groups of families may claim to be descended from the same real or mythical ancestor, and may form the basis for political or religious groupings within a larger society. These groups are often called clans, or lineages, depending on how the groups are set up, or what kinds of relatives they contain.

In small-scale societies, the family is the basic social and economic unit. Labor is divided between men and women. Even in modern societies, this division has tended to persist. Families can take on other types of economic functions as well. In many societies, including our own, families own land and other property. Sometimes a group of relatives acts like a corporation, managing the holdings of all the members together.

For the majority of us today, the most important aspect of the family is probably the warm circle of loving people who cared for us as children. They not only cared for our physical needs, but also gave us those vital intangible things—love and education—that enabled us to grow up to function as members of their group.

It is mostly through the family that a child learns who he or she is, and forms some sort of identity. The child does this by responding to how he or she is treated by others, learning what sorts of social "power" he or she has.

Social Groups & Identity

In Japan, for example, the seven-year-old daughter of a Samurai was taught extreme obedience and self-control, having to memorize extensive lessons and write for hours in frigid rooms, kneeling unmoving in the cold. For her discipline and sacrifice, however, she received lavish praise and the reassurance that she was a superior person, a future priestess. All of us can recall the parental demands, the punishments and praise surrounding our daily activities, which told us when to feel good about ourselves—and which sometimes contradicted our own feelings about what was "good" for us.

The way we see our families treated by other families and groups is another way we form ideas about "who we are." In this way, people create ideas about their race, their economic group, their religion. In our society and others, because the family mediates between the wider social world and the individual, its role in forming identity remains of great importance. What a child learns from its family will depend in some fundamental ways on the kind of social situation that the family is in. If parents and relatives feel helpless, trapped, or frustrated with their world, their experiences will affect their children—just as successful experiences will. So "the survival of the family" is more than an academic concern for the future.

People also derive feelings of identity and security from participation in other kinds of groups outside their families. In some groups, participation is required for all men, or all women, or all boys of a certain age. In other groups, participation is a question of personal choice. Some Indian groups have "societies" for those who wish to heal, or to hunt. In modern societies, immigrant groups may form clubs (to mention only one kind of the many clubs we can think of). Some of these associations are aimed, often with elaborate ritual, at strengthening the identification of the members with the group. Other clubs may provide more limited gratification and enjoyment, or they may be simply educational. Still others may be intended for self-preservation. All of these groups try in some way to enhance the self-image of the participants, and many may meet other needs as well. Anyone who has joined a childhood "secret club" knows that many groups are based on sets of myths, common beliefs and heroes, or a common language. These common symbols express and represent the group.

The identity that comes from the common cultural experiences of a group is called *ethnicity*. In modern societies, ethnicity can be a basis for clubs and "societies," and a basis for political action as well. Relationships among different ethnic groups within a wider society form an important area of political concern for governments today. In Chapter 14 we will examine the question of ethnicity as a social and political issue.

Chapter 13

Kinship & Marriage

JIVARO HOUSEHOLDS OF ECUADOR

NATIVE NAME: Shuara (Jívaro, the more commonly known name, is a Spanish word meaning "uncivilized").

POPULATION: 20,000 as of the 1960 census.

ENVIRONMENT: The lower eastern slopes of the Andes in Eastern Ecuador, South America, a region known as the montaña, characterized by tropical rain forest. Garden crops such as manioc are cultivated by the Shuara, and they also eat fish and wild forest fruit and game.

FIELDWORK: Data on the Shuara were collected during 1956–57 by means of interviewing and direct observation of life.

ETHNOGRAPHIC PRESENT: 1956–57.

Most Jívaro households are very close-knit economic and social units, in contrast to the neighborhood and tribal society as a whole. Each house, averaging about nine occupants, is usually isolated a half-mile or more from the next; but sometimes two, or rarely three, houses may be located within three hundred yards of one another. Adjacent houses, when they occur, invariably belong to

Source: From *The Jívaro: People of the Sacred Waterfalls*, by Michael J. Harner, copyright © 1972 by Michael J. Harner. Reprinted by permission of Doubleday & Company, Inc. Pp. 78–81.

close relatives, usually one being that of a middle-aged man and the other(s) of his son(s)-in-law. Even such limited concentrations are not very permanent, due to such factors as quarreling between the neighboring relatives or the gradual depletion of the local wild game supply.

A household tends to have a typical composition of: one man, two wives, and seven children; or a man, one wife, and three children. Often another relative, such as the widowed mother or an unmarried brother of the head of the household, also resides in the dwelling. Upon marriage of a daughter the house's population is augmented by the son-in-law (*awe*), who will tend to remain until the birth of his wife's first child. Thereafter, according to the norm, the son-in-law and his family dwell in a new house nearby.

Sometimes matrilocal residence [living with wife's parents] is avoided altogether when the suitor substitutes the gift of a shotgun to his father-in-law, instead of performing the more common bride-service [groom works for wife's kin group for a period of time]. This substitution of bride-price [payment made by groom to bride's kin group] for bride-service tends to occur in cases where the suitor feels that a period of matrilocal residence would be a liability, rather than an asset to him, e.g., when his bride's family lives in a neighborhood containing a number of enemies of the suitor's family or when he is already married and must take his bride home with him.

The man is formally head of the household and also informally seems generally to dominate his family. He is responsible for protecting his wife (wives) and children, for hunting and fishing, for clearing the forest for garden plots, and for cutting and bringing in fire logs. He also does some very limited garden chores and weaves the family's homemade garments. His wife (wives) is responsible for the overwhelming majority of the agricultural tasks, as well as for cooking and beer preparation, pottery making, and tending the children, chickens, and pigs, if any. When a son-in-law is resident in the household or living nearby, he helps his father-in-law at his various tasks, and also contributes game and firewood to his father-in-law's household. The son-in-law's wife also often helps her mother, even when resident in another neighboring house. A man and his son(s)-in-law normally consider themselves mutually obligated to defend each other's households from enemies.

Men strongly prefer to have two or more wives. The subsistence productivity of the household closely correlates with the number of wives possessed by a man, because the women are responsible for most of the agricultural production. Thus, a satisfactory household production of food and the important manioc beer is dependent upon polygyny [man has more than one wife at a time].

The most common number of wives for a man to have is two, or three, in that order. The emphasis on polygyny, in part, reflects the fact that the ratio of adult females to adult males is approximately 2:1, largely as a consequence of the attrition of the adult male population through killing. The demand for wives nevertheless exceeds the supply, as evidence by the common practice of "reserving" a prepuberty girl as a future wife by giving gifts of featherwork and trade goods to her parents. Not infrequently, her future husband then takes her home with him to raise her in his house prior to the actual consummation of the marriage. The extreme nature of the demand for wives is illustrated by the fact that men sometimes get a pregnant woman and her husband to agree to "reserve" the unborn child for him if it should be female. Needless to say, these practices result in marriages in which the husband is often substantially older.

An unmarried girl of post-puberty age is normally courted and involved in the decision to become a wife. The suitor, after he informally ascertains her willingness, sends a close male kinsman of his own generation to act as a go-between to sound out the girl's father who, in turn, consults with the girl and her mother. If the go-between reports back to the suitor that there is no opposition, then the latter goes late one afternoon to the house of the girl and her parents, and sleeps that night in the men's end of the house. Before dawn, he leaves the house with a blowgun and goes hunting, attempting to kill a large number of birds and monkeys in order to impress the girl's parents with his competence. When he returns, he offers the game to the girl to cook and he awaits her final decision. If she has decided to marry him, she will squat down beside the suitor when she serves the cooked food and join him in eating it. From that moment on, they are considered husband and wife and will sleep together that night.

The importance of wives in producing food and beer goes far beyond the subsistence requirements of the household itself. Plural wives assure a surplus production which will make possible adequate entertainment of visitors from other households. The Jívaro place a high value on drinking beer and eating (perhaps in that order), so that one's status in a neighborhood is greatly affected by one's generosity with beer and food. No one can expect to have many friends unless he is a good host; and he cannot easily meet the requirements of good hospitality without plural wives as a labor force.[1]

The Jívaro of Ecuador's Amazon Basin have managed to resist domination by the Spanish colonists and their descendants for 400 years. They have also resisted attempts at domination by other Indian societies, including the once mighty Inca of Peru. Among the Jívaro, identity is crucial. A person is either "known" or "unknown." A known person may be either friend or enemy; an unknown person or stranger is usually assumed to be an enemy. For the Jívaro, knowing how to tell the difference may be a matter of freedom or slavery, life or death. Of all the people known by the Jívaro, the most significant are those who fall into that special category known as *kin* or *relatives*. This is true not just of the Jívaro, but of most societies.

A person's primary identity is intimately linked with and expressed in family terms. In American and Canadian society one's last name immediately confers family identification. Knowledge of kinship identity often helps to avoid uncomfortable ambiguities in relations with other people. This knowledge of where one "stands" in relation to others allows an individual the

---

1. From *The Jívaro: People of the Sacred Waterfalls*, by Michael J. Harner, copyright © 1972 by Michael J. Harner. Reprinted by permission of Doubleday & Company, Inc. Pp. 78–81.

In La Paz, Bolivia, it is appropriate for a wife to bring lunch to her husband at the construction site where he works. She and their child keep him company while he eats.

option of conforming to the rules or expectations of proper behavior held by the society for the occasion. Although a person may have several identities in his or her culture, such as shaman, midwife, or songwriter, kinship status is often the most significant one.

In the small-scale societies studied by most anthropologists, where settlements are sometimes sparsely populated and people see relatively few outsiders, most kin are well known. This is also true in small communities in industrialized societies—a small town in the United States, for example. Even in heterogeneous and impersonal urban environments, people recognize their relatives as categorically different from nonrelatives. This differentiation is universal—present in all cultures. It forms the basis for many patterns of behavior.

For example, there are always things that can be done with a relative that cannot (or should not) be done with a nonrelative. Lending money or offering aid in harvesting a crop might be two such activities. There are also some things that cannot be done with relatives that can be done with nonrelatives. With some exceptions, in most cultures closely related persons such as brothers and sisters may not engage in sexual intercourse or *incest*. The exceptions to this incest prohibition are rare: brothers and sisters of the Hawaiian royal family did engage in sexual relations, a practice in accordance with their religious beliefs. Although behavior considered appropriate for relatives differs widely from one society to the next (appropriate behavior between a brother and sister in the United States might not be the same behavior considered appropriate in the Jívaro culture), what *is* universal is the fact that there are different rules for rela-

tives and nonrelatives.

The Family

There is no single, universally accepted definition of a family. Some anthropologists define the family simply as a "kinship group"; this is correct so far as it goes, but it is not very specific. A more widely accepted definition is that the family is "a social unit minimally consisting of a married couple and the children that couple may have."[2] This, as we shall see later in this chapter, conforms to the way Americans define family, but the definition has some problems. For one thing, it does not include the practice found in many societies in which a husband has several wives at one time and each of these wives has several children; a husband and several wives are not a "married couple," as the definition implies. Also, the definition does not take into account the functions performed by the family that distinguish it from any other group of people.

Before trying to formulate a more inclusive definition of the family, let us look at the simple set of biological circumstances that dictates the development of families as social units. If the human species is to survive for more than the brief flicker of one generation, children must be born and raised to maturity so that the cycle will continue and the species and a particular society will perpetuate itself. Human infants are helpless at birth; human babies are born with a sucking reflex, the

2. Carol Ember and Melvin Ember, *Anthropology* (New York: Appleton-Century-Crofts, 1973), p. 545.

ability to cry, and all the potential of a human adult—if the baby lives long enough. Human potential, whatever genetic imprint the child carries, is developed primarily through learning and growing. This means that *at least* two preconditions are essential: (1) the child must be kept alive, and (2) someone must see to it that the child learns those things sufficient for its survival and well-being in its own society. Taking the above into consideration, we could then define family as the group that keeps the child alive and teaches it.

Compared to nonhuman primates, *Homo sapiens* takes a long time to mature physically. In most groups humans take even longer to mature socially, that is, to reach a point at which they are considered responsible for their own lives and behavior. A Jívaro is regarded as a socially mature man at age 16. In American society women and men are considered socially mature when they have left home, are making their own living, and no longer depend on their parents for support. In Ulster and the Republic of Eire, on the other hand, many rural men are not regarded as socially mature until they marry and have a farm of their own; because of the nature of the inheritance system, this might not happen until age 40. One major task of families, then—in the Amazon Basin, the United States, Ireland, and elsewhere—is not only to raise the child physically but also to be responsible for that child's proper behavior until the child reaches the age of social maturity and becomes a responsible adult member of society.

Types of Families

In a study of kinship relations in the United States, David Schneider found that most Americans define a family as a unit that contains a legally married man and woman who are the mother and father of their child or children.[3] However, for a variety of reasons, men and women have lived together, brought forth and raised children, and even observed all the customary behavior of American family life, without ever having engaged in a marriage ceremony. Since the terms "husband" and "wife" imply legal matrimony, we would be forced, using the common understanding in America, to say that these people did not constitute a family. However, common sense seems to have prevailed over legal definitions with the recognition in our legal system of common-law marriage.

The American concept of what constitutes a family, that is, a father, mother, and their children who reside together, is called a *nuclear family*. However, in non-Western societies the social roles played by the father in a nuclear family may not correspond to those of the American father—such roles, for example, as "mother's spouse, as mother's sexual partner (and begetter of children), as provider, as disciplinarian, [and] as legal guardian."[4] All these social roles, except spouse and sexual partner, are assumed by the mother's brother in some societies. Therefore, it is not possible to make the assumption that if the basic family unit in a society is the familiar nuclear one, the way in which the members in such a family will relate to each other will be the same as that in the American nuclear family.

---

3. David M. Schneider, *American Kinship: A Cultural Account* (Englewood Cliffs, N.J.: Prentice-Hall, 1968).

---

4. Roger M. Keesing, *Kin Groups and Social Structure* (New York: Holt, Rinehart and Winston, 1975).

Although she is part of a polygynous household, this Upper Voltan woman retains ties to a more extended family. Here she brings one of her sons to visit his grandfather.

A second major family type found in most societies is the *extended family*. An extended family is a group of people who reside together either in one house or in a cluster of houses, some of whose members are related. Most often, an extended family will consist of at least two nuclear families: a married couple and the families of one or more of their married children. Everyone shares in the work and profits as well as the joys and sorrows that inevitably occur in family life.

The nuclear family ends as a unit when the children grow up and leave home, or because of death or divorce. In the extended family, in contrast, there is provision for replacing members who die or move out. These family types should not be considered absolute, however. In every society families are characterized by a development cycle. A family at its formation may be "nuclear" and at another stage in its history, "extended." A third family type, the polygamous family, will be discussed later in the chapter.

As an adaptive device that relates people to their physical habitat, the extended family is quite efficient, especially in agrarian communities. The extended family has more members than a nuclear family, hence more workers to help plant and harvest the crops. This is especially important in places where mechanized agriculture is not practiced. If the extended family is large enough, some members may specialize in certain skills and crafts, such as horseshoeing, caring for livestock, cooking, and so on.

There are times and situations, however, in which the nuclear family is the superior adaptation. In preliterate societies dependent upon hunting and gathering, families often move frequently because they deplete the food supply in an area. A small group is more readily mobilized than a large one. More important, the relatively small size of the nuclear family, as compared with an extended family, means that there will be fewer mouths to feed and the little group can subsist more easily in an environment with limited food supplies. The nuclear family in industrialized societies is also a successful adaptation. In an urban setting, a family's subsistence is achieved through wage earning. There is no need for the many hands necessary on a farm. Families in industrialized societies may also move frequently because of the job requirements of the major breadwinner. Indeed, the high cost of urban living, as well as the increasingly limited amount of available living space in cities, makes the large extended family, unless extremely wealthy, a less rational adaptation.

However, it has been argued that it is the presence or the absence of money that explains the prevalence of either the ex-

tended or the nuclear family.[5] Thus, if a married couple work for wages they can buy the goods and services provided in an extended family. On a large, modern farm, for example, equipment and labor can be bought, dispensing with the need for relatives. Money, though, is not the only means of replacing the services of family members. Social services outside the family, such as education, public health, roads and sewers, may be provided by the society. Furthermore, not every family has the money to buy needed services. Many nuclear families in the United States, for example, expect to care for elderly parents because their members do not have the means to buy this service.

The Household

A household is a residential arrangement in which an assortment of people live and work together. It is not synonymous with a family, because members need not be related to each other in any way. Widows, bachelor uncles, orphaned children, and others may work together as a group. The Jívaro of Ecuador, described in the capsule ethnography, live in households. In the United States, college students sharing an apartment would be said to comprise a household. The people in a commune residing together and sharing work, food, and shelter would also constitute a household. As in the case of the extended family, the household performs an adaptive function, helping people to cope with economic needs. Cooperation centers on the performance of domestic tasks and the pooling of resources.

Households are found everywhere. Among the Jívaro, a large household assures an adequate supply of labor for the task of raising and harvesting crops. The Jívaro also hunt wild animals for food, but

5. Carol Ember and Melvin Ember, *Anthropology*, 2nd ed. (Englewood Cliffs, N.J.: Prentice-Hall, 1977).

the staples of their diet are manioc and other vegetables grown in garden plots. A Jívaro man's prestige is measured in part according to the size of his garden plots. Because Jívaro culture allows men to have more than one wife at a time, and because women perform most of the agricultural tasks, the more wives a man has, the more land his household will be able to cultivate and the greater his ability to provide the hospitality on which his prestige depends. For the unmarried persons in societies such as the Jívaro, membership in a household is an advantage. It assures them protection, economic support, and more food on a more regular basis than they might be able to produce alone.

Functions of the Family

That the family in its varied forms exists throughout the world indicates that it is functionally necessary; families exist as social units to do something. Although the specific behavior within a family varies from one society to another, there are four functions that families everywhere fulfill:

When food preparation is arduous and time-consuming as in this Senegalese village, two wives can profitably share the responsibility for feeding a household.

the economic functions of work and consumption, the function of regulating sexual relationships, the function of raising and educating children, and the function of providing a social status and an identity for each member of society.

Economic Function

Among the Jívaro, as we have seen in Michael Harner's account, each family constitutes an independent economic unit that provides for its own subsistence. The more numerous the working members, the greater the surplus produced and the wealthier the unit. The male head of the family, as we have seen, supervises production for the group, provides game and fish for the table, clears the land for agriculture, and brings in firewood for cooking and heat. His wife or wives are the major producers of food, which they cultivate in their garden plots. Clothing is woven by the man and sewn into clothes by the women. Pottery is made by women. Thus, the little unit is a self-sufficient one in respect to most of their needs for food and shelter.

Indeed, probably the most important function of a family, even above the nurturance and education of the children, is that of providing the necessities of life to its members. In any society, including our own, a single, independent person may have a difficult time securing a livelihood. Indeed, in most preliterate societies there is no social category for a single person. Everyone is attached to a larger household. In hunting and gathering societies, a single person could not possibly survive for very long alone. In peasant, agricultural societies, single, landless individuals will seek a household to which to attach themselves, there to work as hired hands and receive food and shelter for their labor. In such societies a woman alone is almost unheard of. She must marry and live with her own family, or if she is old, live with her children and contribute to the household.

Not only is the economic well-being of the participants an important function of family life, but the marriage of a son or daughter becomes an economic and political matter in most societies. All family members have something to gain, for example, from an alliance with a powerful family in the community.

Some social scientists claim that the economic function of the family has declined in urban industrial societies. However, it is not that the family is ceasing to function as an economic group but instead, that the visibility of the function being carried out is decreasing. For example, many rural families in Latin America are migrating to urban centers. All family members who are old enough to work find jobs and the income is pooled for mutual use. The father may drive a taxi, the mother may work as a maid, and the children may shine shoes, sell newspapers, or do odd jobs whenever they can find them. However, family members in cities rarely work together as a unit, as they do in rural settings. In industrialized societies, many wives work outside the home to provide a portion of the family income and, increasingly, husband and wife share the responsibility and the work, both inside and outside the home.

Enculturation Function

The family unit is responsible for training the children to participate properly in the life of their society, a process called *enculturation*. It is from the family that a child learns much of his or her social behavior. In societies where formal schooling is rare or nonexistent, the family must teach the child how to behave in relation to others, how to develop the skills needed for survival and for a future occupation. An example from Tikopia illustrates this point:

> Instruction in Tikopia [Polynesia] in matters of etiquette and decorum in the house begins at a very early age, almost before the child can fully understand what is required of it, but as the essence of the system for the young is quietness and self-effacement, the general lesson is soon learned. As always, instruction is given in relation to concrete situations rather than to abstract principles. For instance, to pe tua (throw the back) to people of superior status is bad manners. Firimori was sitting thus . . . facing away from his grandfather, the chief. Nau Nukanefu, his father's brother's wife, spoke to him sharply, "Do not turn your back on your grandfather," whereupon he shifted round slightly. So children learn.[6]

Where formal schooling is available, the schools share some of the burden of enculturation, but the prime responsibility still rests with the family.

Regulation of Sexual Relationships

The sexual function of the family unit is to regulate, through enforcement of a variety of cultural norms, sexual relations between certain categories of people. In no known society is there completely unregulated sexual activity. The most common rule enforced by the family is the almost universal prohibition of incest, sexual relations between individuals considered

---

6. Raymond Firth, *We, the Tikopia* (Boston: Beacon Press, 1963), p. 137.

by their society to be too closely related. The incest prohibition is so widespread as a principle that the overwhelming majority of people in the world are brought up to regard incest, however defined by their culture, to be wrong. The two most common incest prohibitions forbid sexual relations between parents and their children, and between brothers and sisters. This does not mean that it does not occur. But it does mean that to engage in incest is regarded in most societies as one of the most serious sins a person can commit.

Many societies, however, encourage a marriage arrangement between individuals who would be defined by Americans as "first cousins." Incest as a taboo, therefore, is culturally defined. A relationship, for example, between a woman and her mother's brother might be considered incest and forbidden in one society and be acceptable in another.

There are many theories regarding the reason for the near universality of incest prohibitions. One theory is that unrestricted sexual access between family members would lead to disruptions in family life that, if allowed to continue, would destroy the family as a viable social unit. For example, the rivalry between a father and his son for the sexual favors of the woman (or women) in the family could lead to fights between the men which could disrupt the bonds of cooperation needed for economic activities such as hunting or farming together.

Another theory, widely held by the American and European public, is that the children of incestuous matings might somehow be defective. However, in many smaller societies—island populations, for example, or people who follow cousin marriage—there is obviously consistent inbreeding. And there is no generally available evidence to show that such populations suffer from genetically caused disorders. E. B. Tylor, who wrote in the late nineteenth century, explains the incest taboo not biologically but culturally in terms of social relationships. Tylor stated his theory as "Marry out or die." [7]

Lévi-Strauss [8] explained that it was only by exogamy, marrying outside the immediate group, that human society became possible. Exogamy facilitated the establishment of social contracts with neighboring bands; intermarriage between groups created regional political interdependence. The invention of the incest taboo thus forced the men of a group to maintain reasonable relations with their neighbors in order to obtain a wife. According to this view, the women already given in marriage to a neighboring group were, in a sense, hostages—another factor insuring friendly relations with outsiders. The important principle concerning marriage rules and the incest taboo is that each rule has different implications for the structure of economic, ritual, and political relations between intermarrying groups, as well as for the internal organization of the exogamous group, *however* it is defined.

Identity Function

The fourth function of the family is to provide a social identity for each member.

7. E. B. Tylor, "On a Method of Investigating the Development of Institutions, Applied to Laws of Marriage and Descent," *Journal of the Royal Anthropological Institute* 18 (1889): 245–272.

8. Claude Lévi-Strauss, *Elementary Structures of Kinship* (Boston: Beacon Press, 1963).

Role behavior throughout life is always affected, and to some extent even determined, by kinship or nonkinship status vis-à-vis others. The simplest external sign of identity, for example, is the kinship title. A small boy learns that this person is "father," this one "sister," and that one "uncle." The boy, in turn, is seen by these others as "son," "brother," and "nephew," respectively. Note, however, that these are Euro-American divisions of kinship. A mother's or father's brother in our system may be called a father in another system, with corresponding authority over a child. In the Trobriand Islands, the mother's brother, the maternal uncle, is the chief authority figure, the head of the extended family, the one who leaves his property to his *sister's* children. The biological father, on the other hand, is the children's pal, the one who opens his arms to them and

A woman and her two sons near Lima, Peru.

is never the disciplinarian.

In addition to one's kinship title, one's name is also a symbol of identity. In the American, Canadian, and Western European systems, a child usually takes the surname of his or her father. In Spain and Portugal, a person carries the surnames of both father and mother. For example, Pablo Aceves Prados is the son of Buenaventura Aceves Rubio (his father) and Benita Prados Gallego (his mother). He takes the surnames of both his parents. In Spain and generally throughout Hispanic cultures, a woman does not take her husband's surname at marriage. Thus Benita Prados Gallego retained her name and did not append her husband's surname. When it was necessary for her to be identified as Buenaventura Aceves's wife, she would be called *señora de Aceves*, which freely translates as Mrs. Aceves. In Arabic cultures a person may be named as the son or daughter of a certain person; hence, Mohammed ben Yusef would be Mohammed the son of Yusef. This usage also has vestigial remains in English, Scottish, and Irish cultures in such names as Richardson, McDonald, and O'Leary.

In contemporary American society an increasing number of women are keeping their maiden name. This is particularly true of professional women who achieve some measure of reknown prior to their marriage. The anthropologist M. Estellie Smith is married to an anthropologist, Charles Bishop, but retains her maiden name for her professional identity. At home she is Mrs. Bishop; at work she is Dr. Smith. Currently in the United States, some married couples are using both the husband's and the wife's surname. Thus, John Doe and Susan Jones may call themselves John Doe-Jones and Susan Doe-Jones, respectively. Whatever the specifics of the system of naming, the name is a symbol not only of individual identity but of identity with a kin group as well.

Kinship and Descent

In the small-scale societies the family, because of its variety and the particular connotations it bears in our own society, is usually referred to as a *kinship group*. At birth, each person in a society is classified as a member of a certain kinship group or groups according to the cultural rules determining the kinship relations of that society. These rules determine who stands in what relationship to whom. For example, people in all societies have created systems of labeling to identify an individual in terms of sexual availability or role in child-rearing. In the United States a woman who physically bears a child is known as the "mother" of the child. Two siblings who share the same mother know each other as "brother" and "sister." We refer to the sister of the woman who bore the children as the "aunt" of the children. In another society with different labeling customs, she might be regarded by the children as a mother, the same title accorded the woman who gave birth to them. The titles in themselves are not of great importance; what is important is the *behavior* associated with the title. What does an aunt or a sister or a mother do? What is the appropriate behavior that a son should exhibit toward his mother as opposed to his aunt?

Some societies have ritualized behavior between certain classes of relatives. One such behavior is *in-law avoidance*. Among some Apache Indian groups in the United States, for example, the husband must never be alone with his mother-in-law, never touch her or her possessions, speak to her only if necessary and then through a third party. This extreme avoidance must be observed even if the two people like each other. Similar avoidance behavior is also shown between the wife and her male in-laws. Thus, in marriage and alliance, as in some other situations, each society develops cultural norms governing the social behavior between people in a variety of different kinship relations.

Joking relationships are the opposite of in-law avoidance taboos, but they also seem to be designed to promote harmony. Persons related by marriage may be obliged to show extremely friendly behavior toward each other, often marked by sexually oriented horseplay (flirting, making mildly obscene remarks). An especially friendly relationship often exists between children and their grandparents; the child may address these elders in terms that would be disrespectful if applied to other members of the group.

Joking relations between a wife and her brothers-in-law, or between a husband and his sisters-in-law, are commonplace in societies that practice the custom of the *levirate*, the required remarriage of a woman to her deceased husband's brother. Where the custom of the *sororate*, the remarriage of a man to a younger sister, prevails, a joking relationship may exist between a wife's sisters and her husband. Since a man may wind up marrying one of his sisters-in-law and a woman might have to marry one of her brothers-in-law, the liberties of the joking relation have a meaningful and adaptive purpose. Another function of joking is that it serves to ease tensions where interpersonal relations might be or might become socially disruptive.

A person is taught proper kinship behavior according to the status he or she holds in relation to other kinfolk. This in-

Going everywhere on her mother's back, an Upper Voltan child learns all about adult life.

volves knowing the proper terminology to apply to kin. No kinship system has a term for every possible relationship. All systems merge or lump some relatives of differing genealogical statuses into single categories that have a single kinship term. Among the Comanche, for instance, the same term is used by a male to refer to his mother, his mother's sisters, his mother's female cousins, and his father's brother's wife. Comanche terminology, however, differentiates between a male's mother's sister and father's sister, relatives that the system in the United States lumps together and calls

Chapter Thirteen

aunts. The various systems of kinship terminology are discussed in Appendix B.

The Formation of Kinship Relationships

From the viewpoint of the individual, there are three ways in which he or she may be related to other members of society. These are kinship, affinal, and descent relationships.

Kinship has been used as a general term to sum up all three. It also refers to the parent–child relationship, several of which may create a network of links between people in a society. These relationships are ones we in North America and Europe conceive of as "blood ties," given at birth and unchangeable. Not all societies think of them quite this way. Kinship in the narrow sense of "blood ties" contrasts with the relationship created through marriage between two individuals and their families, called *affinity*. Relations by marriage are then called *affines*. Affinal relatives are those that result from a contractual agreement. A husband–wife relationship is the prime example of this type of tie. In almost all societies the contract can be broken, as by divorce. Relatives we refer to as in-laws are also considered affinal kin. The third kind of relationship is called *descent*, which is defined with reference to a common ancestor. We will discuss this type of relationship later in this chapter.

FICTIVE KIN. In most societies there are people who are treated as kin but who are not, in fact, related in any way to those who so treat them. In Western society, for example, we may call close friends of our parents by the kinship terms "uncle" and "aunt" as signs of our affection and respect for them. People may, for a variety of reasons, find the necessity to consider, for all practical purposes, an unrelated individual to be a family member. A familiar example is *adoption*, a process by which a child not born to the wife can acquire the legal rights and obligations of a natural child. Blood brothers and godparents are other examples of fictive kin. Fictive kin provide a means for maintaining and insuring a person's participation in such matters as controlling and/or acquiring wealth, property, or power. Fictive kin can also support and enlarge a family's resources. In some cases, fictive kin need only provide the idea of continuity or solidarity.

IMAGINARY FICTIVE KIN. In many parts of East Africa where women dominate trade in local markets, it is necessary for a woman to have a husband since she cannot by rights consider her income strictly her own—such independence being culturally forbidden. Such a woman may have had a husband who died, and she may choose not to remarry for a variety of reasons. It is possible for her, then, to marry an *object* that is considered to be a symbolic equivalent of a husband. Some women have married trees, others have married their own hand. Widows of childbearing age may take such an imaginary "husband" and have children by other men, but the children regard the symbolic object as their fictive father for purposes of familial identity and inheritance.

The Nuer of the Sudan allow a woman to marry another, usually wealthy, woman, giving the wealthy woman the symbolic status of a male and father. Nuer lineage maintenance is so important that persons may marry a ghost of one of the community's former members if necessary. An old Nuer woman may also, if her lineage is about to die out, see to it that a woman of her lineage is married to the ghost or name of a dead male of her lineage. The new "wife" then has intercourse with some unrelated male, observing lineage exogamy, and her children become heirs to the old woman's lineage property and rights.

Some anthropologists object to calling these arrangements kinship. But if the arrangement is created by the people as a marriage or a kinship tie, and if the participants act accordingly, then for all practical purposes it is a kinship tie. The practitioners of a fictive relationship know well the fictitious nature of what they are doing. No Nuer woman is going to confuse a ghost with a live male. However, a fictive husband provides her with a way to preserve her lineage and to pass on her property. Kinship ties are of such importance to the orderly functioning of human social life that any number of arrangements, however nonsensical any particular one may seem to an outsider, have been found which are used to preserve and maintain social relationships.

THE COMPADRAZGO. One of the best-known forms of fictive kinship is the *compadrazgo* (*padre* means father in Spanish; hence a *compadre* literally means a cofather), the ritual godparenthood or coparenthood association typically found in Roman Catholic and Eastern Rite Catholic areas. The term is Spanish, but non-Spanish cultures have the same practice. For example, in parts of the Balkans, the term *kumstvo* (from the Greek *kum* meaning godfather) is used.

The ideological basis of this association is the precept that parents provide the proper religious education for their children. To insure that the child will receive this education in the event of the death or incapacity of the parents, godparents are expected to assume the duties of the child's religious well-being. While the origin and overt significance of the custom are related to a religious belief system, in practice the godparents have an important secular role to play. In the event of a serious quarrel between an adolescent and the parents, for example, a godparent may be called upon to intercede on the child's behalf. Godparents are expected to remember the child at gift-giving times, such as birthdays and Christmas. A godparent, especially the godfather, is often expected to aid the child to get a job or to secure some benefit such as admission to a university. Indeed, many parents select their *compadres* and *comadres* with an eye to the future.

Wealthy landowners and persons of power and influence in the society are sought out as godparents, and it is not uncommon for such people to be godparents of a number of children of different families. For example, in Mexico there are marked divisions between the wealthy and the poor, between the *hacienda* owner and the peons. For a peon to have the *patron* as his *compadre* is for him to have an almost guaranteed friend in high places. For his part, the high-ranking godfather enjoys playing this role to many families. The cost to him in monetary terms is small; what he receives is the support and allegiance of his *compadres*, whom he can count on for extra work when needed or for services that another peon might disdain to perform.

By treating the *compadrazgo* association in familial or kin terms, the participants show that it is an important association and one that is expected to endure for life. The bringing of a person into the family, however symbolically, indicates the significance the society attaches to such an association.

Descent

The reckoning of membership in a kinship group can be a complicated matter. In our own society, unless large sums of money are involved in a litigation over an inheritance, the ties between affines and kin relatives may depend to a greater extent on personal likes and dislikes than on a relationship determined by rules. A person may have a lifelong friendship with a second cousin because of a closeness in age, interests in common, and residence in the same area, whereas the same individual may see her own brother only at weddings and funerals. Are the ties in a particular American family closer to the mother's relatives or to the father's family? The answer may depend on personal and idiosyncratic variables.

In most small-scale societies it is otherwise. Kinship is a serious matter and there are what to us may seem complex rules, called the rules of descent, for determining membership in a kinship group. One rule of descent common to all systems of reckoning kinship is that members of a kinship group share one ancestor in common. Descent systems differ in the way in which that ancestor is determined. Since each person has any number of ancestors there is a variety of possibilities.

UNILINEAL DESCENT. A *unilineal* kinship system is one in which descent is reckoned through one line, either the male or the female parent. There are several systems for calculating descent relationships. *Patrilineal* systems count only links through males (for example, all people with the same father's father's father may be considered related). *Matrilineal* systems count only links through females (for example, all people with the same mother's mother's mother may be considered related).

In unilineal systems, family obligations may be more clear-cut than in a cognatic system (discussed in the next section). For one thing, the distinction between kin and nonkin is sharply drawn. A person's obligations are primarily to those people defined as kin. The clear definition of line of descent provided by the unilineal system not only serves to place an individual within a group but also promotes solidarity among the members of the group. Such solidarity leads, in turn, to a certain amount of autonomy, which is particularly useful under certain conditions: in a war, groups with strong identities can be easily mobilized; when population is too dense, the apportionment of land can be carried out in an orderly manner if groups have clear visibility. Among the Yanomamö, for example, an exact knowledge of one's relationship to another, as we saw in Chapter 1, may be a matter of life or death.

COGNATIC DESCENT. In recent years anthropologists have clarified the classification of groups who followed neither the patrilinear nor the matrilinear pattern and called such groups *cognatic*; that is, they followed a descent pattern in which neither the mother's nor the father's family dominated. The residence of a given couple, whether near the wife's family or near the husband's, might be a determining factor. Another circumstance might be one in which the husband quarreled with members of his family and chose to go and live with his wife's family. Among the Kwaio of Melanesia, every couple may live in the territory of any group of relatives they choose. If they participate in the affairs of the group, they have equal rights with any adult members. The circumstances of life and of the interests of any particular man will lead him to decide which group he will join. Or, as Keesing points out, he may live with a number of different groups during a lifetime.[9] What follows is a brief summary of the types of descent systems outlined in this chapter. Kinship of one person—called *ego*—is defined for each system.

1. *Patrilineal descent*: Ego is related to men and women by descent from a common ancestor by means of a series of male links, i.e., the ancestor's son, his son's son, and so on.

2. *Matrilineal descent*: Ego is related to men and women by descent from a common ancestress by means of a series of female links.

3. *Cognatic descent*: Ego is related to men and women by descent from a common ancestor or ancestress through a series of male or female links or a combination of both.

The Lineage

A kinship group organized on a unilinear basis "whose members trace their descent from a known ancestor and know the genealogical connection to that ancestor"[10] is called a *lineage*. A lineage unites many people over several generations. In societies that practice ancestor worship, the lineage may even include deceased ancestors. Land is often owned by the lineage as a whole, with rights of use allotted to various members who work the land.

The lineage has proved to be an adaptive

---

9. Keesing, *Kin Groups*, pp. 91–93.

10. Keesing, *Kin Groups*, p. 31.

solution to the problem of defining rights over land and other resources across the generations. The lineage provides a clear definition for a society as to who belongs to which group, and what rights and property belong to the group. It also defines who receives what within each group. The problem of the maintenance of order between groups, and the forging of ties between groups in a society characterized by lineage, has been solved by the almost universal practice of *exogamy*, that is, marrying outside the lineage. (The practice of marrying within one's own group is called *endogamy*.) It is this practice that brought lineage groups into alliances that form a broad social base for a society interwoven with kinship ties.

Marriage

In the United States and Canada marriage is viewed as a private matter: who marries whom is of major interest only to the two people concerned; the only acceptable reason for a marriage between two young people is that they love one another. To us, such a view seems reasonable and natural. Anthropologists, who hesitate to regard any behavior as natural unless they can see a clear biological foundation for it, have found few societies that share this viewpoint with us. Indeed, a marriage is usually considered to be of such importance to the family and the community that it is seldom left to the preferences of the young people involved.

The most essential function of marriage is to create bonds between individuals and between kinship groups. Marriage in all societies creates affinal kin, relatives who can be counted as allies economically and politically. The networks of kinship form the fabric of social ties that make a society possible. In hunting and gathering societies, kinship traced through mother and father fosters unity within a small society. In agricultural societies, alliances by means of marriages between kinship groups become the major organizing principle in a society. The rights to land, livestock, and other property are controlled by kinship groups, insuring, to a great extent, peaceful relations within and between groups. In modern industrial societies, however, property rights and social control are not always dependent on membership in a kinship group. Although kinship may play an important role in an individual's personal life, as a form of organization it has been replaced by ties of class, occupation, and community.[11]

Marriage Forms

In every society, marriage is regulated in some manner. Because marriage affects every person in a society and is of vital importance in social interaction, rules pertaining to it exist everywhere. For example, all societies have some regulations about who may or may not marry. In the United States, a 1972 Texas court decision ruled that members of the same sex may not marry. Some homosexual marriages have been performed by Houston and Dallas clergymen, but these are not recognized as legal by the state. Almost all societies have some age limit with regard to marriage; people younger than the stipulated age normally may not marry. The Australian Tiwi are one notable exception to the general rule of age limitation. In their complex system wherein women are a form of property, a female infant may be legitimately married at birth, generally to a man who is already an adult.[12]

Most of the marriage rules with which we are familiar merely prohibit us from marrying certain types of people—people who are younger than a certain age, or the same sex as ourselves, or related to us as siblings, parents, children, or first cousins. These prohibitions still leave us with a vast number of people from whom to choose a spouse. We are used to choosing our mates based on loose and largely personal criteria such as appearance, intelligence, social background, and the like. But in many of the societies anthropologists study, marriage rules are more specific than that, narrowing down the choice of an appropriate mate to members of a limited group of people.

In a number of places in Southeast Asia, such as among tribal peoples of highland Burma, the marriage rule states that all women who, to a particular man, are classified as "mother's brother's daughters" are affines and thus potentially marriageable. In certain places in Australia, South America, and elsewhere, communities are linked by twos in marriage alliance relationships called *moiety systems*, whereby men of Community A will marry women of Community B, and women of Community A will marry men of Community B. In Australia anthropologists have found some of the world's most complex marriage rules. Some tribes are divided into as many as eight subgroups, called marriage "sections" by anthropologists. Everyone in the society belongs to one or another

---

11. Keesing, *Kin Groups*, p. 8.

12. C. W. M. Hart and Arnold Pilling, *The Tiwi of Northern Australia* (New York: Holt, Rinehart and Winston, 1960).

of these eight sections, and must marry a person of the opposite sex belonging to only one of the other seven sections.

Polygamy and Monogamy

Not only may marriage rules specify *whom* one ought to marry, but they may also specify *how many* mates a person may have. Some 80 percent of the known societies in the world permit the practice of *polygamy*, having more than one spouse at a time. The most common form is *polygyny*, whereby a man has more than one wife at a time. Islamic law, for example, allows a man to have up to four wives at the same time. *Polyandry* is the marriage of one woman to several men at the same time. This practice is extremely rare, but it is found in part of Tibet and among the Toda of South India and some other Indian hill tribes. Generally, in a polyandrous union, all the husbands are brothers, and in many cases female infanticide is practiced.

A polygynous family in Upper Volta. A prosperous-looking man, his two wives, and their eight children pose for a family portrait.

In polygamous societies, especially in polygynous ones, the social structure allows a greater set of alternatives regarding whom a person may marry. The Jívaro, being polygynous, allow a man the alternative of having just one spouse or several spouses, a choice that by law and custom is denied Americans.

In reality, most people practice *monogamy*, whereby a person has only one spouse at a time. Even where polygyny, as among the Jívaro, is permitted, most people are actually monogamously married. There are some practical reasons for this. First of all, wives are expensive both to obtain and to maintain and, therefore, only wealthy men of high status can afford more than one wife. Second, the sex ratio—the number of males born compared to females born in a year—is roughly one to one. Thus, if a few men monopolized all the women, there would be a severe disruption in the society, and probably the unmarried men would revolt in order to cause a more equitable distribution of women.

An unusual and admittedly extreme case of a society in which almost all women are married to only a few men is the Tiwi society, located on two islands off Australia's northern coast. Tiwi men compete for prestige and influence, and it is by means of women that prestige and influence are obtained. Among the Tiwi, every female member of the society must be married. The Tiwi explain this behavior on the basis of a belief that any female is liable to become impregnated by a spirit at anytime, and therefore must always have a husband. A female child is married at birth, almost always to an old man with a high degree of prestige in the community. The little girl lives with her parents until she is old enough to move into the household of her husband. Since the possession of many wives is a mark of high status among Tiwi men, fathers of girls strengthen or create alliances with prestigious elder men by giving them their infant daughters as wives. In return, the elder usually reciprocates by giving up a daughter to the original donor.

One of the results of using women as a sort of "special-purpose money" (see Chapter 11) is that a few old men have a large number of young wives, and many of the younger men might have none at all. As one might predict, the young wives and the young men without wives frequently engage in sexual relations. An old husband does not become overly concerned. For him, the most important thing is that he control the children, especially the female children who can be married to men of influence, thus enhancing his status among the Tiwi.[13]

Two other examples of groups that practice polygamy are the Temne and the Likouala of Africa. A survey taken of 284 married Temne males in the late 1950s showed that 162 had only one wife, 84 had two wives, 24 had three, and 13 had four or more. Of 140 married Likouala males surveyed around 1960, 80 had one wife, 34 had two, 12 had three, and the remaining 14 had four or more.[14] In these groups, just as among the Tiwi, a man's status and prestige in his community are reflected by the number of wives he maintains and often, by the number of children he sires.

---

13. Hart and Pilling, *The Tiwi*, p. 14.

---

14. These data were provided in a National Science Foundation-sponsored Institute in Anthropology held during the summer of 1964.

There are some disadvantages in having many wives. One problem is that jealousies may develop between the women as each tries to have her children favored over those of her co-wives. Some societies practice *sororal polygyny*—that is, the wives that a man marries are sisters. The presumption here is that sisters, knowing each other, will be less jealous and more cooperative. The tendency in societies that practice polygyny is for a woman and her children to form a tightly knit group (the so-called elemental family); in this situation, the child may love the mother but only have "respect" for the father.

Brideprice

Brideprice, sometimes called bridewealth, is the payment by the man of an amount of money or goods to the family of his intended bride. This does not mean that a man "buys" a wife. Different groups offer various explanations for their custom of brideprice. The brideprice appears to be compensation to the girl's family for the loss of her services. The exchange is often viewed as a legal mechanism for cementing the alliance between the wife and the husband's kin groups and as a means of making the marital union "legal." There is also an important symbolic aspect of brideprice. It expresses the value of a wife to her husband and may serve to confirm his intention to stay married. It also rewards the woman's family for releasing authority over the girl. The brideprice, which some anthropologists call "progeny price," also may in effect compensate the bride's family for the loss of the children she will bear, children whose labor would have been useful in the bride's parents' economic activities.

Brideprice is not restricted to small-scale societies. This practice can also be found in such African cities as Mbale and Nairobi. Among European feudal societies, the dowry was given with a daughter in marriage. In many peasant cultures a young woman herself worked to acquire a dowry consisting of household goods to use in her own household after she married. Middle-class women in the United States as recently as World War I had "hope" chests filled with linens which constituted their dowries.

A brideprice is generally arrived at by negotiations between the two families— sometimes involving just the nuclear families, oftentimes the extended families. The following illustration from Uganda shows how a brideprice negotiation might be conducted. The episode is described by the bridegroom.

> I got a team together to go to J's father's house to talk about the marriage. My father, his brother, my cousin (his father's brother's son), and myself. My cousin was the spokesman. I didn't say anything, and I'm not supposed to do any bargaining, nor is my father, only my spokesman. So we went to be introduced.
>
> J's father also had a team. Besides the father there was his eldest brother, who was too old to say anything, another uncle, and J's brother, who would become my brother-in-law. We went to J's house and entered. We sat on one side and they sat on the other side. J's uncle began by welcoming us and asking what we wanted. My spokesman then answered, as though he wanted to marry J instead of me, 'It's very cold at night and I have been looking for a warm blanket and I have seen a beautiful one in this house and I have come to get it.' The uncle then said, 'That is good and well spoken. The

blanket is beautiful. It has many decorations.' That means that J [the fiancée] had been to school in the U.K. [Great Britain]. The uncle continued, 'I will be very sorry to see it go, and I think you should contribute towards its decorations, since you are taking it away and I may never see it again.' My spokesman said, 'Agreed. What is the contribution?' Her uncle said, '2,500/=' ($350). I was shocked by that figure. I expected about 1,000/= ($140). J, who was sitting outside, yelled in, 'Father, do not sell me. My husband needs the money to begin life with.' Then my spokesman said to the uncle, 'That is well spoken. We have come here to discuss the contribution and I hope that we can speak at leisure and reach a compromise. 2,500/= is very much, I would like to contribute 800/= ($112).' The uncle said, 'Well, you have come here and we will discuss: 2,000/= ($280).' My spokesman said, 'I am glad to see that you have come down, and we will go up: 1,000/= ($140).' The uncle said, 'Well spoken, and I am glad that you have come up; we will come down: 1500/= ($210).' My spokesman replied, 'Well spoken.' Well, I was prepared to pay 1,000/=, so I leaned over to my spokesman and said, what's 200 more shillings, go to 1,200/= ($168). My spokesman turned to the uncle, 'We will go up to 1,200/=.' The uncle said, 'Well spoken, you have come up. 1,200/= is agreed.' Then we all had a feast and drank. (Did you pay then?) No. Even if I had it then, I wouldn't have paid for it. J's family now knew me, but my family had to meet hers. Later they came to my house, had a feast, and were presented with the money.[15]

Suitor service is the practice in some societies, whereby the husband must work for a certain period of time for his wife's kin group instead of paying a designated sum. Men usually dislike this arrangement because they must be in close association with the wife's family. This is sometimes an unpleasant situation, since the parents-in-law make heavy demands on his time and labor, and the husband often feels insecure away from his blood kin. The custom of suitor service either supplants or supplements brideprice.

Residence Patterns

The issue of "where shall we live?" is one that faces all newly married couples. In

Dakar, Senegal: A man, his young wife, and their new baby dress up for a special occasion.

15. David Jacobson, *Itinerant Townsmen: Friendship and Social Order in Urban Uganda* (Menlo Park, Calif.: Cummings, 1973), pp. 42–43.

American society, the married couple usually set up housekeeping in a residence apart from both sets of parents. This is called *neolocal residence*, because the couple establish a new residence of their own and do not live with either set of parents. In a society that stresses individualism, personal autonomy, and both social and physical mobility, as American society does, this type of residence is most common. However, neolocal residence as a general practice is found only in about 5 percent of all known societies. Most of these have money-based urban-industrial economies such as are found in North America, Europe, Japan, and the more developed parts of South America and Africa. In these economies, young people can earn wages and be independent of their parents.

The practice whereby a married couple live with or near the husband's kin is known as *patrilocal residence*. This is by far the most common form of residence pattern, although it is found primarily in nonindustrial societies. Patrilocal residence is more favorable for the husband because he can remain with his kin. The wife is

Where large families live together in one place, the women of all ages usually share the tasks of child care.

the stranger, removed from her own family, and she must adjust to an often subservient and inferior status in the midst of her husband's kin. Patrilocal residence is usually the rule in societies where descent is reckoned patrilineally. Patrilocal residence is also adaptive in hunting societies, where it is of utmost importance for men to be thoroughly familiar with the territory and its resources.

Patrilocal residence seems to be associated with a variety of economic factors. Where cooperation between men is necessary, such as in societies that practice extensive plow agriculture or the pastoral herding of animals, it insures that the male will remain as a member of his kin group's labor force and will not be lost to them by moving to a new residence. Patrilocal residence is also common where men have greater social prestige than women, such as in traditional India.

When Jívaro men marry, they may go to live with the wife's kinship group. This custom is known as *matrilocal residence*, and it is usually found in societies that reckon descent matrilineally. Here, the husband is at a disadvantage because he must live with the wife's kin group, who may not treat him as well as his own group does. Where women have a relatively high status, such as among the Zuni or the Hopi of North America, matrilocal residence is often the preferred custom. Economic conditions that help foster matrilocal residence involve the cooperative work of women, as, for example, in horticultural societies.

Matrilocal residence is a less common practice than patrilocal residence. George Peter Murdock, who amassed data on 565 societies for comparative purposes, showed that only 14 percent of known societies have matrilocal residence, whereas 55 per-cent have patrilocal residence rules.[16]

In the Trobriand Islands of the Pacific and in parts of Africa where the mother's brother is the authority figure for a child and the source of a child's inheritance, the newly married man will take his wife to live with or near his mother's brother. This is called *avunculocal* residence.

A number of societies, such as the !Kung bushmen of Africa, the Nambikwara of Brazil, and the Dogrib Indians of Canada, do not have any fixed pattern or type of marital residence. Some married couples may live with the husband's kin group, others in the same society will live with the wife's kin group, and yet others may live neolocally.

Whatever manner developed within a particular society for naming and behaving toward kin, there is in all societies a primary group of people—a family—toward which an individual has responsibilities and from whose members an individual can seek help. Americans tend to underestimate the wisdom of the family as a social institution because of our deep-rooted respect for the supremacy of the individual. Moreover, in the United States and Canada, as in the other industrialized countries, such functions of the family as teaching children, tending the sick, and making a living are generally controlled by other institutions. It is sobering to examine the societies in which politically and economically controlled institutions do not reach into the home—where the family remains the basic unit of social organization. For those of us who seek freedom from family ties and family obligations,

16. George P. Murdock, "World Ethnographic Sample," *American Anthropologist* 59 (1957) : 664–687.

the lesson is clear. No individual is completely self-sufficient. When we find ourselves free of family control, we must look to the larger, impersonal institutions not only for the homes we live in, the bread we eat, but even for a place in which to die.

Summary

1. In most societies, the most significant people in any person's life are those whom he or she considers kin or relatives.

2. One definition of the family is "a social unit minimally consisting of a married couple and the children that couple may have." This corresponds with our American notion of the family, and is called the nuclear family. Another family type is the extended family, which may include at least two nuclear families residing together.

3. The family has a number of functions. It is commonly the important economic unit; it may regulate sexual relationships; it is usually the unit responsible for the raising of children; and finally, it provides its members with social status and identity.

4. Relationship terms, such as "mother," "uncle," and so on, are associated with particular patterns of behavior deemed appropriate for each kinship role. Examples of ritualized forms of behavior between relatives are in-law avoidance and joking relationships.

5. There are three ways in which an individual may be related to other members of society: by kinship, affinity (marriage), and descent.

6. Fictive kinship relationships, such as adoption and the *compadrazgo*, also exist, and

have economic as well as social significance.

7. In most small-scale societies, complex rules of descent determine one's membership in kinship groups. There are two types of descent groups: unilineal (both matrilineal and patrilineal) and cognatic.

8. A lineage is a kinship group whose members trace their descent from a known ancestor via specific, known genealogical links. It is often land-owning and exogamous (out-marrying).

9. Few societies view marriage as Americans often view it—as a private matter between two people. Marriage creates important bonds between individuals and also between kin groups, in most societies.

10. Rules concerning marriage exist in every society. These rules state whom one may and whom one may not marry in each society. Factors such as the sex, age, or kin relationship of the parties involved may be referred to in these rules.

11. Polygamy is a form of marriage in which one may legally have several spouses at a time. Monogamy—marrying one spouse at a time—is the most common form of marriage, however.

12. Residence may be neolocal, as in the United States, or either patrilocal (living near the husband's kin), matrilocal (living near the wife's kin), or avunculocal (living near the mother's brother). Forms of residence are related to the type of descent system, and usually relate to the economic needs of the new family and how these are met in their particular society.

13. Brideprice is a payment by the husband and his family to the family of his intended bride. It is a legal mechanism for cementing the alliance between the kin groups of the husband and the wife created by the marriage, and has symbolic importance as well. Suitor service, where the husband works for his in-laws, may supplement or supplant brideprice in some societies.

Review Questions

1. What are the functions of the family? Give examples of each. Do you think that these functions are still important in industrial society?

2. Make a list of the relationship terms you use (for example, "mother"), and then list the behavior you associate with each term.

3. What are the differences between kinship, affinity, and descent? These ways of tracing relationship are not mutually exclusive, however: your father's brother's daughter may be related to you in all three ways simultaneously. Explain this statement. (Hint: For affinity, assume that your society is matrilineal.)

4. How is marriage in the United States a personal relationship? How is it a relationship between two families?

5. How may the economic needs of new families affect their choice of residence? Why is our most common form of residence in the United States neolocal?

6. What is brideprice? What is suitor service? Is there any equivalent to these in our society?

Suggested Readings

Fox, Robin. *Kinship and Marriage.* Baltimore: Penguin Books, 1967.
This book is for the more advanced student who would like to know more about kinship systems. The first part of the book is an introduction to how families develop. The latter part of the book deals with the specifics of unilineal kinship systems.

Hart, C. W. M, and Pilling, Arnold. *The Tiwi of Northern Australia.* New York: Holt, Rinehart and Winston, 1960.
This ethnography outlines the intricate kinship system of the Tiwi in a readable fashion. Of special interest is the Tiwi practice of betrothing infant girls to older men at birth.

Pasternak, Burton. *Introduction to Kinship and Social Organization.* Englewood Cliffs, N.J.: Prentice-Hall, 1976.
This is a clearly written outline of the anthropological approach used to determine kinship and to analyze kinship terms.

Schneider, David M. *American Kinship: A Cultural Account.* Englewood Cliffs, N.J.: Prentice-Hall, 1968.
A brief but sophisticated examination of what Americans mean by the term "relatives."

Schusky, Ernest L. *Manual for Kinship Analysis: A Study in Anthropological Method.* 2nd ed. New York: Holt, Rinehart and Winston, 1972.
One of the clearest presentations of kinship available today. Well worth reading.

FIELD PROJECT
Family and Kinship

Most of the societies discussed in Chapter 13 were small-scale societies. In societies such as that of the Jívaro, described in the capsule ethnography, kinship and family determine much of social life. Most groups, such as the groups in which people work or eat, and most activities, such as political meetings or religious ceremonies, are predominantly or exclusively kin groups. In our society, the formation of social groups is not usually based on kinship. Many of the economic, political, and other roles that kinship plays in societies such as that of the Jívaro are taken by institutions like schools, governments, churches, and businesses. Nevertheless, the people to whom we are related are important in many contexts. In this project, you will explore the role of kinship and family relationships in your own life.

Before beginning the project, however, think about the following:

1. What does "being related" mean to you?

2. Can it apply to someone you have never met?

3. What obligations and expectations do you have with reference to relatives? Are they the same for all relatives?

The most important kinship unit in our society is often the *nuclear family*—that is, a married couple and their children who live and eat together. Is your family a nuclear family? If a grandparent or other relative or unrelated person lives with your parents and siblings, then your family is an *extended family*. Based on the following questions, make a list of the functions your own nuclear or extended family fulfills or is obligated to fulfill, giving concrete examples of each function from your own experience.

1. Is food grown by members of the family for family consumption, or is food purchased? How frequently is food prepared "from scratch" and how frequently is "prepared" food bought?

2. Are clothes bought or made at home?

3. Are or were children taken care of at home by a family member? By whom? Or were they taken care of by a hired helper? In a day-care center? Are or were any grandparents cared for by family members? By a nursing home? Are family members responsible for the support of children and grandparents? For how long?

4. Do several family members work for wages or salaries to support the family, or only one

of the members? Who works? Do they work together or at unrelated jobs? Do they own property together?

5. Do all members of your family vote the same way or belong to the same political party? Do they ever engage in political activities as a group?

6. Are all members of your family of the same religion?

Think of as many important services as you can which family members are expected to provide for each other, and activities in which they participate together.

Not all families in our society are nuclear families, and many families which are nuclear at one point in their history may not be at another point. These changes over time in the composition of the family are called its *developmental cycle*. For example, a newly married couple might live with the young husband's or wife's parents until they find a place of their own in which to live. In the later stages of a family's developmental cycle, an elderly parent might come to live with the family, or a sister or brother of one of the parents might live with the family.

Select a sample of friends and, if possible, a few people with whom you are acquainted who come from other countries. Using them as informants, try to discover what differences exist among them in family type and family history. Ask them:

1. Who lives together? Note their ages, sex, and relationship to one another.

2. Have these people always lived together in that place? Where and with whom have current coresidents lived in the past? If some family members are no longer living together (for example, because of divorce, growing up, etc.), where are they living now? What was the reason for their moving away?

3. What rights and obligations do family members have to each other (for example, economic support, inheritance, attendance at family celebrations or religious ceremonies, etc.)?

Now we turn to the wider kinship context of the family. In Chapter 13, we discussed several kinds of kin groups. In the United States and Canada, our family names are inherited patrilineally, i.e., the family name is that of the father. Our kinship system is also *ego-centered*. That is, each person, or ego, has his or her own set of people who are the most important kin.

Begin this part of the project by constructing a kinship chart, using the following symbols:

△ male   = married

◯ female   ≠ divorced

▢ person of unknown sex   ◯△ children of the same parents

⧄ deceased person

▲ or ● ego (person from whose point of view the chart is to be read)

For example, the nuclear family may be represented like this:

ego's father △=◯ ego's mother

△   ◯   ●
ego's   ego's   ego
brother   sister

Construct a kinship chart, asking your parents for help if necessary, and try to include as many people as you and your parents consider related to you. Label yourself "ego" and label all others with their names and relationship to you (i.e., Elizabeth Thomas, mother's brother's wife). Anthropologists use the following shorthand:

sister	z	wife	wi
brother	b	husband	hu
father	f	son	s
mother	m	daughter	d

Elizabeth Thomas would be your mbwi.

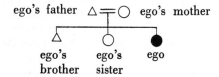

Find out the following information for as many people on your chart as possible:
1. Name
2. Birthdate and place
3. Marriages and divorces

4. Where does the person live now? With whom?

5. How often have members of your family seen or heard from the person? Once a week? Once a month? Once a year?

6. Where and at what does the person work?

7. Are there celebrations or ceremonies—religious, familial, or secular—where all or most of the people on your chart participate together, i.e., weddings, funerals, birthdays? What are some examples?

8. Have any members of your family helped financially or been helped by people on the chart? Who was involved and on what occasions? Was anyone expected to help who did not meet the expectations others had of them? Why?

9. If possible, question a cousin or aunt or uncle about which of their relatives they see or hear from the most frequently. You might find that they call certain people relatives whom you do not consider related to you.

In looking over your own chart, what can you say about the reasons why your family is in closer contact with some relatives than others? Is closeness of relationship the important factor?

Is closeness of residence the important factor? Does your family have a closer relationship with your mother's or your father's side of the family? Does your family depend in important ways on their relatives? In what ways? Could nonfamily institutions substitute for all these functions today? If not, do you think nonfamily institutions ever could? Compare your kinship chart with those of others in your class. Some people with tightly knit families will have been able to collect more information than others. Kinship relationships are more important for some people than for others. Compare the rights and obligations listed by people with large kinship charts and with smaller ones: are they different?

Chapter 14

Cultural Identity & Ethnicity

THE SPANISH-AMERICANS IN NEW MEXICO

POPULATION: Three and one-half million people with Spanish surnames were listed in the 1960 U.S. Census as living in the states
of California, Texas, New Mexico, Arizona, and Colorado. There
were 10 million Spanish-American people in the United States as a
whole in the 1970 Census. Spanish-Americans make up 28.3 percent
of the population in New Mexico. This represents a decline in the
state since 1940, when they comprised over 50 percent of the population.

RESEARCH: Historical and contemporary written sources were used
to present a synthetic account of existing institutions and as a basis
for further research.

PERIOD COVERED: 1950s to the present

. . . a sociological study of Albuquerque made by Carolyn Zeleny
in the early 1940's, noted that Spanish-Americans were almost
totally excluded from fraternal orders such as the Elks, Greek letter
societies on the University of New Mexico campus, the Rotary Club,
and the Junior Service League. Some societies maintained separate

Source: From Nancie L. Gonzalez, *The Spanish-Americans of New Mexico: A Heritage
of Pride*, rev. ed. (Albuquerque: University of New Mexico Press, 1969), pp. 108–111.
Copyright © 1969 by Nancie L. Gonzalez. Reprinted by permission of the University of
New Mexico Press.

chapters which segregated Anglos from Hispanos. This was true for one social organization on the University of New Mexico campus—Phrateres—and was also generally the custom in the veterans' organizations as well as in the churches. . . .

There is no doubt but that prejudice against persons of Spanish or Mexican ancestry was particularly rife during the 1930's and early 1940's and that discriminatory practices affected Hispanos at every level of the social scale. Most informants can cite cases of individuals who sought membership in such groups but were blackballed—presumably because of their ethnic background. However, it should also be noted that the majority of Hispanos probably were not interested in belonging to such clubs, which served somewhat different functions than the Spanish-American dominated groups mentioned above. Certainly the Anglo fraternal orders may also be interpreted as mutual-aid societies, but the aid proffered to individual members is most frequently of a non-material nature. Membership in these groups is most often used as a means of establishing or reaffirming one's social position in the middle- and upper-middle-class business and professional world dominated by Anglos. As such, most Hispanos in the state during the 30's and 40's would have been excluded on other than ethnic grounds. It should be remembered that lower-class Anglos are also rigidly excluded.

However, the total situation has changed in Albuquerque in the past twenty years. Today, almost every voluntary association one cares to mention has at least one person of Spanish descent on its roll, and some have a great many. This includes such prestigious organizations as the country clubs, the Junior League, the Petroleum Club, the Albuquerque Symphony Women's Association, the Rotary, Kiwanis and other service clubs, and sororities and fraternities on the University of New Mexico campus. It is true that participation in these groups by Hispanos is very low, but this would seem to reflect economic status as much or more than ethnic position. The formal and informal financial obligations imposed upon members by these groups would exclude a great many persons. It is likely that there may be persons of Spanish origin who can well afford to belong, and who might very well be acceptable to the other members, but who do not seek membership simply because their world view does not emphasize this type of social participation as a value—in other words, they are not acculturated to Anglo middle-class standards. . . .

This attitude of not seeking membership seems particularly relevant in the case of the men's service clubs, which, like the Chamber of Commerce, are made up primarily of business and professional persons. Throughout the state of New Mexico, while research for this book was being done, it was noted that Spanish-American businessmen in general eschew membership in the Chamber of Commerce, which is open to everyone who cares to join and can pay the fees. The reason for this seems to be that the typical small Hispano businessman continues to conduct business along more personal lines—his clientele comes from among his friends, relatives, *compadres,* neighbors, etc. The advantages of belonging to a group which purposes to increase business in the community at large through quite impersonal means are not readily apparent. At the same time the personal association with other members of the group is similarly only of value to the highly acculturated individual.

There are other areas in which upper-class Hispanos do not highly participate, but this nonparticipation cannot be explained on the basis of prejudice and discrimination. For example, in the 1965 Santa Fe Opera season, out of 554 contributors to the opera, only eight had Spanish surnames—and this in an area of many wealthy and upper-class Hispanos. Similarly, in Albuquerque during the same year, out of 380 listed as "Dons," "Associates," and "Friends" of the Albuquerque Civic Symphony, only eight had Spanish surnames. Two Spanish surnames were found out of forty-one on the Board of Directors, however.

Another intellectually oriented association, the Pan American Round Table, has a high proportion of Spanish-Americans. Thus, in 1965 fourteen of the thirty-seven members were in this category. This women's club, part of a national organization, emphasizes good relations with our Spanish-speaking neighbors south of the border and also stresses the value of Latin-American cultural patterns. Membership is by invitation only, and it is clear from an analysis of the roster that the group constitutes something of an intellectual elite. Local honorary members have included the wife of the president of the University of New Mexico and wives of Latin-American scholars on the faculty. In the Santa Fe chapter the proportion of Spanish surnames is also quite high, but it is interesting to note that in that city many of the members have Spanish surnames through marriage only.

At a somewhat lower level of prestige, there are other clubs with a high proportion of Hispano participants. A key informant estimated that about one-third of the members of the local Elks Club were of Spanish origin. This same informant, himself a recently initiated member, stated that this was a recognized means of gaining prestige among Hispanos striving to achieve middle-class status. Since here again entrance is contingent upon a

360

favorable vote of the membership, the applicant, regardless of ethnic background, will most probably have a world view, way of life, income, education, and ambition similar to that of most of the other members—in other words, his interests and social position will be generally comparable. It is also significant to note that the informant specifically mentioned the fact that the Elks admit only Caucasians and that this provision appeals to those Spanish-Americans who fear being classified with Indians, mestizos, or Negroes.[1]

● ● ● ● ● ● ●

Although kinship relations are the primary source of identity in all cultures, they are not the only source. In all but a few of the most simply organized societies there exist associations, voluntary and involuntary, which serve to unite individuals and provide for them an extrafamilial cultural identity. Ethnicity and ethnic status are other sources of cultural identity for millions of people throughout the world.

According to the distinguished Mexican scholar Miguel Leon-Portilla, cultural identity is a common

> . . . consciousness shared by members of a society who consider themselves in possession of elements and traits that distinguish them from other groups. . . . Principal sources of cultural identity are language, sets of traditions, beliefs, symbols, value systems, a sense of origin, experiences

> . . . shared in common, defined ancestral territory, a world vision and . . . ethos, the moral values and orientation of a culture.[2]

A very basic human question is "Who am I?" The answer can be provided in part by the history of a group of people and the common experience they share. While a person may have as many sources of identity as there are sources of interaction in his or her society, we have selected two areas of life to illustrate the concept of cultural identity: association and ethnic status.

Associations

An *association* may be defined as a group of people organized for the pursuit of one or more interests or goals they all share. Such groupings may be formed voluntarily (a basketball team) or involuntarily (a platoon of Army recruits), and they may be relatively enduring (membership in a uni-

1. From Nancie L. Gonzalez, *The Spanish-Americans of New Mexico: A Heritage of Pride*, rev. ed. (Albuquerque: University of New Mexico Press, 1969), pp. 108–111. Copyright © 1969 by Nancie L. Gonzalez. Reprinted by permission of the University of New Mexico Press.

2. "Leon-Portilla Delivers Fifth Distinguished Lecture," *Anthropology Newsletter* 16, no. 1 (1975): 9.

For the Mossi of Ouahiyagouya of Upper Volta, as for many people, a primary source of personal identity is membership in the family group.

versity alumni association) or short-lived (membership in an anthropology class for one term).[3] It is not necessary that all members know each other, care for each other, or even ever see each other. Indeed, there are associations in which it is impossible (or at least extremely difficult) for all the associates to be acquainted.

Most anthropologists in North America belong to the American Anthropological Association, a formal association of some 6,000 members. Few members know more than a handful of their colleagues in this

organization. Except for annual meetings, members rarely see one another unless they happen to work at the same institution or live in the same town. How, then, is membership in this association of importance to a member's identity?

When an anthropologist performs any professional act—writing an article, pursuing field work, preparing lecture notes—he or she is engaged in behavior common to other members of the association. The anthropologist is concerned with how associates will view these professional actions. The association is the organization to which the member looks for models of appropriate professional behavior. It serves as a reference group that makes certain behavior legitimate or illegitimate; and to a very great extent, it affects the member's self-

3. Michael Banton, "Voluntary Associations: Anthropological Aspects," in *International Encyclopedia of the Social Sciences*, vol. 16 (New York: Free Press, 1968), pp. 357–362.

image as well as the image projected to colleagues.

The role of adaptive associations in providing and maintaining a nonfamilial cultural identity is also quite important. Consider the case described in the capsule ethnography. The practice that existed in Albuquerque, New Mexico, during the 1930s and 1940s, of excluding Spanish-Americans from associations served to reinforce the identity of the Anglo members. It gave the Anglos yet another means of distinguishing themselves from a group whom they regarded as culturally inferior. Spanish-Americans resented the snub, but most felt their cultural identity was based primarily on family ties rather than on associational ties, a feeling that at least partially explains why they protested so little against the discrimination they suffered. Also, they had their own associations, made up exclusively of Spanish-Americans, that served in many ways as substitutes.

The situation has changed today, and Spanish-Americans in New Mexico may now join most of the associations formerly closed to them. Many young upwardly mobile Spanish-Americans find that membership in multiethnic associations helps enhance their status. As the capsule ethnography notes, the Elks Club has been especially important to the ambitious Spanish-American, since there is a great deal of prestige attached to membership in this club in both the Anglo and Spanish-American communities.

FUNCTIONS OF ASSOCIATIONS. Associations may have a number of general functions in any society:

1. They act as agencies of socialization by directing members in appropriate modes of behavior.

2. They provide an identity for members, so distinguishing them from nonmembers.

3. They assist the members in defining and achieving common goals.

4. They provide some degree of social control over members: Members who do not conform to the association's norms may be punished by various means, including expulsion.

5. They may be powerful or influential enough to control the activities of nonmembers who live in the same society. In this sense, an association may be a power group in the society.

6. They provide opportunities for feelings of mutual pride, a sense of belonging, and a chance for expression.

7. They provide mutual aid and protection.

8. They provide heightened status and self-esteem in rank- and class-structured societies.

No single association need perform all of the functions listed above. Not all associations are powerful, for example. Nor does an association have to operate in a formal and highly structured manner, although many do. Still, the list seems to indicate the importance of associations in many different societies.

Clubs and Fraternities

Clubs of varying sorts are commonplace in complex societies such as the United States and Canada. Moose, Elk, Lions, League of Women Voters, Junior League, and the National Organization of Women are just a few of the voluntary associations found in most communities. Equally well known are the fraternities and sororities with active alumni groups that exist on many university campuses. The major difference between clubs and fraternities is the greater

All the men at the left of the photo are members of the same warriors' association of the Crow tribe.

strength of emotional ties between members of fraternities. In many fraternities and sororities, members refer to each other as "brothers" or "sisters." This use of kinship terms suggests that they consider each other to be (ideally, at least) as close as real family members.

Many kinds of voluntary associations exist also in small-scale societies. Some involve secrecy of actions and ritual, some are open to all members of a given group within the society. Secret fraternities generally fall into two categories: those that are an outgrowth of puberty rites that allow all members of a particular group in the society to belong; and those that are limited and selective, to which only a chosen few may belong. In both types, those who have not been initiated into the group are excluded, and members must pledge not to divulge the body of knowledge, tradition, and ritual of the group to noninitiates.

A well-known example of the first type of secret fraternity is the *Poro* fraternity of the Mende of Sierra Leone.[4] All boys, on reaching adulthood, undergo a period of training in a bush school run by the *Poro* fraternity. This training, which may last anywhere from a few weeks to a few months, teaches the youths the skills necessary for survival in their environment. All adult men in Mende society who survive the period of training become *Poro* members. Since the *Poro* fraternity membership is an important step toward being regarded as an adult, the bush school experience is a crucial time in the lives of the young men. Perhaps of greater importance, since

---

4. Kenneth Little, "The Political Function of the Poro," *Africa* 35 (October 1965): 349–365, and 36 (January 1966): 62–71.

364

most boys will have picked up some rudimentary skills such as hunting before going to the bush school, is the training they receive in various rituals of adult Mende men.

The Kpelle people of Africa also have a *Poro* fraternity.[5] Among the Kpelle the *Poro* fraternity dominates and controls more areas of tribal life than it does among the Mende. Other fraternities and clubs exist, but *Poro* membership is a prerequisite for joining these. A man who is not a member of the *Poro* fraternity may not marry. Thus the *Poro* fraternity exercises control even over familial functions.

Examples of the second type of secret fraternity in the United States are the Masons and the Ku Klux Klan. Often such groups are a type of mutual aid society providing for the welfare—spiritual, economic, and/or political—of members and their families. Sometimes such a fraternal group becomes a political force within the larger society. This is the case with the Ku Klux Klan. Since the days of the Civil War, this group has exercised varying degrees of influence and power in the politics of the North, South, and Midwest.

In small-scale societies, exclusive secret fraternities also function as mutual aid societies. In addition, they provide political balance within the larger society by limiting the power of the tribal leader and by preventing anarchy.[6]

5. James L. Gibbs, Jr., "The Kpelle of Liberia," in *Peoples of Africa*, ed. James L. Gibbs, Jr. (New York: Holt, Rinehart and Winston, 1965).

6. H. Webster, *Primitive Secret Societies* (1908; reprint ed., New York: Octagon Books, 1968).

There are other groups that resemble fraternities. In the United States, for example, the Black Muslims are primarily a religious group. They also provide economic and political support for members and have a degree of power in black communities. The Jewish Defense League, primarily a political organization dedicated to the security of the State of Israel, also provides personal assistance to members.

Men's and Women's Houses

Another type of grouping—found in many societies in Africa, South America, Polynesia, and Melanesia—is centered around special houses where same-sex groups live together. Men's houses are common to many societies; women's are relatively rare. There are several reasons for this. Most women marry shortly after achieving puberty, so they are single only a short period of time. In most societies women are under male control and it is typical for a woman, on reaching marriageable age, to pass from the control of her male kinsmen to that of her husband. Also, men are often reluctant to allow unmarried (or married) women an opportunity to achieve solidarity.

Residence in a house provides a form of solidarity among members of the same sex that cuts across other kinship, age, or associational lines. These residential groups, a form of club, serve a number of purposes. In some cases, fugitives can find asylum in the house. In warlike societies, the men's house serves as an armory for spears and other weapons. The age at which men move into the houses varies from place to place. Among the Naga of northwestern India, boys move in at the age of seven. In other societies, such as the Dani of New Guinea, a male may not move in until he has attained adult status.[7]

As a society becomes more complex, the exclusiveness of groups tends to disintegrate. Just as it is adaptively necessary for exclusive groups to reinforce the structure of a small-scale society, so, too, is it necessary that that exclusivity be abandoned in response to new circumstances. This may lead to the weakening of same-sex group bonds. An attitude of equality between the sexes in such matters generally develops in urban and industrial settings where women's active participation is needed outside the home in economic, social, and political activities. Such participation makes women less likely to accept exclusion from all-male groups.

In New York City, all-male clubs for executives are beginning to accept female members. As men and women begin to interact with each other on an equal basis in business, the exclusion of women from these clubs, which provide a setting for business transactions, becomes impractical and dysfunctional.

7. Karl Heider, *The Dugum Dani* (Chicago: Aldine, 1970).

It is common for children of about the same age to form close ties, as is the case with these Dahomians. In some societies, this tendency is further institutionalized by the formal age-set.

Age-Graded Associations

Many associations throughout the world are based on the common age of members. An *age set* is a cohesive group of people of the same age, and usually of the same sex. They move together through some or all stages of life. As P. Gulliver points out,[8] all societies have some way of grouping their members in terms of age. In the United States and Canada, each individual passes through a number of life stages, including teenage, middle-age, and old-age. Each of these positions has its own pattern of activities, rights, and duties, however loosely defined. In many small-scale societies, however, age sets may be more numerous and more rigidly demarcated. The Kikuyu of Kenya, for example, have six age categories for males and eight for females.

The members of each age set in a preliterate society have particular social roles that entail specific rights and obligations. People in the junior age groups, for example, are expected to obey and respect those of senior status. Individuals in senior positions, by contrast, are expected to assist, educate, and lead the juniors. People in the same age set generally play the same kinds of social roles—they engage in similar activities and often cooperate in carrying out the activities. Moreover, they share the same orientation to life, and often the same aspirations. Among the Masai of East Africa, for example, the junior warriors belong to the age grade known as *ilmurran*. These young men have the task of protecting the village and its cattle and carrying messages from one village to another. They also build fences and water the cattle during the dry season. The *ilmurran* are not allowed to marry, nor can they eat meat in public. All individuals of this age set also dress and wear their hair alike and carry similar weapons. Other Masai age grades include the uninitiated youths (*ilaiyok*), the elders (*ilmoruak*), and the oldest elders (*ildasati*). Both the *ilmurran* and the *ilmoruak* are further divided into subgrades. A complex age-set system also exists (although in attenuated form today) among the Swazi of South Africa.[9] When the Swazi were a warfare-based society, the age sets served as military units. Today, the age sets work together in more peaceful pursuits, such as harvesting corn, cutting wood for house poles, running errands, and—most important—participating in the annual rituals designed to "rejuvenate" the Swazi king.

The Nyakusa, a Bantu-speaking people of eastern Africa, have what is perhaps the most highly organized age-set system.[10] Among the Nyakusa, boys live in their father's house until about the age of ten. Then all boys of that age band together and establish a new village where they reside together. As the boys get older, they build better houses for themselves. When the men marry (about age twenty-five), their spouses move into the village with them. Nyakusa society, then, is a collection of age-set villages, with each village com-

8. P. Gulliver, "Age Differentiation," in *International Encyclopedia of the Social Sciences*, vol. 1 (New York: Free Press, 1968), pp. 157–162.

9. Hilda Kuper, "The Swazi of Swaziland," in *Peoples of Africa*, ed. James L. Gibbs, Jr. (New York: Holt, Rinehart and Winston, 1965).

10. Monica Wilson, *Good Company: A Study of Nyakyusa Age Villages* (Boston: Beacon Press, 1963).

posed of men of the same age and their wives and children.

Street Gangs

A common form of association in urban centers throughout the world is the gang— a collection of young men and, sometimes, young women who band together as a social unit. The gang's territorial borders are fixed boundaries such as streets. Control of the gang area, or "turf," is of primary importance. Gang identity is fostered by a gang name, preferably one that sounds ferocious (Cobras, Mean Mothers) or noble (Dukes, Young Lords). Possibly two of the most well known street gangs in America are those from the musical drama *West Side Story*—the Sharks and the Jets. Members wear distinctive clothing, such as a certain style of hat or an embroidered symbol on a jacket. There is a strong sense of group solidarity; this is sometimes reinforced by beatings administered by the gang to deviant members. Nonmembers may be regarded as "the enemy" or at least as undesirables. Some street gangs claim to be exclusive, admitting only the "best" people as members; in practice, gangs actively recruit members and often coerce young men and women in their area to join. Joining a gang may be adaptive for a young person because it can facilitate interaction and provide prestige in an urban environment of alienation and poverty.

Although gangs may engage in criminal behavior—or, more accurately, behavior considered to be criminal by other groups within the society—the members see their gang as a benevolent association devoted to good works on their turf. Their special mission is thought to be the protection of members from the depredations of rival gangs. Puerto Rican and Mexican-American *palomillas* (the Spanish word for gangs) reflect the Hispanic value of protecting women from "dishonor." Members often justify (or rationalize) their actions by claiming that they are performing a needed service.

Membership in street gangs can make young people feel that they belong to something worthwhile. Gang membership may give a person a nickname that imparts stature or uniqueness (Stud, Tiger, etc.); it also provides a meaningful reference group. The group might reinforce a positive self-image that would be difficult for an individual to attain on his own. Gang membership also provides a means to achieve prestige; in fighting gangs, the member's "rep" (reputation) is all-important, so important that many members hide their fears and attempt a brave front in the face of a challenger or enemy, even though they would rather avoid a fight.

Entrance and Transition

In the case of most voluntary and involuntary associations, the initiate or joiner participates in a ritual or ceremony to mark entrance into a new status. In the United States, a child's baptism, a wedding ceremony, a graduation from college, and a funeral are all familiar rituals that mark a transition from one status to another. So, too, are initiations in college fraternities and sororities, and the "prop blast" ceremony that welcomes new paratroopers into the ranks of airborne soldiers. In 1909 Arnold Van Gennep called these rituals and ceremonies *rites of passage*.[11] Van Gennep divided the rites of passage into three basic types: *rites of separation,*

---

11. Arnold Van Gennep, *The Rites of Passage* (1909; reprint ed., Chicago: University of Chicago Press, 1960).

rites of transition, and *rites of incorporation.*

A common element in all rites of separation that mark membership in an association is a "death and rebirth" theme, in which the initiate gives up a past status and assumes a new one. In a number of Roman Catholic convents, prayers from the funeral service are read over nuns taking their final vows, signifying their "death" in the secular world. This service is followed by a form of wedding ceremony in which the nun mystically becomes the bride of Christ and is reborn into a new life, taking a new name and a new costume to signify this.

In military basic-training programs, the male recruit is harshly told by his superiors that his civilian status no longer exists and that he must now learn to be a soldier. Much of the rough behavior that marks basic training is a symbolic (though real) device to "bury" civilian identity as symbolized by hair styles, clothing, choice of food, and so on. These rites of separation are also designed to speed up the process of teaching recruits the new skills and attitudes appropriate to military life. At the conclusion of basic training, the recruit is told by his military superiors that now he is a "real man" or a "real soldier." His new status is ceremonially marked in a rite of transition that grants insignia reserved only for "real soldiers." At this time, the behavior of sergeants toward the individual changes from harshness to relative humaneness. Joking is permitted, and the "new" man may be allowed or even encouraged to insult newly arrived recruits. At one base in the United States, recruits in the last week of training who were sure to "graduate" were allowed, as a special sign of favor by the sergeants, to go to the base reception center to jeer

The hat worn by the Nigerian on the right signifies his membership in a specific group of transportation workers.

at newly arrived recruits just getting off the bus.

The military career of the "real soldier" may be marked by rituals—retreat parades, award ceremonies, etc.—that stress symbolically the cohesiveness of the group. These are Gennep's rites of incorporation; many anthropologists today refer to them as *rites of intensification*, since they seem to function to intensify and strengthen the bonds that link the members to a group.

In small-scale societies, initiates into a secret fraternity may undergo a period of basic training. The *Poro* bush schools mentioned earlier train young men in the things they will need to know as adults. The training is harsh, and some young men may die as a result, but at its conclusion the boys are said to have "died" as children and been "reborn" as adults. "Graduation" from this training serves also to label or identify the boy's radically altered social status.

At the heart of the transition ritual is the need for the new initiate to acquire sufficient skills to function as a member of the society. Depending on the importance of the association to the life of the society, rites of passage are usually preceded by a period of training. Once the individual is socialized into the new status and has an awareness of proper role behavior, the transition is celebrated in the rite. In some cases, such as initiation rites into adulthood in aboriginal Australian tribes and (formerly) in some American Plains Indian tribes, a person takes on a new name and/or title to denote publicly his acceptance into an association and the achievement of a new status.[12]

The prevalence of associations and of rites that mark membership in them suggests that these are adaptive devices. They are adaptive because they provide a means for promoting the stability and survival of a society. Associations serve to complement the existing kinship structure, or to replace it altogether. They also aid a society in further organizing itself in the face of danger or increased complexity, population size, and heterogeneity.

Ethnicity

Ethnicity, according to an interdisciplinary group of social scientists who discussed the problem in 1974, involves a number of variables. A summary of these variables states that ethnicity

(1) involves a past-oriented group identification emphasizing origins;

(2) includes some conception of cultural and social distinctiveness; and

(3) relates to a component unit in a broader system of social relations.

A major difficulty lies in distinguishing ethnicity from other determinants of group formation, such as kinship, locality groups, religion, and social class. Thus, one might add three further criteria:

(4) ethnic groups are larger than kin or locality groups and transcend face-to-face interaction;

(5) ethnic categories have different meanings both in different societal settings and for different individuals; and

(6) ethnic categories are *emblematic*, having names with meaning both for members and for analysts.[13]

Ethnicity is generally defined by social scientists in terms of the cultural ethos— or values, expectations, attitudes, and behavior. Thus, members of an ethnic group have a common genetic and/or linguistic, religious, national, and social background. Ethnic groups are defined both by outsiders (nonmembers), and by insiders, or people who feel that they belong in a particular ethnic category. Cultural ethos is the most important definition of ethnicity. Physical traits are relatively unimportant boundary markers between ethnic groups, except where members and/or nonmembers make them important.

An example of this can be drawn from the authors' own observations in Texas. Under actual and formerly lawful segregation by race in the Texas school system, Mexican-Americans were grouped with whites to distinguish them from blacks.

---

12. Clark Wissler, *The American Indian: An Introduction to the Anthropology of the New World* (Magnolia, Mass.: Peter Smith Publishers, 1957).

13. Wendell Bell, "Comparative Research on Ethnicity: A Conference Report," *Social Science Research Council Items* 28, no. 4 (1974): 61.

Then in the 1960s, a federal court ruled that citizens' committees composed of blacks and whites be formed to advise school authorities on ways to eliminate discrimination. The committees were also to look into possible curriculum changes designed to remove racism. To help attain their own goals of curriculum changes—notably bilingual education—Mexican-Americans claimed a new status: "brown." For educational as well as political reasons, it was expedient for Mexican-Americans to distinguish themselves from the dominant white Anglo population. Because of the unique social and linguistic features of Mexican-Americans, there was never any doubt that they were an ethnic group distinct from whites and blacks. Yet the issue of skin color entered into the distinction only much later—when it became useful to the Mexican-American group to call attention to it.

Ethnicity and Cultural Identity

Creation myths of various ethnic groups suggest how these groups view themselves and how they view nonmembers. (The other social functions of myths are discussed in Chapter 16.) Many ethnic groups have names for themselves which, in translation, mean simply "the people." The now extinct Yaghan of Tierra del Fuego called themselves Yamana, which meant "man," and regarded all other humans as lower animals who quite possibly were not true men.[14] A belief very much like this still exists in the language of the Polar Eskimo and the Navajo. Origin myths sometimes reflect a group's thinking about how the differences between them and the others came to be.

A myth from the North American Creek Indians tells how races were created and how the white man came to rule:

Three Indians were once out hunting. One went after water and found a nice hole of water but was afraid to drink. Another went down to it, dipped his fingers in, and said, "It is good. Let us go into it." So he dived in and came out. When he came out, he was white. From him came the white people. The second dived in and came out darker because the water was somewhat [muddy]. From him came the Indians. The third dived in and came out black because the water was now very [muddy]. From him came the Negroes. Just before the first man dived he felt of the rocks and they rattled. He did not tell the others that this was gold. They went on from there and the Indian found something else. The white man was told about this and he picked it up. It was a book. He asked the Indian to read this book, but he could not. The white man, however, could read it, and it was to tell him about this gold. The book gave him this advantage. "The Nof-filas [whites] were terrible people to take the lead."[15] The Creek myth is a particularly good example of a tale created after contact with black slaves, since the Creek did not know of blacks until well into the seventeenth century.

Ethnic Pride and Solidarity

Ethnic group membership may be a source

---

14. J. M. Cooper, "The Yaghan," in *Handbook of South American Indians*, vol. 1, *The Marginal Tribes*, ed. J. H. Steward (St. Clair Shores, Mich.: Scholarly Press, 1946).

15. John Swanton, *Myths and Tales of the Southeastern Indians*, Bureau of American Ethnology Bulletin no. 137 (Washington, D.C.: Smithsonian Institution, 1929).

of pride to members, even when the group is a subjugated minority. If an oppressed minority is to raise its status in the society, it must have a high degree of cohesion and social solidarity. One way of bringing about that solidarity is the fostering of pride in the achievements of the group and of its individual members. Another is discovering and elaborating on the people's past achievements.

Activists in American Indian "Red Power" movements have sought to instill a sense of pride among their fellow Indians by citing the achievements of their ancestors. The Cherokee, for example, take pride in being the first Indian group north of Mexico to have a written language. Black activists in the United States have stressed the cultural achievements of Afri-

can tribal groups from whom they have descended. They have also complained, with great justification, that the contribution of black Americans has been overlooked in American history books. Mexican-Americans speak with pride of their heritage, although they do not always agree about what that heritage is. Older Mexican-Americans of higher status tend to look back to their Spanish ancestry and their ties, however remote, to the aristocracy of the *conquistadores*. Younger and more militant Mexican-Americans point to the achievements of their Indian ancestry, noting with pride that the Aztec capital of Tenochtitlan was a mighty city at a time in the sixteenth century when Madrid was little more than a collection of adobe huts.

Culture heroes are important as symbols

Every ethnic group prides itself on the details of clothing and architecture that set the group apart from its neighbors.

Cultural Identity and Ethnicity

Even children's games can be a source of ethnic pride that contributes to the group's solidarity.

of group identity and pride. Blacks praise such dissimilar heroes as Booker T. Washington and Malcolm X. Some blacks take a rueful pride in the depredations of Deadhead Dick, a notorious desperado of the post-Civil War American West who happened to be black. Sports have provided a historically rich source of culture heroes such as Jim Thorpe (Indian), Muhammad Ali (black), and Lee Trevino (Mexican-American). Australian aborigines have a sports hero in tennis star Evonne Goolagong, and Brazilians exult in the triumphs of soccer star Péle.

One of the problems and potential pitfalls in understanding ethnic groups is the use of the term "community" to denote ethnic unity. Although phrases such as "the black community" or "white America" are used commonly, it is erroneous to assume that the implied degree of solidarity actually exists. White Americans are divided by a number of factors: age, sex, socioeconomic status, education, occupation, religion, etc. There is not one "black community" but several: middle-class blacks in Atlanta may differ as a group from blacks of Jamaican origin in Miami and these, in turn, may differ from upper-class blacks in Washington, D.C. Lumping American Indians together is a common practice, but separation along tribal lines is still very much a fact—even though there are pan-Indian associations working for the benefit of all Indians.

With worldwide accelerated cultural change and urbanization, more and more people are without the old kinship ties that gave them their primary identity and security. As a result, ethnic associations are becoming more and more numerous. They are particularly widespread in West Africa, where tremendous culture changes have weakened traditional kinship ties. But we can find them in our society, as well: Sons of Norway, Finnish Kaleva, and so on. The functions of these tribal and ethnic voluntary associations range from keeping their members in touch with their traditional culture to providing mutual aid in case of unemployment, illness, or death. Overall, they serve to bridge the gap between two very different lifestyles and are preeminently adaptive.

Ethnicity and Conflict

In almost all heterogeneous societies, membership in an ethnic group may be a source of tension and perhaps violence. Even the

This pageant dramatizing Jewish immigration to the United States was put on by a Zionist group in Milwaukee in 1919. By combining elements of Jewish and American ethnicity, it suggested a way to reduce the traditional culture conflicts of the immigrant. The Statue of Liberty was played by Golda Meier.

most casual observer knows that ethnic strife is a daily feature of North American society. In Canada, French-Canadians and Eskimos are two ethnic groups not well accepted by the dominant Anglo-Canadian group, and vice versa. In Mexico, there are

Cultural Identity and Ethnicity

deep divisions based primarily on cultural differences, between the "pure Spanish," the racially mixed *mestizo*, and the Indian —despite attempts by the government to convince everybody that they are true Mexicans. Some of the same distinctions are found in the southwestern United States.

Ethnic discrimination is not limited to North America. Koreans residing in Japan, black Bantus in South Africa, East Asians in Uganda, Jews in the Soviet Union, and Arabs in Israel all suffer the effects of discrimination based on ethnic status. Nor does membership in the dominant group in a society necessarily spare a person from such discrimination. A white person might encounter prejudice in Harlem, Watts, or the ghetto areas of Chicago. Similarly, an Anglo, who is dominant in the wider society, may find himself a victim of discriminatory practices in the Spanish-American *barrio* of Albuquerque. Furthermore, discrimination is not limited to the majority–minority dimension. There is a good deal of anti-Semitism in black areas in New York and a great deal of antiblack feeling in the *barrios* of the American Southwest.

Nor are conflicts between ethnic groups unique to the United States or even to North America. In Europe, interethnic strife has long been a part of social life. In Wolfsburg, Germany (site of one Volkswagen plant), there have been conflicts among Spanish, Yugoslavian, Moroccan, and Italian immigrant factory workers— and also conflicts between each of them and the Germans. The economic success of Japanese immigrants to Brazil has led to a problem of "the ugly Japanese" in that country, where the immigrants have banded together into groups that refuse to assimilate into the heterogeneous Brazil-

ian culture. The approximately 3 percent nonwhite population of Great Britain, largely clustered in cities, is now a major social problem. Also, the British have taken steps, not always popular with the rest of the world, to shut off emigration—especially by "coloured" peoples—to their islands.

The Conquest Culture

Many of the world's ethnic groups live under a form of *conquest culture*.[16] This is any artificial way of life established by the conquering group to deal with the problems administering a subject population. In such a society, a controlling body, representing the donor culture, attempts to impose its way of life on the subjugated peoples.

A conquest culture is composed of elements taken from both the donor and recipient cultures. For the most part, the conquerors control what will be kept of the recipient culture and what will be transmitted by the donor. In the case of Mexico, the Spanish introduced their version of Christianity and a government system that was quite different from the system used in sixteenth-century Castile. In Castile, each city and major village was virtually autonomous and only rather loosely subject to the rules of the Crown. Obviously, this was no way to govern a colony. Hence, the Spanish monarch borrowed the political ideology and system of feudalism in use in southern and western Spain, an ideology and system quite distinct from the Castilian system. This borrowed system

16. George Foster, *Culture and Conquest* (New York: Wenner-Gren Foundation for Anthropological Research, 1960), pp. 10 ff.

was then modified to fit the requirements of the colonies.

A similar process occurred in North America when black slaves were brought from Africa. The slaves were introduced to Christianity, but only to those elements of Christian doctrine that stressed obedience to the master as a prerequisite for a heavenly reward. Doctrines that might have led the slaves to challenge their masters were not taught—doctrines, for example, that stressed human free will or the equality of all people before God. The behaviors that the slaves were taught were those designed to keep them in a subordinate place.

The conquered peoples, for their part, retain only selected elements of their own cultures, elements which melded into the new way of life thrust upon them. (The bases for accepting or rejecting changes will be discussed in Chapter 18.) In many parts of Mexico, people still pray to the

bines Spanish and Indian elements. Some forms of African music have endured and have served as the base for jazz and blues music of black Americans. Because black slaves were tightly controlled and also were far from their homeland, the source of the original tribal cultures, they have retained less of their original cultures than have the Mexican Indians who, on their home ground, were able to retain a great deal of their culture in spite of Spanish efforts to weaken it.

The "true culture" of an ethnic group probably does not exist. In other words, there probably never was a tightly unified body of beliefs and practices for an ethnic group. What is more likely is that the culture of a group grew out of a number of alternatives from which the members were to some extent able to pick and choose.

Summary

1. Cultural identity is a consciousness derived from a variety of traits and attributes of a human group that make it culturally distinct from other groups. Such traits include language, sets of traditions, beliefs, a sense of origin, and an ethos, which are the moral values and orientation of a culture.

2. An association is a group of people united in the pursuit of a common interest or goal. Associations may be formed voluntarily or involuntarily and may endure for a brief or long period of time. Associations perform a number of general functions: for the members they provide identity, common goals, social control, mutual aid and protection, heightened status, and the opportunity to express feelings of pride. In addition, they sometimes influence the activities of the larger society.

3. Types of associations include secret fraternities, clubs, age sets, and street gangs.

4. Entrance into an association often involves the initiate's participating in a ritual or ceremony known as a "rite of passage." There are three types of rites of passage: rites of separation, rites of transition, and rites of incorporation.

5. Ethnicity is defined in terms of cultural differences; physical differences among ethnic groups are unimportant unless a group makes such differences important as part of its ethos.

6. Conflict between different ethnic groups is found all over the world.

7. Origin myths and culture heroes help foster unity among peoples of a given ethnic group.

8. Many of the world's ethnic groups live, or have lived, under a conquest culture and have been obliged to adapt to the ways of the group that dominates them. Generally the conquerers determine what cultural elements they will transmit to the conquered and what cultural elements of the conquered will be retained.

Review Questions

1. What are the characteristics of an association? List five functions of associations.
2. Name two types of secret fraternity and give an example of each.
3. Van Gennep's idea of the rites of passage is an important anthropological concept. Explain the three basic types of such rites and give an example of each.
4. List a few of the variables of ethnicity.
5. How do members of various ethnic groups promote solidarity among themselves? Give a few examples?
6. Define the term "conquest culture." List its characteristics and give an example of such a culture.

Suggested Readings

Banton, Michael. "Voluntary Associations: Anthropological Aspects." In *International Encyclopedia of the Social Sciences*, pp. 357–362. Vol. 16. New York: Free Press, 1968.
A useful summary of the anthropological perspective on associations. Students who have taken sociology courses will find it interesting to compare the approaches taken by the two disciplines.

Eisenstadt, S. N. *From Generation to Generation: Age Groups and Social Structure.* New York: Free Press, 1956.
An older book, but still one of the best sources of information on age grades.

Friedlander, J. *Being Indian in Hueyapan: A Study of Forced Identity in Contemporary Mexico.* New York: St. Martin's Press, 1975.
Excellent ethnography dealing with problems of changing cultural identity among Mexican Indians today.

Gonzales, N. L. *The Spanish-Americans of New Mexico: A Heritage of Pride.* Rev. ed. Albuquerque: University of New Mexico Press, 1969.
An informative account of the culture of Hispanic peoples in the American Southwest.

Hudson, C. M, ed. *Red, White, and Black: Symposium on Indians in the Old South.* Athens, Ga.: University of Georgia Press, 1971.
A collection of papers on the interethnic relations among Indians, blacks, and whites in the Southern United States. The book looks at these relationships in historical perspective.

PART SIX

A culture expresses its ethos—its character—through its language, art, and religion. These three cultural universals are intricately linked to one another; each depends on the use and understanding of the symbols of the culture. Such symbols, and the ideas that underlie them, are the energies that propel a culture, stamping it with its own identifiable meanings. It is by means of language, art, and religion that a society reveals to the world the adaptations that have enabled it to survive and maintain itself. The rich variety of languages, art, and religions in existence testifies to the many alternative adaptive strategies available to the world's cultures. By studying these adaptations and alternatives, the anthropologist can discover much about the ecological, sociological, and ideological relationships on which a particular society is based.

Probably no other single cultural phenomenon has helped human societies adapt as much as language, the subject of Chapter 15. All other aspects of culture, including art and religion, depend on the ability of the members of a society to communicate with one another. By means of language, individuals transmit information about their thoughts and feelings. Language, moreover, is the medium by which each society accumulates its cultural legacy. Its myths, kinship system, political and economic organization, for example, are passed down from one generation to another by means of language. And language both reflects the society and keeps it running smoothly.

Language must be adapted to many situations in nature—it is necessary for our survival. But as Chapter 15 makes clear, we must also use language to adapt to the social environment: we vary our speech to fit the social context. Thus, we talk to our superiors or employers quite differently than we do to our friends and loved ones. Such social adaptation is carried to an extreme in caste-dominated India, where an upper-class Hindu may have to know four different languages: one for use in religious contexts, and the other three for domestic, business, and educational situations. Within the same society, language reflects the ways individuals from different social classes, different regions, and different lifestyles cope with the natural and social environments.

Just as adaptive to both natural and social environments are art and religion, the respective subjects of Chapters 16 and 17. Art has been defined as the manipulation of the environment to express feelings and beliefs. Art's connection with the supernatural can be seen in the fact that deities, ancestors, and sacred symbols are important parts of many cultural artistic objects

Expressive Aspects of Culture

such as masks, vessels, and funerary items. Most art can be grouped into one of three categories: the visual arts, music, and literature.

Art and religion are so intertwined that many general statements apply to both. Art and religion are adaptive on three levels: the emotional, sociological, and intellectual. On the emotional level, both serve the needs of the individual, helping to reduce anxiety. On the sociological level, both art and religion help foster and maintain social cohesion, stability, and survival. Both promote the success of important social activities such as war, food-getting, marriage and reproduction. On the intellectual level, art and religion provide explanations for life's mysteries—Why am I here? Where did I come from? What happens to me after death? Both art and religion, then, are adaptive in that they help us get through the day, so to speak. In sum, both explain the world and reinforce social values. It follows, then, that it is not easy to understand the artistic and religious expressions of a society if one does not understand the energies that drive it.

An example of the interplay of religion with ecology, population density, and the economy is the sacred cow of India. The Indian cattle, scrawny beasts known as *zebus*, are protected by the Hindu doctrine of *ahimsa*, which forbids the eating of beef. From the culture-bound perspective of the Western observer, the Indians, many of whom are starving, appear to be wasting a valuable resource by not breeding the cattle for food. But anthropologist Marvin Harris, in his study, "The Cultural Ecology of India's Sacred Cattle," has shown that the *ahimsa* taboo is an adaptation to the ecology of the region. First, Indian farmers exist at or near the poverty level because their land is not very productive. The farmers use some of their cattle to pull wagons and plows. These thin cattle are a boon in that they help cultivate the fields but do not consume much food. At the same time, the dung dropped by the beasts is gathered for use as fertilizer in the fields. At certain times of the year, those *zebus* that are employed on farms are allowed to roam the land freely. Some of the wastes dropped by these animals are carried by rains to farms where they manure the crops. Cattle dung is also burned all over India as a source of energy, for cooking and heating. In short, the sacred cow plays an important role in the Indian ecosystem, and the *ahimsa* religious taboo on beef consumption provides the poor farmer with a way of adapting to this ecosystem. Thus does the cow, as symbol and as beast, in an unexpected way play its part in the religion and economy of India.

Chapter 15

Language

MALE/FEMALE LANGUAGE

Sometimes it is easier to observe differences objectively when the subject matter is not our own. This seems to be the case in linguistic studies of male/female language, because the first statement I find with substantial data about these differences is on the American Indian languages, Carib and Arawakan, . . . recorded by Raymond Breton in *Dictionaire Caraibe-Français* [sic] in 1665. Throughout the nineteenth century descriptions are largely on "the women's language" of these . . . peoples. Travelers, historians, and philologists [classical scholars] such as Humboldt enjoyed commenting on these esoteric tribes where the men and women had different languages! It has never been true that males and females had completely different languages, for the societies could not have existed as such.

In this century, language scholars, notably the famous Danish scholar, Otto Jespersen, and the great linguist, Edward Sapir, began more extensive studies of male and female language differences. These scholars, however, were bound by their cultural preconceptions and distortions, as all human beings are, and this is reflected in their otherwise scholarly treatments of "women's language." Jespersen spoke of feminine weaknesses and Sapir

Source: From Mary Ritchie Key, *Male/Female Language* (Metuchen, N.J.: The Scarecrow Press, Inc., 1975), pp. 14–21. Copyright 1975 by Mary Ritchie Key. Reprinted by permission.

included women's speech in his study of "abnormal types of speech." Greenough and Kittredge, highly respected English scholars, spoke of "feminine peculiarities." In discussions of the German language, it was said that, "Women naturally have certain peculiarities in their German as in other languages. . . ."

. . . When Sapir published his study of abnormal speech types of the Nootka language in 1915, he included fat people, dwarfs, hunchbacks, lame people, left-handed people, circumcised males, cowards, baby talk, and women's speech. No one questioned that some of these categories are not abnormal. . . . [But] an enlightened awareness will challenge that kind of classification. Analogous to this is a recent study on mental health that showed double standards being applied in judging for male and female what is normal, healthy behavior. This orientation of looking at language variation as different cultural and sociological types, and the development of linguistics in its maturing stages has led to the establishing of a subdiscipline in linguistics called *sociolinguistics.* This branch of linguistics studies the infinite varieties of language within language: age differences, cultural differences, occupational vocabulary, slang, styles of speech and writing, and many others, but including, of course, sex differences in language. Before the development of sociolinguistics, linguists were not truly ready to talk about male/female differences because none of these differences operates alone and without intricate connections to other variables. The little girl rolling her eyes and inveigling an ice cream cone from a tall adult male, is indeed, using female language, but she is also using pre-school language; familial language (he is her father); and dramatic language (the scene occurs in public). . . .

To show how these concepts can be completely misunderstood even by highly intelligent people, I quote a renowned scholar of the last century. In discussing the Arawak language of Guiana, he noted two genders, which he called masculine and neuter. This kind of linguistic gender classification has nothing to do with diminishing females. Nevertheless, he mistakenly observed:

A peculiarity . . . is that [Arawak] only has two genders . . . masculine and neuter. Man or nothing was the motto of these barbarians. Regarded as an index of their mental and social condition, this is an ominous fact. It hints how utterly destitute they are of those high, chivalric feelings, which with us center around women.

All of the Indo-European languages except Armenian [and Persian] have masculine and feminine grammatical categories of gender in their linguistic systems. In some, . . . the gender system is very predominant—every tree, table, chair, and stone has either a masculine, feminine, or neuter assigned to it. In others, such as English, the gender system is evident only in a few pronouns: she and he, his and her. In order to grasp the significance of gender-consciousness in our world view, it is useful to go outside of the Indo-European languages and see how other people and languages deal with gender. . . . The Aztec language is a good example, because we know something of their ancient beliefs and it is a language which does not have masculine and feminine gender in the grammatical system. The singular pronouns are: *nejua*, *tejua*, and *yejua*, meaning, respectively, first person singular (or I), second person singular (you), and third person singular. This last pronoun cannot be translated into English. It may refer to "he, she, or it." I believe that this is relevant to the concepts which the Aztecs devised for the explanation of their origins. They believed that the origin of the world and all human beings was *one single principle* with a dual nature. This supreme being had a male and female countenance—a dual god who conceived the universe, sustains it, and creates life. This god had the regenerating ability of both male and female. This dual deity, *Ometeotl*, had two different aspects of a single supreme being. Ome = "two" and teotl = "god." The dynamic essence of this divine being was the feminine and masculine nature—a *whole* god.

Ometeotl dwelt in a place called *Omeyocan*: "the mansion of duality, the source of generation and life, the ultimate or metaphysical region, the primordial dwelling place. . . ." This god is spoken of in the singular grammatical form. There is a plural form in Aztec, if the ancients had wanted to use it, but they referred to this god in the singular. At the same time this singular divine being is described as having a partner, which means "equal" or "a thing which fits or adjusts with some other thing" or "that which improves a thing or makes it more complete."

Besides the gender difficulty in rendering these ideas into English, there is the difficulty of the multitudes of gods being *one god*. Do we use "is" or "are"? Note that I have not used either pronoun referent "he" or "she" so far, in reference to this Aztec god. There is nothing in the Aztec language to indicate which gender should be used, and there is simply no way to translate this into English. Nevertheless it is significant that the eminent authorities who discuss Aztec religion all use the pronoun "he" in the discussions. There is no more reason to use the male referent than to use "she." We can substitute the female referent just as correctly: "She is Queen, she is Lord, above the twelve heavens . . . she exercises power over all things. She is Lord and she rules." Also in the translations, the words "wife" and "consort" are used to designate the counterpart, the partner. Again, there is no word in English, unless we use the term "Siamese twin" to refer to this single dual being. This Siamese twin god was referred to as *in Tonan, in Tota, Huehueteotl*, "the Mother, the Father, the old god." In fact, this divine being had many titles:

> Thus the tlamatinime [the sages], anxious to give greater vitality and richness to their concept of the supreme being, gave [the god] many names, laying the foundation for a comprehensive vision of the dual and ubiquitous divinity. And they did this through 'flower and song.'

Thus, attempts at explanations and theoretical discussions continue—and will continue as long as human beings like to talk with each other and ask questions. In reality, what we must deal with now, whether or not we know the explanation, is that for whatever the reasons, male and female linguistic behavior differs one from the other.[1]

● ● ● ● ● ● ● ●

From 3,000 to 6,000 different languages are spoken in the world today. Some of these languages are associated with a single community of speakers, a separate culture and society. Other languages, such as English, are spoken by a great variety of sociocultural groups all around the world. We cannot say whether all languages are dialects of some original tongue—whether, that is, they are historically united. No one knows. But we do know that they form a unity if we think of them as reflections of a characteristic ability of *Homo sapiens*. The ability to learn and use language is universal and uniform in our species. This ability is the same for any infant of our

species, of whatever race or ethnic origin, with regard to any human language. Being born Chinese does not predispose a child to learn Chinese any more than Swedish or Bantu.

Since the ability to learn and use a language is a characteristic of *Homo sapiens*, comparable to the ability to walk upright or the possession of an opposable thumb, it is not possible to rank any particular language. No language spoken on earth today is any more sophisticated than any other. There is no such thing as a "primitive" language. Languages are very different from one another but they require and reflect the same language capacity. Languages spoken by peoples with very simple technologies may be just as complex grammatically, if not more so, and just as expressive, as the languages of industrial civilizations.

Some anthropologists think of this hu-

---

1. From Mary Ritchie Key, *Male/Female Language* (Metuchen, N.J.: The Scarecrow Press, Inc., 1975), pp. 14–21. Copyright 1975 by Mary Ritchie Key.

man capacity for language as having evolved along with the species itself. Because of the importance of language in our lives, we often consider it to be the primary defining characteristic of *Homo sapiens*. All of the major aspects of culture —technology, religion, art, economy, social organization—are difficult to imagine without language. It is as though language made culture in all its aspects possible. It is as though culture as tradition, as human history from the Stone Age to the atom bomb, were made possible by the human capacity for language.

Language and Communication

All living things communicate information. The animal world is full of elaborate communication systems.[2] Birds use intricate songs and dances to establish territorial and mating prerogatives. Fish employ various expressive swimming patterns to communicate with their own and other species. Anyone who has lived with a dog or a cat is familiar with the wide range of messages mammals are capable of sending and receiving. Even plants "signal" to bees that they are ready to spread their pollen by growing flowers—though bees, to be sure, read the signal from their own rather different point of view.

Language as a Communication System

Human language is a *communication system* found in nature, like those we have just mentioned. But it is as different from

2. Thomas A. Sebeok, *Animal Communication* (Bloomington: Indiana University Press, 1968).

Not all forms of communication are verbal. This Senegalese drummer is beating out a message to his audience.

the others as they are from each other. Birds do not grow flowers and plants do not sing. Furthermore, song sparrows do not sing chickadee songs and rose plants produce roses, not tulips. Human language, we are inclined to say, is as unique to our species as are the communication systems of other biological species.

This does not mean that there is no communication between species. We mentioned above that the function of flowers is to attract bees, not to signal other flowers. And pets can be trained to respond differentially to commands in a human language. But does the dog who sits when he hears the distinctive sound "sit" really understand the term as a word in a language? One could easily train a dog to sit when he heard "roll over" and to roll over when he heard "sit." The dog's life would not be appreciably altered. If you tried similar changes on yourself, chaos would be the immediate result. No, like the bee who interprets flowers in terms of his interest in honey, a dog hears something quite different from human language in his master's voice.

Until recently, it was believed that monkeys and apes cannot use human language. However, in the last ten years startling results have been obtained by researchers trying to teach human language to chimpanzees. It remains a matter of controversy how close to human language the chimpanzees have come. But their performance is sufficiently striking to warrant a separate discussion. Before we look at the chimpanzees we must understand some of the basic characteristics of human language as a system of communication. Only then can we evaluate the performance of chimpanzees and determine whether or not human language remains a system of communication unique to *Homo sapiens*.

First we must ask: What are the distinguishing characteristics of language which differentiate it from the many communication systems found in nature? What makes language different from other ways of communicating? Anthropological linguist Charles Hockett answers this question by compiling a list of what he calls *design features* for systems of communication.[3]

He looks at systems of communication as though they were manufactured products designed to a set of criteria. By isolating these criteria from the product itself, he isolates the features of the design.

The design features of communication systems which we will consider are (1) productivity, (2) duality of patterning, (3) displacement, (4) arbitrariness, and (5) transmission by tradition. These design features will serve to distinguish human language as a whole from other systems of communication. Then, when we look at the achievements of the chimpanzees in learning language, we will ask: To what extent do the chimps preserve these design features in their version of human language?

PRODUCTIVITY. Consider this sentence: "John brushes between his toes with Nu-brite." The chances are very slim that you have ever encountered this sentence before. Yet it is as easy for you to understand as a sentence you have encountered before. In fact, some linguists estimate that more than 70 percent of the sentences encountered in a lifetime are entirely novel. It is a remarkable fact about language that original messages are constantly being sent and received in it. This property of language is called *productivity*. A communication system that shows productivity is said to be *open* because there is no limit to the messages it can handle.

Other communication systems in nature fail to show this design feature. A species may be capable of a number of different "signals" or "calls." But no matter how many signals a species uses, it can use each signal only in its appropriate context in the appropriate way. A bird, for example, may have a number of different

---

3. Charles F. Hockett in *Universals of Language*, 2nd ed., ed. J. Greenberg (Cambridge, Mass.: M.I.T. Press, 1962).

characteristic songs. It may use one to attract a mate, one to defend its territory against members of its own species, another to defend against other species, another to call to its young, and still another to signal a general alarm. But no matter how many signals such a species may use, its members are limited to a set number of *mutually exclusive* signals, each with a set meaning in a set context. When we say that signals are mutually exclusive we mean that signals cannot be combined in a single message. A cat, for example, cannot arch his back (a defense message) and purr (a contentment message) at the same time. The two signals are mutually exclusive. Such a system lacks the design feature of productivity. It is called *closed* because there is a limit to the number of messages it can handle.

Language allows us to compose improbable, original messages. Very few people, for example, are likely to brush between their toes with Nu-brite. Productivity is present in language, as opposed to other systems of communication, because the signals are not mutually exclusive. Language allows us to compose unlikely, even impossible messages because we can combine our signals in a great variety of ways.[4]

DUALITY OF PATTERNING. Imagine that, instead of words carrying meanings, each individual vowel sound or consonant had its own meaning. The sound *a* could mean "help," *o* could mean "thank you," *p* could mean "Tom Seaver is a goodie-goodie," and so on. We can readily see that we would very quickly reach a limit to the number of messages language could handle. The human vocal apparatus is not capable of making an unlimited number of distinct sounds; nor can the human ear reliably discriminate so many distinct sounds.

One of the reasons human language is productive, then, is that it combines simple sounds without meaning into complex sounds with meaning. In a final step, it combines these complex sounds with meaning into messages. From the point of view of writing, which gives us a rough approximation to speech, we can say that letters combine to make words and words combine to make messages. There are two levels of combination, or patterning, in human language. One level combines sounds, and the other level combines meanings. This is what is meant by *duality of patterning*.

Animal communication systems lack this design feature, duality of patterning. Each signal, whether it is a sound, a behavior pattern, or even a smell, means whatever it means in the form in which it exists. An animal signal, it is true, may mean different things in different contexts. A dog may growl in a play situation as well as in a truly threatening situation. But the dog's growl is not made up of meaningless elements which are, in turn, composed into messages. Communication systems without duality of patterning, such as the dogs', are closed systems, since they can handle only the number of messages for which they have distinct signal elements.

DISPLACEMENT. Human beings can communicate about situations other than the one that provides the context for their communication. People exchange informa-

---

4. Fred W. Householder, *Linguistics Speculations* (Cambridge: Cambridge University Press, 1971).

tion about other places and times and even about entirely imaginary places and times. This capacity of a communication system to refer to other times and places is called *displacement*.

It is easy to see what an advantage it is to have a communication system with this design feature. By means of displacement, whole communities are able to share in the knowledge of each of their members. Thus, one person's experience can benefit many other people. The ability to plan for the future and to coordinate a group's activities according to a plan depends upon displacement. Displacement into imaginary realms makes possible the great achievements of art, science, and religion.

But displacement may be a curse as well as a blessing. Telling lies, and perhaps evil itself, depend upon displacement. Lies can be told only about situations other than the one that is the immediate context. The imagination is a place of terror as well as beauty. People may be coerced into working according to plan as well as cooperating to realize one.

Animal communication systems, on the other hand, lack the feature of displacement. Animals communicate only about the immediate context. The sign and its meaning are always simultaneous. Animals have not organized to make something where before there was nothing, as people have throughout history. The innocence of animals is preserved by their systems of communication. They are confined to the here and now without responsibility for the past or future.

ARBITRARINESS. In language the relation between a sign and its meaning is arbitrary. Consider, for example, the sound of the word "cat" and its meaning. Compare that to the sound of the word "buzz" and its meaning. The sound of "buzz" resembles its meaning. The sound of "cat" does not. In language, words such as "buzz" occur infrequently. Most words in the language neither bear resemblance to nor have any necessary relationship to their meaning. This is the design feature called *arbitrariness*.[5]

In animal communication systems, on the other hand, we do not find this feature of arbitrariness. Indeed, the relation between sign and meaning in animal communication systems is designed to be close. Typically the sign is just a particularly noticeable part of the context of a situation. The sign serves as communication because it is noticeable, but it is, actually, only a part of the meaning.

For example, we can say that a dog's growl, or the raised fur on his back, or his stiff-legged walk means that he is communicating a threat. Any of these behaviors *serve* as signs that mean something like "watch out!" But such behaviors are only parts in a complex response to fear which includes an increase in heart rate and blood pressure and a flow of strengthening enzymes to the muscle tissue. These internal responses are not noticeable and therefore do not serve as signs. But, from the dog's point of view, the whole complex is his way of responding to a threatening situation of which the external signs are only a part.

Those parts of a situation that are noticeable and serve as signs have evolved over time. It is adaptive for members of a species to communicate with each other in mating, nesting, feeding, and situations

5. Ferdinand de Saussure, *Course in General Linguistics* (New York: Mc-Graw-Hill, 1966).

of danger. Effective communication promotes survival for those who possess the means for it. Evolution has selected for certain noticeable response elements in situations which are critical for survival. The colorful plumage and elaborate songs of some bird species, the odors deposited in the wake of certain insects, the oversized fangs of many carnivores, the colorful backsides of baboons, and the laughing bark of the hyena all have been emphasized by evolution because they function as signs in the communication systems of these species.

The particular signs in any human language, however, have not been selected by biological evolution. Signs in human languages stand apart from the situation to which they refer. The signs "cat," "gato," and "domestic feline" all refer to the same thing. They do not resemble what they mean, as do "bang," "buzz," or "plop." Their relation to what they mean is fixed only by convention. "Cat" means "cat" because that is a rule of English. When signs are related to their meaning by convention, by rule, they display the design feature of *arbitrariness*.

TRANSMISSION BY TRADITION.
Transmission by tradition refers to that which passes from generation to generation by means of a social learning process. Human languages are acquired. This feature is related to arbitrariness. A rule or a convention is arbitrary. Children are not born with an ability to acquire one language rather than another; they are born with the ability to communicate by means of speech. Particular languages are transmitted by tradition.

By contrast, the communication systems of other species are innately fixed in detail. It does not matter in which environment one raises a duck. If the duck makes any sound at all, it will quack. Ducks are born to quack, and they will not learn to warble like canaries. The ability to communicate in particular ways is fixed at birth in most species.[6]

Notice that we distinguish sharply between particular human languages and human language in general. The ability to learn some human language may be like the duck's ability to quack—inherited at birth. It is the ability to use a particular language that is transmitted by tradition.

Chimpanzee Language: Is It Really Language?
Chimpanzees communicate extensively in the wild by means of gesture. The challenge posed for anthropological linguistics by the efforts to teach chimpanzees a human language is this: If chimpanzees can learn some human language, then perhaps the general ability to acquire some language is not exclusively human. The question is, to what extent have chimpanzees succeeded in acquiring language? We will use Hockett's design features of systems of communication to help us with this question.

In 1966 Allen Gardner and Beatrice Gardner set out to raise a chimpanzee named Washoe in their home for the express purpose of teaching her to communicate by means of language.[7] They were familiar with past efforts to teach chimpanzees to talk. They thought it possible

6. Nikolaas Tinbergen, *The Study of Instinct* (London: Oxford University Press, 1969).

7. Allen Gardner and Beatrice Gardner, "Teaching Sign Language to a Chimpanzee," *Science* 165 (1969): 664–672.

that chimpanzees had failed only because they could not produce the sounds of speech. Perhaps, the Gardners reasoned, a chimpanzee could learn a language if the means of expression were in a more appropriate medium.

Washoe was taught American Sign Language (AMESLAN), the system used by the deaf. Her human companions used only AMESLAN in her presence even among themselves. Washoe eventually gained control of at least 150 different signs. She used them in combinations of up to five signs in length. She initiated conversations in AMESLAN. The Gardners' effort was a spectacular success. By using a manual/visual medium rather than an oral/auditory one, they succeeded in tapping surprising abilities in Washoe. But were these abilities really linguistic in nature? Did Washoe really learn a human language? The use of Hockett's design features as criteria yields mixed results.

Washoe's communication system qualifies as language according to the design feature *productivity*. She understood and produced many original messages. Once, while walking in a park, Washoe and her trainer saw a duck on a pond. Washoe knew the sign for "water" and the sign for "bird." She coined the sign "water bird" spontaneously on this occasion. Thus, Washoe's use of AMESLAN was clearly productive.

The form of AMESLAN that Washoe learned does not display duality of patterning, however. The signs are directly assigned their meanings. There are no "letters" in this language, only direct meanings. From the point of view of the design feature *duality of patterning*, Washoe did not learn a human language. Of course, this is not proof that she could not learn a language that did display this feature. The results on this point are inconclusive.

Washoe also did not show displacement in her system of communication. Her achievements fall short of true human language most strikingly with respect to this feature. She used her version of AMESLAN to communicate in terms of the immediate context or her immediate desires. This is also true of children in the early stages of language acquisition, however. Perhaps Washoe's linguistic abilities are like those of a human being, but only a person who has not yet developed to full human capacity.

With respect to the feature *arbitrariness*, the results are, once again, inconclusive. Some of the AMESLAN signs that Washoe learned were *iconic*. That is, the sign resembled the meaning. In other cases the signs were arbitrarily related to their meanings. But an arbitrary relationship can be the result of an accident as well as of a rule. We saw that the design feature, arbitrariness, was closely related to the design feature, transmission by tradition. Only by looking at this feature can we tell whether a case of arbitrariness is a case of a real rule or only an accidental association.

Unfortunately, on this last crucial design feature, *transmission by tradition*, we have no information. Washoe was taught AMESLAN under artificial circumstances. Perhaps the most intriguing question about the chimpanzee's language achievements is left open. Would chimpanzees use language among themselves if they were taught it? And most important, would they pass it on to their offspring if left to their own devices? The behavior of a "talking ape," Lucy, with her pet kitten was certainly provocative. Not only did she try to toilet-train the cat but she seemed to be trying to teach it sign language. Research projects on the transmission of language by apes are underway. We can only wait and see.

Other research on chimpanzee language has been carried out using various formats. One chimpanzee, Lana, has learned to communicate using buttons on a computer console as her signs. Another, Sara, uses chips of different shapes and colors which she sticks to a magnetic board. Both Lana and Sara have surpassed Washoe in the number of signs they use and in the complexity of the combinations they can understand and produce. But Sara and Lana use their versions of language only in the training context. Their use of language is much more elaborate, but it is also more like a circus trick. Washoe's ability to transport her use of AMESLAN into all sorts of circumstances reminds us more vividly of human language ability.

To the extent that Washoe and the others succeed in learning human language, they contradict the belief that language ability is unique to *Homo sapiens*. Their success would suggest that human language is not innate, not a special genetic endowment of our species. If that is so, then language is very different from other communication systems found in nature. To the extent that the chimpanzees fail to learn language we will be encouraged to believe that language *is* unique to *Homo sapiens*. If this is so, it probably has an innately determined physical basis in the human brain and body.

The Physical Basis for Language in Humans

The view that the human capacity for language is innate receives support from a study of the parts of the human body that appear to be designed especially for language. We feel entitled to say that *bipedalism*—the capacity to walk on two legs—is innate because the feet, legs, pelvis, spine, and even the position of the head all contribute to the capacity for bipedalism. Human beings are designed physically to walk and run just as birds are designed physically to fly. Is there evidence that human beings, and they alone, are equipped physically for language? [8]

The evidence for an innate physical basis for human language falls into two categories. First, there is evidence located at the *periphery* of our anatomy. Second, there is evidence located at the *center*, in the brain itself.

The best evidence at the periphery is found in the *vocal tract*. The vocal tract is the area of the mouth and throat, from the lips to the larynx, which is involved in producing speech. We mentioned in our discussion of chimpanzee language that efforts to teach chimps actually to speak have failed. One reason they have failed is that chimps lack the physical structures in the vocal tract that are required to produce speech sounds. The vocal tract of *Homo sapiens* has those specialized physical structures.

The *larynx* is the "voice box" in the throat. It contains the *vocal chords* whose vibrations cause the sound that is the human voice. The human larynx is much simpler than the voice box of other primates. It is shaped so as to accelerate the flow of air with minimum loss of energy. It is positioned so as to allow air flow to both the nasal cavity and mouth. The vocal chords themselves are suspended in such a way as to yield maximum stability of pitch and volume.

The human mouth is surrounded by a delicate network of muscles in the lips and

8. Eric H. Lenneberg, *Biological Foundations of Language* (New York: John Wiley, 1967).

cheeks. These muscles govern the shapes taken by the lips during speech. They are not found in other primates. The human tongue is a more supple instrument than the tongue of other primates. This suppleness is used in speech. The human tongue can bulge and change shape to modify the amount of space in the oral cavity during speech. The tip of the tongue is capable of a large number of rapid, delicate operations.

When we look at the peripheral anatomy of an animal, it is relatively easy to discover function: hands are for holding, noses for smelling, and teeth for biting. But it is not so easy to know what function the various parts of the brain perform. In spite of this problem, there is a way to discover the functions of different parts of the brain. When a certain segment of the brain is damaged by accident or disease, or at birth, we can look to see what functions are impaired. If every time a brain is damaged in a certain area a person loses the use of his left thumb, we can infer that that part of the brain controls the left thumb. The evidence we have for a central physical basis for human language, however, is much more vague and general.

The most striking evidence is very general indeed. It is called *lateralization* or *cerebral dominance*. The human brain is divided down the middle into two halves, or *hemispheres*. In the vast majority of individuals, language is controlled by the left hemisphere. Damage to certain areas of the left hemisphere impairs language functioning. Damage to corresponding areas of the right hemisphere does not. *Homo sapiens* is the only species known to display the phenomenon of lateralization.

A final form of evidence of an innate physical basis for human language should be mentioned. This evidence is much less concrete. It is only an analogy based on an impression of the biological process known as *maturation*. Maturation is the universal process of growth of living creatures from conception to maturity. A fixed pattern of physical maturation is innately determined for each species. Each species follows its own characteristic sequence of stages to maturity.

Children acquire language through a sequence of stages which has reminded some scholars of maturation. All children go through a "babbling" stage before certain sounds come to have meaning; words are spoken before short phrases; short phrases before sentences. No matter what language children acquire, they seem to go through very similar experiences in the process. Children learning English, for example, go through a stage where they say "foots" and "mouses." This stage of *overregularization* is characteristic of the way all children learn any language. Perhaps it is because the stages are determined by a biological process of maturation.

Most anthropologists believe that human culture is not determined by biology. Most anthropologists believe that human society and culture form a level independent of biology, with a history of its own which began when *Homo sapiens* evolved as a species. Is human language a part of this independent cultural level? Or is human language a capacity that evolved biologically along with *Homo sapiens* as a species? This is the still-unanswered question addressed by the chimpanzee studies, the study of the physical basis for language, and the effort to place human language among the other communication systems found in nature. Now let us look at the *structure* of language, as an objective way of describing language as speech.

This sketch of Mayan glyphs, from the field notebook of a scientist on the Tikal project, may provide the key to deciphering a language only imperfectly understood.

The Structure of Language

Most people think of grammar as a set of rules that *ought* to be observed—somewhat like table manners. We are brought up to believe that saying "ain't" is bad grammar just as eating mashed potatoes with your fingers is bad table manners. From the point of view of social acceptability, grammar is like table manners. There is good and bad grammar. But linguists and anthropologists do not make value judgments about grammar. To a scientist who studies a language, a *grammar* is a set of rules that describe the way a particular language or dialect is put together. People who say "ain't" say it just as regularly as people who say "isn't" and "aren't"; they are just using a different rule.

Descriptive Linguistics: The Study of Grammar

Descriptive linguistics is the scientific study of the expression of language.[9] Its goal is to produce grammars. In the study of a particular language, the judgment of what is correct is left to the native speaker. For example, a linguist shows the native speaker a sentence constructed according to the linguist's grammar and asks, "Is this okay?" If the native speaker says "No,"

9. Henry A. Gleason, Jr., *An Introduction to Descriptive Linguistics*, rev. ed. (New York: Holt, Rinehart and Winston, 1961).

Deciphering ancient written languages calls for a lot of detective work. Here an archeologist examines writing on the walls of a building in Tikal.

then the grammar recorded by the linguist must be changed.

Ultimately, a grammar—that is, the linguist's theory of the way the language works—should meet the following goals: (1) Every sentence the grammar allows should be acceptable to a native speaker. (2) There should be no sentence acceptable to a native speaker that is not taken into account by the grammar. If these rules are met, then the grammar is successful.[10]

A grammar has two ingredients. It consists of the *elements* of a language and the *rules* that govern the combinations of elements into words and sentences. Grammars are traditionally divided into three levels. Each level has its own elements and its own rules.

The first level, called *phonology*, is concerned with the sounds in a language. The second level, *syntax*, deals with how words are combined into sentences. Syntax includes morphology. *Morphology* deals with how simple words or meaningful syllables combine to make complex words, such as "re-claim-ed." The third level of grammar deals with the meanings of sentences. It is called *semantics*.[11]

PHONOLOGY, THE SOUND OF LANGUAGE. Japanese speakers of English, unless they are very skilled, will not differentiate between the sound of *l* and the sound of *r*, a difference very striking to native speakers of English but almost imperceptible to a Japanese speaker. The sound *l* and the sound *r* do not contrast with each other in Japanese. There are no pairs of Japanese words such as right/light and rust/lust which are distinguished only by the difference between *r* and *l*. To a Japanese speaker they are the same sound.

If you listen very carefully you will discover that an English speaker will emit a little puff of air after the *p* in the word "pot," but not with the *p* in "top." English speakers think both *p*'s are the same. In English there is no *contrast* between the two sounds. A pot is a pot whether you puff air after your *p*'s or not. But to speakers of Hindi the difference is significant. In

10. Noam Chomsky, *Syntactic Structures* (The Hague: Mouton, 1957).

11. Noam Chomsky, *Aspects of the Theory of Syntax* (Cambridge, Mass.: M.I.T. Press, 1965).

that language, there are many pairs of words which are distinguished only by that difference. English speakers of Hindi make many hilarious errors. They cannot detect the difference between the two kinds of *p*'s any more than a Japanese can detect the difference between *l* and *r*.

In the Japanese language, *l* and *r* are variants of a single phoneme. In English they are separate phonemes. In English, *p* and *ph* are variants of a single phoneme. In Hindi they are separate phonemes. A *phoneme* is defined as the minimal unit of sound capable of distinguishing meaning. Words that differ only by one phoneme, such as light/right, are called *minimal pairs*. They provide the classic test for discovering phonemes.

Phonemes are the elements of the phonological level of a grammar.[12] Different languages have different numbers of phonemes. But all languages construct their phonemes out of a limited set of possibilities. The limits are set by the human vocal tract, which can make only so many distinct sounds. The limitation on phonemes has made it possible to create special descriptive concepts. The International Phonetic Alphabet (IPA) grew out of the work of early anthropologists doing fieldwork in societies without written language. It is now possible for anthropologists to record the speech of native peoples so that other anthropologists can understand it. The IPA contains a symbol for every sound that occurs in every known language, even including the exclamation mark (!) for the Hottentot click.

The phonological rules of grammar state

---

12. Roman Jakobson and M. Halle, *Fundamentals of Language* (The Hague: Mouton, 1956).

what combinations of phonemes are permitted in a particular language. The words of a language are selections from the combinations that the phonological rules permit. However, the rules of grammar are acquired on an unconscious level. Native speakers cannot tell you the rules; they only know "the right way to say it."

SYNTAX. Compare the words "out," "kicked," and "blueberry." They are all perfectly good English words but their internal structure is different. "Out" is simple. It has no components. On the other hand, "blueberry" has two components, each of which is a word like "out." Finally, "kicked" has two components, like "blueberry," but only one of them is a word like "out" or "blue." The other component is not really a word. The component "ed" is meaningful but it never appears as an independent unit.

The basic elements of syntax are defined so as to cover all the elements just introduced. *Morphemes*, the elements of syntax, are defined as the minimal meaningful units of a language. "Out," "ed," "blue," and "berry" are all morphemes. Some words consist of more than one morpheme. Others have only one. Some morphemes can never appear as words but only in combination with other morphemes to make up words.

Syntax, then, takes morphemes for its basic elements. The rules of *syntax* govern the combinations of morphemes into words, words into phrases, and phrases into sentences. No mention has yet been made of *meaning*. Meaning is the province of our next level of grammar.

SEMANTICS. " 'Twas brillig and the slithy toves / Did gyre and gimble in the

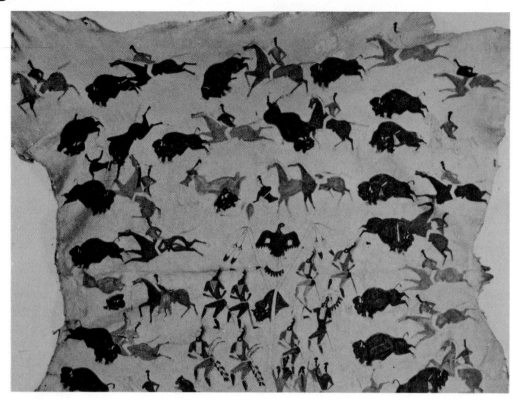

This Shoshone elk skin suggests the laboriousness of communication in the absence of a written language. Instead of writing, "Washakie killed 28 buffalo," the artist had to depict the scene 28 separate times.

wabe."[13] What are "slithy toves" and how do they "gyre?" "Slithy tove" is allowed by the phonological (sound) and syntactic (structural) level of grammar, but not by the semantic (word) level; "slithy" and "tove" are not morphemes in English. In other words, the sentence violates the semantic rules of English. More important, no English speaker would utter such a sentence. *Semantics* deals with the elements of meaning and the rules for their combination. Semantics in a descriptive linguistic account records what native speakers say and the meaning of what they say.[14]

Language, History, and Society

Anthropologists and linguists are also interested in how particular languages work in everyday life. We have considered some

13. From Lewis Carroll, "Jabberwocky," in *Through the Looking Glass* (1871; reprint ed., New York: St. Martin's Press, 1927).

14. Stephen Ullmann, *Semantics: Introduction to the Science of Meaning* (New York: Barnes and Noble, 1962).

questions about language in general, about language as one among many communication systems in nature, and about language as a problem in the description of an important component of a culture. Now we will consider the use of particular languages over time as part of people's lives.

Historical Linguistics

All languages are in constant flux. New languages develop and spread and old languages die out. Just as people have histories, so the languages they speak have histories. *Historical linguistics* is the study of how the world's languages have changed over time. The goal of historical linguistics is to construct a map of the world's languages, a map with a time dimension showing the historical relationship between the languages.[15]

Historical linguists can reconstruct a completely forgotten language by examining its existing descendant or *daughter* languages. These reconstructed languages fill in the time dimension on the historical linguist's map of the world's languages.

In 1786 William Jones, a British linguist, published a study showing grammatical similarities between Sanskrit—the language of ancient India—and Greek and Latin. Building on his work, historical linguists have reconstructed a long-forgotten language called Proto-Indo-European. They have shown this language to be the ancestor of a huge family of languages in Eurasia, including all those descended from Greek, Latin, and Sanskrit, as well as the Slavic and Germanic languages. Achieve-

15. Holger Pederson, *Discovery of Language: Linguistic Science in the Nineteenth Century* (Cambridge, Mass.: Harvard University Press, 1932).

ments of this kind are made possible because languages change in regular and predictable ways. The historical method works because linguists can reconstruct these changes from the study of existing languages.

The study of language change—historical linguistics—is related to descriptive linguistics because language changes are described in grammatical terms. Language changes are observed on the very levels that grammars describe. The historical method consists of looking for similarities and differences between languages in the terms created by descriptive linguistics. Then, with the aid of theories of language change, judgments are made about the historical relations between languages.

SOUND CHANGE. On the phonological level, as on the other grammatical levels, it has been discovered that languages change systematically. Jacob Grimm in 1822 formulated the Law of Phonetic Change which made possible the designation of the Indo-European language family. He noticed that the differences of pronunciation between languages are not random. The number of systematic *sound shifts* displayed between two languages is a clue to how closely related they are.

Portuguese and Spanish are very closely related. They display a large number of obvious sound shifts. For example, where the diphthong *ue* is used in Spanish, the vowel *o* is used in Portuguese words of similar meaning. We have fuego/fogo (fire), puerco/porco (pig), puerto/porto (door), etc.

Sanskrit and English are distantly related languages. The shifts they display are not so obvious. We have a shift, for example, from Sanskrit *p* to English *f*—pitar/father and pat/foot. Here, other sound changes make the shifts less noticeable. In addition, only a few basic vocabulary items display the shift. *Basic vocabulary* includes the names of things that are common to all peoples. These basic words are less susceptible to change than other words because their meanings have held constant through history. Such facts as these indicate to linguists that there is a more distant relationship between the languages.

GLOTTOCHRONOLOGY. *Glottochronology* [16] is the study of linguistic time depth. A technique called *lexicostatistics* has been devised to date the time of divergence for related languages. This technique is based on the assumption that the rate of change of the basic vocabulary is constant for any language. The basic vocabulary consists of names of processes and things—such as parts of the body—which history does not change.

The rate of change for basic vocabulary has been estimated to be 19 percent per 1000 years. That is, 19 percent of the basic vocabulary changes 1000 years after daughter languages begin to diverge from their origin. Estimates of time of divergence for languages that are related but for which no historical records exist can be made using this method. Of course, it is always more reliable to use other evidence as well, if possible. Nevertheless, glottochronology, although controversial, has proved useful to anthropological linguists in the study of histories of unwritten languages.

BORROWING.   Languages show histori-

cal relationships that do not bear on questions about their origin or degree of divergence. Languages provide clues to the histories of the people who spoke them. Languages, especially in their vocabularies, show the effects of contact between cultures through migration and conquest.

English, for example, is syntactically and phonologically very close to the Germanic languages. Yet it has a Latinized appearance. This is almost entirely a result of the incorporation of great numbers of French words into English after the Norman conquest of 1066. We have already mentioned that the Germanic and Latinate languages are ultimately related. They are both descendants of an ancient Proto-Indo-European. With the French influence on English we see a case of *convergence*. Two languages that had themselves diverged long ago are reunited by history to affect each other anew.

The modern world, with its mass transportation and instant communication, shows many examples of borrowing. In the United States, things are often "chic" or "super," while in France they sell aspirin at "Le Drugstore." Borrowing disrupts the neat map of evolutionary development for the world's languages that historical linguists would like to construct. But it provides clues to aspects of history that are not just linguistic. It encourages us to look at language not only as a problem in itself but also as an avenue to the larger social context.

Sociolinguistics

Sociolinguistics is the study of how people use their language in a social context. It is concerned with cultural or subcultural patterns of speaking and how a speaker varies his or her speech to suit different social contexts. For example, what do you

16. Morris Swadesh, "Glottochronology," in *Readings in Anthropology*, vol. 1, ed. Morton Fried (New York: Thomas Y. Crowell, 1968).

talk about to a stranger? to an intimate? In what social situations do you remain silent? How do you address different people? This usually reveals a great deal about the status of the people involved to the sociolinguist. "Baby talk" is a special vocabulary in many languages and is used by adults with infants and young children. Status differences are mirrored in the differing positions in the society of each speaker in a conversation. One speaks differently to one's boss, to a subordinate, to an intimate friend.

Language provides sociolinguists with a window on society. Subtle and not-so-subtle linguistic differences are closely correlated with social differences. We are all sensitive to the language styles of different groups in our society. People from different regions, from different strata, from different lifestyles reveal their origins in their speech. Sociolinguists study the way language differences represent and maintain social structure.[17]

Sociolinguists take subtle differences in vocabulary seriously. The denial of the female aspect of the unisex god of the Aztecs presented in the capsule ethnography by an early anthropologist is an excellent cross-cultural example. A man in a society like our own, which has long denied equal status to women, is culturally blind to the conception of a god who embodies attributes he considers female. An examination of the English language and English usage readily reveals male and female status inequalities.

Social structure is expressed by speech between social groups as well as within them. Status differences are mirrored in prerogatives of language use—who speaks first, who uses first or last names, who gives orders, who makes requests, and so on. Sex differences are recognized in language. Men and women and boys and girls communicate among themselves very differently than they do across sex lines. Elaborate linguistic taboos interact with rules of etiquette, morality, religion, and ritual. Language is sensitive to all the fine distinctions between people and situations which constitute social structure.

A simple example of language that expresses social distinction is familiar to anyone who has studied French or Spanish. These languages have two forms of the English pronoun "you" and two ways of conjugating verbs corresponding to the two forms. The French "vous" and Spanish "usted" are formal terms of address. "Tu" is the familiar form in both languages. Javanese incorporates a similar distinction much more elaborately, a distinction related to social status. In this language, three separate dialects express three different social strata. Grammatical and vocabulary differences permeate the language and are systematically correlated with one's position as aristocrat, landowner, or peasant.

Language, then, is sensitive to the social context of its use. When the sociocultural situation is extremely complex, the need for communication forces a variety of solutions on the people involved. An upper-class Hindu citizen may have to master four different languages for use in religious, domestic, business, and educational contexts, respectively.

Sometimes, in geographical areas where historical circumstances cause linguistic chaos, people settle on a single tongue to effect communication. This language need

17. J. B. Pride, *The Social Meaning of Language* (London: Oxford University Press, 1971).

not be native to any of its users. In large areas of Africa, for instance, French or English is used as a common language between tribes that speak different native languages. When the common tongue used in such situations is an established language, it is called a *lingua franca*. At times the common tongue used in such situations is a contrived blend of two or more established languages. Such blends are called *pidgins* or *creoles*.

Sociolinguists study particular languages in relation to specific historical and social circumstances. Another aspect of language which interests anthropologists is its relation to culture and cognition. Again we are concerned with correlations between particular languages and particular circumstances. This time, however, the circumstances do not have to do with social relationships or historical development, but with how people view and interpret their experience in the world.

The Cherokee Indian Sequoyah invented an alphabet with which to write his tribe's language.

Language, Cognition, and Culture

Eskimos have over twenty words for snow. Each word corresponds to slight differences in the texture, amount, disposition, and so on, of the snow. The Navajo language has a single term that applies to the colors blue, green, and purple. Chinese verbs are not marked for tense. Do Eskimos actually perceive snow differently than do speakers of, say, English? Do blue, green, and purple look the same to a Navajo? Do Chinese people have a different time sense than speakers of tensed languages?

The question of the relation between thought and language is an old one. We have cited some examples of the ways in which anthropologists have formed the ques-

tion. For example, does language determine how people see and think about the world? Anthropologists Edward Sapir[18] and Benjamin Lee Whorf[19] answered this question in the affirmative. They believed that the thinking of individuals is a microcosm of their culture and that language not only embodies the culture but, more important, determines the way people within a culture think. Most linguists, psycholo-

18. Edward Sapir, *Selected Writings in Language, Culture, and Personality*, ed. D. G. Mandelbaum (Berkeley: University of California Press, 1949).

19. Benjamin Lee Whorf, *Language, Thought and Reality* (New York: John Wiley, 1956).

gists, and anthropologists today would not agree with Benjamin Lee Whorf, however. Certainly, language facilitates ways of seeing and thinking about the world, but it does not determine what is seen or thought by the individuals who use it. Just because we might call both crows and sparrows "birds," that does not mean we cannot see the difference, although many experiments in psychology suggest that people would perceive the differences between different birds more clearly if they were acquainted with the labels "crow" and "sparrow."

The vocabulary of a language may also reflect everyday distinctions in the society. Those aspects of culture that are especially important to a people tend to receive greater attention in the language. It has been suggested, for example, that the heavy emphasis on verbs in the Navajo language is connected to their nomadic lifestyle over centuries. The Eskimo vocabulary for the concept "snow" is indicative of their concern with their own special environment. Perhaps you are, or know someone who is, expert in some specialized area—someone who can repair car engines, read music, or forecast the weather. Such a person will be familiar with a technical vocabulary which will represent subtle distinctions in his field of expertise. If one points at random under the hood of a car and asks, "What's this?" one person will say "the engine," whereas another will say "the distributor." Certainly a specialized vocabulary will help a person maintain perceptual and cognitive distinctions.

It remains true that in our daily lives we take for granted the distinctions and assumptions of our language and our culture. We bear within us a vast and complex structure of unconscious guidelines that we follow without resisting. It takes a conscious effort for an English speaker to distinguish the twenty kinds of snow an Eskimo distinguishes automatically. It is this kind of subtle distinction in language that is an aid to the anthropologist in understanding another culture. Language does, indeed, reflect culture.

Summary

1. The 3,000 to 6,000 languages spoken today can be classed into groups of related languages, or language families.
2. The ability to learn some language is universal and uniform in our species. The capacity for language is a primary identifying characteristic of *Homo sapiens*.
3. Particular languages are transmitted by tradition.
4. The languages of nonliterate peoples are not "primitive."
5. Most forms of life communicate information.
6. Charles Hockett identifies certain "design features" which distinguish the human use of language. These include (1) productivity, (2) duality of patterning, (3) displacement, (4) arbitrariness, and (5) transmission by tradition.
7. The communication of most nonhumans lacks these features. Generally, their communication is genetically evolved and controlled.
8. Chimpanzees can learn to use human language symbols. Their communication appears to lack certain of the design features of human language.
9. There is evidence that the human capacity for language is innate.
10. Descriptive linguistics is a study of the rules that govern language.
11. Grammar is a set of rules that describes how a certain language or dialect is put together. Judgment of what is correct is left to the native speaker.
12. Grammars are divided into three levels, each containing elements and rules for com-

bining the elements, phonology, syntax, and semantics.

13. Linguists who study the history of language change use analyses of sound changes, glottochronology, and borrowing.

14. Sociolinguistics is the study of the use of language by different groups within a social system. Language usage varies according to the social context and the social group of both the speaker and the audience.

15. A lingua franca is a language used as a common tongue under historical circumstances that throw people of different languages together. It may not be the native tongue of those who use it.

16. Language facilitates certain ways of seeing and thinking about the world, but does not determine them.

17. The Whorf–Sapir hypothesis asserts that language determines the way people think, but their hypothesis is no longer accepted by linguists. Specific vocabulary, however, does aid thinking by providing words for making discriminations.

18. The language of a people reflects their culture.

Review Questions

1. Why is the capacity for language often considered to be a primary defining characteristic of *Homo sapiens*?

2. What are the criteria for a successful scientific grammar? How does a grammar constructed by a linguist differ from the grammar taught in elementary school?

3. What is a lingua franca? How might one develop?

4. Why should linguistic differences reflect social differences? Give an example from American culture.

5. "Language facilitates certain ways of seeing and thinking about the world, but it does not determine them." Do you agree? Explain your answer.

Suggested Readings

Burling, Robbings. *Man's Many Voices: Language in Its Cultural Context*. New York: Holt, Rinehart and Winston, 1970.
Introduces the major issues confronting the anthropological linguist.

Gudschinsky, Sarah C. *How to Learn an Unwritten Language*. New York: Holt, Rinehart and Winston, 1967.
This is a basic and readable introduction to the technicalities that concern anthropologists.

Hall, Edward T. *The Silent Language*. Garden City, N.Y.: Doubleday, 1959.
This book, which became a popular as well as a scholarly success, introduces the reader to the area of nonverbal communication.

Hymes, D. H., ed. *Language in Culture and Society*. New York: Harper and Row, 1964.
A useful compendium of articles dealing with the relationship between language and culture.

Spradley, James. *You Owe Yourself a Drunk: An Ethnography of Urban Nomads*. Boston: Little, Brown, 1970.
This readable book about down-and-out people in Seattle is a good illustration of the use of language in studying culture and learning how an emic perspective is used in gathering data.

Chapter
16

ARTIST AND CRITIC IN AN AFRICAN SOCIETY

NATIVE NAME: Tiv

POPULATION: approximately 800,000, according to the 1960 census

ENVIRONMENT: Northern Nigeria on the Benue River in West Africa in wooded and deforested grassy plains and foothills varying between 350 and 4,000 feet above sea level

FIELDWORK: numerous field trips by Paul and Laura Bohannan during the 1950s. Data gathered by participant observation and interviewing.

ETHNOGRAPHIC PRESENT: 1950s

The viewpoint of Westerners, interested primarily in creativity, is completely different from that of the Tiv. . . . Tiv, indeed, use the word "create" (*gba*) for working in wood—its only other use is for God's creation of the World. But the primary field of Tiv interest is not on the verbal notion of *gba* or creation, but rather on the objects which are the result of it. Tiv are more interested in the ideas conveyed by a piece of art than they are in its manufacture, just as in their religion they are far more interested in the

Source: From Paul Bohannan, "Artist and Critic in an African Society," in *The Artist in Tribal Society: Proceedings of a Symposium Held at the Royal Anthropological Institute*, ed. Marian W. Smith (New York: Free Press, 1961), pp. 85–94. Copyright 1961 by Royal Anthropological Institute of Great Britain and Ireland. Reprinted with permission of Macmillan Publishing Co., Inc.

Creation than in the Creator.

This capacity on the part of Tiv to come to grips with a piece of art as it is in itelf rather than as a tangible result of creation, gives their critical ideas a forthrightness which we might well envy; it resembles that "firm and sure judgment in artistic matters . . . never raised to the level and consistency of a theory" which Croce ascribes to the ancients before they were bothered by the Christian notion of soul.

My most vivid encounter with such art criticism among the Tiv came when I was watching an artist—not a very good one—carve a wooden figure of a woman. The carving, which I had commissioned from him, was about eighteen inches high and, like all African sculpture, was worked from a chunk of log while it was still green. As he worked, and I sat by silently watching, a youngster from his compound appeared.

The youngster said, by way of greeting, the equivalent of "Grandfather, you are carving [creating—*gba*] a woman."

The old man replied that such was indeed the case.

"What are those three bumps on her belly?" the youngster asked.

The old man laid down his adze and eyed the youngster who had interrupted him. "The middle one," he said impatiently, "is her navel."

The boy was silent for a moment but spoke again just as the old man reached for his adze, "Then what are the other two bumps?"

The old man barely concealed his contempt for questions about so obvious a point. "Those are her breasts."

"Way down there?" the youngster asked.

"They've fallen!" the artist fairly shouted.

"But, grandfather, even if they had fallen, they would not . . ."

The old man grabbed up his adze. "All right, all right," he muttered, and with three perfectly aimed blows the three bumps came off.

I noted, when I wrote up this incident, that the youngster, who had been three years in school, had acquired an aesthetic of naturalism, and that the elder had not. I was annoyed that my carving was no longer "purely" Tiv and failed to consider the incident as an interaction of artist and critic.

When the artist had finished his work, and I had paid him for it, his only comment was, "It did not turn out too badly" (*iduwe vihi yum ga*). I recorded this comment at the time only because I did not really agree with it.

This incident should have told me that Tiv, in many instances at least, care who creates a given object as little as they care about the creative process. Art is, among them, an epiphenomenon to play, religion, prestige and most other aspects of life. Indeed, much of it is a sort of "community" art, a true folk art in which the artist is as unimportant as the composer of folk music.

It was several months later, in another part of Tivland altogether, that I became fully aware of this communal aspect of Tiv art, and that I again noted the phrase, "It didn't turn out too badly." This new area was swampy, and I cut myself a stick to help me traverse the slick swamps without falling. After a week or so, a young man from a nearby compound told me that I must not use that stick any longer: it was an old woman's stick and did not become a man of my position. When I asked what sort of stick I should have, he replied that he would make me one which was suitable. A few days later, he returned with a staff which he called a "stick of a young elder." It was about six feet long; on it were several bands blacked with soot which he had set with the sap of the *ikpine* tree. Into the black, he had carved several series of designs.

The stick was very handsome, and before long almost every male in the countryside was making himself a stick of this sort. I copied several of the designs and watched a number of them being made. The most astounding feature, to me, was that comparatively few of the designs were made by a single individual. As I sat watching a young man of about thirty carve a stick one day, he was called away. He laid aside his stick and the double-edged knives with which he was cutting the design. A guest came in a few moments later, picked up the stick and added a few designs. A little later, he handed it on to someone else. Four men put designs on that stick before the owner returned and finished it. When he had done so, he held it out for me to copy and said, "It turned out pretty well, didn't it?"

This "communal" aspect of all work, whether artistic or utilitarian, showed up again when I bought a couple of adzes, got some wood and tried to make sculpture of my own. Since I have no talent whatever for sculpture, I was very soon disgusted and turned to making stools and chairs instead. But I was not allowed to do it myself. The moment I rested, some bystander would take up the adze and get the work a little farther forward. I, in Western tradition, had a feeling of complete frustration because my "creativity" and my ability were being challenged. For a few days I tried to insist that I wanted to do the work myself, but soon had to give it up because everyone thought it silly and because no one could remember my foible. Eventually several of our chairs and stools "didn't turn out too badly." I had a hand in all of them, but they are not my handiwork—the whole compound and half the countryside had worked on them.

Most Tiv men are competent at turning out these chairs, stools, walking sticks and the like. They appreciate a "good one" but they take comparatively little pains to plan them so that they will be good. There are, however, a few men who work alone and insist on doing all the work; they are regarded as specialists. I knew one man who made chairs from *gbaiye* wood, when he could get it. He refused to let anyone else touch a piece he was working on. He charged about ten shillings each for making a larger Tiv chair; the price was very much higher than usual, but the chairs always "came out well," as was recognized throughout the countryside.

Weaving, like stick carving, is very often a communal activity. However, preparing the cloth for resist-dyeing [tie-dyeing] is not. Tiv today sew patterns into the cloth with raffia rather than tie them as they did when Mr. Murray made his observations. Although some men sew their designs in a pre-planned fashion, many others do not. The first time I saw a man sewing raffia almost at random on to a cloth he was preparing for resist-dyeing, paying attention to a political discussion rather than to any pattern and obviously having no plan, I was upset. I finally interrupted the business at hand to ask him why he did not pay attention to what he was doing. He told me, and though I understood his words I did not grasp their full meaning until later, that one does not look at a pattern until it is finished: then one looks to see if it has come out well. If this one does not come out well, he said, "I will sell it to the Ibo; if it does, I shall keep it. And if it comes out extraordinarily well, I shall give it to my mother-in-law."

Figure carvings are almost always made by an individual artist. In their religious rituals, Tiv need a certain number of stakes to represent females and another sort to represent males. The only requirement is that the stake be of a particular shape (pointed for the female principle, rounded for the male), and that they have representational eyes and mouth. Some people, even today, however, pay comparatively large sums (up to ten shillings) to artists to make figure carvings to be used as such representational stakes. The figurine, of course, is ritually no more effective than a stick with three holes gouged in it, but figurines bring prestige to the owner and, even more importantly, they "please the eye."

In the criticism of these pieces, two points are stressed: first, that the owner was thoughtful enough to want to please himself and everyone else, and second that it makes a "better" stake (*ihambe*). I have little doubt that had I asked questions and primed conversations, I could have gathered (from some people at least) lists of traits and characteristics which were approved and reasons why they were approved. Unfortunately, I did not do so. With my own cultural biases, I thought this was the sort of question one asked artists.

My most revealing experience in the matter of art criticism among the Tiv passed, like some of the others, in misunderstanding and a minor annoyance. A man named Akise, who was of my true age-set (not one of the men some fifteen years older with whom I was associated, by Tiv themselves, on a prestige basis), told me that his kinsman from central Tivland was coming to see him and to sell decorated calabashes in the local market. I said I would like to meet the kinsman and watch him work. Akise told me to come up to his compound the evening before market.

The artist kinsman was friendly, but not very communicative about his work. He showed me his tools and his wares. He reconvinced me of something I knew already: Tiv designs have no mystic or religious symbolism, and are at most only a stylization of natural elements like lizards, swallows and drinking gourds. When asked when he worked, he said, "When my heart tells me"—a standard Tiv answer for anything they do which they have not particularly thought about. When I asked him what his favorite design was, he said that he usually liked the one he was working on, so he liked them all. When I asked him why he carved calabashes instead of carving wooden figures, he replied that he did not have any talent or training for carving wood (literally, he did not "know the root" of it), and in any case wooden carvings were sometimes used by the *mbatsav*, or witches, and carved calabashes were only used as gifts to girl friends. This man, I decided, had no aesthetics.

At the time, I was a little put off by Akise, who insisted on breaking into the conversation. During my questioning of his kinsman, he carried on a long harangue about which of the calabashes he liked best, and which one least, and placed the two dozen or so in a row, in order of merit. I asked the artist if he agreed in Akise's judgment. He said he probably did, but he liked them all well enough. I noted (without realizing its full implications) that Akise considered himself a considerable art critic, and I finally turned to copy some of the designs and some of the reasons why he liked them. We were unfortunately interrupted when I had completed only one copy, and we never returned to the subject.

The design on the calabash was divided into quarters, for which Akise expressed different preferences. One, he said, was best because the black spots (made by burning with the flat of a hot knife) were in the right place. Another was least good because there were too many black places and they did not balance. The artist agreed but said that if you removed any of the black it would be worse. The lid, as a whole, was considered better than the calabash itself, because the balance of black was better and because the two sides were alike.

Either in my notes or in my memory, I have other references to people who have expressed choices and criticism, giving reasons: I have on several occasions heard winnowing trays praised for a tasteful pattern in the weaving or because they were absolutely round. I have also, on one occasion, heard a man say of a winnowing tray (which I also admired) that it was attractive because it had a very fine bulge on one side. I have heard people praise Tiv chairs because of their symmetry, but also because interesting shapes in the wood were retained.

Tentatively, from what I remember, it seems to me that Tiv admire symmetry, but also admire what they consider tasteful asymmetry. They admire pieces of sculpture which make an idea more intense. Further than this, I would not want to go until I have returned to Tivland to discuss the matter.

However, I did learn this: I was wrong in my field work because, Western fashion, I paid too much attention to artists, and when the artists disappointed me I came away with nothing. When I return, I shall search out the critics. And in Tivland, almost every man is a critic. Because there are no specialists in taste and only a few in the manufacture of art, every man is free to know what he likes and to make it if he can. It seems to me that as many Tiv are aware of why they like something as are aware of the implications of any other aspects of their culture. In all spheres, this is a faculty which varies greatly from person to person. There are as many reasoned art critics in Tiv society as there are reasoned theologians or political theorists, from whom we study Tiv ideas about their religion and politics.

Problems of creation in primitive societies are interesting; but they may be overshadowed, from the standpoint of their significance in the societies concerned, by the problems of criticism. We can arrive at an aesthetic for a people by studying the relation of criticism among them to the art objects somewhat more successfully than by studying the relation of creation to the art objects.[1]

●　●　●　●　●　●　●　●

Is this art? Do we judge by the finished product, or the artist's intention to communicate, or the audience's response to the communication?

Humans are complicated animals. They not only live in nature, but they transform it in ways that go far beyond the needs of survival. One of the most consistent features of all human groups is the expression of feelings and beliefs through the manipulation of the concrete world—the creation of art. To accomplish this, people everywhere have made use of similar aspects of their environment. They have embellished physical materials to make visual forms of art. They have fashioned patterns out of sound to create music and patterns of bodily movement to create dance. They

1. From Paul Bohannan, "Artist and Critic in an African Society," in *The Artist in Tribal Society: Proceedings of a Symposium Held at the Royal Anthropological Institute*, ed. Marian W. Smith (New York: Free Press, 1961), pp. 85–94. Copyright 1961 by Royal Anthropological Institute of Great Britain and Ireland.

The Arts

have made language into verbal forms of art that use words as tools to express their hopes and fears and desires and, above all, their ideas about the meaning of life itself. All of this behavior involves four basic elements—a physical medium, a skill applied to the medium, an underlying purpose, and a particular style or format.

Since art is a universal fact of human life, it might seem to offer an avenue for immediate understanding among people of different cultures, a way of reaching across barriers. Nothing could be farther from the truth. Not only do the arts vary from society to society more than any other aspect of culture, but the variations often reflect profound differences in experience and outlook. The arts of a society do not exist in splendid isolation, and artists never merely are expressing themselves. Both are intimately related to a society's culture, which provides the means of expression and regulates the way emotions, sentiments, and ideas are expressed. To an outsider, the arts of another culture are a closed book unless and until their meaning for the people living in that culture can be penetrated, a meaning growing out of a shared past and embedded in the intricate web of relationships and attitudes that dominate their lives. Most art can be classified into one of three broad categories—the visual arts, music, and literature. How are these arts manifested in preliterate societies, and in what ways do they vary from culture to culture?

The Visual Arts

To say that art varies in terms of the culture that shapes it does not mean that similarities as well as variations are not apparent. Cultures display common features;

This recent painting on a wall in Accra, Ghana, is part of a 50,000-year tradition of visual art.

human beings share basic capacities and needs. As we have pointed out, people everywhere have exploited similar aspects of their world to express the sentiments and beliefs specific to their experience. One medium they have employed for this purpose universally is the physical material present in their environments, using it to create visual objects of unique significance to themselves and their fellows.

Cave Arts

As long as 40,000 to 50,000 years ago, early humans were producing visual art. Whether or not they were also creating art in other media—music, dance, oral literature—we shall probably never know. But the evidence of their early stone etchings, paintings, and sculpture is preserved on the walls of caves in southeastern France, Spain, and other areas around the Mediterranean that have been almost miraculously protected from the ravages of time. The Paleolithic arts, it is estimated, flourished for some 20,000 years. They varied from rather sketchy outlines to realistic polychrome paintings of remarkable skill. They also included relief sculptures and female figurines. The later examples of this work, produced from 15,000 to 8,000 B.C., display a polished naturalism and sense of movement that more than match the best efforts of today's artists.

Why did the cave-dwellers of Paleolithic times create this art? Obviously, the best answer we can hope for must be an educated guess. But most experts are in considerable agreement on it: they point out that the hunting scenes were linked to religious rites aimed at securing success in the hunt by invoking magical control over the prey, since the paintings and reliefs almost invariably depict hunting scenes dominated by the figures of the animals under attack by men. Moreover, many animals are shown penetrated by spears and other weapons, and some of the animals are unmistakably pregnant. Finally, in the great majority of cases, the paintings are not located at the front of the cave where the ancient people lived, but were in nearly inaccessible regions deep inside. Sometimes, the caves containing the paintings were not lived in at all, but were used as shrines of some sort. The reliefs include small portable sculptures representing stylized female figures. These female figures, it is argued, probably played a role in fertility rituals.

However, Peter Ucko and Andrée Rosenfeld[2] disagree with this hypothesis.

These investigators believe that hunting magic was not the only reason behind the cave art because this theory fails to explain why animals are depicted in such different but carefully selected proportions. In some caves, for example, only male animals are shown, whereas other caves contain representations only of female animals. Nor does the hunting magic thesis explain the representations of humans and part humans. These authors hold that the cave art may have served as background scenery for some kind of Paleolithic "theater." Ucko and Rosenfeld notwithstanding, a tie-in of art with religion or magic is a theme that reappears again and again throughout the varied array of preliterate art.

The Sculpture of Yoruba

We have already seen in the capsule ethnography how the visual arts fit into Tiv culture: art in Tivland is very much a communal affair, pervading the everyday as well as ceremonial life of the people and yet taken with considerable casualness. There are very few specialists in the making of art among the Tiv. Those that do produce art objects for pay are carvers of ritual figures. And although well-wrought figurines are by no means necessary for ritual purposes, the Tiv are willing to spend comparatively large sums on them, basically for aesthetic reasons. Nevertheless, the Tiv could not be described as an art-centered people, nor do they produce "great" art.

On the other hand, their neighbors, the Yoruba, do produce great art and have done so at least since the early 1400s.[3] At

2. Peter J. Ucko and Andrée Rosenfeld, *Paleolithic Cave Art* (London: World University Library, 1967).

3. William Bascom, "Folklore," in *International Encyclopedia of the Social Sciences*, vol. 5 (New York: Free Press, 1968), pp. 496–500.

The Arts

This double face mask from the Ivory Coast comes from a tradition akin to the humanism of Yoruba art.

at the end of the nineteenth century. But an intensive concentration on the arts remained a continuing tradition among the Yoruba. They have been called "the largest and most prolific of the art-producing tribes of Africa." [4]

This is a culture where specialization in the arts has developed to a high degree— a culture marked by a dense population, a clear-cut division of labor, and a defined social hierarchy. Its arts are highly developed in a variety of areas: weaving, dyeing and embroidery, pottery and calabash carving, leatherworking and beadworking, metalworking, and woodcarving. Interestingly, the designs that appear in its art objects show the characteristics that have been associated with populous, hierarchical societies in general. They frequently feature clusters of animal and human figures and all-over geometric patterns. The style of Yoruba art differs from that of the Tiv in another respect: it is relatively naturalistic.

Moreover, Yoruba art is characterized by its humaneness, and the tendency of the artists to honor their gods through the natural human form. Only rarely do they employ abstraction, surrealism, or expressionism. The Yoruba also are unique in their use of sculpture to tell a story, a trait that undoubtedly arises from the desire of the artists to express the tribal values through homely scenes of daily life. The significance of human relationships is a key value for the Yoruba, so it is not surprising that they should develop a humanistic art. Tiv art, on the other hand, is highly abstract, typical of African tribal art. It is stark and expressionistic, with its figures

that time their ancient capital city of Ife in what was then the kingdom of Benin, had already developed into a flourishing art center, where highly skilled professionals worked in bronze, stone, and terracotta. For example, they produced masterpieces of realistic, portrait-style sculpture in bronze that portrayed ancestors, royalty, and other people of high authority in fine detail. The highly sophisticated technique employed by the artists of that early period is still used by Yoruba sculptors working in bronze today. The kingdom of Benin fell into decline; its magnificent bronze heads were carried off to England

4. William Bascom, *The Yoruba of Southwestern Nigeria* (New York: Holt, Rinehart and Winston, 1969).

Chapter Sixteen

squarely facing front and a total disregard for the natural proportions of the figure.

But what a wealth of objects are produced by the Yoruba woodcarver of religious art! For example, a spearlike staff kept in the shrines of several deities is carved with standing or kneeling figures in low or high relief perched one atop the other. Carved stools are made for some initiation ceremonies and an inverted mortar decorated in low relief is used in others. Wooden trays used by diviners are carved in low relief with the face of a deity and with combinations of animal figures and geometric patterns. The sacred palm nuts of a major deity are stored in cups carved to represent a wide variety of animal forms and human activities. Wood masks used in the rituals of several cults are carved with such figures as a monkey's head, a snail, or the face of a worshipper. Carved figures are placed in one of the shrines of many deities as votive offerings; usually they represent worshippers or the individual making the sacrifice. One votive sculpture, for example, depicted a woman carrying a baby on her back; it had been given by the mother in thanks for the birth of her son.

Non-Western Music

The poet who wrote that "music hath charms to soothe the savage breast" was stating a profound truth, and also giving expression to a widely shared misconception. The truth is that everywhere in the world and among all peoples, music provides a mechanism for the release of feelings and the sharing of experience at levels rarely reached by other forms of communication. The misconception lies in the belief that music is a thing in itself, operating on universal principles, with the power to achieve its effects across differences of tradition and culture. In reality, the meaning of a particular kind of music is as inaccessible to an outsider as the meaning of the verbal symbols that make up an unfamiliar language. Each culture forms an arbitrary sound system from a wide range of possible patterns, and then employs it in ways that are unique to its own social world. The music that soothes the savage breast is the music of its own culture—even when that savage breast is our own.

THE FUNCTIONS OF MUSIC. Perhaps more than the other arts, music can serve many purposes. Some of these purposes are apparent in all cultures. Moreover, some functions are emphasized in some cultures more than in others, and some are unique to particular cultures. Music, for instance, expresses religious sentiments among all peoples, but in ways that are often distinctive. Among many North American tribes, gaining possession of a magical song in a vision or dream, for example, is a prerequisite for full adult status for the men of the group. The use of music as a means of communication also appears in a range of forms. Some African tribes use the drum to convey the sounds and meanings of the spoken language.

Music may enter into the life of a group as a concrete object having independent powers of its own. Among the Apache Indians it is employed to cure sickness—not merely in an incidental way but as a direct therapeutic agent. Healing songs are learned through a process involving a personal ordeal and supernatural help by individuals who become ceremonial practitioners. When a sickness is to be cured, a ceremony attended by the entire community is held. The music, accompanied by drums,

*For the Tuareg, who must transport all of their possessions on their long
annual migrations, a musical instrument is a real luxury.*

is chanted by the medicine man and all
who know it. Certain types of songs are
specific to particular ailments. The chants
bring power to the patient and to all who
attend, and are believed to cure directly.
David P. McAllester notes that from our
point of view, such a conception of music
appears superstitious or magical.[5] However,
he adds, when our knowledge of music
therapy becomes more advanced, we may
no longer feel so superior about the Apache
notions of music's healing powers.

The far-flung functions of music are
pointed up in an analysis by Dennison
Nash, who finds the role of music a central
factor in maintaining social groups.[6] Music,

5. David P. McAllester, "The Role of
Music in Western Apache Culture," in
*Men and Cultures: Selected Papers of
the Fifth International Congress of Anthropological and Ethnological Sciences,*
ed. F. C. Wallace (Philadelphia: University of Pennsylvania Press, 1960),
pp. 468–472.

6. Dennison Nash, "The Role of the
Composer," *Ethnomusicology* 5 (1961):
81–94.

Chapter Sixteen

for example, promotes the success of vital social activities. Thus, different cultures employ music for war, for procuring food and natural resources, and for courtship and marriage. Music may promote the goals of a society and strengthen its beliefs and system of social relationships. In Russia today it is deliberately employed to define what the society requires of its members; the same end is achieved by songs in Dahomey which "glorify the names and deeds of kings and living chiefs."[7] Nash points to many other functions of music. Among them, its use in socialization (in rites of passage and children's lullabies, for example) and in dealing with disruptive behavior. The use of music for social control can be seen in a number of forms. For example, it permits the harmless expression of forbidden impulses by means of songs of insult and songs of love, which provide an outlet for frustrated feelings. Songs have also been used in several cultures to ridicule evildoers and so strengthen the hold of law and order in the community. As we shall see, some forms of the spoken arts perform the same functions.

The music of non-Western societies illuminates the variations that are possible and that actually exist in the creation of an art out of sound. Not only does non-Western music differ from the music familiar to us, but there are great differences among non-Western societies themselves. The contrasting traditional music of China, India, and sub-Saharan Africa is a case in point. In this music there is a connection with the common experience of the group that is not found in the music of our own culture. The traditional music of non-Western cultures is a means for linking oneself to

others and to nature, rather than a medium for the expression of individual experience. This point will be shown in the following discussion, which is drawn from the work of Elise Euverard.[8]

The Music of China

Chinese classical music usually sounds dull and bland to Western ears. In the monosyllabic style used in traditional ceremonial music there is exactly one note and one word in each measure; in the melismatic style used in popular music and in the Chinese opera, the single note becomes embellished. All Chinese music is program music, with each piece telling a story or offering a description. Through China's long imperial history, music was intimately linked to a system of ethics and to the Confucian ideal of harmony between heaven and earth, ruler and subject, father and son. The instruments used in Chinese music produce sounds that are unfamiliar to outsiders. The stone gong, for example, produces a gentle, brittle sound with no equivalent in Western music. One distinctive element of Chinese music, originating in the conception of music formulated by Confucius and his disciples, is its slow beat and uncomplicated rhythm. The rhythm derives from the structure of the Chinese language, in which each character has only one syllable of sound.

Chinese opera, originating around 1000 B.C., is one of the deep-rooted and ancient forms of music in the society. It reached its peak of development in the traditional

---

7. Nash, "The Role of the Composer."

8. Euverard, Mother Elise, "Non-Western Music," in *Music*, ed. Arthur Daniels and Lavern Wagner (New York: Holt, Rinehart and Winston, 1975), pp. 476–495.

Peking Opera, which was performed by an artistic elite and attended by the intellectuals through the long centuries of Manchu rule. It deals with the human side of life, which it portrayed in all of its breadth, treating of corruption, cowardice, and selfishness, as well as gentility, honesty, and humor. Performers were rigorously taught a precise way of moving and vocalizing, in a learning process that started during childhood. Under the Communist regime, the rich heritage of the traditional opera was not discarded but adapted to the goals and beliefs of the new order. Now opera has become a symbol of the people's revolution; its stories deal with the struggles of peasants against landlords, or of the Chinese against the Japanese, rather than official and upperclass family life.

The Music of Africa

Music is an integral component of the day-to-day existence of African tribal life, a part of the environment from the time an individual first comes into the world. Babies strapped to their mothers' backs hear the songs of their people and become accustomed to the rhythms of the music to which they will be exposed for the rest of their lives. Small African children can clap rhythmic patterns of such complexity that the most highly trained Western musician would find it difficult to imitate them. As children grow up, songs, dances, and the beat of a wide variety of percussion instruments accompany the great and small occasions of their lives—from festivals and ceremonies to the performance of household chores. Women of the Hausa tribe, for example, prepare their common food, *fufu* —made of yam, cassava, or plaintain— with the pounding of a heavy stick in a strict and intricate rhythm.

Rhythm is the central feature of African music and the drum its major instrument. The drum is also a sacred object. To make a drum involves invoking the spirit of the tree from which it is formed and which will thereafter express itself in the sounds that are produced. Drums of various types are employed at every kind of occasion— child-naming ceremonies, puberty rites, purely social events, and other ceremonies. There are many types of drums varying in materials, shape, and size, but the most distinctive type are the talking drums that are used to send messages and which duplicate the tones and rhythms of speech. Two kinds of talking drums are found in Africa. The Yoruba of Nigeria and the Ashanti of central Ghana use a single drum made of a piece of wood shaped like an hourglass. The second kind of talking drum consists of two pieces, "husband and wife" drums. They operate on the same principle as the single hourglass drums, but each produces a different pitch. One observer has reported seeing a talking drum convey a complicated message to a member of the Yoruba tribe, instructing him to pick up a pair of eyeglasses from the seat of a bus parked nearby.[9]

African music is not easily adaptable to the Western mode of musical production. One reason is that Africans do not have a system for writing down their music; it has been passed on from one generation to the next through tribal traditions. Recently Western musicians have attempted to record the music of Africa using our notation system, but the results have fallen short of success. Reproducing the rhythmic complexities of African music and the fine subtleties that enter into its performance

---

9. Euverard, "Non-Western Music," p. 486.

with the techniques currently available has proven difficult. It is interesting to note, however, that African music was an important influence on American jazz.

The Traditional Music of India

Four thousand years of history lie behind the traditional music of India. It is an art that has been transmitted from guru to apprentice in a system that is only now beginning to change. The music is a specialized art form embedded in the most basic traditions of an ancient people. Its subject matter is drawn from the Hindu religion with its vast literature of epics and tales, and its spirit expresses this rich tradition. To perform it is a sacred act and to listen to it is a deeply meaningful personal experience for those with knowledge of its form and intention. Recently, the classical music of India has gained an attentive audience in the United States through the performances of Ravi Shankar. It is extremely doubtful that many of the people attending such concerts possess the technical and spiritual knowledge essential for understanding the music.

The musical form of Indian classical music is the *rāga*, performed by three musicians: one playing a stringed instrument—either the *sitar* or the *vina*—another playing a drum, and the third playing the *tambura*, or drone, which maintains the composition's basic note in the background. The *rāga* consists of a lengthy—sometimes four-hour long—composition improvised on the basis of three elements in conformance with formalized principles. These elements are the *rāg*, the *rasa*, and the *tala*. The *rāg* is a musical pattern of five to nine notes following a regular order of ascent and descent; the notes are taken from a scale of twenty-two sounds. The composition made from a particular musical pattern is called a *rāg*. There are a great many *rāgs* and musicians must be able to elaborate on several of them, never repeating any of them exactly. The *rasa* is the mood, sentiment, or emotion created by the *rāg*. The *rasas* may evoke such feelings as serenity, horror, heroism, hopelessness, or amorousness. The *tala* is the rhythm. It is composed of three different patterns of beats which may be combined in a variety of ways for a particular *rāga*.

The object of a performance is the achievement of a state of deep meditation, for musicians and listeners alike. To bring this about, the musicians fast before playing. In addition, a prayer may precede the performance and incense may be burned while it is taking place. The *rāga* represents the high musical art of India. It was supported by the upper castes, which financed the apprenticeship system and provided an audience for the long, demanding performances. Unlike our own "serious" music, Indian classical music is thoroughly understood and appreciated by the people of all strata in the society. Classical music in India, in fact, has much in common with its popular music. Today, the *rāgas* are performed, often in shortened form, for radio audiences.

Oral Literature

Most small-scale societies do not have systems of writing; their oral literature is transmitted from one generation to the next by word of mouth. The Homers of such societies—the poets and the storytellers—typically memorize the body of oral literature and perform their art before live audiences.

The verbal arts include narratives (myths, legends, folktales), poems, drama, jokes, ballads, proverbs, riddles, tongue twisters, and toasts. The following discussion will focus on the narrative genre—the myths, legends, and folktales.

Myths

Myths are accounts of important events that are supposed to have occurred sometime during a culture's formative years. From the viewpoint of the individuals in the society, myths are considered to be absolutely true, authoritarian, and frequently sacred. The events related in myths typically occur in a supernatural, or otherworldly, setting; the characters, though not human, do possess human attributes.

The subject matter of the myth is vitally important to humans, dealing as it does with such cosmic subjects as the origin of the world, the reason for human existence and death, the nature of good and evil, time and eternity, rebirth, destiny, and so forth. These narratives may also describe events in the lives of gods—their love affairs, wars, victories and defeats, and their family lives.[10]

An example from our own culture of a creation myth is found in Genesis, the first book of the Old Testament, which details the creation of the earth, humans, and animals by God. In the Popul Vuh, the great mythological book of the ancient Maya, the creation of the earth begins as follows:

> *Before the world was created, Calm and Silence were the great kings that ruled. Nothing existed, there was nothing. . . . In this darkness the Creators waited, the Maker, Tepeu, Gucmatz, the Forefathers. . . . Then let the emptiness fill! they said. Let the water weave its way downward*

so the earth can show its face! Let the light break on the ridges, let the sky fill up with the yellow light of dawn! Let our glory be a man walking on a path through the trees! "Earth!" the Creators called. They called only once, and it was there, from a mist, from a cloud of dust, the mountains appeared instantly. At this single word the groves of cypresses and pines sent out shoots, rivulets ran freely between the round hills. The Creators were struck by the beauty and exclaimed, "It will be a creation that will mount the darkness!" [11]

As Malinowski[12] points out, myths are important because they provide a charter for the affairs of our societies. Myths also express what Clifford Geertz[13] calls the *world view* of a people—their "picture of the way things in sheer actuality are, their concept of nature, of self, of society. It contains their most comprehensive ideas of order." For example, the Kwakiutl myth entitled "The Rival Chiefs" demonstrates that this northwest coast tribe believes themselves to be violent, extravagant, and possessing a great zest for life.[14] Similarly,

10. Bascom, "Folklore."

11. Ralph Nelson, trans., *Popul Vuh* (Boston: Houghton Mifflin, 1976).

12. Bronislaw Malinowski, *Magic, Science, and Religion, and Other Essays* (New York: Free Press, 1948).

13. Clifford Geertz, "Ethos, World-View and the Analysis of Sacred Symbols," *Antioch Review* 17 (1957): 421–437.

14. John Bierhorst, *The Red Swan: Myths and Tales of the American Indians* (New York: Farrar, Straus and Giroux, 1976).

a number of Aymara Indian narratives (The Fox and the Condor, the Vixen and the Gull, for example) tell of conflict between different species of animals who do not ordinarily prey on one another. Such conflict has been interpreted as a metaphor for the conflict that exists among different Aymara kinship groups which have marriage arrangements with one another.[15]

Legends

Like myths, *legends*, too, are considered to be true by the society that perpetuates them. But legends typically are set in a definite time and place; they describe wars, migrations, the history of noble and royal families, and the exploits of cultural heroes. The chief characters of legends are, in effect, cultural symbols, and their deeds— like the deeds of George Washington, Abraham Lincoln, and Benjamin Franklin in our culture—serve as standards of behavior for the rest of society. Legends are also used to explain many of the beliefs and practices that prevail in the society; they are frequently told to children as a way of inculcating in them cultural values.

Among the legends of the Kiowa Indians, for example, is the story of how their Trickster Hero, Saynday, brought the sun to the Great Plains. In the legend, entitled "How the People Caught the Sun," Saynday conspires with a deer, a magpie, and a fox to steal the sun from the camp of the sun people who live to the east of Kiowaland. Outwitting these people, Saynday and his friends stab the sun with a spear and run with it in relays to Kiowaland. Once there, however, the sun's intense heat and light become unbearable. But the hero neatly solves this problem by tossing the sun into the sky and ordering it to spend half of its day in Kiowaland and half of its day with the people on the other side of the world. When Saynday completed his work among the Kiowa, he vanished, leaving behind only the print of his hand—the five stars of the Pleiades—as a symbol of his eternal presence in Kiowa affairs.[16]

As this example illustrates, it is sometimes difficult to distinguish legend from myth, in that both may deal with the same kinds of superhuman characters and events.

Folktales

Folktales, known as *Märchen* in German and sometimes *fairy tales* in English, differ from both myths and legends in that they are secular and regarded as fiction by those who treasure them. Folktales describe the deeds of humans, animals, monsters, and occasionally gods. Examples of this genre in our own culture include Grimm's fairy tales, the Uncle Remus stories, and the tales of Hans Christian Andersen.

Folktales are full of animals who can appear and behave either as humans or beasts, or both. Wild adventures, sexual promiscuity, gross exaggeration, clever tricksters, numbskulls, and miraculous physical transformations of humans, animals, and objects are common in folktales.

An outstanding characteristic of the folktale is the basic pattern, or motif, which runs through many tales from the same cul-

15. Weston Le Barre, "The Aymara," in *The Anthropologist Looks at Myth*, ed. Melville Jacobs and John Greenway (Austin: University of Texas Press, 1966).

16. Alice Marriott and Carol Rachlin, *Plains Indian Mythology* (New York: Thomas Y. Crowell, 1975).

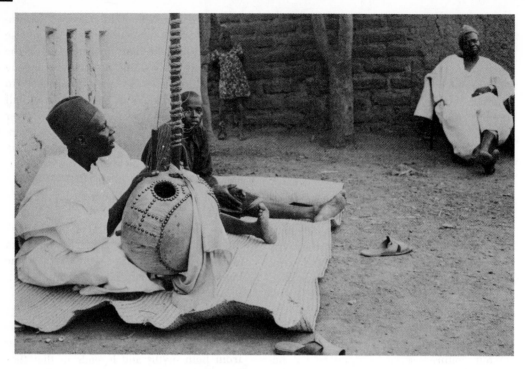

In Ghana, the musician often holds an honored place in society, for he is the keeper of an extensive oral tradition.

ture area. Many West African storytellers, for example, relate slightly different versions of the same tale about the munificence or skulduggery of spiders, hyenas, and other animals. Similarly, in many tales of the Plains Indians of North America, the trickster–hero, Old Man Coyote, is an oft-recurring character. In one Shoshoni version of a common folktale, for example, Old Man Coyote, bedraggled, powerless, and at the end of his days, begs a virile young buffalo bull for some of his power. When the buffalo grants the request, the coyote is made young again. However, the buffalo warns him that even though he has the outward appearance of a strong young buffalo, the coyote will remain old on the

inside. For four years, the newly reborn buffalo Calf–Coyote "really has himself a time. He was a young bull buffalo, growing up, and he felt wonderful. He ran and he wallowed in the shallow ponds, and he met a young buffalo woman, and made love to her. My, he was happy!" [17]

One day, the Calf–Coyote meets an old coyote, a wretched creature who reminds the young bull of his own state before he received the buffalo power. The tattered old coyote begs the young Calf–Coyote for

---

17. Marriott and Rachlin, *Plains Indian Mythology*, p. 74.

Chapter Sixteen

some of his rejuvenating force. When the younger animal agrees and attempts to transmit his virility to the oldtimer, he is again transformed into his former state—"an old, hungry, poor coyote." The motifs of this tale are the coyote's quest for power and regeneration, the fact that he receives only the external appearance of power, and his return to his former debilitated state when he attempts to bestow the power on another creature. These are common threads which run through numerous Plains Indian tales about Old Man Coyote.

Folktales—which frequently contain riddles, proverbs, and tongue twisters—are intended chiefly to entertain and amuse listeners. Another function is education. Proverbs, for example, contain the wisdom of many generations, whereas riddles teach children about plants, animals, and the way society works.

Proverbs, riddles, and folktales can be utilized for social control—to censure social deviants or to praise people who follow society's rules. At the same time they also provide a psychological release from the pressures to conform. Thus, the characters in folktales (and myths) often behave outrageously, flaunting authority and breaking all the rules. American Indians who observe mother-in-law avoidance, for example, think it hilarious when the hero of a folktale has sexual relations with his mother-in-law.

By fulfilling all of these functions, folktales (and other forms of the verbal arts) assure the stability and the continuity of the culture: they teach youngsters socially approved beliefs and practices, reward or punish adults for their behavior, and offer an avenue of escape from the rigors of daily life.[18]

18. Bascom, "Folklore."

Art and Society

Behind all art is order—the attempt to make some sense from the enormous diversity of experience. Viewed in this light, art may also be defined as an ordering of experience,[19] including an understanding

19. Geertz, "Ethos, World-View and the Analysis of Sacred Symbols."

According to Kwakiutl myths regarding the origin of houseposts such as these, the posts have the power of speech and will warn the owner of the house of impending danger.

of the human emphasis on symbol and meaning. The symbols, and the ideas behind them, are the energies which drive each culture, stamping it with its own particular patterns.[20]

How do a culture's symbols fit in with its art? In preliterate cultures, the art symbol becomes social fact, or reality. Not only does the symbol represent some aspect of reality, but it defines and manifests this reality at the same time. Art reinforces the values of the society, while it broadens and unifies the perceptions of its members.

In this sense, then, one cannot ask a member of a preliterate culture the meaning of a particular piece of art. To such an individual, the meaning is so obvious—from an aesthetic, moral, and ontological point of view—that he will probably wonder at the naïveté of the question. (*Ontology* refers to questions about existence—where we came from, why we exist, how we relate to other beings, for example.) For the tribal member, art objects both stand for and are part of a coherent view of reality; they are simultaneously pictures of the way the universe is thought to work and reflections of the way the individual fits into this universe. Thus, art is an important means of communication; it has its own language which is understandable by all members of the society. It should come as no surprise, then, that primitive art is heavily bound up with tradition, repeated generation after generation with little change.

Art, Religion, and Politics

As far as the content of art is concerned, religion was undoubtedly the most potent single influence in the premodern world, with social status becoming increasingly important as societies grew more complex. In terms of the design and style of a society's art, several factors may be at work. The economic organization of a society, the density of its population, the nature of its physical environment, and the image of the universe underlying its belief system all can be seen contributing to the kind of art it produces.

From the beginning, the relation of people to the supernatural has furnished a major motivating drive for the transformation of physical materials into objects with symbolic meaning. This was as true of our earliest forebears as it was for succeeding generations, for those living in cultures with rudimentary technologies to the elaborate civilizations of the ancient and medieval worlds. Gods, ancestors, sacred symbols appear in a wide variety of ritual objects in preliterate cultures throughout the world—sculptured figures, masks, food vessels, ceremonial posts, funerary equipment. Even the widespread art of body decoration often has religious meaning. In the Sun Dance of the Cheyenne Indians, for instance, dancers seeking the power of the sun painted their bodies with symbols of the sky. In more complex civilizations, art and wealth were lavished on massive pyramids, ornate temples and altars, and a proliferation of sacred statuary, painting, and ritual ornaments.

The element of status, reflecting the power structure of a society, is most evident in the art of cultures living beyond a subsistence level and marked by a fairly complex division of labor. Here will be found

20. Charlotte M. Otten, Introduction, in *Anthropology and Art: Readings in Cross-cultural Aesthetics*, ed. Charlotte M. Otten (Garden City, N.Y.: Natural History Press, 1971).

authority figures making a prominent appearance in the pictorial and three-dimensional art forms of the society—the ruler, for example, appearing conspicuously in scenes where he is shown much larger than his attendants; realistic sculpture portraying royalty and notables of the realm. This kind of subject matter—the representation of the elite—was prominent not only in the traditional civilizations of the Far and Middle East but in the more complex African societies as well. The court art of Ife and Benin, for example, idealized and extolled the rulers. Even today, art in China and Russia is used as an agent of political propaganda. Where distinct differences in power and prestige mark a society's social system, they are almost invariably reflected in the content of the art that is produced. But even in small-scale cultures, status differences show up in the visual arts, often appearing in forms of dress or personal decoration denoting high rank. Thus, among the Indians of southeastern Alaska, men of renown wore pieces of wool or small feathers in tiny holes along the outer edges of their ears, a symbol of rank that marked them off from the ordinary members of the group. Another kind of linkage between culture and art—in this case, visual art—shows up at a more subtle level in conventions of design and style. Hunting and gathering cultures, for example, have tended to depict or to symbolize individual people and animals in their visual art. Such art, typified by that of the African Bushman, tends to be naturalistic. In marked contrast, the visual art of agricultural societies with larger and denser populations is *conceptual*—it is marked by the use of geometric, repetitive designs of an abstract character. It has been suggested that the repetitive designs of agricultural cultures may reflect the desire for an abundance of crops or the awareness of the numbers of people in the surroundings.

Variations in the design features of the visual arts produced by different societies have also been attributed to differences in social stratification. According to one theory, egalitarian societies, typically small, self-sufficient, and isolated, tend to use designs that repeat simple elements of equal importance surrounded by considerable areas of empty space.[21] Designs of this type are found in the art of American Indian groups such as the Ojibwa and the Sioux, where few members hold positions of higher authority than others. On the other hand, highly hierarchical societies, encompassing a number of social groups unequal in rank, privilege, and resources, tend to produce art combining several design elements and little empty space. As one example, the art of India displays complex and highly intricate designs with clearly defined units that are carefully balanced but always distinct and separate—a reflection, according to the theory, of India's caste system.

CHANGES IN TRADITIONAL ART. If art reflects the culture that produces it, then it goes without saying that as the culture changes the art will change. Exactly that is happening today with the visual arts of preliterate and traditional societies, as beliefs, technologies, and institutions undergo sometimes drastic transformations under the pressures of modernization resulting from increased contact with the industrial West. What this has meant in Yoruba is a serious decline in the art of

---

21. John L. Fischer, "Art Styles as Cultural Cognitive Maps," *American Anthropologist* 63, no. 1 (1961): 79–93.

sculpture. Why should this be so? Is it because the skills of Yoruba sculptors are inadequate to compete with artists in advanced societies? Far from it. Other Yoruba arts continue to thrive—weavers, dyers, blacksmiths, leatherworkers, and potters seem able to meet the competition of factory products from Europe and Japan. Yoruba's sculpture, however, no longer meets the need it previously filled because the traditional religions have lost much of their hold on the people who have converted to Christianity and Islam in large numbers. The result—Yoruba's woodcarvers and bronze casters have lost too many customers for these skills to survive in their former glory. The traditional sculpture of Yoruba now seems destined for museums and special projects conducted under government sponsorship or with subsidies from patrons of the arts.

Change has affected the arts of preliterate societies in a variety of ways. By and large the most conspicuous development has been the redirection of art products toward outside markets. So-called primitive art sells well in Europe and the United States, a situation that has spurred the production of visual art by groups who had never produced much of it before. In several cases, the result has been the creation of art objects judged superior in quality to what the group had created before. The sculpture now being produced by the Eskimos of Canada is perhaps the most striking example. Faced with the destruction of their traditional economy, these Eskimo people turned to the production of soapstone carvings and lithographic prints that have received an enthusiastic reception in the art world of the West. Ironically, this work does not come out of the traditional communities whose way of life it reflects, but is produced in centers formed by an artificial regrouping of the Eskimo population. It has been charged that Western insistence on the "primitive" is turning these artists away from the kind of art that reflects their authentic experience and the current realities of their societies.[22]

Art in Modern Society

By and large, art in modern industrial societies does not support societal values. Nor does it typically have intimate connections with religion. A painting by American artist Jackson Pollock, for example, does not convey American ethos (the quality and character of our life) and American world view (our ideas about ourselves, our society, and the natural world) in the same simple and direct way a Tiv sculpture transmits ideas about the ethos and world view of the Tiv. Much contemporary Western art cannot be immediately appreciated by all members of the culture. Indeed, not all members of industrialized society are even interested in art. For many people, art is useless or unintelligible, with no direct bearing on their lives. To a society such as the Tiv, which sees art as sacred, such a view would seem blasphemous.

In our society, those who are interested in art expect that experts—art critics—will first examine and explain a painting, sculpture, or poem so that it can be fully appreciated. This situation perhaps arises from the idea of "art for art's sake," a notion which emphasizes originality, individuality, and escape from tradition. Modern Western artists, seeking to be as original as possible—to execute art that has

22. Jacqueline Delange Fry, "Contemporary Arts in Non-Western Societies," *Artscanada*, December 1971–January 1972, pp. 96–101.

never been done before—create work that in some cases cannot be understood even by fellow artists.

For us the artist is the free spirit personified. Bound by neither convention nor tradition, artists possess special gifts and an obligation only to express their uniqueness. The great artist is the innovator, exploring undreamed-of approaches that are often far in advance of what even the most sophisticated audience can appreciate.

Furthermore, art in general is something separate from the routine course of our lives. We take time out from our more pressing concerns to hear music performed by professionals in a concert hall, attend a dance performance in which we occupy the role of observers, visit a museum or art gallery to look at what others have created, and perhaps read a poem or novel written by persons gifted with words who offer us their special slant on life. Most of us, then, are consumers of an art that speaks to us on a person-to-person basis.

Another peculiarity of art in Western society—especially in the United States—is the sharp distinction between the popular arts and art that is considered truly creative, high art. We are not the only kind of society to make this distinction, but we are probably more extreme than others. We see popular art as inferior because it is "commercial"; perhaps we view popular art this way because it is more readily understood by the general public. Certainly because it appeals to a mass audience, rather than a small elite. In one respect, however, popular art and high art in our society are alike in being the product of specialists cut off from an audience of passive consumers, selected for public consumption by experts in taste, and emphasizing something new under the sun rather than continuity with the past.

Needless to say, the separation of art from the community was not true of pre-industrial Western art. The Gothic cathedral of the Middle Ages, or the religious paintings of the Renaissance, for example, is full of symbolism that was easily comprehended by all members of society. Like their counterparts in small-scale cultures, preindustrial Western artists were working in a definite tradition, using widely recognized symbols embedded in subject matter that had moral, aesthetic, and ontological meaning for nearly every member of society. Scenes from the life of Christ or the saints, for instance, fulfilled the same functions that art does in preliterate cultures—to explain the world, to reinforce social values, and to hold up models of behavior. The originality of the artist was unimportant. Indeed, to this day, the architects of most medieval cathedrals remain anonymous. It was only with the advent of modern society and the triumph of secularism—starting in the seventeenth century—that the intimate link between art and religion was broken.

It is clear, then, that if we are to understand the role of art in organized human life we shall have to clear our heads of preconceptions arising—as they inevitably do—from what we know of art in our own society. What we have encountered is not art as it must always be or as it should be, but as it has developed in one particular culture because of the conditions and values dominant in that culture. We are the heirs of a tradition that emerged with the Industrial Revolution, the Protestant Reformation, and the birth of capitalism, which is as limiting as any inherited set of beliefs and customs regulating preliterate societies. It is a tradition centered on the individual rather than the group, on personal achievement rather than on communal bonds. Such a cultural system produces the kind of art with which we are familiar; in other cultures art assumes a different character. This point leads naturally to the topic of ethnocentrism.

Ethnocentrism and "Primitive" Art

As in other areas of culture, Westerners tend to classify the art of preliterate societies as "primitive." The very term springs from early ethnocentric notions about evolution and the superiority of Western civilization over all others. In the eyes of the European colonialist, the preliterate societies were considered to be at the bottom rung of the evolutionary ladder. Because of their lowly station, these cultures were thought to be savage, incapable of providing "fine" ideas or art. Accordingly, one should expect to find savagery and primitiveness in their art. For example, the German Expressionist painter Emil Nolde observed: "It is in fear and trembling that man can rediscover primitive authenticity and permit to well up within himself the signs of exorcism that savages still know." [23]

---

23. Emil Nolde, quoted in Fry, "Contemporary Arts in Non-Western Societies."

Summary

1. Among the most universal of human features is the expression of feelings and beliefs through the manipulation of the world—the creation of art.
2. Most art can be placed into one of three categories: visual arts, music, or literature.
3. Examples of the visual arts date back 40,000 to 50,000 years to Upper Paleolithic cave art.
4. A prime example of visual arts among preliterate peoples is Yoruba sculpture. These art objects, done in wood, are characterized by their humaneness and the tendency of the artists to honor their gods through the natural form.
5. Music has many functions. It expresses religious sentiments, serves as a means of communication, and in some societies may have magico-religious powers.
6. Rhythm is the central feature of African music and the drum is its major instrument. The subject matter of Indian music is drawn from the Hindu religion. The musical form is called the raga.
7. Oral literature includes myths, legends, and folktales. A myth tells the story of an important event that is believed to have occurred during the formative years of a society.
8. Legends, too, are considered to be true happenings, but they deal with the exploits of a society's cultural symbols.
9. Folktales are secular and are regarded as fictional by those who perpetuate them. A feature of the folktale is the motif which runs through many tales from the same culture area.
10. Art involves working with natural materials in which socially meaningful form is imposed on the materials.
11. Art among preliterate peoples is inextricably bound up with religion. It is simultaneously a picture of the way the universe is thought to work, and a reflection of the way the individual fits into this universe.
12. Unlike preliterate art, the art produced in modern societies is not necessarily laden with symbolic meaning which operates simultaneously on moral and aesthetic levels. Nor does it support societal values as it does in preliterate cultures.
13. The Western eye is usually ethnocentric when it judges preliterate art, seeing and choosing only the art deemed beautiful in itself regardless of its original context.

Review Questions

1. The visual arts of the Yoruba and the Tiv have both similarities and differences. Name a few of each.

2. What are some of the functions of music? Of oral literature?

3. Define the terms myth, legend, folktale. Give an example of each, either from a pre-literate culture or from our own heritage.

4. In small-scale societies, art is said to be closely linked to the culture. Can you explain what this means?

5. List five ways in which preliterate art differs from art produced in modern societies.

6. What purpose does art serve in preliterate societies?

Suggested Readings

Boas, Franz. *Primitive Art*. New York: Dover Publications, 1955.
First published in 1927, this classic work explores the nature, fundamental characteristics, and functions of preliterate art, and includes separate discussions of literature, music, and dance.

Kurath, Gertrude K. "Panorama of Dance Ethnology." *Current Anthropology* 1 (1960): 233–254.
An outstanding summary of the dance as it is performed around the world. The article also contains valuable discussions of the techniques of recording dances, including methods used to teach anthropologists how to gather data on preliterate dance.

Merriam, Alan P. *The Anthropology of Music*. Chicago: Northwestern University Press, 1964.
An excellent work on the social aspects of music, analyzed from an anthropological point of view.

Otten, Charlotte M., ed. *Anthropology and Art: Readings in Cross-cultural Aesthetics*. Garden City, N.Y.: Natural History Press, 1971.
A well-balanced collection of twenty-five articles, both theoretical and methodological, that offers a broad perspective on many aspects of art from numerous culture areas.

Wingert, Paul S. *Primitive Art: Its Traditions and Styles*. New York: Oxford University Press, 1962.
A thoughtful introduction to preliterate art that explores the place of artistic expression in societies from Oceania, North America, and Africa.

Chapter 17

DISEASE AND DEATH AMONG THE PITAPITA

NATIVE NAME: Pitapita

POPULATION: 200 (much reduced because of European contact)

ENVIRONMENT: Boulia district in Northwest Central Queensland, northern Australia, an area of approximately 10,000 square miles. People gather seeds and roots, as well as hunt and fish.

FIELDWORK: Notes collected during tenure as Surgeon to the Boulia Hospital from 1894 to 1897. The information was collected in the native language by interviews and observation.

ETHNOGRAPHIC PRESENT: 1894–97

Ethnics [nonliterate peoples] the world over developed certain methods and techniques designed to cure illness and to prevent death. A ready, and seemingly reasonable, explanation for the innumerable curing means reported is that, in the absence of scientific medical knowledge, disease was a great unknown quality enveloped with fear and danger. The tendency among ethnics, as among ourselves, was to try both natural and supernatural cures

---

Source: From Walter E. Roth, *Ethnological Studies among the North-West-Central Queensland Aborigines* (Brisbane: Edmund Gregory, Government Printer, 1897).

in the hope that at least one technique would be effective. Naturally-derived aids were enlisted when the illness was of a known and curable nature, but for maladies with nonlocalized or vaguely manifest symptoms, it was common to seek a supernatural cause and treatment. A person who employed his knowledge to help individuals who were ill is termed a shaman. The word "shaman" was used among a Siberian people, the Tungus, to mean a person who is a specialist in supernatural matters and derives his, or her, power from nonnatural beings. A shaman cures, foresees, predicts, and aids, whereas a sorcerer employs his supernatural powers to cause illness, disease, and death. An individual might be a shaman and also a sorcerer, depending on the manner in which he employed his power in any particular set of circumstances; in such a case the person generally has been termed a shaman.

A shaman among the Pitapita was always a male, and he obtained supernatural powers by one of a number of means. One avenue to this power was through a magical snake. Unknowingly a man who was fishing might have a bone pointed at him by a huge, supernatural water snake. Later, as evening approached and the man continued to fish, he would see what he thought to be the snake coming across the water, and he would run away as quickly as possible. The following morning he would feel ill, and his condition would worsen until some four or five days later when a shaman would be called in to remove a foreign object by sucking it from his body. The substance removed was said to have been a piece of bone, a pebble, or a stone flake which had been magically inserted into his body by the water snake. The patient was thus cured and in turn became a shaman himself. Shamanistic power might also be gained as the result of a revisitation from the soul of a deceased person, or a child might have a piece of bone magically inserted into him by a shaman and in later years become a practitioner. The most common means to become a shaman, however, was for a person to wander about until he was exhausted, at which time a supernatural object would be placed in his body by *Mulkari,* a beneficent supernatural. Each shaman, irrespective of how he gained his power, was in theory an equal to all others for doing social good or evil, and on occasion they aided one another in the performance of their tasks. Shamans participated in the same daily routine as ordinary persons, and were distinguished from others only in their possession of certain objects which were tangible representations of their extraordinary powers. The objects possessed included small pieces of bone, strangely shaped stones, crystals, pebbles, and other unusual forms derived from Mulkari or from the water snake.

Among the Pitapita objectively derived means for prolonging life are clearly set forth and relatively few in number, whereas supernatural curing methods were much more complex and more frequently used since most illness was thought to be of supernatural origin. If a disease or discomfort were considered of secular origin, the cures tended to be straightforward. A broken limb was bound with splints for a month or two, small balls of mud or clay were swallowed in order to cure diarrhea, and a plant was steeped to produce a tea for curing colds and coughs. Any grass or shrub growing near the water was less reasonably used to relieve pain associated with urinating. Rational and supernatural techniques seem to have been combined in a single method of treatment for a nonfatal snakebite. After being bitten, the victim watched the snake reenter its hole, and he then covered the entrance. Using his belt of hair or any other piece of cord that was convenient, he bound the limb above and below the bite and then sucked the wound. The man's wife or anyone else near at hand rushed off to consult the nearest shaman and then returned to dig a large pit close to the site of the accident. A fire was built in the hole, and stones were heated in it. As the flames died they were sprinkled with water, and newly cut boughs and branches were placed on the embers. The afflicted person lay down on this warm bed for two to three hours. Full recovery occurred only after the consulted shaman came to the area and completed the treatment. He dug out the snake and hit it with stones, which are said to have made it decrease in physical size. After the snake was inert, the shaman peeled half of its skin back; filling this skin sheath with water ended the curing process. It would appear that the binding and sucking of the wound were fully rational techniques to remove the venom, and steaming the victim might also have been efficacious physically. The activities of the shaman, however, could only have rendered psychological service.

If a person drowned, the death usually was attributed to a supernatural water snake; if an individual disappeared forever, another supernatural was held responsible. Men had little or no control over events such as these, but they were directly responsible for other types of death and for most serious illnesses. If a person became ill and could not explain his affliction in ordinary terms, he sooner or later concluded that a death bone had been pointed at him. "Bone-pointing" was a ritual performed by a sorcerer acting either on his own behalf or, more likely, on behalf of a client who wanted an enemy killed or injured. A death bone was fashioned from a human forearm or from an emu bone and was ground to a point at one end. Attached to the opposite end was a piece of string, from four to fourteen feet in length, which was extended through a short, hollowed-out section of human arm or leg bone and cemented to the pitch used to seal the end. When the victim was a short distance away, a sorcerer secretly placed the bone cylinder upright in the ground, and sitting on the ground, he placed one foot in the direction of the victim. Using his big toe and the one next to it, he held the pointer facing the potential sufferer. By magical means the sorcerer sent a foreign material into the body of the victim, and the victim's blood flowed magically into the pointer and then along the string to the bone cylinder.

The bone-pointing ritual was employed by men in order to produce either the illness or death of another person. It is reported that occasionally a person who learned a bone had been pointed at him abandoned his will to live and soon died. If he did not abandon hope, he sought the aid of a friend or relative to find out who had plotted his downfall. If the victim's friends and relatives could not help him, he might dream of the identity of the person or sorcerer. The final means for determining the cause of one's illness, if all else had failed, was to consult a friendly shaman for treatment and to request that he learn the identity of the enemy. The shaman usually worked over the patient and appeared to remove a foreign substance from his body by massaging the afflicted area, blowing on the patient's chest, and finally sucking out the material magically without breaking the surface of the skin. He examined the foreign body that he had removed, and after consulting his fellow curers in secret, he determined the guilty individual. Even when in possession of this knowledge, the half-well victim acted with caution. He might cripple the enemy and his agent, the shaman, with a weapon, but he would be careful not to kill them because they still had his blood in their bone-pointer case, and if they died the murderer would surely die as well. His more likely recourse was to enlist the services of another shaman to point a bone at his opponent and the opponent's shaman in retaliation. After obtaining the opponent's blood, they went off alone and built a fire over which they heated the bone cylinder containing the blood. This done, the original victim went off and talked with his opponent, and if the latter admitted that he did not feel well, this was taken as evidence that the pointing had succeeded. If no sign of his illness could be detected, the shaman washed out the container with water, and the bone-pointing ritual began again. If it succeeded this time, the enemy came under the power of his intended victim and might be made ill by heating the blood or killed by burning the blood-filled container. If neither man died during these procedures, they would sooner or later confront one another, and their differences were then brought out in the open. Mutual exposure tended to resolve the problems, and the vessels said to contain their blood then were washed with water, and the episode was concluded.

The bone-pointing complex among the Pitapita raises a number of meaningful questions about the honesty of shamans. Did a typical shaman really believe in his power? The answer seems to be clearly that he did. There were no doubt a few charlatans in the fraternity of shamans, but it appears that most often these men genuinely believed in their supernatural powers. How could this be? Imagination, personal conviction, the powers of suggestion, and above all else, the need for a method of handling that which was unknown, the nature of certain diseases. Did a shaman really believe that he could capture the blood of an enemy in a bone container? Probably not, since he could actually see into the container, but he probably did believe that he could gain and control some magical essence of a person's blood. Did a shaman deceive his clientele? Yes, in some respects he tricked them, but in this capacity he was more a magician than a trickster. Thus, the Pitapita shamans were extraordinary persons who served genuinely important functions: they were able to explain in absolute terms that which was otherwise unexplainable. Their actions brought the people a sense of confidence and knowing which better enabled them to deal with the world in which they found themselves.[1]

●　●　●　●　●　●　●　●

Human experience includes many inexplicable events. We must all live with the knowledge of death, but even that ultimate reality is somewhat unbelievable. The moment of birth is so beautiful that it, too, has a quality of the impossible; conception is an understood biological fact and still an apparent miracle. All human societies develop systems of ideas to deal with these mysteries. The Pitapita blame drowning on a supernatural watersnake. Other deaths are attributed to the bone-pointing of a sorcerer. According to the ethnographic account, a person who knows a bone has been pointed at him may abandon his will to live and die. Bone-pointing obviously has profound meaning for the Pitapita and not only can explain illness or death but can even convince someone to give up life.

Religious symbols, like all cultural symbols, are meaningful only to those who understand them. The Pitapita bone cylinder has no inherent power. Its meaning has

1. From Walter E. Roth, *Ethnological Studies among the North-West-Central Queensland Aborigines* (Brisbane: Edmund Gregory, Government Printer, 1897).

been defined by the culture. Two crossed sticks, likewise, have no inherent power, and yet, think of the wealth of meaning they have to Christians the world over. It is characteristic of human beings to attribute meaning to symbols. In fact, *symbolic behavior* is one of the things that distinguishes us from other primates.

Jane Van Lawick-Goodall[2] has observed chimpanzees preparing sticks to be used to dig termites out of their hills, which indicates that these animals are able to conceptualize a practical implement, but that is not quite symbolic. She has also observed a strange performance during rainstorms, when groups of male chimps run frantically down a hillside waving sticks and swinging around tree trunks. Is it a ritual with some symbolic meaning? Probably not, though like other chimp behaviors it is tantalizingly close. There is no evidence for symbolic behavior among prehuman primates before Neandertal man. Fossil Neandertals, however, have been found with remnants of what could only have been religious rituals of one sort or another. At one Neandertal site seven bear skulls had been sealed in a rectangular pit covered by a large slab.[3] At Shanidar in Iraq, several Neandertal burials were accompanied by mounds of flowers. Their discoverer thinks we ought not to mind an ancestor "of such good character, one who laid his dead to rest with flowers."[4] It is the symbolic behavior, not the aesthetic sensibility, that establishes the ancestry. Only humans are capable of concern with an afterlife and only humans surround their dead with things they have imbued with meaning.

All people deal with the inexplicable. All societies have religious systems just as they have kinship systems and economic systems. It is not difficult to understand that people define differently who are relatives and who are not, but it is a problem of another order to accept definitions from other cultures of that which is not even concrete—the supernatural. Religion, however, is universal and it is universally concerned with phenomena that cannot be observed. And although religions may differ greatly from culture to culture, all religions have certain things in common.

Religion: A Cultural Universal

Cultural anthropology may seem to be concerned primarily with differences, but it is concerned with differences in order to find similarity. If all the variations on a certain institution show an underlying pattern, this tells us something about the human potential. That is why we pursue minimal definitions and try to make general statements that have relevance to many different cultural examples.

What Is Religion?

Edward B. Tylor, the nineteenth-century evolutionist, defined religion as *animism*, the belief in spiritual beings.[5] Animism is

2. Jane Van Lawick-Goodall, *In the Shadow of Man* (New York: Dell Publishing, 1971).

3. Clifford J. Jolly and Fred Plog, *Physical Anthropology and Archeology* (New York: Alfred A. Knopf, 1976).

4. Ralph S. Solecki, *Shanidar: The First Flower People* (New York: Alfred A. Knopf, 1971), p. 270.

5. Edward Burnett Tylor, *Primitive Culture*, vol. 1 (New York: Harper and Row, Harper Torchbooks, 1958).

Praying Moslems on Friday, the holy day, in Ouagadougou, Upper Volta.

a belief in spirit beings, such as gods, ghosts, animal spirits, angels, trolls, and the like. Human characteristics, including a soul, may be attributed to animals, rocks, plants, and other natural phenomena. Animism involves a personification of the elements of the universe. Thus, the Zuni asked forgiveness of the deer they had just killed because they believed the deer was like themselves in that it possessed a soul. The Papago thanked the plant spirit for stems picked for a basket. Among the Eskimo, the wife of the head whale hunter would give the dead whale a symbolic drink of water so its spirit would go back to the whale village unangered. Thus, in addition to spirit beings, animism includes the notion of a soul for many of the natural items of the physical world.

Tylor's monumental work, *Primitive Culture*, published in 1871, was actually a cross-cultural study of religion in which he argued that all cultures belonged to a "complex whole" that could be shown to have developed from the simple to the complex. Tylor and other evolutionists claimed that culture evolved from the simple to the complex by assuming that contemporary small-scale societies represented the early stages of cultural evolution. The small-scale societies Tylor had read about represented for him the earliest cultures. He said that in these early cultures there was only a belief in souls; that later cultures believed in many spiritual beings, including souls and deities; still later cultures, in pantheons of powerful deities; and, finally, among the most highly developed cultures, there was a belief in one god—what we call *monotheism*.[6]

Tylor thought all humans were rational. He believed that animism was a reasonable response to certain unavoidable problems of human existence: "What makes the difference between a living body and a dead one? What causes sleep, trance, disease, death? What are the human shapes which appear in dreams and visions?"[7] In all cultures there is a belief in spiritual beings because all people have to deal with these problems. Religion is thus seen as a rational approach to dealing with a reality that includes some things that are other-

6. Anthony F. C. Wallace, *Religion: An Anthropological View* (New York: Random House, 1966), pp. 6–7.

7. Edward Burnett Tylor, *Primitive Culture*, vol. 2 (New York: Harper and Row, Harper Torchbooks, 1958), p. 12.

wise not possible to explain.

Tylor's student, Robert Marett, questioned Tylor's evolutionary sequence and pointed out that in many religions, including those of Oceania, there was a belief in an impersonal, supernatural power called *mana*.[8] Marett called such beliefs, which did not include the idea of soul or spiritual beings, *animatism*, and suggested that animatism, rather than animism, characterized the earliest religions. Though we no longer believe it necessary or possible to describe the earliest cultures and therefore the earliest religions, it is worth adding Marett's recognition of impersonal power to any general definition of religion.

It is also worth appreciating that the behavioral aspects of religion, that is, religious ritual, are as important as its rationale for existing. In other words, though Tylor and Marett and other evolutionists gave a possible explanation for the existence of religion in early cultures, they failed to discuss the effect of participation in actual religious ritual and its dynamic, functional role in society. A contemporary anthropologist, Anthony F. C. Wallace, has defined religion as "that kind of behavior which can be classified as belief and ritual concerned with supernatural beings, powers and forces."[9] This is a useful working definition because it combines Tylor's supernatural beings and Marett's powers and forces with an emphasis on behavior. Religion is belief and ritual. This may not be an acceptable definition for people who think it is possible to be religious without participating in any ritual (without belonging to a church or temple, for instance),

but it makes a great deal of sense anthropologically where religion is considered as group, not individual, behavior. It is also useful because it is general enough to include behavior that involves the supernatural but may not appear, in a formal sense, to be strictly religious. In closed societies —that is, societies which are relatively small and isolated from the rest of the world —dealings with the supernatural permeate daily life. To talk about religious behavior in such societies as something separable from economic behavior or even kinship is practically impossible. Our inclination to discuss institutions separately may actually distort the social realities of other cultures. Religion is a way of dealing with the supernatural, and in some cultures the other-worldly is as much a part of daily life as the worldly.

Magic

As we have seen, the evolutionists considered religion a rational response to certain human problems. Sir James Frazer, following the tradition of Tylor, constructed an evolutionary sequence, but his sequence did not begin with even a simple form of religion. Frazer believed that the earliest societies used magic to deal with the unpredictable world. He distinguished between magic, which supplicates no higher power, and religion, which is based on powers superior to humans. Magic follows the order of nature, whereas religion makes the assumption that the order of nature is controlled by superior beings. Frazer believed that religion succeeded magic and that science would eventually succeed religion.

Bronislaw Malinowski approached the distinction between magic and religion differently. As a functionalist and a fieldworker, Malinowski was concerned primar-

8. Wallace, *Religion*, p. 7.

9. Wallace, *Religion*, p. 6.

A Catholic priest says Mass in Ghana. The Catholic ritual has retained its essential elements through the centuries and remains the same all over the world.

ily with how magic and religion functioned in living societies, not how they originated. He saw that religious rites had no immediate ulterior purpose, whereas magical rites were performed to attain a specific goal.[10] Such a goal had both psychological and social implications. For instance, Malinowski observed a magician ordering a hurricane to stop and assuring the natives that no harm would come to the village.[11] The magician's performance calmed people's fears and provided leadership in a time of crisis. Malinowski noticed that among the Trobriand Islanders,[12] elaborate magical rites were associated with the dangerous open-sea fishing, but none was associated with lagoon fishing. Magic was deemed necessary only when dangers were anticipated that were beyond human control. According to Malinowski, the Trobrianders did not think the rites would change nature,

10. E. E. Evans-Pritchard, *Theories of Primitive Religion* (Oxford: Clarendon Press, 1965).

11. Abraham Kardiner and Edward Preble, *They Studied Man* (New York: Mentor, 1961), p. 155.

12. Bronislaw Malinowski, *Magic, Science, and Religion* (Garden City, N.Y.: Doubleday, Anchor Books, 1948).

but they recognized human limits and performed magic to give themselves a sense of security in a basically uncontrollable world. Malinowski did not think magic was wrong or evil. He believed it was a way of dealing with real dangers in life. In the ethnographic capsule, a Pitapita man who has been bitten by a snake does various things that presumably help the wound (binding, sucking, heating), but a shaman is summoned to dig out the snake, kill it, and fill its peeled back skin with water. Though killing the snake may be effective in a practical way, its relationship to curing the victim can be only psychological. Magic, for Malinowski, was based primarily in psychological needs. In fact, most theorists until the time of Malinowski explained all dealings with the supernatural as related to human insecurities. Religion, however, was distinguished from magic. Religion gave supernatural and public sanction to the social system. This perspective was first stated in the work of the French sociologist, Emile Durkheim.

Durkheim: God Is Society

Durkheim claimed that what people worship is society itself; their gods are created in their own image.[13] This thesis is illustrated by the totemic religion of the Australian aborigines which Durkheim described in *The Elementary Forms of Religious Life*, first published in 1912. *Totemism* is a system in which kin groups or clans are identified with a plant or animal. Among Australian aborigines, the animal is set apart, treated in a special way, made sacred in contrast to things considered profane. Members of the clan claim descent

from the animal or plant, abstain from eating it except once a year, and paint themselves to resemble it on special occasions. Durkheim claimed that the totem, which, after all, is a profane creature, having been raised to the level of the sacred, in fact represents, and is symbolic of, the society. Thus, the totem is an objective representation of not only the collective society but all its rules and regulations. In taking the totem as god, which Durkheim implied, there is divinity in each worshiper because each worshiper is part of that which is worshiped, society itself.

Freud's Patricide

Freud interpreted totemism differently. To Freud, the totem, or god, was a projection of the father figure. Freud emphasized that totem animals, though not eaten most of the time, were consumed once a year. He thought that the totem animal represented the father whom each person had come to hate jealously as well as to love and identify with.[14] The guilt attendant on the conflict accounts for the reverence to the totem. Freud proposed that after deposing and killing the dominant father, the primordial horde—that is, the earliest peoples—instituted a taboo against eating the totem out of guilt, but broke the taboo once a year to renew their guilt.[15] The feared and revered father became the god, and worship was continued out of guilt for acts that Freud seems to have believed actually took place.

Freud's god and Durkheim's god are of

---

13. Evans-Pritchard, *Theories of Primitive Religion*.

14. Wallace, *Religion*, p. 18.

15. Sigmund Freud, *Totem and Taboo* (New York: W. W. Norton, 1952).

human invention. But there the similarity ends. Freud offers a psychological explanation for religion, and Durkheim, a sociological one. According to Freud, individuals continue to believe in a god out of guilt because of a personally experienced conflict of hate and love of their own fathers. Thus, God is dependent on individual psychological experience. In Durkheim's explanation, God endures because as the object of worship, God is the symbol of society.

Thus, people worship as members of a group and they believe in a god that represents the group. Durkheim's explanation is sociological, since group processes rather than those of individuals are emphasized. It is also significant that societies in which women have influence often have female deities: the Changing Woman among the Navajos, the Three Sisters for the Iroquois, for example.

Witchcraft

A belief in gods does more than soothe people's fears. It also enables people to feel at one with the society and to have ready explanations for what is otherwise mysterious. *Witchcraft* provides a means for explaining events without placing blame on specific individuals. The belief in witchcraft among the Azande is an example of the power of this kind of explanation in a nonscientific context. The Azande are an African group who were studied by the British anthropologist E. E. Evans-Pritchard.[16]

---

16. E. E. Evans-Pritchard, "The Notion of Witchcraft Explains Unfortunate Events," in *Witchcraft, Oracles and Magic among the Azande* (Oxford: Clarendon Press, 1937), part 1, chap. 4.

For the Azande, witchcraft is an everyday occurrence. It explains anything that is unusual or has unfortunate consequences. If a boy hits his foot against a stump and the wound festers, it is attributed to witchcraft. The witchcraft did not put the stump in front of the foot, but somehow brought that particular boy and that particular stump together to cause that particular wound. If the work of an expert potter or woodcarver cracks, it is witchcraft because such skill is taken for granted and the artisans could not be held responsible for the flaws. Evans-Pritchard's most interesting example is that of a granary falling down on people's heads. The Azande know that old granaries occasionally collapse when termites eat away their supports. The Azande also know that people sit under granaries in the summer heat to keep cool. However, when an old granary falls on the people it is blamed on witchcraft. As with the boy and the stump, it is the combination of the particular granary and the particular people at the particular time that is explained by witchcraft.

Our culture does not recognize witchcraft as a cause by means of which a combination of events can be explained. But we recognize the problem. People overburdened with personal tragedies wonder why they have been selected. "Why me?"

Myth and Ritual

Claude Lévi-Strauss has suggested that *myths*, those traditional stories handed down from generation to generation, of heroes, ancestors, and supernatural beings, represent another sort of attempt to deal with the unavoidable but very real fears and mysteries of human life. Lévi-Strauss believes that it is a characteristic of humans to create myths in order to explain phe-

In a government school in Bolgatanga, Ghana, the day starts with a prayer in the Christian fashion despite the fact that some of the children are Moslem and a few are believers in animism.

nomena in the world about them.[17] For example, in a number of Pueblo Indian myths, a threefold distinction is made between grass-eating animals, ravens, and predatory animals. The grass-eaters are, of course, vegetarians; the predators always kill for meat; but the ravens eat meat but do not need to kill for it—they are in between. Lévi-Strauss interprets the symbolism of the ravens as a denial of the association of death with life. It is an imaginative way of making people feel better about the inevitable but unacceptable fact of death. Lévi-Strauss has stressed elsewhere the intellectual needs and expressions of all societies: he suggests that by providing explanations for some of life's mysteries, myths help to alleviate fear.[18]

Victor Turner similarly has pointed out the complexity of *ritual*, the prescribed ceremonials of a religion.[19] He finds intel-

17. Edmund Leach, "Lévi-Strauss in the Garden of Eden: An Examination of Some Recent Developments in the Analysis of Myth," *Transactions of the New York Academy of Sciences* 23 (1961): 386–396, and Claude Lévi-Strauss, "The Structural Study of Myth," *Journal of American Folklore* 67 (1955): 428–444.

18. Claude Lévi-Strauss, *The Savage Mind* (Chicago: University of Chicago Press, 1966), chap. 1.

19. Victor Turner, "Themes in the Symbolism of Ndembu Hunting Ritual," in *The Forest of Symbols: Aspects of Ndembu Ritual* (Ithaca, N.Y.: Cornell University Press, 1967), pp. 280–298.

lectual meaning in ritual, as well as the more obvious psychological and sociological meaning. In his analysis of Ndembu hunting ritual, for example, he shows that a forked stick, peeled of its bark to show the whiteness of the wood, stuck in a fragment of a termite's nest with a bit of grass, not only is a ritual which symbolizes strength and success in the hunt, but also is related to the whole kinship system. In addition, the ritual symbolizes the hunter's relationship to his ancestors, to his instructor, and to the sacredness of the age and sex distinctions in the culture. Turner analyzes ritual not only on the level of what people say the ritual signifies, but on the level of what people do with rituals and how these are related to other cultural symbols. For Turner, ritual is not a simple-minded outlet for simple-minded people. It is a complex system that uses the intellectual capacities of humans to deal with the omnipresent complexities of human life.

If all religions have anything in common, it is their attempt to provide explanations. Much behavior having to do with myth and ritual is an effort to fill in the gaps in human understanding. Religion may be interpreted psychologically as serving individual needs, or sociologically as serving the needs of the society, but an equally important element is a philosophical interpretation—that is, religion provides a rationale for the meaning of life.

Rites and Practitioners

Anthropologists have analyzed the beliefs and rituals of small-scale societies differently, the various interpretations usually reflecting the intellectual climate of the period in which they were made. What do the people think who practice the customs?

Do the Ndembu really believe that a forked stick has anything to do with success at the hunt? Why are the Trobrianders calmed by a shaman's assurances during a storm? Do they actually think he has the power to stop it? What about the shaman himself? Does he think he has real influence over the weather or the forces that produce storms? According to the capsule ethnography, the Pitapita shaman, for example, believes in his power but does not believe it extends to the capture of the blood of the enemy.

There is no question that religious rites and ideas are associated with anxiety-provoking events and problems. Religion prevents the chaos that Clifford Geertz claims would otherwise break in upon humanity "at the limits of his endurance, at the limits of his analytic capacities, and at the limits of his moral insight." [20] Religious symbols, ideas, and rites exist because they must, according to Geertz. Humans are incomplete without symbolic inventions.

Rites of Passage

Birth, puberty, marriage, and death are the events in the life of an individual that most cultures acknowledge in formal ways. The rituals that accompany these major transitions in the life cycle are called *rites of passage*. Anyone who has participated in a funeral can appreciate the funeral ritual, which not only automatically provides something to "do" at a difficult time, but seems to mark the event in an appropriate fashion. A funeral is also a reaffirmation of life, in the sense that it brings the living

20. Clifford Geertz, "Religion as a Cultural System," in *Anthropological Approaches to the Study of Religion*, ed. Michael Banton (London: Tavistock Publications, 1965).

together and reaffirms their ties to one another.

Puberty and marriage are happy times in most societies. When a member attains adult status, the society welcomes the new member to carry on its traditions. The male or female initiate not only becomes eligible for marriage but takes on adult economic responsibilities. In the United States, puberty is celebrated by various religious groups in different ways, but marriage is the more generally accepted initiation into the economic realities of adulthood. Birth is also joyous, but tempered by worries over the well-being of mother and child.

Cross-cultural research has turned up interesting similarities in the human response to these life transitions. Many are associated with *taboos*—restrictions affecting eating habits, sexuality, and even freedom of movement. By observing taboos, people feel they have some control over their most important goals: healthy children, productive adult lives, fruitful marriages, and a dignified death.

CHILDBIRTH AMONG THE SIRIONO.

Following the birth of a child, the Siriono of Eastern Bolivia practice a series of observances and rites called the *couvade* for three days. Similar activities related to childbirth have been observed among many groups. While the Siriono woman is in labor, the father goes out to hunt for a name (the first animal killed in the day's search). The mother waits for him to return to cut the umbilical cord, which he does with a bamboo knife. He first cuts off a piece about 6 inches long which is tied to the underside of the hammock to "prevent the infant from crying." He then returns to his hammock to begin observance of the couvade, the purpose of which is to protect the life of the infant and insure its good health.[21]

During the observance of the couvade, both parents confine their activities to the house and are subject to a number of food taboos—no jaguar or coati, lest the infant break out with sores all over its body, no paca or the infant might lose its hair, no

---

21. Allan R. Holmberg, *Nomads of the Long Bow: The Siriono of Eastern Bolivia* (Garden City, N.Y.: Natural History Press, 1969), pp. 179–180.

Dancing at a naming ceremony (referred to locally as a baptism) in Thionck-Essyle, Senegal.

At the naming ceremony, the people are Moslem, but the drumming and dancing are in the local tradition.

papaya, lest the infant contract diarrhea. On the day after birth, both parents are scarified on their upper and lower legs with the eyetooth of a rat or squirrel. The Siriono say that the purpose of this practice is to get rid of old blood which might cause the child to be sick—a kind of purification rite.[22] On the second day after birth the parents are decorated with multicolored feathers. This ornamentation is extended to

22. Holmberg, *Nomads of the Long Bow*, p. 181.

co-wives and potential spouses as well, thus generalizing the relationships of the newborn child to co-parents.

On the third day the couvade is completed with a ceremonial walk into the forest. The mother weaves a few baskets out of palm leaves which are filled with ashes from a dying fire. She then places the baby in its sling for the first time and follows the father, laden with bow and arrows, down the trail. The mother slowly scatters the ashes to purify the trail and carries a calabash of water in the other hand. After about a five-minute walk, the mother sits down to weave another basket while the father hunts for firewood. The firewood is placed in the basket and the party starts home. When they get inside the hut they kindle a new fire with the new wood and the infant is given a bath in the water that the mother has been carrying in the calabash. Thus ends the couvade.

Social paternity has been established and the health of the child protected. What do we know of the relationship of the couvade to the child's well-being? We know that the mother and the father have fulfilled their obligation to the new member in the eyes of their own people. Were they not to do so, there is no doubt that harm would befall the newborn. The society not only has gained a new member but has been strengthened by the performance of the couvade according to their tradition. No doubt there is much satisfaction among the tribal elders with each renewal of the traditional ritual.

NUER GAR: INITIATION. Initiation rites are common in small-scale societies, sometimes affecting both girls and boys, but more often affecting one or the other. Among the Nuer of Africa, a severe operation is performed called *gar*. Boys between the ages of fourteen and sixteen are initiated in groups. Their brows are cut to the bone from ear to ear in six long cuts. The scars remain for life and may even be detected on a Nuer skull. The initiates are kept in seclusion while the wounds heal, observe certain food taboos, and are instructed in adult male activities. A festivity celebrates the end of their seclusion, marked by licentious horseplay and the singing of lewd songs. This ceremony obviously has sexual significance. Boys are becoming men and are expected to behave like men. [23]

The severity of the operation may reflect the severity of a Nuer man's life. The climate is difficult (see Chapter 11), alternating between a hot, dry season and a rainy season during which much of Nuer land is flooded. As herdsmen, not only are these people constantly ministering to their cattle in a hostile environment, but they are also involved in frequent warfare. Gar may reflect cattle markings or may be a symbolic initiation into the trials that must be endured by an adult male Nuer. For the Nuer the initiation is necessary in order that a male be considered adult. A boy requests that the operation be performed on him so that he can prove his competence.

INITIATION FOR GIRLS.   For girls, initiation frequently is associated with the first menstruation. Among the Maroni River Caribs of South America, a girl is confined to a small room in the house for eight days. She is not permitted to go to the river or forest, where spirits dwell which cannot stand the smell that these people think is associated with female reproductive processes.[24] The girl lives mainly on porridge made from manioc cake and small fish, as there are taboos against eating large things. The only activity she is permitted during her seclusion is spinning cotton in order to make a hammock for her father or brother.

On the eighth day the girl's mother invites an old man and an old woman who have reputations for industriousness to the house. The mother has bits of cotton fluff ready and the father has collected a large bowl of ants. First the girl bathes; then the old woman takes bits of cotton, lays them on the open hand of the girl, and sets fire to them. The girl must throw the burning cotton from one hand to the other in order to avoid being burned herself. This signifies that in the future her hands should never be at rest.[25] The old man puts the girl's hands into the bowl of ants. These large, biting ants are a reminder to her that as an adult woman she must be as industrious as an ant. At the end of this day a feast is held which marks the completion of the girl's initiation. The symbolism in this ceremony is considerably less subtle than among the Nuer, since the people themselves articulate the lesson of the burning cotton and the ants to the young girl.

It has been suggested that female initiation in this group is related to matrilocal residence and the economic importance of

23. E. E. Evans-Pritchard, *The Nuer* (Oxford: Clarendon Press, 1960), pp. 249–250.

24. Peter Kloos, "Female Initiation among the Maroni River Caribs," in *You and Others: Readings in Introductory Anthropology*, ed. A. Kimball Romney and Paul L. Devore (Cambridge, Mass.: Winthrop Publishers, 1973), p. 235.

25. Kloos, "Female Initiation among the Maroni River Caribs," p. 236.

women to the society.[26] The Maroni River Carib women contribute a major part to subsistence (the cultivation of manioc) and remain with their parents at least for some time after marriage. Thus, the initiation serves both to initiate a young girl into the adult role and to teach her the most important aspect of that role—hard work.

In closed societies, people seem to participate automatically and willingly in traditional rituals. There is no choice—to become a Nuer man, a boy requests permission to suffer the painful gar operation; a Siriono would not dare to ignore the couvade. Rites and rituals serve more than one function. What about religious practitioners in such small-scale, closed societies? Do they have more than one function? How do they perceive their work? How do they make good their claims to special powers and unique control over the outcomes of the lives of their fellows?

Shamans

The way in which a Pitapita man becomes a *shaman* (often called a medicine man or witch doctor) is described in the capsule ethnography. Although in a number of societies only men are permitted to be shamans, there are many cases in which women also assume that role. The recognition of what we refer to as a religious "calling" or "vocation" varies from society to society. Among the Tapirape of central Brazil, frequent dreams indicate shamanistic potential, while among the Chuckchi of Siberia, anyone who is able spontaneously to enter a trance is required to become a shaman. As with

26. Judith Brown, "A Cross-cultural Study of Female Initiation Rites," *American Anthropologist* 65 (1963): 837–853.

the Pitapita, recovery from serious illness, as well as survival of an accident, may also be considered indicative of a special power. In some societies, especially in central and northeast Asia, shamans are recruited on a hereditary basis. Depending on the belief system and the power and prestige associated with the role, a person may ignore his or her calling in one society or undergo all sorts of ordeals to qualify for the position in another.

The duties of shamans vary, but the curing of illness is the most common. Since in many societies the cause of disease is often ascribed to foreign objects or spirits in the patient's body, the problem for the shaman may be their removal. The shaman accomplishes this by such means as quick hand movements, sucking, massage, smoking, bleeding, or the like. The shaman who sucks out the cause of disease may produce the object, show it to the patient, and then claim credit for removing the aggravating agent. The object sucked from the patient's body probably has been hidden in the shaman's mouth and produced for effect. Is he then not faking?

A Kwakiutl Indian text collected by Franz Boas contained an autobiographical account of a skeptical man named Quesalid who became a shaman in order to prove his suspicions that shamans had no special power or connection with the supernatural. According to the text, Quesalid learned to simulate fainting and nervous fits; he learned the traditional sacred songs, as well as a technique for inducing vomiting and the use of "dreamers," spies who supply the shaman with the origins and symptoms of diseases he is asked to cure. He even learned how to hide a little tuft of down in his mouth and at the proper moment, produce it, covered with self-induced vomit and blood, as the pathological foreign cause of the disease.[27] Quesalid's suspicions were confirmed, and yet he administered to the sick with outstanding success and became a celebrated shaman.

Quesalid realized that the methods worked, and not only did they work but they were superior to methods used by shamans in other Indian groups. Quesalid could attribute his success, to an extent, to psychological factors, but he also had to deal with the fact that not all psychological methods were equally effective. He had learned a shamanistic tradition that was not a fake in terms of results.

Quesalid's insights probably can also be applied to other shamanistic activities. A shaman says he is exorcizing evil spirits, and he is if the people believe they are gone. He says he is dispatching the souls of dead persons, and he is if they do not trouble anyone again. If he claims to control the weather or guarantee the food supply he is on shakier ground. If he accuses a person of bringing some misfortune upon the community he must be reflecting public opinion. To go against public opinion would be a risk of his own position and even, in some cases, of his life. The shaman, then, is not functioning as much out of supernatural sanction as out of societal sanction. The sick are cured because the culture has defined what will constitute cure and the shaman is the master healer.

Priests

Like the shaman, a *priest* is a ceremonial practitioner, but priesthood is a full-time job. Individual calling or experience is not the only qualification for becoming a priest. More important is the learning of a standardized body of knowledge and ritual. The priest stands apart from the rest of the people and in a special relationship to those things considered sacred by the society. He (or she) is an intermediary with the gods who are accessible only to those knowledgeable in the appropriate ritual. A priest does not usually perform rituals for individuals as do shamans, but, more commonly, officiates at public rites and ceremonies for the benefit of a whole village or community.[28] The priest is supported by the community, which looks to him or her to inspire the values and behavior that will best serve the community's interests. A shaman will not usually give reassurance to his people on the occasion of a storm. A priest, however, is a constant source of interpretation and explanation for the people, and derives his power from the office he holds in the religious establishment rather than from any personal charisma.

It is clear from the few rituals and practitioners we have discussed that religion is more than a system of ideas and practices meant to deal with the supernatural. It is also more than a system of ideas and practices meant to allay human fears and provide explanations of the unknown. Religion is an ideological system that reaffirms the values of a culture. For example, among the Siriono, hunting is essential for survival. When a Siriono child is born, the father "hunts" for a name; such a ritual makes

27. Claude Lévi-Strauss, "The Sorcerer and His Magic," in *Structural Anthropology* (Garden City, N.Y.: Doubleday, Anchor Books, 1967), pp. 161–180.

28. William A. Lessa and Evon Z. Vogt, eds., *Reader in Comparative Religion: An Anthropological Approach*, 2nd ed. (New York: Harper and Row, 1965), Introduction to chap. 10, pp. 451–452.

sense to a hunting society. The Aztecs sacrificed a perfect individual to epitomize the society's idea of perfection.[29] Religious ideas reflect and affirm what the society considers "good." Religion makes life on earth seem "right" as well as making it endurable.

Economics and Religion

If we accept that dealings with the supernatural have psychological and social functions for a group, we can then ask whether they have, in addition, any more practical effects. Religious practice gives members of a society confidence, dispels anxieties, and reinforces ideologies, but does it keep people from starving? Religious ideas legitimate economic systems by justifying the existing social order, but can they also serve specific economic purposes?

Pigs in New Guinea

Roy Rappaport thinks the answer to this question is "Yes." He claims that the ritual cycles of the Tsembaga of New Guinea help maintain the communities within their territories, redistribute land among people and people over land, and limit the frequency of fighting.[30] The Tsembaga say

---

29. Bernardino de Sahagún, "Aztec Sacrifice," in *The Florentine Codex*, Book 2, trans. A. J. O. Anderson and C. H. Dibble (Santa Fe, N.M.: Museum of New Mexico, 1951).

---

30. Roy A. Rappaport, "Ritual Regulation of Environmental Relations among a New Guinea People," in *Man in Adaptation: The Institutional Framework*, ed. Yehudi Cohen (Chicago: Aldine Publishing, 1971), pp. 227–228.

they perform the rituals in order to improve their relationships with the supernatural world.

One such ritual is "planting the rumbim," which is done at the close of hostilities between two groups. The group whose territory has remained intact performs the ritual (every man puts his hand on the ritual plant as it is put in the ground). The rumbim is then dug up at the pig festival (the *kaiko*), which is held when there are enough pigs for sacrifice. The period between the close of hostilities and the festival continues for about a year. There are no battles fought during that time, but friendly groups are occasionally entertained. Visiting dancing contingents are taken as a measure of available fighting forces, so the period serves to consolidate alliances for the next conflict.

Kaiko concludes with major pig sacrifices (as much as 7,000 to 8,500 pounds) when the meat is distributed to other local groups. The killing of so many animals at once is actually necessary, as pigs, though highly valued, invade gardens on whose produce the Tsembaga also depend. The pig population actually must be kept below carrying capacity because of this problem. The human population must also be kept low, as too many gardens in proximity make it impossible to keep any pigs at all. Rappaport, therefore, sees the whole ritual cycle as serving these very practical economic purposes, although the participants may not necessarily take the same view.

Mayordomia

Another case in which economics and religion interact may be seen in the Latin American fiesta cycle. In Mexico it is called the *mayordomia system* and involves the sponsorship by a person or small group of people of ceremonies relating to an image or to a church building or chapel. For the period of one year, masses are paid for, food served on ritual occasions, and images carried in processions. The sponsors are accorded respect and high status for their leadership but the undertaking is, needless to say, a financial drain. This system was originated by Catholic missionaries and, according to George Foster,[31] was meant to reflect the Spanish idealistic system in which religious and civil activities were merged in one endeavor.

In Latin America it served for a long time—it is now breaking down—to impoverish the population. If one person accumulated more wealth than other members of the community he was the obvious candidate to assume ritual sponsorship. The participants did not recognize that mayordomia kept them poor, nor did they realize that it provided a constant leveling mechanism, keeping everyone poor whenever an individual or a group accumulated more wealth than the others.[32] On the contrary, service in the community was valued highly as a religious duty and was considered an honor as well as a pleasure, despite the necessary financial sacrifices.

Revitalization Movements

When traditional values and beliefs cease to have relevance to a changed and harsh economic reality, a new religion may arise. The energy and activity involved in the creation of such a new religion has been called a *revitalization movement*,[33] and usually is a reaction to a situation of economic and social distress. Revitalization movements usually are led by a prophet who claims to have received ecstatic revelation and who promises new and more effective rituals for salvation and a new and more promising culture.

In 1870, a Northern Paiute called Wodziwob became the leader and prophet of a new religion. This was a time on the Great Plains of the United States when white settlers were moving westward and railroads were being built to link the West to the East. There was no place for the Indians in the building of America; they were in the way of progress. The attitude of the government and of most people toward the indigenous population was that the Indians should be eliminated. One response by native Americans to this total disruption was a revitalization movement called the "Ghost Dance," led by Wodziwob, the prophet of a new religion. Wodziwob claimed that a great explosion would announce the return of his dead ancestors by a big train.[34] He also proclaimed that all whites would be miraculously swallowed up, leaving their goods behind for the Indians who joined the cult. Earth would become heaven and the Great Spirit would come to live among the Indians. Ritual in the cult involved dancing around a pole and singing the songs that had been revealed to Wodziwob during his vision.

In 1890, Wovoka, another self-pro-

31. George Foster, *Tzintzuntzan: Mexican Peasants in a Changing World* (Boston: Little, Brown, 1967), p. 196.

32. Beverly Chiñas, *The Isthmus Zapotecs: Women's Roles in Cultural Context* (New York: Holt, Rinehart and Winston, 1973).

33. Wallace, *Religion*, p. 158.

34. Peter Farb, *Man's Rise to Civilization* (New York: Avon Books, 1969), p. 334.

Shoshone Sun Dancers dance toward the center tree. Today many native Americans seek not to adapt to American culture, but to maintain their own tribal life and customs.

claimed prophet, appeared. Wovoka's Ghost Dance spread from Nevada across the Plains finally to the Sioux, who confused his teachings and came to believe that dancing not only would bring back the ancestors but also would bring back herds of bison and exterminate the whites by causing a landslide.[35] They also believed that their

35. Farb, *Man's Rise to Civilization*, p. 337.

dance shirts—ghost shirts—were impenetrable to the white man's bullets, a myth the massacre at Wounded Knee brought to an abrupt end. The Indian populations had been decimated, their cultures disrupted, and their values disregarded. They could make no sense out of what had happened. The Ghost Dance and other such revitalization movements are attempts to bring back control over the circumstances of daily life.

The cargo cults of Melanesia following

World War II reflect similar economic stress. During the colonization of many areas by Europeans, a plantation economy and the zeal of Christian missionaries disrupted the traditional values and economies of many groups. These indigenous people responded with religious movements of their own to gain back some measure of power over their lives. People abandoned their old ways of life, destroyed their material possessions, and prepared for the delivery of shiploads of goods analogous to those that arrived for the Europeans in their midst. During World War II, American G.I.'s who landed in the New Hebrides found the people furiously at work preparing airfields, roads, and docks for the magic ships and planes they believed were coming from "Rusefel" (Roosevelt), the friendly king of America.[36] When cargo did not arrive, they developed rituals in imitation of the European customs they believed contained the "secret" to cargo. For instance, people would sit around tables with bottles of flowers dressed in European clothes, or would write on magic pieces of paper. They saw Europeans writing and gaining power while their own hard work went relatively unrewarded, and it was this which led to such imitative behavior. Cargo cult rituals were not only believed to bring material benefits but would include the return of the ancestors and a paradise on earth—no death, old age, or evil.

Wallace classifies revitalization movements into four types: revivalistic, assimilative, utopian, and expropriative.[37] The Ghost Dance was *revivalistic*, as it sought to restore a Golden Age. Cargo cults are *expropriative* in that they aim to import many of the customs of the alien group but to combine them with native customs and expel the alien persons. Wallace would classify the American civil rights movement as *assimilative*, in that the goal was to enjoy the rights and customs of the dominant group. The Jesus Freaks of the 1960s and 1970s and the various Eastern religious sects can be interpreted as *utopian*, defined as aiming to achieve a Golden Age believed to lie in the future. Jesus Freaks emerged during the Vietnam War, a period of serious political disillusionment, at least among some segments of the population in America.

Wallace suggests that revitalization movements are fostered by widespread disillusionment and alienation, that sense that one is a stranger in a no longer familiar world. The traditional institutions are perceived to be disorganized and inadequate; crime, illness, and asocial responses on the part of affected individuals have increased sharply in frequency.

Summary

1. All people create religions to cope with the unexplainable aspects of human existence. Behavior in relation to the supernatural attempts to fill in the gaps in human understanding.
2. Only human beings create systems of religious symbols.
3. Each set of religious symbols has meaning only to those who believe them, even though

---

36. Peter Worsley, "Cargo Cults," in *Conformity and Conflict: Readings in Cultural Anthropology*, ed. James P. Spradley and David W. McCurdy (Boston: Little, Brown, 1974).

---

37. Wallace, *Religion*, p. 164.

religion is a cultural universal.

4. Early anthropologists such as Tylor and Marett defined religion as the belief in souls, or in supernatural power. They saw religion as a rational way to deal with the unknown.

5. Frazer distinguished between magic, religion, and science, which he saw as an evolutionary sequence of explanations for the world.

6. Malinowski thought that religious behavior served psychological needs. It relieved people's anxieties about dangers they could not control, and offered reassurance in their efforts to cope with the world.

7. Other social scientists took symbolic approaches to religion. Durkheim saw it as a symbolic representation of society itself. Freud saw religion as expressing universal psychological conflicts and the belief in God as a way of maintaining the social order.

8. Witchcraft and myth are other kinds of explanations of the unknown. Witchcraft often serves to explain unfortunate occurrences and to channel interpersonal conflicts. Myths may deal with the mysteries and contradictions of everyday life in the form of stories, teachings, and entertainment.

9. Rituals which celebrate major transitions of life cycles are called rites of passage. They include birth, puberty, marriage, and death. Some rituals may be painful and harsh; others are joyful. Rituals are often associated with taboos.

10. People who are felt to have supernatural powers are often called shamans or medicine men. They are frequently healers. Priests are people who have special knowledge and training with respect to religious belief and ritual. They officiate at public ceremonies on behalf of the group.

11. Religion also may be seen as an ideological system which affirms the values of a culture, reflecting what is considered good and bad according to the values of the group.

12. When cultural values lose their relevance in a changing economic and social situation, revitalization movements may arise. They are frequently led by a prophet who promises a better life by means of new rituals and beliefs.

Review Questions

1. What are some of the characteristics of religion?

2. There are other kinds of explanations for unexplainable events. Describe two of them.

3. What is a shaman? Are a shaman's cures effective? Why?

4. Religions may affirm the values of a culture. Give an example of religious symbolism in the United States and describe the values which are emphasized. How do they relate to the other institutions of the society?

5. What is a revitalization movement? Why do you think that it might develop?

Suggested Readings

Lessa, William A., and Vogt, Evon Z., eds. *Reader in Comparative Religion*. 2nd ed. New York: Harper and Row, 1965.

The leading reader in the field. The contents deal with a variety of religious phenomena of interest to the anthropologist. Important papers by Durkheim, Kluckhohn, Geertz, and others are included.

Malinowski, Bronislaw. *Magic, Science, and Religion*. New York: Free Press, 1954.

A classic account of belief systems in small-scale societies by one of the world's great anthropologists.

Wallace, Anthony F. C. *Religion: An Anthropological View*. New York: Random House, 1966.

A modern textbook that explores the anthropology of religion.

PART SEVEN

For humanity, adaptation is more than a built-in biological response to an ecological niche. As we have seen, human beings can adapt to all sorts of environmental situations. People survive in the frozen wilderness of Alaska and in the desiccation of the Kalahari Desert. People transform poisonous plants into edible ones, dry lands into cultivated fields, wild animals into domesticated creatures. Culture, not biology, is the basic human instrument of adaptation. It is cultural inventions that make it possible to live in such diverse environments. It is cultural inventions that have freed much of humanity from lives taken up solely with the pursuit of enough food to eat.

We usually think of adaptation as the ongoing positive process that has engendered cultural evolution. More efficient technologies are invented; social systems change to accommodate the technology; and belief systems make it all seem morally right. As agriculture was developed and settled communities were organized, people began to "own" the world and accumulate possessions. Differences in status and wealth became appropriate. An example of adaptation and change in our own time is the invention of the birth control pill. Partly as a result of this invention, sexual relations became less restricted; people's attitudes about sex became more liberal, and women came out of the kitchen and the nursery to demand good jobs and equal pay.

The adaptive capacity of human groups is phenomenal. There is a capacity for improvement and endurance. In his book *The Mountain People*, Colin Turnbull has described an African people who have lost their traditional hunting territories and are starving. The culture has adapted, but not in a positive way. There is neither love nor nurturing. Children are turned out to fend for themselves at the age of three; old people are abandoned mercilessly, their suffering a source of amusement. There really is no society left, just people struggling against each other for survival. Adaptation to less than pleasant circumstances is the subject matter of much of contemporary anthropology. We are no longer dealing with isolated populations in happy equilibrium with generous environments. Instead we are dealing with such subjects as peasants exploited by market systems, newcomers to the city living in poverty.

In a justly famous article, "Peasant Society and the Image of Limited Good," George Foster has suggested that peasants, cross-culturally, share a view of the world. Foster calls this view the "image of limited good." All the desired things in life, such as land, wealth, health, friendship and love, security, and safety, exist in finite quantity and are always in short supply. Not only are these quantities limited but there is no way directly within peasant power to increase them. This is very different from our own view of the universe which sets no limits on expansion. We can get more love, more money, more status. We just have to work at it. When the good is viewed as finite there is no reason to work harder. There is no reason to adapt to new technology,

Contemporary Dimensions of Anthropology

whether it be for raising the standard of living or lowering the rate of dying. Foster uses the image of limited good to explain behavior that had otherwise seemed irrational. Peasants risk money on the lottery because it is a source outside their limited world, the only hope for change. The image of limited good is actually a very rational way to deal with the peasants' real situation. In other words, it is adaptive. No matter how hard peasants work, their efforts will not benefit them or their community. They rarely own their own land, and certainly do not control what they get for their products in the marketplace. They are often exploited and indeed the good available to them in the world is limited.

What, then, should the role of the anthropologist be in studying these exploited people? Should we develop models to describe their behavior and leave it at that? Gutorm Gjessing, in his article, "The Social Responsibility of the Social Scientist," argues that such a limited view of anthropology is irrelevant. The argument is that relevance is important for science because (1) as a social activity it entails responsibility to society; and (2) as a search for truth it cannot survive in isolation from reality. The reality of our subject matter is that the ability to adapt has led people into many unfortunate circumstances. People have adapted to rural poverty, to urban slums, to racist ideologies, to the homelessness brought on by war. The problem for anthropology is whether it is adequate to just describe those circumstances. Don't we have to say something about the systems that create them?

During the Vietnam War, many professional societies were challenged to pass resolutions against the actions of the United States government. When such a resolution was introduced at the American Anthropological Association meeting in 1966, it was ruled out of order because it did not "advance the science of anthropology" or "further the professional interests of anthropologists." Only when a member rose and said, "Genocide is not in the professional interest of anthropologists," was the resolution accepted by most members.

It has recently become clear how much funding and government interests have influenced the development of anthropology. It may have been in that light that some anthropologists were against a resolution that condemned the United States government. The early evolutionists described savages who should be brought under the control of enlightened colonial powers. The functionalists described the way cultural systems worked so that this control could be realized. Recently, anthropology has emphasized cultural change as more and more people are brought into the world economic system. But if anthropology is to be revelant and responsible, it must consider the disruption that cultural change has brought to people who do not control their economic situation. In the following chapters we consider possible ways to meet that responsibility.

Chapter 18

Culture

Change

AGRICULTURAL CHANGE IN EL PINAR

NATIVE NAME: El Pinar (Spanish for "the pine forest," the products of which are the major source of wealth for the village)

POPULATION: 2,320 as of January, 1967.

ENVIRONMENT: The west central part of Segovia Province, on the northern plateau of the Iberian Peninsula. The climate is harsh: summers are short and very hot, and winters are long and cold. An extensive forest of pine trees provides materials for the village's principal industry, the production of resin and wood products. The sandy loam soil is poor for farming, but cereal grains, and some fruits and legumes, have been traditionally grown on a subsistence basis by dry farming techniques.

FIELDWORK: Data were gathered during extensive fieldwork in 1966–67 and 1969 as well as short trips in 1968, 1970, 1972, and 1973. Information was gathered by participant observation, interviews, and research in local archives.

ETHNOGRAPHIC PRESENT: 1966–1969.

Source: From Joseph B. Aceves, *Social Change in a Spanish Village* (Cambridge, Mass.: Schenkman Publishing Company, Inc., 1971), pp. 93, 95, 99, 100, 101. Copyright © 1971 by Joseph B. Aceves. Reprinted by permission of Schenkman Publishing Company, Inc.

Sugar beets were readily accepted by the farmers of the *comarca*. There were several reasons for this: first, many men had worked in France in the sugar beet areas and were familiar with the crop; secondly, the crop was profitable and provided a source of income during the winter months when it was harvested. Unlike the French farms, there is little mechanization in sugar beet production in El Pinar, the planting, weeding, and harvesting being done largely by hand.

Most who accepted the crop planted it in plots near the river bottoms, especially near the Rio Chico.

The second new crop introduced into the *comarca* was tobacco, the so-called "black" variety commonly used in Spanish cigarettes. Tobacco requires far more care than sugar beets but the economic rewards are much higher and there are no acreage allotments nor restrictions on production. Some men from the village were taken by the Agricultural Extension agents to Talavera de la Reina in Toledo, where the government maintains a demonstration area for new crops, and there they saw tobacco growing and became interested.

Tobacco seed was procured with government aid; a number of farmers planted the crop and the first year brought successful harvest. Seven tobacco drying sheds were built in El Pinar; these were brick buildings of considerable size to allow for the open air curring of the leaf. The second year the crop was attacked by the Blue Mosaic plague which destroyed most of the plants. No remedy for the plague could be found and, except for a very few small plots, tobacco is no longer grown in the *comarca*. The drying sheds were converted to other uses, some became cattlebarns, others became storage places, and a few just remain empty and unused.

While the crop failed, the enthusiasm of the farmers did not. Failure was due to natural causes understandable to all farmers and they would gladly resume growing tobacco if a cure of the Blue Mosaic plague were found. . . .

The agency that bears the major responsibility for improving the quality of Spanish agriculture is the *Servicio de Extensión Agraria*— the Spanish equivalent of the American Cooperative Extension Service. The S. E. A. is a direct copy of the American Service and was first established in Spain in 1956. In 1966 there were 396 branch offices in operation and today there are over 500.

Agencies are located in *comarcas* which usually include from 10 to 20 villages each. In the El Pinar area, there are four agency offices: Villa Roman, Los Incierros, Fuentesol, and Villa Real. The agency in Villa Roman which services 14 villages, including El Pinar, has two agents. The offices in Villa Real and Fuentesol have more agents, but these *comarcas* are more dependent upon agriculture than El Pinar since they are not in the pine forest belt and have no resin industry.

Agents are never assigned to their own home towns, and generally not to any agency within 40 or 50 kilometers of it. Don Manuel, of the Villa Roman agency is from the province of Guadalajara. Don Francisco, the agent-in-charge is from another part of Segovia. Even though not assigned to their home towns, whenever possible agents are assigned to their native region. My assumption was that this was done because the agent would be familiar with the basic agriculture of the region, but Don Manuel was most emphatic in denying this. The reason is that the agent knows the *character of the people.* Spain has a variety of regional and sub-regional subcultures and one does not change agriculture until he first changes the farmer. And this cannot be done without a knowledge of people. Thus a Castillian is assigned to Castile, a Gallego to Galicia, a Basque to the *Vascongadas*, etc., whenever possible. . . .

The S. E. A. agent is one of the most respected persons in the village; his profession entitles him to the *Don* status but his clients are simple farmers and he must be able to communicate effectively with them. In addition to working directly with agriculturalists, the agent has to deal with the local power structure of each village in their *comarca*, know the local political situation inside out, and be able to converse with industrialists, bureaucrats, merchants, schoolteachers, priests, and the local police. I never met an agent who did not realize that successful human relations was his most important tool and weapon and that people came before plants in importance. These agents are not merely "playing a role" but are genuinely concerned with the welfare of their clients and of their towns. The farmers seem to recognize this also; after a short course in San Juan, the farmers gave both Don Manuel and Don Francisco a young lamb apiece as a token of thanks. When hardbitten farmers in a poor village do things like this, it is a sure sign of the effectiveness of the S. E. A. agents.

The agents use a variety of methods to get across their point. One of the most common is the use of the short course on a specific subject of local interest. Usually these courses are held during the winter months or sometimes during summer evenings—the time depending upon when most farmers can arrange to be present. The courses range from irrigation techniques, animal nutrition, soil conservation, and the like to occasionally more theoretically oriented material such as farm record keeping and business practices. In most cases the emphasis is upon practical application rather than upon abstract theory. Often the agents will give slide lectures or show motion pictures on agricultural topics. Attendance is usually good although in some villages, notably El Pinar, sometimes only ten farmers would show up. . . .

To introduce a new technique, the agents set up demonstrations on land loaned by a local farmer. Seeds, tools, fertilizer, and other special equipment is procured by the agents either from their Service or from other government agencies, but the farmer must use his own land and do all the work himself. If the farmer wishes to adopt a new seed or requires some special equipment, the agents will act as intermediaries for him in his dealings with other agencies.

In the course of a normal day's work, Don Manuel and Don Francisco make a number of calls at farms, sometimes by invitation and sometimes just as an informal visit. Farmers often telephone or write the office for advice or come by personally. The average work day for the agent may begin at sunup and not end until late at night, and they work six days a week and sometimes on Sundays. In addition to the visits and courses, S. E. A. publishes a variety of literature written expressly for the farmer and given him free. The basic approach of the S. E. A. agents is to have the farmers discover for themselves the value of a new technique, and the only way to do this is by example. If a farmer sees that a new seed or a new fertilizer brings better results—either in higher crop yield or in a lesser work load for himself—he may well become an adopter.[1]

● ● ● ● ● ● ● ●

The processes of change, both in technology and behavior, are the most common form of adaptation. Choice is a precondition for change. Change comes about when alternatives, new or old, exist within a society. The mere act of selecting an alternative modifies the social situation, at least temporarily, and thus change has taken place. Sometimes an old alternative exists half-forgotten until it is resurrected. In the United States, nineteenth-century court rulings have recently surfaced in civil rights cases and so have helped to cause change in the twentieth century. Without the ability to adapt to new circumstances, the human species would die out. Without innovations, human cultures would remain static forever.

1. From Joseph B. Aceves, *Social Change in a Spanish Village* (Cambridge, Mass.: Schenkman Publishing, 1971), pp. 93, 95, 96, 99, 100, 101. Copyright © 1971 by Joseph B. Aceves. Reprinted by permission of Schenkman Publishing Company, Inc.

Chapter Eighteen

Processes of Culture Change

Changes in the social or technological elements of culture generally come from one or more of three processes: invention, discovery, and diffusion.

Invention, Discovery, Diffusion

Invention is the process whereby something that has not existed before is brought into being. The product of invention can be a device, an activity, or a way of thinking. *Discovery*, on the other hand, is the process whereby something is found that has been in existence but unknown. Electricity was discovered, but the electric light was invented.

In practice, it is often difficult to make distinctions between an invention and a discovery. Many anthropologists prefer to combine the two concepts under the term *innovation*. An innovation is any idea, process, or device that is new to a culture. Innovations may be tangible, such as a pollution control valve in an automobile engine, or intangible, such as new theological concepts. Forms of social activity, such as games or any of the practices deriving from norms that govern behavior, are generally inventions. Indeed, norms themselves are inventions.

Not all inventions are the result of a deliberate planned effort. In small-scale societies, inventions are more likely to come about by accident. For example, the invention of the wheel was probably the result of an accidental application of the physical laws that were unknown to the inventors. In more complex societies, especially urban-industrial societies, inventions frequently are the result of direct efforts to find a better way to perform a task. Thus, the printing presses that produced this book were developed in an attempt to speed up the process of handcopying documents to produce multiple copies of them.

The presence of similar cultural elements in diverse parts of the world has led to speculation about the way innovations spread. For example, the Mesoamerican game of *patolli* is very similar to the game of *pachisi*, an ancient Indian board game resembling backgammon.[2] Did the games originate independently of one another, or was the game invented in one location and somehow brought to another? The process by which an innovation is taken from one place to another, known as *diffusion*, is a major method of cultural change.

Diffusion is the most common way for a culture to acquire an innovation. Isolated societies, such as the Negritos and the Yanomamö, receive less cultural input from other societies and thus tend to have a relatively unchanging culture. Societies that are physically accessible to other peoples, such as those societies on the border of the well-traveled Mediterranean Sea, are quickest to know of innovations and are most apt to accept new elements into their way of life. It is interesting to note that there are substantial cultural differences between Arab societies on the southern border of the Mediterranean and those located near Christian societies to the north. Because of their location, Arabs may be exposed to many innovations all at once, but they might not all be exposed to the same innovations. Or again, the Arab groups might each be presented with the same innovation, yet assimilate it in a different manner.

2. E. B. Taylor, "On the Game of Patolli in Ancient Mexico and Its Probable Asiatic Origin," *Journal of the Royal Anthropological Institute of Great Britain and Ireland* 8 (1879): 116–129.

When an innovation enters a society, the people affected by it must learn how to use and cope with it and its results. This is true in the case of artifacts, such as the automobile and the airplane, as well as in the case of behavioral innovations, such as the current practice in a number of societies of unmarried men and women living together. The process by which a group learns to adapt to an innovation and assimilate it into the existing culture is known as *acculturation*.

Most anthropologists use the term *acculturation* when discussing adaptation to innovations that diffuse into one culture from another. For example, the adoption of new religious beliefs, such as those described in Chapter 17, requires that the people accepting the new beliefs become acculturated to them. This means that people have to adjust much of their way of life to conform with their new beliefs. On the other hand, the form, meaning, and even the function of the innovation may be

The arrival of a Singer sewing machine on the banks of the River Niger. The impact of such a technological change can be infinite.

modified by the recipient people so that the innovation fits into their existing customs and beliefs. For example, when the Shoshone, an Indian tribe of the North American Plains, adopted the Sun Dance ritual from the Arapaho, they changed it dramatically. Among the Arapaho, medicine bundles and the military society of the individual sponsoring the ceremony were important elements in the ritual. But the Shoshone had neither military fraternities nor priests possessing medicine bundles. The tribe therefore shifted the emphasis of the dance, looking upon it as a curing ritual which supposedly improved the prosperity of the group.[3]

In the early days of anthropological study, many scholars believed that everything originated in a single location and then spread to other places and to other cultures. One school of thought held that Egypt was the source of all civilization, which diffused from there to other parts of the world. Current thought suggests that independent invention and independent discovery by different individuals in different places are as important a culture change as diffusion.

Every culture has within it elements that are the result of local innovation and elements that came to it by the process of diffusion from other cultures. Ralph Linton, in a delightful article entitled "One Hundred Percent American," shows the elements that have diffused into American culture. Speaking of food, Linton says:

Here a whole new series of foreign things confront the American. His food and drink are placed before him in pottery vessels, the popular name of which—china—is sufficient evidence of their origin. His fork is a medieval Italian invention and his spoon a copy of the Roman original. He will usually begin the meal with coffee, an Abyssinian plant first discovered by the Arabs. The American is quite likely to need it to dispel the morning-after effects of overindulgence in fermented drinks, invented in the Near East; or distilled ones, invented by the alchemists of medieval Europe. Whereas the Arabs took their coffee straight, he will probably sweeten it with sugar, discovered in India; and dilute it with cream, both the domestication of cattle and the technique of milking having originated in Asia Minor.[4]

One of the most noticeable examples of diffusion in the United States is in the language, which contains many foreign words—for example, "sirocco," "rodeo," "milieu," etc. A comparable development has taken place in France, where people speak of "le weekend," "le sporting," and "le striptease."

Factors Affecting the Acceptance of Innovations

Acceptance or rejection of any innovation will vary from society to society, as well as from person to person within a given society. The more open a society is, and the more alternative ways it has of explaining phenomena—the more likelihood there is that it will assimilate new elements of culture. The acceptance of a new element, whether it is introduced by invention, dis-

3. L. Spier, *The Sun Dance of the Plains Indians*, Anthropological Papers, vol. 16, part 7 (New York: American Museum of Natural History, 1921).

4. Ralph Linton, "One Hundred Percent American," *The American Mercury* 40 (1937): 429.

464

covery, or diffusion, is always uneven. It depends on the perceptions, predispositions, and values of the recipient peoples. It is not really "a culture" that accepts or rejects changes, but rather the individual people who share the common culture. So in speaking of culture change we are really speaking about a series of episodes and effects stemming from the experiences of individual human beings. Only later do the results become norms that affect the entire society and its culture.

In order to further examine the processes of change, we will use a series of principles regarding change formulated by Leonard W. Doob, a psychologist and specialist on African cultures.[5] These principles have been shown to hold true and to be widely applicable to groups of people as diverse as Spaniards, Africans, or natives of highland New Guinea. Each principle is illustrated with ethnographic data from the El Pinar ethnography that opens the chapter.

1. *People are most likely to accept a change when it does not conflict with their traditional values, as long as these traditional values are proving satisfactory to them.* In El Pinar, traditional values held by the people disposed individuals to favor the use of machinery as a substitute for human and animal labor. They were also

---

5. Leonard W. Doob, "Psychological Aspects of Planned Development Change," in *Perspectives in Developmental Change*, ed. Art Gallaher, Jr. (Lexington: University of Kentucky Press, 1968), pp. 36–70. An extended discussion of innovation may be found in H. Barnett, *Innovation: The Basis of Cultural Change* (New York: McGraw-Hill, 1953).

disposed to favor employing efficient means of agriculture to make a profit. When tractors, gang plows, and new crops such as sugar beets and tobacco were introduced into the area by agents of the Spanish government's Ministry of Agriculture, adoption of the innovations was rapid. It was hindered only by the fact that many people did not have the capital to invest in new machinery or in the drying sheds necessary for the tobacco.

The goals of the people of El Pinar can be summed up quickly: in economic matters, they wanted more income with less work; in social life, however, they wanted tranquility. Unfortunately, it was difficult to attain both at the same time. Adoption of new seeds and techniques did indeed bring increased economic prosperity and less work. Tranquility, however, was another matter.

The people of El Pinar saw the world (to use a metaphor) as a deep pool filled with *lios* (troubles), covered with a thin sheet comprising manners and customs. The ice—the social veneer of manners and customs—could be broken at any time by any improper behavior that violated the village norms.

To stimulate modern agrarian technology, the Spanish government encouraged formation of farm cooperatives. Through these, men could pool land and money to buy machinery. They would then work together and split the profits in proportion to the amount they had invested. But in El Pinar there were no norms to cover long-term, contractual associations with nonkin. The men especially liked to think of themselves as individualists, and everyone assumed that fellow villagers felt the same. Although friendships existed among the villagers, no one wanted to trust his property and his livelihood to an association of individuals who were likely to do as they pleased. The people of El Pinar were well aware that there had been a number of cooperatives formed in the neighboring villages, but many of these were racked by internal dissension.

In sum, to join a cooperative meant to the villagers the possible loss of individualism as well as a figurative foot through the thin ice that would land them in trouble. Thus, while sharing a common goal—more money and less work—they could not bring themselves to accept the best means to that goal, cooperation. What is described here is the *emic* point of view: that is, what the villagers said of themselves. In this case, it corresponded with the anthropologist's own (*etic*) perceptions of them. Ironically, the villagers realized that cooperation was best but just could not risk getting into trouble they were sure existed in cooperatives.

2. *People are likely to accept a change when it appears to have advantages that can be intelligibly demonstrated in the present or that are anticipated in the future.* Proof that an innovation will be of value is crucial when people are being introduced to a change. The inhabitants of El Pinar, with access to the communications media, knew that tractors and other machinery had demonstrated worthwhile advantages. Tractor-drawn grain harvesters in use elsewhere in the region had cut the wheat harvest time from ten days to three days per farmer. In addition, the harvesters required much less labor than the traditional method using the scythe. The Agricultural Extension Service farmed a number of demonstration plots where farmers could go and observe and determine for themselves the advantages of new

On a street in Dakar, Senegal, human beings and artifacts seem violently dissonant.

crops and planting techniques.

3. *During the process of change, people are likely to experience discrepancies among their beliefs and values, which may result in additional change.* Before the agricultural improvement came to El Pinar, the economic system of El Pinar operated almost on a subsistence level. Farmers used what they grew and had little surplus to sell for cash. As a result, they had developed a belief in the necessity of enduring hardships. Deferred gratification became the rule. For example, instead of adding a new room to the house, a family would

crowd into existing rooms. There was a respect for book learning, although most farmers read little, and economic necessity required that young sons be taken out of school and put to work on the farm as soon as they were old enough to be helpful.

With increasing prosperity due to the changes occurring in agriculture, the people of El Pinar began to have doubts about the need for delayed gratification. Purchases on the installment plan, at first reserved for farm implements, began to include other items, notably television sets and home furnishings. Most houses improved their heating systems instead of putting up with the traditional one, which had never been adequate for the cold winters.

Children were encouraged to stay in school long enough to complete elementary school. Secondary-school enrollment also increased. With mechanization, more leisure time was available and people began to think of taking vacations. Farmers who would normally have been in their fields had more spare time to sit in the cafes with other townspeople. Recreation and leisure became important for the first time. Past beliefs about spare-time activities and leisure began to give way to new ideas.

4. *While changing, people are likely to be discontented.* Dissatisfaction may be exhibited throughout the course of an adopted change. Farmers who used new types of wheat seeds were apprehensive and worried at first about possible crop failures. The men who worked at extracting resin from the pine tree, the *resineros*, had been shown a more efficient technique that involved placing dilute sulphuric acid in the cut in the tree from which the resinous sap flowed. The *resineros* feared that the acid would ruin the trees, which were the basis of their livelihood. Their wives were unhappy because the acid solution damaged the men's clothing, so more

Not only the television set itself, but all the images it brings into people's lives may have far-reaching consequences. This is just as true in suburban Boston as in downtown Dakar.

money was spent on work shirts and trousers. Perhaps the greatest discontent was due to an ever-present fear that the innovation might fail and wreak economic havoc among an already poor people.

The four principles stated thus far concentrate upon the innovation itself. The next four principles concentrate more directly on human factors. In studying culture changes, the anthropologist must take into account not only the nature of the technological or social innovation but also the nature of the culture into which change is introduced.

5. *People are likely to accept an innovation when it is proposed or introduced by people whom they consider important and competent.* In El Pinar, the majority of major changes were brought about by government agencies. The agents of change —people like those in the Agricultural Extension Service—were men and women whose competence was made clear to the villagers as they watched these agents demonstrate new techniques. When these innovations were spoken of highly by local people whose opinion was valued, the chances increased that others would adopt them. In this particular case, Aceves himself became a participant in the process of change. The new acid technique had been pioneered in the United States, in part at the University of Georgia, with which Aceves was affiliated at the time of the study. He requested informational brochures from the University of Georgia and showed them to local *resineros*, explaining how the technique had benefited people in the United States. This action helped to persuade a number of the *resineros* to look at the innovation with an open mind.

6. *People are likely to accept a change when it involves components with which they are already familiar or which they feel confident they can learn.* The new acid resination technique required that the *resineros* learn relatively few new skills. They felt they could learn these easily in special night courses set up by the government. Since most farmers were capable mechanics already, the new machines did not require learning a whole new set of techniques.

7. *While in the process of change, people are likely to unite with, or seek support from, groups or other persons whose point of view about change is similar to and supportive of their own.* In El Pinar there were no organized groups proposing or rejecting changes. Indeed, the family is the basic unit of social life there, and few forms of organization exist beyond the family. Seeking support, then, was restricted to family members and friends. Farmers sought the advice of other farmers, *resineros* of other *resineros*, and some sought support from the Agricultural Extension agents. The key phenomenon here is that nobody wished to be alone in trying out or accepting an innovation. A person who did so and failed would be seen as a fool by the community. But if many people together tried and failed, the individuals would not bear such a heavy social burden for their failure.

8. *Beyond their immediate effects, planned or unplanned changes are likely to have additional consequences which may be unforeseeable.* One of the unforeseen consequences of the programs for change in the El Pinar area was emigration to the cities. Programs had been designed to improve rural life and to make farming more profitable and more attractive. Spain's cities are already overcrowded and there is a serious unemployment problem everywhere in the country. However, benefi-

Culture Change

Tourism, commerce, and programs such as those of the Peace Corps cause profound cultural change, not only in the hosts, of course, but also in the visitor from a fully industrialized society.

ciaries of the rural development programs often learned new skills (motor mechanics, plumbing, electrical installation and repair, bricklaying) through participation in adult education classes held in the villages. They then took themselves and their new skills to the city where they hoped to find higher-paying jobs. Machinery did make farming easier, but it also left the farmer with children who were now not needed to work on the farm. Large families were no longer required. Children became eco-

nomic liabilities rather than assets. Indeed, today there is a marked decline in the birth rate in El Pinar and the neighboring villages that corresponds almost exactly— and causally—with the introduction of technological changes.

While the lower birth rate takes the pressure off overcrowded cities and re-solves the problem of "excess" children in farm families, the reduction has been ac-complished largely by means of contracep-tion techniques and devices forbidden by the Roman Catholic Church. Since everybody in El Pinar is Catholic, this decline in the birth rate means that some drastic new ideas about church teachings are beginning to filter into people's minds. This is definitely *not* what the government that sponsored the changes had intended.

Apathy and Failure to Accept Innovation

There are occasions when innovations, especially planned innovations, are not accepted by a people. Some of the most frequently cited "reasons" for a people's resistance to adopt an innovation or failure to accept it on a permanent basis are: poverty, distrust of an authority known to exploit people, ignorance, illiteracy, social-class antagonisms, religious fatalism (in certain societies), and apathy. We would hesitate to call any of these "reasons" for failure. They may be important factors and influences, but they are rarely determinative. These are usually given as reasons for the failure of an innovation when in fact the real reason might be the ineptness of the agent calling for change.

Apathy is a particularly interesting phenomenon in the change process. It cannot legitimately be given as a reason for the nonacceptance of an innovation. If a person is not at all interested in an innovation it may well be that he or she prefers some other mode of action, *probably the traditional one.* Thus, so-called apathy is a culturally patterned response to a situation, motivated by the prevailing values and beliefs of the respondent's social group. In other words, what appears to be apathy may actually be a logical activity in terms of the person's value system. The stare of the South American Indian, the muttered *in'sha'Allah* of the Arab peasant, do not represent apathy. They *do* represent a choice of response, and any expression of choice is in itself activity. When it comes to a matter of survival, no one is apathetic, and those who apply the term are showing an ethnocentric bias. They are arguing that failure to act as *they* would is somehow an admission that a person does not care about his or her fate.

Alternatives

Change is essentially a process of ever-expanding modes of response to situations. Where there is no choice, there rarely is change. Choice, however, need not be from among only pleasant alternatives. Nor does change imply that life will necessarily be "better" or "worse." It simply means that a situation will be "different." In the history of the United States the American Indians were faced with an unjust and harsh choice: extermination or incarceration on a reservation. Many died, and for those who lived, reservation existence was a radical change. A current example is that of Jews living in the Soviet Union. They have a choice either to live in a repressive society with the threat of imprisonment or death if they are outspoken, or to go into exile and settle elsewhere.

The presence of many alternative modes of action may in itself be a source of problems for the people undergoing changes. Arden King, in a paper provocatively entitled "The Anthropology of Evil,"[6] argues that the opening up of new alternative ways of perceiving the world may be a source of trouble or "evil." He maintains that the point at which knowledge has

---

6. Arden King, "The Anthropology of Evil" (Paper presented at the Third Annual Meeting of the Southern Anthropological Society, Gainesville, Fla., March 1, 1968).

Emma Kickapoo, a native American.

uals involved in the change. Cross-cutting socioeconomic lines, Holmes found a strong link between life changes—such as death of a spouse, change in financial state, outstanding personal achievements, and even vacations—and such minor medical problems as headaches, stomachaches, backaches, and colds.[7] Though the study was done in the United States, Dr. Holmes notes that similar supporting data have been found in Denmark, Sweden, Japan, and San Salvador. Change, especially rapid social change, has its effects on health. Literally, change can be a pain in the neck.

Evolution and Revolution

Most social change is evolutionary in nature. The changes came about relatively slowly, and people are able to make a series of adaptations to each successive change without major disruptions in their way of life. In societies like the United States and Canada, where rapid social change is the normal way of life, people are generally tolerant or welcoming of innovations. Indeed, it would probably seem strange to an average American or Canadian if life remained the same for long periods of time. Revolutionary change is much more dramatic. By revolutionary change we mean abrupt major shifts in lifestyle brought about by political actions, including warfare. Revolutions come about when power relationships between the controlling groups in a society and the masses being controlled are badly out of balance. When the group without power realizes that

increased sufficiently to force the people into a conscious examination of their basic values and beliefs is also the point at which evil will appear.

The whole notion of evil is wrapped up in metaphysical speculations and is hard to put into everyday terms. Change, however, does produce some visible signs of trauma. A Seattle psychiatrist, Dr. Thomas H. Holmes, has produced evidence that indicates that change, pleasant or unpleasant, has an effect on the health of individ-

7. T. S. Holmes and T. H. Holmes, "Short-term Intrusions into the Life-Style Routine," *Journal of Psychosomatic Research* 14 (1970): 121–132.

it has alternatives, that there are ways to bring about a change in its status, revolution becomes possible.[8]

The round of legislative and civil disorders affecting black Americans since the first sit-ins in 1960 are part of what can validly be called a "Black Revolution." This revolution encompasses activities that range from legal suits by the National Association for the Advancement of Colored People (NAACP) to the terrorism employed by some Black Panther groups. Even the shift in language which substitutes "black" for "Negro" is part of this set of revolutionary changes. Any revolution must have visible symbols to help unite its adherents and, in some instances, to threaten its opponents. Culture heroes such as Malcolm X and Martin Luther King emerge. In life these men were charismatic leaders; in death they serve as symbols of martyrdom to a cause.

Although revolutions involving political action are often fought in the name of an oppressed mass of people, they are generally led by people of higher social status. In urban situations, the leaders are almost always from the middle and upper-middle classes. Furthermore, revolutions are more likely to take place in urban areas than in rural ones.

An example of a person of higher status leading a revolution is that of Miguel Hidalgo, a Mexican priest who led a peasant army against the Spanish colonial government of Mexico in 1810. The revolt was initiated by the *criollos*, a group of people born in Mexico but descended from Spaniards.

The Spanish kings had always passed them over when filling positions of authority, preferring, instead, to name men born in Spain. By themselves, the *criollos* could never have formed an adequate fighting force. The peasantry, mostly Indians, also had grievances against the colonial authorities, but lacked the knowledge needed for effective political action to remedy their situation of landlessness and poverty.

Hidalgo, a well-educated man, was highly regarded by the peasants for his dedication in helping them out of their misery. He was equally respected by the *criollos* for his learning and for his ideas on political reform. The *criollo* revolutionaries placed Hidalgo at the head of their ragtag army, since he was the only one who could explain to the peasants the political ideology underlying the revolution. Hidalgo was able for a time to bridge the gap between the *criollos* and the peasants, but in the end, the superior military power of the Spaniards, combined with the *criollos'* distrust of the peasants, led to the ultimate failure of the revolt.[9]

Throughout the world, peasants tend to be ill treated and abused, yet they rarely revolt. (Sporadic strikes such as have taken place in rural areas are not really revolutions but small-scale and localized gestures of protest.) Eric Wolf has examined the phenomenon of peasants' resistance to revolutionary actions. Noting that peasants do perceive injustices and do wish to obtain justice (if not revenge), Wolf claims that they have difficulty in passing from passive recognition of wrongs to political participation as a way of re-

8. W. Laquer, "Revolution," in *International Encyclopedia of the Social Sciences*, vol. 13 (New York: Free Press, 1938), pp. 505–510.

9. Parkes, Henry B., *A History of Mexico*, rev. ed. (Boston: Houghton Mifflin, 1960).

Road-building in Peru—community development as a community activity.

dressing those wrongs. He cites five reasons for this:

> First, *a peasant's work is more often done alone, on his land, than in conjunction with his fellows. Moreover, all peasants are to some extent competitors for available resources within the community as for sources of credit from without.* Second, *the tyranny of work weighs heavily upon peasants: their life is geared to an annual routine and to planning the year to come. Momentary alterations of routine threaten their ability to take up the routine later.* Third, *control of the land enables him (the peasant), more often than not, to retreat into subsistence production should reverse conditions affect his market crop.* Fourth, *ties of extended kinship and mutual aid within the community may cushion the shocks of dislocation.* Fifth, *peasant interests—especially among poor peasants—often cross-cut class alignments. Rich and poor peasants may be kinfolk, or a peasant may be at one and the same time owner, renter, sharecropper, laborer for his neighbors, and seasonal hand on a nearby plantation.*[10]

10. Eric Wolf, "Peasant Problems and Revolutionary Warfare" (Paper presented at the Third Annual SSC Meeting, New York, September 10, 1967).

Chapter Eighteen

Lenin in Russia and Mao Tse-tung in China discovered that peasants in their countries were both culturally and politically conservative. In both countries peasants and urban workers were believed by the ideological leaders of revolutions to have common interests. Unhappily for these ideologies, the peasants were less tractable than the city dwellers. This phenomenon has turned up time and again in places as diverse as Mexico, Vietnam, France, and Spain. Even in the United States, where historical factors are such that a true peasantry never developed, the Black Revolution and the Chicano Revolution did not get started until both groups were urbanized. The most reticent followers of these revolutions have been the rural blacks and Mexican-Americans. Wolf makes a final point that is worth noting: ". . . past exclusion of the peasant from participation in decision-making beyond the bamboo hedge of his village deprives him all too often of the knowledge needed to articulate his interests with appropriate forms of action." [11]

Revolutionary change, then, while it may affect large numbers of people from the lower social strata, is based largely upon the ideologies of a middle and/or intellectual class and is almost always led by members of these groups. More data are urgently needed to increase our understanding of the dynamics of revolution. [12]

11. Wolf, "Peasant Problems and Revolutionary Warfare."

12. Students who wish to pursue the study of revolution would do well to read Eric Wolf, *Peasant Wars of the Twentieth Century* (New York: Harper and Row, 1969).

The Costs of Change

Anthropologists, in spite of their accumulated knowledge about change, are not oracles and can claim no unique insights into the future of humanity. Yet few anthropologists, regardless of their subdisciplinary specialty, fail to look toward the future and to ponder the ultimate fate of the human race. Evolution of the species and of culture is a continuing process, the end of which is not yet in sight—although the means for ending the process seem to be within the grasp of humankind. A level of weapons technology has been achieved that ensures the demise of *Homo sapiens* and of the various cultures of the human species if those weapons are used to their fullest capabilities. Yet humankind continues to look to the future, believing that humanity will endure. Perhaps this optimism has its roots in culture.

Technology and Change

In 1929 the sociologist William Fielding Ogburn coined the term *culture lag* to describe the condition wherein human social institutions and behavior patterns are not well equipped to cope with changes in human technology. In other words, behavior and ideology within a culture sometimes cannot keep up with the technological or material advances of that culture.

The sheer speed with which technological innovations seem to come can create feelings of anxiety and inadequacy in the most "progressive" of peoples. When the crossbow was invented during medieval days, many thoughtful people saw in it the seeds of destruction of the world as they knew it. Today atomic weapons exist and strategists project that an atomic war would be "successful" if "only" 60 percent of the "winning" nation's population were annihilated! Behind progress lies the ever-present, gnawing fear of what has been developed. Sometimes there is doubt that the new way is any better than the old.

Human "progress" seems enormous when measured in terms of sheer mechanical efficiency, elaborate means of energy production, or other technological criteria. Yet, in terms of process, there is really no essential qualitative difference between a two-million-year-old hand-ax and the latest IBM computer. In human beings the development of a large cerebrum with elaborate associational areas capable of generating and mixing symbols made possible the production of the hand-ax as well as the computer. Both items are implements in the tool kit of humankind that have made possible both physical and cultural adaptation. Often the quantitative difference between two such items is emphasized: it is worth noting the qualitative similarity of the mental activities that created them.

The effects of technology upon the human spirit (if we may be permitted to use an unanthropological term) are a source of concern and a cause for debate among many people today. Some would say that it is amazing that the world has survived, given the capacity for destruction that exists within the cultures of its progressive

After the traditional market day, a Peruvian woman is ready to return to her home. The automobile has shortened her trip and lightened her load.

societies. With an increasingly man-made environment, people are becoming aware of a growing separation from their natural environment and of an increasing alienation from each other. As technological innovativeness outstrips the sociocultural mechanisms necessary for adapting to innovations, the criteria for judging these new items of culture are not available. For example, of what use is medical technology that allows the prolongation of life artificially while the world is already overpopulated? What justifies extending the quantity of life without improving its quality?

In his 1954 book, *The Human Use of Human Beings: Cybernetics and Society,* Norbert Weiner pointed out that by its inventiveness, humankind is mortgaging itself to technology, a mortgage that must be paid off in three currencies: interdependence, information, and time. Let us briefly examine each of these.

INTERDEPENDENCE. Members of societies with cultures based on a complex technology are dependent to a high degree upon the goods, services, and even the protection of others. Unlike small-scale societies in which most people have at least a basic knowledge of their technology, few members of complex industrial societies have more than a nodding acquaintance with the technology upon which they depend. Most individuals cannot build a betatron, a microwave oven, or a transistor radio. Indeed, people in the United States and Canada joke about the skill required to put together children's toys that are packaged unassembled with a set of instructions which might read "insert tab A into slot B using bolt X and nut Y as explained in diagram Z." We are all dependent upon other people who have special

This young woman of Upper Volta seems well acculturated to the best of both worlds.

skills to build and repair these devices.

Not only are we dependent on one another, but we are increasingly dependent on one another's products, a large percentage of which nowadays is machinery. Machines are being built to operate themselves, to function automatically without direct human supervision. This automation has been feared by many people; the growing dependence on machines that can run by themselves may put them out of work altogether. For the most part this fear has proved unfounded. Although each new machine puts some people out of work, it also creates new jobs. The computer, for example, has spawned an entire new industry.

Culture Change

Sometimes a trend toward automation can be partially reversed. When the automobile replaced the horse, blacksmiths became a disappearing breed. Many became auto mechanics. Now, with the widespread use of automobiles, one would think that there would be little call for shoeing horses. But there has been a marked increase in the use of horses for recreation. No longer a beast of burden, the horse has become a beast of play. Horseowners today face a shortage of blacksmiths, and a number of universities now offer smithery as a major field of study.

An effect of mechanization more subtle yet more serious than unemployment is emerging. Unlike the work of the blacksmith, many jobs today cannot be understood by the people performing them. A worker on an assembly line places bolt number 551 into nut number 551 without seeing how this relates to the whole operation. If the worker does this work long enough, he or she may, in a sense, *become* bolt 551. As a result, there is evidence that many people find the work they do emotionally unsatisfying, unchallenging, and unimportant.

In addition, the mechanistic perspective is spilling over from the factory into other areas of life. In large, overcrowded hospitals phrases such as "we have an appendix in OR," "there's a previa in OB," or "get that hot gallbladder to surgery" are common. The child with appendicitis who suffers and cries becomes "an appendix in OR."

All social life to some degree overlaps with the products of technology. In complex technological societies such as those of the United States and Canada, the degree of overlapping and the degree of danger that attends such overlapping is much higher since people are so dependent upon machinery and upon an artificial environment for sheer survival.

INFORMATION. Interdependence requires information. The accumulated material culture must have a foundation of information or, to use a related term, knowledge. Beyond the mere accumulation of existing knowledge is the fact that new information or knowledge is constantly being produced. Some estimates, based on a number of publications in various scientific fields, claim that by the time a person born in 1974 reaches the age of fifteen, 97 percent of the raw knowledge in existence will have come into being during his or her lifetime. But raw information is relatively useless unless it is interpreted or "filtered" into terms the public can understand. Of critical importance to a society will be the interpreter of such information and that interpreter's use of the knowledge at his or her command. The control of societies may well rest in the hands of those who control the flow of information and the interpretation of that information to the masses. The control of information may lead to a form of mind control as an inevitable consequence of an expanding technocratic culture that demands highly specialized skills, a need for quick operational decisions, and a minimum of social frictions. Control of information also means a *de facto* control over most innovations, with the controllers in the position of being able to stifle change or to bring about only those changes they see as desirable.

TIME. The third currency in which humanity will pay its cultural debts, according to Weiner's thesis, is time itself—always in short supply. As we review the history of humankind, progressing from a subsistence level to a bartering system, to money, and finally to credit, we are drawn to speculate about the future. Increasingly time and money are being equated. Imagine a day when technological developments have made communication and transportation instantaneous. Under these conditions, individual worth or "buying power" could be determined by the length of time required to render services or make goods. As more things become available to more and more people with less individual effort, the quest for acquisition will turn into a quest for time to enjoy these new material acquisitions. In the words of the saying, "time is money." If this attitude becomes dominant, as current trends indicate, our whole economic system in both its formal and substantive aspects will undergo wrenching changes in content and style. Even today individuals are faced with decisions about whether to spend money to save time, or to perform a task to save money.

The relationships between interdependence, information, and time need more study, for it is upon their interrelationship that the nature of any culture will largely be determined. A question exists regarding the order of priorities—and the method for determining these priorities—for change. As the villagers of El Pinar discovered to their chagrin, some changes may entail such high social costs that they become threats to the quality of life envisioned as desirable. Such changes may never take place. In programs of planned change, including technological and behavioral change, the agents promoting change (as well as the change itself) should be carefully evaluated by those whose lives would be affected.

Adapting to Change

A further ramification of technology concerns the concept of adaptation. Though small-scale societies still exist in the world today and adaptation to physical surroundings is still taking place in all cultures, societies are increasingly confronted with the necessity of adapting to power as well. A few societies exist—among them the United States and the Soviet Union—who possess the size, wealth, and technology that enable them to exercise control, authority, and influence over smaller, less well developed societies. In order to promote their own identity, well-being, and survival, some of these smaller societies are "adapting" to the larger societies.

The Arab countries, for example, are using their natural resources to deal with both the United States and the Soviet Union and cannot really be said to be dominated by either. Cuba, on the other hand, has adapted by aligning itself ideologically with the Soviet Union, although Cuba and the United States are beginning to adapt to each other today. Israel, among others, looks to the United States for support. A number of African, Asian, and Latin American countries (among them Indonesia, Turkey, and Ecuador) have informally aligned themselves with each other to form a bloc called the Third World. In the United Nations, for example, they vote as a unit in order to maintain their self-determination without having to align themselves with either the United States or Russia.

To be sure, there are small societies in remote areas of the world that remain untouched by the activities of large societies. But the isolation of some of these societies is already crumbling. In Brazil, for example, where a road-building campaign was begun in the late 1960s to facilitate tapping the country's natural resources, Indian tribes are being discovered that had never before had contact with non-Indians. Among these tribes are the Kreen-Akarores and their enemies the Txukahameis.[13] The Brazilian government has set up a foundation to handle the task of introducing these simple societies to the modern world and shielding them from inevitable dangers. It has been found, for instance, that these tribes have little immunity to certain diseases. A national park is being used as a reservation for these people to keep them relatively safe. The Indians are now confronted with a situation wherein they must adapt to other tribes, some of whom were enemies, and to the larger, modern, baffling society as well. Clearly, then, a particular group's isolation is no longer guaranteed or inevitable.

The powerful societies themselves must adapt to each other or face the possibility of a major conflict possibly leading to nuclear war. Although it is true that some societies have always been more powerful than others, such power had not been global until the development of nuclear weapons in the mid-twentieth century. How societies adapt to each other on this level could determine whether humanity will survive or perish.

13. W. Jesco von Puttkamer, "Brazil's Kreen-Akarores: Requiem for a Tribe," and "Brazil's Txukahameis: Good-bye to the Stone Age," *National Geographic* 47 (1975) : 254–269, 270–283.

Summary

1. Choice is a precondition for change. Change comes about when alternatives, new or old, exist within a society.

2. Invention is the process whereby something that has not existed before is brought into being. Discovery is the process whereby something is found that has been in existence but unknown.

3. The process by which a group learns to adapt to an innovation and assimilate it into the existing culture is known as acculturation.

4. The most common way that a culture acquires an innovation is through diffusion.

5. The acceptance or rejection of an innovation will vary from society to society and from person to person within a society.

6. Leonard Doob's widely applicable principles regarding change are as follows: (1) People are likely to accept change when it does not conflict with traditional values that are proving satisfactory. (2) People are likely to accept change when it appears to have advantages that can be intellectually demonstrated in the present or that are anticipated in the future. (3) During the process of change, people are likely to experience discrepancies among their beliefs and values, which may result in additional change. (4) While changing, people are likely to be discontented. (5) People are likely to accept innovation when it is proposed by people whom they consider important and competent. (6) People are likely to accept change when it involves components with which they are already familiar or that they feel confident they can learn. (7) While in the process of change, people are likely to unite with others whose points of view about change supports their own. (8) Planned or unplanned changes are likely to have unforeseeable consequences beyond the immediate results.

7. The aid of anthropologists has often been sought by the agencies of societies seeking to

Chapter Eighteen

institute social or technological changes.

8. Technological change, though materially beneficial, also has its social costs. These costs must be paid off in three currencies: interdependence, information, and time.

Review Questions

1. What are some possible causes of culture change? Give an example of a change in your society, with your thoughts about the reasons for the change.

2. What is the most common way in which cultures acquire new elements? Can you think of a change that was adopted in this way?

3. According to Doob, when are people most likely to accept change?

4. When, or why, would people resist change? From your experience, can you give an example of people who refused to accept a change?

5. Can we predict the consequences of planned or unplanned changes? Elaborate your answer, giving an example from contemporary life.

Suggested Readings

Aceves, Joseph B. *Social Change in a Spanish Village*. Cambridge, Mass.: Schenkman Publishing, 1971.

The source of this chapter's capsule ethnography, the book describes and analyzes the types of changes introduced into a Spanish village through a series of government-sponsored development plans.

Bodley, John J. *Victims of Progress*. Menlo Park, Calif.: Cummings Publishing, 1975.

This book looks at the impact of change on simple societies and poses a series of questions about what social costs a people should be made to pay when changes are brought into their traditional culture.

Eisenstadt, S. N. *Modernization: Protest and Change*. Englewood Cliffs, N.J.: Prentice-Hall, 1966.

A good overall view of change in complex societies and comments of a theoretical nature on the processes of modernization.

Lerner, Daniel. *The Passing of Traditional Society: Modernizing the Middle East*. New York: Free Press, 1958.

An older book, but a worthwhile one that examines the effects of the diffusion of Western culture to the traditional culture of the Middle East.

Niehoff, Arthur H., ed. *A Casebook of Social Change*. Chicago: Aldine, 1966.

This collection of case studies of social change in a variety of countries throughout the world is an excellent source of comparative data on the way changes come about.

Chapter
19

Medical & Urban Anthropology

DEATH IN TEPOZTLÁN, MEXICO

Death apparently inspires no undue fear or preoccupation. Old people freely speak of death, using the expressions, "when I am dead," or "when I am underground." Perhaps because from childhood Tepoztecans have not been protected from the facts of death, they see it as a natural occurrence. Display of grief is restrained at a death, although it varies according to the age and status of the deceased. Suicide is uncommon, and in no case has anyone killed himself because of the death of a loved one. When a Tepoztecan dies soon after the death of someone close to him, however, it is often said that he died of *sentimiento* or grief. The death of an old person or of an infant causes relatively little emotional disturbance.

Tepoztecans are concerned with the release of the soul from the body at death and with its journey to heaven. They say that those who have led wicked lives have difficulty giving up their souls and take a long time to die. They say also that often children "cannot die until they receive a benediction from their parents or godparents" and that a father or a mother "cannot die if their children cry too much." In such cases the children are taken away to hasten the death. When death comes, the soul leaves the body and may be seen

Source: Oscar Lewis, *Tepoztlán: Village in Mexico* (New York: Holt, Rinehart and Winston, 1960), pp. 84–85. Copyright © 1960 by Holt, Rinehart and Winston. Reprinted by permission of Holt, Rinehart and Winston.

as a white, foamlike figure which resembles the deceased and which walks without touching the ground but disappears after leaving the house.

When a person is at the point of death, he is taken from his bed and placed on a *petate* [palm mat] on the floor. With death the body is dressed with clean clothes, covered with a sheet, and placed on a table. A newspaper is spread on the *petate* and a cross of sand and lime is fashioned on the paper. Flowers are placed above the cross, and a candle, kept burning day and night for nine days, is placed at the head of the *petate.* If the deceased is a man, his sombrero and huaraches [sandals] are laid next to the candle; if a woman, her *rebozo* [shawl]. All the clothes of the dead person are washed and ironed and also laid on the *petate.* A *rezandero* [professional prayer]is hired by the bereaved family to come to the house to pray twice a day for nine days. The women of the house are required to be present on these occasions and to kneel in prayer. A wake is held day and night, and coffee, alcohol, bread, and cigarettes are provided for those who come to keep vigil. Close relatives may help with the expenses. At the death of a young godchild, most godparents fulfill their obligations to provide a coffin, burial clothing, and perhaps music.

The next day a few men go to the cemetery to dig the grave. The deceased is placed in a coffin and, accompanied by the mourners, is carried to the cemetery. If the deceased is a prominent person or a member of the *Acción Católica,* the funeral procession may enter the church for a benediction before proceeding to the burial place. The church bells will be rung if a special fee is paid. On the ninth day or *novena* the ceremony of the raising of the cross of lime and sand takes place at a night wake similar to the one held on the day of the death. This time, however, an offering of tamales, *mole verde,* oranges, chocolate, and bread is left for twelve hours on the altar in the home in order to provide the deceased with food for each month of the year.

For the raising of the cross, a boy and girl who are not relatives are selected to act as *padrinos* [assistants]. Accompanied by the *rezandero* and carrying flowers, the two children walk toward the *petate* which holds the cross of lime and sand. Prayers are first recited and the children are then given new brooms with which they sweep the sand and lime onto a tray that is later carried to the grave. The clothes of the deceased are also raised. As each article is picked up, the *padrinos* recite a prayer. The ceremony closes with the singing of hymns in honor of the dead. A year after the death another wake may be held, a special Mass arranged and the grave revisited.

A child's funeral is somewhat different. Because the child's soul goes directly to heaven, it is supposed to be a joyous occasion, and gay music is played. The child is dressed like San Jose if a boy, like the Virgin of Guadalupe if a girl. A crown of paper flowers is placed on the head, the face covered with a veil, and the feet fitted into socks and sandals lined with gold paper. When the body is laid out, the hands and feet are tied together with ribbons, which are untied at the grave. A small painted gourd, placed beside the body, is believed to provide the soul with water during its journey to heaven. The litter is carried by children of the same sex as the deceased and, as the body is taken out of the house, the barrio chapel bell is rung.[1]

● ● ● ● ● ● ● ●

In the capsule ethnography, anthropologist Oscar Lewis shows how death is dealt with in the small Mexican village of Tepoztlán. He describes how the villagers have adapted to this biological universal by devising certain rituals. The ways different cultures treat sickness and death is the subject of the growing anthropological subdiscipline of *medical anthropology*.

Lewis has also studied what happens to inhabitants of small villages, such as Tepoztlán, who move to an urban environment, such as Mexico City. Indeed, as more and more of the world's peoples migrate from rural and tribal environments to cities, the city is becoming increasingly important as a phenomenon that must be adapted to. The study of adaptation to modern cities is the subject of *urban anthropology*.

Medical and urban anthropology have become two important concerns of applied anthropologists—anthropologists involved in trying to solve some of the problems that have been identified by their more theoretical colleagues. In this chapter we will look at some aspects of both medical and urban anthropology.

Medical Anthropology

In a very real sense, health and disease (as well as the death rate) are measures of the effectiveness with which human groups combine biological and cultural resources in order to adapt to their environments. The fact that health and disease are related to cultural as well as to biological factors underlies the combining of medicine and cultural anthropology.[2] Although

1. Oscar Lewis, *Tepoztlán: Village in Mexico* (New York: Holt, Rinehart and Winston, 1960), pp. 84–85.

2. Richard Lieban, "The Field of Medical Anthropology," in *Handbook of Social and Cultural Anthropology*, ed. John J. Honigmann (Chicago: Rand McNally, 1973), pp. 1031–1071.

modern scientific medicine has a primarily biological orientation, concern with the social, cultural, and psychological aspects of health and hygiene is deeply rooted in medical history and practice. Today, as antibiotics and vaccines are found that can cure or eliminate diseases caused by viruses and bacteria—such as pneumonia, polio, smallpox, and measles—medical attention is turning to disorders caused by economic, social, political, and cultural factors. *Medical anthropology* combines both biological and cultural approaches in its study of the human struggle with disease, sickness, and death. It is also concerned with the medical adaptations devised by all human groups for dealing with these common realities.

Much of the development in the field of medical anthropology has taken place since the end of World War II. Before that time, most ethnologists recorded details about the medical practices of the people they were studying as a matter of course during their observations of everyday behavior. Usually they included lists of medicines, descriptions of personnel involved in the healing process, and subjective impressions about dying and illness. Specialized interest in medicine and health was relatively rare among anthropologists. Since then, however, the situation has changed considerably. A great deal of interest in the medical practices of small-scale societies and their replacement with Western scientific methods was stimulated by the development of the World Health Organization in the 1950s. Many medical anthropologists now specialize in the study of traditional medical systems and the effect of cultural change upon them. More recently, physical anthropologists and archeologists have become interested in *paleopathology*, the study of disease and its effect upon past populations as revealed by human fossils and archeological remains. Thus, such conditions as osteoarthritis, syphilis, rickets, and other diseases involving the skeleton have been studied, as have the blood and tissues of Egyptian mummies dating back to the sixteenth century B.P.

The Adaptive Approach to Sickness and Death

In any culture, illness gives rise to adaptive cultural phenomena which always include knowledge, beliefs, roles, practices, and organized social behavior. In any culture, for example, there are illnesses about which there is certain *knowledge*—diagnoses, remedies, and treatments which have a high degree of success. In addition to specific knowledge, there is a *system of beliefs* about the general nature of illness and curing practices. Every culture includes *roles* for healers, patients, and their families. There are *practices* that are believed to heal illness, and there is in each culture *social behavior* that is considered to be appropriate for coping with illness. For example, in our society we whisper in the sick room. In other societies there may be drumming or dancing in the presence of a sick person. In order to illustrate the cross-cultural approach of medical anthropology, we will use the example of the treatment of sickness in rural Mexico.

Pathogenesis and Sickness in Rural Mexico

Pathogenesis is the study of the origin of diseases. It usually includes a complex system of beliefs about the cause or causes of a particular disease, as well as the signs and symptoms that indicate its presence. In both complex and technologically primitive cultures, disease is recognized by ob-

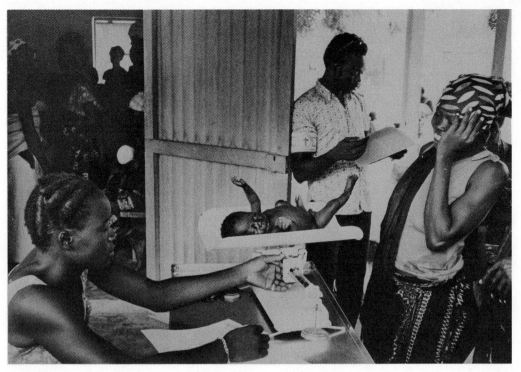

Medical anthropologists study traditional medical systems and the ways cultural change affects them. Here, a mother seems surprised at her baby's weight at an early childhood clinic in Upper Volta, Africa.

servable physical signs such as fever, rash, or swelling, and by behavioral symptoms such as malaise, pain, or irritability. All societies work out adaptations to disease because it interrupts normal activities.

In any culture, people cope with illness, as they do with death, in a manner generally consistent with their knowledge and beliefs about the causes and nature of disease. In most of rural Mexico, for example, disease is regarded as disequilibrium. Health and general well-being are associated with equilibrium, as they are in many societies where order and balance are considered natural. The equilibrium that must be maintained consists of a deli-

cate balance among many sets of opposites. One such set of opposites is that of good and evil, where good is seen as order and evil as disorder in the natural scheme of things. Associated with good in this folk tradition is the principle of warmth, against which is counterposed cold, or the absence of warmth. Thus, an effective treatment for a fever would be to cool the patient until a more natural distribution of cold and heat results. Chills are treated by keeping the patient warm. These two symptoms, incidentally, are treated the same way by modern medical specialists.

This opposition of cold and heat in Mexican pathogenesis is characteristic of most Central American traditional folk medicine. Many peasants in rural areas classify not only diseases but foods, medicinal plants, and modern medicines according to this conceptual scheme. The cold/heat opposition may have existed among the prehistoric peoples of Mesoamerica, and in more recent times, has been clearly influenced by Spanish medicine. This technique of treating illness and maintaining health by prescribing medicines, treatments, or foods with warm or cold qualities first appeared in the writings of Greek physicians, notably Hippocrates in the seventh century B.P. According to Hippocrates, there are four primary and opposite fundamentals: fire (hot), air (cold), water (wet), and earth (dry). These elements and qualities of paired opposition—hot/cold and dry/wet—constitute all matter. The four humors or liquids of the body—blood, phlegm, black bile, and cholera, or yellow bile—each possess these fundamental qualities in different combinations. Blood is hot and wet, yellow bile is hot and dry, phlegm is cold and wet, and black bile is cold and dry. The health or equilibrium of an individual can be maintained only when the balance between hot and cold, wet and dry is not upset. Humoral medicine spread from Greece to Rome and the Arabic world. It was practiced all over Europe during the Middle Ages and the Renaissance. It was introduced into Spain during the Moorish occupation, and was brought to the New World by the Spanish during their conquest of Mexico in the sixteenth century.

Humoral qualities are also associated with various foods. However, a "hot" (in the humoral sense) food is not necessarily a spicy one. And a "wet" food may not have an especially high water content. Instead, various foods and medicinal plants are assigned a humoral quality that refers to their innate character or essence. Different foods, therefore, are used to treat different illnesses. For example, foods or plants with "cold" properties are fed to feverish individuals. Michael H. Logan reports that in Guatemala:

> On several occasions, . . . hospitalized patients running high fevers refused to take the prescribed vitamin and protein supplements given to them daily. . . . Upon questioning, a few confessed that it would be best not to use vitamins at that time because vitamins, like their fever, are katan, or very hot.[3]

The patients reasoned that taking a vitamin that they considered to be "hot" would only worsen their condition by increasing the level of heat in their bodies. They felt that the only proper treatment for their fevers would be food or medicine "cold" in nature, such as cool drinks or penicillin. Vitamins were temporarily rejected by patients as long as their fevers continued, because vitamins are not considered to be appropriate medicine for fever.

In most cases, treatment of illness in rural Mexico consists of the application or prescription of hot or cold foods. Considerations of wet and dry are rarely mentioned. Among the things a successful therapist or physician must know are the thermal properties of foods used to restore the balance of temperature within the

---

3. Michael H. Logan, "Humoral Medicine in Guatemala and Peasant Acceptance of Modern Medicine," *Human Organization* 32, no. 4 (1973): 385–395.

body. For example, hot items include beef, pork, ice, honey, peanuts, garlic, avocado, tobacco, figs, and orange blossoms; whereas such items as rabbit, chicken other than hen, beer, milk, eggs, tomato, salt, and maize are considered cold.

Classifying Disease

Any healing system, primitive or modern, makes use of a *taxonomy*, or a system of classification, of disease. Diseases must be recognized according to their most important features so that the best therapy may be selected. In rural Mexico, two kinds of diseases, natural and supernatural, are recognized. Each requires different treatment, personnel, information, and approach. Natural diseases are easily recognizable to the Mexican rural practitioner. They are caused by a local maldistribution of heat. For example, heat generally attacks the body in the course of ordinary daily life: exposure to open flame or the sun; overconsumption of any of the items listed in the preceding paragraph as hot; or undue amounts of emotional turmoil or excitement. *Susto*, or fright, is a common disorder believed to have a harmful effect because fright is a hot emotion that overconcentrates heat in the chest and head.[4]

Similarly, cold may also cause a thermal imbalance. Cold is transmitted through an *aire* (ay-e-ray) which displaces heat and causes it to be compressed into the remainder of the body. Developing a fever as a result of wet feet, for example, is explained by an upward displacement of the heat by the *aire*.

---

4. Douglas Uzzell, "Susto Revisited: Illness as a Strategic Role," *American Ethnologist* 1 (1974) : 369–378.

Individuals going about their daily tasks are sure to be exposed to alternating heat and cold (walking outside, cooking over open fires, using cold metal implements, eating the wrong foods, etc.). The likelihood that a portion of the population will be ill at any given time is thus explained. The ability to resist illness after such exposure requires a knowledge of what conditions call for special care so that one may take prophylactic (preventive) measures. For example, since heat is an important property of blood, women who are menstruating are subject to a great deal of heat loss. Knowing this, they are careful to avoid drafts, cold objects, getting wet, etc. It is believed that the body will reestablish its own equilibrium if allowed to do so.

A second category of diseases, more dangerous and less easily dealt with, are those that arise from other than natural causes—that is, caused by supernatural forces. Such diseases are believed to be due to the malevolent glance of a witch (*bruja*), particularly one possessing the evil eye (*mal de ojo*), which has the capability of centralizing heat, and thus producing disease. It is worth mention that there is often an element of retributive justice associated with these diseases; perhaps the stricken individual is being punished for some wrongdoing. In such instances, attempts to effect a cure may place the sufferer in greater danger by upsetting the overall balance of good; equilibrium will be reestablished if the patient endures the punishment.

Therapeutic Personnel

In the system of medicine practiced in rural Mexico, certain people have special knowledge of various aspects of disease and appropriate therapies. These are not

In many cultures, individuals who specialize in medicine are thought to have special powers. This healer from the African country of Mali proves his abilities by passing a flame over his body.

dissimilar to specialists in Western medicine. The principal figure is the *curandero* (curer), who is a diagnostician, pharmacist, and practitioner. The *curandero's* first task is the differential diagnosis of the disease, that is, the assignment of the disease to either a natural or supernatural cause. This classification is based upon the ready availability of natural explanations, such as information about what the patient has eaten, whether he or she has gotten wet, etc. If a natural cause cannot be found, the *curandero* will rely upon knowledge of the patient's emotional state, knowledge of who the patient's enemies are, etc. In general, the *curandero* will try to determine if the principle of limited good is in operation. Perhaps the *curandero* will advise the patient that he should wait until the body restores its own equilibrium, and that to attempt a cure would be dangerous.

A few anthropologists have likened this method of curing to situations in Western medicine in which the doctor credits the patient's recovery to spontaneous recovery or unknown causes. In each culture this allows medical practitioners to preserve their credibility and authority, although they are unable to achieve a therapeutic result.

Often the rural Mexican medical system includes an *adivino* (diagnostician) who may be called in to distinguish natural from supernatural diseases. The *adivino* may be a man, but more often this role is filled by a woman. The services of an *adivino* are usually less costly than those of a *curandero,* whose arsenal of techniques includes purgatives, bleeding, dietary manipulations, and sometimes topical surgery. *Curanderos* sometimes manipulate emotional states—anger, fear, shame, etc.—to achieve desired thermal response by methods that can be likened to psychotherapy. *Adivinos,* on the other hand, usually perform spiritualistic rituals and interpretations of dreams or visions that are rather standardized.[5]

Adaptive Features of the Mexican Healing System

In order to maintain its existence over the years, despite the inevitable occasional failures encountered by all systems of medical practice, such a system of curing must be adaptive within the context of the larger society; it must not contradict religious beliefs, the local technology, or the economic realities. Perhaps the best evidence of the adaptability of the rural Mexican system of healing—aside from its comprehensiveness—is its ability to accommodate elements, techniques, and medicines from other medical systems. The following examples illustrate this accommodation.

Throughout rural Mexico, the idea of flame-sterilization was acceptable to the people when introduced, not because rural *curanderos* came to appreciate the value of heat in killing germs—after all, germs are invisible and what is invisible does not exist—but because a metal blade, which has cold properties, loses some cold after exposure to heat. Thus, application of a heated blade would discourage an *aire* more readily than an application of an unheated blade. George Foster[6] cites an example of patients whose fingers were pricked for blood samples. Usually some antimalarial quinine tablets were given to the patients at the same time. However, the assumption of the local people was that the pills were provided to keep an *aire* from entering the hole left by the pin-prick.

Balms and certain drugs were assigned thermal properties on the basis of their effect on the patient, and were added to the list of hot and cold items. Logan lists the following as either hot (H) or cold (C): aspirin (H), Alka-Seltzer (C), vitamins (H), Vicks Vapor-Rub (H), tetracycline (C), antiseptic creams (C), and menthol (H).[7]

The extent to which alien elements can be incorporated into the system offers almost limitless flexibility. The system is adaptive, however, in a more general fashion; because the rural Mexican pathogenesis is not based upon knowledge of the more complex physiological and ana-

5. Irwin Press, "The Urban Curandero," *American Anthropologist* 73 (1971): 742–756.

6. George Foster, *Tzintzuntan: Mexican Peasants in a Changing World* (Boston: Little, Brown, 1967).

7. Logan, "Humoral Medicine in Guatemala and Peasant Acceptance of Modern Medicine."

tomical relationships of Western medicine, it lends itself to explanations which "make sense" in terms of everyday experiences. Furthermore, the equation of good and warmth allows ideas about sickness and health to be integrated into social values and the overall social fabric. For example, the distribution of disease, illness, and health in rural Mexico can be seen by the local people as analogous to the distribution of cold and heat in the human body, offering both an explanation for the state of public health and a societal goal—that is, that a balanced distribution of good and health is desirable for all members of the society.

The Cross-Cultural Perspective

For many anthropologists, a cross-cultural study of disease seems to reveal that with modern scientific medicine the medical profession has succeeded in setting illness apart from the rest of behavior. Since most diagnoses in the modern tradition determine disease on the basis of clusters of biological features—such as blood sugar, enzyme values, and blood chemistries—and patterned changes within those categories, it becomes easy to talk about disease apart from the changes in such nonphysical aspects of a patient's life as emotional states, financial problems, or kinship ties. In other words, the disease is extracted from its social framework. For example, physicians commonly discuss the physiological state, symptoms, and prognosis of terminal cancer patients without taking into account the financial drain on the patients' families, the emotional upheaval and suffering involved, or even the thoughts or feelings of the patients themselves. Physicians in our culture are able to act in this fashion because in modern medical science disease

has assumed the status of an entity separate from that of the patient.

The *curandero* of rural Mexico, on the other hand, takes care on almost all occasions to treat the diseased individual within the context of the family. Each member of the primary group is given special ritual tasks to perform. These may include chanting, manipulating amulets or fetishes, or preparing special foods. The treatment prescribed will, of course, depend upon whether the disease is natural or supernatural, but in either case, the final appeal is to God. When the *curandero* handles a case, the overall response to the disease calls for social restructuring of the primary group in which the patient becomes the important person. The real thrust of the therapy is aimed at a diseased person, not a disease.

When a person becomes ill in our society, he or she is often removed from the family setting and placed in a hospital. This is consistent with our beliefs about infection, proper care, and medical technology. Even though receiving the best of care, a patient may feel isolated from the moral support of loved ones. Such a psychological state may result in a slower recovery or healing, and in many cases, fear, withdrawal, and despondency, and the consequences of such emotions on health.

Some similarities that rural Mexican and modern Western societies such as ours share are:

1. In both small-scale and industrial societies, disease and death call for knowledge, beliefs, special organized behavior, specialized roles, and specific curative practices.

2. Explanations of disease and death are consistent with the overall value system.

3. Disease is perceived as having social consequences.

4. Theories of disease and death are usually "accommodative," i.e., they are adaptive or flexible enough to withstand or accommodate new concepts or knowledge.

Disease in the Social Context

As Robin Horton points out, many traditional societies view disease as being linked to disturbances in the social fabric.[8] Throughout tribal Africa, sick individuals consult diviners for answers about the causes of their troubles. Typically, the diviner tells the afflicted person that a god or other spiritual being is the cause. The remedy usually involves propitiating the spiritual agent by an offering or the performance of a ritual. But the diviner also must explain what caused the spirit to bring misfortune on the sick person. Usually, the diviner will indicate that some event in the world of visible happenings is ultimately responsible. If the diviner tells his patient, for example, that witchcraft is causing the illness, he usually also points out that human jealousies, hatreds, or misdeeds led to the witchcraft. Among the Ndembu of northwestern Zambia, for example, headaches are thought to be caused by *chisaku*, which denotes anything afflicting a person, including illness. *Chisaku* is also equated with a grudge, which a person holds secretly

8. Robin Horton, "African Thought and Western Science," in *Rationality*, ed. Bryan Wilson (New York: Harper and Row, 1970).

Figure 19–1   *A cross-cultural perspective illuminates the alternatives that exist among the approaches that different cultures have toward disease and sickness. Major differences in the adaptive ideologies in rural Mexico and in modern Western scientific societies are summarized below.*

RURAL MEXICAN SOCIETY	MODERN INDUSTRIALIZED SOCIETY
1. Disease seen as a part of social behavior.	1. Disease abstracted from social behavior.
2. Pathogenesis which equates ill health with a state of disequilibrium.	2. Pathogenesis based upon germ theory, trauma, etc.
3. Strong supernatural component in cause and cure.	3. Lack of any concern with the supernatural.
4. Disease seen as a "condition" or "state" of a person.	4. Disease seen as a tangible entity.

against another.[9] Indeed, the Ndembu believe that all ailments are caused by "little grudges."

Alternately, the diviner may find that an ancestor of the patient caused the illness because the patient has breached some code regarding kinship relations. Not surprisingly, the treatment for diseases among many small-scale societies often includes rituals aimed at appeasing ancestral spirits. Thus, it is thought that members of a social group who disturb the strength and unity of the group deserve to be punished. Disease and misfortune are the punishments visited upon the offenders.[10]

The therapies suggested by the African diviner often fail to have any effect on the patient. For example, the Ndembu treatment for hemoptysis (a lung disease characterized by spitting of blood) includes administering to the patient roots from the nest of the red ant, the diaphragm of the great anteater, and the scale of the scaly anteater. Yet, such treatments continue to be practiced. As Victor Turner observes, one reason for the persistence of the therapies is that "they are part of a religious system which itself constitutes an explanation of the universe and guarantees the norms and values on which orderly social arrangements rest."[11] Such therapies can bring relief to many patients for this reason.

Even in those instances where some microorganism brings on the disease, the theories of small-scale societies about the cause and treatment of the illness can be valuable. To take a not uncommon occurrence, one man may steal the wife of another. This situation is bound to place a great deal of stress on the wife, the wife-stealer, and the husband, not to mention the relatives of the three parties. Such stress can lower resistance to disease. Horton observes: "In these circumstances the traditional healer's effort to cope with the situation by ferreting out and attempting to remedy stress-producing disturbances in the patient's social field is probably very relevant."[12]

Then again, as Horton points out, many tribal communities are small and self-contained social units that exist in equilibrium with the diseases that afflict them. New diseases are rarely encountered. Thus, any given social group has been coexisting with a given group of diseases over generations. For example, largely as a result of natural selection, many African tribes have built up a resistance to typhoid, malaria, smallpox, dysentery, and other serious diseases. Thus, in Chapter 6, we saw how some African populations have a genetic resistance to a certain kind of malaria. Because these groups lack modern antibiotics and other medicines, what happens to tribal members depends largely on other factors, usually social in nature, that add to or subtract from their resistance to disease.

9. Victor Turner, "Lunda Medicine and the Treatment of Disease," in *The Forest of Symbols*, by Victor Turner (Ithaca, N.Y.: Cornell University Press, 1967).

10. Horton, "African Thought and Western Science."

11. Turner, "Lunda Medicine and the Treatment of Disease," p. 356.

12. Horton, "African Thought and Western Science," p. 138.

Urban anthropology has recently become a major subdiscipline of anthropology, largely because many rural and tribal peoples are migrating to cities. Shown here is a congested street in Lagos, Nigeria.

Urban Anthropology

Social arrangements, both orderly and disorderly are also the subject of the other important concern of applied anthropology—urban anthropology. From its nineteenth-century beginnings, anthropology has concentrated on rural peoples and largely ignored urban peoples. Anthropologists went into the field to study people, who frequently lived in remote areas. They went by canoe, small aircraft, or on foot slogging through forests and jungles. The scope of anthropology did not include the urban landscape with the researcher going off to the field by subway or bus. This is no longer true, however. In Chapter 1, we saw how two anthropologists

studied the social interactions that took place in Brady's Bar, for example.

There are a number of reasons for the dramatically increased interest in urban culture. First, large numbers of the people who have been studied by anthropologists have moved into urban environments from rural areas. Anthropologists are studying what happens as these people make the transition to urban life.

Secondly, the city has increasingly become the place where the people are, and anthropologists are drawn to study these people. Here human problems exist in abundance. In the United States, for example, over 73 percent of the population lives in urban areas.[13] However, African cities such as Mbale, Uganda, share the same problems as those that are found in American urban areas. Inferior housing, unemployment, crime, and overcrowding exist in Mbale as they do in Detroit or New York City. The core of human social problems is poverty. Urban anthropologists study how groups of people cope with urban poverty and how they utilize the cultural heritage of their origins to adapt to the problems presented by the urban environment. The city is an arena which presents many modes of behavior and social organization; these new urban dwellers must adapt by choosing from among alternatives which are not usually present in a homogeneous village or tribal settlement.

Kenneth Moore, an urban anthropologist, points out that the urban adaptations required of city dwellers must take into account the fact that city life is highly intense in its diversity:

> The city derives from a central attribute which is that all the things man does are done here more intensively, more precisely, more profoundly, and in more varied ways, because of the profusion of alternate choices. . . . Never was culture more adaptable, more seething with creative promise, and more demonstrative of human accomplishment than in this cauldron of creative change that we refer to so vaguely as the urban milieu. . . .[14]

But such intensity and profusion of choices can also take its toll on the city dwellers' psyche. Indeed, in a large city like New York, such richness can be damaging. For example, social psychologist Stanley Milgram found that as a result of overcrowding, New Yorkers are continuously overloaded with external stimulations and must continuously adapt to this stress.[15] Most New Yorkers, says Milgram, have learned to tune out much that goes on around them in order to get through the day. A derelict lying sick on the sidewalk of a busy street, for example, is casually ignored by streams of people passing by him. Some New Yorkers maintain unlisted telephone numbers in order to avoid talking to unwanted callers, while others keep their telephone receivers off the hook for hours at a time. Thus, says Milgram, harried New Yorkers have become less courteous toward one another and thus more isolated and alienated.

City Life Versus Village Life

What are the essential characteristics of the city that make it so bewildering to the newcomer? Louis Wirth[16] in 1938 suggested that city life could be understood on the basis of three variables: (1) population size, (2) density of settlement, and (3) heterogeneity of the urban population. A village, on the other hand, is small, with little crowding and a homogeneous population—family and neighbors who know each other well. In cities

13. U.S. Bureau of the Census, *Statistical Abstract of the United States: 1976* (Washington, D.C.: Government Printing Office, 1976).

14. Kenneth Moore, "The City as Context: Context as Process," *Urban Anthropology* 4, no. 1 (1975): 19–20.

15. Stanley Milgram, "The Experience of Living in Cities," *Science* 167 (March 1970): 1461–1468.

16. Louis Wirth, "Urbanism as a Way Life," *American Journal of Sociology* 44 (1938): 1–24.

most of the workers are specialized in their jobs and are economically dependent on the productive skills of others. In villages and tribal units, the division of labor is based for the most part on sex and age, with some workers skilled at special jobs. In Tepoztlán, for example, men do most of the work in the fields, while women's work centers around the maintenance of the house and family. Still, a few individuals specialize in certain tasks, such as carpentry, shoemaking, ironworking, teaching, and baking.

Robert Redfield made the classic distinctions between the folk and urban ways of life. Redfield describes a folk society:

> Such a society is small, isolated, non-literate, and homogeneous, with a strong sense of group solidarity. The ways of living are conventionalized. . . . Behavior is traditional, spontaneous, uncritical, and personal; there is no legislation or habit of experiment and reflection for intellectual ends. Kinship, its relationships and institutions, are the type categories of experience and the familial group is the unit of action. The sacred prevails over the secular; the economy is one of status rather than of the market.[17]

It is a major upheaval for an individual to leave the familiar village life where most all of the residents are family, friends, and neighbors, where, for the most part, little that happens is unexpected and where there is a traditional answer for life's crises. For such a one the city is uncaring, impersonal, and frightening.

---

17. Robert Redfield, "The Folk Society," *American Journal of Sociology* 52 (1947): 293.

Why Do They Go?

People migrating to cities apparently see a comparative advantage in urban living and a comparative disadvantage in rural living. One way to look at this is to call the opportunities in the city a "pull" factor in migration, and the hardships in rural areas a "push" factor. A widespread cause of migration to the cities is the fact that incomes there are generally higher, even for unskilled labor. Public education has often made young people dissatisfied with village life and has resulted in the migration of large numbers to the cities, where they hope to find nonagricultural employment or continue their education. Education is the most influential factor in the migration of young people to the cities of the Ivory Coast. In 1968, more than 60 percent of the young persons who had completed primary school had left the rural sector. Many of the others told social investigators that they were waiting for an opportunity to move to Agidjan or another urban center.

Around the world, this situation has led to cities being inhabited by a preponderance of males. This distortion of the sex ratio is due to the masses of male peasants flocking to the city for work and hoping to earn enough to send for their wives and children. Since infant mortality is high among poor urban immigrants, the city population does not increase from within, but from constant additions from without.

The International Labor Office has found that in most countries agricultural incomes are lower than other incomes and do not rise so fast. These push and pull factors are strong economic reasons for migration. In Nigeria, for example, an unskilled worker earns more than twice as much as a farm worker.

Rural and tribal people who move to urban areas sometimes live in temporary quarters just outside the city. Houses of this temporary camp, called Pueblos Juvenes near Lima, Peru, have walls made of burlap mats.

The lure of higher income is not the only factor responsible for migration to the cities. Strong pull factors for many young people are the opportunities in cities to complete secondary schooling and to obtain white-collar work. For educated young people, these pursuits are much more prestigious and higher paying than agricultural work. Another pull factor may be the individual's preference for the comforts of city life. He or she may have discovered a liking for these while in military service or while seeking employment in the agricultural off-season.

On the other hand, individuals who own no land and see no opportunity to obtain land are frequently motivated by the push factor of landlessness. Drought and soil exhaustion are also responsible for pushing people into the stream of migration. Lack of services such as water, electricity, roads, markets, credit, schools, and hospitals adds to the discontent of many rural people. Civil strife, which disrupts rural economic activity and poses a threat of physical violence against which rural people are helpless, has also been a strong push factor at times. In such cases some flee to the hills, others to the city.

How Do They Cope?

The migration of rural people to urban cities is a worldwide phenomenon which has been documented in many areas

Chapter Nineteen

by anthropologists. Michael Whiteford studied Barrio Tulcán, an urban neighborhood on the fringes of the city of Popayan, Colombia.[18] His study showed how the people of the barrio, most of whom were migrants from rural Colombia, depended upon wage labor, small-scale trade, and odd jobs to make a living. It also showed that the barrio's people relied on the city for the education of their children, for health services, and for entertainment. Whiteford found that the basic social organization in the barrio conformed primarily to a village model of social interaction. Within the barrio people knew one another as they did in their villages. Life was still organized in family and kinship groups. It was like a large village transplanted to the city. Herbert Gans, a sociologist, in a study of Italians living in Boston in the 1960s, found a similar pattern. He called the people he studied "urban villagers."[19]

Claudio Esteva Fabregat[20] has followed the careers of migrants from rural central and southern Spain who came to Barcelona seeking a better life. In many cases, the migrants had friends or relatives in Barcelona who had migrated to the area earlier and had become established in jobs and housing. The newer migrants received some aid, such as temporary lodging and leads on job opportunities, from established migrants. Once settled and working, these new migrants, in turn, helped friends and kin to join them. This chain migration is a pattern that is common throughout the world; indeed, much the same pattern characterized migration to America by Europeans in the nineteenth and twentieth centuries.

A general pattern of adaptation to urban life—whether in Barrio Tulcán or Boston, Barcelona, or Mbale—is discernible at least in its major details. Immigrants come to the city seeking improved living conditions. Socially, they usually settle in areas of low-cost housing where they can also be near people from their native village or area. Most immigrants have little education and most often find employment in the most menial and lowest-paying occupation—street cleaning, unskilled construction work, and the like. Because the complexities of urban life are frightening to them, and because they are often discriminated against by city dwellers who are well established in the social hierarchy, migrants re-create in their neighborhoods forms of social organization familiar to them from their life in villages.

Two processes are at work: the slow acceptance by the migrant of an urban way of life and world view; and, paradoxically, the "ruralization" of a part of the city as migrants re-create the social patterns of village life with which they feel comfortable. The continued existence of "ethnic neighborhoods" in urban America illustrates that this pattern of social organization is present in highly industrialized countries as well as in less developed societies.

In some large cities, such ethnic neighborhoods are broken up by the building

---

18. Michael Whiteford, "Barrio Tulcán: Colombian Countrymen in an Urban Setting" (Ph.D. diss., University of California, Berkeley, 1972).

19. Herbert J. Gans, *The Urban Villagers* (New York: Free Press, 1962).

20. Claudio Esteva Fabregat, *Antropología Industrial* (Editorial Planeta, 1973).

of huge housing projects in slum areas without regard for the existing socially adaptive subcultures. New York City is a good example of this practice. The city planners have failed to consult anthropologists and other social scientists before erecting the housing. Not surprisingly, the results of such social disruption have not been good. They include individual depersonalization, apathy, and violence in the form of vandalism.

Network Analysis

As a result of their study of urban living, anthropologists have developed a number of new techniques. One of these is *network analysis*, which is the study of concrete interpersonal relationships linking individuals with other individuals in complex societies.[21] The aim of network analysis in social anthropology is to analyze and describe those social processes that join different social groups, particularly in urban environments. The study of such networks should reveal the structure of each group. Thus, the network is valuable for analyzing those situations where the individual is involved in interpersonal relations which cut across the boundaries of his village, subcaste, or kin group.

As a result of large numbers of individuals moving to the cities, network analysis has become an increasingly important tool. It is helpful in large cities where there is high population density,

21. J. A. Barnes, "Networks and Political Process," in *Social Networks in Urban Situations*, ed. J. Clyde Mitchell (Manchester, England: Manchester University Press, 1969).

Rural immigrants usually settle in areas of the city where housing is inexpensive and where they can live near people from their native village or area. Shown here is one such enclave in Lagos, Nigeria.

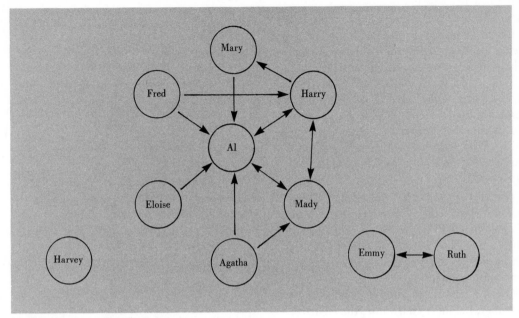

Figure 19–2   *Network analysis reveals patterns of social interaction and group dynamics among individuals in large urban areas where traditional methods of kinship analysis fail.*

ethnic heterogeneity, increasing social and economic differentiation, and high residential and occupational mobility.[22] In such an environment, lasting groups, such as kin groups, have not formed and people interact daily with numerous other strangers. In so doing, they must continuously make choices about whom they should turn to for help, leadership, guidance, and information. Such analysis is not necessary among traditional societies, such as that of the Nuer or the Ndembu,

where the institutional structure of the kinship system provides a framework into which all the daily activities of the people and their relationships with one another can be fitted and studied. In more complex nonstructured urban societies, network analysis helps identify the roles of the participants in a given social situation, sorting out the leaders and the followers, the popular and the unpopular, the socially active and the socially inactive.[23]

In network analysis, individuals are typically represented by nodes, and the complex relationships between them as lines, as in Figure 19–2. This diagram

22. A. L. Epstein, "The Network and Urban Social Organization," in *Social Networks in Urban Situations*, ed. J. Clyde Mitchell (Manchester, England: Manchester University Press, 1969).

23. Barnes, "Networks and Political Process."

was obtained by asking each of the individuals depicted to name those people with whom they interacted most in their daily lives. Questions might have included "Whom do you work with? Vacation with? Party with?" or, "To whom do you look for leadership? Whom do you turn to in times of illness and other emergencies? Whom do you ask for help or guidance when you have problems with your spouse?"

In this figure, the directions of the arrows show who interacts with whom. Double-headed arrows represent mutual interaction. The pattern of social relationships within the group is shown by the lines interconnecting the group members. In the figure, Al may be the most popular member, the most charitable, the smartest, or the leader, depending upon the questions asked in constructing the network. It is obvious that Harvey is either a loner, a staunch individualist, or a social outcast, whereas Emmy and Ruth appear to form their own mutual admiration society, since they interact only with one another.

Thus, network analysis in urban situations can reveal much about group structure, group dynamics, and group cohesion in the absence of the kind of rules that govern social interactions in small-scale societies.

Summary

1. Medical anthropology combines both biological and cultural approaches in its study of the way humans handle illness and death.
2. In any society, illness and death produce adaptive cultural responses that include knowl-edge, beliefs, roles, practices, and organized social behavior.
3. All cultures deal with illness and death in a manner consistent with their knowledge and beliefs about the causes and nature of sickness and death.
4. All healing systems classify diseases so that the disease can be identified and treated. Thus, in rural Mexico, two kinds of disease are recognized: natural and supernatural.
5. The cross-cultural study of disease has revealed that modern scientific medicine sets the illness of an individual apart from the rest of his or her behavior.
6. As more and more rural and tribal peoples move to cities, anthropologists are beginning to focus on the ways the immigrants adapt to urban life.
7. Some anthropologists believe that a city is marked by three outstanding characteristics: large population, dense settlement, and heterogeneous population.
8. Those who immigrate from rural areas to cities typically follow a general pattern of adaptation to their new environment. They usually settle in areas of low-cost housing, obtain menial, low-paying jobs, and re-create in their neighborhoods the forms of social organization that prevailed in their native villages. In other words, poor rural people have almost always wound up as poor urban people.

Review Questions

1. What is the subject matter of medical anthropology? What are some of the cultural phenomena that are employed to adapt to illness?
2. In most of rural Mexico, disease is regarded as an imbalance in the natural order. Explain the meaning of this statement.

3. Rural Mexican society and modern Western societies share a number of similar attitudes toward illness and death. Discuss two or three of these.

4. Why has urban anthropology become increasingly important in recent times?

5. Compare folk and urban society in terms of some of their identifying characteristics.

6. Those who immigrate from rural or tribal communities to urban areas usually follow a general pattern of adaptation to their new homes. Describe this pattern.

Suggested Readings

Eddy, Elizabeth M. *Urban Anthropology: Research Perspectives and Strategies.* Southern Anthropological Society Proceedings, no. 2. Athens, Ga.: University of Georgia Press, 1968.
This small volume contains ten essays by anthropologists on the problems, both theoretical and methodological, of urban life.

Fabrega, Horatio, Jr. "The Need for an Ethno-medical Science." *Science* 189 (1976): 969–974.
A concise overview of medical systems in cross-cultural perspective. Includes a discussion of the problems encountered in defining disease more broadly.

Lewis, Oscar. *The Children of Sanchez: Autobiography of a Mexican Family.* New York: Random House, 1967.
This book, which won popular and scientific acclaim, is a searing account of poverty in a Mexico City slum. It is one of the works that triggered the interest of contemporary anthropologists in urban social problems.

Mumford, Lewis. *The City in History: Its Origins, Its Transformations, and Its Prospects.* New York: Harcourt Brace Jovanovich, 1961.
A scholarly, well-written study of the role of the city in human history. Mumford traces the development of the city from its beginnings to its future, covering virtually every aspect of the urban phenomenon.

Sudnow, David. *Passing On: The Social Organization of Dying.* Englewood Cliffs, N.J.: Prentice-Hall, 1967.
A thorough treatment of adaptive values, practices, personnel, and other factors involved in death and terminal illness, as seen in a comparison of two American hospitals.

Chapter 20

READINGS
LA Victoria China RESTAURANT
ESPECIALIDAD EN COMIDAS CHINAS Y LATINAS
CHINESE & SPANISH FOOD
TAKE OUT ORDERS

Anthropology & the Future

PROGRESS

Americans, and most Europeans in fact, believe in something called "progress." Many of them hold the firm conviction that the history of the world can be viewed as an ascent from worse to better. Moreover, this progression is viewed as inevitable and irreversible. "You can't stop progress" is a phrase much used by every real estate developer, timber cutter, highway builder, or community booster in the nation. But is there such a thing at all? What evidence shows that we have become one whit better than we were two million years ago? Are we kinder to our fellows? Indeed, we do not sacrifice them on sacred altars anymore, but we do see the highways strewn with bodies and still we clamor for ever more powerful automobiles.

Are we more concerned today for the aged or infirm? I doubt it. True enough, we have improved medical technology and have invented institutions such as Social Security and Medicare to help us bear the burden of the old. But these are only institutional variations. The most savage of people rendered their elders esteem and emotional support and the care permitted within their means and institutions. There is ample evidence that we have regressed rather

Source: From James F. Downs, *Cultures in Crisis*, 2nd ed. (Beverly Hills, Calif.: Glencoe Publishing, 1975), pp. 139–141. Copyright 1971, 1975 by James F. Downs. Reprinted by permission of Glencoe Publishing Co., Inc.

than progressed in this respect—witness the hopelessly lonely pensioners in any park in America. Compare their plight to the proud security of the last years of a Navajo grandmother, to gauge our progress in caring for the old. Great numbers of our old people have one role left in our society—to die with as little disturbance to the rest of us as possible. How unthinking and unkind such treatment would seem to the Semang or the Washo or the Bushmen of the Kalahari.

Have we developed means any more effective than in the past to control our aggressive urges? In the feudal ages, when war was glorified and almost continuous, fighting was suspended on Sundays and Wednesdays and eventually on Fridays and Saturdays as well. The rules of war, observed at least in the early years of feudalism, provided that the peasant and the serf, who had traded freedom for security in a great historical bargain, were not to be harmed by the warring nobility. Can we say that we have progressed very far, remembering the bombing of Berlin and Coventry and Hiroshima and Nanking and still living with refugee camps created after World War II?.

Let me hasten to say that I am not condemning our society as hopelessly rotten but rather suggesting that we may be easily deceived by the technological achievements we see around us into accepting without question the idea of progress. Far from being a natural law of history, that idea may be simply an artifact of Western culture along with baseball, the cowboy, or the drive-in bank. There is no empirical evidence to suggest that humans have progressed since they became human, except in one area. It is almost everywhere apparent that technologically, or materially, we have improved and become more complex. Our ability to kill each other has increased enormously—how frustratingly difficult it must have been for cavemen with nothing more efficient than a stone ax. Our transportation allows us to traverse great distances. Our medicine is better, our houses more permanent and healthy. Our ability to construct dams and stadiums and highways and buildings has, indeed, improved. We have devised ingenious ways to harness energy to do all kinds of tasks beyond our own physical powers. We have flown to the moon and back and we are able to produce more food per acre and per work-hour than ever before. In short, the history of our material development is indeed an upward curve, ever more steep, of increasing mechanical efficiency and complexity. However, this can only be said of our material history. To a degree, our social history reflects the increasing complexity of our efforts to keep abreast of our material development. But it is debatable whether a modern factory represents progress over a craftsman's shop, if we evaluate the two activities in terms other than mechanical or economic efficiency.

Essentially, in transferring the empirical reality of technological progress to all spheres of life, we have created a theme or cultural idea of progress which is not really supported by the evidence of human history. As human beings we are not really better than we once were. Our institutions are more complex, but they do only what human institutions have always done. In many cases, they do it much less efficiently—considering the lack of human warmth that characterizes some of them. We have elaborate systems of insurance to protect the widow or orphan, but are these really advances over ancient systems in which a widow or an orphan was cared for emotionally as well as physically by other members of the tribe or village as a matter of course? Our society provides us with a measure of financial security through a government pension or a social security payment (which stops if a widow remarries). In a tribal system, the widow may be expected to marry a brother of her dead husband and thus is assured of human companionship as well as membership and a role in an ongoing human institution. I raise these questions, again, not to decry our society but to suggest that there is some confusion in our thoughts about it. *Progress* is a term applied to material developments in human history. To the degree that progress can assist us in having a more rewarding and meaningful life, it is worth exporting to the rest of the world. On the other hand, to the degree that it produces miners with black-lung, or a clutter of tasteless hotels and cheap gimcrack shops to mar an area of natural beauty like Waikiki in Hawaii, then its value for the rest of the world is open to serious question.[1]

● ● ● ● ● ● ● ●

The methods and theories of anthropology were developed to study small-scale, isolated societies. With difficulty, anthropology has expanded to include peasant peoples and even urban populations, but what was specific to anthropology—an interest in technologically simple, non-Western cultures—has become less and less possible. Few people remain in today's world who have not been influenced by the larger industrial nations. Fewer still are the simple technologies that have been left intact since improved material goods seem to be welcomed wherever they are introduced. The state in which to study cultural variation is no longer a state of self-contained isolation. The influence of industrial

1. From James F. Downs, *Cultures in Crisis*, 2nd ed. (Beverly Hills, Calif.: Glencoe Publishing, 1975), pp. 139–141.

Anthropology and the Future

technology, with its potential for raising the material standard of living, is omnipresent. It is the function of the anthropologist to observe its influence and perhaps even influence its direction.

What Is Progress?

All human beings are concerned with material needs. All cultural adaptations provide for the material necessities—food, shelter, reproduction, security. There is no reason why those needs should not be satisfied as efficiently as possible, freeing people to use their energy and creativity on pursuits above and beyond mere subsistence. Some question exists, however, as to whether material progress, as it has been achieved, represents progress in all spheres of life. In the research report that begins this chapter, Downs decries the ugliness that has accompanied the material developments of industrialized technology. He points to the insensitivity of Western institutions to such natural things as old age, death, and even work. As more and more non-Western cultures turn to industrialism, we may ask whether progress must always be only material. Could it not include more humane ways of living with each other? Couldn't anthropologists contribute some ideas to this challenge? Kathleen Gough has asked, "Who is to evaluate and suggest guidelines for human society, if not those who study it?"[2] What we consider here is how progress has been defined, how it might be defined, and how a

redefinition might be more consistent with the original intent of anthropology—which was the understanding and explanation of human potential.

Human Vulnerability

From a purely zoological viewpoint, human beings are not very impressive. It is our cultural capacity, not our physical endowment, that enables us to survive. As we have seen, human cultural innovations have been wonderfully varied. We make up for our vulnerable physical condition with all sorts of inventions: not one kind of boat but boats from bark canoes to nuclear submarines, not one kind of house but houses from grass lean-to's to marble palaces, weapons from sharpened sticks to atomic bombs, transportation from the backs of animals to jet aircraft. We feed ourselves, warm ourselves, transport ourselves, entertain ourselves in a rich variety of ways. The more technologically complex the solution, the more satisfactory the comfort provided.

But many of our material comforts have been attained at the expense of other human needs. As Downs points out, our warfare is more time-consuming and life-consuming than the occasional warfare of the Middle Ages. Our houses are warmer but our environment is polluted and our resources running out. The urban sprawl that is swallowing up every acre of open space represents expansion, but at the same time, it is a contraction of natural beauty. What is usually considered progress is only material progress and it is not clear that that is enough.

"Culture against Man"

Jules Henry has argued that it is not only modern industrial societies that ignore certain nonmaterial human needs. All cultures

---

2. Kathleen Gough, "World Revolution and the Science of Man," in *To See Ourselves*, ed. Thomas Weaver (Glenview, Ill.: Scott, Foresman, 1973), p. 158.

ignore them and are, in that sense, "against man." "Man has been so busy finding ways to feed himself and to protect himself against wild animals and against the elements and against other men that in constructing society he has focused on these problems and has let even sex (not marriage) take care of itself." [3] Henry indicts American culture for creating a tension between drives and values. Our drives are toward achievement, competition, profit, mobility, security, and a higher standard of living, while our values include gentleness, kindness, generosity, love, fun, contentment, and honesty. Not always compatible, the values too frequently are sacrificed to the drives, leaving individuals confused and unsatisfied. In simpler societies, there is no discrepancy between what people do and what they value. "People do the kinds of things they do, not because somebody just thought up that kind of thing, or because anybody ordered them to do so, but because it seems to the people to flow from the very necessity of existence that they do that kind of thing." [4] People also repeat the behavior patterns of the past because they are ethnocentric, or because ancestor worship works against change. For such people, the moral order is embedded in the technical order.

The Moral Order versus the Technical Order

Robert Redfield defines the *moral order* as the "organization of human sentiments into judgments as to what is right." [5] The *technical order,* as opposed to the moral order, is the necessary organization of work that is involved in survival. Redfield proposes that only in civilized society can the moral order be separate from the technical order. A Siriono man may leave an ailing wife behind to die alone in the Bolivian forest without thinking it is wrong. It is necessary, which at the same time is "right." It is only with the civilized perspective that other alternatives make it possible to judge that to leave one's wife alone in the forest is "wrong." With civilization came the development of the idea of reform, the idea that humans can control their own destinies, and carve out an ever better future. Redfield claims that the West invented progress, an idea which is inconceivable in cultures where alternatives do not exist. Small-scale societies see the future as a reproduction of the immediate past. People's children will do what they did because that is the way life is and they do not know people who live otherwise.

For Redfield, a moral order that is separate from the technical order represents an advance. Civilization is an improvement on preliterate society. It means that humans can strive for what is right with a comparative knowledge of the possibilities. Torture can be eliminated, disease can be humanely dealt with, violence toward the human body can be tempered. There can be an ever-growing concern for the welfare and dignity of others. Redfield knew that technological progress did not necessarily mean moral progress, but he saw the possibility for moral progress only with civili-

3. Jules Henry, *Culture against Man* (New York: Random House, 1963).

4. Robert Redfield, *The Primitive World and Its Transformations* (Ithaca, N.Y.: Cornell University Press, 1953), p. 14.

5. Redfield, *The Primitive World and Its Transformations,* p. 20.

zation in which time and energy can be turned to the matter of humaneness. He was not afraid to abandon his cultural relativism and say the civilized way was better because it had potential to bring about significant change.

The Past Is the Key to the Future

Stanley Diamond thinks anthropologists are most "appropriately engaged" as "hunters on the track of human potential and human necessity." [6] If our civilization falls short of ideal, we have the information to suggest improvements that will benefit humankind. We know what has been—lessons which might be brought to bear on what is to be. Diamond quotes Lamartine: "History teaches us everything, even the future." [7] He then lists the typical attributes of preliterate society. These should be considered not as a model for retreating into the past, or for grafting onto civilized cultures, but as characteristics to be pondered when conceiving of new, more adequate, contemporary societies. The preliterate attributes have served humankind well for most of its history, and therefore should be taken into account in the creation of any enduring future.

What are these attributes? First is economic communalism, an economic system in which no person exploits the labor of another. There is no money, but an emphasis on reciprocity. Second is the fact that leadership is communal and no force is needed to back it up. "Obeisance [toward leaders] is symbolic, a sign of respect toward one's tradition, and thus of self-respect." [8] Not surprisingly, there are no laws. Informal regulations and customs are enough to make people do what is best for the society. There is little conflict of the sort that might lead to social disorganization. The clashes that do arise are settled in institutionalized ways. Fourth is the high degree of integration between religion, the social structure, economic organization, and technology. All the components of a culture make a unified whole.

Because of this integration, an individual's life is coherent rather than segmented. The ordinary member of a small-scale society participates in many more aspects of the economy than the ordinary member of industrialized society. Fifth, society is personal, most activities being discharged within kin groups. These characteristics make preliterate society essentially different from civilized society; yet we recognize in them a reflection of human needs. What Stanley Diamond is saying is that in proposing a new social order, we should arrive at a union of the "primitive" and the "civilized," and use what we know to make more than material progress.

Applied Anthropology

In *The Primitive World and Its Transformations*, Robert Redfield argues that civilization has brought moral progress. This is not to say that the potential for reform is

6. Stanley Diamond, "Primitive Society in Its Many Dimensions," in *The Critical Spirit: Essays in Honor of Herbert Marcuse*, ed. K. H. Wolff and B. Moore, Jr. (Boston: Beacon Press, 1968), pp. 418–424.

7. Diamond, "Primitive Society in Its Many Dimensions," p. 419.

8. Diamond, "Primitive Society in Its Many Dimensions," p. 420.

totally lacking in primitive society. In fact, Redfield tells a moving story of a young Pawnee Indian who tried to prevent the annual sacrifice practiced by his people. The son of the chief, Petalesharoo, stepped forward just as the victim (a young girl from another tribe) was about to be killed, declared that it was his father's wish to abolish the sacrifice, and requested that his own life be taken in exchange or the victim be released. Redfield admires Petalesharoo's independence, but points out that even if he stopped the sacrifice that year, the practice would undoubtedly be resumed the next. In admiring Petalesharoo, Redfield is making a judgment, a judgment he claims it is hard to avoid. He is against human sacrifice and sees the attempt to end it as courageous and humane. In so doing, he is repudiating the anthropological doctrine of *cultural relativism*, which states that "the values expressed in any culture are to be understood and themselves valued only according to the way the people who carry that culture see things." [9] Thus, Redfield can be considered to be engaging in *applied anthropology*, which uses the knowledge and methods of anthropology to solve practical problems. In this sense, the chief goal of this subdiscipline is planned or directed change.

No applied anthropologist can claim to be a true cultural relativist. Applied anthropologists are concerned with "processes of social and cultural change, particularly as they bear on planned improvements in such fields as agriculture, health and medical services, educational systems, social welfare programs, community development,

and the like." [10] They assist and support innovations intended to raise and change the standard of living of traditional and peasant peoples, as well as effecting change in industrial societies. For example, researchers in one branch of applied anthropology, medical anthropology, might study the hierarchy and relationships that exist between doctors, nurses, administrative staff, and patients in a hospital and suggest methods of reorganization to deliver better patient care. One important principle of applied anthropology is that in introducing change, an effort should be made to disrupt the culture as little as possible— to preserve those characteristics that have given the culture its unique meaning and completeness. Researchers in this branch of anthropology anticipate—or try to anticipate—the possible consequences that might follow after change is introduced.

The History of Applied Anthropology

Originally, applied anthropology served colonial administration. Its inception has been dated to 1908 when Northcote W. Thomas was appointed as British Government Anthropologist in Nigeria, where he was instructed to study the Ibo- and Edo-speaking peoples of that country to "facilitate the extension of the then new colonial philosophy of 'indirect rule.'" [11] The following thirty years of British anthropology

---

9. Redfield, *The Primitive World and Its Transformations*, p. 144.

10. George Foster, *Applied Anthropology* (Boston: Little, Brown, 1969), p. viii.

11. Allan H. Smith and John L. Fisher, "Anthropology and the Problems of Society," in *Anthropology*, ed. Allan H. Smith and John L. Fisher (Englewood Cliffs, N.J.: Prentice-Hall, 1970), p. 426.

were directed toward problems of colonial administration.

In the United States, few anthropologists worked in administrative situations prior to World War II, although they were consulted by the Bureau of Indian Affairs when it joined hands with the Soil Conservation Service to promote conservation measures in the Southwest.[12] During World War II, however, anthropologists were involved in many government activities: in the War Relocation Authority which resettled 100,000 Japanese from California in camps east of the Sierras; in the Foreign Morale Division of the Office of War Information on "psychological warfare"; in training officers bound for administrative posts in newly occupied areas; and in the preparation of "survival handbooks" which told downed fliers how to live off the land.[13]

Directed Change

The postwar surge of developmental efforts in new countries gave birth to a new kind of applied anthropology. Today, work in applied anthropology is concerned primarily with the social problems that accompany technological change and modernization in developing countries.[14] Again, it is cultural relativism that makes anthropologists useful. They understand that a culture is an integrated system whose various parts are so intricately connected that a change in any

one of them will affect many other aspects of the system. Thus, applied anthropologists can anticipate the effects produced by a change in any part of the system. For instance, an attempt was made in one Mexican village to upgrade hygiene by building a wash house which had showers on one side and a row of washtubs for laundering clothes along the opposite back wall. The women of the village refused to use the washtubs even though their alternative was to carry their laundry a long distance to the river, where, on their knees, they would wash their clothing in cold water. They refused because they did not want to face a wall, as if they were children being punished in school. Actually, an anthropologist was able to see that the real reason for their resistance was the unsociable design of the wash house. The layout restricted them from chatting away the tedium of the job—something they could do with ease at the river. Only when the washtubs were repositioned to face each other in pairs were they adopted.

Another technological improvement with social ramifications was the installation of a flush toilet in the house of a rather well-to-do Mexican villager. The woman claimed that she preferred to return to the public latrines because there she could meet her friends once or twice a day and spend a leisurely social hour talking and smoking cigarettes. In that particular town, smoking among women was frowned upon and could be done only in this situation without fear of censure.[15]

Most programs of directed change involve raising the level of agricultural production. In Nepal, foreign agricultural

12. Smith and Fisher, "Anthropology and the Problems of Society," p. 427.

13. Smith and Fisher, "Anthropology and the Problems of Society," p. 427.

14. Foster, *Applied Anthropology*, p. viii.

15. Foster, *Applied Anthropology*, p. 11.

specialists introduced a Japanese rice that would yield 200 percent more than the native rice. Though perfectly receptive to improved production, the people found the crop unacceptable because it grew on a dwarf stalk which provided much less fodder for their animals. Moreover, the seeds clung tightly to the stalks, requiring a special threshing machine usually not available to farmers.[16]

According to Charles Erasmus, a new crop or any new idea will not be adopted unless there is clear and immediate proof of its effectiveness and desirability.[17] Erasmus points out that new crops are generally more successful than soil conservation programs because the results are more immediately apparent.

Innovations that are likely to be most successful are those for which the people perceive a need before they are introduced. In one case, for example, a government-sponsored agency in Latin America instituted a program enabling farmers to build new houses and improve their farm structures. The theory underlying the housing program was that more sanitary living conditions would result in more able-bodied farmers and eventually, in higher production.[18] The farmers, however, did not think anything was wrong with their personal living conditions and took advantage of the government subsidy to improve only their farm structures.

The task of the applied anthropologist is to understand the people's viewpoint and, when necessary, to explain the value of a proposed program in terms they will appreciate. One issue that has recently been raised is that anthropologists must not only know the people for whom planned change is intended, but they must also know the bureaucracy that is introducing the change, to avoid exploitation. "Barriers to change are as prevalent in the structure, values and operating procedures of bureaucracies and in the personal qualities of the change agents as in the target cultures or subcultures."[19] Our reluctance to realize that failure may be as much our own fault as the fault of the target culture is indicative of our own ethnocentrism. When people resist what we regard as progress, we blame their conservatism.

The Vicos Project

A famous example of planned change in which anthropologists not only advised but directed the program is the Vicos Project. In 1952, the Cornell anthropologist Allan Holmberg became the *patrón* of a Peruvian *hacienda* called Vicos. Vicos consisted of over 30,000 acres in the highlands of northwestern Peru. It was inhabited by 2,000 Quechua-speaking Indians who had very little contact with modern civilization. When Holmberg took control, the standard of living was at a bare minimum, health and nutrition were extremely low, educational facilities were lacking, resistance to the outside world was high, and attitudes to-

16. Foster, *Applied Anthropology*, chap. 1.

17. Charles Erasmus, "An Anthropologist Looks at Technical Assistance," in *Readings in Anthropology*, 2nd ed., vol. 2, ed. Morton H. Fried (New York: Thomas Y. Crowell, 1968), pp. 565–582.

18. Erasmus, "An Anthropologist Looks at Technical Assistance," p. 570.

19. Smith and Fisher, "Anthropology and the Problems of Society," p. 430.

ward life were static and pessimistic.[20]

Five years later, at the end of the project, Holmberg himself reported great improvements. The organization of the *hacienda*, in which peones had been employed without pay, had been abolished. It became a community-controlled organization with shared interests and local control. The Peruvian government had been asked to expropriate the land in favor of Vicos residents. A board of delegates, elected from each of the six zones of the old *hacienda*, had assumed legal responsibility for the direction of community affairs. Whereas in 1952 there had been no source of income, in 1957 lands were farmed for the public good and provided a steady income for the payment of lands and development of public services. The small school of one teacher and ten to fifteen students had been replaced by a structure with a capacity of four hundred that was already serving two hundred students and employing nine teachers. The value of production per hectare of land had risen from $100 to between $400 and $600. (A hectare is a metric measure of area equal to about two and one-half acres.) A health center had been built and a clinic was open twice a week with a public health program under way. When the Peru–Cornell project left, Vicos was an independent, locally controlled community, that was even in a position to lend another *hacienda* money

to take control of their own lands and lives.[21]

Throughout the project, Holmberg recognized the precariousness of his position both as community patrón and as anthropologist. Had he failed the community, they would have had even less faith in the outside world. Moreover, his already skeptical colleagues would have held him in disgrace for taking on the responsibility in the first place. Holmberg says that he took these risks because he believed that "everyone, if he so desired, should at least have the right and the opportunity, if not the responsibility, to participate in the decision-making process in the community, to enjoy a fair share of its wealth, to pursue a desire for knowledge, to be esteemed by his fellow men, to develop talents to the best of his ability, to be relatively free from physical and mental disease, to enjoy the affection of others, and to command respect for his private life." [22] Holmberg obviously believes in a broader kind of progress than just improved technology. He also had faith that the people of Vicos could be induced to participate in his notions of how to improve their lot. Morton Fried has said, "Without raising the vexing question of ethnocentrism, it may be agreed that an increase in the food supply and a reduction of the death rate are regarded

20. Garth N. Jones, "Strategies and Tactics of Planned Organizational Change: Case Examples on the Modernization Process of Traditional Societies," in *To See Ourselves*, ed. Thomas Weaver (Glenview, Ill.: Scott, Foresman, 1973), pp. 450–457.

21. Allan Holmberg, "The Research and Development Approach to the Study of Change," in *To See Ourselves*, ed. Thomas Weaver (Glenview, Ill.: Scott, Foresman, 1973), pp. 464–470.

22. Holmberg, "The Research and Development Approach to the Study of Change," p. 466.

as good in all known cultures." [23] The Vicos project went much further and with impressive success.

Science for What Purpose and for Whom?

Applied anthropology explicitly serves the cause of economic development. Whether applied anthropologists like it or not, their efforts not only help the people for whom "planned change" is intended, but they also help the sponsoring organization, be it the U.S. Government, a Latin American state, or, more rarely, a community-based group. Anthropologists may claim to be "apolitical," but their actions affect the polity of a culture. In the last ten years the people being "helped" have started to say something about the good intentions of anthropologists. The anthropological community itself has had to examine its motives and consider the implicit politics of a discipline which makes the claim that it is pure science. No science of man can exist, says Kathleen Gough, if it no longer pursues the goals on which it was based. Those goals—"to help men live more fully and creatively and to expand their dignity, self-direction and freedom"—are dismissed as irrelevant to the scholarly pursuit of knowledge by some, and held as essential to the survival of an interesting and responsible anthropology by others. We therefore ask the question, "Science for what purpose and for whom?" [24]

Reactions of Those Studied

Vine Deloria, Jr., an Ogala Sioux, has attacked American anthropologists with candor and distressing insight. He claims that whether anthropologists are engaged in "pure research," for which he does not have much use, or applied work, their fundamental thesis is that "people are objects for observation, people are then considered objects for experimentation, for manipulation, and for eventual extinction." [25] Some anthropologists tell Indians what "real" Indians are like and run workshops in which they blame Indian problems on being "caught between two worlds." To be "real" Indians is to dance, exhibit warlike tendencies and drink; to be "caught between two worlds" is to do nothing about their situation. No matter how well-meaning, these anthropological insights are irrelevant to Indian needs. "How," Deloria asks, "can the Ogala Sioux make any headway in education when their lack of education is ascribed to a desire to go to war? Would not perhaps an incredibly low percapita income, virtually nonexistent housing, extremely inadequate roads, and domination by white farmers and ranchers make some difference? If the little Sioux boy or girl had no breakfast, had to walk miles to a small school, and had no decent

23. Morton H. Fried, Introduction to "An Anthropologist Looks at Technical Assistance," in *Readings in Anthropology*, 2nd ed., vol. 2, ed. Morton H. Fried (New York: Thomas Y. Crowell, 1968), p. 565.

24. Gough, "World Revolution and the Science of Man," p. 162.

25. Vine Deloria, Jr., "Anthropologists and Other Friends," in *Custer Died for Your Sins* (New York: Avon Books, 1969), p. 86.

514

clothes and place to study in a one-room log cabin, should the level of education be comparable to New Trier High School?"[26]

Deloria does not put the full blame on anthropologists. He blames Indians for listening, which is considerably easier than organizing to do something about their conditions. Nor has he given up on anthropologists. He asks that they "get down from their thrones of authority and pure research and begin helping Indian tribes instead of preying on them."[27]

Most of the people anthropologists have studied are nonwhite groups under the domination of the governments of industrialized societies.[28] The anthropological dedication to leaving those people alone, that is, respecting their traditional cultures as working systems, sounds to some of their members like a dedication to condemning them to eternal poverty and powerlessness. Not only has anthropology been concerned largely with nonwhite peoples, but it has been concerned with poor, nonwhite peoples. Practically none of those peoples are now ignorant of the Western world. Peasant peoples are an integral part of modern nation–states—the impoverished part. What is being asked by some Indians, peasants, and others the anthropologist studies is, why can't anthropologists do

something about this poverty? There is yet another aspect of the "white anthropologist versus poor, nonwhite subjects" situation: anthropology will not really come of age until small-scale societies in New Guinea, Melanesia, native America, and elsewhere produce their own anthropologists who will analyze the Western white societies as they themselves have been studied.

Women—A Case in Point

The questions anthropologists ask reflect certain unconscious, cultural assumptions. Those unconscious assumptions then determine, to an extent, what will be known about whatever is being studied. Just as the politics behind anthropology have often gone unrecognized, the cultural bias, in many instances, has also gone unrecognized. Recent work has shown that male domination of the field has tended to distort our understanding of certain cultural phenomena. For instance, a famous article on human evolution, "The Evolution of Hunting," by Sherwood Washburn and C. Lancaster,[29] proposes that most of the characteristics we consider specifically human can be causally related to hunting.[30] Early man, and they mean only man, hunted in order to support his dependent wife and children. While the dependents remained at camp he went out with other men, learned to cooperate, communicate and even create

26. Deloria, "Anthropologists and Other Friends," pp. 95–96.

27. Deloria, "Anthropologists and Other Friends," p. 104.

28. William S. Willis, Jr., "Skeletons in the Anthropological Closet," in *Reinventing Anthropology*, ed. Dell Hymes (New York: Random House, 1972), pp. 121–152.

29. Sherwood Washburn and C. Lancaster, "The Evolution of Hunting," in *Man the Hunter*, ed. Richard Lee and Irven DeVore (Chicago: Aldine Publishing, 1968), pp. 293–303.

30. Sally Linton, *Woman the Gatherer* (Boulder, Colo.: University of Colorado, 1971).

An outdoor market in Ouagadougou, Upper Volta. The merchandise clearly evidences the impact of modern technology, but the social and cultural style of the market remain relatively unchanged.

the first artistic objects (hand-axes). Selection pressure favored these abilities and led to modern *Homo sapiens* who, according to Washburn and Lancaster, still exhibit the adaptive characteristics of their ancestors (that is, modern men still hunt). The trouble with the theory is that it leaves out the other half of the human species. Sally Linton has pointed out that the male bias in anthropology led male anthropologists to give all the credit to men. Looking at the same data another way, Linton arrives at a totally different interpretation. Females prob-ably supported their children by their own food-gathering activities, says Linton. Like higher primates, they probably had male consorts rather than permanent mates and they may have supported them too. Food sharing, therefore, may have been a female-centered, rather than a male-centered, activity. Cooperation and communication would have been just as necessary to females as males, and hand-made objects could as easily have been slings for carrying babies or gathered food as hand-axes. There is actually more support for Linton's

516

argument than for Washburn and Lancaster's. In modern hunting-gathering societies, for example, women gather between 60 and 80 percent of the food consumed. The male hunters often come home empty-handed, or carrying a few specimens of small game. Hunting is important, but by no means the most important source of subsistence. It is interesting that even in light of controverting facts it is hard to give up the "man, the hunter" version of human evolution. We are so steeped in a male bias that it seems "right."

If our view of something as distant as earlier human evolution has been contaminated by male bias, has the study of contemporary cultures been equally contaminated? When anthropologists first became aware of their unconscious biases they wondered if there were not some female-dominated societies after all. Early anthropologists such as Morgan and Maine had proposed that matriarchal societies preceded patriarchal ones, but no convincing ethnographic evidence was ever produced. Recent work has suggested that there are some truly egalitarian societies and there are some in which women have considerable social recognition and power, but none has been observed in which women have more publicly recognized power and authority than men.[31]

Strictly biological reasons for the inequality of men and women have pretty much been eliminated. It is, therefore, in social structure that we expect to find the answers. A change in the status of women has been noticed among the !Kung Bushmen. The !Kung, who have been hunters and gatherers in the Kalahari Desert of South Africa for 11,000 years, have recently begun to live in agricultural villages near the neighboring Bantu.[32] In the new situation, !Kung women are losing their egalitarian status, children are no longer brought up to be nonaggressive, and the birth rate is going up.

When the !Kung were hunters and gatherers, women gathered at least 60 percent of the food consumed. They were as mobile as the male hunters and no more limited to home base than the men. Whoever did not go out to obtain food on a particular day stayed home with the children, be it man or woman. Because their nomadic bands were small, children rarely had playmates their own sex and age. They were, instead, part of groups containing both sexes of varied ages. They did not play competitively probably because it would not have been possible in such a mixed group, and also because ever-watchful adults discouraged aggression of any kind. In addition, there were no models for competition and aggression. Instead, the adults, who typically did not quarrel, were models for cooperation.

In the agrarian villages, women are no longer involved in food gathering. Their duties are confined to home base where the community is large enough to contain companions for them and for their children. Boys and girls learn the roles of their parents early, the girls staying at home

31. Michelle Zimbolist Rosaldo and Louise Lamphere, "Women, Culture and Society," in *Women, Culture and Society*, ed. Rosaldo and Lamphere (Stanford, Calif.: Stanford University Press, 1974), pp. 219–222.

32. Gina Bari Kolata, "!Kung Hunter-Gatherers: Feminism, Diet and Birth Control," *Science* 185 (September 13, 1974): 932–934.

and the boys going off to do agricultural work with their fathers. Men are much more mobile and must learn the Bantu language of their bosses. The Bantu, therefore, only communicate with !Kung men. These changes have severely affected women's status. They are no longer equal members of the community but are relegated to child care and housework, with an accompanying drop in recognition for their efforts. Children do have playmates their own age, do compete, and do exhibit aggression.

The !Kung example is one in which we can see clearly the effect of a number of factors on the status of women: their involvement in the productive economy, their freedom of movement, and their enculturation as children. Previous theories have emphasized the economic sphere as the determinant of female status, but such ideas have not been supported by cross-cultural data. Even in class-structured societies, women may hold property and bring in an income, but still do not enjoy the respect allotted to their male counterparts.[33] With

33. Karen Sacks, "Engels Revisited," in *Women, Culture and Society*, ed. Rosaldo and Lamphere (Stanford, Calif.: Stanford University Press, 1974), pp. 324–332.

A performance of traditional dance and song for tourists at the Polynesian Cultural Center in Hawaii. Such efforts to preserve and exhibit "native culture" often smack of commercial exploitation.

Anthropology and the Future

all the ethnographic studies that have been done, there are still not enough data to explain the position of women. The ethnographers certainly encountered as many women as men, but the male bias in anthropology prevented them from asking the questions, or even making the observations, that might have been relevant to solving the problem.

The Future of Anthropology

There are few isolated societies left to describe in the world. Most peasant peoples are subject to one industrial power or another, and some are in the throes of their own revolutionary movements. Such populations make an apolitical anthropology an impossibility. Does the reality of the modern world mean the doom of anthropology altogether? Most anthropologists believe that cultural variation is part and parcel of the human condition. Therefore, such variation will always exist, if only among subcultures of larger society. There is also a great deal of data, already collected, to analyze in terms of questions that are relevant to the contemporary scene.

Urban Ethnography

One problem is the understanding of poor people in urban situations, a condition in which more and more people find themselves. In some cases, these are the very same people anthropologists studied in the idyllic isolation of their traditional cultures. Charles and Betty Lou Valentine, who have done years of fieldwork in a ghetto in the northeastern part of the United States, complain that there are bodies of recorded data on the poor, but all from an outlook that

is external to the people.[34] Participant observation has not worked as a data-gathering method for people who are not able to identify with the groups they are attempting to study. Moreover, it has not been risked by social scientists afraid to enter areas torn by racial tension and political unrest, with only their white faces and field notebooks to protect them.

It has been suggested that this kind of ethnography can best be done by insiders. Anthropologists have always intended to become insiders, but a white anthropologist, no matter how well trained, can never feel like a black American, equally well trained, studying his or her own people. The results will not be objective, but they will reflect the observations of one who knows how it feels to be black in this society.[35] Native or urban ethnographers might become a completely different force in anthropology, consisting intentionally of minority-group members with explicit political objectives. The criterion for choosing research problems would be the sociopolitical significance of a problem.[36] Such

---

34. Charles Valentine and Betty Lou Valentine, "Making the Scene, Digging the Action, Telling It Like It Is: Anthropologists at Work in the Dark Ghetto," in *Afro-American Anthropology: Contemporary Perspectives*, ed. Norman E. Whitten, Jr., and John F. Szwed (New York: Free Press, 1970), pp. 403–418.

---

35. Delmos Jones, "Toward a Native Anthropology," *Human Organization* 29, no. 4 (1970): 251–259.

---

36. Willis, "Skeletons in the Anthropological Closet."

people would not be objective observers but dedicated activists.

The Valentines are a good example of this kind of ethnographer. Their study of the community they fictitiously call Blackston was done to contribute techniques to urban anthropology and to advance theory about complex societies. But more important, it was carried out because they believe "the fortunes and interests of the minority poor—indeed the poor in general—should be rapidly and radically advanced." [37] They went to live in Blackston in order to see what minority poverty was in a United States ghetto, whether it at all conformed to traditional theories advanced about poverty. According to these theories (which have been advanced by white social scientists), the urban poor are thought to be apathetic—they do not belong to organizations established to help the community. Indeed, the few such organizations that do exist are considered facades because the community poor refuse to invest time and energy to help transform the society. Nor, these theories hold, do the urban poor trouble themselves to vote. For this reason, the poor remain outside the mainstream of American life, living marginal lives, with no power to change their lot.

The Valentines established rapport by being active members of the community. This meant joining demonstrations in which they risked arrest, sharing illegally obtained food supplies, lending and trusting their car to a neighborhood where car guttings were common, having all their possessions stolen, and even writing up their

preliminary findings in anonymous pamphlets to combat incorrect reporting of certain local events in the press.

Their preliminary results did not seem to support the culture of poverty thesis. They found community members very active in the major institutions of the society, certainly in the welfare system, clinics and emergency wards of hospitals, the mass media, and the national and local elections of November 1968. Their community friends had possessions, shopped once a week, had bank accounts; some even had a little land somewhere in the South. They generally shared the same economic values as the rest of the society, though they were intertwined with values that supported extensive networks for obtaining and distributing illicit resources.

They did not find the apathetic poor hopelessly adapted to circumstances of marginality in Blackston. Though very poor, the people were struggling for institutions they believed all Americans had a right to—decent health care, adequate schools—institutions they knew were better in affluent, white neighborhoods. The insiders' point of view gave a very different picture from that produced by earlier, white social scientists.

Sociobiology

Contemporary anthropology is currently witnessing a trend away from ethnographic-based study to an alliance with other scientific fields. Though great cultural variations have been recorded by anthropologists, no integrating, explanatory theory has been produced to account for it. One contemporary school of thought that attempts to fill this gap is known as *sociobiology*, which treats *Homo sapiens sapiens* as just

37. Valentine and Valentine, "Making the Scene," p. 404.

one of many animal species and tries to explain culture within a biological, evolutionary framework.

In keeping with Darwinian evolutionary theory, sociobiology emphasizes the survival and transmission of genetic materials from parent to offspring. The name of the game of evolution, then, is the perpetuation of one's self by transmitting genetic material to descendants, no matter what the cost. Where sociobiology parts from accepted Darwinian theory, however, is in its insistence that behavior, too, is passed on. This new theory holds that the behavior of all animals—human and nonhuman— is based on inherited "programs" which have been fairly well established during the course of evolutionary development. Any behavior that helps individuals to survive the struggle for life is passed on through such genetic programs to their offspring.

As Lionel Tiger and Robin Fox [38] put it, the genetic material carries from parent to offspring a program that includes not only body shape, color, sense of smell and other characteristics, but behaviors as well. Even our sense of morality and justice have evolved with us and are passed from generation to generation through the genes. These investigators write:

> . . . living involves successful programs and . . . successful behavioral programs are as much a result of natural selection as the opposable thumb and the reproductive differences be-between men and women.[39]

---

38. Lionel Tiger and Robin Fox, *The Imperial Animal* (New York: Holt, Rinehart and Winston, 1971).

---

39. Tiger and Fox, *The Imperial Animal*, p. 18.

Where does cultural variation fit into all this? One of the founders of this new approach is E. O. Wilson, a biologist who specializes in the study of bees.[40] Wilson asks whether humans are genetically "wired" to enter certain social classes and to play certain roles. He uses the example of conquest to illuminate this aspect of his theory. When one group conquers another, for example, the genetic differences of the two are preserved by a variety of techniques. Among these are the raising of class barriers, racial and cultural discrimination, and the establishment of physical ghettos which separate those perceived as undesirables from the elite and other strata of the new amalgamated society. Thus, descent from one group or another would put an individual in line to receive one or the other set of traits. Those who descended from the upper classes, for example, would inherit genetic material from a superior gene pool. The reverse would be true for those who occupied the bottom rungs of the social ladder. In reality, however, such differences have not been observed in groups such as the different castes in India that have remained relatively genetically "pure" for centuries.

A less testable hypothesis of Wilson's is that a genetic predisposition to aggression led to hominid expansion, and is, therefore, at the base of human culture. He argues that "if any social predatory mammal attains a certain level of intelligence . . . one band [of such mammals] would have the capacity to consciously ponder the significance of adjacent social groups and to

---

40. Edward O. Wilson, *Sociobiology* (Cambridge, Mass.: Harvard University Press, Belknap Press, 1975).

deal with them in an intelligent, organized fashion." [41] Thus, a band might conquer a neighboring band, seize its territory, and by interbreeding, spread its genes throughout the conquered group. This process would be repeated; the victors would always represent the more aggressive group, or the group most able to sidestep genocide by making some form of peaceful settlement, which Wilson also thinks represents mental and cultural advance.

Our ethnographic knowledge of hunting-gathering peoples, however, does not indicate that one group was in any hurry to force itself on another. In fact, hunters and gatherers are extremely nonwarlike and even tend to minimize conflicts within their own small bands.

Sociobiology tends to interpret all social occurrences in terms of what are presumed to be their underlying motivations. [42] In other words, it tries to supply biological reasons for all behavior. If there is conflict, it is an expression of aggression. If there is food-sharing, it is an expression of altruism. Marshall Sahlins has pointed out that people do not go to war because they are aggressive. In fact, many unaggressive people go to war for all kinds of reasons: love of country, humaneness (compared to brutality attributed to the enemy), honor, self-esteem, guilt, to appease the ghosts of one's ancestors, to save the world for democracy. [43] The reasons are cultural as the wars are cultural.

An aboriginal chief of the Tiwi tribe in Australia's Northern Territory.

The accumulation of anthropological data on many different cultures suggests that cultural phenomena are considerably more complex than the biological interpretations thus far offered by sociobiology. The new theory is in trouble for other reasons as well. In a period when anthropologists are particularly sensitive to the political and ethical implications of their work, they find in sociobiology a sense of social Darwinism, not to mention male chauvinism. Sociobiology provides biological reasons for behavior that anthropologists

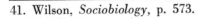

41. Wilson, *Sociobiology*, p. 573.

42. Marshall Sahlins, *The Use and Abuse of Biology* (Ann Arbor: University of Michigan Press, 1976).

43. Sahlins, *The Use and Abuse of Biology*, p. 8.

Anthropology and the Future

and other social scientists have always considered to be socially conditioned. Indeed, its gospel of genetic determinism has come under fire for feeding other social theories based on genetics, including racism.

Erich Fromm has written about human destructiveness: "Modern society, with its almost limitless readiness for destruction of human lives for political and economic ends, can best defend itself against the elementary question of its right to do so by the assumption that destructiveness and cruelty are not engendered by our social system, but are innate qualities in man." [44] It would be equally evasive to excuse the exploitation of one class by another—as well as the unequal treatment of individuals of a certain race or sex—on biological grounds.

An Ethical Anthropology

Though anthropology is ostensibly an academic discipline, a science of culture, it has many practical applications, as we have seen. We have also seen that objectivity is impossible in a field in which one human being studies other human beings. A basic premise of our own discipline, i.e., that human perception is culturally conditioned, rules out complete objectivity. We cannot even formulate questions that are not a reflection of the culture from which we come. Perhaps this will change as members of the Third World and other minority groups begin to produce anthropologists.

But beyond the shortcomings of individual anthropologists are the politics of the field. Anthropologists have been asked to participate in espionage activities be-

cause of their expertise with small-scale societies. A few years ago, the U.S. Department of Defense sponsored a vast program, Project Camelot, which would have used anthropologists and other social scientists to find out the causes of social unrest leading to armed insurgency. The program caused an international scandal and was never carried out. Anthropologists also were used in Thailand to advise counterinsurgency efforts. This use of anthropology jeopardizes any future fieldwork. Increased literacy has made it possible for formerly isolated peoples to know what is going on in the world and what anthropologists are saying about them. Rightfully, the subjects will not tolerate people who win their confidence and then use it against them.

There is some sentiment that all fieldwork in other cultures should be abandoned because of its implicit political implications. Others feel that cross-cultural research must continue because it is the essence of anthropology. Yet, anthropologists cannot ignore the political situation in which they find themselves. Gutorm Gjessing has eloquently stated, "If we must choose between the immediate interests of the oppressed and those of the oppressor, there can be no doubt that our responsibility is first and foremost to the former; for it is here that our special competence lies." [45]

This means we must find ways to study accurately the poor in our own country as well as in others. We must combat the ideology of racism with our knowledge of the physical basis of race. We must teach

44. Erich Fromm, *The Anatomy of Human Destructiveness* (New York: Holt, Rinehart and Winston, 1973).

45. Gutorm Gjessing, "The Social Responsibility of the Social Scientist," *Current Anthropology* 9, no. 5 (1968): 402.

about the differences in culture that celebrate the potential of the human species. Nor should we forget that small homogeneous cultures have much to offer their industrialized counterparts, practices which can help solve some of our own problems. For example, taking a leaf from the preliterate book, we could break our crowded urban areas into smaller, more manageable autonomous communities. Something like this is already underway in such cities as New York, where block members or other smaller urban groups have out of necessity taken over the functions which the financially pressed city could no longer afford to provide. Other customs we might borrow from the small-scale society are child-rearing practices that emphasize cooperation, respect for the individual, and nonaggressive techniques for settling differences.

And, of course, we must continue to search for solid theories to explain cultural variation.

Summary

1. Although humans have made enormous strides in material progress, they are far behind in realizing certain nonmaterial needs.
2. American culture creates a tension between drives and values; often the values are sacrificed to the drives, leaving individuals confused and unsatisfied.
3. Only in industrial societies is the moral order—the organization of sentiments into judgments as to what is right—separate from the technical order—the organization of work that is involved in survival.
4. The attributes of preliterate society could be included in all designs for new, contemporary societies.
5. Applied anthropology uses the knowledge and methods of anthropology to solve practical problems in all areas of social life.
6. Modern applied anthropology is concerned with the social and cultural problems that accompany technological change and modernization in developing countries.
7. Most anthropological studies have been concerned with poor, nonwhite peoples. Many of these peoples now resent the fact that the anthropologist does nothing to help alleviate their poverty.
8. Recent work has shown that male domination of anthropology has tended to distort our understanding of certain cultural phenomena which involve women.
9. The future of anthropology is very much alive, and includes new problems to pursue and new methods to refine. One such problem is the understanding of poor people in urban situations.
10. A current trend in anthropology is toward alliance with other scientific disciplines. Sociobiology, for example, attempts to explain the enormous cultural variation of humankind in terms of its biological basis.
11. Ethical anthropology has many tasks. Among these are the accurate study of the oppressed, the continuation of the fight against racism, and the search for theories to explain cultural variation.

Review Questions

1. Many investigators believe that progress, as it is defined in today's industrial societies, has not been all that good for humankind. Do you agree or disagree? Explain your answer.
2. Two important anthropological ideas are Redfield's concepts of the moral order and the technical order. Explain each of these ideas in your own words.

3. List four characteristics of preliterate societies. How are these manifested in modern industrial cultures, if at all?

4. What is applied anthropology? Give an example.

5. Cultural bias often distorts what we know about the subject being studied. Give an example of such bias in anthropology.

6. What is sociobiology? Give an example. What are its shortcomings?

Suggested Readings

Clifton, James A., ed. *Applied Anthropology: Readings in the Uses of the Science of Man.* Boston: Houghton Mifflin, 1970.

The best available reader on applied anthropology. Includes case studies.

Henry, Jules. *Culture against Man.* New York: Random House, 1963.

A critical study of American institutions from a Marxist-anthropological point of view.

Rosaldo, Michelle Zimbalist, and Lamphere, Louise, eds. *Women, Culture and Society.* Stanford, Calif.: Stanford University Press, 1974.

One of the few available good readers on women in cross-cultural perspective.

Weaver, Thomas, ed. *To See Ourselves: Anthropology and Modern Social Issues.* Glenview, Ill.: Scott, Foresman, 1973.

A comprehensive collection of articles on issues that have caused controversy in anthropology in recent years.

Appendix A

ARCHEOLOGICAL METHODS

Archeology, a subdiscipline of anthropology, studies prehistoric cultures. Archeology involves the analysis of cultural material in the absence of observable behavior. It concentrates on the study of material remains from particular sites in order to reconstruct the cultures of the people who lived at those sites. A major problem of this subdiscipline is to squeeze from material remains enough information to actually portray a culture. The stone tools, potsherds, projectile points, bone objects, and other things left behind by ancient cultures—discussed in Chapters 5, 7, 8, and 9—have been neither described nor catalogued for us by their makers. They can only be reconstructed from what is preserved.

By reconstructing certain aspects of these past cultures, we can learn what the people were doing, which is as close to live culture as we can get in an archeological context. It is exciting that a vanished society can be brought back to life. Such resurrection is to the archeologist what participant observation is to the ethnographer. Indeed, it may be said that archeology is an attempt to add prehistoric cultures to the inventory of cultures considered by anthropologists.

The challenge of archeology, then, is to learn as much as possible about past cultures. To reach that goal is, in great part, a methodological problem. We have to ask the right questions. But beyond that, we have to develop procedures to begin to approach the answers. Three such procedures are preliminary investigation, excavation, and analysis.

Preliminary Investigation: Finding a Site

The basic unit of archeological fieldwork is the *site*, which is any location that contains the remains of past human activity. How do archeologists find sites? How do they determine past human behavior from what is there? Written documents help them find historic sites, such as those in Egypt, Greece, or Italy. Maps, histories, literary works, and hearsay define the general area of an historic occurrence or community. The ancient Greek city of Troy, for example, was discovered in the last century by Heinrich Schliemann, who located the city by studying Homer's *Iliad*. Even with such information, however, it is not always easy to pinpoint the exact location. But there are no documents at all for prehistoric sites. That is, initially there are no documents. An investigator approaching a new area, of course, looks in the archeological literature—the professional journals and books—for reference to previous excavations that may have been done there.

If there is nothing in the literature, there are other ways of finding a site. One of these is simply to look in those areas that one thinks may have been inhabited in the past. A researcher interested in the cultural remains of hunters would know that these groups lived in small camps and moved often as they followed game. The sites of such groups would have been near water, game, and possibly some source of fuel. An investigator studying early farming communities (as in Chapter 8) would know that farmers inhabited permanent settlements that were near arable land.

One general rule for locating a site is to be on the alert for anything that looks out of place. A hill that has an unusual shape, soil that is different in color from other soil in the area, vegetation growing in a peculiar fashion, or growing where it shouldn't—all are giveaways to an archeological site. For example, grass growing higher and fuller on the edge of a rectangle may form the boundaries of a prehistoric house or ditch.[1]

No matter how the archeologist decides where to look for a site, the first investigator in a new area must rely on being able to identify definite signs of past human occupation. This is done first by examining the surface of the site—by making a survey, which may involve some subsurface testing, and by noting the artifacts and features that occur at or near the surface.

The Survey

Archeological surveying is a systematic approach to the location of sites. The archeologist divides the area in question into a number of squares, or grids. He or she then systematically walks over the grid, examining the ground for past cultural remains. More recently, archeologists have located sites by aerial photography, sometimes using infrared film. Such film records heat absorbed by the earth and man-made features on the earth. Different materials absorb different amounts of heat,

---

1. Frank Hole and Robert F. Heizer, *An Introduction to Prehistoric Archeology*, 3rd ed. (New York: Holt, Rinehart and Winston, 1973).

and these variations show up on the film as contrasting darker or lighter areas. Most archeological sites, for example, absorb more heat than the earth around them. As a result, they appear darker on infrared film than surrounding areas.

A survey may be done for a variety of reasons. Ideally the archeologist has a research problem in mind which calls for the study of certain kinds of sites. For example, Richard MacNeish believed the earliest corn would be found in a particular environment south of Mexico City (see Chapter 8). He surveyed several valleys before finding what he was looking for in the Tehuacán area. Sometimes survey is for the more general purpose of seeing what kinds of sites are in a given area in an effort to reconstruct the cultural history of the region. Archeologists are interested in *settlement pattern* in relation to the environment—that is, how people adapted to the different topographical features (flood plains, river banks, mountain slopes, for example) in their surroundings. Investigators may also do a survey to get some idea of the *demography*—or the size, density, and distribution—of an ancient population. Finally, a survey can also provide information about the links that may have joined different prehistoric populations. All these problems may be at least initially approached by surveys. For the archeologist, then, it is not simply a matter of finding artifacts, but of finding meaning in their distribution.

Limited subsurface testing of the site may also be part of a survey. For example, small shovel tests or holes made with an auger to the subsoil may reveal the outlines of features or concentrations of artifacts. This kind of testing is very important in *public archeology*, which is that paid for by public tax dollars or corporation funds. Federal legislation now requires that federally funded projects which may disturb historic or prehistoric cultural remains must allot a certain amount of their budget to archeological survey and, if necessary, excavation.[2] More often than not, highways, sewers, dams, and the like are constructed in areas that have been disturbed previously by human settlements. In most cases, the location of archeological remains can rarely be done by mere surface examination. Systematic, subsurface testing is often necessary in the earliest stages of a survey. Because so many surveys are required by law, there is great potential for a dramatic expansion of our knowledge of cultural history. Surveys, then, even when they do not lead to full-scale excavation, can contribute to our understanding of behavior.

Artifacts and Features

Two kinds of cultural remains that may be found during the survey are artifacts and features. An *artifact* is anything that has been made or modified by humans. Artifacts found on the surface of a site are assumed to represent material from all periods of its occupation. Many sites extend tens of feet into the earth and have been occupied over hundreds of thousands of years by different groups. Olduvai Gorge, mentioned in Chapter 5, is 300 feet deep and contains numerous layers holding the physical, and possibly the cultural, remains of our ancestors.

---

2. Thomas F. King, Patricia Parker Hickman, and Gary Berg, *Anthropology in Historic Preservation: Caring for Culture's Clutter* (New York: Academic Press, 1977).

Archeologists have learned that it is not always practical to collect every artifact on the surface of a site. Instead, the investigator may gather only a random sample of artifacts. This is done by placing an imaginary grid over the site and picking up pottery and other objects only from certain grid squares. As we shall see, sampling can also indicate material beneath the surface.

The location of features without excavation is an even more difficult problem. A *feature* is some structural remnant of past human activity, such as a hearth, a wall, an irrigation ditch, or a canal. Aerial photos can help locate subsurface remains. For example, on such photography, plant growth may show up differently where moisture has collected in abandoned canals, or where buildings stand. Plowlines, old trails, and other features that are not easily discerned on the ground are often visible from the air. Another useful instrument for locating foundations is the *proton magnetometer*. This device measures the intensity of the earth's magnetic field. The presence of underground features directly below is signaled by changes in the strength of the field.

Excavation

Excavation is the essence of archeology. All anthropologists are interested in human behavior, but for the archeologist there is a particular fascination in finding its remnants in the ground. It is obviously impossible to dig up an entire past way of life. Only a small proportion of the material remains can be dealt with, and that only in fragmentary form. The archeologist must therefore be very careful about how he or she approaches excavation. It is physically hard work and intellectually challenging.

Stratigraphy

The first problem in an archeological excavation is to figure out the stratigraphy —the order and content of the earth layers at the site. For example, the investigator must find out if any variations in soil composition and color in different layers are the result of past human occupations. Some sites, such as an infrequently visited hunting camp, are very small. Stratigraphy at such a site would at least be limited spatially. At larger sites— mounds, villages, shell heaps, for example —the stratigraphy may vary from one place to another and present a greater problem. At the beginning of an excavation, digging is approached very delicately: the researcher notes every change in soil color and composition as he or she progresses from top layers to bottom ones. This gives the researcher a fairly accurate picture of how many strata are at the site and which contain cultural items. The interpretation of stratigraphy is an ongoing problem in excavation and the key to understanding past cultural events.

Sampling

Since an archeological site is rarely fully excavated, some procedure for sampling its cultural remains must be adopted. As a matter of fact, it would not be desirable to excavate a whole site even if possible. This is so because archeology is necessarily destructive. The aim of the good archeologist is to leave as much information as possible in the ground for future generations of archeologists who may have developed better techniques for recovering cultural remains. The archeologist, then, tries to destroy as little as possible by sampling intelligently.

Another important consideration in sampling is the research interest of the investigator. What is he looking for? Is he trying to solve some particular problem? For example, a researcher looking for signs of fortification does not concentrate on what he or she believes to be the center of the site, but instead samples the area around the edges. Conversely, the archeologist looking for the overall settlement pattern of an ancient society must sample the entire area in a systematic way.[3]

Mapping

Sampling is based on a graphic representation of the site. A *datum point* is established and a map made on which all excavation units are measured with reference to this point (see Figure A–1). The datum point may be anything as long as it is permanent: the edge of a structure or a road, for example. The purpose is to tie the map to a point that can be located by future investigators.

After the datum point has been fixed, one or two base lines are drawn through it to provide the outline for a grid on which all excavation is made. A grid is then placed over the site, dividing it into a number of grid squares, or excavation units. The units can then be identified by their distance east or west, and north or south, from the datum point.

The grid need only be hypothetical. A sample number of units are then excava-

---

3. Charles Redman, *Archeological Sampling Strategies*, Module in Anthropology, no. 55 (Reading, Mass.: Addison-Wesley, 1974), pp. 3–34.

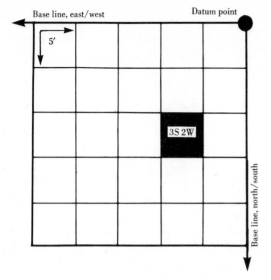

Base line, east/west

Datum point

5′

3S 2W

Base line, north/south

FIGURE A–1. A typical site map showing datum point and excavation grids, each of which is 5 feet on a side. Darkened grid square is marked 3S 2W, meaning that it is 3 squares south and 2 squares west of the datum point.

ted and recorded in great detail. All artifacts are related to the level at which they have been found and sometimes even mapped and photographed where they lie. Features are drawn and described. Excavation generally continues to the level of subsoil that contains no human cultural or physical remains.

Archeologists are not only digging to find artifacts. They are digging in a highly controlled way to find any and all indications of past human behavior. They are interested in individual cultures, not in a mixture of every culture that has ever inhabited a site. This means that different periods of occupation must be recognized and kept separate to be analyzed as separate cultural occurrences. The purpose of archeology, it should be remembered, is to add to our knowledge of all cultures, not to confuse the record with unreal mixtures that do not represent any specific cultures.

Analysis

Provenience—which refers to the exact location at which an object is found at a site—is of utmost importance in archeological analysis. It is absolutely essential that every artifact, every bone, every remnant of human behavior be identified as to the specific location at which it was discovered. Objects found at the site that are to be brought back to the laboratory for analysis are transported in bags that are marked with all information relevant to the provenience of the contents. The name of the site is on the bag, the location of the excavation unit, the stratum within the unit, the depth of that stratum, the date, and probably even the names of the people who excavated that particular grid square. When the material is taken out of the bag it is washed and marked with a number that indicates its exact provenience. Only then can materials be grouped and compared for other kinds of analysis.

Typology

Artifacts are generally classified into types. A *type* is a particular kind of artifact in which several attributes combine or cluster with sufficient frequency or in such distinctive ways that the investigator can define and label the artifact and can recognize it when he or she sees another example. In Chapter 7, for example, we saw how the Mousterian tools were arranged into types according to use. The shape, material, or method of manufacture of projectile points found at a site may allow the investigator to group these artifacts into separate categories. He may find that 20 percent of the points have a channel running down the center, whereas 70 percent may have the same shape but no channel. If radically different types of the same kind of projectile point (or other artifacts) are found at different contemporaneous sites in the same region, it may be inferred that the sites were inhabited by two different cultures. Types are useful in that they enable researchers to organize large collections of artifacts. The establishment of types also makes it easier for the archeologist to compare objects from one site to objects from other sites.

Because all artifacts collected at a site have been marked with a number indicating provenience, it is possible to determine if certain types are characteristic of certain time periods or locales within the site. Perhaps certain types of pottery are consistently found with certain types of projectile points. These combinations may be found at other sites, too, which increases the probability that they were manufactured by the same culture. A problem with typology has been a tendency to give types misleading names. Thus, not all projectile points are projectile points. Some are knives, some scrapers. Determining the use of an object is quite different from classifying it typologically.

Functional Analysis

The shape of an artifact gives some indication of its use. But this may not be accurate enough. Because some ancient tools are not so different from modern ones, the investigator can infer how the former were used. Ethnographic examples may also be helpful. More recently, investigators have begun to examine artifacts under the microscope to deduce wear patterns. This method was used to determine that the flint sickles, discussed in Chapter 8, were actually employed to harvest grain. The context in which an artifact is found is also important in determining its function. For example, artifacts called *banner stones* in the eastern United States were once believed to be used for ceremonial purposes. Then, it was noted that these objects were consistently found in association with antler pieces now identified as parts of throwing sticks (atlatls). This information led archeologists to conclude that the banner stone was part of the atlatl.

Some archeologists believe that once a group of artifacts is placed into functional categories, the use of a site at which they were unearthed becomes much clearer. Howard Winters, for example, devised ten such categories in his study of the Riverton Culture in Illinois: weapons, general utility tools, domestic implements, fabricating and processing tools, woodworking tools, agricultural or digging implements, ornaments, ceremonial artifacts, recreational equipment, and fire-making equipment. Thus, the discovery of a high percentage of weapons suggests a hunting camp, whereas large numbers of general utility tools and domestic equipment point to a habitation site. Winters does not argue that each individual artifact can be absolutely identified, but that classes of artifacts will emerge and provide clues as to how the site was used. He does not define sites only in terms of artifact categories either. He uses all available information—whether it be climatic, geologic, or faunal—in combination with artifacts and other archeological data, to come up with the most complete explanation of a site possible.[4]

Food Remains

All archeologists have come to appreciate the significance of nonartifactual materials for reconstructing past cultures. Thus, animal and plant remains are saved when they are recognized, and methods for saving even that which is not immediately apparent in the field are being developed.

It is useful for the archeologist to be able to identify faunal remains, but a zoologist must often be consulted to assure accuracy. Once sorted, bones can be a key to understanding the diet, hunting preferences, and other aspects of prehistoric cultures. This is particularly true in reference to the hominids discussed in Chapter 5 because the addition of meat to their diets had important implications for human evolution.

The presence of certain animal species in cultural remains says something about the meat-eating of early peoples. But one must calculate the number of animals killed before he or she can estimate how vital meat was to the group. The calculation of meat consumed is not easy because some bones deteriorate and others represent the inhabitants of archeological sites rather than hunted creatures of times past. Rodents, for instance, may have died natural deaths exploring ruins. On the other hand, large game animals until recently were considered the only prey of early humans. This assumption led archeologists to ignore the remains of humbler species. But our knowledge of modern hunters and gatherers, combined with more thorough analysis of the archeological context, has led to an appreciation of the importance of smaller animals in the diet of early peoples.

Plant remains also present problems for archeological analysis. Seeds are rarely noticed in the field and larger, charred remains such as corn cobs are easily lost in handling. To overcome some of the problems in recovering even microscopic plant remains, a technique known as *flotation* has been developed. Soil samples from archeological sites are brought back to the laboratory, where water and fine sifting equipment (screens, for example) separate plant remains from the dirt. The remains are then identified, by a botanist if necessary. This procedure has become particularly important in determining whether or not prehistoric people practiced agriculture (the subject of Chapter 8). Other ways of assessing the importance of cultivated plants in the diet have also been developed. Pollen from plants may be analyzed and compared to the modern flora in the area in order to construct a local sequence of plant history. This is then used for dating as well as identification. In the capsule study for Chapter 7, for instance, we saw how the analysis of pollen grains contributed to our knowledge of Neandertal burial practices.

The diet of prehistoric peoples may also be determined from the microscopic analysis of *coprolites*, the preserved remnants of human feces. Fecal matter in very dry climates can preserve certain bones of

4. Howard Winters, *The Riverton Culture: A Second Millennium Occupation in the Central Wabash Valley*, Illinois State Museum Reports of Investigations, no. 13 (Springfield, Ill.: Illinois State Museum and Illinois Archaeological Survey, 1969), p. 30.

small mammals and fish, as well as insects, seed, and other vegetal matter.

Food remains provide information on more than diet. They also offer clues about the climate, and even the very season during which a site was used. If caches of ripe seeds are found, for example, the archeologist can infer that the site was inhabited during the harvest season. If animals of a certain age predominate, it may indicate a seasonal hunting period. Even mollusk shells can tell the investigator the season at which they were collected. Thus, archeology has become more than just the analysis of people-made objects. It is the analysis of artifacts in conjunction with all the other information which is so important to a reconstruction of a living society.

Dating

Typology, artifacts, and floral remains have been used to date archeological sites. If an archeologist finds a type of projectile point that has been found at twenty other sites dating between 14,000 and 11,000 B.P., he or she tentatively assumes that the new example is also a product of this period. Various absolute and relative dating techniques were discussed in Chapter 5. Other methods available primarily to the archeologist include seriation, archeomagnetism, and dendrochronology.

SERIATION. The times that the same site was inhabited by different cultures may be relatively determined by *seriation*. Seriation is based on the fact that the life spans of artifacts follow certain popularity curves. When an object is first introduced —say the steam locomotive—it is found only in a few places. Gradually, it catches on and numerous such artifacts are produced and purchased. Then, after a number of years, the popularity or usefulness of the item begins to decline until it is finally no longer produced. Such was the fate of the steam locomotive. Using this information, an investigator can compare the various periods during which the object was popular—from its introduction to peak popularity to decline. A cultural sequence based on this change in use can then be constructed. Seriation is most often used in dating pottery.

ARCHEOMAGNETISM. Artifacts made of fired clay can occasionally be dated by a method called *archeomagnetism*. This technique is based on the fact that unfired clay contains certain iron minerals whose grains are aligned randomly in the clay. When the clay is fired the grains align themselves with the magnetic field surrounding them. This magnetic field has been shown to change at different periods of time. The periods when the changes occurred are known for some areas. If the magnetic changes are known for an area in which the clay has been fired, the exact date of its manufacture can be established. This method has limited application, however, because the records of magnetic variations are rarely available for areas in which archeological sites are located.

DENDROCHRONOLOGY. Another exact method of dating which is also limited in its application is *dendrochronology*. More commonly called *tree ring dating*, this technique is based on the fact that trees growing in temperate zones have clearly defined annual rings of growth. The cross-section of a tree trunk reveals this rate of annual growth preserved as a series of concentric rings. The basic operating principle is that each year of a tree's growth produces a band different from that of the preceding year. Since the yearly variation is usually due to climate or moisture in the entire region, the band of all trees of the same species in a single region will be roughly identical for any one year. Thus, it should be possible to identify, say, a band for the year 1925 on all trees of the same species that were alive in the region in 1925. Usually it is not just one band, but a series or sequence of bands, that helps identify the year the tree was felled. By working carefully backward in time from band sequences whose absolute dates are known, archeologists have created a master series of bands for several different species in the American southwest, series extending back to about 5,000 B.P. By comparing the band pattern of, say, a sapling used as a roof support in a pueblo with the master sequence or master series for the same species, archeologists can pinpoint the probable date the sapling was cut by the pueblo builders. But this technique can work only on trees from the same species and region.

Once a date for cultural remains at a site has been established, the investigator is then ready to take the next step in analysis. What does all of this mean, he may ask himself. What definite things can be said about this long-vanished society? In short, the archeologist is now faced with the most important task of the project— interpreting the remains of a past society.

Interpretation

The major organizing principle in modern archeology has been evolutionary theory, discussed in Chapters 4 and 12. This kind of thinking is appropriate to archeology because of its emphasis on economic and technological developments. According to this theory, all societies are interpreted as representing one of four levels of sociocultural integration: band, tribe, chiefdom, or state. Each level can be characterized as to population, subsistence, social organization, and political organization. Consequently, much effort has been spent developing techniques that will adequately estimate prehistoric populations, subsistence, and sociopolitical organization from archeological data.

Population

One approach to population estimates has been to calculate how many houses there were at a site and how many people would have inhabited each. R. Naroll gathered data on eighteen societies from various parts of the world. His analysis of this data led him to the conclusion that there was one person for every 1,000 square feet of floor space at any given site in the societies studied.[5] William Haviland has estimated Mayan populations by assuming that prehistoric families had adapted to their environment in much the same manner as modern Mayan families. So Haviland multiplied the number of houses by the assumed family size to arrive at a population estimate. Of course, not every house has been excavated.[6]

---

5. R. Naroll, "Floor Area and Settlement Population," *American Antiquity* 27 (1962): 587–589.

---

6. William A. Haviland, "Family Size, Prehistoric Population Estimates and the Ancient Maya," *American Antiquity* 37 (1972): 135–139.

Ethnographic examples can help. Iroquois longhouses were inhabited in historic times. When calculating the number of prehistoric residents per longhouse, archeologists assume two families used one hearth as they did in the historic period. Numbers of burials can also be used to estimate population. The ages of buried individuals are calculated and compared with the normal age distribution in a population living under similar circumstances.

Detailed analysis of environmental factors is being employed more and more for reconstructing prehistoric populations. By estimating the food, water, fuel, and other resources that may have existed in the ancient environment, researchers can arrive at some idea of the number of people such resources could have supported.

Social Organization

Social organization is an even more subtle problem in archeological interpretation than population. One of the most inventive and stimulating studies in reconstructing prehistoric social organization was James Deetz's work on ceramics manufactured by the Arikara, a tribe of North American Plains Indians.[7] Deetz showed that the characteristics of pottery manufactured by the Arikara were related to the shared behavior that results from the social solidarity of the group. He demonstrated that matrilocal potters who resided together in the same tribe shared certain pottery designs that differed from those of other kin groups in the tribe. Moreover, the designs of pottery made by female potters decreased in number as the matrilocal families ceased being the primary social unit. Deetz's conclusions were corroborated by historical data.

In another example, Robert Whallon[8] interpreted increased stylistic, ceramic homogeneity within Iroquois villages in New York State as a reflection of decreasing contact between villages. Earlier, the villages had been in contact and had exchanged pottery and other goods. But when they became agriculturalists, territoriality increased, fortifications were built, and peaceful interchange was reduced.

Status differences among individuals have always been noted by archeologists. It was the tombs of the Egyptian upper classes, for example, that filled our museums with beautiful objects. Now, however, social status is noted on every level. Archeologists are interested in the status distinctions among burials, among houses, among sites, even among entire archeological zones. It is from such distinctions in social standing that archeologists can begin to understand not only political organization but the entire society of long-dead cultures.

7. James Deetz, "The Inference of Residence and Descent Rules from Archeological Data," in *New Perspectives in Archeology*, ed. Sally Binford and Lewis Binford (Chicago: Aldine Publishing, 1968).

8. Robert L. Whallon, "Investigations of Late Prehistoric Social Organization in New York State," in *New Perspectives in Archeology*, ed. Sally Binford and Lewis Binford (Chicago: Aldine Publishing, 1968), pp. 223–243.

Appendix B

KINSHIP TERMINOLOGY

Imagine that an anthropologist from the Crow Indians set out to study the kinship system of some large American city. Imagine further that he overheard a churchgoer refer to her pastor as "father" and to other members of the congregation as "brothers" and "sisters." Would the foreign scholar conclude that all these people belonged to one big family? If he asked these people specific questions about their relatives, would he be surprised to learn that Americans do not distinguish between the mother's brother—the maternal uncle—and the father's brother—the paternal uncle? And how would he react when informed that we do not even bother to differentiate between the children of our uncles and aunts, not even on the basis of sex? To us, these individuals are simply lumped in a single category and called "cousins." To the visiting anthropologist, such a practice would seem illogical, perhaps even immoral. Doesn't one's descent group—the matrilineage or patrilineage—have any significance in our life, he might ask. How do we know our rights and obligations with respect to our kin if we lump them together like this? Worse yet, he might wonder, how does a person know who his or her eligible marriage partners are?

Questions such as these undoubtedly ran through the minds of the earliest English and American anthropologists as they began scrutinizing the kinship systems of small-scale societies. These pioneers were amazed to learn that some preliterate peoples lumped their fathers together with their paternal uncles, using a single term to refer to both. Similarly, mothers and maternal aunts received the same label. Stranger still was the practice of referring to infants with labels suitable for parents, and to cousins with terms appropriate for offspring, for brothers and sisters—and even for the offspring of brothers and sisters. The first thoughts that occurred to these investigators may have been obvious ones such as, "Don't these people know who their fathers and mothers are? Can't they keep track of the identities of their own children?"

It should come as no surprise, then, that the world of *kinship terminology*—the labels used by societies to designate their relatives—is an intricate one. Despite this complexity, however, anthropologists have managed to ferret out the mechanisms behind most kinship systems—and their social implications. They have found only six basic kinds of terminological systems. These are the Eskimo, Hawaiian, Sudanese, Iroquois, Crow, and Omaha. Each is distinguished from the other on the basis of the way cousins are labeled. Let us examine these systems, focusing on the way cousins—and uncles—are classified in each.

ESKIMO TERMINOLOGY. We shall start with the Eskimo system of kinship terminology because it is the one we are most familiar with—it is our own. Eskimo terminology, so called because it is found among most Eskimo groups, is a *linear system*—it separates *linear relatives* (those, such as one's parents, grandparents, and children, who are either ancestors or descendants) from *collateral relatives* (all other biological relatives including brothers and sisters, aunts, uncles, nieces, nephews, and cousins. The Eskimo system is shown schematically in Figure B–1. In this figure, ego is the speaker, the person through whose eyes we are viewing the kinship web. As the drawing shows, the Eskimo system emphasizes the nuclear family by giving each member of this group his or her own term. On the other hand, ego's uncles, whether they be father's brother or mother's brother, are all lumped together under the same term. The same is true for the aunts. And the children of these collateral relatives are not even dis-

tinguished by sex—they are simply designated "cousins."

The Eskimo system is usually found in cultures where the nuclear family, rather than the descent group, is the chief productive unit. Thus, groups of hunter-gatherers, such as the Eskimo, and very complicated societies, such as our own, use this type of kinship terminology. In such cultures, the nuclear family lives apart from other relatives and typically does not depend on them for social or economic support. Indeed, the only occasions on which members of such families come together may be funerals, weddings, and other important family events. Since one's collateral relatives from both sides of the family are perceived as equals, the Eskimo system typically is found where a cognatic kinship system prevails. It is the third

FIGURE A–1. The Eskimo system of kinship terminology focuses on the nuclear family, each member of which is labeled by a separate term. In this figure, triangles symbolize males and circles are females. Vertical lines stand for descent, identifying relationships between ancestors and descendants. Horizontal lines link collateral relatives. Fa = father, Mo = mother. Br = brother, and Si = sister.

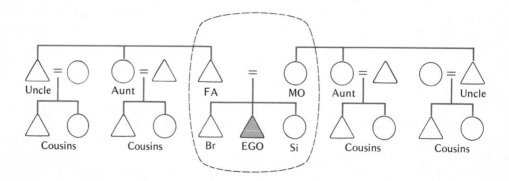

most common type, used by 16 percent of the world's cultures.

HAWAIIAN TERMINOLOGY. The Hawaiian system of kinship terminology, so called because it is found in Hawaii and other Malayan–Polynesian societies, is the simplest to describe because it has the least number of terms. As Figure A–2 shows, all members of Ego's parental generation are called by one of two terms, depending on their sex—mother or father. Roughly translated, these terms mean "male member of my parent's generation," and "female member of my parent's generation." Similarly, in Ego's own generation, all cousins are distinguished by sex alone and are called either brother or sister. This makes sense because these are children of individuals whom Ego calls mother and father. Because it lumps members of the same generation and sex under the same label, the Hawaiian system is a *generational* one.

As is the case with other systems of kinship terminology, the Hawaiian scheme reflects some important fact of social organization. That is, if an anthropologist knew nothing else about a society that classified kin in this way, he would immediately be tipped off that the chief means of social organization was cognatic descent, usually expressed in the form of the extended family or the ambilineal descent group. In a cognatic descent system, Ego traces descent through both her mother's and her father's side of the family. Thus, as in the Eskimo system, paternal and maternal relatives (aunts and uncles and their offspring) are perceived as being equal both to Ego and to Ego's parents, and are treated as such. Found in 32 percent of the world's societies, the Hawaiian is the most common form of kinship terminology system.

SUDANESE TERMINOLOGY. The Sudanese system can be considered the opposite of the simple Hawaiian system in that it distinguishes every member of the paternal and of ego's generation by his or her own term, thus mother's brother.

FIGURE B–2. The Hawaiian system has only four terms which distinguish individuals by sex and generation. Ego calls all of his cousins "brothers" or "sisters."

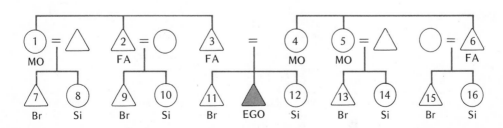

Each of the paternal and maternal aunts and uncles is labeled separately, as are their offspring. Such a system is known as a *bifurcate–collateral* one because ego's collateral relatives are separated (or bifurcated) from lineal relatives and from each other as well. Thus, it is quite exacting in its terminology. The Sudanese system is quite rare: only 8 percent of the world's cultures use it.

IROQUOIS TERMINOLOGY. The Iroquois system, named after the North American Indian tribe, is an example of a *bifurcate–merging* system. That is, some uncles and aunts are terminologically bifurcated, or separated, from ego's parents, whereas others are terminologically merged, or equated, with the parents. As Figure B–3 shows, ego's mother and the mother's sister are both referred to as "mother." Similarly, the father and the father's brother are both called "father." By contrast, ego's mother's brother and the father's sister are distinguished and given

their own labels. The same pattern prevails in ego's generation. Thus, the sons and daughters of the mother's sister, as well as the sons and daughters of the father's brother—ego's *parallel cousins*—are respectively referred to by ego as brother or sister. As in the Hawaiian system, this is so because these individuals are the offspring of men and women whom ego calls mother and father. By contrast, ego's *cross cousins*—offspring of the mother's brother and offspring of the father's sister—are called cousins, without regard to sex. This arrangement reflects the fact that these people are the children of ego's maternal uncle and paternal aunt.

The Iroquois system, the second most common form of kinship terminology, is usually found in those cultures where the unilineal descent group prevails. Such groups can be either patrilineal or matrilineal in form.

CROW TERMINOLOGY. The Crow system, together with its mirror image, the

FIGURE B–3. The Iroquois system shows the influence of both the patrilineal and the matrilineal descent group. Mother and mother's sister are merged, but father's sister is separated. Similarly, father and father's brother are lumped, but mother's brother is distinguished.

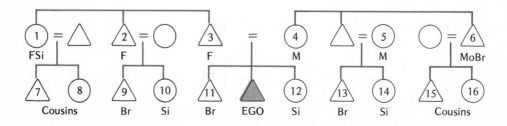

Omaha system, are the most complex for the Western mind to come to grips with. This is so because at first blush they seem to contain several illogical elements. Like that of the Iroquois, the Crow system is a bifurcate merging one which separates some individuals and merges others. But unlike the Iroquois, it does this without regard to generations. An examination of Figure B–4 will illuminate this point. As the figure shows, the members of the parental generation are labeled just as in the Iroquois system. For example, ego's mother and her sister are merged under the same term, but the father's sister is distinguished by her own term. The same is true for ego's father, the father's brother, and the mother's brother.

The Crow system differs from the Iroquois in the way certain members of ego's generation are labeled. As the figure indicates, the son and daughter of ego's father's sister are merged with the ego's parents' generation and given the same

names as their parents—the sons are called "father" and the daughters, "father's sister." At the other end of the figure, in ego's generation, is another unusual labeling—at least to our eyes. Here, the children of the mother's brother are merged with the generation of their parents, being called "son" and "daughter."

All this may seem terribly complex to us. But to our hypothetical Crow anthropologist, it is extremely logical, elegantly simple, and easy to explain. The Crow scholar would start by telling us that the arrangement is based on the fact that the Crow system is found in matrilineal societies in which the individuals of the father's matrilineage are terminologically separated from those of the mother's. Membership in the matrilineage far outweighs one's actual biological position or one's generation. In a matrilineage, as we saw in Chapter 13, ego's rights and duties are bound up with the members of his or her mother's descent group. Ego lives with these people,

FIGURE B–4. The Crow system shows the alliance of two matrilineages, each of which is kept terminologically distinct. In the father's matrilineage, each male who is called "father," regardless of generation, is a potential husband for ego's mother, and so addresses her as "wife."

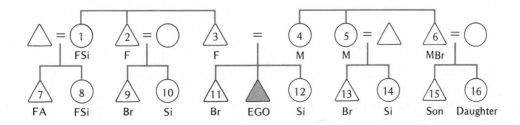

interacting with them on a daily basis. Indeed, one's mother's brother in such a descent group is more important than one's own father.

The Crow anthropologist would also tell us that it is the alliance between one matrilineage and another that is important in any marital union, rather than any romantic notions about love and personal relationships that the married couple may hold. How are these social facts reflected in Crow kinship terminology?

In this system, ego's mother's sister is better thought of as "female member of my mother's matrilineage," and his maternal uncle is "a male of my mother's matrilineage." Ego refers to the offspring of his mother's brother as "son" and "daughter." This is so because of the peculiarities of the marriage arrangement in matrilineages. In such groups, ego is theoretically permitted to carry his mother's brother's wife, should her husband die. Indeed, ego refers to her as "wife." Therefore, he refers to the offspring of this

couple as "son" and "daughter." The same is true for ego's mother—she is called "wife" by all the male members of his father's matrilineage because any of them can marry her, regardless of generation, should her spouse die.

The father, the father's brother, and the father's sister and her offspring are all members of the father's matrilineage. Therefore, these individuals are distinguished only by sex and are merged across generations. Thus, the father's sister's son is referred to as "father," and the daughter is called "father's sister." The sons and daughters of the father's brother, by contrast, ego calls "brother" and "sister," because they were produced by a man whom ego calls "father."

Thus, as illogical and complicated as it may seem to our minds, the Crow system keeps this matrilineal culture running smoothly. The Omaha system is the patrilineal counterpart of the Crow arrangement. It is shown in Figure B–5.

FIGURE B–5. The Omaha system is the patrilineal counterpart of the Crow matrilineal system. Again, the patrilineage of ego's mother and the father are kept distinct. In ego's mother's descent group, any female called "mother" is a potential wife for any male called "father" in the opposite group.

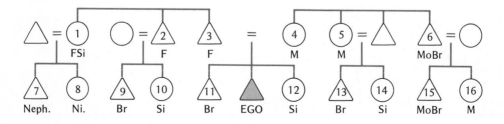

Glossary

Absolute dating   Any technique for determining the exact age of a fossil or other material excavated from the ground. Sometimes called chronometric dating.

Acculturation   Change resulting from contact between two or more autonomous cultures.

Acheulean   A tool tradition, dating from around the Middle Pleistocene and usually associated with *Homo erectus*. Its chief product is the hand axe.

Achieved status   A status acquired during one's lifetime.

Adaptation   The physical and behavioral responses of organisms to changes in the environment. Cultural adaptation is the process by which a human group adjusts to its environment through cultural means.

Aegyptopithecus   Extinct form of ape that lived in the Fayum area of Egypt about 29 million years B.P.

Affinal relationship   A marriage relationship, as opposed to a consanguinal or blood relationship.

Agriculture   The cultivation of plants carried out by means of plows, draft animals, and fertilizers.

Allele   Each of the pair of genes that govern any given trait in an individual.

Allen's rule   The principle that limbs and other exposed appendages of a species will be shorter and thicker in cold-stressed populations.

Animism   A belief in spirit beings, such as ghosts, animal spirits, or angels, that are thought to give life to nature.

Anthropoidea   A suborder of primates that includes monkeys, apes, and humans.

Anthropological linguistics   The study of languages that have no written form, by means of analysis of the sound system and grammatical structure of languages; also includes the study of historical relationships among languages.

Archeology   The scientific study of the written and unwritten history and cultural heritage of a people based on the excavation and analysis of material remains.

Artifacts   Material objects made or modified by a member of the human family, such as tools, housing, or works of art.

Ascribed status   A status into which one is born.

Aurignacian   An early culture of the Upper Paleolithic in Europe and the Near East, dating between 35,000 and 20,000 B.P.

Australopithecus   A hominid genus that dates back between 5½ million and 1 million B.P.

Australopithecus africanus   The most primitive species of *Australopithecus*, with dentition similar to modern *Homo*, and a cranial capacity ranging between 428 and 485 cc.

Australopithecus boisei   The most evolved species of *Australopithecus*. This form approached modern *Homo* in body size and inhabited East Africa.

Australopithecus robustus   A species of *Australopithecus* that was more evolved than *A. africanus*, this form inhabited South Africa.

Band   A small, autonomous, egalitarian group related by kinship and prevalent among hunter-gatherers.

Barter   The direct exchange of one commodity for another.

Bergmann's rule   The principle that within a mammal species, the breeding populations will be distributed so that groups with larger body size will be found in colder regions.

Biface   A stone tool produced by removing flakes from both sides of a core, or nucleus.

Binomial nomenclature   A system of naming living organisms, developed by Linnaeus, in which each species of animal or plant receives a name of two Latin terms, the first identifying the genus to which it belongs and the second the species.

Biological determinism   The belief that differences in ability and personality are innate, and that there is a tendency toward biological uniformity in behavior.

Bipedalism   A means of locomotion by which an animal habitually walks upright on two feet.

Brachiation   A means of arboreal locomotion in which an animal, suspended below the branches of a tree, uses its hands and arms to swing from one hold to another.

Brideprice   Payment by a man of an amount of money or goods to the family of his intended bride. Also called bridewealth.

Carnivore   An organism that consumes mainly meat.

Caste system   A hierarchy of ranked endogamous groups, with each individual assigned a group at birth.

Cercopithecoidea   A superfamily of anthropoids that consists of Old World monkeys.

Chromosome   Threadlike structure that contains the genes, found in pairs in the cell nucleus.

Clan   A group of kinspeople who trace their descent from a common ancestor, but are not certain of all the links that join them to the ancestor. Clans typically are united by a name, totem, or other symbol.

Cognatic descent   Descent pattern in which the individual traces his roots through both sides of the family equally.

Compadrazgo   A form of ritual co-parenthood between a child and a nonrelated adult sponsor established in the rite of Catholic baptism.

Creole   A blend of two or more established languages such as French and Spanish. Also called pidgin.

Cross-cultural method   The method by which cultural anthropologists compare practices in one society with those in other groups.

Cultural ecology   A school of thought pioneered by Julian Steward that is concerned with the way cultural systems adapt to their total environment as well as the way institutions of a given culture adapt to one another.

Cultural materialism   A school of thought begun by Julian White and based on the Marxist idea that the economic base of a culture supports its sociological bases. Thus, culture, and cultural change, depend upon a society's economic, or technological, factors.

Cultural relativism   The concept that the culture of another people should be approached with respect.

Culture   In anthropology, learned human behavior that is transmitted down the generations.

Cuneiform   The earliest known writing, using wedge-shaped characters, invented about 5000 B.P. by the Sumerians.

Deme   One of several local breeding populations of a species.

Deoxyribonucleic acid (DNA)   The master molecule containing the genetic code that directs the manufacture and distribution of proteins in all living things.

Descent   Origination from an ancestral line that determines membership in a kin group as well as the inheritance of property and social position.

Descriptive linguistics   The scientific study of the ways languages are structured (sound, meaning, and structure) and used.

Deviance   The labeling of certain individuals within a society because the individuals are judged as having broken the rules and sanctions of the society.

Diffusion   The spread of various elements of a culture—behavioral and material—from one human group to another.

Division of labor   Determination within a society of who is to do what kind of work, for whom, and in what manner. May be based on sex, age, caste, or other factors such as degree of specialization.

Domestication   The cultivation of plants and animals.

Dominant allele   The allele of a heterozygous gene pair that is expressed in the phenotype of the individual.

Dryopithecus   A fossil genus of hominoid (ape) that lived in Europe, Africa, and Asia during the Miocene period.

Economic anthropology   The study of how a society determines—by written and unwritten laws—who has the right to own resources and tools, and how labor and the products of labor are to be distributed.

Economy   The system in a society by which labor is organized and goods are produced and distributed.

Enculturation   All those learning processes by which a human being, as a member of a given society, obtains a working knowledge of the culture of that society.

Endocranial cast   A mold of the inner surface of an animal's skull that reveals such features as its brain size, shape, or pattern of blood vessels.

Endogamy   The custom requiring marriage within one's own social group.

Ethnocentrism   The assumption that one's own way of living is better than that of another group or society, and that one's own moral philosophy should form the basis for judging that of other groups or societies.

Ethnology   The comparative study of the similarities and differences among the world's cultures.

Evolution   The process whereby plants and animals change physically and behaviorally as they adapt to the environment.

Exogamy   The practice of marrying outside one's group.

Extended family   A group of people, consisting of two or more generations or two or more sets of parental generations, who reside together and who are related by blood or marriage.

Family   A social unit minimally consisting of a married couple and their children.

Feuding   A state of conflict between two kinship groups, usually initiated as a means of revenge, and lasting a relatively long time.

Formalism   The point of view of those economic anthropologists who study the economy from the standpoint of the individual, who must decide what work to do and what goods to produce.

Fossil   The remains or impression of an ancient animal or plant that has been preserved in the earth's crust.

Fossil record   The arrangement of known fossils in a time sequence relative to one another, based on both relative and absolute dating techniques.

Functionalism   The point of view in anthropology that each trait and institution within a culture performs a specific task which serves to hold the social system together.

Gene   Portion of the DNA molecule that is responsible for the manufacture of a given protein. The individual chemical unit of heredity.

Gene flow   The introduction of new alleles into the gene pool of a population as a result of the mating of individuals of the population with those of another.

Gene pool   All of the genes and alleles of a given population; the collective genotype of a population.

Generalized reciprocity   The free giving of gifts without conscious thought on the part of the giver of receiving something in return.

Genetic drift   The chance deviation, up or down, in the frequency of alleles in a small population.

Genotype   The genetic makeup of an individual.

Geographical race   Two or more local races grouped together and isolated reproductively from other similar groups by a major geographic boundary.

Gloger's rule   The principle that the breeding populations of bird and mammal species that inhabit the warm areas of a geographical range are darker in color than populations living in cooler regions of the range.

Glottochronology   A statistical method that determines the time during which two or more languages evolved separately from a common source.

Grammar   A set of rules to describe the way a particular language or dialect is put together.

Gravettian   A culture of the Upper Paleolithic, dating from 27,000 to 17,000 B.P., that appeared chiefly in eastern Europe.

Herbivore An organism that consumes only plants.

Heterozygote An individual in whom the alleles of a gene pair for a particular trait are different.

Hominid Any member of the human family, including modern people and their immediate ancestors, and including *Australopithecus* and probably *Ramapithecus*. Also called *Hominidae*.

Hominoidea A superfamily of anthropoids that includes the fossil and living apes and hominids—that is, the families Hominidae, Pongidae, and Hylobatidae.

Homo A hominid genus that may have appeared about 3 million B.P. It includes *Homo erectus, Homo sapiens neandertalensis*, and modern humans, or *Homo sapiens sapiens*.

Homozygote An individual in whom the alleles of a gene pair for a particular trait are the same.

Horticulture Farming carried out with simple tools and techniques; that is, lacking plows and draft animals.

Hunter-gatherers Small social groups, usually seminomadic bands, who use simple tools to hunt animals and collect plant foods as a means of subsistence.

Ideal culture The embodiment of the ideals and values that determine what ought to go on in a society.

Incest Sexual intercourse between persons defined as being closely related. Taboo in almost all societies.

Initiation rite Rite of passage observed in some societies, usually to mark puberty.

Innovation Any idea, process, or device that is new to a culture.

Insectivore An organism that consumes only insects.

Intensive agriculture An agricultural adaptation characterized by plows, irrigation, fertilizers, etc.

Ischial calliosities Tough skin on the buttocks of Old World monkeys that allows the animals to sit comfortably for long periods.

Kinship group All the individuals to whom one is related.

Learned behavior In anthropology, behavior that the individual derives from the cultural traditions of the group.

Levallois technique A method of manufacturing stone tools developed during the Acheulean period, probably by *Homo erectus*. This technique allowed the tool-maker to obtain flakes of predetermined form from a shaped core.

Levirate In some small-scale societies, the required remarriage of a woman to her deceased husband's brother.

Lexicostatistics Statistical technique devised to date the time of divergence of related languages.

Lineage A kinship group organized on a unilinear basis whose members trace their descent from a common known ancestor.

Lingua franca A language used in common among peoples of diverse languages.

Llano A tool-making tradition associated with Paleo-Indian hunters of the southwestern United States and dating from around 11,500 to 9000 B.P.

Magdalenian Late Upper Paleolithic culture of western Europe, dating from 17,000 to 10,000 B.P., and distinguished by antler and bone barbed harpoons.

Magic The use of means, such as charms, spells, or rituals, believed to control supernatural forces.

Market-exchange economy An economy in which the exchange of goods is by means of a general-purpose money, with the prices of goods set by the relationship between their supply and the demand for them.

Matrilineal descent A form of unilineal descent that includes links only through females.

Matrilocal residence Residence pattern in which a newly married couple live with or near the wife's kinship group.

Mayordomia The sponsorship by a person or small group of people of ceremonies relating to a religious image or to the building of a church.

Meiosis A process of cell division resulting in the production of reproductive cells (egg or sperm), each of which receives half of the chromosomes possessed by the parent.

Melanin Dark skin pigment in human populations that acts as a screen against the ionizing effects of ultraviolet radiation.

Mesolithic Age The Middle Stone Age; a period in the development of human culture marked by the establishment of small, prehorticultural villages. Lasted from 14,000 B.P. to about 12,000 B.P.

Mitosis Process of cell division which produces two new cells, each of which receives the same number of chromosomes possessed by the parent.

Moiety system A system of marriage in which communities are linked by twos in marriage alliance relationships, whereby men of Community A, for example, will marry women of Community B and women of Community A will marry men of Community B. Also a descent grouping within a community.

Monogamy Marriage in which a person has only one spouse at a time.

Monotheism Religious system built upon the belief in one god.

Morpheme The smallest unit of meaning in a language.

Mousterian Tool-making tradition of Middle Paleolithic period usually associated with Neandertals.

Mutation A random change in the genetic material of an individual that results in a new gene.

Natural selection The mechanism of organic evolutionary change as proposed by Charles Darwin. This mechanism provides that those individuals in a population who are better adapted to a given environment survive and outreproduce others in the population, so passing on their genes to the next generation.

Negative reciprocity An exchange of items in which one person tries to take advantage of another in the trade relationship.

Neolithic Age The New Stone Age; a period in the development of human culture marked by the domestication of plants and animals. Began about 10,000 B.P. in the Old World and 7000 B.P. in the New World.

Neolocal residence   Residence pattern in which a newly married couple set up housekeeping in a residence apart from both sets of parents.

Nomadism   A means of exploiting the environment by moving from place to place, never establishing a permanent settlement.

Norm   A social value or standard that shapes behavior in a particular society.

Nuclear family   A mother, father, and their children who reside together.

Omnivore   An organism that consumes both plant and animal substances.

Paleolithic Age   The Old Stone Age; a period in the development of human culture that dates from about 5 million to 14,000 B.P. It includes the cultures of three species of the genus *Homo*: Lower Paleolithic (*Homo erectus*), Middle Paleolithic (*Homo sapiens neandertalensis*), and Upper Paleolithic (*Homo sapiens sapiens*).

Paleontology   The study of the fossil remains of plants and animals.

Pastoralism   Nomadic herding of animals, adopted by some societies as an alternative to agriculture in an environment with a low potential for food production.

Patricide   The murder of one's own father.

Patrilineal descent   A form of unilateral descent that includes links only through males.

Patrilocal residence   Residence pattern in which a married couple live with or near the husband's kinship group.

Percussion flaking   Primitive tool-making technique, dating from Olduvai tradition, in which one stone is struck by another to obtain a sharp edge.

Perigordian   An early culture of the Upper Paleolithic. In Europe, dating between 35,000 and 20,000 B.P., characterized by big-game hunting.

Phenotype   The observable physical characteristics of a plant or animal that are determined by the interaction of its genotype with the environment.

Phoneme   The smallest unit of sound in a language capable of distinguishing meaning.

Phonology   The science of the speech sounds of language, including the history and theory of sound changes in any one language or in two or more related languages.

Plano   Late cultural tradition of Paleo-Indian hunters in North America, dating from 10,000 to 7000 B.P., characterized by unfluted stone points and rudimentary plant-processing tools.

Pleistocene   A geologic epoch, lasting from 2.5 million to about 9000 B.P., characterized by large-scale glaciations in much of the Northern Hemisphere.

Pollen analysis   Technique used by archeologists to identify microscopic pollen grains of plants.

Polyandry   A form of polygamy in which a woman has more than one wife at the same time.

Polygamy   The practice of having more than one spouse at the same time.

Polygyny   A form of polygamy in which a man has more than one wife at the same time.

Polytheism   Belief in, or worship of, many gods.

Polytypic species   A species whose breeding populations differ in genotype and phenotype.

Population   In genetics, a group of organisms within a species that are able to interbreed and reproduce viable offspring.

Population genetics   The study of the way gene pools change from one generation to another.

Potassium-argon dating   Technique for the absolute dating of igneous rocks that are older than 500,000 years.

Prehension   The ability of an animal to use the digits of its hands or feet (or both), or its tail, for grasping and seizing.

Pressure flaking   Precision tool-making technique developed by Upper Paleolithic peoples, whereby small flakes are removed from a stone core by pressing against it with a bone or wood tool.

Protoculture   Rudimentary culture. In primate studies, learned behavior patterns manifested by some higher primates, such as chimpanzees, and passed down from generation to generation.

Radiocarbon dating   Technique for the absolute dating of organic material that measures the amount of carbon-14 remaining in the material. The C-14 method is valid for dating material up to 70,000 years in age.

Ramapithecus   An extinct hominoid genus that ranged throughout Africa, Europe, and Asia about 14 to 12 million years B.P. Considered by some anthropologists to be the first hominid.

Recessive allele   The allele in a heterozygous gene pair that is not expressed in the phenotype of the individual but that is part of the genotype.

Reciprocation   In anthropology, the exchange of support, protection, and food within a society.

Redistributive exchange system   A system in which one person or group accumulates goods for the purpose of subsequently distributing those goods to members of the society, including the initial producers and contributors.

Relative dating   Technique for dating fossils that reveals the age of one fossil or earth layer in relation to another.

Religion   Beliefs and practices organized around supernatural entities. Gives a culture its moral imperatives, world view, and theories about the nature of reality.

Revitalization movement   The creation of a new religion at a time when traditional values and beliefs have ceased to have relevance to a society.

Ribonucleic acid (RNA)   A nucleic acid that carries the genetic code from the DNA molecule in the cell nucleus to the place in the cell where proteins are manufactured.

Rite of intensification   Rite that stresses the cohesiveness of the group.

Rite of separation   A rite of passage in which an individual gives up an old status and assumes a new one.

Rites of passage   The rituals or ceremonies that accompany the major transitions in the life cycle, such as birth, puberty, marriage, or death.

Ritual   A prescribed ceremonial of a religion which reinforces the beliefs of a society.

Role Pattern of behavior expected of an individual.

Sanctions Actions imposed by a society on its members in order to shape their behavior. Sanctions can be negative or positive.

Savanna Grassland containing scattered clusters of trees and found in tropical and subtropical regions.

Sedentarism A settlement pattern characterized by permanent villages or towns.

Semantics The study of meanings in a language.

Sexual dimorphism Physical differentiation, in secondary sexual characteristics, between the male and female of a species.

Shaman A ceremonial practitioner who uses magic to cure the sick, divine hidden facts, or control events. Often called medicine man or witch doctor.

Social Darwinism A social philosophy, modeled after Darwin's theory of evolution by natural selection, which holds that entire cultures are subject to the laws of biological evolution and that the world's cultures can be arranged in a definite hierarchy according to their stages of development.

Social organization The patterns of individual rights and obligations that join people in a given society.

Society A permanent group of people who share a common culture.

Sociobiology A contemporary school of thought that considers a human being as a species of animal subject to the laws of natural selection, and whose behavior patterns are transmitted, along with physical traits, by genes from one generation to the next.

Sociolinguistics The study of how people in the same culture use language in different social contexts.

Solutrean A culture of the Upper Paleolithic in France and Spain, dating from 21,000 to 17,000 B.P.

Sororal polygyny A form of polygamy in which a man has more than one wife at the same time and the wives are sisters.

Sororate The remarriage of a man to the younger sister of his first wife after the first wife has been found to be barren or has died.

Speciation The evolution of one biological species into another.

Species A population of organisms that naturally interbreed with one another.

State A politically organized body of people usually occupying a definite territory. Typically there is high population density, social stratification, complex division of labor, and the exercise of force vested in various branches of government.

Status The position of an individual in the social structure of a society.

Steppe Grassland having few or no trees.

Stratigraphy Technique for the relative dating of fossils, based on the assumption that strata of earth materials are deposited one atop the other, so that the oldest deposits are on the bottom and the newest are on top.

Structuralism The view that subconscious mental processes, or "mental structures," are responsible for human behavior, and that by analyzing the way in which a society uses terms and concepts, the anthropologist can discover its cultural beliefs and social organizations.

Subculture The customs and beliefs shared by a subgroup within a society.

Subspecies A subdivision of a species that differs from other divisions, usually in certain observable features.

Substantivism The point of view of those economic anthropologists who study economy from the standpoint of the society as a whole, and who see the economy as a social institution with the function of providing for the needs of the members of the society.

Symbols Forms, sounds, objects, or ideas created by a society which, through time and experience, come to stand for and evoke meanings beyond the objects or words themselves.

Syntax The way in which words are put together to form phrases, clauses, or sentences.

Taboo Prohibition of an act which, if performed, is thought to bring supernatural reprisal.

Taxonomy The study of the general principles of scientific classification.

Territory That space within a home range that a group of animals will defend against invasion by others of its species.

Totemism Belief in kinship with, or mystical relationship between, a group or individual and a plant or animal that serves as the emblem of a kinship group and often as a reminder of its ancestry.

Tribe A social group comprising numerous families, clans, or generations, together with their dependents or adopted strangers.

Tundra Extensive flat, treeless plains found in subarctic and arctic regions.

Uniface A stone tool produced by removing flakes from only one side.

Unilineal descent Descent through only one line, that of either the male parent or the female parent.

Witchcraft The use of sorcery or magic to bring misfortune to others.

Photo Credits

Cover photograph courtesy of the United Nations.
Chapter 1 Opener, Beryl Goldberg; Beryl Goldberg; Beryl Goldberg; UNICEF photos by M. and E. Bernheim; Beryl Goldberg; Courtesy of The American Museum of Natural History; Courtesy of The American Museum of Natural History; Polynesian Cultural Center; Beryl Goldberg.
Chapter 2 Opener, Beryl Goldberg; Tourist Organization of Thailand; Australian Information Service; Beryl Goldberg; Beryl Goldberg; Beryl Goldberg; Beryl Goldberg; Beryl Goldberg.
Chapter 3 Opener, Beryl Goldberg; Courtesy of the American Museum of Natural History; Courtesy of The American Museum of Natural History; Courtesy of The American Museum of Natural History.
Chapter 4 Opener, Beryl Goldberg; New York Public Library; © M. W. F. Tweedie, 1973, Photo Researchers, Inc.
Chapter 5 Opener, Beryl Goldberg; Courtesy of the Oriental Institute, University of Chicago; Courtesy of The American Museum of Natural History; Copyright National Geographic Society; Copyright National Geographic Society; Courtesy of The American Museum of Natural History.
Chapter 6 Opener, Beryl Goldberg; The National Foundation March of Dimes; New York Public Library; Courtesy of The American Museum of Natural History; Courtesy of The American Museum of Natural History; Dan Klugherz; United Nations; Australian News and Information Bureau.
Chapter 7 Opener, Beryl Goldberg; Spanish National Tourist Office; Courtesy of The American Museum of Natural History; Courtesy of The American Museum of Natural History; Courtesy of The American Museum of Natural History.
Chapter 8 Opener, Beryl Goldberg; Courtesy of The American Museum of Natural History; Beryl Goldberg.
Chapter 9 Opener, Beryl Goldberg; Oriental Institute, University of Chicago; Courtesy of The American Museum of Natural History; Tikal Project, University Museum, University of Pennsylvania.
Chapter 10 Opener, United Nations; Beryl Goldberg; Polynesian Cultural Center; Beryl Goldberg; Beryl Goldberg; Beryl Goldberg; Museum of the American Indian, Heye Foundation; Australian News and Information Bureau; Beryl Goldberg; Beryl Goldberg; Tourist Organization of Thailand.
Chapter 11 Opener, United Nations; all other photographs by Beryl Goldberg.
Chapter 12 Opener, United Nations; all other photographs by Beryl Goldberg.
Chapter 13 Opener and all other photographs by Beryl Goldberg.
Chapter 14 Opener, United Nations; Beryl Goldberg; Courtesy of Museum of the American Indian, Heye Foundation; United Nations; Beryl Goldberg; Beryl Goldberg; Beryl Goldberg; State Historical Society of Wisconsin.
Chapter 15 Opener, United Nations/Farkas; Beryl Goldberg; University of Pennsylvania Museum; Courtesy of Museum of the American Indian, Heye Foundation; Library of Congress.
Chapter 16 Opener, Beryl Goldberg; Portland Zoological Gardens; Beryl Goldberg; The Museum of Primitive Art; Beryl Goldberg; Beryl Goldberg; Courtesy of The American Museum of Natural History.
Chapter 17 Opener, United Nations/J. P. Laffont; Beryl Goldberg; Beryl Goldberg; Courtesy of the Museum of the American Indian, Heye Foundation; Beryl Goldberg; Beryl Goldberg; Courtesy of the Museum of the American Indian, Heye Foundation.
Chapter 18 Opener, United Nations; Beryl Goldberg; Beryl Goldberg; Beryl Goldberg; Beryl Goldberg; Rodman Wanamaker, Courtesy of The American Museum of Natural History; Beryl Goldberg; Beryl Goldberg; Beryl Goldberg.
Chapter 19 Opener and all other photographs by Beryl Goldberg.
Chapter 20 Opener, Beryl Goldberg; Beryl Goldberg; Polynesian Cultural Center, Hawaii; Australian News and Information Bureau.

Figure Sources

Figure 3-1 adapted from J. R. Napier, "Prospects in Primate Biology," *U.S. National Museum Proceedings* 125 (1968): Figure 1. Washington, D.C.: Smithsonian Institution Press, 1968.
Figure 3-4 adapted from J. R. Napier and P. H. Napier, *A Handbook of Living Primates.* Copyright 1967 by Academic Press Inc. (London) Ltd.
Figure 7-1 adapted from Jacques Bordaz, *Tools of the Old and New Stone Age*, p. 32. Copyright 1970 by Jacques Bordaz. Reprinted by permission of The American Museum of Natural History.
Figure 7-3 adapted from François Bordes, *The Old Stone Age*, pp. 39, 62, 99, 103, 162. Copyright 1968 by François Bordes. Used with permission of McGraw-Hill Book Company.
Figure 8-2 redrawn from Kent V. Flannery, "The Ecology of Early Food Production in Mesopotamia," *Science* 147 (1965): 1247-1255. By permission of the American Association for the Advancement of Science. Copyright 1965 by the American Association for the advancement of Science.

Index

1 2 3 4 5 6 7 8 9–RRD–82 81 80 79 78